Labour Law and Industrial Relations in Recessionary Times

ADAPT LABOUR STUDIES BOOK-SERIES

International School of Higher Education in Labour and Industrial Relations

Series Editors
Tayo Fashoyin, University of Lagos (Nigeria)
Michele Tiraboschi, University of Modena and Reggio Emilia (Italy)

Author
Michele Tiraboschi, University of Modena and Reggio Emilia (Italy)

English Language Editor
Pietro Manzella, ADAPT Senior Research Fellow (*Italy*)

ADAPT (www.adapt.it) is a non-profit organisation founded in 2000 by Professor Marco Biagi with the aim of promoting studies and research in the field of labour law and industrial relations from an international and comparative perspective. Our purpose is to encourage and implement a new approach to academic research, by establishing ongoing relationships with other universities and advanced studies institutes, and promoting academic and scientific exchange programmes with enterprises, institutions, foundations and associations. In collaboration with the **Marco Biagi Centre for International and Comparative Studies** (www.csmb.unimore.it), ADAPT set up the International School of Higher Education in Labour and Industrial Relations, a centre of excellence that is accredited at an international level for research, study and the postgraduate programmes in the area of industrial and labour relations.

Labour Law and Industrial Relations in Recessionary Times: The Italian Labour Relations in a Global Economy

By

Michele Tiraboschi

CAMBRIDGE
SCHOLARS
PUBLISHING

Labour Law and Industrial Relations in Recessionary Times:
The Italian Labour Relations in a Global Economy
By Michele Tiraboschi

This book first published 2014

Cambridge Scholars Publishing

12 Back Chapman Street, Newcastle upon Tyne, NE6 2XX, UK

British Library Cataloguing in Publication Data
A catalogue record for this book is available from the British Library

ISBN (10): 1-4438-5371-2, ISBN (13): 978-1-4438-5371-2

TABLE OF CONTENTS

List of Illustrations

LIST OF TABLES

FOREWORD

In the last fifteen years, and as a result of the passing of the Treu Reform (1997) and the Biagi Reform (2001-2003), Italian Labour Law has undergone a substantial overhaul. The reform process was a fragmentary and turbulent one and was marked by sudden changes of direction and social turmoil, which brought about the assassination of Prof Marco Biagi, immediately after the presentation of the White Paper on the Labour Market that he drafted.

Today, low rates of employment and labour market dynamism mostly affect young people and women. Major inequalities in terms of job opportunities are still prevalent between northern and southern Italy, and traditional phenomena such as precarious employment, over qualification, and graduate unemployment are more pronounced.

Low productivity—coupled with major differences between the labour costs borne by employers and workers' net income—furthers the improper use of contractual schemes in atypical and temporary work, quasi-salaried employment, joint ventures as well as the recourse to contractual arrangements to ease integration between learning and working, most notably training and apprenticeship contracts.

Shortcomings in employment services—alongside a failing educational system which is far from meeting the employers' needs—produced an attitude on the part of workers and trade unions towards employment aimed at safeguarding individual jobs, rather than guaranteeing overall occupational levels. In turn, this state of play results in increasing levels of dependence on the government—by way of income support measures which are provided on a permanent basis—thus discouraging processes such as restructuring, redundancies, and vocational training. The system of safety-net measures is not designed to promote access to employment of workers made redundant and their participation in training or retraining schemes.

Undeclared work in Italy, which is reported to be twice or three times higher than in other European countries, is indicative of two aspects which are intimately intertwined. While acknowledging considerable levels of backwardness and illegality, one might also note the dynamic nature of an ever-growing society which strives to adapt to sudden changes in the world of work. Yet such attempts prove unsuccessful, for—as the recent reforms exhibit—extant legislation fails to keep pace with these changes and clings onto traditional contractual arrangements—e.g. permanent and salaried employment.

Accordingly, the fact that today Italian Labour Law is faced with much uncertainty should come as no surprise, as labour legislation is devoid of an underlying approach and fails to keep up with real production processes. Compounding the picture is the crisis of the industrial relations system at a national level. The reform issued by the Monti's Government in 2012 did not provide a solution to unravel some major knots in the Italian labour market, the consequence of certain historical events that took place at a national level.

Indeed, the parties to the employment relationship are not satisfied with the watered-down and fragmentary nature of labour legislation. Workers feel more insecure and precarious. Employers reckon that the regulation of the employment relationship is not in line with the challenges posed by globalization and the emerging markets. Such profound dissatisfaction with labour laws is apparent even in the aftermath of recent reforms, as labour legislation is regarded as complex and consisting of too many provisions, thus not providing safeguards to workers and disregarding current production processes and work organization.

We are of the opinion that some of the major issues in the recent reforms of labour laws in Italy are to be explained by the nature of the debate among lawmakers and trade unions, which is still parochial and self-referential. This is what emerges—yet partly—from the debate among legal scholars, which is still dominated by excessive attention to the formal aspects of the legal process resulting from high levels of state regulation, for central government still plays a major role in regulating the employment relationship.

The present volume includes a number of papers written in English and published in the last fifteen years in which the Italian labour market underwent many changes. The intent here is not only to provide the international readership with a frame of reference—in both conceptual and legal terms—that helps to appreciate the Italian Labour Law currently in force. The real goal of this volume is to contribute to move beyond the self-referential nature of the Italian debate on the reform of labour laws. This would supply the reform process of the Italian labour market with an international and comparative dimension which—in accordance with the programmatic approach of Marco Biagi—should also feed the debate at a national level.

PART I

ECONOMIC CRISIS AND LABOUR LAW REFORMS: MODELS AND SCENARIOS

CHAPTER ONE

YOUNG WORKERS IN RECESSIONARY TIMES: A CAVEAT TO (CONTINENTAL) EUROPE TO RECONSTRUCT ITS LABOUR LAW

1. Introductory Remarks[1]

Policy makers, social partners, and the public opinion monitor with interest and growing concern the steep increase in youth unemployment, in Europe more than elsewhere.[2] Indeed, all the main international institutions[3]—supported by the analysis of labour market experts[4]—seem to uphold that young people have been hit the hardest by the "great crisis" that began in 2007 with the collapse of financial markets.

---

[1] The present contribution was previously published in 2012 in the *E-Journal of International and Comparative Labour Studies* 1, No. 1-2.

[2] In other areas of the world, especially in developing countries, the cultural lens through which the problem of youth unemployment is explored might be different. See on the issue Senatori, I., and M. Tiraboschi. "Productivity, Investment in Human Capital and the Challenge of Youth Employment in the Global Market. Comparative Developments and Global Responses in the Perspective of School-to-Work Transition," 5th IIRA African Regional Congress, IIRA Cape Town, South Africa 2008.

[3] See, by way of example, ILO. 2012. *World of Work Report 2012. Better Jobs for a Better Economy*. Geneva: International Labour Office; ILO. 2010. *Global Employment Trends for Youth.* Geneva: International Labour Office; Martin, J. 2011. *Unfinished Business: Investing in Youth.* OECD Employment Outlook, Paris: OECD; OECD. 2010. *Off to a Good Start?* Jobs for Youth, Paris: OECD.

[4] See Verick, S. 2009. "Who Is Hit Hardest during a Financial Crisis? The Vulnerability of Young Men and Women to Unemployment in an Economic Downturn," IZA Discussion Paper, No. 4359. Bonn: IZA. For a different perspective and some valid criticisms on this shared opinion see O'Higgins, N. 2012. *This Time It's Different? Youth Labour Market During the Great Recession*, IZA Discussion Paper, No. 6434, in particular, par. 2. Both papers are available at www.bollettinoadapt.it, A-Z index, *Lavoratori giovani*.

It is only natural then that in a time of ongoing recession and many sacrifices demanded of workers,[5] feelings of apprehension and hope arise with regard to the future, therefore involving younger generations and their employment prospects in the years ahead.

The notion of "unemployment" has long become less and less appropriate to frame the critical aspects of the interplay between young people and employment.[6] Of equal importance, as well as extensively discussed and highly controversial, are those phenomena accompanying young people in their school-to-work transitions, particularly inactivity, precarious employment and low wages.[7]

Nevertheless, unemployment still remains a main indicator, as it supplies clear and immediate evidence of the vulnerability of young people in the labour market, also for those who are not experts in the field. According to relevant data,[8] in most countries—whether industrialised or non-industrialised ones—high levels of youth unemployment have been reported long before the onset of the recent economic and financial crisis, to the extent that many specialists made use of the term *déjà vu* to refer to the phenomenon.[9]

Accordingly, the concern resulting from high youth unemployment rates is not a novelty. What appears to be new here, at least within the political and institutional public debate taking place in recent years, is the emphasis placed by Europe on the future of younger generations and how this issue is taken as an excuse to justify—or perhaps to impose—major labour market reforms and deregulation on nation States overseen by central institutions, which will also limit their sovereignty.[10]

---

[5] Particularly relevant in this respect is the study presented in the *World of Work Report 2012* of the ILO (*op. cit.*, note 2) on the measures that affected workers in terms of protection reduction.

[6] On this topic, see Marchand, O. 1999. "Youth Unemployment in OECD Countries: How Can the Disparities Be Explained?", *Preparing Youth for the 21st Century—The Transition from Education to the labour Market,* OECD, (Paris: OECD), 89.

[7] This issue has been extensively discussed in Tiraboschi, T. 2006. "Young People and Employment in Italy: The (Difficult) Transition from Education and Training to the Labour Market," *IJCLLIR*, 81 ff.

[8] See, among others, N. O'Higgins, *op. cit.*

[9] Bell, D.N.F., and D.G. Blanchflower. 2010. "Youth Unemployment: Déjà Vu," IZA Discussion Paper, No. 4705. Bonn: IZA, at www.bollettinoadapt.it, A-Z index, *Lavoratori giovani*.

[10] In this respect, see Baylos, A. 2012. "Crisi del diritto del lavoro o diritto del lavoro in crisi? La riforma del lavoro spagnola del 2012", *Diritto delle Relazioni Industriali*, No. 2.

Put differently, labour law rules—chiefly concerning high levels of protection against termination of employment—would explain high youth unemployment rates as well as the increasing recourse to atypical, non-standard or temporary employment arrangements.

Indeed, there is little wonder about this issue, save for the fact that—in a time of severe crisis and ongoing recession—fathers are now called to make a lot of sacrifices that are deemed to be "acceptable", for they contribute to provide their sons with better employment prospects. In this sense, the "great crisis" has acted as a catalyst[11] for long-awaited labour market reforms and liberalisation processes, which however have never been fully implemented so far due to a lack of adequate political and social consensus.

Of particular significance in this respect is an interview with the President of the European Central Bank, Mr. Mario Draghi, which appeared in the *Wall Street Journal*.[12] In the midst of the international crisis and in the name of younger generations, Mr. Draghi questioned the future sustainability of the "European Social Model", urging a major overhaul of national labour regulations in Europe, which are currently more favourable to labour market insiders, i.e. adult workers.

This is what occurred in many European countries between 2008 and 2012[13] with the introduction of a number of unpopular measures aimed at reducing workers' protection that have been imposed on increasingly disoriented and helpless citizens, and presented as an unavoidable sacrifice required by the current macro-economic situation with a view to improving employment and retirement prospects (also) of younger generations.[14]

---

[11] See OECD. 2012. *Economic Policy Reforms. Going for Growth*. Paris: OECD.

[12] Interview with Mario Draghi (Interview Transcripts), in Blackstone, B., M. Karnitschnig, R. Thomson. 2012. "Europe's Banker Talks Tough", *The Wall Street Journal*, 24 February 2012, available in the *Adapt International Bulletin*, No. 7.

[13] For a review of the main actions taken by national governments in Europe, with or without the support of social partners, see Simms, M. 2011. *Helping Young Workers during the Crisis: Contributions by Social Partners and Public Authorities,* European Foundation for the Improvement of Living and Working Conditions. Dublin: Eurofound, in particular 20 ff., at www.bollettinoadapt.it, A-Z index, *Lavoratori giovani*. See also ILO, *World of Work Report 2012. Better Jobs for a Better Economy,* cit.

[14] As far as Italy is concerned, see Prime Minister Monti's Inaugural Speech to Parliament on http://www.governo.it/. Reference to future opportunities of younger generations is a *leitmotiv* of Government discourse. See, in particular, Monti, M. 2012. "Italy's Labor Reforms Are Serious and Will Be Effective", *The Wall Street Journal*, 6 April 2012, also in the *Adapt International Special Bulletin*, No. 1.

This trend has not been witnessed only in Europe, since 40 out of 131 countries—as are the Members of the International Labour Organization (ILO)—have reduced their standard employment protection levels.[15] This aspect is particularly apparent in industrialised countries, and chiefly in central and southern Europe, where 83% of anti-crisis reforms focused on employment protection, with particular reference to the regulation on dismissal for economic reasons.[16]

In view of the above, and in the context of a dramatic deterioration of the economy and lack of public resources for subsidies, this paper sets out to understand whether job-creation policies, employment incentives,[17] and deregulation of labour laws in Europe—in particular in relation to unfair dismissal—could really provide a possible (if not the only) solution to cope with the issue of youth unemployment.

2. The Issue of Youth Unemployment: The New Perspective Provided to Labour Lawyers by a Comparative Study

Intuitively, it could be argued that high protection levels provided to labour market insiders may discourage or pose an obstacle to outsiders, thus including young people. Drawing on this assumption, at the end of the last century, the OECD started implementing a set of measures collected in the well-known *Jobs Study*.[18] The studies that followed have

---

[15] See ILO. 2012. *World of Work Report 2012. Better Jobs for a Better Economy*, cit., 35 ff. With particular reference to the measures adopted in favour of youth employment, see Ha, B., C. McInerney, S. Tobin, and R. Torres. 2010. "Youth Employment in Crisis", International Institute of Labour Studies Discussion Paper, No. 201, at www.bollettinoadapt.it, A-Z index, *Lavoratori giovani*.

[16] See ILO. 2012. *World of Work Report 2012. Better Jobs for a Better Economy*, cit.

[17] The relevant literature, as well as having highlighted "pitfalls" and "risks" of public subsidies to youth unemployment and inactivity, has long discussed the shortcomings of job creation policies, that produce limited (if not negative) effects in terms of cost-benefit analysis. On the subject, see Ryan, P. 2001. "The School-to-Work Transition: A Cross-National Perspective: Corrigendum", *Journal of Economic Literature* 39, No. 3, 767 ff., and Boone, J., and J.C. Van Ours. 2004. "Effective Active Labor Market Policies," IZA Discussion Paper, No. 1335. Bonn: IZA. For a general overview see Tiraboschi, M., *Young People and Employment in Italy: The (Difficult) Transition from Education and Training to the Labour Market*, *op. cit*.

[18] OECD. 1994. *The OECD Jobs Study. Facts, Analysis, Strategies*. Paris: OECD.

questioned the role of workers' protection in terms of total and youth unemployment.[19]

Limited data reveal increased youth employment prospects in countries with a deregulated or flexible labour market. To the contrary, many studies show that higher workers' protection actually favoured, at least in the medium term, youth employment during the "great crisis".

Likewise, straightforward is that in deregulated labour markets with higher flexibility in hiring and dismissals, youth can be discouraged or find themselves in a less favourable position compared to adults, due to a lack of work experience, no well-established connections or relations helping them in the job search, lower productivity, lack of expertise and skills, and competition with migrant workers, who are more inclined to take up jobs and withstand employment arrangements deemed unacceptable by the local population.[20]

Labour lawyers, like the author of the present paper, have limited knowledge of technical and conceptual instruments to take part in a debate—that is also very controversial among labour economists—on the effects of the regulatory framework on the labour market organisation and regulation. Because of the thorough knowledge of the regulatory and institutional framework, labour lawyers can however present economists with a different interpretation of the potential impact of protection measures on youth unemployment rates.

This is the real challenge to take on, as pointed out also by the International Labour Organization over the last decade. According to the ILO, the current available indicators are perfectly suitable to afford an analytical framework through which detailed information about the condition of young workers in the labour market in the different areas of the world might be given. It is still the ILO, which stresses that the real

---

[19] See Nickell, S. 1997. "Unemployment and Labor Market Rigidities: Europe versus North America", *Journal of Economic Perspectives* 11, No. 3; Baker, D., A. Glyn, D. Howell, and J. Schmitt. 2004. "Labor Market Institutions and Unemployment: A Critical Assessment of the Cross-Country Evidence", *Fighting Unemployment: The Limits of Free Market Orthodoxy*, ed. Howell D., Oxford: Oxford University Press; Nickell, S., L. Nunziata, and W. Ochel. 2005. "Unemployment in the OECD Since the 1960s: What Do We Know?", *The Economic Journal* 115, No. 500; Bassanini, A., and R. Duval. 2006. "Employment Patterns in OECD Countries: Reassessing the Role of Policies and Institutions", OECD Social, Employment and Migration Working Paper, No. 35. Paris: OECD.

[20] With reference to internal and external labour market, see Bell, D.N.F., and D. G. Blanchflower, *op. cit.*, 2. In the same vein, see also ILO. 2010. *Global Employment Trends for Youth,* cit.

difficulty is rather to identify the tools to improve employment conditions by means of existing indicators.[21]

Fig. 1-1. Relative Youth Unemployment Rate (2008 and 2010)

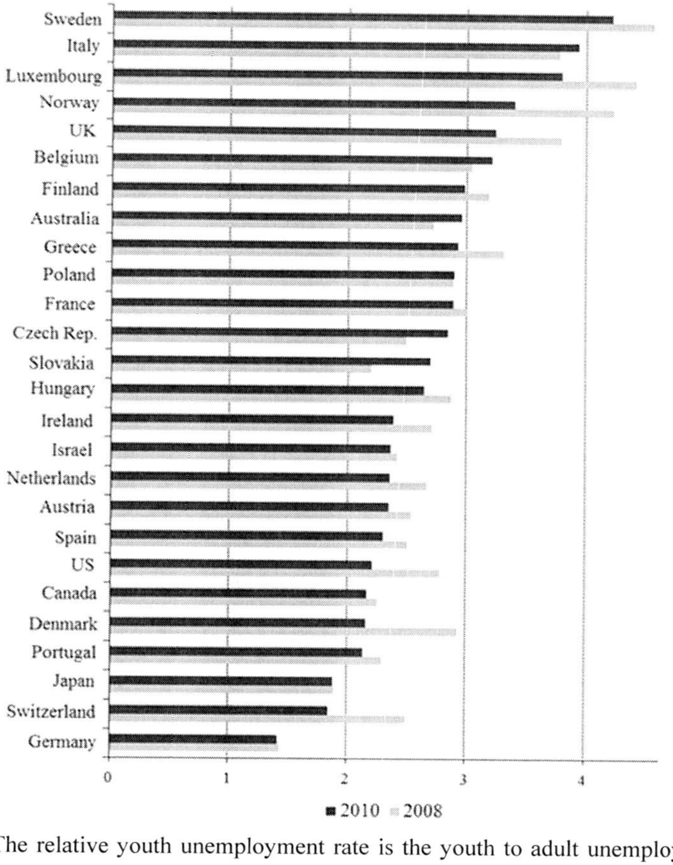

Note: The relative youth unemployment rate is the youth to adult unemployment ratio.
Source: Own Elaboration on OECD data

What labour economists may interpret by simple facts empirically proven—if not even the outcome of their investigation—is seen by labour

[21] ILO. 2006. *Global Employment Trends for Youth*. Geneva: International Labour Office at www.bollettinoadapt.it, A-Z index, *Lavoratori giovani*.

law experts, especially if a comparative perspective is taken, as some useful insights to better assess the efficiency of labour market institutions and, in particular, the impact of protection measures on youth unemployment.

Fig. 1-2. Youth Unemployment Rate 2010

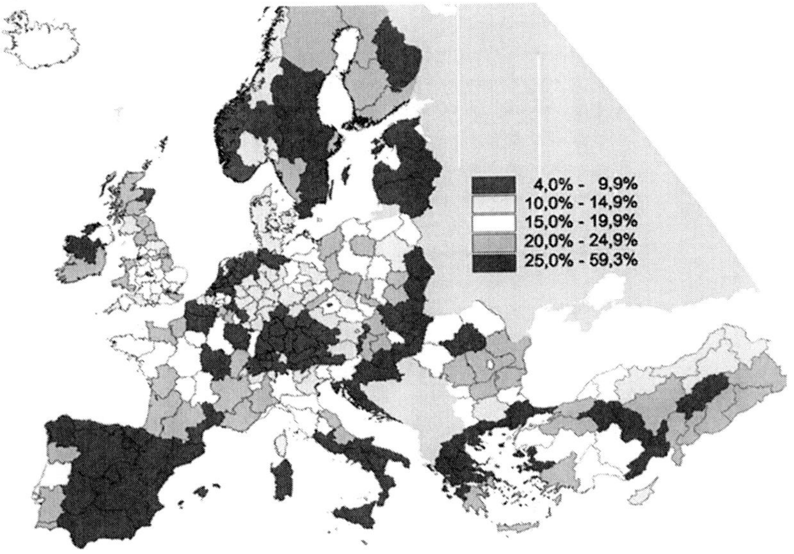

Source: Eurostat Data

From a comparative analysis of the labour market indicators—before and after the "great crisis"—what emerges is the different ratio between youth and overall unemployment rates (see Fig. 1-1). Of particular interest to a labour lawyer is that in some countries youth unemployment is broadly in line with that of adult workers (Germany, Switzerland), whereas in other countries, regardless of its level, youth unemployment is about twice (Portugal, Denmark, Spain, the United States) or three times as high as that of their adult counterparts (Italy, Greece, the United Kingdom, Sweden).

At first glance, a "geographical" representation of the different youth unemployment rates intuitively shows that youth unemployment is not much of a problem in those countries (or in those legal systems, as a labour lawyer would put it) which make extensive use of apprenticeship, and which consider this tool not merely as a temporary contractual scheme, but rather as a lever for placement[22] to achieve better integration between education and training and labour market (Fig. 1-2).

The same holds true for inactivity, most notably the issue of the NEETs (not in employment, nor education or training), which is less serious in countries where apprenticeship is resorted to as a means to obtain secondary education (Fig. 1-3). However, there is more. The best performing countries in terms of youth employment, such as Austria and Germany report high levels of workers' protection, especially against unfair dismissals (see Fig. 1-4). By contrast, countries with more liberal legislation on dismissals, such as Denmark, the United Kingdom and the United States, account for high levels of youth unemployment. Evidently, they do not fall within the European countries with the worst youth employment outcomes, such as France, Italy and Spain, but youth unemployment is still twice as high as that recorded in the best performing countries.

This simple and straightforward empirical observation seems therefore to uphold the assumption that major difficulties for the youth entering the labour market are not caused by inadequate regulations, but rather by inefficient school-to-work transition processes as well as by the failure to properly match labour demand and supply. A good match between labour demand and supply is, however, not to be intended in static terms as merely dependent on more or less effective employment services—be they public or private—but rather in relation to the devising of academic careers which are consistent with current and future labour market needs in terms of training and skills acquisition.

[22] See in this connection the article by Ryan, P. 2011. "Apprendistato: tra teoria e pratica, scuola e luogo di lavoro", *Diritto delle Relazioni Industriali*, No. 4, analysing the German "ideal" model, as opposed to the lack of transparency of market-oriented systems and to Italy and the United Kingdom, where apprenticeship is an employment contract.

Fig. 1-3. NEET Rates 2010

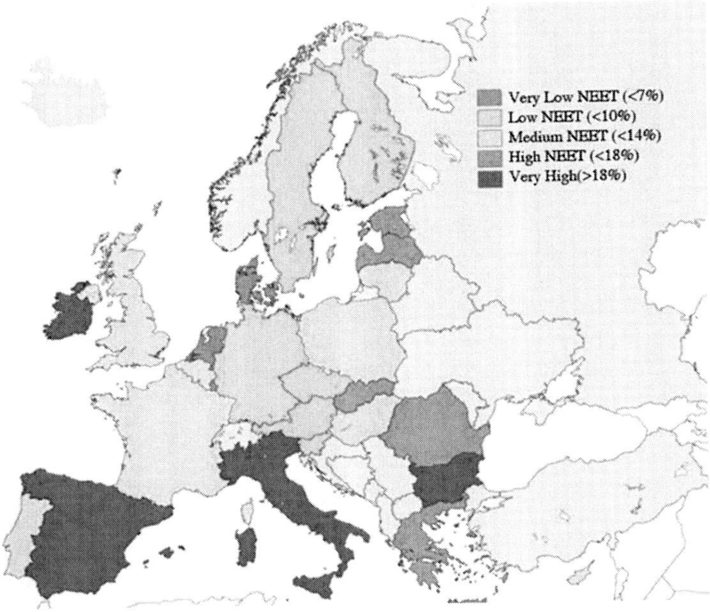

Source: Eurostat data

Fig. 1-4. Overall Work Protection and Work Protection against Individual Dismissal (0 = less restrictive; 4 = more restrictive)

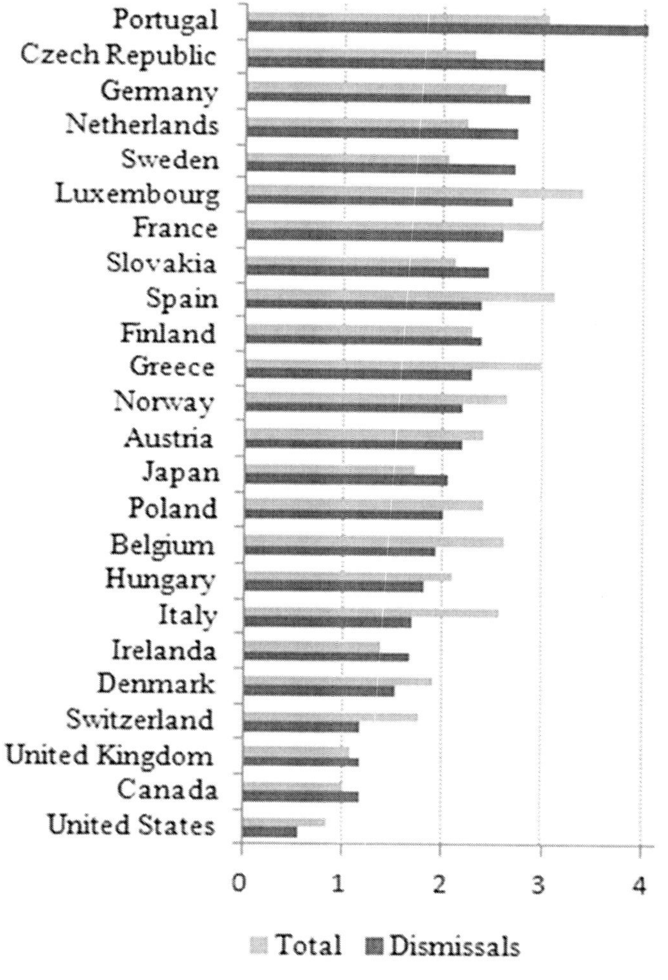

Source: Own Elaboration on OECD data

3. *Flexicurity* and Apprenticeship: the Limits of the Proposal for the so-called "Single Employment Contract"

Countries embracing the *flexicurity* model as strongly recommended by the European institutions[23] report positive outcomes in terms of youth employment, with high employment rates and low unemployment levels (see Fig. 1-5).

Fig. 1-5. Youth Employment and Unemployment Rates 2010

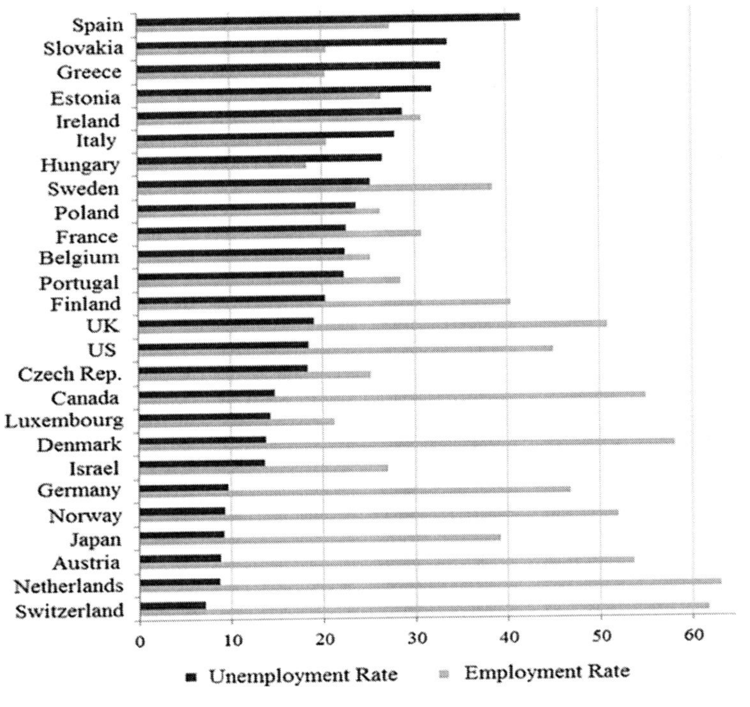

Source: Own Elaboration on OECD data

[23] See the Green Paper of the European Commission: European Commission. 2006. *Modernising Labour Law to Meet the Challenges of the XXI Century* (COM(2006)708 final). Brussels: European Commission; and the Communication of the European Commission of 27 June 2007: European Commission. 2007. *Towards Common Principles of Flexicurity: More and Better Jobs through Flexibility and Security* (COM(2007)359 final). Brussels: European Commission.

This led many experts to put forward the introduction of a "single employment contract" both in central and southern European countries. In some of these, including France,[24] Italy[25] and Spain[26] attempts have been made to adopt new legislative provisions favouring a "single"—or at least a "prevailing"—contract for salaried workers, generally open-ended and with significantly reduced workers' protection against unfair dismissal, to be offset by a higher degree of protection in the labour market, no longer provided by the contract itself, but rather by a more generous universal system of unemployment benefits, that can support workers during unavoidable and increasingly frequent occupational transitions.

The misleading charm and the limits of the proposal for a "single employment contract"—rest on the irrational belief, not even put forward in Fordism, with standardised production and work organisation models, that the duality of European labour markets can be overcome by reducing the multifaceted and diverse reality of modern work and production to fixed contractual arrangements, through one single contract of employment, abolishing self-employment and coordinated and continuative collaborations (quasi-subordinate work) also in their most genuine forms. This is achieved by reducing to a limited number of cases the scope to lawfully resort to temporary work, by prohibiting it also when

---

[24] Blanchard, O., and J. Tirole. 2004. "Contours of Employment Protection Reform", *Macroeconomic Theory and Economic Policy. Essays in honour of Jean-Paul Fitoussi*, ed. Velupillai K. V., New York: Routledge; Cahuc, P., and F. Kramarz. 2005. "De la précarité à la mobilité: vers une Sécurité sociale professionnelle", *La Documentation Française*, Paris.

[25] See in the literature Boeri, T., and P. Garibaldi.2008.*Un nuovo contratto per tutti*, Milano: Chiarelettere. Among the numerous draft laws, see Senato della Repubblica, Draft Law No. 1873 of 11 November 2009, ddl No. 1873, *Codice dei rapporti di lavoro. Modifiche al Libro V del codice civile*; Senato della Repubblica, Draft Law No. 1481 of 25 March 2009, *Disposizioni per il superamento del dualismo del mercato del lavoro, la promozione del lavoro stabile in strutture produttive flessibili e la garanzia di pari opportunità nel lavoro per le nuove generazioni*; Senato della Repubblica, Draft Law No. 2000 of 5 February 2010, *Istituzione del contratto unico di ingresso*; Camera dei Deputati, Draft Law No. 2630 of 22 July 2009, *Disposizioni per l'istituzione di un contratto unico di inserimento formativo e per il superamento del dualismo del mercato del lavoro*; Camera dei Deputati, Draft Law No. 4277 of 8 April 2011, *Deleghe al Governo per l'adozione di norme in materia di disciplina dei rapporti di lavoro, di formazione e di misure di protezione sociale per favorire l'accesso dei giovani al lavoro*.

[26] Andrés, J., S. Bentolila, J.J. Dolado, and F. Felgueroso. 2009. *Propuesta para la reactivación laboral en España*. FEDEA.

plausible technical, organisational and productive reasons are in place, by disregarding the educational value of access-to-work contracts directed to disadvantaged groups as well as of apprenticeship contracts for youth, with a view to favouring a pure and poorly balanced type of flexibility, where freedom of dismissal is easily granted upon payment of severance pay.

On close inspection, a solution of this kind would damage not only employers, but also the workers themselves, most notably young people and those forced out of the labour market, who, in all likelihood, would bear the heaviest brunt of the reform, as they would no longer be doomed to "precarious", but rather to "illegal" employment in the shadow economy. Not only would they have no access to internships, job-training contracts and project work, but they would also be denied protection resulting from employment stability, at least during their first years of work for the same employer or client.

This explains why the proposal for a "single employment contract" was soon dismissed in all the countries where it had been put forward, replaced—at least in France[27] and Italy[28]—by a major overhaul of the apprenticeship system, as well as of those schemes (of contractual of non-contractual nature) promoting labour market access for entrants, including internships, training and guidance. This can be seen as a reasonable trade-off based on the need to reduce the mismatch between labour demand and supply. A solution that is supported, in the author's view, by the evidence that *apprenticeship* countries (as defined in par. 1) coped better with the crisis,[29] reporting a significantly lower increase in unemployment (see Fig. 1-6), and in some cases, a reduction in the unemployment rates (see Fig. 1-7). This aspect can be appreciated in comparison with *flexicurity* countries, which, by contrast, proved to be more vulnerable in the recession.[30]

---

27 Law No. 2011-893, so-called "Cherpion Reform".

28 Legislative Decree No. 167/2011. See in this connection Tiraboschi, M., ed. 2011. *Il Testo Unico dell'apprendistato e le nuove regole sui tirocini. Commentario al decreto legislativo 14 settembre 2011, n. 167, e all'articolo 11 del decreto legge 13 agosto 2011, n. 138, convertito con modifiche nella legge 14 settembre 2011, n. 148*. Milan: Giuffré.

29 See Simms, M. *op. cit.,* in particular 24 ff.

30 See Andersen, T. M. 2011. "A Flexicurity Labour Market in the Great Recession: The Case of Denmark", IZA Discussion Paper, No. 5710, Bonn: IZA. For a comparative evaluation, see Spattini, S., and M. Tiraboschi. 2012. "Labor Market Measures in the Crisis and the Convergence of Social Models", *W. E. Upjohn Institute for Employment Research*, 2012.

Fig. 1-6. Youth Employment Rate in 2010 and Percentage Variation between 2007 and 2010

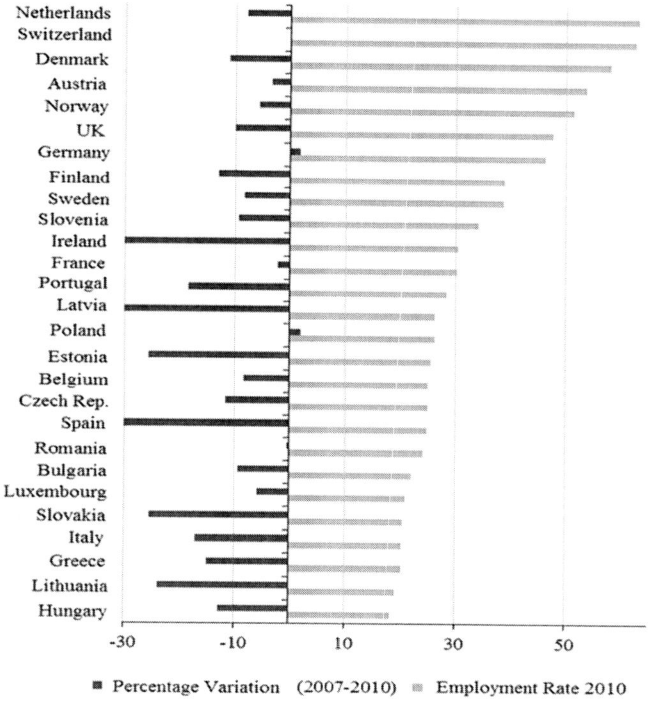

Source: Own Elaboration on Eurostat data

Fig. 1-7. Youth Unemployment Rate 2007 e 2010

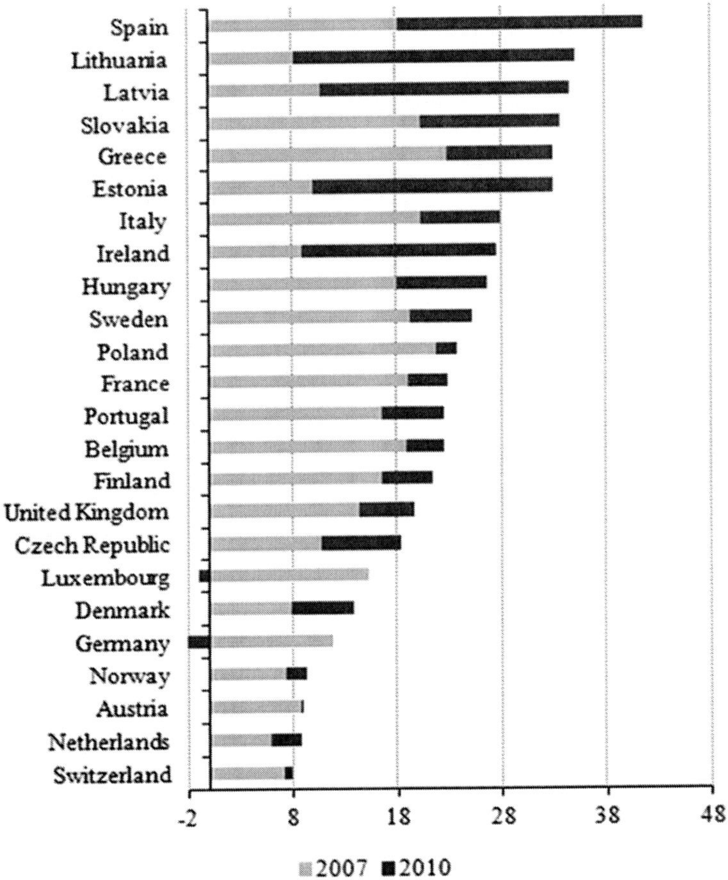

Source: Own Elaboration on Eurostat data

4. The (Main) Determinants of Youth Unemployment: Education Systems, School-to-work Transition, Labour Market Institutions, Industrial Relations Systems

The existence of a sound dual system of apprenticeship cannot be the only reason for low levels of youth unemployment in countries such as Germany, Switzerland, and Austria, and in more general terms, nor the cause of what has been defined as the "German labour market miracle during the great recession".[31]

Without assuming a direct causal relationship between labour market institutions and the policies in place in the different countries, it seems however possible to identify a number of specific determinants of youth unemployment that show how limited and partial an intervention of a purely regulatory nature would be in tackling the problem of youth employment, all the more so if an institutional approach would probably be more effective.

According to several comparative analyses, youth unemployment trends are not only—or not much—affected by labour market rules with regard to hiring and dismissing, but rather by a series of factors including the quality of the education system, an effective school-to-work transition, the integration between school and vocational training, the quality of the industrial relations system, and the functioning of labour market institutions.

The table that follows classifies some European countries and the United States considering the unemployment rate for youth aged 15-24 years old, providing an overview of the determinants of positive or negative youth employment outcomes based on three factors: education and training, industrial relations and employment protection legislation (see par. 4). The comparative overview supplied in the foregoing table is based on a series of indicators collected from authoritative research and international studies and shows in particular that different priority issues must be taken into account to effectively tackle youth employment, and that labour market reform is not enough.

---

[31] See on the issue Burda, M. C., and J. Hunt. 2011. "What Explains the German Labor Market Miracle in the Great Recession?", IZA Discussion Paper, No. 5800. Bonn: IZA.

Table 1-1. Characteristics of Labour Market Institutions and Youth Unemployment in Europe and in the United States

Youth Unemployment Rate 2010		Training and School-to-work Transition						Industrial Relations System		Employment Protection Legislation	
		Quality of education	Apprenticeship			School-to-work Transition					
			As flexible employment	As a form of training	Low pay, more training	School Placement	Efficient employment services	Cooperative Ind. Rel.	Wage Flexibility	Flexibility in Hiring	Flexibility in Firing
Austria	9%	x		x	x	x	x			x	
Netherlands	9%	x			x	x	x	x	x	x	
Germany	10%	x		x	x	x	x	x	x	x	
Denmark	14%	x				x	x	x		x	x
USA	18%	x				x	x		x	x	x
UK	19%	x	x			x	x	x	x	x	x
France	23%				x		x			x	
Italy	28%		x							x	
Spain	42%		x							x	

Source: Own Elaboration

At the time of addressing interventions, priority should be given to the education system, focusing on the shift from school to work. Indeed, education policies are not only applied during crises, but also as structural measures, and it is no coincidence that countries with good youth employment outcomes have high quality education and training systems. As pointed out in Table No. 1, the higher quality of education is related to lower youth unemployment rates. For reasons of simplicity, the table presents a general indicator describing the "quality of the education system" taken from the *Competitiveness Report* of the World Economic Forum[32] where in an executive opinion survey it was asked "How well does the educational system in your country meet the needs of a competitive economy?" [1 = not well at all; 7 = very well].

Countries with low youth unemployment rates (light and medium grey in the table) are those where the quality of education perceived by corporate executives is high. Although this indicator is probably subjectively biased, it can be particularly useful in that it gives the standpoint of labour market operators, not merely focusing on education *per se*, but taking into account the extent to which education and training meet the skills and vocational requirements of a competitive economy.

In the context of education and school-to-work transition, apprenticeship plays a substantial role also in cultural terms, providing effective training and work-based learning and being acknowledged in the literature as one of the most valuable means for an effective school-to-work transition.[33] However, not all apprenticeships are equal in terms of investment in training, which is the fundamental feature of a true apprenticeship.[34] Moreover, not all apprenticeships carry the same value in terms of youth employability, and if there is no investment in "genuine"

---

[32] Schwab, K. 2011. *The Global Competitiveness Report 2011-2012*. Geneva: World Economic Forum. The X indicates that the country ranks among the first 30 out of 140 countries in relation to the *Quality of education* index.

[33] See the review on school-to-work transition systems, with particular reference to the superiority of the dual apprenticeship model in Quintini, G., and T. Manfredi. 2009. "Going Separate Ways? School-to-Work Transitions in the United States and Europe", OECD Social, Employment and Migration Working Papers No. 90, and in Quintini, G., J. P. Martin, and S. Martin. 2007. "The Changing Nature of the School-to-Work Transition Process in OECD Countries", IZA Discussion Paper No. 2582. Bonn: IZA. In the Italian literature, see Bertagna, G. "Apprendistato e formazione in impresa," Tiraboschi, M. ed., *op. cit.*

[34] According to Ryan (in *Apprendistato: tra teoria e pratica, scuola e luogo di lavoro, op. cit.*), "ideal" apprenticeship is not only a work-based learning opportunity, but should rather provide part-time vocational training as well as work experience, leading to the acquisition of a formal vocational qualification.

training on the part of the company, what remains is the mere use of cheap labour. For this reason, in the table below, apprenticeship schemes are divided according to the (effective, and not just theoretical as required by law) provision of training. Although a number of legal provisions establish compulsory training during apprenticeship, reality is often very distant from the ideal apprenticeship model, and this tool becomes a mere instrument of exploitation of a flexible and cheaper labour force. Apprenticeship schemes in Germany and Austria include part-time formal schooling, whereas in Italy and in the United Kingdom, apprenticeship is not only a "flexible" or "subsidised" employment contract, but it is often devoid of real learning contents, if we consider that the share of apprentices receiving formal training is lower than 40%.[35]

This is also the reason why the third indicator, i.e. pay levels of apprentices with respect to skilled employees, was included in the table. By analysing the level of pay granted to apprentices, one might quantify the exchange value of training, and it follows that the higher the investment in training, the lower the apprentice's remuneration defined in collective agreements; whereas, apprentices are paid almost the same as skilled workers when training is neglected. It is significant, as the following table clearly shows, that German and Austrian apprentices receive lower pay and learn more. The dual system distinguishes itself from how apprentices' pay is defined, since it is considered an allowance (*Vergütung*) rather than wage in a strict sense, as is generally referred to in the United Kingdom and in Italy. In Austria and Germany, as well as in the Netherlands and France, apprentices receive less than the half of the wage of a skilled employee, whereas in Italy apprentices' pay can reach up to 80% of the full wage of a skilled worker.

[35] Ryan, P., K. Wagner, S. Teuber, and U. Backes-Gellner, *Trainee Pay in Britain, Germany and Switzerland: Markets and Institutions*, SKOPE Research Paper, 2010, n. 96. See also M. Tiraboschi, *Ragioni e impianto di una riforma*, in M. Tiraboschi (ed.), *op. cit.*

Table 1-2. Apprentices' Pay as a Percentage of the Wage of a Skilled Worker

		Manufacturing	Services	Other Sectors	
United Kingdom	2005	46%	70%	Da 45% (hair-dressers) a 60% (trade)	
Germany	2007	29%	34%	27%	
Switzerland	2004	14%	17,5%	18%	
Ireland	2009	30% (I year), 45% (II year), 65% (III year), 80% (IV year)			
France (% minimum wage)	2010	25% (under 19 years old), 42% (20-23 years), 78% (over 24 years old)			
Italy	2010	72% (2 levels below the final employment grade)	from 70% to 80% (2 levels below the final employment grade)	Craftsmanship: from 55% to 90%	Construction: from 60% to 85% (over 3 years, + 10% per year)

Source: ADAPT, Giovani e lavoro: ripartiamo dall'apprendistato, in fareApprendistato.it, 10 May 2011

Besides the proper use of contractual (and non-contractual) arrangements, an efficient school-to-work transition should rely on a placement system able to develop synergy between "knowledge" and "know-how"—i.e. schools and businesses—by fostering a systematic collaboration based on an ongoing information exchange that builds a bridge between labour demand and supply, as well as in light of future prospects, exploring training and skills needs required by the market and providing the training centres with relevant information.[36]

In countries where there is a well-established school and university placement system, the relationship between training centres and businesses is—in their mutual interest—of a cooperative nature. Students' CVs, as

[36] Tiraboschi, M. 2006. "*Il problema della occupazione giovanile nella prospettiva della (difficile) transizione dai percorsi educativi e formativi al mercato del lavoro*", *Scuola, Università e Mercato del lavoro dopo la Riforma Biagi. Le politiche per la transizione dai percorsi educativi e formativi al mercato del lavoro,* eds. Reggiani Gelmini, P., and M. Tiraboschi, Milano: Giuffrè; Spattini, S., and M. Tiraboschi. 2011."La revisione dei regimi di autorizzazione e il rilancio del placement universitario", *La riforma dei rapporti e delle controversie di lavoro. Commentario alla legge 4 novembre 2010, n. 183 (cd. Collegato lavoro),*eds. Tiraboschi, M., G. Proia, Milano: Giuffrè; Spattini, S. "Riforma dell'apprendistato e nuovo placement", ed. Tiraboschi M., *op. cit.*

well as job posts are freely available on the universities websites and in placement offices and schools are actively involved in the job-matching process and are aware of the skills required by the market.

In countries such as the United Kingdom and the United States, this synergy results in a smoother youth labour market entry and lower youth unemployment rates. Inefficient placement offices and inadequate placement employment services—both public and private—make job search for young people even more difficult. So much so that, as shown in Table 1-1, in countries where employment services are efficient, young people tend to rely more on them during their job search, increasing the chances to find employment. By contrast, EUROSTAT figures show that in countries with higher unemployment levels, youth rely less on employment services, and resort to informal methods (such as friends and social connections) acquiring less information and thus adding further barriers to the traditional difficulties in labour market entry resulting from asymmetric information.

Not only does this first proposal represent an alternative to Labour Law reform as the only solution to youth unemployment. It can also contribute to preventing the increase in youth unemployment, by setting the stage for the acquisition of marketable skills for the job market, bringing young people closer to the labour market by means of apprenticeship and other relevant tools, and creating a network among the institutions involved.

The idea that Labour Law reform is not the only way to reduce youth unemployment is reinforced by the awareness that new policies and regulations are adopted only when problems have already arisen and they cannot fully solve the difficulties that youth face in the labour market.

The second important area of intervention to focus on is the quality of the industrial relations system. As provided in Table No. 1, two factors falling under the rubric of industrial relations could particularly contribute to promoting youth employment and to creating a more inclusive labour market.

In countries where industrial relations are more cooperative, where collective bargaining is decentralised and wage determination is flexible, the production system is efficient and new opportunities for youth can easily arise. By contrast, in countries where social partners do not act cooperatively and where the bargaining system is highly centralised, the voice of labour market insiders, i.e. adult workers with stable employment, prevails over the voice of outsiders and of the unemployed or inactive.

Among industrial relations indicators, particularly relevant is the extent to which industrial relations can be considered cooperative, and wage determination flexible. Both indicators are drawn from the *Competitiveness Report*[37] with a view, once again, to looking at reality rather than providing a theoretical perspective based on laws and contracts. The World Economic Forum classification and the analysis of youth unemployment rates seem to be in line with the idea that cooperative industrial relations and flexible wage determination mechanisms can contribute to building a more inclusive productive system.

However, the debate at a European level is moving away from the notion of "concertation", with employment protection legislation that is considered almost unanimously the main cause of youth unemployment.[38] As previously noted, labour economics literature has not universally established the effects of employment protection systems on unemployment, while there is overwhelming agreement only on the fact that these effects are ambiguous. In this connection, Table No. 1 shows that higher flexibility in dismissals perceived by labour market operators is not related to lower youth unemployment levels, since, as noted, in Austria, the Netherlands and Germany it is not as easy to dismiss workers as in *flexicurity* countries or in those countries with a free market economy, despite reporting lower youth unemployment rates.

5. Future Prospects for Interdisciplinary Research

The main economic studies on the subject agree that a central role in terms of youth employment promotion policies is played by aggregate demand. It remains crucial, therefore, in the fight against unemployment in general, and youth unemployment in particular, to adopt sound tax and monetary macro-economic and sectoral policies.[39] Particularly relevant, today and more so in the future, is the role of demography, both for the sustainability of retirement and welfare systems and for the effects on the labour market and business organisation models.

---

[37] Schwab, K. *op. cit.* The X indicates that the country is ranking among the first 30 out of 140 countries with reference to the *Cooperation in Labour-employer Relations* and *Flexibility of Wage Determination* indexes.

[38] Tiraboschi, M.2012. "I paradossi di una riforma sbagliata (e che si farà, anche se non piace a nessuno)", and Tomassetti, P. 2012."Riforma del lavoro: una sconfitta della concertazione o delle relazioni industriali?", *Lavoro: una riforma a metà del guado. Prime osservazioni sul DDL n. 3249/2012, Disposizioni in materia di riforma del mercato del lavoro in una prospettiva di crescita,* eds. Rausei, P., and M. Tiraboschi, Adapt University Press, at www.bollettinoadapt.it.

[39] ILO. 2012. *World of Work Report 2012. Better Jobs for a Better Economy*, cit.

The present article has aimed to point out the marginal role played by labour market liberalisation reforms, showing instead that institutional factors are of fundamental importance when concerning youth employment. These factors include the quality of the education system, apprenticeship as a work-based training opportunity, efficiency and quality of the industrial relations system and more generally, of labour market institutions. There is therefore scope for a new strand of research based on a cross-sectoral approach and intended to verify the assumption presented in the previous paragraphs and focusing on the determinants of youth employment and related problems in an interdisciplinary fashion.

To those who are aware of the complexity of the subject, these issues cannot be addressed and solved with legislative interventions alone.

CHAPTER TWO

ANTI-CRISIS LABOUR MARKET MEASURES AND THEIR EFFECTIVENESS BETWEEN FLEXIBILITY AND SECURITY

1. Introduction[1]

Following the GDP decrease resulting from the economic crisis, the EU Member States experienced a higher level of unemployment and a decline in terms of employment rates. However, the implementation of so-called anti-crisis measures limited such increase—in some cases not to be as high as expected—in the majority of the EU Member States.

With the view to minimise the impact of the downturn in social terms and support both companies and employees, the European Union took a number of actions to drive the economic recovery and coordinate EU Member States public interventions,[2] with Member States adjusting existing labour market policies and/or introducing new ones. In this connection, the majority of Member States launched *ad-hoc* and comprehensive "anti-crisis packages" consisting of a variety of measures to cope with the recession and resulting in a wide range of public policy tools aiming at reducing the impact of the crisis on the labour market.

The aim of this paper is to analyse the relation between different labour market policy combinations issued by Member States and their social protection systems and employment protection legislation, also considered as a combination of flexibility and security tools, and to try to assess their effectiveness in tackling the crisis. The results could be useful when considering possible changes of social protection systems or social models with the purpose of balancing flexibility and security.

---

[1] The present contribution has been produced in collaboration with Silvia Spattini and was previously published in Davulis, T., and D. Petrylaite. 2012. *Labour Regulation in the 21st Century: In Search of Flexibility and Security*, Cambridge Scholars Publishing, Adapt Labour Studies Book Series No. 2, 163.

[2] European Commission. 2008. *A European Economic Recovery Plan*, COM (2008)800. Brussels: European Commission.

2. The Crisis in Figures

The starting point of the analysis is the set of figures describing the changes in the European labour market during the crisis.

Between the second quarter of 2008 and the second quarter of 2009, the real GDP in the EU (27 Member States) fell by almost 5%.

Fig. 1-8. GDP—Percentage Change on Previous Period

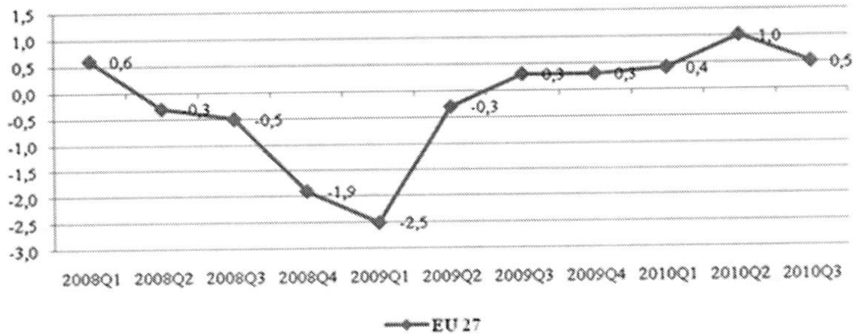

Source: Eurostat, seasonally adjusted and adjusted data by working days

- The fall in GDP caused a reduction of labour demand and, accordingly, an increase in unemployment and a decrease in employment.
- The figures show a considerable difference in the impact of the crisis on the 27 EU Member States, particularly if one compares unemployment rates in July 2008—that is before the crisis—and July 2010.
- Although regarded as emerging economies before the downturn, countries such as Spain and Ireland reported a significant increase in unemployment. More specifically, the levels of unemployment almost doubled in a two-year span, with this issue becoming a serious concern.

The same happened to the Baltic States (Estonia, Lithuania and Latvia), which experienced the highest rates of unemployment in Europe (Fig. 1-9).

Looking at the trends in Fig. 1-10, Latvia, Estonia, Lithuania, Ireland and Spain also recorded the highest decrease in terms of employment rates. A case in point was Denmark, which, before the crisis, had a low level of unemployment, and during the economic downturn experienced a worsening of labour market situation. Here, despite the unemployment levels (7.3% in July 2010) were not very high and lower than the EU average (9.6%), such levels experienced a critical increase and doubled in a two-year period. At the same time, the employment rate dropped by 2%, which was more than the EU average.

The situation of the labour market is less worrying in countries like Germany, Austria, Belgium, the Netherlands and Italy, where the rise in unemployment rates was in no case higher than 1.7%, with the decrease in employment rates not being as significant as in the countries mentioned above.

Indeed, Germany represents a unique case: after a very limited increase in unemployment (0.4% in July 2009 compared to July 2008), an unexpected reduction was reported in 2010, with concurrent growth in the levels of employment.

Fig. 1-9. Unemployment Rate Change and Unemployment Rate 2010/07

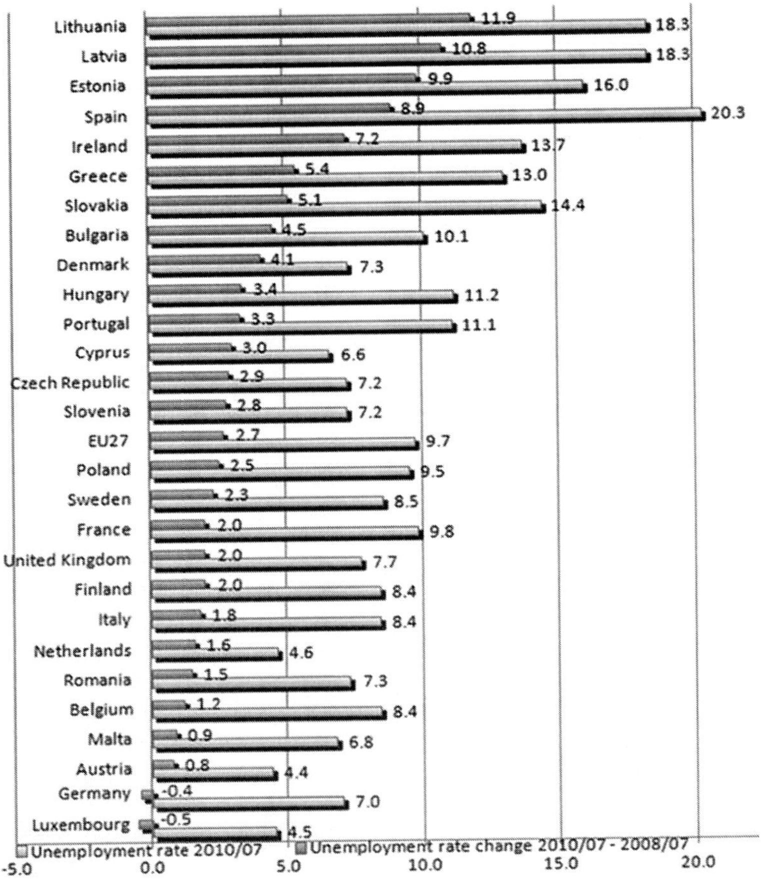

Source: Own Elaboration on Eurostat data

Such variability among European countries, and the little impact of the recession on some of them, is not coincidental.

Although it is "too early to draw final conclusions",[3] there is evidence that the different performance levels within national labour markets result

[3] European Commission. 2010a. "Short Time Working Arrangements as Response to Cyclical Fluctuation", European Economy, Occasional Papers No. 64. Luxembourg: European Commission.

from the diversified nature of labour regulation and existing labour market policies, along with new measures taken by governments to combat the crisis.

Fig. 1-10. Change in Employment Rate 2010Q2-2008Q2

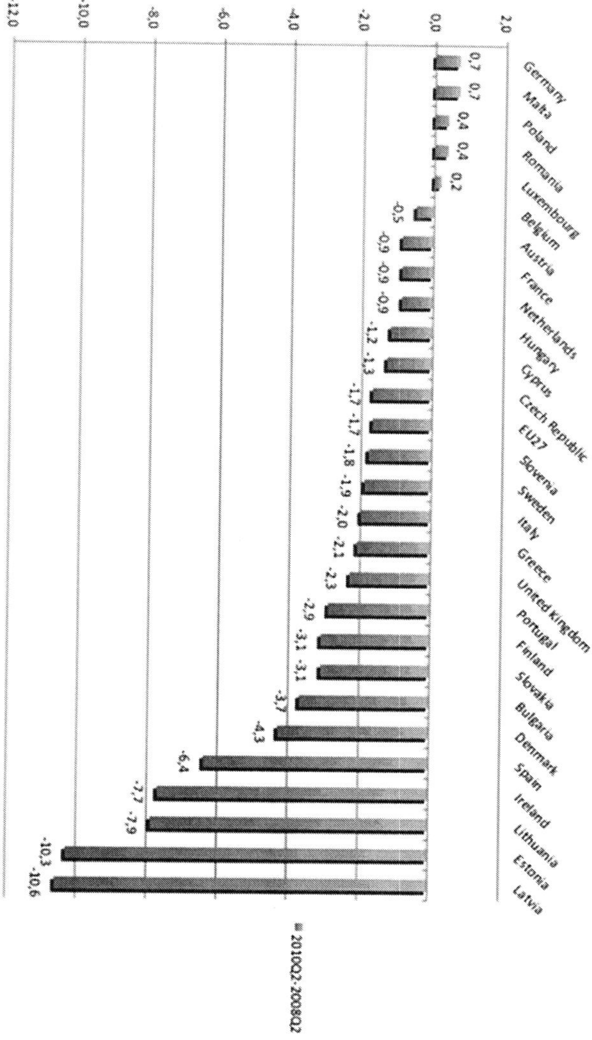

Source: Own Elaboration on Eurostat data

3. Anti-crisis Measures across Europe

The combination of several factors at a national level actually produced 27 different ways in which the economic downturn hit the EU Member States. In addition, there were 27 different responses to the crisis. Each country has adopted a set of measures—therefore not a single initiative among which it is possible to identify the most frequently implemented ones.[4]

In order to assess the effectiveness of these policies, it is necessary to review existing legislation and classify measures implemented by every European country, in accordance with a simple scheme.

Moreover, it is necessary to take into consideration that labour market policies adopted by national governments vary considerably especially in terms of issues concerning the role played by social partners in each country.

Their participation in the development and implementation of anti-crisis measures and to the adjustment of existing labour market tools differs across Europe also if one considers the level and the extent of their involvement in public policy design. This depends on the diversity of functions performed by social dialogue over the time, and the power of each government to operate in the present situation.

In Austria, Belgium, Italy, Germany and the Netherlands—countries with a well-established social partnership—agreements among social partners significantly contributed to the drawing up of stimulus packages.

As regards collective bargaining, opening clauses allow company-level agreements to derogate from sectoral collective agreements in order to cut costs and safeguard employment (i.e. derogation to the general framework). These agreements usually envisage the extension of working time without full compensation in pay or cuts in working time, cuts in benefits or delays in agreed pay increases.

The classification of policy measures is a preliminary step to verify whether—at least intuitively and while waiting for empirical evidence—there is a relation between patterns of labour market policies adopted by Member States and the trends of the national labour market during the crisis.

To date, key reports from the European Commission, OECD and EU institutions have analysed public interventions in the labour market. In particular the European Foundation for the Improvement of Living and

---

[4] European Commission. 2009. *Recovering from the Crisis—27 Ways of Tackling the Employment Challenge*. Luxembourg: European Commission.

Working Conditions (from now on Eurofound) has provided a useful classification of crisis-related measures implemented in the EU Member States.[5] This classification is based on three different types of interventions: 1) measures to create employment or to promote re-insertion, 2) measures to maintain employment, 3) income support measures for the unemployed.

3.1. Measures to Create Employment and to Promote Re-insertion

Measures to create employment aim at promoting the hiring of employees by means of economic incentives, mainly consisting in a reduction of non-wage labour costs and wage subsidies, or public sector job creation. In some countries (France, Germany, Italy, Portugal, Slovenia, Sweden), economic incentives for companies are provided to hire special target groups. Support measures for self-employment, based on the provision of consultancy and training (Bulgaria, the UK) or the reduction/defer of social security payments also fall within this category. Several Member States (Austria, Italy, Lithuania, Portugal, the UK) have introduced or extended subsidies for start-ups.

Measures to promote reintegration into employment, put into action by employment services, try to enhance the transition from unemployment to employment by addressing job mismatch, supporting job matching by means of counselling, career guidance, job-search assistance, activation measures and by increasing employability through training. Efforts have been made to improve and adapt public employment services in order to manage the higher number of "clients" (for example hiring additional staff, as in Germany, Norway, Spain, and the UK) and to financially support private employment agencies through economic and/or normative incentives (the Netherlands, Italy). In the same vein, and with the view to make workers more willing to accept a new job, mobility grants are envisaged (the Czech Republic, Lithuania, Slovakia). In Belgium, for instance, employees that agree to move their residence in order to accept a job offer obtain tax benefits.

---

[5] Mandl, I., and L. Salvatore. 2009. *Tackling the Recession: Employment-related Public Initiatives in the EU Member States and Norway.* Dublin: European Foundation for the Improvement of Living and Working Conditions. Hurley, J., I. Mandl, D. Storrie, and T. Ward. 2009. "Restructuring in Recession", ERM Report 2009. Dublin: European Foundation for the Improvement of Living and Working Conditions.

3.2. Income Support for Unemployed People

Income support for unemployed people mainly comprises unemployment benefits, provided to reduce the socio-economic consequences of job loss.

Unemployment benefit schemes exist in every EU Member State, even though amendments (in some cases temporary) have been made at a national level to their regulation in order to respond to the increased number of unemployed people resulting from the crisis. Relevant changes concerned the following aspects: eligibility criteria, amount, duration of entitlement, and beneficiaries. More specifically, some countries relaxed the rules for entitlement to unemployment benefits (Finland, France, Sweden), while others extended their duration: Romania has envisaged an extension of 3 months, Latvia extended such period to 9 months and in Poland it passed from 12 to 18 months. In the Czech Republic, the Government has opted for an increase in the amount of funds, while Italy introduced special benefits for quasi-subordinate workers, yet to be provided on a temporary basis.

3.3. Measures to Maintain Employment

Measures to maintain employment have the purpose to prevent dismissals and preserve existing jobs. Among them, mention should be made of short-time work arrangements and compensation.

4. Short-Time Work Schemes

Short-time work may take the form of a temporary reduction in working time or a temporary lay-off. In both cases, the employment relationship between employers and employees persists and the arrangements have a limited duration.[6]

Compensation for income loss is usually envisaged in case of short-time work, in the form of social security payments, to be either state-funded—by means of taxes—or based on social security contributions.

Nevertheless, short-time work compensation systems across Europe differ considerably from one another in terms of: procedures, involvement of trade unions, "back-to-normal" plans, coverage, compensation,

---

[6] European Commission. 2010a. "Short Time Working Arrangements as Response to Cyclical Fluctuation", European Economy, Occasional Papers No. 64. Luxembourg: European Commission.

eligibility criteria. Moreover, it is possible to distinguish between well-established systems and innovative schemes introduced to face the crisis.

In the first case (which includes Germany, Austria, Belgium, France, and Italy), the compensation system is part of the unemployment benefit system, in that employers and employees pay social contributions to a fund or to the unemployment insurance system so that in the event of short-time working or temporary lay-off, employees are covered by these funds for the lost income as a consequence of the working hours reduction.

Conversely, in Member States (e.g. The Netherlands, Poland, Hungary, Slovakia) that introduced, whether temporary or not, short-time work compensation as a new measure during the crisis, such new arrangements are not part of the unemployment insurance system and therefore they are funded by the State through taxes.

Short-time work compensation can be classified also on the basis of its function. In some national systems, it takes the form of part-time unemployment benefits.[7] This means that employees in working hours reduction or in temporary lay-off are regarded as people working on a part-time basis seeking full-time employment and, in some cases, they have to be available for a new job despite the employment contract with their employer is still in force.

In the majority of EU Member States, even if short-time work schemes envisage lost income compensation within the unemployment insurance system, they represent a form of job protection against dismissal.

With reference to this measure, it is possible to point out that it might be of benefit to different actors involved in the national economic arena. Needless to say, employees benefit from short-time work schemes since measures of this kind avoid dismissal and help maintaining existing jobs, at the same time ensuring income support by compensating lost income.

However, short-time work schemes have many pros for employers. First of all, these arrangements allow companies to preserve human capital and skills that will be necessary in the recovery phase. This also translates into saving potential costs related to personnel turnover, dismissal, recruitment process, and training.

Short-time work compensation is a convenient measure also from the viewpoint of governments, as it helps to maintain social peace and cohesion in that employers and employees share the impact of the downturn. Finally, such arrangements represent a flexible tool for

---

[7] European Commission. 2010a. "Short Time Working Arrangements as Response to Cyclical Fluctuation", European Economy, Occasional Papers 64. Luxembourg: European Commission.

governments that are able to somehow control the adjustment of the labour market.

5. Policies Mix Adapted or Adopted by the EU Member States

In order to analyse the relation between different combinations of labour market measures implemented by Member States and their social models, it is necessary to consider *in toto* the set of labour market policies—both new or amended ones—that the EU Member States put into action to face the crisis.

Table 1-3 represents the measures adopted or adapted (if already existing) by each EU Member State against this background. The EU countries have been singled out by increasing unemployment rate growth (considering the difference between July 2010 and July 2008), ranked from the best to the worst performer.

Although at the early stages of the analysis, it is possible to point out that the countries with the most significant increase in unemployment rates did not envisage or did not amend existing short-time work schemes.

On the contrary, EU Member States with good labour market performances, such as Austria, Belgium, Germany, Italy, and Luxembourg, had already issued measures of this kind in their system, yet making them more flexible in the last years, in consideration of the needs of the moment, and improved or adapted by combining them to training and/or to activation measures. Other countries, such as the Netherlands and Romania, have introduced (even on a temporary basis like the Netherlands) short-time work schemes to face the recession.

The next step is to contextualise such different combinations of policies in the wider regulatory framework of the national labour markets, taking into consideration the relevant social model.

There are two main social models in Europe: the new welfare system model and the flexicurity model.

The first one is characterised by rigid employment protection legislation (particularly in the event of dismissal), an ungenerous unemployment benefit system, a minimum level of implementation of active labour market policies and activation policies through public employment services. We decided to term this model "new" welfare system, as a way to distinguish it from the traditional one, in which active labour market policies and activation policies were usually in a very limited manner.

On the other hand, the flexicurity model is based on a generous unemployment benefit system, high levels of implementation of active labour market policies and activation policies, and efficient public employment services.

Examples of the first model can be found in countries like Germany, Austria, Belgium, and Italy, while Denmark has always been the model of flexicurity, together with Finland, Sweden, Norway and the Netherlands.

Even in this case, by looking at the labour market performance of these countries, and also by considering their social model, it clearly emerges that countries resorting to the new welfare system model had a lower increase in unemployment rates, while flexicurity countries, especially Denmark, experienced a more significant rise.

Table 1-3. Measures Adopted by EU Member States

	STW Compen-sations	Training activities during the time off/ Training Support for Employees	Reduction/ deferral of non-wage labor costs	Public Expen-diture	Income tax cut	Incentives to employ additional workers	Direct Enterprise support (loan guarantees, low interest loans)	Mobility Grants	(Re-) Training of unemployed people	Improving employment services	Unemployment benefits (amendments)
Germany	+	+	+			+	+			+	
Luxembourg	+	+							+		
Malta		+									
Austria	+	+							+		
Romania	new		+				+			+	+
Belgium	+	+	+					+			
Netherlands	new	compulsory	+			+	+		+	+	
Italy	+	+							+		
Finland									+	+	+

United Kingdom		+				+				+	+
France	+	+		+		+	+		+		+
Sweden			+			+				+	+
Poland	new				+		+		+		+
EU 27											
Czech Republic	new	compulsory	+					+			+
Portugal	+	+	+			+					
Slovenia	new	compulsory				+	+				
Hungary	new	compulsory	+			+	+				
Cyprus		+									
Denmark											+
Bulgaria	new		+			+				+	
Greece		+				+					
Slovakia			+					+			
Ireland		+							+		+
Spain				+					+	+	
Estonia					+		+		+		+
Lithuania		+			+		+	+			
Latvia		+			+		+		+		+

Source: Own Elaboration

6. The Effectiveness of Labour Market Measures

This analysis tries to identify which system and policies seem to provide a higher level of effectiveness in tackling the crisis and to collect information that could be useful on a general basis while deciding which labour market policies to implement.

It is generally acknowledged that it takes time to evaluate the effectiveness of the labour market measures. Indeed, and with specific reference to the crisis-related measures, the European Commission itself points out that it is too early to draw final conclusion or to provide an overall assessment.[8]

However, the European Commission and the Employment Committee tried to provide in a joint paper some evidence on the effectiveness of the main labour market policies adopted and implemented by EU Member States during the crisis and, more generally, they review evaluations of the effectiveness of similar measures implemented in the past.[9] The OECD, on the other hand, gives evidence of the effectiveness particularly of short-time work schemes applied during the recession.[10]

Considering the three different types of labour market policies taken into consideration in this paper (measures to create employment or to promote re-insertion; measures to maintain employment and income support for the unemployed), measures to maintain employment in the form of short-time working arrangements, wage subsidies, and non-wage cost reductions are deemed to have successfully limited the decrease in employment rates[11] and the rise of unemployment, by preventing lay-offs.

Among measures of this kind implemented by the Member States, some of them—particularly short-time work schemes—have been crucial in preserving jobs[12] proving more effective than others.[13]

---

[8] European Commission. 2010a. "Short Time Working Arrangements as Response to Cyclical Fluctuation", European Economy, Occasional Papers No. 64. Luxembourg: European Commission, 6.

[9] Employment Committee, European Commission. 2010. *The Choice of Effective Employment Policies Measures to Mitigate Jobless Recovery in Times of Fiscal Austerity*. Brussels: European Commission.

[10] OECD. 2010. *Employment Outlook, Moving Beyond The Jobs Crisis.* Paris: OECD, 11, 56 ff.

[11] European Commission. 2010b. *Employment in Europe 2010.* Brussels: European Commission, 11.

[12] OECD. 2010. *Employment Outlook, Moving Beyond The Jobs Crisis.* Paris: OECD.

Nevertheless, commentators point out the most critical issues related to short-time work arrangements, that is the fact that they may artificially maintain employment in declining industries instead of allowing an efficient reallocation of employment. There is agreement about the negative impact associated with the deadweight, substitution and displacement.[14] In order to face these distortions, some countermeasures can be taken, in particular short-time work schemes need to be provided for a shorter period and arranged on the basis of more precise criteria, notably eligibility conditions and limited duration of the scheme.

With reference to measures to create employment, job subsidies consisting in hiring incentives or reduction of non-wage labor costs are effective in terms of job creation, but they are costly measures and can lead to negative consequences in terms of deadweight effects. At the same time, public sector job creation is less likely than other policies to provide a positive impact.[15]

As regards measures to promote re-insertion, training has a little impact on employment and it is more likely to be associated with times of high unemployment. In general, then, positive training effects become evident in the long run.[16]

On the contrary, job search assistance and activation measures have a positive impact on employment and are effective in the short run, but they need an economic context characterised by growing or stable labour demand. Only if there is labour demand, is it possible to support job search and matching and help workers' re-insertion in the labour market. For this reason, such measures are mainly adopted in the recovery phase.

Generally speaking, income support for the unemployed has a negative effect on unemployment, since it discourages job search and re-insertion in the labour market. In order to reduce the negative effects in terms of efficiency, some adjustments can be made, such as decreasing the amount of benefits and reducing the period through which such support is provided. Besides, unemployment benefits are linked to activation policies, which require active job search from jobseekers, and sanctions

---

[13] Employment Committee, European Commission. 2010. *The Choice of Effective Employment Policies Measures to Mitigate Jobless Recovery in Times of Fiscal Austerity*. Brussels: European Commission.

[14] OECD. 2010. *Employment Outlook, Moving Beyond The Jobs Crisis.* Paris: OECD.

[15] Kluve, J. 2007. *The Effectiveness of European Active Labor Market Policy.* Bonn: IZA.

[16] Ibid.

are applied in case of refusal to actively search for work and to accept suitable job offers.

6.1. Public Expenditure on Labour Market Policies

The question of effectiveness of labour market policies is fundamental not only with reference to crisis-related measures, but also for EU Member States following an increase in budgetary constraints.

In 2009 (and most likely even in 2010), the European Commission reported that EU countries increased their expenditure on labour market interventions and income support by 0.7% of annual GDP, while before the crisis, public expenditure on labour market policies experienced a decline. In fact, in 2008, public expenditure on labour market policies in the European Union amounted to just 1.6% of total EU-27 GDP, though there were considerable variations between the Member States (Fig. 1-11).

For this reason, EU governments need to be aware of the most effective policy mix in order to direct public expenditure.

It seems interesting to compare data on labour market policies expenditure and the trends of the unemployment rate during the crisis. The data on public expenditure for all countries are available only 18-20 months after the reference period, thus at the moment Eurostat only provides data for the year 2008.

In any case, considering that the labour market policies impact on the labour market itself is not immediate, but requires a period of time to become evident, it seems reasonable to compare data on public expenditure for 2008 and the unemployment rate growth over the last two years.

Member States with the lowest increase in the unemployment rates in 2009 compared to 2008, were the same that in 2008 reported considerable high labour market policies expenditure, notably Belgium, Germany, the Netherlands, and Austria with more than 1.8% of their GDP.

This trend is confirmed even if one compares the growth in the unemployment rates between 2008 and 2010 and the labour market policies expenditure for 2008.

Fig. 1-11. Total LMP Expenditure 2008 and Unemployment Rate Growth 2009/07-2008/07

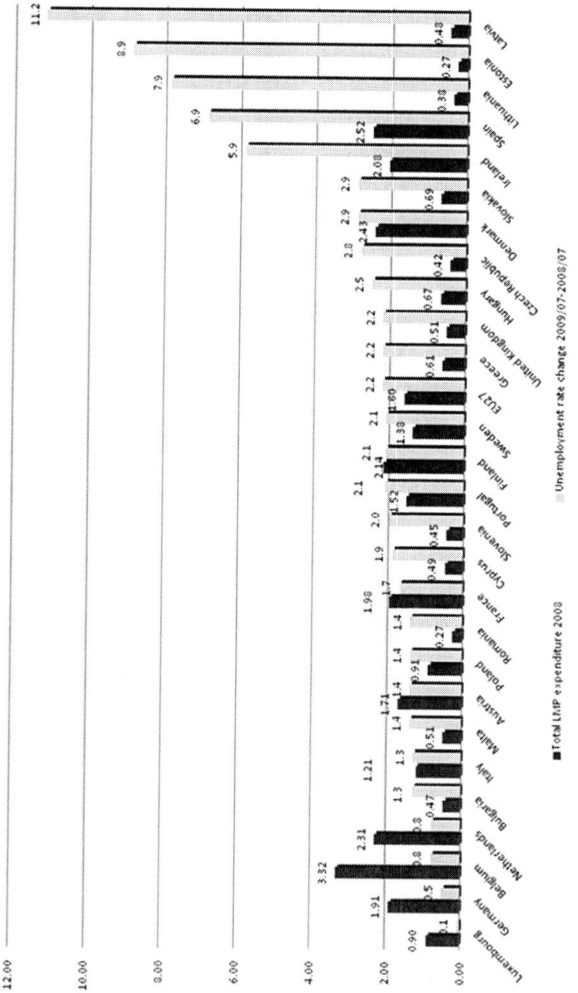

Source: Own Elaboration on Eurostat data

Fig. 1-12. Total LMP expenditure 2008 and Unemployment Rate Growth 2010/07-2008/07

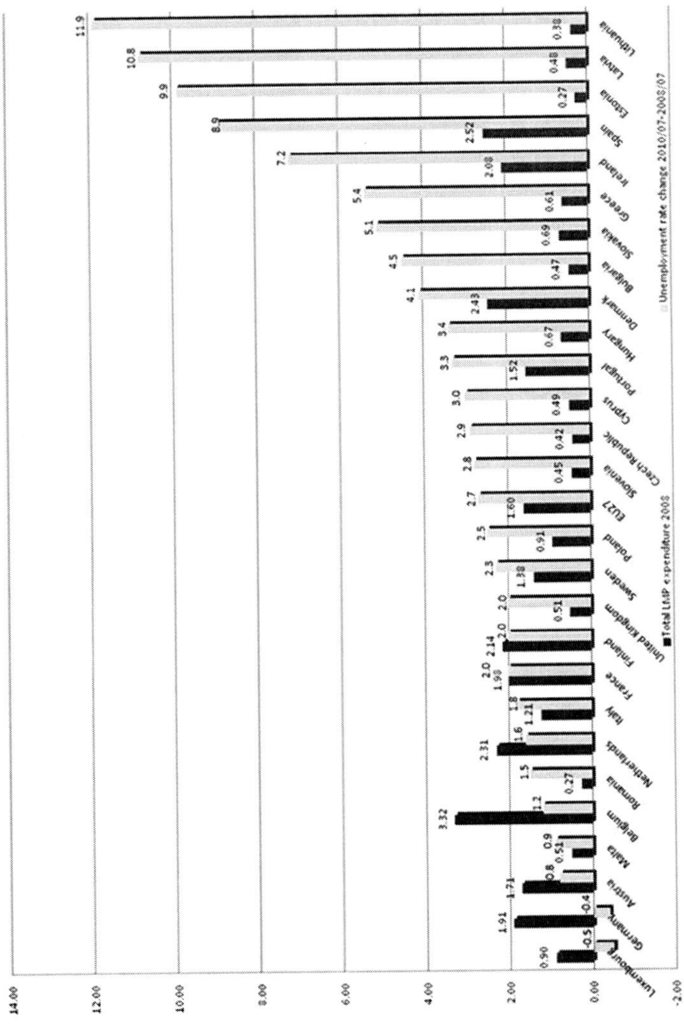

Source: Own Elaboration on Eurostat data

6.2. The Effectiveness of the Social Model

These figures give the opportunity for further observations and remarks. In Denmark, total public expenditure on labour market policies in 2008 was quite high (as it traditionally is). It was the third highest spending country among those surveyed. Nevertheless, the rise in the unemployment rates was high. This situation suggests looking at the types of policies implemented and at the social model adopted in Denmark.

Indeed, this country has been and still is an interesting case with reference to the performance of the labour market during the crisis. It is regarded as a role model of flexicurity (see below), characterised by: non-restrictive dismissal protection legislation, generous unemployment benefits, consistent adoption of active labour market policies, and efficient public employment services. Before the crisis, this system ensured low unemployment rates and a quick re-insertion of jobseekers in the labour market. During the crisis, however, this system proved to have some shortcomings, and Denmark had doubled the levels of unemployment: from 3.2% in July 2008 to 6.5% in September 2009 (the highest level was reached in April 2010: 7.4%).

The aim of this system is not to prevent dismissal but rather to support a quick transition between jobs and re-insertion in the labour market. Nevertheless, if labour demand is low, workers' reinsertion is not possible or is very difficult.

In addition, Denmark does not envisage a "real" short-time work compensation system, even though companies may use short-time work arrangements and employees involved are eligible for part-time unemployment benefits. They must fulfil the contributory requirements for eligibility to total unemployment benefits and have to be available for a new occupation despite the employment contract with the same employer is still in force. In practice, it seems that this provision is not strictly applied, if the employee has the possibility to stay in the company.

Looking at the labour market performances of the EU Member States, taking into consideration the two different social models adopted in Europe, some interesting remarks are possible.

As regards the growth of the unemployment rates during the crisis, Austria, Belgium, Germany, and to some extent Italy, are regarded as countries with the lowest increase. The social model of all these EU Member States can be classified as a new welfare system.

Table 1-4. Comparison between the New Welfare System and the Flexicurity Model

Systems	Employment protection legislation	Unemployment benefit	STW compensations	Effective in the crisis
New welfare	Stringent dismissal protection legislation	Non generous: • Short duration • Low replacement rate	Yes	More effective (Germany, Austria Belgium, Italy)
Flexicurity	Non-restrictive dismissal protection legislation	Generous: • Long duration • High replacement rate	No or very limited as partial unemployment benefit	Less effective (mainly Denmark, Finland, Sweden, the Netherlands)

Source: Own Elaboration

On the contrary, as mentioned, Denmark, which is the reference model for flexicurity, experienced a high increase in unemployment.

Also Finland, Sweden, and the Netherlands (and Norway, though not a Member State) are considered as countries adopting the flexicurity system, but they had better labour market performances than Denmark during recession, even if they reported an increase of the unemployment rates amounting to more than two percent.

Actually, there is an important variation factor between Denmark and the other flexicurity countries, due to employment protection legislation. In fact, Denmark adopts liberally-oriented employment protection legislation, while the other countries have more stringent rules.

Table 1-5. OECD EPL Index

Countries	OECD EPL index
Germany	2.63
Luxembourg	3.39

Malta	-
Austria	2.41
Romania	-
Belgium	2.61
Netherlands	**2.23**
Italy	2.58
Finland	**2.29**
United Kingdom	1.09
France	2.90
Sweden	**2.06**
Poland	2.41
European Union	2.41
Czech Republic	2.32
Portugal	2.84
Slovenia	2.76
Hungary	2.11
Cyprus	-
Denmark	**1.91**
Bulgaria	-
Greece	2.97
Slovakia	2.13
Ireland	1.39
Spain	3.11
Lithuania	-
Latvia	-
Estonia	2.39

Source: OECD

Among flexicurity countries, the Netherlands is the only country characterised by a lower rise in the unemployment rate. In this case, it is worth pointing out that the Netherlands introduced short-time work compensation of a temporary nature, while Finland has a system similar to the Danish one and Sweden does not envisage any.

On the basis of these observations and considering evidence from labour market policies effectiveness, the new welfare system model appears to be more adequate in facing the crisis, while the flexicurity system, as seen, had and still has difficulty in this connection, and turns out to be less effective in controlling the increase in unemployment.

It is not completely clear whether this is due to short-time working arrangements or to the presence in the new welfare system model of a stringent regulation against individual or collective dismissal. It might probably depend on both aspects, also because they are related.

Now, in considering social models and labour market policy combinations applied by the EU Member States, there is not a unique "best solution" to tackle "different variety" of economic recessions. It is also important to understand the context and the legal framework in which any possible solution has to be implemented.

7. Active and Passive Labour Market Policies between Flexibility and Security

Over the last two decades, and with reference to labour market policies to be implemented by countries, the international institutions (OECD and the European Commission, among others) put emphasis on active labour market policies rather than passive ones, therefore addressing public interventions mainly towards active measures.

Looking from this standpoint at the policies packages applied by the EU Member States, at the beginning of the crisis there was a critical approach towards short-time work arrangements. Observers and commentators constantly pointed out the labour market distortions and limitations associated with these schemes. A reason for that, since they are income support measures, could be the passive nature of labour market policy.

But recently, and perhaps thanks to the effectiveness in tackling the crisis, it seems that authors look at these schemes in a different way.

Indeed, a recent report of Eurofound,[17] describing the effectiveness of short-time work schemes, tries to link these measures to the flexicurity principles, by stressing how they serve the implementation of flexicurity.

In examining the functioning of short-time work schemes, it is easy to see them as a tool for flexicurity, combining internal flexibility and job and income security. In fact, the scope for a reduction of working hours (till zero hours) allows internal flexibility for employers (based exactly on flexible working time arrangements). At the same time, this provision prevents dismissals and helps employees to stay in their current position, enhancing job security. Moreover, wage compensation linked to short-time work arrangement ensures income security for the employees, thanks to the continuity of income, granted through either remuneration or unemployment benefits.

Among the other types of labour market policy measures mentioned above concerning flexicurity, those which promote re-insertion and create employment are fundamental resources for guaranteeing employment security, that is continuity of employment, not necessarily within the same employer.

On the other hand, income support for unemployed people has the obvious purpose of ensuring income security in case of dismissal and can be seen as complementing external flexibility.

8. Concluding Remarks

While wondering if and which changes may be necessary in the national system—intended as a combination of the social security system—employment protection legislation, the public employment services system and labour market policies applied, it can be probably useful to take into consideration the different aspects highlighted.

The crisis has created a sort of *laboratory* in which it was somehow possible to conduct experiments on the functioning of different national system.

Before the crisis, European and international institutions took in great consideration the flexicurity principles dominated by external flexibility and employment security based on non- or low-restrictive employment protection legislation (and dismissal rules), supported by a generous unemployment benefit system, efficient public employment services, and

---

[17] Mandl, I., J. Hurley, M. Mascherini, and D. Storriel. 2010. *Extending Flexicurity—The Potential of Short-time Working Schemes*. Dublin: European Foundation for the Improvement of Living and Working Conditions.

high level of active labour market policies. From this point of view, the prevailing measures should be those aiming at creating employment or, to be more precise, at promoting workers' re-insertion, giving momentum to transition between jobs. By launching the EU flexicurity strategy, the European Union promoted internal and external flexicurity "accompanied by secure transition from job to job".[18]

Before the crisis, the shift of the old model towards the flexicurity one became a matter of urgency. However, the economic downturn raised awareness on the fact that this formulation was suitable for a period of economic growth and to face structural unemployment, which need in particular measures to support workers' re-insertion by addressing job mismatch, and to promote job matching by means of counselling, career guidance, job search assistance, activation measures and employability through training.

Indeed, a flexicurity strategy based on external flexibility and employment security, as described above, was not able to stand the impact of the recession. In such a situation, and in order to limit the related socio-economic consequences, policy measures to maintain employment and keep employees at work proved to be indispensable.

Therefore, in an attempt to plan an appropriate combination of the above mentioned elements, it is necessary to balance the different kinds of flexibility and security and to bear in mind that measures and tools should be put into place both in a period of economic growth and recession.

References

Employment Committee, European Commission. 2010. *The Choice of Effective Employment Policies Measures to Mitigate Jobless Recovery in Times of Fiscal Austerity*. Brussels: European Commission.

European Commission. 2007. *Towards Common Principles of Flexicurity: More and Better Jobs through Flexibility and Security*, COM (2007)359.

—. 2008. *A European Economic Recovery Plan*, COM (2008) 800.

—. 2009. *Recovering from the Crisis—27 Ways of Tackling the Employment Challenge*. Luxembourg: European Commission.

—. 2010a. "Short Time Working Arrangements as Response to Cyclical Fluctuation" European Economy, Occasional Papers 64.

[18] European Commission. 2007. *Towards Common Principles of Flexicurity: More and Better Jobs Through Flexibility and Security*, COM(2007) 359. Brussels: European Commission.

—. 2010b. *Employment in Europe 2010.*
Hurley, J., I. Mandl, D. Storrie, and T. Ward. 2009. "Restructuring in Recession," ERM Report 2009. Dublin: European Foundation for the Improvement of Living and Working Conditions.
Kluve, J. 2007. *The Effectiveness of European Active Labor Market Policy*. Bonn: IZA.
Mandl, I., and L. Salvatore. 2009. *Tackling the Recession: Employment-related Public Initiatives in the EU Member States and Norway.* Dublin: European Foundation for the Improvement of Living and Working Conditions.
Mandl, I., J. Hurley, M. Mascherini, and D. Storriel. 2010. *Extending Flexicurity—The Potential of Short-time Working Schemes*. Dublin: European Foundation for the Improvement of Living and Working Conditions.
OECD. 2010. *Employment Outlook, Moving Beyond the Jobs Crisis.* Paris: OECD.

CHAPTER THREE

ITALIAN LABOUR LAW AFTER THE SO-CALLED MONTI-FORNERO REFORM (ACT NO. 92/2012)

1. The Reform of the Labour Market in Italy: Main Reasons and General Framework[1]

Prompted by the main European and international financial institutions, and in response to a particular—and in many respects unique—institutional and political scenario, the technocratic government led by Mario Monti carried forward an impressive reform of the Italian labour market just a few months after its appointment.

This state of affairs gave rise to an array of interventions across all economic and social sectors that—albeit long-awaited[2]—previous administrations have been unable to put in place. Act No. 92 of 28 June 2012 was preceded by an even more substantial and widely debated overhaul of the pension system[3] and was intended to amend the regulatory framework of the Italian labour market. Once the newly installed

---

[1] The present contribution was previously published in 2012 in the *E-Journal of International and Comparative Labour Studies* 1, No. 3-4:47-86.

[2] See *The White Paper on the Labour Market*, which was drafted by Marco Biagi on 3 October 2001 under the Berlusconi Government. Significantly, most of the objectives set down by Mr. Monti and the Minister of Labour Elsa Fornero were already outlined by Prof Biagi ten years ago. An English version of the document is available in Blanpain, R., ed. 2002. "White Paper on The Labour Market In Italy, The Quality of European Industrial Relations and Changing Industrial Relations", *Bulletin of Comparative Labour Relations*.

[3] For an overview of the reform of the pension system in the context of the so-called "Decree to Save Italy" see *Monti's £30 billion survival plan,* on *http://www.eurofound.europa.eu/eiro/2012/01/articles/it1201039i.htm* (last accessed: 1 October 2012).

government took office, and straight from the inaugural address, the measure was presented for public opinion as a matter of urgency. In discussing the current macro-economic context, the reform of the national labour market was portrayed as an inevitable move to secure the future of younger generations—most notably in terms of job opportunities and pension entitlement—as they have been hit the hardest by the crisis that was caused by the collapse of the financial markets.[4]

This is consistent with the view—not prevailing, although well established among European commentators and decision-makers—that high unemployment rates, chiefly among young people, coupled with the steady increase in atypical and precarious employment, have been brought about by the high levels of protection for workers in salaried employment.

An authoritative indication of this line of reasoning is the move made during the financial downturn by the President of the European Central Bank, Mario Draghi.

In order to safeguard the future of the youngest generations, Mr. Draghi openly questioned the long-term sustainability of the European social model. In this sense, he prodded European law-makers into reviewing national labour laws, deemed to be unbalanced in favour of adult workers (the insiders), particularly in the current recession.

The Italian Government followed Mr. Draghi's advice carefully, fuelling a polemical discussion concerning the European Central Bank and some other European bodies allegedly placing Italy under special administration. This state of play *de facto* impinged on the effort—to date successful—on the part of both trade unions and pro-labour political parties, to counter the decisions made unilaterally by the Government.[5]

---

[4] For an in-depth analysis on the reasons for the reform, particularly to offset the levels of protection offered to young people against those supplied to their adult counterparts see Tiraboschi, M. 2012. "Young Workers in Recessionary Times: A Caveat to (Continental) Europe to Reconstruct its Labour Law?" in this book.

[5] At the time of Silvio Berlusconi's last term in office, trade unions were definitely given more room to manoeuvre following the passing of Article 8 of Legislative Decree No. 138/2012 on the reform of the labour market. Then as now, the Government was prompted by the European institutions to take action. It thus empowered collective bargaining at company and territorial level to implement certain employment safeguards by way of derogation from national bargaining, in order to cope with the crisis and favor economic growth. Of course the levels of protection set down by the international Conventions, Community legislation, as well as certain limitations concerning labour issues imposed upon by the Italian Constitution were still valid. On that occasion, social partners succeeded in challenging the measures put forward by the Government. See various comments in *Diritto delle Relazioni Industriali*, No. 3, 2012 (under *Ricerche*).

As will be discussed further, Act No. 92/2012 (hereafter the Monti-Fornero Reform) has introduced numerous innovative measures. This aspect could be observed, as this substantial piece of legislation consists of 270 controversial paragraphs, yet grouped into four articles to expedite the approval process. For different reasons, the reform was hailed with outright hostility by the social partners (see par. 6). Such a reaction pressured the Legislator to promptly amend the provision, with a number of changes that were already foreseen by the Parliament and took place one month after its enforcement.[6]

The reform greatly impacted the main aspects of Italian labour law, namely the legal procedures to establish and terminate the employment relationship. It also deals with the sources of labour law; this is because of the preference that has been given to the norms of a compulsory character, which narrows down the role of trade union law, particularly company customs. In addition, social concertation—once pivotal in the evolution of labour law in Italy—played a peripheral role while the provision was being devised.

In contrast to what occurred in some other European countries—most notably in Spain[7]—the reform does not touch upon internal flexibility that is the set of legal provisions governing the employment relationship (personnel and job classification, working hours, job description, absence from work, and so forth). These aspects—which are clearly of great importance—still fall within the province of collective bargaining or are subject to mandatory forms of regulation that date back to the 1970s, such as Law No. 300/1970 (the Workers' Statute).

This approach further upholds the trend towards legal abstentionism in labour relations, all the more so if the drafters of the reform also refrain from amending the structure and the functioning of collective bargaining.[8]

---

[6] See Act No. 134 of 7 August 2012.

[7] Ley No. 3/2012, *de 6 de Julio, de medidas urgentes para la reforma del mercado laboral*. For a reconstruction of the provisions laid down by the reform of the labour market in Spain, see Martín Hernandez, M. L. 2012. *La última fase de la evolución del derecho del trabajo español: las reformas laborales del bienio 2010-2012*, Bollettino Speciale Adapt No. 17; Navarro Nieto, F. 2012. "Spagna - La riforma del quadro giuridico della contrattazione collettiva", *Diritto delle Relazioni Industriali* No. 3; Baylos, A. 2012."Crisi del diritto del lavoro o diritto del lavoro in crisi: la riforma del lavoro spagnola del 2012", *Diritto delle Relazioni Industriali* No. 2; García Viña, J. 2012. "Il sistema di relazioni industriali in Spagna dopo la riforma della contrattazione collettiva. L'impegno per il contratto d'azienda", *Diritto delle Relazioni Industriali* No. 1.

[8] As a result, and in line with the Italian experience, collective agreements in the private sector are regarded within the common-law framework still governed by

Indeed, the Parliament just delegated to the Government the power to deal with issues concerning economic democracy and workers' participation. Drawing on the German model of co-determination (*Mitbestimmung*), and by means of special provisions that introduced certain participation schemes, the attempt of Italian law-makers has been to move away from the current industrial relations model—which is of a more adversarial nature—to a more cooperative and collaborative approach. The proposal was met with approval by the most reformist unions (the Italian Confederation of Workers' Union—CISL—and the Union of Italian Workers—UIL), whereas both the more antagonist General Confederation of Italian Workers (CGIL)—and the most influential employers' associations (e.g. Confindustria) firmly opposed this approach.

As far as the overall structure of the reform is concerned, the Government's original intentions were to favour more flexibility in hiring by way of open-ended contracts, an aspect that makes the dismissal easier—mainly for economic reasons—concurrently scaling back the scope of atypical and temporary work, both in salaried and quasi-subordinate employment.

One might note, however, that the give-and-take accompanying the approval of the Monti-Fornero Reform and subsequent amendments—e.g. Act No. 134/2012—prejudiced the foregoing plan.[9]

In fact, just a few weeks after the passing of the reform, a number of amendments were made to the provisions on contractual schemes and on the remedies put in place in the event of failing to comply with provisions regulating dismissals for economic reasons. In some respects, the amendments to the reform made it more complicated to conceive the overall structure of the proposal put forward by the Government, as well as the guiding principles underlying the reform process.

The same holds for the reform of the labour market safety-net measures, which, based on the model of Danish flexicurity, could play a key role in enhancing the transition between occupations, as well as

---

the Civil Code of 1942, which, at least in formal terms, are binding on the contracting parties only if they are members of employers' associations and trade unions.

[9] In actual terms, such a proposal would concern only large-sized enterprises, for the vast majority of small and medium-sized companies in Italy already enjoy higher levels of flexibility in dismissals. This is a further explanation of the strong opposition to the proposal on the part of several representative associations (artisans and small employers in the commercial and tertiary sectors), for it reduces the levels of flexibility in hiring without any gains in terms of flexibility in dismissals.

leading to a more adequate balance between flexibility in hiring and flexibility in dismissals. However, a watered-down compromise was eventually reached, since the early proposals made by the Minister of Labour to introduce the guaranteed minimum wage and, above all, to repeal traditional forms of income support were firmly opposed by both social actors and the governing parties.

The review of the safety-net measures introduces a number of significant amendments (see par. 5), yet representing a case of "old wine in a new bottle". In other words, the provision of unemployment benefits funded by social contributions—and not by the general system of taxation, as it was hoped for—is already a well-established practice in Italy. On top of that, this system will only be fully implemented in the years to come, for its effective sustainability—alongside macroeconomic compatibility—will be monitored by the social partners and dependent upon the development of the crisis.

In an awareness of the foregoing issues, the Legislator outlined the reasons and the purposes of the reform, reasserting the central role played by full-time open-ended subordinate employment, also with regard to the apprenticeship contract, which remains the most widespread contractual scheme for those who enter the labour market for the first time. Indeed, the preference for this contractual arrangement is not to be ascribed to a decrease in the labour costs for open-ended contracts, nor to certain simplified procedures that favour their implementation. Rather, there has been a concurrent, and in some respects radical, dwindling of the regulatory mechanisms and contributions to be borne by employers for contractual arrangements in temporary work, self-employment, and quasi-salaried employment (continuous and coordinated collaboration contracts).

The explicit intention here is to overcome the duality between insiders and outsiders—e.g. stable workers and precarious workers—of the Italian labour market. Nevertheless, the issue is dealt with in a contradictory manner. In fact, the introductory paragraphs of the document clearly state that—pending a future and uncertain harmonisation process—the reform only concerns the private sector. Accordingly, the public sector does not fall within the scope of the provision, primarily because of higher rates of trade union representation that ensure protection in terms of stability of employment.

Yet early commentators[10] have pointed out another contentious issue, which has been acknowledged by the Minister of Labour in a number of

---

[10] See the contributions in Magnani,M., and M. Tiraboschi, eds. 2012. *La nuova riforma del lavoro—Commentario alla legge 28 giugno 2012, n. 92.* Milano: Giuffrè.

public statements. The move on the part of the Government aimed at narrowing down the use of flexible and atypical work—especially in recessionary times—might foster another dualism that is peculiar to the Italian labour market, viz. that existing between regular and irregular employment. This is particularly the case if one considers the telling arguments put forward at an international level,[11] according to which the extensive hidden economy in Italy—amounting to between 23% and 27% of Gross Domestic Product (GDP), that is twice or three times that reported in France and Germany—alongside a sound set of safety-net measures[12]—now called into question (see par. 5)—helped Italy tackle the crisis originated in 2007 following the economic turmoil.

The creation of a regular monitoring system to assess the impact of the reform on the labour market on the part of the Legislator should be deemed of particular significance. The development of a system for monitoring purposes should be the domain of the Minister of Labour and Social Policies,[13] who should also oversee the evaluation of the implementing stage of the reform programme, its effects in terms of efficiency and employability, and the mechanisms for entering and exiting the labour market. The results of this monitoring activity might be useful to take cognizance of the amendments to be made to the provisions laid down by the reform.

2. Flexibility in Hiring: The Tightening Up of Atypical and Flexible Work and the Revival of Apprenticeships

2.1. Fixed-term Contracts

Following the reform of 2001, which implemented the EU Directive No. 1999/70/CE, Italian legislation allows for the issuing of employment

---

[11] See Monteforte, F. 2012. *The Paradox of Italy's Informal Economy,* Stratfor.

[12] For a reconstruction—from an international and comparative perspective—of the system of safety-net measures which traditionally consists in a scaling back of working hours through various forms of income support, see Tiraboschi, M., and S. Spattini. 2012. "Anti-crisis Labour Market Measures and their Effectiveness between Flexibility and Security", *Labour Regulation in the 21st Century: In Search of Flexibility and Security,* eds. Davulis, T., and D. Petrylaitė, ADAPT Labour Studies Book Series, No. 2, (Cambridge: Cambridge Scholars Publishing), 163 ff.

[13] Article 17 of Legislative Decree No. 276/2003 (the Biagi Reform) already made provisions for a careful monitoring system that evaluates the effectiveness of the legislative measures put in place. Regretfully, this system was never implemented.

contracts of a definite duration, although this must be linked to the presence of technical, productive or organisational reasons, even in relation to the everyday activity of the employer.

Although questioned by a number of case law rulings on matters of fact, the aim of the Legislator was to normalise the recourse to fixed-term contracts, which up until then could be used only on a temporary basis and under special circumstances.

In an attempt to stress the pivotal role played by open-ended salaried employment, the document of the reform states that, "full-time open-ended subordinate employment is the standard form of employment". In the aftermath of the reform, this contractual arrangement was widely used, whereas fixed-term contracts were once again seen as being entered into only in certain circumstances, while still regulated by Act No. 230/1962 and, before that, the Civil Code of 1942.

With a view to moving beyond this hard-and-fast distinction, the Monti-Fornero Reform opens the possibility of two additional forms of temporary employment.

In the first case, fixed-term contracts without indicating the justifying reason can be issued, that is irrespective of the temporary nature of the assignment or the organisational needs of the employer. This employment contract can be concluded between an employer (or a user-company) and a job seeker who is hired for the first time and for a limited time up to a period of twelve months, in order to perform any kind of task. Unlike the past, an employment relationship of this kind can thus be established for the first time regardless of the tasks to be carried out by the employee and without the obligation upon the employer to provide technical and organisational reasons, even in cases of substitute work. The only requirement is that the employment relationship lasts for less than twelve months.

Alternatively, the reform specifies that workers can be hired under fixed-term contracts for an indefinite period without the need on the part of the employer to give details about the reasons for hiring, provided that the following conditions are met:

- this clause must be agreed upon in collective agreements;
- it must involve not less than 6% of the workers of each production unit;
- it must be carried out in certain organisational processes (start-ups, the launch of new products, technological changes, further stages of a research project, renewal or extension of a job assignment).

It must be said that this route can be pursued only if agreed upon during collective bargaining, with the opportunity to resort to this flexible form of work in the relevant industry that might be taken into account.

As far as the first option is concerned, the Legislator appears to run into a contradiction. This is because after reasserting the major role played by full-time open-ended subordinate employment, a major exception is introduced to this proposition that impinges on the logic of national labour law, although limited to the first employment contract that is entered into.

In the second case, and save for a few exceptions, employers' associations will be loath to enter into agreements of this kind, as employers are now allowed to wait twelve months before recruiting a worker for the first time, also taking account of the limitations posed by collective bargaining. In addition, the reform reveals a tendency to move away from a decentralised industrial relations system which marked earlier provisions at a national level. This is because only company-wide and interconfederal (national multi-industry) agreements are regarded as valid in this case, with decentralisation that takes place in the presence of delegation from national collective bargaining.

The unwillingness to make use of regulated forms of temporary employment is further exhibited by another aspect. Starting from 2013, the employer who decides to recruit a worker on a fixed-term contract will be required to pay an additional contribution amounting to 1.4% of pension-qualifying income, in order to finance an occupational fund (*Assicurazione Sociale per l'Impiego,* see par. 5). Employers will be reimbursed this contribution—up to a maximum of the last six months' pay—if the employment relationship will be converted into full-time open-ended employment, or that the worker will be hired within six months of the termination of the fixed-term employment relationship. Due to the particular nature of this form of employment, this additional contribution is not to be paid in the event of workers taken on under fixed-term contracts for seasonal and substitute work.

Still on fixed-term employment contracts, further interventions concern the continuation of the employment relationship after the expiration of the terms, the procedures to dispute its validity, and the forms of compensation in the event of transformation into salaried employment.

With reference to the first point, employees can provide their service for the employers up to a maximum of 30 days—and not 20 days as previously set—from the date of the expiration of the employment contract, if the employment relationship has a duration of less than six months. For employment contracts lasting more than six months, this threshold has been raised from 30 to 50 days. Contracts which are extended longer than these terms will be converted into an open-ended employment relationship.

The Legislator also regulates the interval between fixed-term contracts to re-employ the same worker. If the previous employment relationship had a duration of less than six months, the lapse of time between the two employment contracts should be of 60 days, and not 10 days, as it was in the past. However, 90 days rather than 20 days should have elapsed between one employment contract and the other in cases in which the first employment contract lasted more than six months. Nevertheless, collective agreements concluded by the most representative trade unions and employers' associations at a national level, are allowed to reduce these intervals. More specifically:

- up to 20 days if the first employment contract has a duration of less than six months;
- up to 30 days if the first employment contract has a duration exceeding six months, particularly in the event of hiring resulting from certain organisational processes (start-ups, the launch of new products, technological changes, further stages of research projects, renewal or extension of a job assignment).

The scaling back of the minimum period between the two employment contracts applies to seasonal work and in all cases laid down in collective agreements concluded at a national level by the most representative trade unions.

The reform also introduces a statute of limitations for disputing the termination of the fixed-term contracts. Workers can appeal against the termination that is invalid for reasons related to the date of expiry after appraising the employers, also by means of out-of-court procedures, within 120 days of the termination of employment, thus raising the previous 60-day time limit. After lodging the complaint, workers should initiate legal proceedings within the following 180 days and not 270 days, as it was originally set down.

As for employment cases, the law now reviews compensation to be paid by the employer in the event of a ruling in favour of the worker and the resulting conversion of the fixed-term employment contract into an open-ended one. Statutorily, the sum to be paid by the employer amounts to 2.5 to 12 months' pay, considering the last salary. The novelty lies in the fact that this sum of money is now regarded as full compensation for any loss suffered by the worker, thus including entitlement in terms of pay and social contributions from the termination of the employment contract and the decision made by the tribunal. Therefore, following the ruling on the part of the courts, the employer—whether or not fulfilling the obligation to re-engage the worker—is required to provide arrears of pay and relevant contributions.

2.2. Temporary Agency Work

The intentions on the part of the Legislator to stress the pivotal role played by full-time and open-ended subordinate employment as the most widespread form of employment in Italy are patent if one looks at the interventions made to the provisions regulating temporary agency work.

At the outset, it should be noted that the proposals laid down seem to be insufficient. Most importantly, they show a tendency away from the efforts made since 2003—and in line with international experience—to single out agency work as a form of work facilitating the matching of supply and demand for labour, especially if compared to atypical and temporary employment.

Within the Italian legal system, agency work was originally regarded as particularly useful in organisational and managerial terms, benefitting labour flexibility and contributing to the modernisation of the productive system. This is also because certain mechanisms of contractual integration between undertakings and certain processes—namely staff-leasing, and in-sourcing, co-sourcing, net-sourcing, selective sourcing, multi-sourcing, back-sourcing, co-specialisation and value added outsourcing—to be overseen by high-qualified operators within the labour market, as is (presumably) the case of work agencies.

However, the Monti-Fornero Reform puts fixed-term employment on the same footing as agency work, thus taking a step back in time of at least ten years, as the proposals detailed in the reform programme scale back the scope of application of this form of employment. Further, according to the reform, the recourse to agency work is possible by providing a justifying reason, save for two cases.

In the first case, the employer and the agency worker can conclude an employment contract for the first time and with a maximum duration of 12 months, without specifying technical, productive, organizational reasons, nor whether the worker will be engaged in substitution work, which, as a rule, should be included in the particulars of the employment contract. It seems worth pointing out that the wording "the very first employment relationship between the employer/the user company and the employee" used in the text of the reform attempts implicitly, yet in an ambiguous manner, to confine this exception to the first employment contract entered into, and not to the relationship between the employment agency and the worker.

Alternatively, the conclusion of the employment contract between the employer and the agency worker does not require any justification, nor do these contracts have limitations in terms of number and duration, whereas the following conditions are met:

a) this exception is agreed upon during collective bargaining;
b) it must involve at most 6% of the workers of each production unit;
c) in the event of hiring resulting from certain organisational processes (start-ups, the launch of new products, technological changes, further stages of research projects, renewal or extension of a job assignment).

None of the exceptions allows for an extension of the employment contract, once ended.

In the author's view, the recourse to agency work devoid of a justifying reason might on first approximation facilitate the task of temporary work agencies and reduce the rate of employment disputes, particularly if compared to that of the previous years. However, in the long- and medium-time frame this state of play will debase the role of temporary work agencies as qualified operators in the labour market in terms of improvement of human capital and specialization of production, limiting their function to the mere provision of workers on the basis of the employer's needs.

The reform also specifies that, for the purposes of calculating the maximum duration of fixed-term contracts—in any case not exceeding 36 months—it is necessary to count towards the time needed to perform the same task—e.g. with the same job description—carried out by workers with the same qualification. Agency work is thus once again likened to fixed-term employment, with this provision that is far from securing stable employment. In addition, it acts as a disincentive for the work agency, which is therefore loath to provide training and special skills for agency workers. As already discussed above, this aspect is further confirmation of the marginal role allocated to this form of employment.

In addition to this, the reform regulates employment agency apprenticeships. Employers are still prohibited to hire apprentices on a temporary basis. However, it is possible to utilise the services of apprentices who are employed by an agency work for an unlimited period (staff leasing) in all the productive sectors that is when a commercial contract of an indefinite term between the user company and the employment agency is concluded. An obstacle to the implementation of this provision might arise from the fact that the reform repealed certain norms laid down by the Biagi Reform in 2003. In particular, in compliance with European Directive No. 2008/104/CE, the Biagi Law set forth a derogation from the principle of equal treatment between agency workers and other employees, if the recourse to agency work is made for training purposes or aims at easing access to labour market. This aspect might affect the procedures to determine remuneration for apprentices hired by the employment agency, as it is usually equal to pay for employees of a lower grade, or to a certain percentage of remuneration provided to more trained and qualified workers.

Distinct from what was laid down in previous interventions, the Monti-Fornero Reform also makes provisions for a longer interval between fixed-term employment contracts at the time of rehiring the same workers. In this connection, the lapse of time to issue a new limited-term contract should be of 60 days if the previous employment contract has a duration of less than six months, or 90 days for fixed-term contracts lasting longer than six months. A literal interpretation of the norm suggests that the relationship between the work agency and the worker falls outside the scope of application of the provision, while doubts arise in reference to the relation between the work agency and the user company. Perhaps this can be explained by the attempt on the part of the Legislator to prevent the abuse or the repetitive use of fixed-term contractual arrangements ("chains" of contracts). Should this be, the work agency is either allowed to send the same worker to different user-companies on a permanent basis, or to the last user-company the worker provided his/her services to, for the latter upon compliance with terms of renewal statutorily laid down.

After an inspection of the reform, one might also note a shrinking of the funding allocated to employment agencies to promote active labour market policies, training, and retraining of temporary workers. In this sense, the law provides that starting from 1 January 2013; employers have to pay an additional contribution corresponding to 1.4% of pension-qualifying income for salaried workers hired on a temporary basis. As for the employment agencies, this sum is partly offset by a reduction in the contribution paid to a training fund for agency workers that is equal to 4% of aggregate salary.

2.3. Apprenticeship, Access-to-Work Contracts, and Placements

The Monti-Fornero Reform sets much store by the apprenticeship contracts, regarded as a privileged channel for helping young people to enter the labour market. In the context of this paper, it might be useful to point out that a comprehensive reform of apprenticeships already took place in September 2011, and included a number of agreements concluded over the two years prior to the reform between the Government, the Regions, and the social partners.[14]

The reform reasserts the pivotal role carried out by apprenticeship as the main contractual arrangement for first-time entrants to the labour market. This approach stands in line with the proposal of many academics—particularly economists—for a "single employment contract" for people starting their first job. One might note, however, that some critical aspects of apprenticeship—e.g. the training content—still remain unsolved. Accordingly, the widespread use of apprenticeship for first-time entrants into the labour market is to be attributed mainly to provisions, which scaled back the recourse to other contractual schemes for this category of workers. This is particularly the case of access-to-work contracts—introduced by the Biagi Law in 2003 and now repealed—project work and placements.

In consequence, although welcomed in principle, the proposal of apprenticeship as the main contractual scheme to enter the labour market is, in general terms, far from being realistic. In fact, nearly one year after the enforcement of legislation regulating apprenticeship, the devising of a system which considers the needs of productive sectors and the differences at regional level has not yet been fully envisaged. The setting-up of a national system of vocational standards to validate and certify one's vocational skills as laid down by the relevant provisions in 2011 has never been implemented either. Therefore, only in formal terms can the apprenticeship contract be classified as full-time open-ended subordinate employment and be freely terminated at its end. In practice, it is to be considered a fixed-term contract devoid of the training content and not in line with the German dual model system to which the Legislator claimed to have referred to.[15]

Of significance is the innovation concerning the increase of the number of apprentices that can be recruited by the employer, which is determined by the number of qualified workers in employment. Starting from 1 January 2013, the ratio of apprentices—to be hired either directly or through open-ended employment agency contracts—to qualified employees will be 2 to 3. Notwithstanding specific more favourable conditions laid down for the artisan sector, the ratio is set at 1 to 1 for employers with less than ten workers, while employers with no qualified

[14] See Tiraboschi, M., ed. 2011. *Il Testo Unico dell'apprendistato e la nuova disciplina dei tirocini formativi*. Milano: Giuffrè.
[15] Supra, par. 3.

staff or with less than three specialized workers will be allowed to take on up to three apprentices.

In addition, for the purposes of the reform, employers with at least ten employees are allowed to hire apprentices on the condition that they had recruited at least 50% of apprentices whose contract ended in the past 36 months. This percentage has been reduced to 30% in relation to the 36 months subsequent to the enforcement of the reform. As the provision expressly laid down, the employment relationships terminated over the probationary period, or due to resignation or just cause dismissal are not to be included in the foregoing calculation. Apprentices recruited in violation of these conditions are to be considered salaried employees hired on open-ended contracts entered into force since the employment relationship was established. In the event of non-compliance with this ceiling, it is possible to recruit another apprentice who adds to those already employed. The same goes in cases in which no apprentice has already been hired upon termination of the apprenticeship contract. The statutory 50% is a minimum threshold and applies to all productive sectors. For this reason, it might be amended upward, depending on the applicable collective agreements.

In order to ensure adequate training, the reform also sets forth that apprenticeship contracts should have a minimum duration of 6 months, with the sole exception of seasonal work, for which it is only possible to issue vocational apprenticeship contracts.

Also in consideration of the widespread recourse to apprenticeship, the Monti-Fornero Reform provides delegation of certain tasks to the Government, also with a view to narrow down the recourse to placements and prevent their improper use. This can be done only upon an agreement concluded between the parties involved (the State and the Regions) which sets down guidelines on training and placements for career guidance purposes, to be implemented at regional level. In this connection, the reform programme also lays down a number of criteria that foresee more stringent rules to regulate this contractual scheme. An example is the obligation on the part of the employer to provide remuneration to the trainees for the work performed.

2.4. Part-time and On-call Work

The reform introduces a number of major changes to part-time work which concern certain clauses (*clausole flessibili ed elastiche*) allowing the employer to either modify the time and increase the hours agreed upon in the employment contract to perform a given task.

The conditions and the specifics to carry out the working activity are not determined by the employer and the employee directly, but they should be set down during collective bargaining.

In order to encourage the proper use of part-time work as a flexible form of employment, the Monti-Fornero Reform specified that it is for collective agreements to envisage the procedures enabling workers to repeal or amend these clauses. Therefore collective agreements will detail the cases in which workers might opt for a review of the employment contract in relation to the foregoing clauses.

Furthermore, the reform also provides the opportunity for some categories of workers who already agreed on these clauses to reverse their position, most notably working students, workers with oncological conditions, and the category of workers listed in collective agreements.

More radical changes have been made to on-call work (zero-hours contracts), that is the employment relationship—either of a definite or indefinite duration—in which the workers agree to provide their services to the employers, who in turn make use of their performance on the basis of what has been laid down by the law or collective agreements.

The reform made provisions particularly in relation to its scope of application. In this sense, it sets forth that—without prejudice to the cases specified in the collective agreement—work on an intermittent basis can be performed by workers over the age of 55—thus raising the 44-year-old threshold set by the Biagi Law in 2003—and by workers up to the age of 24, provided that the tasks are carried out before attaining the age of 25.

The reform also repeals the clause allowing the carrying out of on-call work in certain times of the week, month or year agreed in advance in collective bargaining, and sets down some measures to raise the levels of transparency.

More specifically, it places an obligation upon the employer to notify relevant authorities (*Direzione Territoriale del Lavoro*) before the embarking on a job task—or a series of job tasks totalling less than 30 days—on the part of on-call workers. The notification can be made by text (Short Message System), fax, or simply by email. Upon fulfilment of this obligation, the employment relationship can be concluded, with the employer who is required to notify the relevant authority every time the worker is called out to work.

2.5. Coordinated and Continuous Collaborations (Quasi-subordinate Employment)

The Monti-Fornero Reform made profound amendments to quasi-subordinate employment. This is particularly the case concerning project work, that can be loosely defined as an employment relationship between the employer and the employee, which takes place on a coordinated and continuous basis, characterised by an absence of subordination relating to the completion of the project.

Unlike what was laid down by the Biagi Law in 2003, the employer is relieved from the obligation to provide a work schedule of the project—or project phases—to be implemented. As a result, the existence of an employment relationship of this kind will only be determined for specific projects.

The project to be carried out needs to be related to a given end result, which cannot consist in the mere employer's company purpose and cannot include repetitive tasks.

The reform clarifies the meaning of the provision laid down in the Biagi Law in 2003 according to which professions for which enrolment in special registers (*albo professionale*) is required are excluded from the scope of application of project work. It seems important to point out that this exception is limited to quasi-salaried employment in the form of intellectual work, the nature of which is the same as that performed by professionals who need to comply with registration procedures.

In consequence, professionals who are enrolled in these special registers, operate for one client and carry out tasks which are not related to their trade will be regarded as engaged in project work. This applies also in cases in which professionals operate simultaneously for more than one client. However, whereas the employment tribunal ascertains that there exists a relationship between the work performed and the trade carried out, the employment relationship is converted into salaried employment, as a project justifying the recourse to project work has not been provided.

These measures are intended to prevent the fraudulent use of project work, particularly to mask salaried employment. One might note, however, that this goal has not been achieved through a set of repressive measures to combat fraudulent practices, but rather because of the unwillingness on the part of employers to make use of project work. This is exhibited by an increase in the labour costs for project work—that will be the same as those for salaried employment by 2018—and by the provision of more stringent regulations to assess whether project workers are hired on salaried employment contracts.

The reform also posits that there is a legal presumption in favour of the existence of salaried employment without the opportunity to provide rebuttal evidence in cases in which the lack of the project to be implemented at either formal or substantial levels has been ascertained by the courts.

On the contrary, there shall be a presumption of salaried employment with the opportunity to supply rebuttal evidence in cases in which the working activity is performed along the same lines of that carried out by salaried employees, thus not taken into account tasks which require high levels of skills on an exclusive basis.

As for the termination of the employment relationship, it is still possible to discontinue the contract for just cause before it ends, yet pursuant to the reform the parties are not allowed to freely terminate the employment relationship. The employment contract can be brought to an end by the employer only when there is an objective lack of fitness of workers which endangers the fulfilment of the project. For their part, workers hired on project work contracts can discontinue the employment relationship by giving notice, only if this clause is expressly laid down in the contract.

The reform introduced major amendments also with regard to remuneration. Notwithstanding that the amount paid should be proportional to the quality and quantity of the work performed, it also specified that workers should be remunerated at a rate which is not less than the minimum wage set on a sectoral basis. Further, the system of remuneration should also consider the employment grading methods set up for each sector and the minimum wage levels set down for similar tasks for salaried employees. Wage setting is agreed upon in collective agreements concluded by the most representative trade unions and employers' associations at national, inter-sectoral, and sectoral levels, also by means of decentralisation by way of derogation clauses. In the absence of specific collective agreements, reference should be made to the minimum wage provisions specified in the national collective agreements for workers operating in the same sector and with the same employment grade as project workers.

2.6. Self-employment

The Monti-Fornero Reform narrows down the scope of application of self-employment in a considerable manner. This is due to the prevailing legal presumption that autonomous workers are hired on salaried employment contracts, to be applied in the cases provided by the law.

There are three criteria to establish whether an individual claiming to be self-employed is actually presumed to perform salaried employment on an open-ended contract. For the sake of clarity, it should be noted that the provision makes use of the wording "continuous and coordinated collaboration". Nonetheless, pursuant to Italian labour law, a contractual arrangement of this kind lacking a specific project is reclassified as open-ended salaried employment. For an individual to be regarded as a salaried employee on an open-ended contract, at least two out of three of the conditions listed below must be met.

The criteria laid down by the law are factual situations pertinent to the running of the employment relationship, which, besides its classification at a formal level, help determine the coordinating and continuing nature of the work performed. The criteria laid down by the Legislator are:

1) the duration of the employment relationship, whereas lasting for more than eight months for two consecutive years;
2) the provision of services to one client on an exclusive basis, provided that the turnover of the self-employed earned while operating for the same client—or for a permanent business establishment—over a period of two consecutive years amounts to 80% of his/her total earnings.
3) the presence of a fixed workstation at the client's premises, where "fixed" means that it is non-movable or temporary.

The legal presumption of open-ended salaried employment does not apply in cases in which the tasks to be performed require high skill levels or "practical skills acquired through experience". This is conditional on the fact that the average annual earnings of autonomous workers are equal to or higher than a certain sum statutorily determined. Another exception—which works as an alternative to the foregoing—concerns, for instance, a professional self-employed individual performing his/her job upon membership to professional associations (special registers, professional bodies, and so forth).

2.7. Special Forms of Joint Ventures

The reform also makes provisions for special forms of joint ventures, whereby an associating party grants an associated party a share in the profits of the business or of one or more transactions on the basis of an agreed upon contribution. This is known in Italy as *associazione in partecipazione* (literally, joint venture partnership). Over the years, an increase in the misuse of this contractual scheme has been reported, particularly in clerical work or manual labour in the building industry.

The Monti-Fornero Reform amends previous legislation governing this contractual arrangement, and specifies that it is possible to have up to a maximum of three associated parties engaged in the same activity if the contribution provided also includes the work performed. This applies regardless of the number of associating parties, with the sole exception of an associated party being a spouse, a family member up to the third-degree of kinship or a second-degree ascendant. In the event of non-compliance with this clause, the associated parties who provide a contribution in the form of work performance will be considered as salaried employees on an open-ended contract. The legal presumption in favour of salaried employment thus does not allow for rebuttal evidence to demonstrate the genuine nature of the employment relationship.

Prior to the enforcement of the reform, the setting-up of a number of joint ventures to deal with the same business or transaction did not impinge on the validity of the contract, save for cases in which at least one of them is established at a later stage (unlike otherwise agreed, the associating party cannot grant other individuals a share in the profits of a business or a transaction without the consent of the former associated parties).

As already pointed out, the reform tightens up the regulation for this special form of joint venture. For the contract to be valid, it is possible to have up to a maximum of three associated parties engaged in the same activity, except in cases of family members or ascendants.

The reform also sets down certain cases of legal presumptions of salaried employment, against which evidence can however be provided. A contractual arrangement concluded to set up a joint venture is presumed to be salaried employment in the following cases:

- if the associated party does not have a share in the profits of the business run by the associating party;
- in the event of failing to report the associated party on the activity carried out (by way of a report on the annual management if the activity has been performed for more than 12 months);
- in the event that the agreed upon contribution on the part of the associated party corresponds to "unqualified" labour, that is neither characterized by theoretical knowledge acquired by specific training nor by practical skills acquired in the same job.

In addition, in order to restrain the recourse to this form of joint venture, the reform sets forth an increase in the social contributions for the associated parties. In this sense, the cost of labour will rise at 1% every year until 2018, totalling a contribution rate of 33% for those who are not covered by any other form of public retirement scheme.

2.8. Occasional Work of an Accessory Nature

The reform foresees a thorough review of regulations governing occasional work, that is work provided without concluding and employment contract and by means of a particular payment system, namely vouchers for an amount of 10 Euros per hour.

Already in 2003, the Biagi Law made provisions for workers on this contractual arrangement based on remuneration. In this sense, the Biagi Law also detailed the category of workers who can engage in occasional work (young people, housewives, and retired people) as well as its scope of application (domestic and agricultural work, and light housework).

Contrary to what was laid down in 2003, the Monti-Fornero Reform now specifies that occasional work only include work performed on an occasional basis, which generates a total income of €5,000 in a calendar year. Significantly, this sum corresponds to the sum earned from the services provided to all the client firms, marking an important difference with the past. Occasional workers can still carry out working activities up to a maximum of 2,000 Euros per annum to be paid by different client firms, if their services are rendered to entrepreneurs and professionals.

Another relevant measure—which will certainly facilitate the recourse to ancillary work without any consequence in legal terms—is that the recourse to this form of employment is allowed for all working activities and irrespective of the workers' personal characteristics.

Some special regulations have been laid down which scale back the use of occasional work in the agricultural sector to the following cases:

- agricultural work of an occasional nature performed by retired people and by young people who are less than 25;
- agricultural work provided to farmers which generates a turnover of 7,000 Euros per annum, with the exception of farmers enrolled in special registers for the previous year.

Public bodies are still allowed to make use of occasional work, as long as they comply with regulations to contain personnel costs and, whereas in force, budgetary stability pacts. In the same vein, recipients of social security benefits who are entitled to a maximum of 3,000 Euros for the year 2013, can perform occasional work in both private and public bodies and in all productive sectors to supplement their monthly wage or any other form of social aid.

3. Flexibility in Dismissals: Remedies for Unfair Dismissals and New Rules on Collective Dismissals

In the Italian legal system, the termination of open-ended and salaried employment contracts can only take place for just cause—thus not allowing for the continuation of the employment relationship—or for justified reasons. If the latter, the employment contract can be discontinued because of a serious violation of the worker's contractual obligations (that is for "subjective reasons") or justified by needs related to production and its functioning, or organizational choices made by the employer (that is for objective reasons). In the event of an unjustified dismissal, Italian legislation provides a set of remedial measures traditionally consisting in the worker's reinstatement—in the event of large and medium-sized companies—or a compensation award—if concerning small-sized companies.

Reinstatement takes place in cases of unfair dismissals, in businesses employing more than 15 employees in the productive unit where the unfair dismissal occurred—or more than 5 for employers who run a farm—or in businesses with more than 60 workers altogether, whether operating in the same productive unit or not. By virtue of this remedy the employment contract is not regarded as interrupted, thus the employee can ask to return to the same job and to demand unpaid salary. With regard to remedies in the form of compensation, it concerns the productive units and the employers not falling within the foregoing cases. It does not invalidate the effects of unfair dismissal, but it places an obligation upon the employer to choose between reinstating the workers and granting them a sum of money ranging from 2.5 and 6 months' pay.

By regarding as unfair the dismissal delivered without a reason, the reform amends the Italian remedial framework, seen as "anomalous" if compared to that of other countries, as producing discouraging effects on foreign investors in our country and penalising local employers at an international level.

As a result, extant legislation now regulates unfair dismissals taking account of the underlying reasons and the employers' liability. In this sense, there are different employment safeguards that apply in accordance with the reasons and depending of the type of dismissal, viz. discriminatory dismissals, disciplinary dismissals and dismissals for justified objective reasons.

3.1. Discriminatory Dismissals: Remedies including Reinstatement and Compensation

Discriminatory dismissals take place when employees are removed from their position—irrespective of the employer's will—on the grounds of religion, political, and personal belief, age, disability, gender, sexual orientation, race, language, and trade union affiliation. The reform does not make significant changes to the regulation of discriminatory dismissals. Regardless of the reasons provided and the number of workers employed, the ruling handed down by the employment tribunal making the dismissal of employees or executives null and void places an obligation upon the employer to reinstate the workers.

This remedy now also includes dismissals nullified because in violation of the rule which prohibits one to discharge workers who are on maternity or parental leave or on the grounds of marriage. In addition, dismissals that are statutorily regarded as null and void are also considered discriminatory dismissals. By way of example, this includes workers who are removed from their position after being given training leave, or leave for particular circumstances. The same holds for dismissal resulting from illegal practice, such as the so-called "retaliatory" termination, that is illegal and arbitrary action taken against an employee who did not commit any misconduct.

Workers are entitled to reinstatement also in the event of a dismissal that is null and void because notified orally and not in writing, regardless of the number of employees.

As a result of the order of reinstatement ruled by the tribunal, the employee should return to work within 30 days from the employer's communication. Alternatively, and without prejudice to the employee's right to compensation for any loss suffered, the dismissed workers might ask for payment of up to 15 months' pay, considering their last salary.

The judge might also order the employer to pay compensation for the damage suffered from unfair loss of job, the amount of which is arrived at by calculating the last salary paid to the worker—e.g. to which he would have been entitled if not discharged—from the date of dismissal up to the date of effective reinstatement. The earnings resulting from working activities performed during the dismissal period should be deducted (*aliunde perceptum*).

Under any circumstances compensation for unfair dismissal can be less than five months' pay, with the employer also obliged to pay social contributions and compulsory insurance for the entire period the worker has been away, including premiums for occupational injuries and diseases.

It is also implied—the law remained silent on this point—that the employer is obligated to pay a fine for non-payment or delayed payment of social contributions.

3.2. Dismissals for Disciplinary Reasons

The reform also makes provisions for dismissals for disciplinary reasons, that is termination of employment due to a breach of contractual duties or serious violations on the part of the worker. These specifics are also grounds for dismissal for justified "subjective" reasons and just-cause dismissal, respectively. There are three remedies following a finding of unfair dismissals and they depend on the seriousness of the circumstances.

The first case occurs when the employment tribunal ascertains that the dismissal is null and void for a lack of a justified "subjective" reason or just cause, because there is no case to answer, or because the violation falls within those for which measures short of dismissal can be imposed on the employee, in line with what is laid down by collective agreements or codes of conduct.

In this case, the tribunal nullifies the unfair dismissal, ruling that the employer should reinstate the employee—or alternatively and on the employee's request, he should pay a compensation award amounting to 15 months' pay. The judge also specifies that the employment contract is terminated whereas the workers fail to return to work within 30 days from the employer's communication, or they do not claim for compensation.

It is also implied—the law kept silent on this point, too—that the employer is obligated to pay a fine for non-payment or delayed payment of social contributions.

The employee is also entitled to the payment of compensation which is equal to remuneration accrued from the date of dismissal to the date of effective reinstatement—which cannot exceed 12 months' pay—from which earnings resulting from working activities performed during the dismissal period should be deducted (*aliunde perceptum*), as well as potential wages earned if the worker had found a new occupation. The ruling that the dismissal is unfair also places an obligation upon the employer to pay social contributions and compulsory insurance for the period the worker has been away, including premiums for occupational injuries and diseases. Distinct from what happens in the event of discriminatory dismissal, social contributions must include the interests legally accrued without taking into account sanctions for non-payment or a delay in the payment on the part of the employer.

The second case concerns the event when the employer tribunal rules in favour of a lack of the justified "subjective" reasons or just cause put forward by the employer. Under these circumstances, the dismissal, if unjustified, is not regarded as null and void and the judge orders the termination of the employment contract from the date of dismissal. If this is the case, the worker is entitled to full compensation—in the sense that it also includes social security contributions—ranging from 12 to 24 months' pay considering the last salary, and some other criteria (length of service, number of employees, the size of the business—as well as the conduct and the conditions laid down by the parties, the latter requiring a written statement explaining the reasons for such conduct).

The last case refers to the discriminatory dismissal that is null and void because of a violation of the requirement to provide justification or because of a procedural defect, which is typical of disciplinary dismissals. Under these circumstances, the dismissal is null and void and the employer is bound to pay full compensation—including social security contributions—ranging from 12 to 24 months' pay considering the last salary, depending on the seriousness of the violation of the employer, with a duty to provide motivation in writing.

3.3. Dismissals for Justified Objective Reasons

The other case of dismissal is that taking place for justified objective reasons. In this respect, a review of extant legislation redesigned the remedial framework and introduced two new measures in procedural terms.

The reform specifies that in notifying the worker of the dismissal, the employer must also provide the reasons causing the decision. This requirement marks a difference with the past, as previous legislation only specifies that such justification could be provided upon the former worker's request within 15 days from being given notice.

A further innovation concerns the discontinuation of the employment relationship for economic reasons. More specifically, the requirement to attempt conciliation has been introduced as a pre-requisite to further action to be taken with regard to the dismissal. This initiative, which is of an experimental nature, does not apply to small-sized enterprises as previously defined.

The notification to be filed by the employer must specify the intention to terminate the employment contract for objective reasons, the justification for the dismissal and the measures to be taken to help the dismissed worker find alternative work. Once notification has been handed in, a special body appointed by the Ministry of Labour (*Direzione Territoriale del lavoro*—Provincial Labour Direction), summons the employer and the dismissed worker to a hearing before the local conciliation board within seven days from the delivery of the communication. If members of a union, both parties can appoint or mandate a union delegate, a lawyer or an employment consultant to represent them at the hearing, which can be postponed for a maximum of 15 days only in the event of a serious and certified impediment.

The aim of conciliation is to find an alternative route to the termination of the employment contract. However, this procedure cannot last more than 20 days from the date the parties were called on to meet, unless they agree to further discuss the issue until a settlement is achieved.

Whereas the recourse to conciliation is not effective, or the Provincial Labour Direction fails to convene a meeting with the parties within 7 days of the delivery of the communication, the employer can dismiss the worker by giving notice. Conversely, if the attempt at conciliation is successful and the contract of employment ends by mutual agreement, the law provides for the implementation of safety-net measures, as will be seen further on. It could also be the case that employment agencies are appointed to help the worker re-enter the labour market.

In order to encourage conciliation, it is also specified that in the event of a further appeal, the attitude of the parties will be taken into account—as resulting from the minutes of the hearing—as well as the proposal put forward by the local conciliation board to settle the issue. Based on these elements, the judge will rule in favour of the prevailing party to be awarded the court costs, and decide the amount of compensation resulting from the dismissal that is null and void as devoid of an economic or productive reason claimed by the employer.

There are four circumstances, which in turn, give rise to four types of remedies. The forms of compensation laid down are thus related to the seriousness of the flaws at the time of terminating an employment contract.

3.3.1. Remedies including Reinstatement and Compensation

This remedy concerns the situations in which the dismissal for objective reasons is unfair as justified on the grounds of physical or mental unfitness of the workers. This case also refers to an employment contract that is discontinued before expiration of the time granted to workers on sick or parental leave to maintain their post, or when the organizational and productive reasons claimed by the employer are not grounded.

In all these cases the dismissal is null and void and the employer is obliged to reinstate the dismissed worker, who is also entitled to a sum of money corresponding to a maximum of twelve months' pay considering the last salary, deduced from what was earned from the workers when they were dismissed and what should hypothetically be paid to them if still in employment in that period, including social contributions and interests. In essence, remedies are the same as those laid down in the event of disciplinary dismissals that are held as unfair.

3.3.2. Reinstatement in the form of Compensation without Reintegration

This remedy refers to all those cases not falling under the label of dismissal for justified objective reasons. Like the previous case, the reason justifying the dismissal is not grounded, or not in a patent manner. Accordingly, the dismissed worker is not entitled to reinstatement, but simply to a sum of money amounting to 12 to 24 months' pay considering the last salary and arrived at by taking into account a number of factors (length of service, number of employees, size of the business, and the attitude and the conditions set by the parties). The judge here acts as if he had to deal with unfair dismissal for just cause or justified objective reasons.

3.3.3. Dismissals for Justified Objective Reasons: The Case of Discriminatory and Disciplinary Dismissals

Another case is when the dismissed employee claims that the dismissal for justified objective reasons is the result of discrimination or unfair disciplinary action. If the employment tribunal finds the complaint well founded, remedies for unfair discriminatory or disciplinary dismissals apply.

3.3.4. Dismissals for Justified Objective Reasons and Non-Compliance with Formal Requirements

Dismissals for justified objective reasons must be initiated in accordance with certain formal requirements. Failing to provide justification for the dismissal or to comply with the obligation to seek conciliation will make the dismissal null and void. Being characterized by a procedural defect, they stand upon an equal footing with unfair dismissals resulting from disciplinary action. Accordingly, relevant legislation provides for termination of the employment contract, along with the supplying of an award amounting to six to twelve months' pay to be granted to the dismissed workers, depending on the seriousness of the procedural defect.

3.4. New Rules on Collective Dismissals

Besides making amendments to existing rules on individual dismissals, the Legislator also put forward some new legislative measures concerning the regulation of collective redundancy.

One aspect concerns the obligation to give early notice placed upon the employer who decides to dismiss employees for reasons of redundancy. The innovation lies in the opportunity to overcome the non-compliance of this requirement by signing an agreement concluded with trade unions during the redundancy procedures.

Amendments have also been made to the obligation to communicate to relevant authorities or trade unions the list of workers made redundant or on mobility schemes. Information for each worker should include personal details, employment grade, as well as a detailed explanation of the criteria adopted to identify the workers to be made redundant. As for the time requirements, such communication should take place within seven days from—and no longer concurrently to—the notice of dismissal delivered to the employees. With regard to remedies in the event of collective dismissals that took place in breach of agreed procedures, they rest upon the seriousness of the breach, which might give rise to the inefficacy of collective dismissals (in the event of failing to notify in writing or to comply with statutory procedures)—or make them void—in cases of violations of the eligibility criteria to dismiss the workers.

3.4.1. Remedies in the Form of Compensation and Reinstatement

In the event of collective dismissals not notified in writing, the worker is entitled to reinstatement and to a compensation award. The employment tribunal nullifies the dismissal and, concurrently, rules that the employees return to the same job, entitling them to a sum of money for the damage suffered. The amount of money to be paid is arrived at by calculating the wages and the social contributions from the date of the dismissal to the ruling of the courts—in any case not less than 5 months' pay—which should be reduced by what has been earned by the employer whereas performing another working activity over the same period.

3.4.2. Remedies in the Form of Compensation without Reinstatement

If collective dismissals have been found to be unfair because of a violation of the collective agreements, the tribunal orders the discontinuation of the employment contract that is effective from the date of the dismissal. It also entitles the employee to a sum of money amounting to 12 to 24 months' pay considering the last salary and arrived at by taking into account the worker's length of service, the number of employees and the size of the business, the attitude and the conditions set by the parties, with an obligation to specify the reasons in this connection.

3.4.3. Remedies including Reinstatement and Special Forms of Compensation

In the event of non-compliance with the criteria laid down to identify the workers to be made redundant, the most comprehensive forms of remedy apply. In other words, the employment tribunal nullifies the unfair dismissal and the employer is obliged to reinstate the dismissed workers and to grant them a sum of money amounting to a maximum of twelve months' pay considering the last salary from the date of dismissal to the date of reinstatement. The total sum should be reduced by the earnings resulting from other working activities performed by the workers while dismissed, as well as what was earned if they had been committed to seeking a new occupation. The employer is also under the obligation to pay social contributions for the same period, increased by the interests accrued until the date of reinstatement and without including penalties for non-payment or delayed payment of the amount due. This sum—yet lower than what entitled to the worker if not dismissed—is equal to the difference between contributions accrued following the dismissal and those paid to the employer as a result of other working activities performed by the workers during the time they were dismissed.

4. Undated Letter of Resignation and Termination by Mutual Consent

The reform makes provision also with regard to the dismissal procedures. More specifically, special sanctions have been put in place for employers who ask workers to sign an undated letter of resignation and use them at a later stage, further dismissing the workers but claiming that they have resigned or freely terminated the employment contract.

To combat this illegal practice, the law provides that resignation handed in by some categories of workers has to be validated by special bodies. This concerns women workers during pregnancy or workers who are fathers of children—through birth, custody, or national or international adoption—up to three years of age, thus extending the previous age limit of one year.

Another innovation lies in the requirement to assess whether the resignation was really intended, which now applies to cases of voluntary resignation in a strict sense and to all cases of consensual termination other than those resulting from maternity or paternity.

The genuine nature of both voluntary resignation and termination by mutual consent will be assessed through two distinct procedures, and their validity is thus conditional upon the outcome of this review process.

Validation of resignation is not required in cases in which the discontinuation of the employment contract is the result of a staff reduction agreed upon by unions or relevant bodies, which are assumed to take all necessary steps to assess whether the workers consented to the discontinuation of the employment relationship.

Procedures for validating workers' resignation or termination of the employment contract can be carried out by the Provincial Labour Direction (*Direzione Territoriale del lavoro*), the local employment services, or by any other body listed in collective agreements and agreed upon by the most representative trade unions at a national level.

Alternatively, the parties might issue a written statement to be appended to the notification of the termination of the employment relationship that has been sent to the employment services. Simplified criteria to ascertain the accuracy of the date and workers' statement are to be detailed in a Ministerial Decree.

There are also certain obligations placed upon the employer in the event of non-compliance with the requirement of validation or the issuing of the foregoing statement. The employer has to send the worker a formal request to report to the evaluating bodies or to produce a statement to be added to the notification sent to the employment services that the employment relationship has been brought to an end. This must be done within 30 days of the date of resignation or termination by mutual consent.

Within seven days from the request and in the event of failing to fullfil these two conditions, the employment contract is dissolved in cases in which workers:

- did not report to the Provincial Labour Direction or the local employment services in charge of ascertaining the voluntary nature of resignation;

- did not produce the foregoing statement in writing;
- did not revoke their resignation or intention to end the employment contract.

The last aspect concerns the tightening up of the sanctioning mechanism and the devising of administrative fines—ranging from 5,000 to 30,000 Euros—that apply in the event of employers making use of undated letters of resignation, without prejudice to their criminal liability, if any. It is the Provincial Labour Direction that has to determine the employers' liability and the statutory amount to be paid.

5. Reforming the System of Safety-Net Measures

A key aspect of the Monti-Fornero Reform concerns the safeguards provided to workers in cases of loss of employment, as a means to strike a more effective balance between flexibility in hiring and flexibility in dismissals. Although the ambitious proposals originally put forward by the Minister of Labour, the reform does not impact on the system of safety-net measures, which does not distance itself from the protection supplied to the worker in cases of partial or total unemployment.

In the event of partial unemployment, that is suspension or reduction of the working time, workers might rely on certain forms of income support, with the reform that has widened their scope of application also by means of the setting-up of bilateral funds, which might also include ad-hoc funds for lifelong learning for employees of small-sized companies not covered by income support schemes. This money is made available by sectoral employers' associations and unions with the purpose of promoting workers' further education, and is usually used to devise training schemes organized by the employers subsidising the fund. At present, income support measures only cover workers operating in the manufacturing sector, or those in some other industries with a certain number of employees. By way of example, in the commercial sector only businesses with more than 50 employees can apply to such funds.

A wide-ranging reform was put forward in relation to the employment safeguards in case of total unemployment. In this connection, provisions have been introduced to supply protection to workers in a more thoughtful manner by means of Social Insurance for Employment (*Assicurazione Sociale per l'Impiego, ASpI*)—now regarded as the only form of income support in the event of loss of employment. The Social Insurance for Employment will be implemented in place of the unemployment benefits—granted to workers at the end of the employment contract, in cases of dismissal and special instances of resignation—and redundancy allowances—income support provided to workers who have been made redundant or are registered as unemployed in special lists—previously supplied. Finally, the scope of application of traditional forms of income support measures has been widened, with the sole exception of those allocated to workers in the agricultural sector who are enrolled in special registers.

In the event of total and involuntary unemployment, income support measures are envisioned through the Social Insurance for Employment starting from 1 January 2013 to all those eligible after that date. The eligibility criteria are similar to those laid down to access the unemployment benefits currently in place. Most notably, only workers who lose their occupation are entitled to these benefits, with inactive people or those who want to re-enter the labour market following a period of inactivity being excluded from them.

This aspect is noteworthy as it shows that this set of safety-net measures is not universal in scope, pointing out that long-overdue equality in the provision of welfare is not yet ensured.

The system will be fully implemented starting from 2016, subsequent to a round of consultation between the Government and the social partners to assess its sustainability in relation to public expenditure and the transition period between the old and the new system. From 1 January 2014 and throughout the transitional phase, unemployment benefits will gradually increase in duration, whereas redundancy schemes will decrease until their depletion, yet not later than 31 December 2016.

In order to fund the Social Insurance for Employment, the reform imposes an obligation upon the employer to pay a certain amount of money in cases of termination of the employment relationship other than resignation (Article 2, par. 31 of Act No. 92/2012). Payment to the fund in the event of the foregoing conditions will take effect from 1 January 2013 and the sum is arrived at by calculating 50% of the monthly unemployment benefits for each 12 months' seniority over the last three years.

Besides the Social Insurance for Employment, the reform also introduces another type of unemployment benefit, addressing those workers who meet only some of the social security requirements to fully enjoy these forms of income support, which is known as partial unemployment benefits (*Mini ASpI*).

Similarly, to the redundancy schemes previously in place for this category of workers, in order to be entitled to partial unemployment benefits, workers must have paid social contributions amounting to only

13 weeks (78 days) in the 12 months preceding redundancy. However, the difference lies in the fact one of the eligibility criteria—e.g. 2 years' seniority—has been removed, fulfilling the goal of further widening the number of prospective recipients of the employment safeguards. Partial unemployment benefits are supplied for a period amounting to half the number of weeks for which contributions have been paid in the last year, deduced by previous benefits, if any.

5.1. The Conditionality of the Unemployment Benefits

With a view to help jobless people adequately re-enter the labour market—most notably those who are in receipt of unemployment benefits—the Legislator has long since laid down a number of conditions that need to be satisfied in order to gain or maintain the status of unemployed, and thus being granted unemployment entitlements. These conditions mainly concern the attitude of recipients of benefits in relation to active labour policies—taking part in interviews, training, active job-search—or their status at the time of accepting an offer of work. In reality, this system has never been implemented, nor have there been any reported cases in which unemployment benefits have been suspended or terminated.

An attempt to make this conditionality more effective is that of raising the eligibility requirements. In this sense, recipients of unemployment benefits lose such entitlement if they perform a working activity resulting in annual earnings that are higher than the individual minimum income excluded from taxation. In a similar vein, the duration of contracts in salaried employment causing the termination of the unemployment benefits has been reduced to 6 to 8 months. Furthermore, unemployment benefits might be terminated on the grounds of a refusal to respond to an offer of work, either open-ended or fixed-term ones and irrespective of the duration of the employment contract.

Along the same lines, with a view to encourage benefit recipients to actively seek work, help them to re-enter the labour market and make the conditions to supply income support more stringent, unemployment benefits—provided to both unemployed and inactive people—are terminated as a result of an unjustified refusal to take part in initiatives in the area of social policies or those promoted by relevant services. The same applies in cases of individuals occasionally taking part in such initiatives, or job seekers who forgo job offers for which they are paid at least 20% of the gross amount of the benefit granted.

If still in employment, the provision of unemployment benefits is terminated in the event of a refusal to attend training or retraining courses or even to take part in them on an irregular basis without a justified reason. In this sense, only working activities, training and retraining courses carried out within 50 Km of the individual's residence—or that can be reached in at most 80 minutes by means of public transport—pertain.

5.2. Lump Sum Benefits for Workers in Quasi-Salaried Employment

The government has committed to provide income support to workers in quasi-salaried employment (continuous and coordinated collaborators). This category of workers is regarded as distinct from that of autonomous workers—as they operate in absence of financial risks and without making use of site machinery and equipment—and salaried employees—for differences arising in terms of organisational autonomy, and no rights to exercise managerial and disciplinary power on the part of the user-company. This move is intended to supply forms of income protection to all economically dependent workers, irrespective of the degree of autonomy or subordination.

Indeed, the Legislator in 2008 moved along the same lines—although on an experimental basis—envisioning a lump-sum allowance for workers on quasi-salaried employment who operate for one client in the event of a shortage of labour.

The reform programme is intended to safeguard this category of workers, as they do not fall within the scope of application of Social Insurance for Employment, which only addresses salaried employees. Accordingly, starting from 2013, a lump-sum allowance will be granted to workers on quasi-salaried employment who have only operated for one employer in the previous year, if they pay contributions to the National Social Insurance Fund on an exclusive basis and in accordance to a special scheme (*Gestione Separata*).

In order to be eligible, workers on quasi-salaried employment contracts must meet certain conditions in terms of income and contributions. The lump sum benefit amounts to 5% of the minimum taxable income paid for social security purposes, multiplied by the lowest remuneration received on a monthly basis in the previous year—at least four months' pay—and remuneration not subject to contributions. The lump sum allowance is granted in a single payment whereas lower than 1,000 Euros, or in monthly rates amounting to 1,000 Euros or less if lower than 1,000 Euros.

6. A Preliminary Assessment of the Reform: The Omnipotence of the Law, the Demise of Concertation, and the Debased Role of Collective Bargaining

Reviewing the legal framework of the employment relationship has never been an easy task, in Italy more so than elsewhere. This is exhibited by the wave of terrorist attacks against drafters and practitioners who have engaged in the reform of labour law in our country. Accordingly, the efforts of those who undertake this task, which is as complex as crucial for the Italian labour market should be acknowledged. All the more so as this is done in an awareness of the delicacy of the matter and the political, economic, and social implications that entail. Indeed, innovative and forward-looking ideas have never been lacking in Italy.

As recalled by Prof Marco Biagi ten years ago—the last victim of terroristic attacks linked to labour issues—there is a need to move beyond ideological blinkers and social tensions that prevent the devising of reforms necessary to keep up with the changes currently underway. His teachings are still relevant today, and the passing of Act No. 92 of 2012 on the part of the Monti's Government demonstrates for the first time that it is possible to overcome legal constraints and limitations that have long penalized Italy in the international and comparative context. On close examination, this is the most relevant aspect the Government and Elsa Fornero—the tenacious Minister of Labour—should be credited for.

Nevertheless, the reform came under heavy criticism for a number of reasons, even prior to the amendments made by the Government and the Parliament approval. This might be ascribed also to the fact that Italy is lacking of an *ex ante* evaluation system that foresees the economic and social impact of newly issued provisions. This state of affairs of course acts as a hindrance to the reform process and gives rise to a number of objections devoid of solid grounds.

Indubitably, the reform drafted by the technocrats currently in office does not appeal to labour lawyers nor to operators in the labour market. The few proponents of the reform programme are mainly experts in the field who perform a dual role—they are both academics and members of the Parliament—and contributed to issue and approve the reform.

Employers' associations and trade unions are likewise discontent, albeit for opposite reasons. From where the employers stand, the narrowing down in the use of atypical and fixed-term contracts is unacceptable, especially for small-sized enterprises, which unlike large and medium-sized companies, did not benefit from provisions concerning flexibility in dismissals.[16]

Trade unions for their part oppose the deregulation of provisions on dismissals for economic reasons in open-ended employment. The remedy of reinstatement in the event of unfair dismissal, (rightly or wrongly) perceived as peculiar to Italy within the international context, has been limited only to certain cases (see par. 3.4.3.). As for compensation, it has been extended also to large-sized enterprises, yet the relevant procedures remain unclear.

Trade union leaders, yet this view is also shared by most academics, signal that the shift from property rule to liability rule with regard to dismissals will undermine the position of workers who, primarily during an economic crisis, will be forced to take jobs with low levels of protection and remuneration.

Academics also maintain that the reform is inadequate in technical terms and much groundwork is needed. Nevertheless, there is a need to avoid the tendency, which is peculiar to Italy, to reject any attempt to change *a priori*, that is without carefully entering into the merits of the proposals that are put forward. Arguing against the mechanics and the underlying principles of a proposal—as is the case of the Italian reform—is often done in support of ideologies and lines of thought arguing in favour of the relationship between capital and labour.

Indeed, the Treu and the Biagi Reforms[17] have shown that substantial pieces of legislation can be appreciated only after a relatively long period that is after an implementation period and a harmonisation process with the extant legal framework.[18] As a result, Mr Monti is absolutely right in telling the *Wall Street Journal* that the reform deserves "a serious analysis rather than snap judgments".[19]

However, the lack of an adequate evaluation system in Italy that helps to predict the impact of the provisions put in place questions the unfaltering assertion made by the Italian Prime Minister and reported by

---

[16] Supra, note 7.

[17] See Tiraboschi, M. 2005. "The Italian Labour Market after the Biagi Reform", *The International Journal of Comparative Labour Law and Industrial Relations* 21, No. 2: 149-192.

[18] In a similar vein, see Tiraboschi, M. 2008. "The Reform of the Italian Labor Market over the Past Ten Years: A Process of Liberalization?", *Comparative Labor Law and Policy Journal* 29, No. 4, 2008, 427-458.

[19] Monti, M. 2012. "Italy's Labor Reforms Are Serious and Will Be Effective", *The Wall Street Journal, April 7, p. A14.* See also in Adapt International Bulletin, No. 14, 2012, at *www.adaptbulletin.eu.*

the same newspaper, according to which the reform "will have a major and positive impact on the Italian economy".

The major problem of the Italian labour market is not the (vast) amount of provisions enacted nor their technical content, but their full implementation and effectiveness.

Experience clearly indicates that many legislative measures remain only on paper. This is the case of a number of proposals envisioned in the reform of the labour market of 2003 (the Biagi Reform), among others the national employment information service, the access-to-work contracts addressing women living in the South of Italy, the apprenticeship contracts providing an alternation between school and work and modelled after the German system, forms of cooperation between public and private operators, the accreditation system of employment agencies, the suspension of the unemployment benefits for those who refuse training or an adequate offer of work underpinning an innovative system of safety-net measures.

These institutions have gained momentum, or have been amended by the newly issued reform, yet they are bound to remain unenforced without the involvement of social and political parties, operators of the labour market and actors of industrial relations.

Accordingly, if one considers the two principles underpinning the reform—higher flexibility in dismissals and lower flexibility in hiring—the amendments made to the contractual arrangements appear to be inappropriate (supra par. 2). Paradoxically, unfulfilled promises of stable employment and the limitations placed upon project and temporary work come to penalise not only compliant employers, but also precarious workers who are not offered stable occupations at the end of the 36-month period until which fixed-term contracts can be extended. This aspect contributes to raise the rate of undeclared work, which is another major problem of the Italian labour market, which in turn, might bring about a tightening up of the sanctioning system, as well as an increase in the cost of labour and bureaucracy. This state of play will jeopardise the successful effort made in the last twenty years with the Biagi and Treu Reforms to regulate jobs performed in the hidden economy, restoring the recourse to undeclared work, and encouraging precarious employment and processes of delocalisation.

Neither telling are the arguments put forward to modify Article 18 of the Workers' Statute (Law No. 300/1970), a cornerstone of Italian labour law. According to this provision, employers with less than 15 employees are under the obligation to reinstate workers who are found to be unfairly dismissed. The issue has attracted wide media coverage at both national and international level but produced a result that goes in the opposite direction to that expected by those who argued in favour of its repeal or a narrowing down of its scope of application. Once again, it would have been sufficient to refer to the teachings of Marco Biagi, who always argued for the need to resort to common sense in envisaging interventions that would not affect the modernisation of the labour market or jeopardize the dialogue between lawmakers and social partners. He used to say, "Why didn't I make reference to Article No. 18? The reason is quite simple. The White Paper made a passing reference to Article 18, but it was not regarded as a key aspect, even though it shows a bias towards its amendments. I think that reinstatement is no longer applicable. It is just a sort of symbol, a deterrent measure with no power of discouraging dismissals. Indeed, its deterrent nature lies in the fact that it promotes fraudulent practices. Worldwide, unfairly dismissed workers are entitled to compensation. This is done under civil law, pursuant to which the only way to deal with the damage suffered by workers is to grant them the payment of a compensation award—regardless of the amount and the waiting time.

Notwithstanding its marginal role, one might ask why we still discuss Article 18. Actually, I do not think that this topic should be discussed. We had better focus on some other, and far more relevant, issues".[20] The struggle over Article 18 of the Workers' Statute allowed the Government to repeatedly—and perhaps naively—assert the effectiveness of the reform, on the assumption that, if the reform is criticized by everyone, it means that a balance has been stricken between different interests. This is the position of the Minister of Labour Elsa Fornero prior to the passing of the reform, while from the *Wall Street Journal* a rather confident Prime Minister Mario Monti maintained that "the fact that it has been attacked by both the main employers' association and the metalworkers union, and part of the leading trade union confederation, indicates that we have got the balance right". In the author's view, this is the heart of the problem.

The idea that a reform is balanced because it makes everyone unhappy is paradoxical.

The assumption that changes to the existing legal framework are necessary to keep up with "new needs arising from a different context"—as reported in the report accompanying the legislative text—was not followed up with a careful reading of the new conditions, leading the reform to promote once again the same pattern of open-ended employment

[20] Biagi, M. 2002. "Non fissiamoci sul 18," intervention made to CNEL, November 2001, *L'Espresso,* 18 April 2002, p. 56.

relationships which characterized Taylorism and Fordism over the last century.[21]

The peripheral role allocated to the consultation process with social partners on the part of the Government led some to talk of the demise of concertation. However, there is more than meets the eye.

Aside from the marginal role carried out by employers' associations, and above all trade unions, in devising the reform, it is beyond dispute that mandatory provisions play a major role whereas limited room to manoeuvre is left to collective bargaining and social partners.

Accordingly, rather than the method of concertation, it is the principle of subsidiarity and the role of decentralized collective bargaining that are penalised the most, along with the trust placed in an autonomous model of industrial relations and a bilateral approach, so far the privileged channel for the regulation of the labour market.

The truth is that the Monti-Fornero Reform is not poorly made or technically inadequate, as maintained by some labour law scholars, but simply conceptually wrong because it draws on the assumption that it is possible to deal with diversified production and work processes by way of a single (or prevailing) and open-ended employment relationship, which for Mr. Monti himself no longer exists and is labelled as "boring".

In practical terms, this will act as a hindrance to the recourse of quasi-salaried employment (coordinated and continuative work) or autonomous work. In addition, temporary work is limited to exceptional cases and to temporary needs, and incentives for access-to-work contracts for disadvantaged workers will be repealed. Further, the use of part-time work and other forms of employment relationships (including the use of the voucher system and on-call work) will also be limited, although over the years, they contributed to legalize undeclared work.

On reflection, however, the ongoing change of the economic context provides for a major overhaul of flexible, quasi-salaried, and temporary employment only on condition that flexibility in dismissals is increased, and if accompanied by a review of the safety-net measures.

A halfway solution, such as the one put forward in the reform would end up penalizing employers, but above all workers. Younger workers and those currently forced out of the labour market will bear the brunt of the

---

[21] Some critical remarks on the central role of open-ended salaried employment in relation to the transposition of the 1999 Directive on fixed-term work, of a more general nature, can be found in Tiraboschi, M. 1999. "Glancing at the Past: An Agreement for the Markets of XXIst Century," *The International Journal of Comparative Labour Law and Industrial Relations* 15, No. 2: 105-120.

reform and, accordingly, they will no longer be pushed towards precarious employment but rather towards illegal and undeclared work.

For the most part, workers feel more insecure and precarious than in the past. Employers believe that the regulatory framework is unsuitable to face the challenges posed by globalisation and new markets.

There is profound dissatisfaction with a very complex body of law that does not provide workers with the necessary protection, hampering the dynamism of production processes and labour organization. Against this background, it would be foolish to push for a radical reform of the labour market that will probably just remain on paper.

Overindulging in reforms is certainly a lesser evil than partisanship and ideological blinkers that marked the last ten years in Italy, yet at the end of the day, it is perhaps just as damaging and counterproductive.

Today workers and businesses need a very simple regulatory framework, with effective rather than formal rules, to be complied with by everyone as contributing to foster mutual trust and active collaboration at the workplaces. A competitive economy must rely on highly motivated workers, who give their best, invest in their skills and adaptability, rather than on an overly rigid protection system. This is what stability of employment really means, a kind of stability based on mutual advantage rather than on norms that are statutorily imposed.

The fact that the reform of the labour market leaves everyone unsatisfied should not be regarded as a positive feedback, rather as a serious weakness of a provision imposed by the Government, which reduces the role of the social partners and moves away from an autonomous system of industrial relations to regulate employment relationships at all levels.

The attempt to strike a balance between flexibility and security caused this reform to be incomplete, a halfway reform that oscillates between a dangerous past and a future that is still to be planned.

The risk that "growth" would only be a word in the title of the legislative text is thus far from being unlikely.

CHAPTER FOUR

THE ITALIAN LABOUR MARKET AFTER THE BIAGI REFORM

1. The Reasons for the Reform[1]

With the entry into force of Act No. 30/2003, and the decrees implementing the Act, Italy has initiated an ambitious process for the radical reform of the labour market.

The reform project outlined in the White Paper on the Labour Market published in October 2001[2] has encountered considerable difficulties along the way, and this helps to explain why the Italian legislator has provided quite a long interim period,[3] in order to enable the transition from the old to the new legal framework to be carried out gradually by means of a series of experimental stages. The opposition of part of the trade union movement to Government proposals to suspend or repeal, even only on an experimental basis,[4] certain consolidated elements of Italian labour law—in particular, Article 18 of the *Statuto dei lavoratori* that dates back to 1970 and deals with the protection of the worker in the case of unjustified dismissal—gave rise to a long period of tension and social conflict that had a strong impact on the approval of a range of measures, even though they are largely a continuation of those adopted during the previous legislature, and in particular the Treu measures introduced in 1997.

---

[1] The present contribution was previously published in 2005 in *The International Journal of Comparative Labour Law and Industrial Relations* 21, No. 2:149-192.

[2] Available *at www.adapt.it*, selecting *Riforma Biagi* from the list of contents A-Z.

[3] For a reconstruction of the transitional legal provisions and an assessment see Tiraboschi, M. ed. 2004. *La riforma Biagi del mercato del lavoro, Prime interpretazioni e proposte di lettura del d.lgs. 10 settembre 2003, n. 276. Il diritto transitorio e i tempi della riforma*. Milano: Giuffrè.

[4] The reform makes provision for a two-year experimental period (October 2003—October 2005), after which by means of negotiation the Government and the social partners will ascertain which norms to confirm, and which ones to amend or repeal.

Nor should it be forgotten that the confrontation between the Government and the social partners was dramatically altered—and contaminated—by a sudden revival of domestic terrorism with the assassination by a group of terrorists on the evening of 19 March 2002 of Prof. Marco Biagi, who had drafted both the White Paper and the related delegating legislation.[5]

Only in the early months of 2003—in the wake of the tripartite agreement of 5 July 2002 (known as the *Patto per l'Italia* or Pact for Italy) signed by 36 employers' and trade union organisations (with the sole exception of the CGIL)[6] and following the entry into force of Act No. 30/2003[7]—was it possible to proceed with a legislative intervention aimed at reorganising the labour market,[8] together with the reform of the Labour Inspectorate and the supervisory functions relating to employment and social insurance.[9] In relation to the programme outlined in the White Paper, the parts that still have to be introduced are the new safety-net measures—that are incorporated, together with the proposal to modify Article 18 of the *Statuto dei lavoratori*, in a proposal for delegating legislation currently under discussion in Parliament—and, at a later stage, a *Statuto dei lavori* or Work Statute.[10] The Government intends this to be a single piece of legislation consolidating all the norms relating to labour law, so that the current reform becomes part of an organic and unitary framework. The reform of the labour market—quite rightly dedicated to Marco Biagi[11]—should not be seen as the final stage of a reform programme that can trace its roots a long way back. Rather, the legislative decrees implementing Act No. 30/2003 represent a starting point, an essential step that is not sufficient in itself to bring about a complex redefinition and rationalisation of the rules governing the labour market.

---

[5] News reports and articles on the various stages of the reform are available at *www.adapt.it*.

[6] See *www.adapt.it*, list of contents A-Z, *Statuto dei lavori*.

[7] See *www.adapt.it*, list of contents A-Z, *Riforma Biagi*.

[8] See Legislative Decree No. 276/2003, as amended by Legislative Decree No. 251/2004, at *www.adapt.it*, list of contents A-Z, *Riforma Biagi*.

[9] See Legislative Decree No. 124/2004, at *www.adapt.it,* list of contents A-Z, *Servizi ispettivi*.

[10] See *www.adapt.it*, list of contents A-Z, *Statuto dei lavori*.

[11] The polemical discussion about the authorship of the reform appears to have been rather futile. For a collection of drafts and norms that provide incontrovertible evidence of the fact that the reform was designed by Marco Biagi, see Tiraboschi, M. 2004. "La riforma Biagi del mercato del lavoro: il lungo percorso della modernizzazione", *Quaderni AGENS*, No. 1, available at *www.adapt.it,* selecting *Riforma Biagi*.

This is not just because the necessary preconditions are now being put in place for a codification of a *Statuto dei lavori* or Work Statute, laying down a body of fundamental rights for all workers, and not just those in the public administration or in large and medium-sized undertakings, in order to overcome once and for all the dichotomy between those with a particularly high level of protection and those with hardly any safeguards at all, resulting from an ill-conceived and short-sighted distribution of employment protection rights. What is even more decisive, in this transition period between the old and the new legal frameworks, is the role of the social partners and, in particular, of the bilateral bodies[12] provided in the new legislation as the forum for the regulation of the labour market and for balancing the interests of the two sides. The reform assigns a central role to the social partners, as shown by the 43 references to collective bargaining in the decree law. Collective bargaining is therefore intended as the means for dealing with the various matters covered by the reform.

Any assessment of the implementation of the reform therefore needs to be based on a careful monitoring of collective bargaining, as this is essential for the implementation of the measures laid down by the national legislation. However, this will only be possible at the end of the transition period, and in particular only once the functions to be performed by the social partners have been implemented not only in the various productive sectors but also in individual undertakings and above all at a local and regional level.

On this basis, in order to describe the most important developments and the changes taking place in the regulation of the Italian labour market since the enactment of the Biagi reform, it is necessary to provide an outline of the reasons for the reform, reasons that are evident if we consider the poor performance of the Italian labour market in comparison not just with that of the United States and Japan, but also with other European countries.

Over the years, the Italian economy has been characterised by low employment levels in relation to economic growth, also due to the significant barriers that limit access to the regular labour market, as shown in Fig. 1-13.

---

[12] See De Lucia, D., and S. Ciuffini. 2004. "The System of Bilateral Bodies in the Artisan Sector: The Italian Experience in the Context of European Social Dialogue", *IJCLIR* 20, No. 1:133.

Fig. 1-13: Growth in GDP and employment trends in Italy

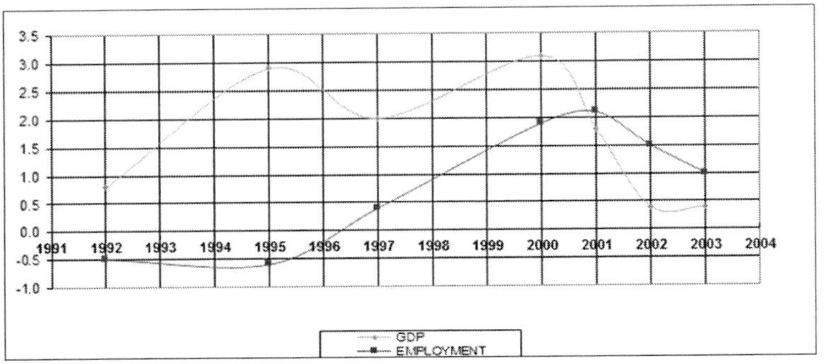

Source: Graph based on ISTAT figures

What is particularly serious is the shortfall compared to the employment objectives laid down in Lisbon, most notably the target of 70 per cent employment for all the European economies. In spite of the positive trend over the past three years (with a 2.5 per cent increase), in 2003 the regular employment rate stood at just 56 per cent of the total population, the worst performance in Europe. The female employment rate, at 42.7 per cent, is also clearly insufficient, and the same may be said for those over the age of 55, at just 30.3 per cent. Activity and employment rates for men and women are shown in Fig. 1-14.

Fig. 1-14: Rates of activity (A) and employment (E) for the 15-64 age range, 2002-2003

	2002				**2003**			
	Men		**Women**		**Men**		**Women**	
	(A)	**(E)**	**(A)**	**(E)**	**(A)**	**(E)**	**(A)**	**(E)**
North	76.0	74.0	55.7	52.5	76.6	74.6	56.5	53.4
Centre	74.0	70.5	50.8	46.0	74.9	71.4	51.8	46.9
South	71.4	61.2	36.8	27.0	71.4	61.4	36.3	27.1
Italy	74.0	68.8	47.9	42.0	74.4	69.3	48.3	42.7

Source: National Employment Plan 2004 based on ISTAT figures

In addition, the duration of unemployment is one of the longest in Europe: more than 5 per cent of the workforce has been unemployed for at least a year, compared to the EU average of 3.8 per cent. The statistics are even more alarming if we shift the focus from the national to the regional figures, and consider the territorial differences between the North and the South of Italy. The shortage of workers in the North-East is the counterpoint to the high level of unemployment and the limited prospects for growth in the *Mezzogiorno*. In recent months, unemployment in the South has fallen below 20 per cent, but the chronic inefficiency of the public employment services tends to aggravate the long-term structural problems rather than alleviating them.

Together with a regular employment rate that is one of the lowest in Europe, Italy is characterised by an enormous submerged or hidden economy, especially in the South, that is estimated to account for 23-27 per cent of GDP,[13] twice the European average. This may be seen as a national emergency that concerns a vast number of people: more than four million workers, who are employed outside of any regulatory framework. There is also an extensive grey area, between self-employment and salaried employment, often consisting of forms of employment that are based on a legal fiction of self-employment when they are not actually *contra legem*.

It is well known that in the late 1990s, various forms of employment not leading to a stable and regular occupation gradually degenerated, giving rise to a kind of quasi-salaried employment known as *collaborazioni coordinate e continuative.* Many undertakings made widespread use of this form of employment in a vain attempt to meet the demands of competition, in an increasingly international market, simply by reducing costs instead of aiming to improve the quality of labour by investing in human capital. This model of employment contract is associated not just with genuine forms of self-employment, but also with precarious forms of employment that give rise to situations of illicit work and the evasion of social insurance contributions, which until recently was widely tolerated. The fact that such practices are firmly rooted in the Italian labour market goes some way to explaining the lack of flexible forms of salaried employment facilitating access to the labour market on the part of young people and women, and encouraging the participation of older persons.

In the rest of Europe—where quasi-salaried employment in the form of *collaborazioni coordinate e continuative* does not exist—part-time work involves 18 per cent of the workforce (and one out of every three women), and fixed-term contracts almost 13 per cent of the workforce, whereas in

---

[13] Research reports on employment in the hidden economy are available on the website of the Ministry of Labour and Social Policy (www.welfare.gov.it), selecting *Lavoro, occupazione e mercato del lavoro.*

Italy just 9 per cent of workers are part-time, and fixed-term contracts account for just under 10 per cent.

Moreover, the provisions for supporting the transition from full-time education to employment are inadequate. The employment and training participation rate on the part of young people is more than 6 percentage points lower than in the rest of Europe, whereas the unemployment rates for young people, and the long-term unemployment rates for the same category (in the case of young people, more than six months without work or training) are among the highest in Europe.

Italy presents clear and alarming signs of a decline in the quality of human capital also in terms of training for those of working age, in the form of continuing education. Although some informal training is provided in the extensive network of small and medium-sized enterprises, without which it would be hard to account for Italy's competitive position, Italy's performance in terms of lifelong learning is better only than that of Greece and Portugal, even in the enlarged EU with 25 Member States. The European average is almost 10 per cent of the workforce receiving training in the past year (still far short of the target adopted in Lisbon), whereas in Italy it is just 4 per cent.

This figure also reflects a low level of occupational mobility in the Italian labour market, compared to the economies of the UK, the Netherlands and the Nordic countries that have rates that are from five to eight times higher.

Recent surveys[14] have shown that in Italy three out of four enterprises (accounting for 44 per cent of employees) have carried out no training at all. The main factor appears to be the absence of any perception of the need for training or the lack of time on the part of the employees, who are too busy contributing to the production of goods and services. On the other hand, training costs do not appear to be a significant factor for companies, though in this case Italy ranks above the other EU countries, with a cost of €47 per participant against an EU average of €31. Considering the enterprises taking part in the survey, just 18 per cent reported that the training services they required were available on the market, a figure that was well below the EU average of 29 per cent.

From the scenario outlined above it was clear—and continues to be clear—to those drafting the reform that the labour market is not highly developed and is lacking in dynamism, with negative features both in quantitative and qualitative terms, and a low level of investment in human

---

[14] See the bibliography in Sacconi, M., P. Reboani, and M. Tiraboschi. 2004. *La Società attiva.* Venice: Marsilio.

capital. Alongside a group of workers enjoying high levels of protection (some 3.5 million in the public administration and some 8.5 million in large and medium-sized enterprises), there are others with low levels of protection (more than five million atypical or non-standard workers along with those employed in small and medium-sized enterprises), and those with no protection whatsoever (some four million workers in the hidden economy).

The Biagi reform takes as its starting point the need to recognise and deal with the poor performance of the Italian labour market and—as stated in Article 1 of Legislative Decree No. 276/2003—to contribute to increasing the rates of regular quality employment, especially with regard to access to employment for the categories at risk of social exclusion, the so-called outsiders.

2. The Pillars of the Biagi Reform of the Labour Market: Employability, Adaptability and Equal Opportunities

In the light of the overall structure of the labour market outlined above, with all its evident shortcomings, it seems to be misleading to interpret the Biagi reform, as has been prevalently the case until now, as if it were intended to expand the area of precarious employment or, on the basis of political and/or ideological positions, in terms of mere flexibility as an end in itself.[15] It is clear that with some four million workers in the hidden economy and some two million in quasi-salaried employment the Italian labour market has been characterised for some time by the worst forms of precarious employment of a deregulated kind, over which the trade unions are not in a position to exert any influence. Flexibility of this kind is therefore outside the legal framework, with serious consequences in terms of employment protection but also in terms of competition between enterprises, giving rise to a vicious circle that the Biagi reform is intended to break, albeit by means of largely experimental measures that need to be put to the test in practical terms. It is significant that the final article of Legislative Decree No. 276/2003 clearly states the experimental nature of the decree, specifying that in May 2005 a round of negotiations is to take place between the Government and the social partners to assess its impact on the labour market, also with a view to introducing any changes to the legal provisions that may be required.

---

[15] For a survey of the legal issues, see Biagi, M., and M. Tiraboschi. 2004. *Istituzioni di diritto del lavoro*. Milano: Giuffrè.

If the interpretation of the reform as an attempt to introduce flexibility and precarious employment is misleading, in a market that is as dysfunctional as ours is, the key words for interpreting the reform appear to be "employability", "adaptability" and "equal opportunities". These concepts are adopted as labour policy guidelines in the European Employment Strategy[16] and are embodied in the reform in an efficient system of employment services, public and private, authorised and accredited, which, as part of a network creating an online employment database, facilitates the matching of the supply and demand for labour.[17] The various forms of flexibility in this framework are regulated and negotiated with the trade unions, providing an alternative to precarious employment and the hidden economy, and striking a balance between the requirements of the enterprise to compete on international markets, and the fundamental need for employment protection and for improving conditions for employees. Moreover, the framework provides for experimental measures with active "workfare" policies in favour of those groups of workers who today encounter most difficulty in gaining access to regular employment of good quality, with a view to improving job security, achieving a balance between work and personal and family life, meeting the needs of women workers, workers with disabilities, young people and persons over 45/50 years of age, and so on.[18]

Further initiatives include measures to promote and support compliance with the law, rendering effective legal provisions rather than honouring them in the breach, by means of a redesigned Labour Inspectorate and supervisory functions relating to employment and social insurance.[19]

The central aim of the reform, as stated in the technical report accompanying it,[20] is to safeguard the employability of each worker in a context—that of the knowledge and information society—in which the paradigms of economic growth and social development tend to converge and enhance the importance of the individual (in the sense of human capital). In relation to this objective, it is only ideological blinkers that

---

[16] On the relationship between the Biagi reform and the European Employment Strategy, see Biagi, M., and M. Tiraboschi, *Istituzioni di diritto del lavoro,* cit.

[17] For an in-depth analysis, see Olivelli, P., and M. Tiraboschi, eds. 2005. *Il diritto del mercato del lavoro dopo la Riforma Biagi*. Milano: Giuffrè.

[18] For further discussion, see the papers in Tiraboschi, M., ed. *La riforma Biagi del mercato del lavoro,* cit.

[19] For further analysis, see the papers in Monticelli, C., and M. Tiraboschi, eds. 2004. *La riforma dei servizi ispettivi e delle attività di vigilanza,* Milano: Giuffrè.

[20] See *www.adapt.it*, list of contents A-Z, *Riforma Biagi.*

prevent the recognition of the fact that the Italian labour market today is particularly inefficient and lacking in equity, as shown by the extensive areas of social exclusion (evidence for which is to be found in the low employment rates and the abnormal level of irregular employment in the hidden economy) and the precarious nature of much employment arising from low levels of educational achievement and the lack of continuing education and training (see *infra* § 1).

Although there are some gaps that need to be filled (above all the lack of a modern system of safety-net measures), the reform places an emphasis on the central role of persons of working age—considering both their rights and their responsibilities—when it redefines the employment services as a network based on the personal details of the individual worker, to be accompanied by a training portfolio. This concept is further developed in the promotion of an efficient and transparent labour market by means of an online employment database, along with duly authorised and/or accredited employment consultants, and centres for the certification of employment contracts—all of them free of charge for the worker—providing assistance to social actors who in many cases are "weak" due to the lack of adequate information and training. In this way access is provided to information about all the employment opportunities across the country in a transparent and timely manner, so those seeking work can find an employment contract that matches their requirements.

In this connection mention should be made of the reform of safety-net measures currently under discussion in Parliament, which, as agreed in the Pact for Italy of 5 July 2002, extends the period for which unemployment benefit is paid, making it payable for twice as long as at present; in addition it provides for supplementary benefits to be paid by the social partners, and close links between the social partners and the training and career guidance services. This part of the reform will complete the framework of active employment policies required for a modern and transparent labour market capable of identifying and preventing individual social exclusion.

Until this part of the reform is approved, there is a risk that the provisions introduced by the Biagi law risk not being sufficient to revive the Italian labour market and provide support for workers in the transition from one form of employment to another.

Once the system of safety-net measures comes into force, the new contracts[21] introduced by the Biagi law will contribute to an improvement of the employability of the individual. These contracts are intended to

[21] See *infra,* documentation.

combine (genuine) training and (quality) employment, such as the new apprenticeship contracts, that, together with employment access contracts, are a way to allocate economic incentives for employment primarily in favour of weaker groups in the labour market. These are fixed-term contracts, but nobody can consider them to be the cause of precarious employment, since they are not only accompanied by legal provisions aiming at job stability, but they also provide access or a return to the labour market by offering training to those who lack key employment skills, or whose skills are now outdated. The new apprenticeship contracts perform a specific function for those who have dropped out of school, as they are linked to a system of credits to facilitate a return to full-time education.

A significant provision of the reform is the setting up of joint training bodies, providing training for various categories, including apprentices and workers made redundant. Although such bodies are to be found in comparative experience, in Italy they are a significant innovation. In implementing Act No. 388/2000, and in keeping with the aims of the Biagi law, provision has been made to allow enterprises to allocate 0.3 per cent of total payroll costs to the training and retraining of employees. Thanks to the joint training bodies, the social partners now have the opportunity to play a key role in planning and managing a substantial share of the public funding allocated for training. The bilateral approach, directly involving the employers' associations and the trade unions, is the most appropriate way to identify and respond to the demand for continuous education and training, leading to innovative programmes for the management of resources and training schemes. In order to raise the level of continuous education and training, it is essential to facilitate access, to reduce the cost of management of training centres, to disseminate knowledge, and to provide practical, financial and procedural indicators, *ex ante* and *in itinere*, to support the planning and implementation of training schemes.

Mention should also be made of the new approach to the regulation of contracts with non-standard or flexible hours (part-time, job sharing, on-call or zero-hours contracts) that are intended to encourage the mutual adaptation between the requirements of employees and those of the employer by means of contracts aimed at providing stability of employment. When a company decides to increase the number of employees in relation to the same workload, it modifies its organisational structure with lasting effects, leading to more employment in the form of open-ended contracts. Moreover, it is evident that the chance to reconcile work and personal or family commitments facilitates access and continuing participation in the labour market for many men and women who would otherwise not be able to take up employment opportunities. Flexibility is incorporated into these contracts as a means to achieve regular and stable employment, aiming not at the disintegration of stable employment and careers, but rather at providing an effective legal framework for work that would otherwise be carried out in a precarious and informal manner in the hidden economy, that in Italy is estimated to be three or four times larger than in other European countries.

A further objective of the reform is to provide for the appropriate development—and a legal framework in keeping with the demands of the new economy and the need for employment protection—of processes of labour outsourcing (and insourcing), enabling companies to benefit from networking arrangements and from investments in information and communications technology (with the development of facility management, logistics, and so on) in order to deal with fraudulent forms of labour outsourcing.

In particular, employment agency work, including both temporary agency work and staff leasing, though often alleged to be a form of exploitation that reduces the status of labour to that of a commodity, does not reduce the level of protection of the worker and undermine his or her dignity, provided that, for this purpose, a binding contract is agreed on between the employment agency and the worker. In other words, agency work is in itself a neutral procedure that does not determine the nature of the employment relation, but is simply an exchange between a company providing certain services and another company that utilises them. The significant issue is rather that of the legal protection provided for the worker. In this regard, it is highly significant that in Italian case law and legislation, there are continual references to legitimate forms of agency work and illegitimate forms of workforce intermediation.

In this connection, a significant provision is to be found in Legislative Decree No. 276, 10 September 2003, which provides sanctions in the case of illegitimate or fraudulent forms of agency work, thus confirming to all intents and purposes a similar provision in Article 1 of Act No. 1369/1960. In spite of claims that employment agency work was undergoing total deregulation, the provisions regulating employment agencies now take a strong stand on fraudulent dealings, in order to prevent agency work being used in such a way as to harm the rights of employees based on inderogable provisions of law or collective bargaining. At the same time, these provisions aim to clarify the law deriving from the case law interpretations relating to the combined effect of Article 2094 of the Civil Code and Article 1 of Act No. 1269/1960. The aim of the decree is therefore not only to repeal all those norms aimed solely at preventing flexibility in the management of labour, even in cases where labour protection is not at stake, but also at removing obstacles to forms of labour outsourcing that can play a significant role in the context of the new economy.

A further indication that procedures such as staff leasing are not a matter of speculation in the labour market is to be found in the principle of equal treatment laid down in the decree between temporary agency workers and employees of the same grade in the user enterprise (on the basis of the framework laid down in the Treu reforms regulating temporary labour). As shown in comparative research,[22] in the systems where the equal treatment principle is adopted, the net income of the employment agency is not simply based on the difference between the amount received by the agency and the amount paid to the worker: once equal treatment has been assured for the agency employee, the earnings of the employment agency are necessarily based on the capacity of the agency to supply labour in a timely and professional manner that without the intervention of the agency would be uneconomical for the user company to procure, or specialised labour that may not be readily available on the market. In these cases the earnings of the employment agency can be justified as profits arising from a typical business risk in that agency is obliged to offer at market conditions a service which, in terms of the individual worker, is supplied at a higher cost than that which in theory the user company would incur were it to hire the employee directly. On the other hand, the higher costs incurred by the user company that makes use of the services of the employment agency, together with the fact that not all the responsibilities typically taken on by the employer are transferred to the agency, should mean that the user company makes use of agency workers only in the case of objective need. It is for this reason that the use of agency work, especially for an unlimited period (staff leasing), is linked to the presence of technical, organisational or productive reasons laid down by the legislator or delegated to collective bargaining.

---

[22] See Tiraboschi, M. 1999. *Lavoro temporaneo e somministrazione di manodopera.* Torino: Giappichelli, including bibliographical references.

3. Towards an Open, Transparent and Efficient Labour Market

The aim of creating an open, transparent and efficient labour market, that was the fundamental criterion for Act No. 30/2003 on the reform of the labour market, has given rise to the need to provide a clear and explicit organisational model and related regulatory techniques.[23] This task was approached in two distinct ways. On the one hand, a definition was provided of the roles and functions of the various actors taking part in the regulation of the labour market with regard both to the structural norms, that is to say the norms aimed at the organisation of the market, and the regulatory norms, that is to say the norms, including sanctions but above all incentives, aimed at guiding the behaviour of those operating on the market. On the other hand, a definition was provided of the roles and functions of the various operators (both public and private) on the market supplying various types of services and taking part in the management of the relative organisational model.[24]

From the point of view of the regulation of the market, the roles and functions of the various actors reflect the principle of subsidiarity, and are defined in compliance with the powers assigned to the Regions in relation to "employment protection and security" by Constitutional Act No. 3, 18 October 2001, as confirmed by an important ruling of the Constitutional Court in January 2005.[25]

The reform of the labour market undoubtedly poses the delicate problem of the division of powers between the State and the Regions. However, rather than persisting with an exhausting and questionable formalistic division of the two spheres of competence,[26] the reform deals with the question in terms of the functional synergy between State and regional competences, on the basis of the belief that this type of approach leads to more productive results than one that sees the two levels as being in competition with each other, leading to pointless comparisons between the concepts of "civil order" and "employment protection and security".

---

[23] For an overall view of the labour market reform see the contributions in Tiraboschi, M., ed. 2003. *La riforma del collocamento e i nuovi servizi per l'impiego.* Milano: Giuffrè.

[24] See *infra,* documentation, paragraph 1.

[25] Sentence No. 50 deposited on 28 January 2005. See *www.adapt.it*, contents A-Z, *Riforma Biagi.*

[26] See Biagi, M. 2003. "Il lavoro nella riforma costituzionale", *Marco Biagi. Un giurista progettuale. Scritti scelti,* eds.L. Montuschi, T. Treu, and M. Tiraboschi, Milano: Giuffrè.

The initial pronouncements of the Constitutional Court relating to the new Title V suggest that the expression "employment protection and security" should be construed not simply in the strict sense, but rather as a principle protected by the Constitution[27] which, in connection with the regulation of employment services, can fruitfully be translated into an integrated system for supporting the constitutional right of access to work.

On the assumption that the effectiveness of active labour market policies depends on the efficiency of employment services, particular emphasis has to be placed in regulating this matter on safeguarding an essential level of services (not necessarily the minimum level) in all parts of the country with measures for improving access to the labour market, which is the main priority.[28] As a result, the new framework of competences concerning the labour market identifies the following as the responsibility of the national legislator:

- the identification of the fundamental principles and role of coordinating the definition of national standards, also in order to avoid duplicating or making more onerous the duties to be performed by those operating in the market, in a perspective of streamlining and simplifying procedures for matching the supply and demand for labour;
- the determination of the essential level of services concerning civil and social rights, that undoubtedly includes employment services, to be provided in a uniform manner in all parts of the country, constituting the framework and standard, not necessary at a minimum level, of the concurrent legislation;
- the planning of national labour policies, in order to ensure their compliance with EU objectives in relation to employability, as well as in relation to equal opportunities, adaptability, and entrepreneurship;
- the definition and planning of policies for coordinating the various systems, in particular the links between schools, vocational training, employment, and social insurance;

---

[27] See the analysis of Constitutional Court sentence No. 407, 26 July 2002, in Trojsi, A. 2003. *Prime indicazioni su "tutela e sicurezza del lavoro" nella recente giurisprudenza costituzionale,* in *DLM* No. 1:199-205 and Tullini, P. 2005. "Mercato del lavoro, modello organizzativo e livelli di regolazione (ancora dubbi di legittimità costituzionale?)", *La riforma del mercato del lavoro: deregolazione o riregolazione?*, ed. Serra, C., Milano: Giuffrè.

[28] See Sestito, P. 2005."Pubblico e privato nei servizi per l'impiego: quale ruolo per l'operatore pubblico?", *La riforma del mercato del lavoro: deregolazione o riregolazione?*, ed. Serra, C., Milano: Giuffrè.

- the integration and monitoring of regional services;
- the development and management, for monitoring and decision-making purposes, of statistical services and IT systems, in collaboration with the Regions, in support of employment services and policies.

On the other hand, the Regions have responsibility for the following activities:

- the planning regional employment policies, within the framework laid down at national level;
- the management and design of employment incentives within the framework of fundamental principles adopted at national level;
- the design and implementation of active labour policies, in particular training policies;
- the definition of operational parameters (unemployment status, prevention of long-term unemployment, loss of unemployment status, and so on);
- the provision of access by individuals and enterprises to integrated employment services run by public and private bodies;
- the implementation of information networks for public and private bodies and users.

In assigning powers to the State and the Regions, one particularly sensitive matter was the certification of private companies, with regard to agency work (both of a temporary and an open-ended nature) and with regard to intermediation (placement services and career guidance, consultancy services, skills audits and so on).

On the basis of a literal interpretation, as so far adopted under the terms of prevailing legal opinion, of the expression “employment protection and safety”, the matter in question could have been considered to come within the powers of the Regions, with grave risks for the unitary structure of the system. A unitary structure could not have been achieved simply by means of a definition of the fundamental principles laid down by the national legislator. As a result, there were valid reasons, in a perspective of subsidiarity, for safeguarding above all the unitary structure of the system, for allocating the regulation of access to the labour market by private agencies to the national legislator, while sharing certain tasks with the Regions.

With reference in particular to employment agency work, it must be noted, looking beyond the letter of the legislative decree (that made reference to a unified system of authorisation and accreditation) that illegal intermediation in the labour market is still today deemed to be an offence (also of a criminal nature), and bearing this in mind there was no reason to provide, even considering the new constitutional provisions, a system of authorisation that was differentiated in various parts of the country but accompanied by identical criminal sanctions.

Moreover, it is widely recognised in the debate about regulatory techniques for employment agency work that the system of regulation for private agencies is not particularly significant in itself, but exists for the purposes of protecting the rights of workers, so it should be dealt with under the general civil provisions at national level. This approach has been confirmed by the proposed Community directive on the supply of temporary labour, that lays down an obligation on the Member States to abolish all restrictions on the administration of temporary labour, including restrictions relating to the system of authorisation of private agencies, except in cases in which the regulations serve the purpose of protecting the rights of temporary agency workers or of defending interests of a general nature.[29]

On the other hand, if it had been assigned to the regional level, the system of authorisation would have posed the question of mutual recognition between the different regional systems, with a significant risk of social dumping, resulting in the need for an intervention by the national legislator to determine the essential level of services relating to civil and social rights. Pursuant to Title V, these rights must be safeguarded in a uniform manner in all parts of the country (Article 117(2)(m) of the Constitution).

In application of the principles of subsidiarity and adequacy, the authorisation and certification of private undertakings operating in the sector of agency work was therefore assigned to the national legislator, albeit in close cooperation with the Regions, since this is indispensable for it to be effective, considering that the regional level does not appear to be the most effective for dealing with all the issues (legal and organisational) arising from authorisation and certification.

With regard, on the other hand to activities relating to the recruitment and selection of personnel and staff outplacement, the Regions were given the option of issuing authorisation for businesses operating within a given Region. Unlike agency work, where an employment relationship is established between the agency and the worker, and where a high level of protection is required, for the other functions it may be argued that the level of protection required is not so high, since the relation between the

[29] See *www.adapt.it*, selecting *Somministrazione* from the list of contents A-Z.

agency and the worker is one in which services are provided, without a contract of employment being concluded, and consequently the conditions giving rise to the need for regulation at national level, as outlined above, no longer pertain.

Clearly, it is a different matter when dealing with systems for the accreditation of private and other public bodies providing services within a framework of horizontal and vertical subsidiarity, such as career guidance, monitoring, vocational qualifications, and so on. This kind of accreditation is assigned exclusively to the regional authorities. The Regions have the power to adopt, promote and develop models of employment services at territorial level, providing for the transfer of functions to external public and private bodies, recognised as qualified to operate in an integrated manner with the public system. The Regions are therefore empowered to adopt provisions setting up and regulating accreditations and the procedures for issuing them. At the same time, the reform has pursued the objective of safeguarding the homogeneity of the level of services at national level, by identifying principles and general criteria with which the Regions have to comply.

A second significant point is that of the level and type of regulation. The general ineffectiveness of the centralised state-sector model for matching the supply and demand for labour has led to experimentation, where possible, with innovative regulatory techniques or "soft laws" in contrast with the traditional approach based on binding legal provisions. In the employment agency sector, that is characterised by a high level of illegal activity, there was a need to experiment with new forms of regulation, in particular management by objectives, providing an alternative to the enactment of legislative norms seen almost as an end in themselves, with a view to achieving decentralisation, reduced reliance on legislative instruments, and a devolution of the normative sources (with the delegation of certain tasks to collective bargaining and secondary regulations).

In this perspective a particularly important function is the gathering and dissemination of information, and attempts have been made to provide incentives for this function at a normative level, for example by making applications for authorisation and accreditation conditional on the utilisation of IT systems that are integrated with the public employment services, and conditional on supplying all the information required for the labour market to function effectively, and so on. A similar approach has been taken to providing access to employment for disadvantaged groups in the labour market, who are to be assisted also by private employment agencies thanks to financial incentives and normative provisions.

Opportunities for those in disadvantaged groups to enter or re-enter the labour market will be enhanced if private employment agencies also seek to meet their requirements, by means of suitable incentive mechanisms.[30]

A third significant element is the organisation of a national online employment database that is a key resource for governing the labour market and improving the interface between public and private operators. The Biagi law makes provision for the setting up of an Employment Information System with unitary and standardised characteristics, mainly with a view to defining the standards and setting up a unified network linking the various operational levels (national, regional, provincial and local). From this point of view, based on the supposition that it would be less problematic than defining a division of powers between the State and the Regions, while responding to the need to set up a practical and efficient system, it was decided to provide direct access to the customers. This makes it possible to set up an online employment database without any filters or barriers to access,[31] but also to take a radical approach to the problem of State and regional competences, since in this perspective the driving force is the working of market mechanisms, in a framework of total freedom and subsidiarity within the system.

The online database can only be set up in a reasonable period of time if resources are not wasted by the proliferation of different IT systems, and this network is now proceeding according to plan. If this matter had not been dealt with in a timely manner, in keeping with Article 120 of the Constitution that prohibits the placing of limits of any kind on the exercise of the right to work in any part of the national territory, the system would have suffered from various forms of rivalry between the State, the Regions and the Provinces, leaving the market without rules and channels of communication in line with Community, national and regional labour policies.[32]

It is in this sense that it is necessary to interpret the fundamental norms governing the labour market contained in the legislative decree, in particular in the article in which provision is made for the setting up of a national employment database "safeguarding the effective enjoyment of the right to work laid down in Article 4 of the Constitution, and fully respecting Article 120 of the Constitution". In this perspective the national

---

[30] See Olivelli, P., and M. Tiraboschi, eds. 2005. *Il diritto del mercato del lavoro dopo la riforma Biagi*. Milano: Giuffrè.

[31] See Tiraboschi, M., W. Bromwich, O. Rymkevitch, and S. Spattini. *Employment Services and Employment Contracts in the Biagi Law*, paragraph 1.5.

[32] See Tiraboschi, M. 2004. "La borsa continua nazionale del lavoro", *La riforma Biagi del mercato del lavoro*, ed. M. Tiraboschi, Milano: Giuffrè, 573.

employment database is to be directly accessible to workers and employers alike, and it will be possible to consult it from anywhere in the network. Workers and employers will have the right to place jobseekers' notices and vacancy announcements directly on the database without having to go through any intermediaries, using the access points provided by public and private operators who are authorised and accredited.

The network will consist of a series of regional nodes with both a national and a regional dimension.[33] At national level, the focus will be on defining national technical standards for the exchange of information, the interoperability of the regional systems, and the definition of the information resulting in the highest degree of effectiveness and transparency in the matching of the supply and demand for labour. At a regional level, while respecting the competences of the Regions in planning and managing regional employment policies, the focus will be on setting up and integrating public and private systems, authorised and accredited, operating within the region, with a view to designating and setting up employment service models. The Regions will also be called on to cooperate in the definition of national standards of communication.

With regard to the roles and functions of the various operators (public and private) in delivering the different types of services and managing the relative organisational model, the decision was taken to identify certain public functions for which public bodies are responsible, even though at an operational level they are provided by private agencies (accredited or authorised), and certain functions (that are no longer to be defined as public and therefore perhaps better considered to be services) to be provided in a system of horizontal and vertical subsidiarity.

The exclusively public functions continue to be:

- the tracking and updating of the employment status of the worker and the quantitative and qualitative monitoring of labour market operations (personal data, vocational profiles, and communications systems for employees) also for the purposes of setting up and maintaining an employment information system;
- the certification of involuntary unemployment and its duration, for the purposes of providing access to preventive measures and benefits (vocational training, work experience, and so on), tax and contributions relief, and social insurance benefits.

---

[33] See Pirrone, S.2005. "Borsa continua nazionale del lavoro: standard tecnici, flussi informativi di scambio, implementazione e messa a regime", *Il diritto del mercato del lavoro dopo la riforma Biagi*, eds. Olivelli, P., and M. Tiraboschi, Milano: Giuffrè, 629.

The functions and services to be provided in a system of horizontal and vertical subsidiarity on the part of public- and private-sector operators are:

- the matching of supply and demand;
- the prevention of long-term unemployment;
- the promotion of access to the labour market by disadvantaged groups (on the part of public but also private operators, such as personal service agencies, that hire the worker);
- support for the geographical mobility of the worker;
- the setting up of a national employment database providing access that is as universal as possible, promoting an effective matching of supply and demand for labour, and therefore an open market with access for all (public and private service providers and customers);
- the recognition of the role of public operators that can contribute to the efficiency and transparency of the labour market, in particular public bodies and universities that can provide employment services for specific segments of the labour market and also experiment with pilot projects aimed at promoting employability and adaptability, especially by means of local agreements, making full use of the opportunities made available by the legislative decree on the labour market.

The opening up to public bodies such as local authorities, universities and high schools, in particular, is aimed at strengthening and raising the profile of the public operators in the labour market, particularly in the crucial phases of access to employment. These phases do not consist solely of matching the supply and demand for labour, but also of developing and validating the phase in which the employment contract is negotiated, by means of certification programmes.

In this way the unitary structure of the Biagi law is confirmed, as it is not intended to introduce two separate reform programmes, consisting of one setting up the new employment services and another one introducing new forms of employment contracts (such as on-call working or zero-hours contracts, project work, and job sharing) or the reorganisation of existing forms of employment (part-time and agency work).[34] On closer examination, it may turn out to be the case that certification can play a decisive role, linking up the various aspects of the employment relationship and matching various forms of employment protection and market mechanisms pending a comprehensive reform of the entire sector

[34] See *infra,* documentation.

by means of the long-awaited consolidating legislation known as the Work Statute[35] (see *infra*).

4. Quasi-subordinate Employment

Having proposed a new structure for the labour market, the Biagi law aims to deal with the various types of employment by means of a relaxation of the limitations on employment contracts with reduced working hours, or modulated or flexible working hours, together with a reduction of the other areas of quasi-subordinate employment which should pave the way for the codification of the Work Statute mentioned above.

The regulation of quasi-subordinate employment by means of "project work" appears to be the most innovative element—but also the most critical—in the legislative decrees implementing the Biagi law. The rigorous limits laid down by the legislator in the decrees, aimed at restricting the use of quasi-subordinate employment to a significant extent, represents what for many will be an unexpected innovation compared to the existing structure of the labour market, but also in relation to the debate on non-standard or atypical employment. In this debate there may appear to be a clear-cut choice between two alternatives: either granting official recognition to a type of employment that is in between salaried and self-employment, or proceeding with the codification of a Work Statute.

The Biagi law on the other hand favours a different approach, a kind of third way, with the introduction of a series of barriers, consisting of definitions and sanctions, to prevent the improper use of quasi-subordinate employment, and the strategy is therefore to abandon any attempt to consolidate a type of employment contract in a grey area between self-employment and salaried employment.[36]

However, under the terms of the Pact for Italy signed on 5 July 2002, this matter is to be dealt with as part of the overall reform of the labour market known as the Work Statute. The main characteristic of this proposal is that it replaces the traditional dichotomy between self-employment and salaried employment, along with the proliferation of employment contract types, with a series of protections based on

---

[35] With regard to the Work Statute see the collection of papers and draft norms available at *www.adapt.it,* selecting *Statuto dei lavori* from the list of contents A-Z.
[36] See Tiraboschi, M. 2005. "Il lavoro a progetto: profili teorico-ricostruttivi", *La riforma del mercato del lavoro: de regolazione o riregolazione?,* ed. Serra, C., Milano: Giuffrè.

concentric circles (with the highest level of protection in the inner circle) and variable arrangements depending on the forms of employment protection adopted. It may be seen then that Legislative Decree No. 276/2003 does not attempt to impose the same level of protection for quasi-subordinate employment as for salaried employment, nor does it assign to collective bargaining the task of providing such protection.

At the same time, it is not intended to promote autonomous bargaining in an abstract and generic manner regardless of the field of application of project work. Indeed, those who see this Legislative Decree as an attempt to place limits on the autonomy of the parties to collective bargaining tend to overlook the fact that quasi-subordinate employment has so far not been a clearly defined form of employment for bargaining purposes, but rather a catch-all category including a variety of contracts characterised by economic dependency, reflecting an asymmetrical relationship placing the worker in an inferior position to the client firm.

The conceptual choice of considering quasi-subordinate employment as a genuine form of self-employment, in order to prevent the improper use of this type of employment contract, has resulted in a political intervention aimed at moving as many employment contracts as possible, in a gradual manner over a period of time, from the uncertain grey area of atypical employment to the area of salaried employment. This area has now been extended to provide a variety of different forms reflecting the objective of redesigning the forms of protection leading to regulated flexibility subject to the approval of the trade unions. In anticipation of the Work Statute, this operation is intended to replace the ill-defined mass of individual arrangements currently to be found in the grey area with a continuum of employment contract types located between the two extremes of quasi-subordinate employment and salaried employment on open-ended contracts. In other words, this continuum is intended to result in the emergence of irregular employment contracts, and those that are lacking in clarity, with a view to redefining the various forms of employment protection while taking account of the weaker position of the worker. In taking an approach to employment matters that focuses on the various forms of protection, rather than focusing on the definition of the employment relationship,[37] the structure of a Work Statute needs to be placed in a perspective of "economic dependency".

Proceeding with the codification of a Work Statute without first having brought together, by means of new types of employment contracts, the

---

[37] Reflecting the approach of Treu, T. 1997. "Intervento", *Nuove forme di lavoro tra subordinazione, coordinazione, autonomia,* eds. D'Antona, M., T. Treu *et al.*, (Bari: Cacucci), 225.

myriad of employment arrangements located in the grey area and increasingly in the hidden economy, would probably have been an admirable symbolic gesture devoid of any practical effects arising from the legislative intervention. In reply to those who refer to "44 types of flexibility (and even more with the certification of employment contracts) after this reform"[38] it should be pointed out that the proliferation of employment contract types is more apparent than real. The aim of the reform is to make inroads into that vast area of employment that is irregular or located in the hidden economy, for which every employment contract represents a particular type of contractual flexibility, with the result that the codification of a Work Statute without the prior identification and redefinition of types of employment that are adopted at present without the least regard for regulations and trade union negotiation would have given rise to a futuristic project without a solid foundation.

The Italian labour market needs first of all a process of emergence and restructuring, and to this end the diversification of contractual types can be the first phase in the move towards the regularisation, structuring and emergence that would facilitate the introduction of a Work Statute for all types of employment, whether typical or atypical, in the form of self-employment, project work, or salaried employment. With the regulation of quasi-salaried employment by means of project work, a wide range of atypical employment contracts that are difficult to classify (estimated to involve some two and a half million workers) will be clearly defined and brought back within the legal framework.

5. Critical Aspects of the Reform

It needs to be clearly stated that the reform does not deal with all the problems of the labour market and presents certain critical aspects, the most evident of which is the exclusion of the public administration from the application of Legislative Decree No. 276/2003. This is a policy choice that is undoubtedly open to criticism, especially considering the widespread use of quasi-salaried employment and the contracting out of public services, but it may be explained (though not justified) in terms of political and trade union choices with regard to privatising the work of public-sector employees, rather than in technical terms. It is to be hoped

---

38 See the comment by Boeri, T. 2003. "Il co.co.co. dovrà cambiare pelle," *La Stampa,* 8 June, in contrast with those who claim that there has been an increase in rigidity (see, for example, Ichino, P. *op. cit.*).In line with T. Boeri, see Treu, T. 2003. "Statuto dei lavori: una riflessione sui contenuti," *Ildiariodellavoro.it*.

that the Government will maintain the commitment, laid down in the final provisions of the decree, to hold negotiations with the social partners with a view to drafting legislative provisions leading to harmonisation.

A further matter about which no conclusions can at present be drawn is that of part-time work:[39] it remains to be seen whether greater flexibility for the purposes of increasing the take-up of this type of employment will generate more employment opportunities for workers. The reform is not intended to deregulate part-time work, and in any case, such a move would not be possible, due to the provisions laid down at EU level. The approach adopted in the decree aims rather at providing more room for manoeuvre for autonomous bargaining (individual or collective) with a view to providing incentives for consensual part-time working, in compliance with sentence No. 210/1992 of the Constitutional Court that lays down a requirement for the consent of the employee to be obtained whenever working time comes into conflict with personal and family responsibilities.

At the same time as mentioned above in Sections 1 and 2 it cannot be denied that some of the measures aimed at defining an organic set of employment protections in the market, and not just in a given employment relationship, are likely to be less effective due to the failure to include in the decree the safety-net measures and employment incentives, that have been presented as a separate piece of legislation that is currently under discussion in Parliament. But also, in this case, political considerations and the outcome of negotiations with the social partners have prevailed over purely rational and abstract criteria.

In order to appreciate the reasons for certain choices of legislative policy or for the adoption of certain technical solutions, another significant consideration is that this reform is intended to be carried out without resulting in any increase in public expenditure. Article 7 of the Legislative Decree specifies that the implementation of the various measures is to take place without generating additional costs for the State. In the report accompanying the decree of 6 June 2003[40] it was argued with good reason that overall the decree not only would not present problems in terms of costs, but in the medium to long-term it is expected to give rise to significant savings and generate an increase in revenue, by means of:

- a series of measures for regularising employment by means of normative incentives with a view to increasing the number of those in regular employment who pay contributions to the State. With the

[39] See *infra,* documentation, paragraph 2.6.

[40] See *www.adapt.it*, selecting *Riforma Biagi* from the list of contents A-Z.

approval of the decree there is expected to be an increase in regular employment, and in particular with the reform of quasi-salaried employment, and a more widespread use of salaried employment contracts, with the result that many workers will be transferred from contracts giving rise to minimal contributions to others with higher rates of contributions;

- a series of measures for reducing unemployment that will lead to a decline in the number of those receiving unemployment benefit and a lower take-up of certain safety-net measures (workfare programmes, long-term unemployment, workers on mobility schemes, and so on);
- stringent measures aimed at reducing the area of quasi-salaried employment and at scaling back (by means of incentives and sanctions) the illicit use of other contractual types, such as fictitious partnership arrangements, that are at present exempt from contributions. An extremely significant number of quasi-salaried employment contracts with a 12 per cent contribution rate will be converted into salaried employment contracts that are subject to a contribution rate of 33 per cent, even if they are temporary, part-time or job sharing contracts;
- measures aimed at containing occasional or casual employment. The decree provides that every employment relationship that continues for more than 30 days a year, or which generates an income of €5,000 with the same client firm, cannot be considered to be occasional or casual work, but must be regulated by the new project work contracts or as salaried employment. The decree also lays down regulations for occasional or casual work of an accessory nature that at present is in most cases carried out in the hidden economy. In this case, a small contribution is introduced for the industrial injuries fund, INAIL, and the social insurance fund, INPS;
- the widening of the range of flexible contractual types that is likely to lead to a decline in the use of fictitious work training contracts that are at present utilised for the purposes of containing labour costs.

In effect, the Biagi reform aims to increase the levels of regular employment, presumably with positive effects in terms of tax revenues and insurance contributions. Also in the light of previous experience in Italy following the Treu reforms in 1997, the introduction of new forms of flexibility and options for regular employment should result in an increase not only in the potential for growth in GDP but also of overall employment levels in the economy. This objective, over a year after the entry into force of Legislative Decree No. 276 of 10 September 2003, appears to be confirmed by recent ISTAT figures that show an increase in stable employment of good quality and a decline in work in the hidden economy.[41]

However, on the basis of the traditional auditing criteria relating to these provisions adopted by the State accounting department, the legislator issuing the decree was not able to base the calculation of costs on the positive effects mentioned above, that are to be taken into consideration only for the purposes of defining the macroeconomic and financial framework for the coming years, and for economic and financial planning, but not for the drafting of the legislative decree. This aspect of the delegating legislation gave rise to a careful examination, carried out jointly with the Ministry for the Economy and Finance, of the certain and direct effects of the provisions. This had a significant impact on the formulation of Article 13 relating first of all to workfare provisions for those receiving unemployment and similar benefits, that was almost completely rewritten, then to job sharing, that is now limited to two workers per contract, and finally to the definition of the field of application of financial contracts and the new access-to-work contracts.[42]

6. A Preliminary Assessment

In an attempt to draw initial conclusions, it may be said that we are in the presence of a complex process of reform that still presents areas of uncertainty,[43] but which should be construed in a constructive spirit reflecting an awareness of the need for far-reaching reform in the Italian labour market in the interests both of employers and workers.

Although it is now a year and a half since the reform came into force, it still seems to be too early to make an assessment,[44] though it must be mentioned that all the legislative texts pertaining to the Ministry of Labour

[41] The quarterly ISTAT survey of the workforce shows that in the last 12 months almost 200,000 permanent jobs have been created, whereas the number of workers on temporary contracts has fallen by 110,000. See Boeri, T., and P. Garibaldi. 2004. "Nuovi lavori e nuovi numeri", *Lavoce.info,* 28 September.

[42] See Tiraboschi, M., "Employability, Active Labour Policies and Social Dialogue in Europe: Comparison of Experiences", Collana del Dipartimento di Economia Aziendale dell'Università degli Studi di Modena e Reggio Emilia, No. 94.

[43] See European Commission. 2005. *Draft Joint Employment Report 2004/5* and *Second Implementation Report on the 2003-2005 Broad Economic Policy Guidelines*. Brussels: European Commission.

[44] The same view is expressed in the 38th *Rapporto annuale Censis sulla situazione sociale del paese.*

have been produced in a timely manner.[45] However, it is also true that collective bargaining has implemented only part of the provisions, at times in a contradictory and incoherent manner. It should also be noted that the Regions have not intervened in a timely manner to deal with the matters within their sphere of competence, especially concerning the new apprenticeship contracts.

The fact that this is not a deregulation of the labour market is clear to all concerned, but particularly to all those workers who have so far been employed in a context devoid of regulation—in the hidden economy and the area of precarious employment that the Biagi law is intended to combat. It would be easy to point out that the quarterly ISTAT figures released over the past year for the period corresponding to the entry into force of the Biagi law have revealed a constant rise in stable employment, a significant decline in temporary work, and a scaling back of the hidden economy,[46] but this is not the point. It is evident that a year and a half is too short a period to obtain reliable data and to draw conclusions. This is shown by the recent example, albeit less complex, of the Treu reforms of 1997, that started to bear fruit only several years later, mainly with the rise of temporary agency work. This is all the more the case with a measure such as the Biagi law, which, with the exception of the regulation of dismissals, has an impact on all the key aspects of the labour market, making provision for a gradual entry into force, by means of a series of experimental programmes, also with the participation of the social partners. This is the case of quasi-subordinate employment that has become a sort of weathervane for the reform, with the termination of the transitional phase on 24 October 2004, though further extensions are allowed until 24 October 2005 as agreed during collective bargaining. For this reason, for the moment it is not possible to make a realistic and objective judgement about the intention, announced by the Government and supported by the reform of the Labour Inspectorate, of carrying out a drastic reduction of the area of fictitious quasi-subordinate employment. The same applies to the other measures introduced by the reform, that are only now coming into full effect: the new apprenticeship contracts, employment agency work, on-call or zero-hours contracts, certification, work vouchers, and the online employment database.

However, it is also true that a year and a half is a sufficient period for a provisional assessment of the state of application of the reform as a whole. It is not particularly significant that all the regulations for implementing

---

[45] See *www.adapt.it*, list of contents A-Z, selecting *Riforma Biagi.*

[46] See. note 27: T. Boeri, P. Garibaldi, *Nuovi lavori e nuovi numeri,* in *Lavoce.info*, 28 September 2004.

the reforms have been adopted in record time, because the real changes only take place in the hearts and minds of those involved, and cannot be achieved simply by enacting legislation and decrees. As Marco Biagi used to say, the modernisation of the labour market is a particularly delicate matter that requires a constructive approach on the part of all those concerned to reforms that are necessary for governing the changes taking place in economic and social relations.[47] This is an endeavour that requires team spirit, as Luca di Montezemolo, the President of Ferrari and Confindustria, the employers' association, recently remarked,[48] and it is from here that we need to move forward, concluding the experimental phase in a spirit of fairness, before drawing conclusions about a law that is still in its early stages. In the experimental phases that we are now entering, the contribution of the social partners, together with that of the Regional authorities, will be decisive in building on the foundations laid down by the Biagi law to construct a dynamic, flexible and competitive labour market providing adequate levels of employment protection.

7. Documentation: Short Note of Synthesis of the Biagi Law

Employment Services and Employment Contracts in the Biagi Law[49]

7.1. Employment Services

7.1.1. The Network of Employment Services[50]

A fundamental objective of the Biagi Law, Legislative Decree No. 276/2003, is the design and setting up of a network of employment services run by public, private and non-profit bodies, linked together in a national online employment database *(borsa nazionale continua del*

---

[47] See Marco Biagi's articles published in *Il Sole 24 ore*.

[48] See *infra* L. C. di Montezemolo in 2005 (Speech by Luca Cordero di Montezemolo at the Conference on the Italian Labour Market one year after the Biagi Reform), *The International Journal of Comparative Labour Law and Industrial Relations* 21, No. 2: 347-348.

[49] See: Biagi, M., and M. Tiraboschi. 2004.*Istituzioni di diritto del lavoro.* Milano: Giuffrè, and Tiraboschi, M. 2004. *La riforma Biagi del mercato del lavoro,* collana ADAPT-Fondazione "Marco Biagi", Milano: Giuffrè.

[50] See: Olivelli, P., and M. Tiraboschi. 2005. *Il diritto del mercato del lavoro dopo la riforma Biagi,* collana ADAPT-Fondazione "Marco Biagi", Milano: Giuffrè.

lavoro). By means of a register of employees it will be possible to ascertain at any time the position of all those in work and all those in search of employment, also for career guidance and training purposes. Moreover, subject to certain conditions, the new employment agencies can now provide a complete range of services (job search services, recruitment and selection, career guidance and training, and employment agency work).

Local authorities are free to set up their own job matching services, especially to meet the needs of disadvantaged groups. In addition incentives are provided to encourage cooperation between private companies and non-profit organisations to meet the needs of individuals in disadvantaged groups. Trade unions and bilateral bodies (set up jointly by employers' associations and trade unions) are also authorised to run employment services, and provision is made for schools and universities to arrange work experience programmes and job placements for school-leavers and undergraduates. All private employment services are free of charge for the employee, whereas a charge is levied for employers.

Public employment services continue to operate, but in cooperation, and in some instances in competition, with private employment agencies and other authorised bodies. These public employment services are run at a provincial level on the basis of guidelines laid down by the Regions, and are responsible for the employment register, career guidance, matching the supply and demand for labour, preliminary selection procedures, advice for employers, and assistance for people with disabilities or in disadvantaged groups.

7.1.2. Private-sector Services

In the private sector, employment agencies provide a range of services, including both temporary work and staff leasing, job matching, recruitment and selection of staff, and outplacement. In order to perform these activities, employment agencies require a specific authorisation. The Ministry of Labour and Social Policy issues authorisations only to private-sector agencies that meet the following conditions:

- the registered office must be located in Italy or another EU member state;
- the agency must have suitable premises;
- the agency must comply with data protection requirements;
- the staff of the agency must have approved qualifications;
- the directors and managers of the agency may not have a criminal record;

- the agency is required to be linked to and share data with the online national employment database.

Once an agency has obtained an authorisation, it is entered in an official register (*Albo delle agenzie per il lavoro)*[51] in one of the following five categories:

(1) employment agencies *(agenzie di somministrazione)*, dealing with both temporary work and staff leasing, that may also provide job matching services, recruitment and selection, and outplacement services. In particular, they are required to have a paid-up capital of at least €600,000, to carry on business in at least four regions and to pay contributions to a training fund and an income support fund for agency workers. In addition they have the right to run their own training, work access and retraining programmes for disadvantaged workers;

(2) staff leasing agencies, dealing only with this activity;

(3) job matching agencies *(agenzie di intermediazione)*, that are required to have a paid-up capital of at least €50,000, and to carry on business in at least four regions. They also have the right to run recruitment, selection and outplacement services;

(4) recruitment and selection agencies *(agenzie di ricerca e selezione)*, that are required to have a paid-up capital of at least €25,000;

(5) outplacement agencies *(agenzie di supporto alla ricollocazione del personale)*, that are required to have a paid-up capital of at least €25,000. (Articles 3-7, Legislative Decree No. 276/2003).

The Regions are responsible for the accreditation system of employment agencies, enabling them to take part in the network of employment services and providing support for disadvantaged people to enter or return to the regular labour market.

7.1.3. Authorised Bodies

The work of the public employment services and private employment agencies is supplemented by that of other bodies authorised either by law or by registration.

Public and private universities, together with university foundations dealing with labour market issues, are authorised by law provided that:

- they operate on a non-profit basis;

---

[51] See www.welfare.gov.it, selecting *Lavoro* and then *Agenzie per il lavoro -Albo informatico.*

- they link up to and share data with the national online employment database;
- they undertake to provide all the information relevant to employment statistics and labour market policy, pending the completion of the national online employment database.
- Other bodies may be authorised by registration, in particular:
- municipal authorities;
- chambers of commerce;
- schools;
- trade unions, employers' association and bilateral bodies;
- foundations providing labour law advice and consultancy services.

7.1.4. Disadvantaged Groups

Provisions for improving access to employment by disadvantaged groups are laid down in Articles 13 and 14, Legislative Decree No. 276/2003, including specific schemes run by employment agencies that sign agreements with public operators (local, provincial and regional authorities), and incentives for companies that award contracts to cooperatives employing disadvantaged workers. In addition to these specific measures, disadvantaged workers can benefit from access-to-work contracts. The definition of disadvantaged groups is laid down in Article 2, EC Regulation No. 2204/2002.

Employment agencies are authorised to run individual access-to-work schemes for disadvantaged groups on condition that:

- they have drawn up an individual access-to-work or return-to-work plan, with provision for training;
- the worker is assisted by an adviser with suitable qualifications and experience;
- the scheme lasts for at least six months.

Provided these conditions are fulfilled, the employment agency may benefit from certain more favourable conditions than those laid down by general regulatory provisions, in particular:

- a derogation from the principle of equal pay compared to other employees with the same employment grade, allowing for a lower rate of pay;
- deductions from the wages to be paid equivalent to the mobility allowance, unemployment benefit, or any other benefit or subsidy. In this case the contract must be for at least nine months.

Social cooperatives that employ disadvantaged workers benefit from a system of framework agreements providing incentives for companies to award contracts to them. These agreements are concluded with:

- employment services;
- employers' associations and trade unions recognised as most representative at national level;
- associations representing social cooperatives and consortia of cooperatives.

Enterprises that negotiate framework agreements of this type are deemed to have met the requirements for hiring a certain number of workers on the mandatory employment register.

Both of these types of measure in favour of disadvantaged groups are of an experimental nature: at a later stage the Minister of Labour and Social Policy and the most representative employers' associations and trade unions at national level are to carry out an assessment of their impact, after which the Minister will report to Parliament.

7.1.5. The National Online Employment Database

Based on a network of regional nodes, the national online employment database is freely accessible on the Internet. It is an information system intended to increase the transparency of the labour market and to favour the matching of the supply and demand for labour. The intended users are:

- workers and jobseekers, who can reply directly to vacancy notices without having to go through intermediaries;
- enterprises and employers, who can advertise vacancies;
- authorised and accredited public and private operators, who are required to enter into the online employment database all the data they collect from workers and employers.

Anyone in search of employment can access the database either directly or through public employment services or private employment agencies, choosing the level (provincial, regional or national) at which they intend to distribute their jobseeker's profile. Jobseekers can choose either to publish their personal data or to maintain confidentiality.

The matching of supply and demand takes place by means of a computerised procedure for identifying suitable vacancies. The vacancy notices are freely accessible, though job applicants are required to provide identification.

The online database operates at two levels, national and regional, each of which has specific functions:

- the national level defines the technical standards for the exchange of information, for harmonising the regional systems, identifying the information for maximising the effectiveness of the system and the transparency of the matching of supply and demand;
- the regional level is intended to promote cooperation between the public and private systems within the region, to design and implement regional models of employment services, and to cooperate with the national level for the definition of operational standards for communication between the various regional services.

In order to ensure the smooth working of the system, a body responsible for coordinating the national and regional levels is in the process of being set up.

7.1.6. The Labour Inspectorate[52]

With the reform of the labour inspectorate, the Ministry of Labour and Social Policy has taken on a central role in the supervision of labour relations and in bringing employment out of the hidden economy. This function is carried out by provincial and regional labour inspectors, along with inspectors from the industrial injury and social insurance funds.

A central body has been set up by the Ministry to coordinate efforts by regional and provincial labour departments in order to enforce existing regulations in an effective manner. In addition, the inspections carried out by all the relevant bodies are recorded in a section of the national online employment database, containing all the information about the employers inspected, and providing an overview of labour market trends, and training materials for labour inspectors.
The regional and provincial labour departments are responsible for a number of functions such as:

- monitoring the application of employment protection provisions of all kinds;
- monitoring the application of collective labour agreements;

---

[52] See: Monticelli, L. C., and M. Tiraboschi. 2004. *La riforma dei servizi ispettivi in materia di lavoro e previdenza.* Collana ADAPT / Fondazione "Marco Biagi". Milano: Giuffrè.

- monitoring social insurance and pension contributions to be paid by professional associations, and public and private bodies, with the exception of those that are run directly by State, provincial or local authorities;
- carrying out enquiries and surveys as required by the Ministry.

The Biagi law has introduced a new function for the labour inspectorate: in cases in which an employer has not paid wages and salaries in full, the inspectorate has the power to issue an injunction for payment.

2. Employment Contracts

2.1. The Rationale of the New Employment Contracts[53]

The Biagi law aims to (re)regulate certain employment contracts intended to promote access to and continuity in regular employment, particularly for those who need to reconcile working time and family responsibilities, or who need training and retraining, and those with other specific needs.

These employment contracts include an extension of employment safeguards and opportunities for workers while encouraging companies to hire them, overcoming the traditional resistance to the idea of distributing the same workload among a larger number of workers. These contracts are intended to regularise employment and to provide stability for those at present employed on a precarious basis.

The reform is also intended to make it easier to enter or return to the regular labour market by combining work and training opportunities. Training is provided in the form of apprenticeship contracts organised in a flexible manner with the participation of bilateral bodies set up by employers' associations and trade unions.

2.2. The New Apprenticeship Contracts

In apprenticeship contracts the employee receives training at the employer's expense in addition to remuneration. Legislative Decree No. 276/2003 provides for three types of apprenticeship contract:

---

[53] Tiraboschi, M. 2004. *La riforma Biagi del mercato del lavoro.* Collana ADAPT / Fondazione "Marco Biagi", Milano: Giuffrè. Enrico, C., and M. Tiraboschi. 2005. *Compendio critico per la certificazione dei contratti di lavoro. I nuovi contratti—lavoro pubblico e lavoro privato*. Milano: Giuffrè.

- educational training apprenticeships, providing training and access to the labour market for school leavers;
- vocational training apprenticeships, combining on-the-job training with a technical or vocational qualification;
- higher-level apprenticeships, with advanced technical training leading to a high-school diploma or a university-level qualification.

Educational training apprenticeships are designed mainly for 15-18 year olds, whereas vocational training apprenticeships and higher-level apprenticeships are for 18-29 year olds, or for 17 year olds with a vocational qualification (pursuant to the reforms proposed by the Education Minister).

Apprenticeship contracts may be concluded in any sector, including agriculture, but the number of apprentices may not exceed the number of qualified staff in a given firm. Small firms without qualified staff (or with fewer than three) may hire up to three apprentices, and other provisions apply to artisan firms.

With regard to duration, educational training apprenticeships may last for up to three years, depending on the qualification to be obtained, whereas vocational training apprenticeships may last from two to six years, depending on the provisions of collective bargaining, but this type of contract may be used to provide further training at the end of an educational training apprenticeship. As regards training matters, the duration of higher-level apprenticeships is established at regional level, in agreement with the social partners and the educational bodies involved.

Apprenticeship contracts must be issued in writing, specifying the work to be performed, the training schedule and the qualification to be awarded. Remuneration may not be based on piecework, and the pay may not be more than two levels below the level specified in the company-level collective agreement for workers with the same employment grade. The qualification awarded for each of the three levels provides credits for further training and education. During the apprenticeship the employer cannot terminate the contract except for a just reason or cause, but has the right to discontinue the employment relationship when the contract runs out. Social insurance contributions are payable pursuant to Act No. 22/1955.

2.3. Access-to-work Contracts

Access-to-work contracts (Legislative Decree No. 276/2003, Articles 54-59) are designed to enable certain categories to enter or return to the labour market by means of an individual plan for the purposes of acquiring the skills required for a particular working environment. In the private sector these contracts replace the old work training contracts. The following categories are eligible for these contracts:

- 18-29 year olds;
- long-term unemployed 29-32 year olds;
- workers over the age of 50 who are no longer in employment;
- workers who wish to return after a break of two years or more;
- women of any age resident in areas where the employment rate for women is more than 20% less than for men (or the unemployment rate is 10% higher);
- individuals with a recognised physical or mental disability.
- The following employers may make use of access-to-work contracts:
- public bodies, enterprises and consortia;
- groups of enterprises;
- professional, socio-cultural and sports associations;
- foundations;
- public or private research bodies;
- sectoral organisations and associations.

There is no upper limit on the percentage of workers hired on these contracts, except for the limits laid down in national, sectoral or company-level collective bargaining. An employer may only hire new workers on access-to-work contracts if at least 60% of the employees hired in this way whose contracts have run out in the previous 18 months are still employed by the company.

With regard to the field of application, access-to-work contracts may be issued in all sectors, except for the public administration. For the first time the Biagi law permits groups of employers to hire workers on these contracts, thus granting them legal recognition as employers.

Access-to-work contracts can be issued for a period of nine to 18 months (or for up to 36 months in the case of workers with a physical or mental disability), but periods of military or voluntary service, or maternity leave, do not count. At the end of the contract, it is not permitted to continue with another contract of the same kind with the same employer, but the employee may take up work on another such contract with a different employer. Any extensions must be kept within the limits laid down by law (18 or 36 months).

The contract must be in writing, specifying the training to be provided; in cases in which the employer fails to issue a written contract, the agreement becomes null and void and the employment relationship is transformed into open-ended salaried employment.

Remuneration may not be more than two levels below the level specified in the national collective agreement for workers with the same employment grade. These contracts give rise to benefits in the form of tax and contributions relief for the employer.

2.4. Project Work Contracts

These are quasi-subordinate employment contracts relating to one or more specific projects or project phases, managed autonomously by the worker with reference to the end result, regardless of the time required for completion. The purpose of these contracts is to prevent the improper use of quasi-subordinate employment and to provide a higher level of protection for the employee. Contracts of this type may be issued in all employment sectors, but the following are excluded:

- sales representatives;
- professionals obliged to register with professional bodies (that were in existence when the decree came into force);
- board members and company auditors;
- members of panels and commissions (including those of a technical nature);
- people over the age of 65;
- athletes engaged on a freelance basis, even if in the form of quasi-subordinate employment;
- those engaged in quasi-subordinate employment with one client firm for no more than 30 days a year, or earning up to €5,000 with one client firm;
- individuals working for the public administration;
- those in quasi-subordinate employment with recognised sports associations.

The project work contract must be in writing, and provide an indication of the duration of the project or project phase, a description of the project or phase to be implemented, the amount of remuneration or the criteria by which it is to be determined, payment dates, any provisions relating to expenses, methods for coordination between the project worker and the client firm, and any health and safety protection measures additional to those already adopted in the workplace. The remuneration must be comparable to similar work on a freelance basis in the place where the work is carried out.

Legislative Decree No. 276/2003 (Articles 61-69) provides a higher level of protection for these contracts in comparison to quasi-subordinate employment with regard to sickness, injury and maternity. In the case of sickness or injury, the employment relationship is suspended but not extended. In the event of a suspension that is more than one sixth of the duration of the contract (if specified), or more than 30 days, the client firm has the right to terminate the contract, whereas in the case of maternity, the contract is suspended and automatically extended for 180 days. In addition, the project worker has the right to work for other client firms (unless specified in the individual contract that this is not permitted), and may claim patent rights for any inventions arising from the work performed.

2.5. Occasional Labour

Occasional or casual labour is intended for individuals at risk of social exclusion, those who have yet to enter the labour market, and those who are about to leave it. The aim of this type of work is to enable these workers to make the transition from the hidden economy, where they have no protection whatsoever, to the regular economy, as well as to facilitate access to the labour market on the part of disadvantaged groups, enabling them to find work in private households or the non-profit sector. Those who can make use of these contracts are:

- individuals who have been unemployed for over a year;
- housewives, students and retired people;
- people with disabilities and those in rehabilitation centres;
- non-EU citizens with a regular work permit, in the first six months after losing their job. This measure is intended to enable the following to employ help on an occasional basis:
- private households;
- non-profit organisations;
- individuals who are not entrepreneurs, or entrepreneurs not engaged in their main business.

The type of work is intended to be as follows:

- light housework of an occasional nature, including childcare, and assistance for older persons and people with disabilities;
- private lessons;
- gardening, cleaning and maintenance of buildings and monuments;
- social, sports, cultural and charity events;

- collaboration with public bodies and voluntary associations for dealing with emergencies and unexpected natural events.

In the agricultural sector, work performed by family members, unpaid work and work for which only expenses are paid is not deemed to be occasional labour.

The contract may be in the form agreed between the parties, for a maximum of 30 days per calendar year and up to €5,000 per annum.

A particular payment system is provided, with vouchers for an amount established by ministerial decree, to be purchased by the employer in advance. These vouchers are then presented to authorised centres, that deduct a percentage for their services, together with a 13% social insurance and 7% industrial injury insurance contribution, and pay the balance to the worker. No income tax is payable, and the worker continues to be classified as unemployed or not in employment (Legislative Decree 276/2003, Articles 70-74).

2.6. Part-time Work

This is considered to be anything less than full-time working hours. It may be horizontal (a shorter working day), vertical (full time but only on certain days or certain times in the month) or mixed, consisting of shorter working days and a reduction in the number of days worked.

It has been found to be a particularly effective way to increase employment opportunities for particular groups, such as young people, women, older people and retired persons. It provides stable rather than precarious employment, making it possible to reconcile the employer's need for flexibility with the worker's need to deal with family responsibilities or educational requirements. Part-time contracts give rise to salaried employment that may be open-ended or fixed-term. Contracts must be in writing and specify the working hours, the days of the week, the weeks and the months to be worked in the course of the year.

Part-time employees may not be discriminated against in relation to full-time workers, and as a result the hourly rate of pay, and rates for sickness, injury and maternity leave are calculated in proportion to the hours worked, unless the applicable collective agreement makes provision for rates that are more than proportionate. In addition, part-time workers have the same right to annual leave, maternity/parental leave, sickness and injury provisions, and so on.

Compared to the measures previously in force, Legislative Decree No. 276/2003 allows for greater flexibility in the management of working hours and fewer limits on working additional hours, overtime and flexibility or elasticity clauses, for which collective agreements can make provision within the limits laid down for full-time working.

Individual contracts may allow the part-time worker to opt for full-time working whenever the employer intends to hire full-time workers, with the part-time worker taking priority over incoming workers with the same employment grade. In the same way, full-time workers are entitled to be informed of the intention to hire new part-timers and may opt for part-time. Employees who are diagnosed with a tumour may opt for part-time and then at a later date opt to return to full-time working.

The part-time provisions in Legislative Decree No. 276/2003 are immediately applicable, and not subject to tripartite assessment at a later stage, though further provisions may be laid down by collective bargaining.

2.7. Job Sharing

In this contract two workers jointly take on the rights and responsibilities arising from an individual employment contract, and are free to divide up the hours as they choose. The aim of job sharing is to reconcile work requirements with other responsibilities, while striking a balance between the needs of the employer and those of the worker, but it is not permitted in the public administration. In relation to previous provisions, the innovation in the Biagi law consists of limiting this type of contract to two workers at a time.

The job-sharing contract must be in writing, and specify the hours to be worked by each of the employees. They may modify these arrangements as they wish but are required to notify the employer on a weekly basis of the hours each of them intends to work, so that a record can be kept of any absences. The employment contract may be open-ended or fixed-term, and the principle of equal pay and equal treatment with other workers of the same employment grade applies. For the purpose of calculating social insurance contributions, workers on job-sharing contracts are treated like part-timers, but the calculation has to be made on a monthly basis. In the event of the dismissal or resignation of one of the employees, the contract of the other employee is also terminated, though the employer may offer the remaining employee a part-time or full-time salaried position. Moreover, the employer has the right to refuse to take on a third party to fill the position.

2.8. On-call Work

On-call or zero-hours contracts are used when the worker agrees to work intermittently (for activities laid down by national or territorial collective bargaining) or at certain times of the week, month or year. This contract is entirely new in the Italian system and may take two different forms: with or without a stand-by allowance, depending on whether the worker agrees to be bound to accept the offer of work.

The purpose of this new type of contract is to regularise a particular use of payment by invoice, used until now for work of an intermittent nature. It is also intended to be a way of creating employment opportunities for unemployed people trying to find a way into (or back into) the labour market.

On an experimental basis, these contracts may be issued to:

- unemployed workers up to the age of 25;
- workers over the age of 45 who have been made redundant or are on mobility schemes or registered as unemployed.

Companies that have not carried out a health and safety assessment pursuant to Legislative Decree No. 626/1994 are not permitted to issue contracts of this kind, nor is the public administration. In addition, employers are not permitted to issue contracts of this kind to replace workers who are on strike, and they may not be used in companies that have made workers redundant in the past six months, unless provided otherwise by collective bargaining.

Rates of pay are required to be the same as those for comparable workers on standard contracts. In cases in which the worker agrees to be bound to accept an offer to work, a monthly stand-by allowance is made, that may be divided by an hourly rate, laid down by ministerial decree, not payable in the event of illness. An unjustified refusal to respond to an offer of work may result in termination of the contract, the repayment of the stand-by allowance, and payment of damages as laid down in the collective agreement or, in the absence of such a provision, in the employment contract. In the case of on-call working only at certain times of the week, payment is made only when the worker is called out. This type of contract is experimental and subject to tripartite assessment at the end of the trial period.

2.9. Employment Agency Work[54]

This type of work enables a user company to utilise the services of workers (on the basis of temporary agency work or staff leasing) who are employed by an employment agency. It is important to distinguish between two types of contract that are the basis of this arrangement:

- a contract for the supply of labour between the employment agency and the user company, which is a commercial contract, and
- a subordinate employment contract, between the employment agency and the worker.

Each of these contracts may be fixed-term or open-ended. Such contracts are a form of outsourcing (or rather insourcing, due to the fact that workers take their instructions from the user firm), and are intended to enable companies to expand their workforce quickly and flexibly, while providing employment opportunities for the workers hired by the agency.

The law does not place any limits on contracts between employment agencies and user companies, and subordinate employment contracts may be concluded with all categories of workers, not just disadvantaged groups. Open-ended employment agency contracts may be issued for:

- information technology consultancy services;
- cleaning and caretaking services;
- transport and haulage;
- the management of libraries, parks, museums. archives and warehouses;
- interim management services, certification, resource planning, organisational development and change, human resources management, staff recruitment and selection;
- marketing, market research, commercial operations;
- call-centre operations;
- certain tasks in the building industry;
- other functions as laid down in collective agreements concluded by the most representative employers' associations and trade unions.

Fixed-term employment agency contracts may be issued for:

---

[54] See: Tiraboschi, M. 2006. *Le esternalizzazioni dopo la riforma Biagi—Somministrazione, appalto, distacco e trasferimento di azienda*, Collana ADAPT-Fondazione "Marco Biagi". Milano: Giuffrè.

- technical, production, organisational and labour replacement needs, even in relation to the ordinary activity of the user company (Article 20, Legislative Decree No. 276/2003);
- temporary requirements as laid down in existing collective agreements until they run out (Article 86, Legislative Decree No. 276/2003).

An employment contract of this kind can be extended for a longer period by the employment agency, with the consent of the worker and in writing, as provided in the collective agreement applied by the employment agency. The contract between the user company and the employment agency is required to be in writing and contain certain specific indications. However, there are no specific requirements for the form of the contract between the worker and the employment agency.

Employment agency workers have the right to equal treatment with comparable workers in the user company, provided their duties are the same. The user company is jointly liable with the employment agency to pay the worker the agreed remuneration and contributions: as a result, if the employment agency fails to pay the agreed amount, the worker may demand payment from the user company, which is under an obligation to pay the amount due.

In the case of fixed-term contracts, the employment agency is obliged to pay the worker an indemnity as laid down in the collective agreement, but which cannot be less than €350 per month pursuant to a decree of the Minister of Labour and Social Policy.

Open-ended contracts are regulated by the general employment provisions laid down by the Civil Code and special laws, and may be part-time.

Fixed-term contracts are regulated by Legislative Decree No. 368/2001, with certain differences:

- the employment agency may issue a number of fixed-term contracts in sequence without having to comply with the provision requiring an interval between contracts;
- special provisions are made for information and training;
- no percentage limits are laid down for agency work, so an employer may choose to use only agency workers in the undertaking.
- Employment agency contracts may be issued by:
- temporary work agencies, authorised to operate under the previous regulations, as soon as they have submitted an application for authorisation pursuant to the new provisions;

- other operators as soon as they are authorised to operate as employment agencies and register as such (pursuant to Legislative Decree No. 276/2003).

The provisions relating to employment agencies are of an experimental nature and will be subject to tripartite assessment at the end of the trial period.

2.10. Other Employment Provisions

The forms of employment outlined above are intended to illustrate the innovative nature of the Biagi law, and do not provide an exhaustive survey. Mention should however be made of provisions relating to contract work (Article 29), secondment of employees on a temporary basis (Article 30), the continuity of employment in the event of the transfer of an undertaking or part of an undertaking (Article 32), the clarification of the position of workers in cooperatives (Article 9), and finally work experience programmes *(tirocini)* (Article 60) for school-leavers and undergraduates. These programmes are not a form of employment but are intended to provide experience for young people during their secondary or higher education enabling them to take part in training and to make informed choices in the labour market.

3. Certification of Employment Contracts

The certification of employment contracts by bilateral bodies, provincial labour departments and universities registered with the Minister of Labour and Social Policy (Articles 75-84) is a procedure for ascertaining whether an employment contract that is about to be issued complies with the provisions laid down by the law. It is a voluntary procedure that can be adopted only at the request of both parties, the employer and the employee, and is intended to reduce the number of individual employment disputes.

This procedure can be applied to any kind of employment contract. Certification may also be used to deal with any particular provisions, the settlement of disputes between an employee and an employer, and internal regulations in cooperative societies relating to employment contracts issued to worker members.

Certification can be carried out by committees set up by:

- bilateral bodies established by employers' associations and trade unions in a given area or at national level;
- provincial labour departments;
- local authorities at provincial level;
- public and private universities that have submitted an application to be enrolled on the Ministry of Labour and Social Policy register.

The certification procedure is initiated by a joint application submitted in writing by the employer and the employee, and the procedure must be completed within 30 days of submission of the application. In assessing the application the committee must take account of best practices. The procedure is concluded with a deed of certification stating the reasons for the decision and indicating the authority to which an appeal may be presented, the deadlines for submission, and the effects of the certification. An appeal against the deed of certification may be lodged by the employer, the employee, or any interested third party, with the labour courts or the regional administrative tribunal. Applications for certification and the certified contracts must be kept on file by the certifying body for at least five years after their period of validity has come to an end. The certifying bodies also provide advice and assistance to the worker and the employer in relation to the negotiation of the contract and any changes to be agreed on. These provisions are of an experimental nature for an 18-month period, after which a tripartite assessment will be carried out in order to decide whether to continue with these certification procedures.

CHAPTER FIVE

THE REFORM OF THE ITALIAN LABOUR MARKET OVER THE PAST TEN YEARS: A PROCESS OF LIBERALIZATION?

1. The Recent Labour Market Reforms in Italy: A Brief Historical Overview

Over the past decade, the labour market[1] has undergone a process of profound legislative change, not just in Italy.[2]

The constant evolution of the legal framework governing the labour market and the underlying economic and social structures is clearly not a recent phenomenon. Rather, it may be argued that this has been one of the characteristics of labour law since it first emerged as a discipline domain. It is significant that Hugo Sinzheimer, universally recognised as one of the founders of modern labour law, considered this branch of juridical system as the law of the frontier, but also as a frontier of the law.[3] Little or nothing has changed since then, confirming that the essence of labour law still consists of the intrinsic need to remind constantly the jurist of the

---

[1] The term "labour market" is used in the broad sense here, concerning the area of regulation covered by labour law as a whole.

[2] For a comparative overview see Blanpain, R., and M. Weiss, eds. 2003. *Changing Industrial Relations and Modernisation of Labour Law—Liber Amicorum in Honour of Professor Marco Biagi*. The Hague: Kluwer Law International; and, more recently, Blanpain, R., S. Bisom-Rapp, W. R. Corbett, H. K. Josephs, and M. J. Zimmer, eds. 2007. *The Global Workplace—International and Comparative Employment Law*. Cambridge: Cambridge University Press. See also the Report of the Director General of the International Labour Office. 2006. *Changing Patterns in the World of Work*. Geneva: ILO (also available at *www.adapt.it*, index A-Z, under the heading *Statuto dei lavori*.

[3] Sinzheimer, H. 1922. "Über soziologische und dogmatische Methoden in der Arbeitsrechtswissenschaft", *Arbeitsrecht*, 187 ff.

difficult task of classification and qualification of new phenomena, or phenomena undergoing continuous change.[4]

The recent far-reaching changes in methods of production and work organisation, introduced by technological innovation and the globalisation of markets, have if anything contributed to the acceleration of the range and depth of legislative intervention, to a greater or lesser extent, so that the process of reform has had a significant impact on all the main areas of this branch of legal studies.[5]

This has undoubtedly affected the internal dynamics of labour law: over the course of just over a century of development, the driving force of normative innovation has been collective bargaining, and the self-regulating balance of power reflected in it. At the same time, legislative provisions have been assigned a role that is subsidiary—at times even secondary[6]—in labour market regulation, with recourse to the traditional techniques of implementation, consolidation and extension of the provisions of collective bargaining.

The progressive loss of centrality of the system of inter-trade union relations, considered in Italy as an autonomous juridical system distinct from that of the State,[7] has led to profound changes in the traditional sources generating labour law[8] and in their degree of effectiveness in regulating the labour market. The gap between the abstract provisions of inderogable legal and/or collective bargaining norms on the one hand, and the economic and productive system on the other, which is another constant feature of the development of Italian labour law,[9] has never been as wide as it is today, as shown unequivocally by the alarming figures on

---

[4] Giugni, G. 1977. *Introduzione allo studio dell'autonomia collettiva*, Milano: Giuffrè (first published 1960), p. 20.

[5] For a penetrating analysis of the development of labour law that prefigures the recent reforms, see Giugni, G. 1998. "Il diritto del lavoro: ieri, oggi e domani", *Scritti in onore di Giuseppe Federico Mancini* 1, Milano: Giuffrè, p. 287.

[6] In this connection reference should be made to Kahn-Freund, O. 1977. *Labour and the Law*. London: Stevens & Son, (second edition), esp. pp. 1-17 and p. 2 for the citation, where he speaks of the law "as a secondary force [...] in labour relations".

[7] According to the classical study of Giugni, G. *Introduzione allo studio dell'autonomia collettiva*, cit.

[8] See Mariucci, L.2003. *Le fonti del diritto del lavoro, quindici anni dopo*. Torino: Giappichelli.

[9] In this connection see Mariucci, L. 1979. *Il lavoro decentrato. Discipline legislative e contrattuali*. Milan: Angeli, esp. p. 20 and p. 25, putting forward the argument, that is still relevant today, that "the history of labour law largely coincides with the historical reconstruction of the reasons for its ineffectiveness".

employment in the hidden economy. It has been estimated that more than a quarter of the Italian labour market, over four million jobs amounting to 23-27 per cent of GDP,[10] is in the shadow economy, with a consequent lack of legal regulation.[11]

The explosion of the area of atypical employment and the loss of effectiveness of inderogable legislative and collective bargaining norms are clearly not to be found only in the Italian labour market. However, it must be pointed out that the other OECD countries are not characterised by a degeneration of the kind to be seen in Italy, where employment in the hidden economy is estimated to be two to three times higher in percentage terms than the European mean.[12]

The progressive loss of effectiveness of the regulation of labour relations, with its negative impact on the constitutional right to work for all,[13] together with the constant loss of competitiveness of Italian enterprises in the international market, was undoubtedly one of the main reasons that led the legislator to attempt a profound reform of the labour market, though not without opposition from those intent on maintaining the status quo.

It has been argued[14] that the most recent normative developments will tend to undermine the power of the social partners and industrial relations,

---

[10] See Scheneider, F., and D. H. Enste. 2002. *The Shadow Economy: an International Survey*. Cambridge: Cambridge University Press. More limited, but still alarming, are the estimates published by ISTAT. 2004. *La misura dell'occupazione non regolare nelle stime di contabilità nazionale: un'analisi a livello nazionale, regionale e retrospettiva a partire dal 1980*. Rome: Istat, available at *www.adapt.it*, index A-Z, under the heading *Lavoro irregolare*. An influential study is that of Dell'Olio, M. 2000. "Il lavoro sommerso e la lotta per il diritto", *Arg. Dir. Lav.*, pp. 43-53, but see also Sala Chiri, M. 2003. "Il lavoro sommerso e il diritto del lavoro", *Scritti in memoria di Salvatore Hernandez*, *Dir. Lav.*,No. 6, pp. 731-745, and the bibliography therein.

[11] It should be pointed out that this phenomenon is by no means new, and was highlighted in the 1970s and 1980s. See, for example, Giugni, G. 1989. "Giuridificazione e deregolazione nel diritto del lavoro italiano", *Lavoro legge contratti*, ed. Giugni G. (Bologna: Il Mulino), first edition 1986, esp. pp. 350-351.

[12] See Scheneider, F. 2002. "The Value Added of Underground Activities: Size and Measurement of the Shadow Economies and Shadow Economy Labor Force all over the World", World Bank Paper, at www.lex.unict.it, under the heading *Dossier sul lavoro sommerso*. In addition extensive documentation is available at *www.adapt.it*, index A-Z, under the heading *Lavoro irregolare*.

[13] Art. 4 Italian Constitution of 1948.

[14] Cf., by way of example, Bellardi, L. 2005. "La struttura della contrattazione collettiva e il d.lgs. n. 276 del 2003", *Diritto del lavoro. I nuovi problemi—L'omaggio dell'Accademia a Mattia Persiani* 1:339-362.

thus bringing to an end a phase characterised by the devolution of powers and competences to collective bargaining. However, this view is highly controversial, and less linear than it might appear to be from a superficial assessment. It is even possible to argue the opposite: that the significant intervention on the part of the legislator in recent years is due to the persistent inertia of the social partners, who are reluctant to come to terms with changes in the world of work,[15] together with the lack of reform of the industrial relations system and collective bargaining structures.

An analysis of the main national collective agreements unequivocally confirms that certain matters relating to organisational innovation and productivity (working hours, contracting out and outsourcing, job descriptions and grading, training issues, etc.) are dealt with only to a marginal extent by collective bargaining as a way of governing the changes taking place in work and production.

Rather, a prevalent tendency is for trade unions to exercise the power of veto, as shown by the numerous agreements (both at national and company level) aimed at "sterilising", to use the term used by some trade unions,[16] the most recent legislative provisions relating to flexibility and labour organisation.

Arguably, the main aim of reform in Italy is to overcome this logic of conservation and opposition, also trough the resurgence of domestic terrorism, to change. "Of all the mistakes that the unions may be said to have made", wrote in 1980 one of the first victims of the terrorism in the area of employment and social reforms named Walter Tobagi,[17] "the reluctance to come to terms with social transformation is the one requiring the closest attention. It is indicative of the fact that the unions have managed to exercise the power of veto in relation to leading companies and political power, but have not managed to redesign the Italian economic model. And the market powers have found a new point of equilibrium which indeed takes account of the rigidity of the trade unions,

---

[15] This is the view taken ever since his inaugural speech by the CISL general secretary, Raffaele Bonanni. See his remarks at the General Council of the CISL, 27 April 2006, *Bollettino ADAPT*, 2006, No. 25.

[16] The renewal of the metalworkers' national collective agreement, that is influential in terms of pattern setting in Italy, is emblematic: see Tiraboschi, M. 2006. "Metalmeccanici: siglata l'intesa", *Guida Lav.* 5:11. Ample documentation for the arguments put forward is available at *www.adapt.it,* index A-Z, under the heading *Contrattazione collettiva.*

[17] Tobagi, W. 1980. *Che cosa contano i sindacati*. Milano: Rizzoli, reprinted in Baiocchi, G., and M. Volpato, eds. 2005. *Walter Tobagi giornalista*, Associazione Lombarda dei Giornalisti, Milan, esp. p. 226.

but only in order to find a way round it" (our translation). These words appear to be particularly relevant today, and it is significant that this concept underlies the *White Paper* of Marco Biagi (the last victim of the domestic terrorism in Italy)[18] published in October 2001[19] and its attempt—culminating in the reform of the labour market that bears his name[20]—to challenge this equilibrium based on the safety valve of employment in the hidden economy and employment contracts of dubious value affecting vast numbers of individuals who are denied protection and rights.

The need to deal with the extensive area of the informal economy, while governing and shaping the major transformations that are taking place, gave rise to the need to rethink the labour market, in order to provide a systematic reform of legislative provisions that had become increasingly incoherent at the end of the 1970s and the beginning of the 1980s, with the result that they were of little practical value and failed to work together as part of an overall plan. This fragmentary legislation, as has been rightly pointed out,[21] was not based on a coherent and far-reaching vision, and although attempts were made to deal with a range of matters such as the promotion of employment among young people and safety-net measures for the extensive processes of restructuring and reconversion, it was mainly characterised by the resistance to any intervention aimed at introducing systematic change. However, this resistance to innovation, though based on a passive approach providing derogations and exceptions, was accompanied by some initial concessions to market values and the requirements of the enterprise.

It is significant that some analysts have seen Italian labour law as mainly responding to economic crisis or transformation.[22] This approach

---

[18] See Tiraboschi, M. 2002. "Marco Biagi: The Man and the Master", *The International Journal of Comparative Labour Law and Industrial Relations* 3.

[19] See also the EU documents on the modernisation of labour law which the *White Paper* explicitly mentions: in particular the Communication of the European Commission on *Modernising the Organisation of Work—A Positive Approach to Change*, COM(98)592, esp. p. 8, available at *www.adapt.it*, index A-Z, under the heading *Lavoro (organizzazione del)*, and the documentation therein.

[20] On the so called "Biagi reform", reference can be made to the documentation and the bibliography in *www.adapt.it*, index A-Z, under *Riforma Biagi.*

[21] With reference to emergency labour law reforms adopted in the absence of an overall plan, see Romagnoli, U. 1983. "Il diritto del lavoro tra disincanto e riforme senza progetto", *Riv. Trim. Dir. Proc. Civ.*,esp. p. 20.

[22] See Giugni, G. 1989. "Il diritto del lavoro negli anni '80", G. Giugni, *Lavoro legge contratti*. Bologna: Il Mulino, p. 319.

may be said to be conservative, attempting to deal with emergencies[23] in a purely defensive manner, and limiting the social consequences of economic crisis[24] by means of a policy of passive measures with ever-increasing subsidies by the State to enterprises.[25]

Such a traditional conception of labour law gives priority to rigid regulation and extremely high levels of protection, which has become increasingly inadequate for governing a marketplace undergoing drastic and far-reaching changes.

Particularly emblematic, in this connection, is the failure on the part of labour law to provide a strong response to the hidden economy,[26] in which the main intention is to avoid normative provisions and evade social contributions, while paying due regard to the development of modern forms of work organisation. As a result of the traditional approach, certain management techniques and employment models have been considered illegal, solely due to the inadequacy of the Italian legal framework, and its failure to modernise, when compared to provisions adopted in other countries.[27]

Consequently, there is a need to analyse the most recent normative developments in the labour market against the background of a complex historical process, aimed at the rationalisation of a system of labour law

---

[23] The dubious results of the period of emergency labour law are examined in De Luca Tamajo, R., and L. Ventura, eds. 1979. *Il diritto del lavoro nell'emergenza*. Napoli: Jovene.

[24] On this topic see the papers in D'Antona, M., R. De Luca Tamajo, G. Ferraro, and L. Ventura, eds. 1988. *Il diritto del lavoro negli anni 80*. Naples: ESI, vols. 1-2.

[25] On this point see Giugni, G. "Il diritto del lavoro negli anni '80", cit., p. 309, and for a more incisive analysis, Mancini, G. F. 2006. *Democrazia e costituzionalismo nell'Unione Europea*. Bologna: Il Mulino, esp. p. 18. For an analysis of economic policies adopted solely with a view to neutralising or offsetting, in the short term but also in the long term, normative constraints, in the form of the protection laid down by the traditional system of labour law, reference may be made to the study by the present author, 2002. *Incentivi alla occupazione, aiuti di Stato, diritto comunitario della concorrenza*. Turin: Giappichelli, esp. Chap. I.

[26] See the authoritative comments by Giugni, G. "Il diritto del lavoro negli anni '80",cit., esp. p. 329.

[27] Emblematic, in this connection, is the legitimisation of agency work, introduced in France and Germany as long ago as 1972, but introduced in the Italian system only by the Treu measures of 1997. See Biagi, M., and T. Treu. 1998. "Temporary work in Italy", *Comparative Labor Law and Policies Journal.* For an historical and comparative survey, reference may be made to the work of the present author, 1999. *Lavoro temporaneo e somministrazione di manodopera*. Torino: Giappichelli.

which at the end of the 1980s was characterised by successive layers of normative provisions, rigid practices of a corporative nature, and ad hoc legislative measures that were not part of an overall plan.[28]

At the same time, an interpretation in a perspective of pure and simple deregulation—although put forward by many Italian labour law scholars[29]—may be said to be completely inappropriate, and incapable of explaining the overall development of the transformations taking place in recent years in the Italian system of labour law.[30]

It should also be noted that, in normative terms, legislative intervention has not resulted in a significant amount of deregulation or the promotion of free market policies, but has become more intense in recent years, to the point that some scholars have made ironic comments on the amount of space dedicated to labour market reform in the *Gazzetta Ufficiale*.[31]

Rather, it would appear to be more appropriate to speak of legislative innovations inspired by the need for a properly governed labour market, with a view to making legal norms more effective by adopting positive measures and normative incentives, to achieve greater cohesion between abstract normative provisions and the economic and social system they are intended to regulate.

The aim of safeguarding the effectiveness of legal norms would appear to be the main focus for an analysis, albeit problematic, of recent developments in Italian labour law. The system of labour law needs to embrace the values of industrial (and post-industrial) society,[32] pursuing

---

[28] See Giugni, G. "Il diritto del lavoro negli anni '80", cit., esp. p. 304, p. 322 and p. 331. Reference should also be made to Romagnoli, U. "Il diritto del lavoro tra disincanto e riforme senza progetto", cit., pp. 11-23 and Mariucci, L. *Le fonti del diritto del lavoro etc.*, cit., esp. pp. 135-168.

[29] For this view see, among others, Garofalo, M.G. 2006. "Il diritto del lavoro e la sua funzione economico-sociale", *Percorsi di diritto del lavoro*, eds. Garofalo, D., and M. Ricci, eds. Bari: Cacucci, pp. 127-144.

[30] On this point, with reference to the Italian debate on deregulation and the search for alternatives to a legalistic approach to employment relations based on inderogable norms, reference may be made to the study of the present author, *Incentivi alla occupazione, aiuti di Stato, diritto comunitario della concorrenza*, cit., Chap. I, § 2. In the international literature, comparable arguments are put forward by Gaudu, F. 2005. "Libéralisation des marchés et droit du travail", *Droit Social* No. 5, pp. 505-513 esp. 506, where the process of reform of French labour law is placed at the beginning of the 1980s.

[31] This comment about the Biagi reform of the labour law was made by Vallebona, A. 2004. *La riforma del lavoro*. Padova: Cedam.

[32] As advocated in the early 1980s by Giugni, G."*Il diritto del lavoro negli anni '80*", cit., esp. pp. 334-335. This position, for many years neglected or at least

modernisation as an alternative to pure and simple deregulation,[33] while conciliating the traditional objectives of social justice with efficiency and productivity imposed by the transformations taking place in the economy and society, as in the early days of labour law.[34]

2. The Innovations Introduced by the Treu Measures and the Biagi Reform of the Labour Market

The reforms in the 1990s, with the "privatisation" of public-sector employment, the restructuring of employment services and the Treu measures for promoting employment[35] were carried forward with a considerable degree of continuity from one government to the next, though at times there were elements of incongruence[36] and even of discontinuity. In particular, reference should be made in this connection to Constitutional

---

supported only by a minority of Italian labour law scholars, (cf. Mariucci, L. "Il diritto del lavoro e il suo ambiente", *Scritti in onore di Giuseppe Federico Mancini*, cit., esp. pp. 346-348), was advocated again, in a perspective of constitutional recognition of the freedom of private economic initiative, by Persiani, M. "Radici storiche e nuovi scenari del diritto del lavoro", *Diritto del lavoro*, ed. Persiani, M. Padua: Cedam, Padua, esp. p. 91. For a highly critical comment see Garofalo, M. G. "Il diritto del lavoro e la sua funzione economico-sociale", cit., esp. p. 140, who speaks of the "hegemony of the so-called business culture" (our translation).

[33] A strategy for the "modernisation of labour law" as an alternative to a neoliberal approach was proposed in the international literature by Hepple, B. 1997. "Economic Efficiency and Social Rights", *Law in Motion*, ed. Blanpain, R. (The Hague: Kluwer Law International), pp. 867-878 esp. p. 857, and advocated in Italy by Biagi, M. 2003. "Competitività e risorse umane: modernizzare la regolazione dei rapporto di lavoro", *Marco Biagi: un giurista progettuale*, eds. Montuschi, L., M. Tiraboschi, and T. Treu, Milano: Giuffrè, pp. 149-182.

[34] For an attempt to demonstrate that labour law is not solely a unilateral system for the protection of the weaker party, but that since its origins it has also performed other functions, such as the protection of competition among undertakings, the resolution of social conflict, etc., reference may be made once again to the work of the present author, *Lavoro temporaneo e somministrazione di manodopera*, cit., esp. Chap. 3.

[35] Cf., in particular, Act No. 196/1997 and, for a detailed analysis, Biagi, M., ed. *Mercati e rapporti di lavoro etc.*, cit., and in the same volume, in particular, the introduction by Tiziano Treu and Marco Biagi.

[36] The most significant of which is, without a shadow of doubt, the exclusion of the public administration and public-sector workers from the field of application of the Biagi law, except for a generic reference to subsequent harmonisation, that has not led to further measures of any substance.

Law No. 3, 18 October 2001, reforming Title V of the Constitution. In spite of the ambiguous formulation regarding the division of competences relating to the "protection and security of employment" between the State and the Regions, this measure had a significant impact on the regulation of the labour market during the fourteenth legislature (2001-2006). But also in this case the paradigm shift was more apparent than real,[37] as recently confirmed by sentence No. 50/2005 of the Constitutional Court.[38]

Above all the most recent measures[39] were intended to favour the modernisation of the system of labour law as a whole, in an attempt to balance the system of safeguards with the pressure exerted by international competition, in a dimension that transcends national sovereignty.

However, the turning point, in the form of the Treu measures in 1997, was only a partial step, as shown by the significant changes to the initial government proposals introduced by the agreement with the unions and the Act approved by Parliament.[40] Also the ambitious reform proposals announced by the Berlusconi government, with the publication of the *White Paper on the Labour Market* in October 2001,[41] were only partially embodied in legislation with the approval of Act No. 30, 14 February 2003, and the relative implementation decrees.[42]

In line with reforms taking place in other sectors, the substantial changes in the legal framework were adopted with the objective, in line

---

[37] Reference may be made, also for the bibliographical references, to the paper by the present author. 2005. "Riforma del mercato del lavoro e modello organizzativo tra vincoli costituzionali ed esigenze di unitarietà del sistema", *Il diritto del mercato del lavoro dopo la riforma Biagi*, eds. Olivelli, P., and M. Tiraboschi, Milano: Giuffrè, pp. 40-96.

[38] See the comment by Scagliarini, S. 2006. "Competenze dello Stato e competenze delle Regioni in tema di regolazione del mercato del lavoro," note on the Constitutional Court 13-28 January 2005, sentence No. 50, *Dir. Rel. Ind.*, No. 1:182-194.

[39] For an overall assessment, which is beyond the scope of the present study, see Veneziani, B. 2003. "Le trasformazioni del diritto del lavoro in Italia", *Scritti in memoria di Salvatore Hernandez*, *Dir. Lav.*, No. 6, pp.901-922.

[40] See T. Treu, *Politiche del lavoro—Insegnamenti di un decennio*, Il Mulino, Bologna, 2001, esp. p. 26.

[41] See *www.adapt.it,* index A-Z, under the heading *Riforma Biagi.*

[42] In addition to the legislation to be cited below, for an analysis of the reform set in motion by Act No. 30/2003, known as the Biagi law, reference may be made to the extensive documentation available at *www.adapt.it*, index A-Z, under the heading *Riforma Biagi.* See also Tiraboschi, M. 2005. "The Italian Labour Market after the Biagi Reform", *The International Journal of Comparative labour Law and Industrial Relations,* No. 2.

with the European Employment Strategy to which the reforms make express reference,[43] to increase the level of regular employment, to overcome inefficiencies in the labour market, to promote employment of good quality and labour productivity.[44] This was to be achieved also by means of research and experimentation[45]—which was hotly contested by part of the trade union movement[46]—with new normative techniques that were considered to be more effective, in an economic and social framework that had undergone profound change, with a view to conciliating in a pragmatic manner the need for efficiency and competitiveness of the enterprise with the protection of the workers.[47]

However, the recent labour market reform in Italy cannot simply be considered to be based on a policy—or inspired by a philosophy—of liberalisation, even in terms of the final effects rather than the original intentions.

On close examination, both the Treu measures and the Biagi law are part of a complex phase of transition in which, as in any significant reform process,[48] the influence may be seen of political programmes, political cultures and legal traditions that are quite different from each other, and

---

[43] For the fundamental influence of EU employment and competition policy on the reform of the labour market in recent years, reference may be made to the paper by the present author "Riforma Biagi e Strategia Europea per la occupazione", Tiraboschi, M., ed. 2004. *La riforma Biagi del mercato del lavoro—Prime interpretazioni e proposte di lettura del d.lgs. 10 settembre 2003, n. 276*. Milano: Giuffrè, pp. 40-52. With reference to Act No. 196/1997, see Treu, T. "Politiche del lavoro e strumenti di promozione dell'occupazione: il caso italiano in una prospettiva europea", *Mercati e rapporto di lavoro etc.*, cit., pp. 3-20. On the connection between the regulation of national labour markets and the Lisbon strategy, see Ashiagbor, D. 2005. *The European Employment Strategy—Labour Market Regulation and New Governance*. Oxford: Oxford University Press, pp. 242-300.

[44] See in this connection, the provisions of Article 1 (1) of Legislative Decree No. 276/2003, implementing the Biagi law.

[45] Above all the Biagi law was characterised, at least in the intention of the legislator, by the fact that it made provision for experimentation with the measures introduced. See in this connection Article 86 (12), Legislative Decree No. 276/2003.

[46] This matter is dealt with by Iorio, M.R. "Riforma Biagi e conflitto", *La riforma Biagi del mercato del lavoro,* ed.Tiraboschi, M. cit., pp. 731-745.

[47] This overall plan is dealt with in a systematic manner in Biagi, M. *Competitività e risorse umane: modernizzare la regolazione dei rapporto di lavoro*, cit., pp. 149-182.

[48] See in this connection, and with reference to the reform of labour law, Giugni, G. 1970. "I tecnici del diritto e la legge 'malfatta'", *Pol. Dir.*, p. 479.

that at times may even be difficult or impossible to reconcile.[49] As a result, any attempt to identify an abstract structural homogeneity in these substantial provisions is destined to failure. But an even more significant point is that the reform process cannot be said to be complete either at present or in the near future.

Even without taking into consideration the ambitious proposal for structural reform of the labour market—put forward during the thirteenth legislature[50] and then again with the tripartite pact on 5 July 2002—aimed at introducing a Work Statute or *Statuto dei lavori,*[51] the completion of the plan set out in the Biagi Law would require the reform of safety-net measures and the legal framework for employment incentives.[52] Not to mention the implementation at a practical level of the innovations introduced into the legal framework to facilitate company-level bargaining, that at present is held back by the power of veto exercised at the bargaining table both at sectoral and company level.[53]

Evidently, it is by no means easy to identify a unified policy and inspiration in the legislative interventions considered, i.e. the Treu measures and the Biagi Law, but at the same time, it is even more problematic to provide an overall appraisal of these measures. Apart from any other consideration, such an appraisal would be possible only by means of an interpretation—that has been forward by the present author elsewhere—aimed at placing value on and identifying the systematic aspects of the numerous elements of continuity between the thirteenth and the fourteenth legislatures, which may be considered to be a natural

---

[49] This point, with reference to the Treu measures by Montecchi, E. "La legge n. 196/1997: una nuova fase dell'intervento pubblico sui mercati del lavoro", *Mercati e rapporto di lavoro etc.*, ed. Biagi, M. cit., p. 53, is made, with reference to the Biagi law, also in De Luca Tamajo, R. "Dietro le righe del d.lgs. n. 276 del 2003: tendenze e ideologie", *Diritto del lavoro. I nuovi problemi—L'omaggio dell'Accademia a Mattia Persiani*, cit., p. 953.

[50] See Treu, T. *Politiche del lavoro e strumenti di promozione dell'occupazione etc.*, cit., esp. p. 11.

[51] *Infra*,§ 5.

[52] Reference may be made here to the contribution of the present author. 2004. "Il sistema degli ammortizzatori sociali: spunti per un progetto di riforma", *La riforma Biagi del mercato del lavoro*, ed. Tiraboschi M., Milano: Giuffrè, pp. 1105-1121.

[53] On this point see Maresca, A. "Modernizzazione del diritto del lavoro, tecniche normative e apporti dell'autonomia collettiva", *Diritto del lavoro. I nuovi problemi—L'omaggio dell'Accademia a Mattia Persiani*, cit., p. 469-492. For an overview of the implementation of the Biagi law in collective bargaining, see the heading *Riforma Biagi* in the A-Z index at *www.adapt.it.*

progression from the rather confused legislative measures adopted between the end of the 1960s and the end of the 1980s.[54]

3. The Ambiguous Nature of the Expression "Liberalisation Policies" in Labour Market Regulation

The identification of a substantial degree of continuity in the recent labour market reforms makes it possible to refute, as clearly unfounded, the interpretations that, at times in an ideological manner and at times by way of caricature,[55] point to elements of discontinuity in the various legislative interventions which, though substantial, are often extrapolated in an artificial and arbitrary manner from their historical and cultural context.

In this perspective, a line of interpretation that is particularly emblematic is that which, deliberately setting aside the values and principles laid down in the Constitution, maintains that the reform

---

[54] In terms of continuity, see Ichino, P. 2003. "La 'Legge Biagi' sul lavoro: continuità o rottura col passato?", *Cor. Giur.*, pp. 1545-1549; Vallebona, A. *La riforma del lavoro*,cit.; Magnani, M. 2006. *Il diritto del lavoro e le sue categorie—Valori e tecniche nel diritto del lavoro*, Padova: Cedam, p. 35; Napoli, M. 2004. "Autonomia individuale e autonomia collettiva alla luce delle più recenti riforme", *Autonomia individuale e autonomia collettiva alla luce delle più recenti riforme*, Atti delle giornate di studio di diritto del lavoro, Abano Terme-Padua, 21-22 May. Milano: Giuffrè, p. 10; Perone, G. 2005. "Incertezze applicative ... e interpretazioni ragionevoli", *Tutele del lavoro e nuovi schemi organizzativinell'impresa*, ed. Ficari, L., Milano: Giuffrè, p. 107; Sestito, P., and S. Pirrone. 2006. *Disoccupati in Italia—Tra Stato, Regioni e cacciatori di teste*. Bologna: Il Mulino, p. 10. However, this view is not universally supported by legal scholars. Among the many scholars who consider the elements of discontinuity to be prevalent, see Ghezzi, G. 2003. "Mercato del lavoro, tipologie negoziali e definizioni", *Scritti in memoria di Salvatore Hernandez*, *Dir. Lav.*, No. 5, p. 322.

[55] Mention should be made of the argument that the recent labour market reforms have given rise to an uncontrolled proliferation of flexible and precarious types of employment contract. According to a recent study by the De Benedetti Foundation (*Il Sole 24 Ore,* 24 February 2006) there are at least 44 types (and more considering certification) of atypical employment introduced by the Biagi law. As I have argued elsewhere (Tiraboschi, M. 2006. *Precarietà e tipologie di lavoro: la moltiplicazione dei pani e dei pesci*, in *Bollettino ADAPT*, No. 13, the types of employment contract in the entire system, including open-ended salaried employment, amount to just over a dozen.

measures not only contain significant technical defects[56] but also violations of the Constitution.

Indeed this is a feature to be found in many of the criticisms of the recent reform measures: from the reform of temporary agency work to the new provisions on working time, from the reform of the structural rules for the labour market to the regulation of part-time, job sharing and flexible employment contracts.

However, on closer examination, even if the aim is to carry out an abstract appraisal of the measures laid down in the most recent and controversial legislative intervention, the Biagi reform of the labour market, there does not appear to be any evidence to support the argument—which is actually of an ideological nature[57]—that it is part of an overall design clearly based on neo-liberalism inspired by classical macroeconomics.[58] As if to say that today, as in the early days of the industrial revolution, the Italian labour market is left entirely to the free play of market forces, subject only to the common law of contract.

Such a position would fail to take account of the persistent and rigorous safeguards (both legal and contractual) which at least formally, considering the loss of effectiveness of the provisions of legislation and

---

56 The characterisation of the law as 'defective' is by no means original and in fact practically every legislative reform of any substance is subject to the same criticism. See on this point Giugni, G. "I tecnici del diritto e la legge 'malfatta'", cit., pp. 479-480, who rightly notes that every "new law, that has a high degree of technical and juridical content, is by its very nature subject to critical comment" (our translation). There are various reasons for this, even though "it is often and perhaps always the case that the critical comments conceal an underlying political opposition" (our translation) as may be said to be the case with the Biagi reform of the labour market. Reference may be made in this connection to the study by the present author, "Riforma del mercato del lavoro e modello organizzativo tra vincoli costituzionali ed esigenze di unitarietà del sistema",in Olivelli, P., and M. Tiraboschi, eds. *Il diritto del mercato del lavoro dopo la riforma Biagi*,cit., esp. pp. 40-58.

57 The Biagi reform was roundly criticised even before the legislation actually appeared. See in this connection Del Conte, M. "Il ruolo della contrattazione collettiva e l'impatto sul sistema di relazioni industriali", *La riforma Biagi etc.*, ed. Tiraboschi, M., cit, esp. pp. 636, which, on the basis of a presumed (or presumable) political will underlying the reform outlined in the *White Paper on the Labour Market*, describes the "preventive commentary" of a significant number of legal scholars on a legislative text that had not yet been drafted and even less approved by Parliament.

58 In these terms cf. on the other hand De Luca Tamajo, R. "Dietro le righe del d.lgs. n. 276 del 2003 etc.", cit., pp. 953-969, and Mariucci, L. *Le fonti del diritto del lavoro etc.*,cit., esp. p. 152.

collective agreements discussed above (*supra*,§ 1), regulate the matching of the supply and demand for labour, the management of the employment relationship, and above all dismissals.[59] On the other hand, it is evident—even for those who tend to underestimate the extent to which the law reflects labour policy[60]—that the Biagi reform does not affect any of the fundamental features of existing trade union and labour law.[61]

Suffice it to make a comparison, with a minimum of scientific rigour, between the Italian legislation enacted since 2001 and the neoliberal policies adopted in the United Kingdom by the Thatcher and Major governments—and substantially continued by the Blair administration since 1997[62]—to appreciate the fact that, even after the Biagi reform, Italy is by no means characterised by an individualistic ideology based on the self-regulation of the free market, hostile to the intervention of labour law and the State in the regulation of employment relations, with the ultimate objective of dismantling the power and prerogatives of the unions.

---

[59] On dismissal law and the principle of justification see Liebman, S. "Dispute Settlement procedures and Flexibilisation of Employment Relations: Remedies Against Unfair Dismissal Under Italian law", *Changing Industrial Relations and Modernisation of Labour Law—Liber Amicorum in Honour of Professor Marco Biagi*, cit., eds. Blanpain, R., and M. Weiss, pp. 269-276.

[60] Initially this aspect of the Biagi reform did not attract much critical attention either in terms of Act No. 39/2003 or the later implementation decrees. Among the few legal scholars commenting on this aspect, see P. Ichino, "L'anima laburista della legge Biagi—Subordinazione e "dipendenza" nella definizione della fattispecie di riferimento del diritto del lavoro", *Giust. Civ.*, 2005, pp. 131-149.

[61] For an analytical account of the matters not dealt with by the Biagi reform, see Vallebona, A. *La riforma del lavoro*, cit., esp. p. X. The reform is considered to be in a minor key, compared to the plans laid down in the *White Paper on the Labour Market*, also by Alleva, P. 2003. "La ricerca e la analisi dei punti critici del decreto legislativo n. 276/2003 in materia di occupazione e mercato del lavoro", *Riv. Giur. Lav*, No. 1 p. 887, who recognises that in an analytical framework that is strongly critical, the reform may by no means be compared to the vision "of a sociologist or economist espousing neo-conservative theories" (our translation).

[62] See in this connection the powerful analysis by Fredman, S. 2004. "The Ideology of New Labour Law", *The Future of Labour Law—Liber Amicorum Bob Hepple*, eds. Barnard, C., S. Deakin, G. Morris, (Oxford: Hart Publishing), 9-39 and p. 10, where it is argued that "as New Labour labour law demonstrates all too dishearteningly, behind the Third Way rhetoric, neoliberalism has, by stealth, become the dominant ideology, relegating social democracy to the minor partner". See also Deakin, S., and F. Wilkinson. 2005. *The Law of the Labour Market—Industrialization, Employment and Legal Evolution*, Oxford: Oxford University Press.

Rather, it may be said that it makes little sense when considering the Italian labour market to speak of liberalisation in the proper sense of the term. First of all, because such an expression takes on a specific meaning in this particular area of law, with a negative connotation since it is in contrast with the fundamental rationale for the emergence and development of a special and autonomous area of law, albeit not self-sufficient, known as labour law, aimed primarily at striking a balance between the bargaining power of the individual worker and market pressures in the negotiation of, in the course of, and on termination of the employment relation. Second, because, if it is really intended to speak of liberalisation, at least in the experience so far in Italy, these measures should be seen as interventions for modernising and updating the legal framework. In other words, as measures for the progressive rethinking of certain rigidities (often arising from case law interpretation) in the employment of the workforce—that may be seen as part of a policy of deregulation only in improperly speaking[63]—that cannot be justified in terms of the protection of the fundamental rights of the weaker party in the employment relationship[64] but that have a negative impact on the competitiveness of the Italian economy.

The trend towards a scaling back of normative restrictions and the introduction of greater elasticity in the labour market, though now decidedly more evident and explicit should not be confused in a superficial manner with a neoliberal policy based on a return to free bargaining and the self-regulation of the market. Rather, the recent normative interventions may be seen, regardless of their technical and political

---

[63] In this connection see Giugni, G. "Giuridificazione e deregolazione nel diritto del lavoro italiano," cit., esp. p. 349 and p. 353, where he argues that in the Italian tradition deregulation cannot be seen as "the abolition of norms and hence the return to the individual contract, but the introduction of flexibility into the normative process external to it" (our translation). For the view that these policies are tantamount to pure and simple liberalisation, that in our opinion is unfounded and not based on a scientific approach, see Garofalo, M. G. "Il diritto del lavoro e la sua funzione economico-sociale", cit., esp. p. 139-141.

[64] In this connection, see, for example, the use of the term "liberalisation" by Giugni, G. "Il diritto del lavoro etc.", cit., p. 291, with regard to the first cautious measures for deregulating the rigidities of the labour market. In the same vein see Treu, T. "Politiche del lavoro etc.", cit., esp. pp. 26-27, which, with reference to the substantial watering down, during the parliamentary proceedings and the negotiations with the social partners, of a number of innovative proposals in the first draft of the Treu measures, speaks of "the resistance of an ideological kind and on the part of vested interests encountered by deregulation in our country" (our translation).

limitations, as an attempt to deal with certain developments in the labour market and industrial relations, which, as noted above, can be traced back to the period in which labour law had to respond to a situation of emergency and crisis.

In relation to the consolidated structure of the Italian system, the impact of the Biagi reform of the labour market cannot be said to represent more of a break with the past in qualitative or quantitative terms than other recent reforms, in particular the Treu measures. Moreover, it cannot be said to have been introduced without due regard for the negotiating procedures traditionally laid down by the Italian industrial relations system, bearing in mind the tripartite agreement concluded on 5 July 2002, with some reservations,[65] and not without a degree of opposition.[66]

As evidence of a degree of continuity with the past, reference may be made to the tripartite agreement on the regulation of the labour market concluded in January 1983,[67] that was an initial attempt to shake up the outdated public employment services, making provision for more extensive use of fixed-term employment contracts and certain new types of employment such as work training contracts and part-time work. Reference could also be made to the structural measures on employment policy contained in the protocol of July 1993,[68] in favour of the employment of young people, the revival of the labour market and the management of the crisis in employment. More extensive provisions were implemented with the agreement of September 1996,[69] paving the way for the Treu measures, introducing temporary agency work in the face of a

---

[65] See, in particular, Montuschi, L. "Tecniche sperimentali deregolative del mercato del lavoro: un'intesa contrastata",in *Scritti in onore di Giuseppe Suppiey*, cit., esp. p. 717, where he pointed out, in connection with the fact that the CGIL did not sign the agreement, that "the Pact for Italy cannot count on a high degree of social cohesion" (our translation).

[66] See the highly critical comments by Giugni, G. 2003. *La lunga marcia della concertazione*. Bologna: Il Mulino, pp. 112-118.

[67] With regard to the Scotti protocol, reference may be made to Giugni, G. *La lunga marcia della concertazione*,cit., esp. pp. 39-55.

[68] On the labour measures contained in the Giugni protocol, see D'Antona, M. 1993. "Il protocollo sul costo del lavoro e l''autunno freddo' dell'occupazione", *Riv. It. Dir. Lav.*, No. 1, esp. pp. 426-427, where he highlights the limits of a reform project that followed a well-trodden path, starting from the "proliferation of employment contracts of dubious value" (our translation). This criticism is now levelled at the Biagi law, but with a line of reasoning, as we can see, that is not new.

[69] On the 1986 labour agreement see Antonello, M. "Note sulla genesi della legge n. 196/1997", *Mercati e rapporti di lavoro*, cit., pp. 55-57.

certain amount of opposition. The 1996 agreement provided for the introduction of training and career guidance placements, a reorganisation of training contracts, new forms of employment with reduced and flexible working hours, a reform of the sanctions relating to fixed-term employment, the abolition of the public monopoly on employment services, and the recognition of the legitimacy of private employment agencies.[70]

If these measures, representing a clear break with the traditional paradigm of labour law, are not considered to be representative of a neoliberal approach,[71] the same may be said of the recent reform of the legal framework,[72] which responds to the same need for rationalisation of employment safeguards in response to changes that are under way, in particular, the expansion of the hidden economy and irregular employment, the modification of productive processes and organisational innovation due to the use of new technology, the globalisation and internationalisation of markets, the growth of the tertiary sector, the increasing importance in the labour market of workers (especially women and young people) who require flexible working arrangements, particularly in terms of working hours and the possibility of re-entering the labour market after a period away from paid employment.[73]

4. Deregulation, Reregulation, Decentralisation

The recent reform cannot therefore be seen as a process of liberalisation at least in the strict sense, with the negative connotation that

---

[70] An extensive analysis is provided in Biagi, M., ed. *Mercati e rapporti di lavoro etc.*,cit.

[71] This view is expressed by Giugni, G. *Giuridificazione e deregolazione nel diritto del lavoro italiano*, cit., pp. 349-350. Along similar lines,Treu, T. *Politiche del lavoro e strumenti di promozione dell'occupazione etc.*, cit., p. 3.

[72] It is by no means easy to understand why the measures introduced by Treu are for certain legal scholars the "continuation of a long period of reform of traditional practices, of a long-standing commitment to reforms which has the support of the large trade union confederations in person" (Mariucci, L. *Le fonti del diritto del lavoro etc.*, cit. p. 151), whereas the Biagi law, that does not go any further towards a break with traditional labour law practices, is seen as a neoliberal plan for the deregulation of the labour market. However, one author who gives due recognition to the fact that the issues tackled by the most recent labour market reforms can be traced back to the 1980s is Carabelli, U. 2006. "Leggi sul lavoro, ricominciamo da cinque," *Eguaglianza & Libertà* www.eguaglianzaeliberta.it.

[73] In questo connection see Biagi, M.*Competitività e risorse umane: modernizzare la regolazione dei rapporti di lavoro*, cit., esp. p. 151.

the term takes on in relation to the original *raison d'être* of labour law. In addition, it cannot be argued that there has been a de-structuring of labour law or of the fundamental values laid down in the Italian Constitution. In the disciplinary area that studies labour market developments and regulation, it is clearly useful to analyse the evolution of legal provisions in an interpretative framework that makes a distinction between the reregulation (or reformulation) and/or decentralisation (or devolution) of the normative sources on the one hand, and measures that may be considered to be a form of deregulation properly speaking.[74] This is the most favourable perspective for putting to good use the teachings of a leading scholar recently departed such as Matteo Dell'Olio, even though he has raised objections to the recent legislative reforms.[75] "In relation to a law that is in force," wrote Dell'Olio recently[76]—"the approach of the legal scholar should be to make a fair attempt to interpret and apply it in the most rational and reasonable way possible, without 'hunting for errors,' that is of little value," (our translation) and, it may be added, without an ideological response and preconceived ideas.

4.1. The Organisation and Regulation of the Labour Market and Support for Bilateralism

An instance of genuine deregulation did undoubtedly take place in relation to the organisation and governance of the labour market.[77]

However, this occurred from the 1980s on,[78] with measures prefiguring the abolition of the principle of the state monopoly on employment

---

[74] On this point cf. Giugni, G. *Giuridificazione e deregolazione nel diritto del lavoro italiano*, cit., esp. pp. 352-361.

[75] Reference may be made to the critical observations in Dell'Olio, M. 2005. "Ordinamento civile e diritto del lavoro: tecniche, fonti, figure", *Diritto del lavoro—I nuovi problemi. L'omaggio dell'Accademia a Mattia Persiani*, cit., esp. pp. 107 ff. See also Dell'Olio, M. "I rapporti di lavoro atipici nella recente riforma", *Arg. Dir. Lav.*, p. 69-94.

[76] Dell'Olio, M. 2005. "Intervento", *Tutele del lavoro e nuovi schemi organizzativi nell'impresa*, ed. L. Ficari, Milano: Giuffrè, p. 160.

[77] In this case I refer to the labour market in the strict sense, with reference not to labour law as a whole, but to the regulation of hiring and the channels for matching the supply and demand for labour.

[78] See for a brief comment, Giugni, G. 1984. "Giuridificazione e deregolazione nel diritto del lavoro italiano", cit., p. 353. For an in-depth analysis, Ichino, P. "Politiche del lavoro e strategia di deregulation," *Riv. It. Dir. Lav.*, No. 1, pp. 590-598, and Tullini, P. 1992. "La liberalizzazione 'guidata' del collocamento", *Riv. It. Dir. Lav.*, No. 1, pp. 48-81.

services, formally introduced only in the late 1990s.[79] It should be noted that the plan for a public system for matching the supply and demand for labour was never fully implemented, and as a result the subsequent normative changes took the form of a reorganisation of employment services, made necessary by EU policies on employment and competition, and by the reassignment of powers between the State and the regions arising from the reform of Title V of the Constitution.[80]

There seems to be little reason to speak of indiscriminate liberalisation and policy deregulation[81] with regard to a system for matching the supply and demand for labour which, unlike the system in many other European countries,[82] still prohibits private companies from operating on the market unless they have an administrative authorisation that is issued only on the basis of rigorous formal and substantial requisites.[83] Rather, it is the case that the measures taken to improve the fluidity of the labour market, with the transition from the concept of a public function to that of a service, are aimed solely at achieving social objectives by means of private economic initiative,[84] in a far more effective manner than the previous system based on prohibitions that were highly rigorous in formal terms but largely ineffective in practical terms. The primary aim of the reform is to create a properly functioning labour market, so that the right to work becomes

---

[79] Cf., as one of many authors, Ales, E. 1998. "La nuova disciplina del mercato del lavoro tra 'decentramento controllato' e 'liberalizzazione accentrata'," *Arg. Dir. Lav.*, p. 527.

[80] Cf., on this point, Olivelli, P. "Pubblico e privato nella riforma dei servizi per l'impiego", *Il diritto del mercato del lavoro dopo la riforma Biagi*,cit., esp. pp. 7-12.

[81] But on this point see Angiolini, V. "Le agenzie del lavoro tra pubblico e privato", *Il lavoro tra progresso e mercificazione etc.,* cit., p. 36, and Mariucci, L. *Le fonti del diritto del lavoro etc.*, cit. For a more complete and convincing analysis of the Biagi reform of the labour market, highlighting the elements of continuity with the past, see Napoli, M. *Autonomia individuale e autonomia collettiva alla luce delle più recenti riforme*, cit., p. 9 ff.

[82] See the comparative study by Spattini, S. 2006. *Il governo del mercato del lavoro tra controllo pubblico e neo-contrattualismo*, Milano: Giuffrè.

[83] See, for example, Lassandari, A. "L'intermediazione pubblica e privata nel mercato del lavoro", *Mercato del lavoro etc.*, cit., pp. 393-408, and Magnani, M. "La riforma dell'organizzazione del mercato del lavoro",in *Il diritto del mercato del lavoro etc.*, cit., pp. 24-39.

[84] See Liso, F. "Appunti sulla trasformazione del collocamento da funzione pubblica a servizio",in *Mercato del lavoro etc.*, cit., esp. p. 367.

effective[85] in compliance with the principles of subsidiarity, transparency and efficiency,[86] and certainly not liberalisation without rules governing the matching of the supply and demand for labour.

Together with the scheme for the authorisation of private operators,[87] particular importance is given in the context of the reregulation and reformulation of the labour market to regional accreditation schemes,[88] aimed at facilitating the development of an integrated and decentralised network of employment services at territorial level (placement services, the prevention of long-term unemployment, the promotion of access to work for disadvantaged groups, support for the geographic mobility of workers, and so on) based on cooperation and active links between public bodies and private operators.[89]

In connection with the territorial level, mention should be made of the legislative provisions for bilateral bodies[90] as a privileged channel for the regulation and shared governance of the labour market.[91] Comparative experience shows that active labour market and income support policies

---

[85] See Dell'Olio, M. 2002. "Mercato del lavoro, decentramento, devoluzione", *Arg. Dir. Lav.,* esp. p. 176.

[86] For an in-depth study, that is beyond the limits of the present work, reference may be made to the paper by the author, "Riforma del mercato del lavoro e modello organizzativo tra vincoli costituzionali ed esigenze di unitarietà del sistema", *Il diritto del mercato del lavoro etc.*, cit., pp. 40-96.

[87] In this connection see Spattini, S., and M. Tiraboschi, "Le agenzie per il lavoro: tipologie, requisiti giuridico-finanziari e procedure di autorizzazione", *Il diritto del mercato del lavoro etc.*, cit., pp. 127-168, and the bibliography therein.

[88] On the system of regional accreditation, see Rosato, S. "I regimi di accreditamento: profili generali e prospettive regionali di sviluppo",in *Il diritto del mercato del lavoro etc.*, cit., pp. 127-168, and Falasca, G. 2006. *I servizi privati per l'impiego*. Milano: Giuffrè, pp. 103-150.

[89] For an in-depth treatment, that cannot be attempted here, see Tiraboschi, M. "Riforma del mercato del lavoro e modello organizzativo tra vincoli costituzionali ed esigenze di unitarietà del sistema", cit., esp. pp. 74-79.

[90] On this topic, also for a survey of the many normative references to bilateralism contained in the Biagi law, see Proia, G. 2003. "Enti Bilaterali e riforma del mercato del lavoro", *Scritti in memoria di Salvatore Hernandez*, *Dir. Lav.*, pp. 647-657, and Napoli, M. 2003. "Gli enti bilaterali nella prospettiva di riforma del mercato del lavoro", *Jus*, pp. 235-246, and Napoli, M. 2005. "Riflessioni sul ruolo degli enti bilaterali nel decreto legislativo 10 settembre 2003, n. 276", *Jus*, pp. 309-321.

[91] See Article 2 (1) (h), Legislative Decree No. 276/2003.

are particularly efficient and effective when jointly managed, in whole or in part, with the social partners.[92]

In addition, the bilateral approach is associated with an industrial relations model of a collaborative and cooperative type that promotes territorial development and regular employment of good quality. Bilateralism does not eliminate conflict, nor does it alter the function of the trade union with a shift towards a liberal approach to labour market regulation,[93] but may be a useful instrument for the implementation of contractual terms, i.e. the conditions negotiated during collective bargaining, with a view to promoting human capital, in line with developments in employment relations in the matching of the supply and demand for labour, vocational training, the certification of employment contracts and income support,[94] that are particularly suited to modes of production that are increasingly fragmented and intermittent.

4.2. Outsourcing and the Recourse to External Labour Markets

A similar argument can be put forward with regard to the regulation of the outsourcing of labour. The abrogation of Act No. 1369/1960 (followed by the formal abrogation of Articles 1-11 of Act No. 196/1997 on temporary agency work), represents an attempt, at least in the intention of the legislator,[95] to reform an area characterised by antiquated and inderogable legal provisions which over the years had become increasingly inadequate for regulating the new models of production and labour organisation.

In the Italian context the attempt to facilitate the movement of labour between companies and the possibility, within an increasingly complex productive system, to assign the employees of a company to work to be

---

[92] Spattini, S. *Il governo del mercato del lavoro tra controllo pubblico e neo-contrattualismo*, cit.

[93] For an opposing view, Mariucci, L. 2003. "Interrogarsi sugli enti bilaterali," *Lav. Dir.*, 167-177.

[94] On the certification of employment contracts see Pasquini, F. "Il ruolo degli organismi bilaterali nel decreto attuativo della legge 14 febbraio 2003, n. 30: problemi e prospettive", *La riforma Biagi del mercato del lavoro etc.*, cit., pp. 650-678. See also the documentation available at *www.adapt.it*, index A-Z, under the heading *Enti bilaterali.*

[95] For an in-depth analysis of the rationale of the Biagi law in relation to outsourcing and insourcing see the paper by the present author, "Somministrazione di lavoro, appalto di servizi, distacco", *La riforma Biagi del mercato del lavoro etc.*, cit., pp. 205-229.

carried out outside the company has been strongly criticised by a number of legal scholars.[96] Once again, reference has been made to a model of organisation of the productive system that is unequivocally neoliberal in character, aimed at dismantling the existing legal restrictions on decentralisation and contract labour, in order to protect the organisational choices and economic interests of the employers, while defining as illicit "only those processes consisting of fraudulent and anti-labour practices" (our translation).[97]

However, as rightly noted by legal scholars adopting a less ideological stance and paying greater attention to the actual provisions of the law,[98] the abrogation of the outdated legislation that had failed to effectively govern the processes of labour outsourcing and insourcing was not an act of deregulation "but simply the condition for a normative reform of the entire matter" (our translation).[99]

In place of the drastic prohibition of every form of agency work, even when not accompanied by intentions of a fraudulent nature or when detrimental (or potentially detrimental) for the workers,[100] attenuated only

---

[96] See among others, Alleva, P. "La nuova disciplina degli appalti di lavoro", *Il lavoro tra progresso e mercificazione—Commento critico al decreto legislativo n. 276/2003*, cit., p. 166; Chieco, P. "Somministrazione, comando, appalto. Le nuove forme di prestazione di lavoro a favore del terzo", *Lavoro e diritti dopo il decreto legislativo 276/2003*, cit., esp. p. 92; Speziale, V. "Somministrazione di lavoro", *La riforma del mercato del lavoro e i nuovi modelli contrattuali*, eds. Gragnoli, E., and A. Perulli, Padova: Cedam, esp. pp. 277-279, and Scarpelli, F. 2004. "Appalto," ibid., esp. p. 437; Romagnoli, U. 2004. "Radiografia di una riforma", *Lav. Dir.*, esp. pp. 39-38, and Mariucci, L. 2004. "I molti dubbi sulla c.d. riforma del mercato del lavoro", *Lav. Dir.*, p. 11.

[97] See De Luca Tamajo, R. *Tra le righe del d.lgs. n. 276/2003 etc.*, cit., esp. p. 351

[98] Cf. Magnani, M. 2005. "Le esternalizzazioni e il nuovo diritto del lavoro", *Organizzazione del mercato del lavoro e tipologie contrattuali*, eds. Magnani, M., and P. A. Varesi, Torino: Giappichelli, pp. 283-297; Del Punta, R. 2004. "La nuova disciplina degli appalti e della somministrazione di lavoro", *Come cambia il lavoro*, Various Authors, Milano: Ipsoa; Ichino, P. 2004. "*Somministrazione di lavoro, appalto di servizi, distacco*", *Il nuovo mercato del lavoro*, Various Authors, Bologna: Zanichelli, pp. 258-326; Romei, R. "La distinzione tra interposizione e appalto e le prospettive della certificazione", *La riforma Biagi del mercato del lavoro etc.*, cit., pp. 287-306.

[99] See Magnani, M. "Le esternalizzazioni e il nuovo diritto del lavoro," cit., esp. p. 284.

[100] In this connection, for a useful survey of the main opinions among legal scholars and in case law, see Bano, F. 2004. "La somministrazione di lavoro", *Impiego flessibile e mercato del lavoro*, ed. Perulli, A., Torino: Giappichelli, esp. pp. 3-5.

by the derogations and exceptions laid down by Act No. 196/1997, the recent reform introduced a normative framework, in line with a number of case law rulings,[101] that provides a more effective response the needs of the enterprise.

However, workers continue to be protected by a general prohibition on intermediation in employment,[102] and this prohibition has now been made more effective by bringing to light irregular and fraudulent forms of contract labour.[103]

At the same time, the regulation of service contracts and the transfer of undertakings has been reformed, with a view to improving company performance and providing greater safeguards in terms of stability of

---

[101] See Calcaterra, L. 2002. "Il divieto di interposizione nelle prestazioni di lavoro: problemi applicativi e prospettive di riforma", *I processi di esternalizzazione. Opportunità e vincoli giuridici*, ed. De Luca Tamajo, R. Naploli: ESI, pp. 127-181, and, more recently, Luzzana, M. 2005. "*Outsourcing/insourcing*: vincoli e opportunità alla luce dei più recenti orientamenti della giurisprudenza", *Lo sviluppo del 'capitale umano' tra innovazione organizzativa e tecniche di fidelizzazione*, eds. Malandrini, S., and A. Russo, Milano: Giuffrè, Milan, pp. 95-110.

[102] Among legal scholars, see Magnani, M. "*Le esternalizzazioni e il nuovo diritto del lavoro",* cit., esp. p. 284. Case law rulings: Cass. 21 November 2005 (hearing 25 October 2005), No. 41701, Cass. 26 April 2005 (hearing 1 February 2005), No. 15579; Cass. pen. 3 February 2005 (hearing 20 December 2004), No. 3714; Cass. pen. 26 January 2004 (hearing 11 November 2003), No. 2583; Cass. pen. 24 February 2004 (hearing 29 January 2004), No. 7762; Cass. pen. 25 August 2004 (hearing 16 June 2004), No. 34922, all of which are available at *www.adapt.it*, index A-Z, under the heading *Somministrazione*. For one of the first comments Tuffanelli, A. "La somministrazione di lavoro altrui: nuovo quadro legale e regime sanzionatorio" *Il diritto del mercato del lavoro dopo la riforma Biagi*, cit., pp. 461-473, and in particular in relation to Cass. pen. 25 August 2004 (hearing 16 June 2004), No. 34922, cit., and on Trib. Ferrara, sez. pen., 24 December 2003 (*Riv. it. dir. lav.*, 2005, II, p. 726) see the comment by Romei, R. 2005. "L'elisir di lunga vita del divieto di interposizione,"*Riv. it. dir. lav.*, No. 2, pp. 726-736. See also the analysis provided, in the form of *obiter dictum*, in Cass. 1 April 2005, No. 6820, available at *www.adapt.it*, index A-Z, under the heading *Somministrazione*.

[103] For an overview of the problem, and an in-depth treatment that is beyond the scope of this paper, reference may be made to the work of the present author. 2006. "Esternalizzazioni del lavoro e valorizzazione del capitale umano: due modelli inconciliabili?", *Le esternalizzazioni dopo la riforma Biagi*, ed. Tiraboschi, M., Milano: Giuffrè, pp. 1-38.

employment.[104] In this way, there is greater flexibility for undertakings wishing to make use of external human resources, while rethinking their models of work organisation in the belief—shared by the EU institutions[105]—that only by governing change is it possible to maintain and develop the human capital of a given system of production.

In the light of variations in transaction costs in each company and productive sector, regarding the costs arising from decision-making and acquiring experience, management (concerning contracts and labour relations) and change (arising from the transfer from one type of contract to another)[106]—agency work cannot simply be considered as directly equivalent to open-ended salaried employment. Rather, in the provisions laid down by Legislative Decree No. 276/2003, it is seen as a specific organisational and management resource operating in favour of flexibility in employment but also, and perhaps above all, in favour of the modernisation of the productive system—and of the public administration[107]—by means of models of contractual integration between companies coordinated by actors providing a range of services with a high degree of specialisation, as is the case with employment agencies today.[108]

4.3. Human capital, Flexibility in Employment Contracts, Organisational Innovation and the Power of the Employer

Human resource development and organisational innovation also give rise to the need for the reform of the various types of training contracts, atypical work, and the organisation of working hours. In this perspective, the reform of the regulation of fixed-term employment is of central

---

[104] For an in-depth analysis see Del Conte, M. "Rimodulazione degli assetti produttivi tra libertà di organizzazione dell'impresa e tutele dei lavoratori" *Le esternalizzazioni dopo la riforma Biagi*, cit., pp. 419-434.

[105] European Commission. 2002. *Anticipating and Managing Change: a Dynamic Approach to the Social Aspects of Corporate Restructuring*. Brussels: European Commission, esp. p. 2, available at *www.adapt.it*, index A-Z, under the heading *Lavoro (organizzazione del)*.

[106] On this point see Rugiadini, A. 1985. "L'efficienza delle scelte manageriali fra organizzazione e mercato", *Organizzazione e mercato*, eds. Nacamulli, R.C.D., and A. Rugiadini, Bologna: Il Mulino, and Golzio, L. 2005. "L'evoluzione dei modelli organizzativi d'impresa", *Dir. Rel. Ind.*, pp. 313-323.

[107] See Verbaro, F. "Il fenomeno delle esternalizzazioni nella pubblica amministrazione", *La riforma Biagi del mercato del lavoro etc.*, cit., pp. 489-512.

[108] For an in-depth analysis reference may be made to the work of the present author, "Somministrazione di lavoro, appalto di servizi, distacco", *La riforma Biagi del mercato del lavoro etc.*, cit., pp. 205-229.

importance[109] in the modernisation of the Italian labour market, following the Treu measures of 1997.[110] In effect, setting aside the considerable controversy surrounding the "strange case" of Legislative Decree No. 368/2001 implementing EU Directive No. 99/70/EC,[111] the measures taken by the legislator reregulate and reformulate a fragmentary and contradictory legislative framework in which over the years the exception, compared to the rigorous provisions of Act No. 230/1962, had become the rule. The result was that fixed-term contracts had become "not a subordinate but an alternative (and rival) model compared to open-ended employment" (our translation).[112]

The regulatory technique in the case of the legitimate use of fixed-term employment adopted in Legislative Decree No. 368/2001 is undoubtedly innovative. The explanatory memorandum appended to the Decree provides evidence of this,[113] stating that, compared to the previous regulations, "the approach adopted [...] is undoubtedly innovative, simpler and, at the same time, less likely to be subject to evasion by means of fraudulent practices. Rather than stating that fixed-term employment is forbidden, except in the cases explicitly laid down by the law and/or by collective agreements (often subject to specious interpretation), it has been decided to adopt a clear formulation as found in other European systems: the employer may hire employees on fixed-term contracts, on condition that at the same time written motivation is provided of a technical, productive or organisational nature, or for the substitution of personnel" (our translation).

---

[109] Cf. Legislative Decree No. 368/2003 and the papers in Garilli, A., and M. Napoli, eds. 2002. *Il lavoro a termine in Italia e in Europa*. Torino: Giappichelli.

[110] In this connection see Biagi, M. 2002. "La nuova disciplina del lavoro a termine: prima (controversa) tappa del processo di modernizzazione del mercato del lavoro italiano", *Il nuovo lavoro a termine*, ed. Biagi, M. Milano: Giuffrè, pp. 3-20.

[111] The matter is examined by Pera, M. 2001. "La strana storia dell'attuazione della Direttiva CE sui contratti a termine", *Lav. Giur.*, esp. p. 306, with reference to the complex social dialogue leading to a joint agreement (without the signature of the CGIL) and the intention of the Italian legislator concerning the obligations laid down in the Directive. For an overview of this issue see also M. Biagi, *La nuova disciplina del lavoro a termine etc.*, cit.

[112] See Montuschi, L. 2000. "L'evoluzione del contratto a termine. Dalla subalternità all'alternatività: un modello per il lavoro, in Il lavoro a termine", *Quaderni Dir. Lav. Rel. Ind.*, pp. 10-11.

[113] Available at *www.adapt.it*, index A-Z, under the heading *Lavoro a termine (o a tempo determinato)*.

However, at least with regard to the implementation at a practical level of fixed-term contracts, it is difficult to speak of a reversal of previous provisions,[114] resulting in a radical and indiscriminate liberalisation of such contracts.[115] The formal innovations introduced by Article 1(1) of Legislative Decree No. 368/2001, though appearing to be radical on the basis of a purely textual comparison with the wording of Act No. 230/1962, are not actually radical if considered in the light of recent developments in the use of fixed-term contracts.[116]

Evidence in support of this argument is to be found in case law interpretation[117]—but also in the measures adopted by collective bargaining[118]—revealing a considerable degree of continuity with the past "in spite of the innovations and perhaps mainly to counteract the changes considered to be more apparent than real" (our translation).[119] As a result even legal scholars who in relation to earlier changes in the law had spoken of fixed-term contracts as a factor likely to polarise labour law[120] defined the process of reform set in motion by Legislative Decree No. 368/2001 as "the negation of liberalisation" (our translation).[121]

In fact, it may be argued that with the regulatory technique introduced by Legislative Decree No. 368/2001 the Italian system has once more adopted the anti-fraudulent approach of the early regulation of fixed-term

---

[114] In this sense see on the other hand Angiolini, V. "Sullo "schema" di decreto legislativo in materia di lavoro a tempo determinato (nel testo conosciuto al 6 luglio 2001)", available at www.cgil.it/giuridico.

[115] In addition to the author cited in the preceding footnote, see in particular Roccella, M. "Prime osservazioni sullo schema di decreto legislativo sul lavoro a termine,"available at www.cgil.it/giuridico.

[116] For an attempt to provide an analysis, see the paper by the present author: Tiraboschi, M. 2005. "L'apposizione del termine nel contratto di lavoro dopo il decreto legislativo 6 settembre 2001, n. 368", *Compendio critico per la certificazione dei contratti di lavoro—I nuovi contratti: lavoro pubblico e lavoro privato*, eds. Enrico, C., and M. Tiraboschi, Milano: Giuffrè, espec. § 1.

[117] See Senatori, I. 2006. "Gli orientamenti della giurisprudenza di merito in materia di lavoro a termine", *Dir. Rel. Ind.*, pp. 148-150.

[118] See Senatori, I. 2006. "Gli orientamenti della contrattazione collettiva sul lavoro a termine", *Dir. Rel. Ind.*, pp. 231-233.

[119] See Montuschi, L. 2006. "Il contratto a termine e la liberalizzazione negata", *Dir. Rel. Ind.*, pp. 109-129.

[120] Montuschi, L. "L'evoluzione del contratto a termine. Dalla subalternità all'alternatività etc.", cit., p. 9.

[121] See once again Montuschi, L. "Il contratto a termine e la liberalizzazione negata", cit.

contracts,[122] moving away from the extremely rigid practices that had emerged from certain interpretations of Act No. 230/1962 that tended to impose restrictions reducing the flexibility of workforce management, while failing to safeguard the fundamental rights of the worker.[123]

The reform of 2001, that prefigures the contents and methods of the Biagi law, had the objective of curtailing the power of the employer, that would otherwise be discretionary, to place a limit on the duration of the employment contract, while setting aside the traditional prejudice towards temporary work.[124] At the same time, it must be pointed out that the use of fixed-term contracts has not been liberalised but is required to be justified by reasons of a technical, organisational or productive nature, or for the substitution of personnel.

As a result, in terms of safeguards for the employee, the burden of proof concerning the legitimacy of certain organisational and managerial decisions falls on the employer.[125] Along similar lines, with regard to the controversial area of parasubordinate employment *(collaborazioni coordinate e continuative),* the Biagi law takes measures to combat the fraudulent use of these contracts by requiring the negotiating parties to specify in advance how the work is to be organised, in order to ensure that the contract is not used to mask salaried employment.[126] As confirmed by

---

[122] On the original antifraudulent aims of the 1962 law see Giugni, G. 1979. "Intervento", *Il lavoro a termine*, Atti delle giornate di studio di Sorrento 14-15 April 1978, Milano: Giuffrè, esp. p. 125, that makes reference in this connection to Balzarini, G. 1966. *La disciplina del contratto a tempo determinato*. Milano: Giuffrè.

[123] Reference may be made to the paper of the present author, *L'apposizione del termine nel contratto di lavoro dopo il decreto legislativo 6 settembre 2001, n. 368*, cit., and in a comparative perspective, Tiraboschi, M. "La recente evoluzione della disciplina in materia di lavoro a termine: osservazioni sul caso italiano in una prospettiva europea e comparata," *Il nuovo lavoro a termine*, cit., pp. 41-86.

[124] This may be seen also from the abolition of the presumption of the open-ended nature of employment contracts, pursuant to Article 1 (1), Act No. 230/1962, save for the (limited) exceptions permitted by the same law. A presumption which, as pointed out in Giugni, G. "Intervento", *Il lavoro a termine*, Atti delle giornate di studio di Sorrento 14-15 April 1978, cit., p. 126, resulted in Italy being "basically the only country where fixed-term contracts (were) seen as detrimental, as an exception to be allowed only in limited circumstances).

[125] See once again the paper by the present author, "L'apposizione del termine nel contratto di lavoro etc.", cit., esp. pp. 106-109.

[126] See the case law available at *www.adapt.it*, index A-Z, under the heading *Lavoro a progetto* (Trib. Milano, 11 July 2007, Judgment No. 5223.; Trib. Torino 23 March 2007; Trib. Bergamo 22 February 2007; Trib. Bologna 6 February 2007; Trib. Milano 5 February 2007; Trib. Milano 2 February 2007; Trib. Livorno 8

the first court ruling on this matter, "project work" is not a new type of employment contract, but a way to manage parasubordinate employment in compliance with Article 409(3) of the Code of Civil Procedure.[127] However, certain restrictions are introduced in the form of definitions and sanctions in order to limit the use of such employment contracts to genuine self-employment, in which work is aimed at producing a predetermined result, which characterises it and limits its duration.

Also in this instance, as in the case of fixed-term contracts, project work places the burden of proof on the principal, in derogation of the provision of Article 2607 of the Code of Civil Procedure. Thus there is a requirement on the part of the parties to the contract to specify in advance—by identifying a project or programme of work or a particular phase of the project—the result to be achieved in a manner that safeguards the effective autonomy of the worker.[128] In the absence of such a provision, the relation is classified as open-ended salaried employment from its inception.[129]

The aim of dealing with the vast area of irregular or grey labour that is often concealed behind parasubordinate employment contracts, that limits the use of organisational models providing an alternative to policies aimed merely at the containment of labour costs, gives rise to the need for an intervention in the area of subordinate employment in order to provide employers with a valid alternative to the improper use of flexible

---

January 2007; Tar Lazio, sez. I, Ordinance 22 November 2006; Trib. Milano 2 August 2006, Judgment No. 2655; Trib. Torino, 17 May 2006; Trib. Torino, 10 May 2006; Trib. Modena 19 April 2006; Trib. Genova 7 April 2006; Cons. Stato, 3 April 2006, Judgment No. 1743; Trib. Milano 23 March 2006; Tar Sicilia, Catania, 14 February 2006, Judgment No. 202; Trib. Torino, 26 January 2006; Trib. Milano, 10 November 2005; Trib. Ravenna 25 October 2005; Trib. Torino 15 April 2005).

[127] For an analysis of the notion of parasubordinate employment, see Santoro Passarelli, G. 1979. *Il lavoro 'parasubordinato'*. Milan: Angeli.

[128] See Proia, G. "Lavoro coordinato e lavoro a progetto", *Diritto del lavoro. I nuovi problemi—L'omaggio dell'Accademia a Mattia Persiani*, cit., esp. p. 1408, though this author considers project work as a new type of employment contract. For the opposing view, Tiraboschi, M. "Il lavoro a progetto: profili teorico-ricostruttivi", cit., and Napoli, M. "Riflessioni sul contratto a progetto", *Diritto del lavoro. I nuovi problemi—L'omaggio dell'Accademia a Mattia Persiani*, cit., esp. p. 1349.

[129] As confirmed by the first case law rulings, that are available in the monographic issue of the *Bollettino Adapt* dedicated to *Il lavoro a progetto*, cit. in note 145 above.

arrangements in the form of self-employment that result in a form of unfair competition.[130]

This explains the regulation of working time,[131] the redefinition of short-time working, modular and flexible working hours,[132] the introduction of certification for ascertaining the free consent of both parties to the contractual provisions,[133] the reform of the labour inspectorate and labour inspection procedures[134] and, finally, the reform of the various kinds of training contract (apprenticeships, work training contracts, and access to employment contracts),[135] for the purposes of providing effective training programmes in line with the objective of lifelong learning, while at the same time combating the practice, that is quite widespread in Italy, of making improper use of employment training contracts and training funds to provide covert subsidies for undertakings.[136]

---

[130] For this interpretation of the Biagi law and its main provisions, see the papers in Tiraboschi, M., ed. 2004. *La riforma Biagi del mercato del lavoro—Prime interpretazioni e proposte di lettura del d.lgs. 10 settembre 2003, n. 276. Il diritto transitorio e i tempi della riforma*. Milano: Giuffrè; and in particular the introductory paper (also available at *www.adapt.it*).

[131] Cf., for example, the papers in Cester, C., M. G. Mattarolo, and M. Tremolada, eds. 2003. *La nuova disciplina dell'orario di lavoro*. Milano: Giuffrè. See also, although the arguments put forward are not entirely convincing, Carabelli, U., and V. Leccese. "Il sofferto rapporto tra legge e autonomia collettiva: alcune riflessioni ispirate dalla nuova disciplina dell'orario di lavoro" *Percorsi di diritto del lavoro*, cit., pp. 193-224.

[132] See, for example, Voza, R. 2005. "I contratti di lavoro a 'orario ridotto, modulato o flessibile' (part time, lavoro intermittente lavoro ripartito)", WP C.S.D.L.E., No. 37. For a different approach see Russo, A. "La nuova disciplina del lavoro a tempo parziale", *La riforma Biagi del mercato del lavoro etc.*, cit., pp. 179-192.

[133] See the papers in Enrico, C., and M. Tiraboschi, eds. *Compendio critico per la certificazione dei contratti di lavoro etc.*, cit., and the bibliographical references therein.

[134] See the papers in Monticelli, C. L., and M. Tiraboschi, eds. 2004. *La riforma dei servizi ispettivi in materia di lavoro e previdenza sociale*. Milano: Giuffrè.

[135] For further analysis and bibliographical references, see Tiraboschi, M. 2006. "Productive Employment and the Evolution of Training Contracts in Italy", *The International Journal of Comparative Labour Law and Industrial Relations,* No. 4.

[136] On this point, with reference to the debate on precarious employment, see Tiraboschi, M. 2006. "Young People and Employment in Italy: the (Difficult) Transition from Education and Training to the Labour Market", *The International Journal of Comparative Labour Law and Industrial Relations*, No. 1.

It appears to be difficult to claim that these developments subvert the rationale of the protection provided by labour law. The recent reforms go no further than enabling economic operators and legal specialists to strike a balance between productive efficiency, which is essential for the enterprise, and the values of social justice that are at times jeopardised by a line of reasoning that is based on ideological, one might even say theological, considerations.[137]

In this way it becomes clear, or at least clearer than in the past,[138] that management power is not subject solely to internal limits, but also to external limits arising from formal and/or substantial conditions of legitimacy and the countervailing power of the unions, while remaining free of judicial control over company decision-making. This should lead to a reduction in the level of legal uncertainty[139] by limiting control over the legitimacy of company decision-making, while facilitating greater uniformity of judicial decisions, resulting, if not in legal certainty, at least in court rulings that are more predictable.[140]

5. Prospects for the Future

An assessment of the Biagi law and the recent reforms of the labour market is beyond the scope of this study and, at present, it is still too early to attempt such a task.[141] However, it is likely that over the coming years

---

137 For an overview of the problem, see Persiani, M. "Diritto del lavoro e autorità dal punto di vista giuridico", cit., esp. pp. 13, 17-19.

138 The problem of legal certainty is highlighted, among others, by Vallebona, A. 2003. "L'incertezza del diritto e i necessari rimedi", *Scritti in memoria di Salvatore Hernandez*, *Dir. Lav.*, No. 6, pp. 881-900, and in particular pp. 888 et seq. for a discussion of the system of certification of employment contracts introduced by the Biagi law.

139 Reference may be made once again to Persiani, M. 1995. "Diritto del lavoro e razionalità", *Arg. Dir. Lav.*, pp. 1-36, esp. pp. 2-3, where the author examines certain interpretations, ideologically oriented and reflecting vested interests, in support of the theory of internal limits.

140 This matter is discussed in general terms that are still relevant for our line of reasoning in Castelvetri, L. 2001. "Correttezza e buona fede nella giurisprudenza del lavoro. Diffidenza e proposte dottrinali", *Dir. Rel. Ind.*, p. 248. Along similar lines, Ferraro, G. 1991. "Poteri imprenditoriali e clausole generali", *Dir. Rel. Ind.*, p. 169, and Persiani, M. "Diritto del lavoro e razionalità," cit., esp. p. 36.

141 Tiraboschi, M. 2006. "A due anni della Riforma Biagi del mercato del lavoro: quale bilancio?", *Dopo la flessibilità, cosa?—Le nuove politiche del lavoro*, ed. Mariucci, L., Bologna: Il Mulino. See also Tiraboschi, M. 2005. "The Italian

the legal framework will undergo further significant change, above all with regard to flexibility in the termination of contracts (the law on dismissals) and, hopefully, with regard to safety-net measures.[142]

On close examination the controversy surrounding the Biagi law, and before that the reform of the regulation of fixed-term contracts and the Treu measures, reveals the cultural difficulties that still exist in Italy in dealing with the central issue of the modernisation of labour law, which is certainly not the liberalisation of the labour market, but rather, as argued by Matteo Dell'Olio),[143] the progressive reduction of the gap that has arisen "between an area that is heavily laden with protective measures for the worker and an area that is devoid of them" (our translation).[144] The issue to be faced, without further delay, is that of an overall realignment of protective measures, only partially attempted by the Biagi law,[145] in such a way as to overcome the contrast between insiders and outsiders,[146] which is both the cause and effect of the proliferation of atypical and irregular forms of employment and jobs in the shadow economy.[147]

Arguably the most recent reforms, far from promoting a process of unbridled liberalisation of the labour market, have laid down the conditions for reformulating employee protection by means of the codification of a *Statuto dei lavori* or Work Statute,[148] i.e. a body of

---

Labour Market after the Biagi Reform", *The International Journal of Comparative Labour Law and Industrial Relations*, No. 2.

[142] This is the matter that needs to be dealt with in order to complete the Biagi law. Reference may be made to Tiraboschi, M. "Il sistema degli ammortizzatori sociali: spunti per un progetto di riforma", *La riforma Biagi del mercato del lavoro*, etc., cit., pp. 1105-1121.

[143] Cf. Dell'Olio, M. 1998. "La subordinazione nell'esperienza italiana", *Arg. Dir. Lav.*, esp. p. 708.

[144] Dell'Olio, M. "Il lavoro sommerso e la lotta per il diritto", cit., esp. p. 46, and Dell'Olio, M. 1994. "Violazione della legge in materia di lavoro", *Enc. Giur. Treccani*, Rome, vol. 32. Along similar lines, Persiani, M. 2005. "Individuazione delle nuove tipologie tra subordinazione e autonomia", *Arg. Dir. Lav.*, esp. p. 2.

[145] As argued by Treu, T. *Il diritto del lavoro etc.*, cit., esp. pp. 518-520.

[146] This is a point that is rightly underlined by Ichino, P. 1996. *Il lavoro e il mercato.* Milano: Mondadori.

[147] In this connection see Biagi, M. *La nuova disciplina del lavoro a termine etc.*, cit., pp. 18-19.

[148] See, most recently, Proia, G.2006. "Verso uno Statuto dei lavori?" *Arg. Dir. Lav.*, pp. 61-72. On this topic see the draft proposals, the positions of the social partners, and the substantial amount of comment by legal scholars available at *www.adapt.it*, index A-Z, under the heading *Statuto dei lavori.* See also the papers at the conference on *Tutele senza lavoro e lavori senza tutele. Uno Statuto per rimediare?*, Benevento 10 May 2004, at *www.unicz.it/lavoro/BN10052004.htm.* In

fundamental rights for all workers, and not only those in the public administration or in medium-sized and large enterprises, with a view to moving beyond—once and for all—the dualism between those enjoying a high level of protection on the one hand, and precarious employees on the other, resulting from an ill-conceived and short-sighted allocation of employee protection.[149]

In order to be consistent with its original principles,[150] and at the same time to support the development strategies of Italian enterprise, labour law will inevitably need to move beyond the limits of the traditional—yet inefficient—distinction between self-employment and salaried employment in order to bring within its area of application all types of employment contract, in keeping with the most recent developments in EU rulings[151] and constitutional case law,[152] based on a broad definition of employment. The extension of the definition of employment to include all forms of work with an economic value carried out in an organisational context on behalf of others is the first step towards redesigning the system of employment protection—in compliance with the applicable

---

the international debate, in connection with the transition from the *"Statuto del diritto del lavoro"* to the *"Statut de l'actif"*, see Gaudu, F. *Libéralisation des marchése et droit du travail,* cit., esp. p. 513.

[149] This point is made, among others, by Ichino, P. 2000. *Il Contratto di lavoro.* Milano: Giuffrè, p. 59 et seq. In this perspective see Hepple, B. 1986. "Restructuring Employment Rights", *Industrial Law Journal,* p. 74. In the mid-1980s Hepple proposed the adoption of a wider and more comprehensive definition of employment, leading to the identification of a new legal criterion for the assignment of labour protection, including labour of an intermittent or casual nature, and employment relations characterised by the continuity of the work carried out.

[150] On the connections between the essential component leading to the foundation of labour law (the subordinate position of the employee) and the original rationale for the protection of the worker, see Dell'Olio, M. "La subordinazione nell'esperienza italiana", cit., pp. 697-713.

[151] See in particular the Lawrie-Blum ruling of the European Court of Justice, No. 66/85, 3 July 1986, available at *www.adapt.it,* index A-Z, under the heading *Statuto dei lavori*, according to which the essential characteristic of the employment relationship is that the individual concerned supplies labour of economic value to another person under the direction of that person, receiving remuneration in exchange.

[152] C. Cost. 5 February 1996, No. 30, available at *www.adapt.it*, index A-Z, under the heading *Statuto dei lavori*, which speaks of work "intended to be carried out in the context of a productive organisation and with a view to producing a result that the owner of the organisation (and of the means of production) is immediately entitled to utilise" (our translation).

provisions[153]—on the basis of a model of concentric circles underlying certain labour law reform proposals put forward over the past decade[154] and the idea of a *Statuto dei lavori.*[155]

In short, there is a need to identify a fundamental nucleus of universal safeguards,[156] applicable to all employment relations regardless of the classification of the contract as self-employment, salaried employment or parasubordinate employment pursuant to Article 1322 (2) of the Civil Code. The forms of protection that would be included in this area, that would be extensive and without subdivisions, would be, by way of example, freedom of opinion and protection of the dignity of the worker, trade union rights, prohibition of discrimination, health and safety at work, the right to lifelong training, the protection of privacy, access to employment services and employment information services, and the right to fair remuneration. The remaining forms of protection would be determined on the basis of the following criteria, in relation to which the subordinate nature of the employment would continue to be a significant but not an exclusive factor:[157] 1) the degree of economic dependency (an initial indicator of which is whether a person works for one or more than

---

[153] See Treu, T. *Il diritto del lavoro etc.*, cit., esp. pp. 472-473.

[154] See Dell'Olio, M. "La subordinazione nell'esperienza italiana," cit., esp. p. 708, where he identified in the reform proposals "the intention to extend the area of labour law to all forms of work of a prevalently personal nature".

[155] See the documentation available at *www.adapt.it*, index A-Z, under the heading *Statuto dei lavori* and, in particular, the *Relazione Finale* (final report) of the High-Level Commission for drafting a Work Statute set up by Ministerial Decree on 4 March 2004.

[156] In this connection see Zoppoli, L. "Politiche del diritto e ambizioni statutarie", paper presented at the conference on *Tutele senza lavoro e lavori senza tutele. Uno Statuto per rimediare?*, cit. in footnote 165 above.

[157] Dell'Olio, M. "La subordinazione nell'esperienza italiana", cit., esp. pp. 712-713, raises objections to the idea that the proposals for a *Statuto dei lavori* would result in moving forward from the fundamental concept of subordination. However, this is not necessarily the case, considering that this concept would continue to play a key role, supported by other indicators for the purposes of assigning protection. In this connection the English system is particularly significant, as in most cases it is not sufficient—and in other cases it is not even necessary—to be a salaried employee in order to be covered by the legislation granting employment protections. Reference may be made to my paper: Tiraboschi, M. 1996. "Autonomia, subordinazione e contratti di lavoro sui generis: un recente *revirement* della giurisprudenza inglese," *Dir. Rel. Ind.*, No. 2, pp. 153-176.

one employer);[158] 2) seniority of service on a continuous basis (for example, confirmation of the stability of employment as laid down by Article 18 of the Work Statute for all workers who have completed a period of continuous service with the same employer of at least two years); 3) the type of employer (public/private, non-profit sector, etc.) and the size of the company as factors to be taken into consideration, not just in terms of the number of employees but also the volume of business); 4) the subjective or objective conditions of the worker in a perspective of positive discrimination and norms providing incentives for hiring (for example, the long-term unemployed, people with disabilities, immigrants, those in search of employment for the first time, those resident in geographic areas with particularly high levels of unemployment, or low levels of employment); 5) the manner in which work is to be carried out under the contract (for example, the type of work, the degree of management control, whether the work is merely coordinated, continuity over time) or the type of activity (for example, periods of work alternating with training, the need for a high degree of vocational skill or specialisation) or the purpose of the contract (access to employment or a return to the labour market, work of public utility, etc.); 6) other parameters as laid down by collective bargaining or by bilateral bodies in cooperation with employment contract certification agencies.

Alongside employment safeguards that were partially promoted by the Biagi law, the development of labour law requires the construction of a system of protection in the labour market. By way of example: efficient employment services, bilateral bodies, the recognition of training rights for employees (also in the form of training credits), the reform of the system of safety-net measures and incentives, the regulation of labour on the fringes of the market, measures for promoting access to employment after time out from the labour market (similar to those laid down in Articles 13 and 14 of Legislative Decree No. 276/2003), recognition of previous experience and employment in the transition between active, inactive, salaried and parasubordinate phases.

Labour law needs to come to terms in the near future with the redesigning (and certainly not the dismantling) of employment safeguards, and this process needs to take place not just by means of abstract notions predetermined by the legislator, but also by means of the certification of provisions negotiated between the parties. This is the proposal contained

---

[158] On the relevance of the criterion of economic dependency, see Treu, T. *Il diritto del lavoro etc.*, cit., esp. pp. 494-495, who also mentions the use of this criterion in systems as varied as those of Germany, France, the Netherlands and the United Kingdom.

in the *White Paper on the Labour Market* of October 2001, that identified a nucleus of inalienable rights (in addition to universal safeguards and those dependent on status) distinct from safeguards of a non-essential nature, that is to say subject to negotiation during collective bargaining and/or individual agreements supported by certification of the employment contract.

This is the challenge facing the legislator and labour law scholars but also and above all the social partners.

PART II

YOUTH EMPLOYMENT: PROSPECTIVES IN SCHOOL-TO-WORK TRANSITION

CHAPTER SIX

THE CHALLENGE OF YOUTH EMPLOYMENT IN THE PERSPECTIVE OF SCHOOL-TO-WORK TRANSITION

1. Rethinking the Employment of Young People in the Global Market[1]

In a comparative perspective, access to the labour market on the part of young people is a complex issue, and for some time now it has attracted the interest of labour market specialists.[2] In an awareness of this complexity, that is reflected in the relative lack of convincing proposals, even of an experimental nature, on the part of the academic community, and labour law scholars in particular, the analysis put forward in the present paper focuses on certain aspects of youth employment that are only apparently contradictory, not to say paradoxical.[3] These aspects are still in need of in-depth examination, at least in an international context and in the global workplace perspective, reflecting not only the various levels of economic and social development,[4] but also the stage of

---

[1] The present contribution was previously published in Manzella, P., and L. Rustico. 2011. *Productivity, Investment in Human Capital and the Challenge of Youth Employment*. Cambridge: Cambridge Scholars Publishing.

[2] See, recently, ILO. 2010b. *Global Employment Trends for Youth 2010*. Geneva: ILO; OECD. 2010. *Economic Survey of China: a Labour Market in Transition*. Paris: OECD. Among the other authors, Bell, D.N.F., and D. G. Blanchflower. 2010. "Youth Unemployment: Déjà Vu?" IZA Discussion Paper No. 4705. Bonn: IZA.

[3] Or even "deeply ironic", as argued by the International Labour Organization. 2005a. "Youth Employment: From a National Challenge to a Global Development Goal", Background Paper contributed by the ILO to the G8 Labour and Employment Ministers' Conference, London, United Kingdom, 10-11 March 2005.

[4] Since the Industrial Revolution. Lansky, M. 1997. "Child Labour: How the Challenge is Being met", *International Labour Review* 136, No. 2. Malmberg-

development of labour law and industrial relations in the various countries considered in this study. Economists themselves show an increasing interest in youth employment, and in labour market dynamics more generally, as confirmed by the 2010 Nobel Prize that has been awarded to three economists who investigated labour market frictions, namely the imperfect matching between labour demand and supply.[5]

The most advanced economies are characterised, in general, by a progressive raising of the age at which young people enter the labour market, giving rise to significant social and economic problems in a context of overall ageing of the population. The high level of academic attainment and well-being is in some cases accompanied by a significant level of graduate unemployment, together with difficulties on the part of enterprises in recruiting employees with the right skills for positions that tend to be rejected by young people among the local population. The same goes for the management of small or micro enterprises and for the numerous trades taken up by immigrant workers who are willing to learn and hand down trades that are essential for the national economy and that may now be seen as a kind of "endangered species". On the other hand, the economies and societies of the developing countries are characterised by the opposite trend, that may appear to be contradictory or paradoxical,

---

Heimonen, I., and I. Jukunen. 2006. "Out of Unemployment? A Comparative Analysis of the Risk and Opportunities Longer-term Unemployed Immigrant Youth Face when Entering the labour Market", *Journal of Youth Studies* 9, No. 5: 575-592.

[5] Diamond, P.A., Massachusetts Institute of Technology, Cambridge, MA, USA, Dale T. Mortensen, Northwestern University, Evanston, IL, USA, Aarhus University, Denmark, and Christopher A. Pissarides, London School of Economics and Political Science, UK. 2011. *The Prize in Economic Sciences 2010 - Press Release.* http://nobelprize.org/nobel_prizes/economics/laureates/2010/press.html. Their theory on markets with search frictions shows how "unemployment, job vacancies, and wages are affected by regulation and economic policy. This may refer to benefit levels in unemployment insurance or rules in regard to hiring and firing. In fact, on many markets, buyers and sellers do not always make contact with one another immediately. This concerns, for example, employers who are looking for employees and workers who are trying to find jobs. Since the search process requires time and resources, it creates frictions in the market. On such search markets, demands of some buyers will not be met, while some sellers cannot sell as much as they would. Simultaneously, there are both job vacancies and unemployment on the labour market. One conclusion is that more generous unemployment benefits give rise to higher unemployment and longer search times". The theory has been applied to many other areas in addition to the labour market.

bringing to mind the early stages of the Industrial Revolution and the emergence of modern labour law, marked by the large-scale and often brutal exploitation of the young workforce and by child labour.[6] Extremely high levels of unemployment and underemployment lead to large-scale migrations towards the most developed regions[7] that are characterised by a declining workforce, low birth rates, and an ageing population, giving rise to the risk of impoverishing the human capital in the country of origin.[8]

The question of youth employment has therefore become an extremely urgent matter which should be a priority on the agenda of political decision-makers and trade union leaders in all the regions of the world, including the most economically advanced ones. This holds especially true if one considers the financial downturn that affected the global economies during 2008/2009, with an impact particularly on younger people. In this connection, significant developments have been recorded in the countries of the Organisation for Economic Cooperation and Development (OECD). In these countries, although the younger age groups are less numerous and more highly educated than previous generations, there is increasing anxiety about their employment prospects, reflecting the alarming labour market statistics concerning young people in various countries, though these indicators are not necessarily the most appropriate[9] to explain unemployment (Fig. 2-1) and in particular long-term unemployment, among young people (Fig. 2-2). In addition, the issue of segmented labour markets or precarious employment, in the sense of work of a temporary

---

[6] The phenomenon of child labour exists nonetheless within developed countries as well, although in a lesser extent.

[7] United Nations. 2007. *World Youth Report 2007*. New York: Department of Economic and Social Affairs, United Nations.

[8] Docquier, F. 2006. "Brain Drain and Inequality Across Nation", IZA Discussion Paper No. 2440. Bonn: IZA.

[9] See, for instance, Marchand, O. 1999. "Youth Unemployment in OECD Countries: How Can the Disparities Be Explained?", *OECD Preparing Youth for the 21st Century—The Transition from Education to the labour Market,* Paris: OECD Publishing, pp. 89-100, who argues that "the unemployment rate becomes less and less appropriate to describe their situation as the length of time they spent in school increases and the average age at which they start working increases". In similar vein, see Rees, A. 1996. "An Essay on Youth Joblessness", *Journal of Economic Literature* 24, No. 2, pp. 613-28, who suggests using the parameter of joblessness instead of unemployment—undoubtedly more reliable, though not so easy to use in comparative terms—as the main indicator of youth employment problems.

nature and of low quality that is available to young people,[10] is of central importance in the domestic debate in many countries, with an impact on election campaigns both at national and local level.

The problem of youth unemployment takes a totally different form in other regions of the world, particularly Sub-Saharan Africa and South Asia, where the extremely high rates of poverty and low income levels are accompanied by a strong presence of young people, who account for 80% of the young people of the world (Fig. 2-3).

In the African countries, in particular, it is well known[11] that youth unemployment is closely linked with high levels of poverty, reflecting the apparently contradictory situation in which a low level of demand co-exists with the highest participation rates for young people in the world, with high rates of employment in the informal sector, and all the negative consequences that ensue in terms of unemployment, underemployment, lack of education, training and vocational skills.

The global dimension of the problem, arising from the irreversible interdependence between the economies of the world, is reflected in the migration of young people leaving their country of origin to seek better training and employment opportunities abroad (at times unsuccessfully) in what has been called the "battle for brains"[12]—which led analysts to examine the possibility of taking countermeasures on a transnational scale.

Significant steps have been taken in this direction by the International Labour Organization, the United Nations and the World Bank:[13] starting from a comparative study, they have gradually adopted measures to coordinate employment policies designed for young people. These initiatives, such as the *Youth Employment Programme* of the International Labour Organization, adopt measures of the type implemented in connection with the Employment Strategy of the European Union since the end of the 1990s, albeit with limited success. In particular, the approach is that of the Open Method of Coordination (OMC), consisting

---

[10] Booth, A. L., M. Francesconi, and J. Frank. 2002. "Temporary Jobs: Stepping Stones Or Dead Ends?", *The Economic Journal* 112, No.480. Kalleberg, A. L. 2000. "Non standard Employment Relations: Part-Time, Temporary and Contract Work", *Annual Review of Sociology,* p. 26.

[11] International Labour Organization. 2006a. *Regional Labour Market Trends for Youth: Africa,* ILO Youth Employment Programme, Geneva: ILO.

[12] Blanpain, R. 2008. "The End of Labour Law?", *The Global Labour Market. From Globalization to Flexicurity,* eds. Blanpain, R., and M. Tiraboschi, The Hague: Kluwer Law International.

[13] Youth Employment Network, *Millennium Development, Global Employment Trends for Youth.*

of the definition of common guidelines by a supranational body for the Member States, comparing the measures adopted by the various countries, providing for a periodic assessment aimed at identifying best practices, and where possible, their extension to other national settings (benchmarking).

Fig. 2-1. Youth Unemployment (age range 15- 24 years) in a Number of OECD Countries

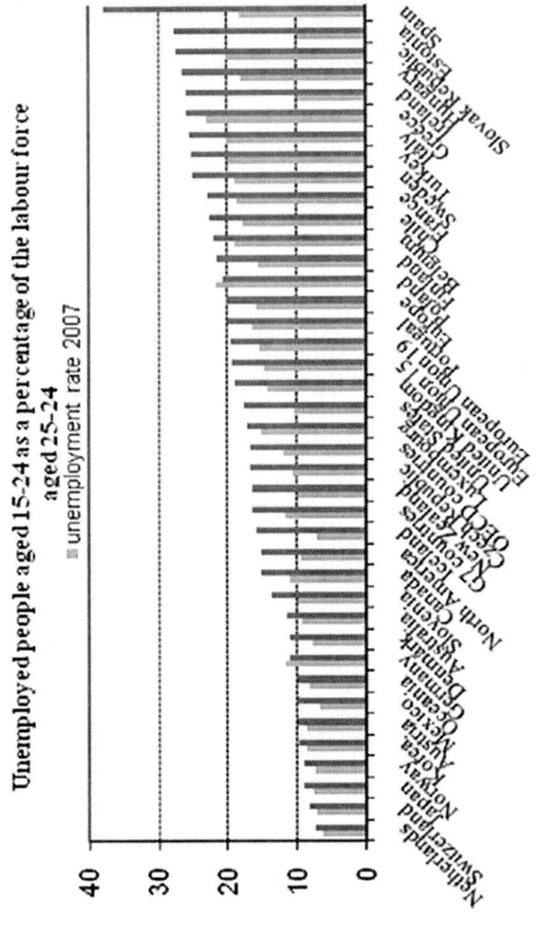

Source: OECD database on Labour Force Statistics

Fig. 2-2. Incidence of Long-term Unemployment among Youth (1995-2009)

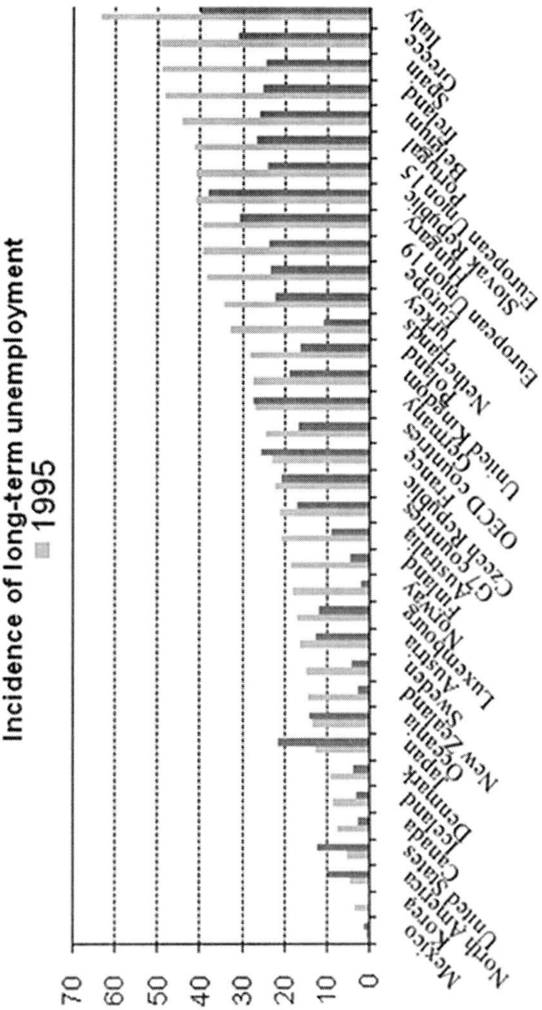

Source: OECD database on Labour Force Statistics

Fig. 2-3. Half of the Global Youth Population Live in Low-income Countries

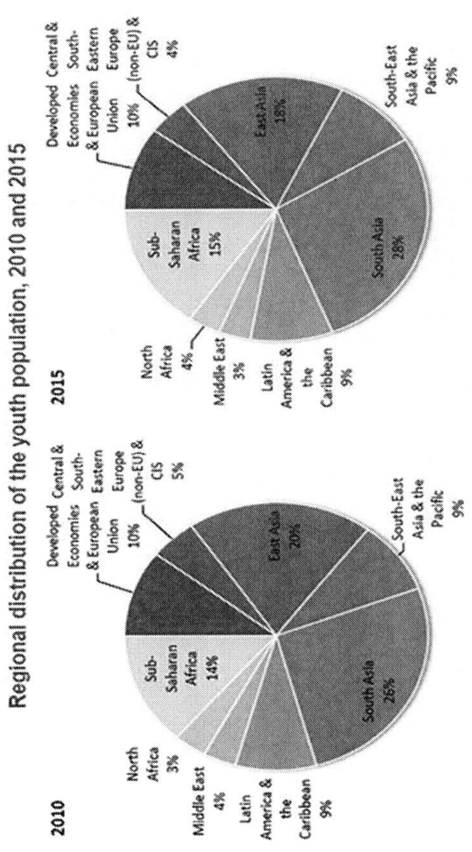

Source: ILO—Regional Distribution of the Youth population, 2010 and 2015

However, the EU experience, together with the pressures exerted by the global economy on national systems, highlights the limits of an approach in which regulatory powers remain in the hands of the nation states, albeit with a certain amount of transnational coordination (that may be more or less strict), without calling this traditional function into question. The attention of institutions and scholars dealing with the legislative implications of economic internationalisation is now shifting from the external sphere of state sovereignty (the soft-law influence of transnational institutions) towards the internal sphere, concerning the national institutions, the actors in the industrial relations system, and the nature of regulatory provisions, based on the idea that in the context of globalisation, effective labour market policies require profound changes in terms of legal practice and fundamental legal principles.

2. Limits of the "Traditional" Approach to Labour Law and Shortcomings in Relevant Legislation. Investing in Human Capital and Increasing Productivity as an Alternative Perspective

When labour law and industrial relations scholars lose sight of the fundamental issues of labour productivity, investment in human resources, and the links between education, training and the labour market, then their main focus is on a formal, conceptual system that is in many cases largely self-referential. As a result, they can make only a limited contribution to labour market institutions and the work of the social partners (both national and international) in their efforts to implement an organic action plan, taking account of the insights provided by the economic disciplines relating to the improvement of employment conditions for young people.[14]

Accordingly, it is possible to point to a plethora of international measures—such as the prohibition of child labour,[15] measures relating to decent and productive work,[16] and the definition of employment contracts as self-employment or salaried employment[17]—that are of great symbolic

---

[14] International Labour Organization. 2010b. *Global Employment Trends for Youth 2010*. Geneva: ILO.

[15] International Labour Organization. 1999. *Convention C182, Concerning the Prohibition and Immediate Action for the Elimination of the Worst Forms of Child Labour*. Geneva: ILO.

[16] See the several references to the concept of a "full, productive and freely chosen employment" included in the International Labour Organization Recommendations R122, *Employment Policy*, 1964; R169, *Employment Policy (Supplementary Provisions)*, 1984; R195, *Human Resources Development*, 2004.

[17] See the Green Paper released by the European Commission. 2006. *Modernising Labour Law to Meet the Challenges of the 12st Century, COM(2006)708final.* Brussels: European Commission, which puts into question the persistent relevance of such a distinction. For an outline of the debate developed throughout Europe on the issue see European Commission. 2007. *Outcome of the Public Consultation on the Commission's Green Paper "Modernising Labour Law to Meet the Challenges of the 21st Century", SEC(2007)1373.* Brussels: European Commission.

value but largely ineffective in terms of their impact on the real economy, both in the advanced countries (that are characterised by high levels of employment protection) and in the developing countries (due to the brute force of circumstances and objective economic conditions).

An important point that could be made in this connection, with all the necessary provisos, is that employment safeguards and standards that are imposed in a mechanical way on developing countries may act as a brake on their economic growth to the benefit of the more developed regions of the globe which, in the course of their development over the centuries, have benefited from the implementation of modern labour law. As a result, though it may appear to be a paradox, bearing in mind the historical role played by labour law, it could be argued that standards of international competition that have been set are disadvantageous for enterprises in the less developed economies.

A paradigmatic case in this connection is that of the countries of East Asia, that have achieved record growth in recent years with the rapid expansion of the Chinese economy. Here, as underlined by the report of the International Labour Organization on *Global Employment Trends2010,* the key cause of concern for the future is the development of human capital and labour productivity and the creation of employment with a high level of vocational skills.

Further, it is crucial to prepare young people for the future through investment in their human capital, as low-cost labour will not continue to be the region's comparable advantage.[18]

The arguments put forward so far should contain all the elements to provide a general interpretation of the problem of youth employment, as indicated in the introduction. The analysis is based on a particular interpretation of the concept of "decent work" that of "employment opportunity", in the sense of employability, linked to the development of human capital.[19]

Of the four dimensions of the concept, as identified by the International Labour Organization (security, opportunities, basic workers'

---

[18] See International Labour Organization. 2010a. *Global Employment Trends January 2010.* Geneva: ILO.

[19] See ILO. 2005c. *Resolution Concerning Youth Employment.* Geneva: ILO. The concept of employability "encompasses the skills, knowledge and competencies that enhance a worker's ability to secure and retain a job, progress at work and cope with change, secure another job if he/she so wishes or has been laid off, and enter more easily into the labour market at different periods of the life cycle".

rights and representation),[20] this one appears to be the most appropriate in the context of the global economy, in that it is the concept that is relevant to all the regions of the world, regardless of their specific characteristics. Whereas the imbalances between post-industrial and developing countries mean that it is unlikely that industrial relations can be coordinated on a global scale for instance in terms of trade union representation and fundamental rights (such as working hours and pay), for which it seems difficult to construct a shared platform, also in consideration of the extremely divergent levels of economic and social development, the problem of employment opportunities is a matter of common interest, as we have argued, for all the regions of the world. This includes the regions where there is a lack of skilled labour, engaged in the "battle for brains", and those with a surplus of young people which, in a global perspective, can transform the dramatic problem of youth unemployment into an unexpected resource for growth and development.

The argument put forward here is in keeping with the widely supported idea that the aim of "decent work for all" can only be achieved by raising productivity.[21] Studies on the relationship between productivity and the quality of employment, in line with the various stages of development that countries around the globe go through, have highlighted the fact that to achieve significant results in terms of long-term growth it may be necessary in the early stages of development to give lower priority to certain factors concerning quality employment.

In some cases, improvements in productivity may have detrimental effects on employment quality, especially in relation to fundamental rights. As shown in recent years by the Chinese experience,[22] the initial phases of development are characterised by factors that provide a competitive advantage, even when this means low labour costs and a lack of attention to labour protection. In these early stages, employment

---

[20] ILO. 2006b. *World Employment Report 2004/*2005. Geneva: ILO, chap. 2: "What society can achieve is to ensure that the worker has a smoother transition and protection in the form of security, opportunities, basic workers' rights and representation, the four main dimensions of decent work".

[21] ILO. 2006b. *World Employment Report 2004/*2005. Geneva: ILO. Preface: "Productive employment is the economic foundation of decent work".

[22] OECD. 2010b. *Economic Survey of China: a Labour Market in Transition*. Paris: OECD. Directorate-General for Employment, Social Affairs and Equal Opportunities, European Commission, The Institute of Population and Labor Economics, and Chinese Academy of Social Sciences. 2010. *New Skills for New Jobs: China and the EU. Shared Labour Market Experiences to Inform the Harmonious and Sustainable Society of the Future*. Brussels: European Commission.

safeguards consist above all of the mental and physical qualities required to deal with the "turbulence" encountered on the way towards economic stability.

Employment opportunities become therefore a priority, rather than a feature of decent work.

Due consideration should be given to the argument that the imposition of strict employment protection measures in the early stages of development of the economy may result in the competitive advantage shifting to the more developed economies, that in an earlier phase went through their own initial stages of development with low levels of employment safeguards, comparable to developing countries today.

According to this argument, the introduction of a high level of employment safeguards would be detrimental to the interests of workers in developing countries in the global economy.

With a view to considering this argument more fully, and to transfer it to a global economic context beyond national boundaries, reference may be made to the classic study *Industrial Democracy* by Sidney and Beatrice Webb (1897), in particular as regards their discussion of standard regulations for labour, with the preferences of individual workers and employers being subject to a "common rule" in the interest of both parties and the nation as a whole. The Webbs advocated the introduction of such regulation not *through* legislative intervention, but as an *alternative* to state intervention in employment relations, by means of a self-regulation of the market, based on collective bargaining as the essential method. In *Industrial Democracy* there are continual references to the regulatory role of collective bargaining, which is seen not as a mere economic tool for determining labour conditions, but as a social instrument aimed at furthering the "interests of Industrial Peace",[23] and promoting "the selection of the most efficient factors of production, whether capital, brains, or labour"; preventing the deterioration of the "capital stock of the nation"; stimulating "the invention and adoption of new processes of manufactures", while eliminating from the market "incompetent or old-fashioned employers", for the purposes of the "nation's productive efficiency" or "industrial efficiency". Just as emblematic are the pages of *Industrial Democracy* dedicated to "industrial parasitism", showing their strong faith in market self-regulation. On the one hand, they argue, the more extensive and effective the mechanism of the "common rule", the greater the proportion of the population protected from the devastating

[23] For this and the following quotations, see Webb, B., and S. Webb. 1897 and 1926. *Industrial Democracy*. London: Longmans, respectively p. 218, 703, 751, 724,728, 732, 766-767, 759, 703.

effects of speculation on the labour of others, whereas on the other hand, in cases in which minimum conditions for the use of the labour force are stable and standardised, qualitative standards will tend to improve, both for labour and the system of production as a whole, thus eliminating from the market parasitic competitors who survive solely by speculating on the cost of labour.

In considering the fundamental role of labour law in regulating the competition between enterprises, it is evident that a mechanical and historically decontextualised application of employment protection measures would have a negative impact on developing economies and ultimately also on the workers themselves, who would be expelled from the labour market.[24]

The creation of employment opportunities, linked to the improvement of human capital, may serve as the key objective for the governance of the intermediate phases of economic development. It may be said that a close match between an increase in productivity and an increase in decent employment can be achieved only in the medium to long term. In the intermediate phases, an increase in productivity, with a shift away from labour-intensive systems of production, can result in a loss of jobs (particularly in low-skilled occupations). Investment in human capital in these circumstances is needed to cope with a fall in employment levels that accompanies the increase in productivity, enabling workers to acquire the skills needed for occupational mobility, both internal and external.

3. Global Perspectives for Future Actions

In the context of the global labour market, an interdisciplinary perspective can turn the apparently insoluble problems of each country into a great opportunity for development and growth in what is by no means a zero-sum game, provided that an integrated and cross-disciplinary approach is adopted. As rightly argued by the International Labour Organization:

> The outflow of young migrants to the developed world presents a number of benefits for both receiving and sending countries. As regards the former, there is evidence that migrants have only slight negative effects on the wages of nationals, and tend to pay more taxes than they receive in tax-supported services. Conversely, little evidence exists that migration leads

---

[24] A different argument could be developed for those multinational corporations which settle in under developed areas only to start activities intended for other markets.

> to a displacement of nationals in employment. Given the current demographic change, young immigrants are also likely to become part of the solution to the employment and welfare problems raised by aging in developed economies. Young migrants can also be a source of funding for development in their countries of origin. Their remittances help cover family expenses and investment for job creation. When they return, they bring back human, financial and social capital, thereby contributing to the development of their home countries.[25]

The present paper, summarising the initial findings of a wider research project currently under way—resulting in a number of conferences and carried out by the International School of Higher Education in Labour and Industrial Relations set up by ADAPT (*www.adapt.it*)—promotes a global approach to analyse this phenomenon as the possible basis for rethinking institutional strategies for the labour market, and in particular the role of the actors in the industrial relations system. This paper will argue that the main limits to the "traditional" approach to labour law are the result of a "static" conception of labour markets on a global scale, whereas forward planning, in the sense of a complete rethinking of the transition and links between education and the world of work on the part of institutions and the social partners, could provide a dynamic contribution to achieve a better and more sustainable balance on a global scale.

For this purpose, it may be useful to adopt a school-to-work transition perspective, a concept that has until now been relegated to a secondary role by industrial relations and labour law scholars. This paper considers the reasons for the lack of attention that an approach of this kind has received. First of all, employment policies adopted so far have had a merely local and/or national application, whereas bridging the gap between the wealthiest and the poorest regions of the world requires a global approach, by strengthening the link between education and training, on the one hand, and the labour market, on the other. The school-to-work transition perspective, applied to industrial relations and labour law, seems particularly well suited to develop more effective policies and policy evaluation tools.

This approach makes it possible to actively involve the various actors dealing with productivity issues, investment in human capital, youth unemployment and underemployment. When applying the school-to-work transition concept to the legal and industrial relations methods in a

---

[25] International Labour Organization. 2005a. "Youth Employment: From a National Challenge to a Global Development Goal," Background Paper contributed by the ILO to the G8 Labour and Employment Ministers' Conference, London, United Kingdom, 10-11 March 2005.

comparative framework, it becomes clear that human capital improvement, work productivity and effective measures to deal with the problem of youth employment can be achieved only if policies are designed to cover the period before entering the labour market, i.e. the education and training phase. In general, labour market policies focus mainly on a given labour force, preventing the solution of the structural problems of youth employment, and particularly their impact on the gap between wealthy and poor regions. On the other hand, a method enabling us to tackle such problems at an earlier stage, dealing with how to design education and training to respond to the demands of the global labour market, might contribute to solutions for the governance of international flows of labour.

This strand of research will only develop its full potential if it succeeds in adopting a holistic vision linking the worlds of education and employment, moving beyond a traditional conception of labour law provisions and industrial relations, and education and training systems, that have until now been considered as two separate spheres, to be studied by specialised research groups who are separate from and not in communication with each other. A modern vision of the relations between education and training on the one hand, and socio-economic development on the other, leads to the development of policies and programmes that take account not only of the demand for labour, but also of the quality of the labour supply.

It is only by means of integration between education and training, and the world of work, that it will be possible to deal in global and pragmatic terms with the problem of youth employment and promote a balanced development of human capital in all the regions of the world. It is undoubtedly the case that the availability of adequate education and vocational training is a key factor in the allocation of resources on the part of investors, and as a result of the quality of employment. Investors do not set up businesses of "good quality" (i.e. not aiming merely to exploit low-cost labour) in regions where there is a lack of personnel with the skills required to run the business. This means that the response to the problem of youth employment must be based on the construction of a system of education and vocational training. These are the real investment assets that generate income, productivity, development, social mobility and, last but not least, decent work.

In the new economy, the main source of the wealth of nations is their endowment with human capital. Indeed, human capital is the key factor for growth and development, and the engine for change. Compared to the European countries and the other western nations with a rapidly ageing population, developing countries and some of the poorest economies in the world are endowed with vast wealth. Therefore, in order to avoid wasting this precious resource, it is necessary to go well beyond a legal regulation that may or may not produce results, undertaking a reform of education and training systems on a global scale that should be entrusted to the social partners. This appears to be possible only if we are prepared to rethink the role and functions of industrial relations, in order to make a contribution to the true modernisation of education and training, closing the traditional gap between school and work.

In this connection, the report by the International Labour Organization on *Global Employment Trends for Youth,* published in 2010[26] provides supporting evidence for this argument. In this report, the ILO underlined that the indicators for youth employment currently available are sufficient to provide an analytical framework on the condition of young people on the labour market in the various regions of the world. In the words of the Report:

> for further expansion of the youth employment knowledge base, the need is not one of developing new indicators, but rather finding a way to make use of the indicators that already exist (labour force participation rates, employment ratios, unemployment rates, employment by status and sector, long-term unemployment, underemployment, hours of work and poverty).

4. A Different Legal, Institutional and Industrial Relations Perspective: Forward Planning and the School-to-work Transition Based on a Modern Conception of Education and Vocational Training

Recent studies have shown that in the debate on deregulation, following on from major developments in the English-speaking countries and from the authoritative recommendations over the past decade of the OECD,[27] there is a tendency to confuse employment policies and labour

---

26 ILO. 2005b. *Resolution on Decent Work for Youth in Africa and the ILO Response, Document GB289/5.* Geneva: ILO.

27 Relying upon the *Job Studies* started since1992—which tended to show a relationship between high levels of unemployment and high standards of work protection—the OECD has set up an action programme (*JobStrategy*), addressed to governments and social partners, founded on ten recommendations. Among those, particular reference should be made to the labour market deregulation for purposes of job creation. Along with the yearly *Employment Outlooks,* see OECD. 1994. *The OECD Job Study: Evidence and Explanations,* Paris: OECD. See also OECD. 1997. *Implementing the OECD Jobs Strategy: Lessons from Member Countries.*

policies that are taken to be one and the same thing.[28] Once the two concepts are confused, there appears to be an inevitable connection between high levels of unemployment (especially youth unemployment) and labour protection. In the same vein, simplistic claims are made that the opposite is also the case: lower unemployment levels in the United States, the United Kingdom, Australia and New Zealand are usually explained in the light of neo-liberal ideas.

The expressions "employment policies" and "labour policies" actually refer to two profoundly different concepts. Employment policies are intended to increase employment levels in a given socio-economic system, and to achieve this objective, they operate at another level in relation to the regulation of labour, by means of measures such as tax and contributions relief, credit and capital markets, investment in infrastructure, the reform of public spending and, of particular interest for the present study, investment in human capital and the modernisation of education and training systems.

Labour policies, on the other hand, are intended to promote jobs for certain groups (the long-term unemployed, those not in employment, workers lacking the skills required by the market, immigrants, women, young people) by means of employment services, schemes providing for alternation between training and work, the elimination of barriers to access to and exit from the labour market, as well as the various kinds of job creation mentioned above. As a result, they only have a marginal impact on total employment levels, while producing more significant effects on the duration and above all on the distribution of unemployment among different groups.

The most recent empirical studies have provided econometric evidence showing the lack of a clear correlation, in terms of cause and effect, between levels of employment protection and levels of unemployment. The OECD,[29] which over the past decade has advocated a neo-liberal approach to labour market policy, has come to the same conclusion that

---

Paris: OECD, and OECD. 1999b. *Implementing the OECD Job Strategy: Assessing Performance and Policy.* Paris: OECD.

[28] Biagi, M., and M. Tiraboschi. 2000. "The Role of Labour Law in Job Creation Policies: an Italian Perspective", *Job Creation and Labour Law,* ed. Biagi, M., The Hague: Kluwer Law International, 179-193.

[29] OECD. 1999b. *Implementing the OECD Job Strategy: Assessing Performance and Policy.* Paris: OECD, especially chapter 2: *Employment Protection and Labour Market Performance.*

many researchers have also reached[30] in that the regulation of employment relations and the introduction of greater flexibility in the regulation of the workforce can, in the best possible case, contribute to creating the preconditions required to make employment policy effective.

The outcome of the current debate on deregulation is that it would be pointless to sacrifice labour law on the altar of employment. It would prove ineffective to assign to labour policy in the strict sense an ambitious role that it is well beyond its scope, especially with reference to the creation of new employment of good quality.

Rather, the route to be taken, also in relation to future research, is that of the modernisation and rethinking of labour law legislation, adopting a less formalistic approach, and assigning a larger role to industrial relations in order to provide a structural solution to the problem of youth unemployment.[31]

It would appear to be far more important to undertake the reform of education and vocational training, and to improve the functioning of the bodies intended to promote the employability of young people, by means of networks, whether formal or informal, between international and local institutions, educational and training bodies, employers' associations, undertakings or trade unions. In this connection particular attention needs to be paid to the alternation of periods of school and work, and especially apprenticeship schemes,[32] as well as institutional mechanisms aimed at promoting the placement of students and the transition from education to employment. As shown in the German and Japanese experience, "labor

---

[30] Regini, M., and G. Esping-Andersen. "The Effects of Labour Market Deregulation on Unemployment. A Critical Review of the Different Research Approaches and of Empirical Evidence", paper presented to the European Commission, Brussels, Belgium, 1998.

[31] Such an argument appears to be in line with the recent statements developed by the International Labour Organization, which draw a distinction between "good" and "bad" labour market institutions for the purposes of social development: Berg, J., and D. Kucera. 2007. *In Defence of Labour Market Institutions: Cultivating Justice in the Developing World.* Geneva: ILO.

[32] In the sense of programmes combining vocational education with enterprise-based training. See Axmann, M. 2004. "Facilitating Labour Market Entry for Youth through Enterprise-Based Schemes in Vocational Education and Training and Skills Development", SEED Working Paper No. 48. Geneva: ILO, par. XII. At a European level, the importance of apprenticeship for youth employability has been highlighted also by the European Parliament; see European Parliament. 2010. "Report on Promoting Youth Access to the Labour Market, Strengthening Trainee, Internship and Apprenticeship Status (2009/2221(INI))" Committee on Employment and Social Affairs.

market programmes come and go. Institutions develop, adapt and, for the most, endure".[33]

Once again, this strengthens the argument about human capital, which has so far been assigned a marginal role both by employment protection measures and by incentive measures.[34] The failure of job creation schemes and of employment protection measures based on non-negotiable conditions to produce the desired results provides reason to conceive the global governance of youth employment in a perspective of productivity and workforce employability.

It is therefore of considerable importance to identify regulatory techniques that are innovative both in terms of method and content. From the point of view of method, there is a need to recognise the limits of traditional techniques imposing norms from outside the employment relationship, that are not necessarily taking account of all the interests of the parties, nor of keeping up to date with changes taking place, and as a result they may not be capable of generating truly effective solutions. The need for "tailor-made regulations" should also be taken into account, especially for those categories of workers who "fall outside the pattern of the traditional employment relationship in a strict sense".[35] In this connection, more fluid and negotiated regulatory processes based on the

---

[33] See Ryan, P. 2001. "The School-to-work Transition: a Cross-national Perspective," *Journal of Economic* Literature 39, No. 1: 34-92. With regard to apprenticeships in Germany and school and university placement services in Japan, Ryan rightly notes that "those institutions have allowed Germany and Japan to avoid mass labour market programs and to concentrate instead on institutional development improving general education, vocational preparation and job placement, and making it easier for low achievers to participate. Although Japanese and German transition institutions have come under strain, they have adapted well and they continue—thus far at least—to function largely intact". For updated sources about Japan, see the *Japan Institute for Labour Policy and Training* http://www.jil.go.jp/english/reports/jilpt_01.html. Among the others, see Hisashi, T. O., K. Koichiro, I. Koh, H. Park, K. Reiko, S. Tomoki. 2010. "The Labour Issue of Youth: Looking Back over 20 Years," *The Japanese Journal of Labour Studies,* No.602. For Germany, see Bundesministerium für Wirtschaft und Technologie. 2010. *Nationaler Paktfür Ausbildungund Fachkräftenachwuchs in Deutschland 2010—2014.* Berlin: BMWi.

[34] United Nations. 2005b. *The Economic report on Africa 2005—Meeting the Challenge of Unemployment and Poverty.* Addis Ababa: Economic Commission for Africa.

[35] Weiss, M. "Realising Decent Work in Africa," Keynote Speech at the Opening Ceremony of the Fifth African Regional Congress of the IIRA in Cape Town, South Africa, 26 March 2008.

active participation of the labour market actors might well be better suited to achieve greater policy coordination, that is essential in dealing with the issue of youth employment, which is of vital importance for every state and region of the world, since no region is immune from external pressures.

However, in terms of content, there is a need to focus more closely on the objectives of the policies to adopt, focusing on the areas where incisive action is required to deal with the structural problems that prevent the qualitative and quantitative growth of youth employment. These elements, in line with the role assigned to productivity as the key to decent work, may be linked to two principles: employability and stability. The first means that the individual is capable of playing a role on the labour market thanks to adequate cultural, vocational and social skills, dealing in a confident manner with transitional phases as they occur. The objective of stability is linked to the concept of productivity and to the level of turnover in the workforce of an enterprise. If there is any truth in the claim set forth in the *World Employment Report 2004/05* of the ILO,[36] that "there is substantial evidence that stability of employment (tenure) is positively related to productivity gains", the stability of the relationship between the employer and the employee should be safeguarded not so much by limits on termination, but rather by placing an emphasis, at the hiring stage, on matching the skills of job applicants to job descriptions.

In this respect, a central role is played by the school-to-work transition, in particular in the economic and sociological analysis, where it serves as an essential tool for gaining a better understanding of the problems of labour market entrants.[37]

This concept, that could be used systematically also in the study of labour law and industrial relations, is particularly important as it:

> draws together in a common arena a previously disparate set of issues in such areas as vocational education and training, youth unemployment, and wage structure. It does so by emphasising process attributes, as individuals flow from full-time schooling to full-time permanent employment, through various intermediate conditions, including vocational education and apprenticeship, fixed-term and part-time employment, and labour market programmes.[38]

---

[36] ILO. 2006b. *World Employment Report 2004/2005*.Geneva: ILO, p. 183.

[37] 2010b. *Global Employment Trends for Youth 2010*. Geneva: ILO, p. 36-43.

[38] See Ryan, P. 2001. "The School-to-work Transition: a Cross-national Perspective", *Journal of Economic Literature* 39, No. 1, pp. 34-92.

The ILO has itself resorted to this concept in examining certain youth employment indicators: the length of the transition from education and training to employment, the age of those entering the labour market, occupational status, the relation between the level of educational attainment and the position taken up in the labour market, income levels, employment sector, and gender inequality. At this point there is a need to complete the process, closing the gap between education, training and the labour market. With regard to the problem of youth unemployment and the quality and productivity of labour, the concept of the school-to-work transition can foster innovation in terms of both method and content, establishing a clear connection not just in theoretical but also in practical and operational terms between education, training and the labour market.[39]

In terms of content, this concept enables us to focus on shortcomings in the "accumulation" of human capital in the phases leading up to the entry into the labour market. The key issues here are asymmetrical information and the mismatch between the supply and demand for labour, resulting in unemployment, underemployment and low-quality employment. Investing in productivity is the key to employment of good quality and means rethinking regulatory instruments (such as employment contracts), and perhaps also the principles underlying training and the interpretation of rules, with a view to improving the match between the supply and demand for labour.

In terms of method, the concept of school-to-work transition requires a highly institutionalised regulatory approach, not based on conditions imposed by an external authority, but on the participation of all the stakeholders (the public authorities, the social partners, education and training institutions). Only a strong institutional structure, actively involving all these actors, can strengthen the links between the various phases of the transition. These links are essential conditions for the development of human capital, leading to increased productivity and decent employment. This is because, on the one hand, they are the actors who are best placed to interpret the employment needs in a given economic situation; and on the other hand, because they play an essential role in monitoring and safeguarding the workforce against irregular practices (to prevent training schemes from being used solely as a means to supply low-cost labour, or as a means to replace adult workers with young people prepared to work for low wages). This could lead to a new

---

[39] United Nations. 2005b. *The Economic Report on Africa 2005—Meeting the Challenge of Unemployment and Poverty.* Addis Ababa: Economic Commission for Africa. Aring, M., and M. Axmann. 2004. "Why Developing Countries Need a School-to-Work System, Now More Than Ever", RTI International.

concept of education and training, no longer considered as a self-referential world of its own, but rather as a resource closely linked to the world of work.

In an industrial relations perspective, and with a view to developing the above mentioned system, all the actors involved are required to provide a more decisive contribution in the design and implementation of education and training programmes in line with the needs of the global labour market, setting up networks and alliances with institutions and bodies in other countries, envisaging forward planning with a view to problem solving. For this purpose, the social partners must take a part in dealing with the school-to-work transition, integrating the formal system of education and training as a unified system of equivalent standing (with the option of taking interchangeable programmes of education to training from the secondary level onwards)—with the labour market (Fig. 2-4) rather than maintaining the traditional division[40] between education and work (Fig. 2-5).

Fig. 2-4. Human Capital and the Labour Market: Our Proposal

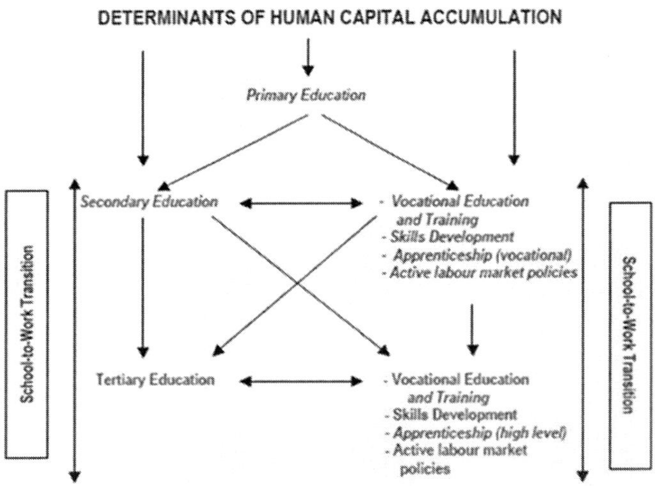

Source: United Nations—Economic Commission for Africa

[40] See for example United Nations. 2005b. *The Economic Report on Africa 2005–Meeting the Challenge of Unemployment and Poverty.* Addis Ababa: Economic Commission for Africa, p. 8.

Fig. 2-5. Human Capital and the Labour Market: the Traditional Pathways

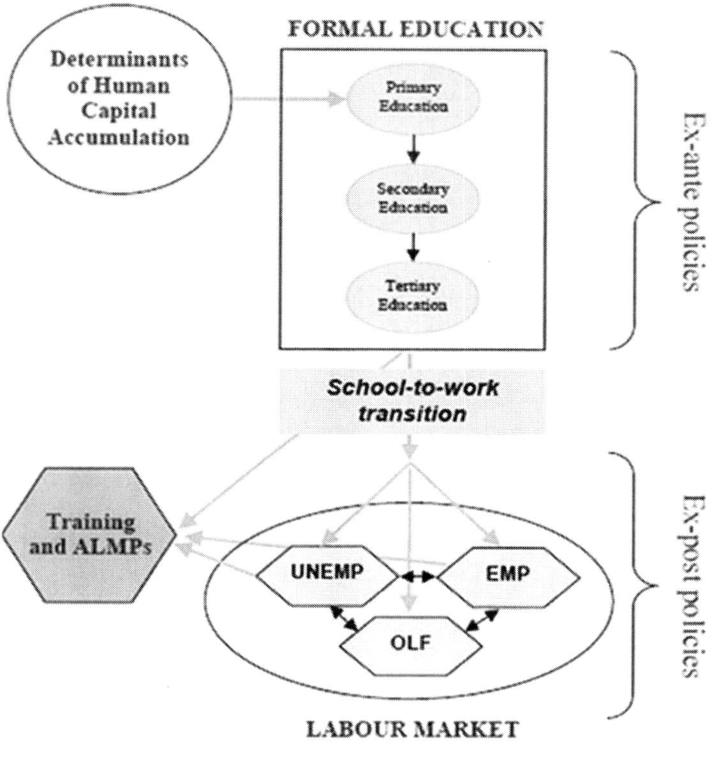

Source: United Nations—Economic Commission for Africa

The importance of this pathway becomes evident only when taking account of the fact that many studies have concluded that the impact of interventions on future employment outcomes of disadvantaged young people diminishes with age.[41] In other words, as recently pointed out by

[41] See among others Martin, J., and D. Grubb. 2001. "What Works and for Whom: A Review of OECD Countries' Experiences with Active Labour Market Policies", IFAU Working Paper No. 14. Institute for Labour Market Policy Evaluation. Heckman, J. J., and L. Lochner. 2000. "Rethinking Education and Training Policy: Understanding the Sources of Skill Formation in a Modern Economy", *Securing the Future: Investing in Children from Birth to Adulthood*, eds. Danziger, S., and J. Waldforgel, New York: Russell Sage Foundation. Garces, E., D. Thomas, and J.

the World Bank in a major study on policies intended to support employment in Sub-Saharan Africa,[42] "addressing potential problems early has a greater return than when young people have left formal education". Also the OECD, in reviewing the evidence, has concluded that:

> the evidence from the evaluation literature suggests the biggest pay-off for disadvantaged youths comes from early and sustained interventions. Such interventions should begin before children enter the compulsory schooling system, and they should be followed by intensive efforts to boost their performance in primary and secondary schooling and reduce drop-out rates.[43]

It is not clear why, after recognising that "any policy advice on addressing youth employment problems should emphasise that prevention is more effective than curing",[44] legal scholars in general have not developed[45] a unitary approach to the relation between education and training and the labour market in a global perspective. It may perhaps be explained by the lack of interdisciplinary study bringing together, in a unified conceptual scheme, the various specific disciplinary competences. However, it is only by means of reconsideration on the part of the institutions and the social partners of education and training pathways that

---

Currie. 2000. "Longer-term Effects of Head Start", NBER Working Papers No. 8054. The National Bureau of Economic Research.

[42] See Rother, F. 2006. "Intervention to Support Young Workers in Sub-Saharan Africa", Regional Report for the Youth Employment Inventory. Washington: The World Bank, p. 3.

[43] See OECD. 2002. *Employment Outlook 2002. A Better Start for Youth,* Paris: OECD, p. 32. See also the country-by-country and transnational programme of the OECD, Jobs for Youth. The European Commission is also addressing child care and early education, and intends to support specific measures to these policy areas, as declared in European Commission. 2011. "Tackling Early School Leaving: A Key Contribution to the Europe 2020 Agenda, COM(2011)", Communication From The Commission To The European Parliament, The Council, The European Economic and Social Committee and The Committee Of The Regions, Brussels: European Commission, p. 18

[44] See Rother, F. 2006. "Intervention to Support Young Workers in Sub-Saharan Africa," Regional Report for the Youth Employment Inventory. Washington: The World Bank, p. 3.

[45] With reference to youth employment in Sub-Saharan Africa see Rother, F. 2006. "Intervention to Support Young Workers in Sub-Saharan Africa," Regional Report for the Youth Employment Inventory. Washington: The World Bank, 3, that without going into detail refers to "practical grounds for limiting the inventory to post-formal-schooling interventions".

a realistic integration with the world of work can be achieved in order to respond to the challenges of globalisation. An integrated system of education and vocational training, in a school-to-work perspective, as well as representing a step towards a solution to the problems of youth unemployment, could narrow the gap in education and training between developed and developing countries, bearing in mind that the expected duration of primary and secondary schooling is only 7.5 years in Africa compared with 12 years for Europe and the Americas.[46] Moreover,

> according to human capital theory, the education acquired by a young person will be remunerated in terms of earnings, with higher wages reflecting higher productivity resulting from more advanced levels of education. Education will also determine the ability to participate in the labour force, not just the level of wages.[47]

In addition, for developing countries and the African countries in particular, the crucial problem is to provide primary education for all. It seems to be unrealistic to maintain a formal traditional system for secondary and tertiary education when in a significant number of cases, the primary level is not completed.[48] In this connection, international experience provides a number of good practices that could be a suitable basis for experimental schemes in developing countries: *1)* a broadening of vocational programmes and qualifications (e.g. a broad construction trades programme rather than separate programmes in carpentry, painting and bricklaying); *2)* the creation of links between general and vocational education, and the combination of work-based learning with continuing school education (e.g. vocational options within upper secondary education, more general education content within vocational training, and a modular approach to general education and vocational training courses, making it possible to combine modules from both); *3)* the creation of pathways from secondary vocational education into tertiary education, consisting of "dual qualification" pathways (qualifying the individual either to start work with technical expertise or to continue into tertiary education) as in Austria, the Czech Republic and Hungary, and supplementary examinations and courses taken in parallel with or after

---

[46] United Nations. 2005b. *The Economic Report on Africa 2005—Meeting the Challenge of Unemployment and Poverty.* Addis Ababa: Economic Commission for Africa, 9.
[47] Ibid.
[48] Ibid., 12.

vocational training qualifications, as in Australia, Austria, Norway and Switzerland.[49]

As highlighted by the OECD,[50] a wide variety of models exist for school-based workplace experience, ranging from unpaid work experience while still at school, to arrangements that combine schooling with half-day, or one-trimester-per-year, paid work. There is some evidence that school-based workplace experience has a positive impact on later labour market outcomes: some studies also suggest relatively good outcomes for students who take part-time or holiday jobs. It is well known that youth outcomes are generally good in countries like Germany and Denmark where a substantial proportion of young people enter work through apprenticeships that, in dual systems, provide an invaluable bridge between school and work. What these arrangements have in common is the benefit derived from contact with the world of work during education and training.

Measures can be taken to implement a major renewal of the systems of education and training that have so far been considered as two distinct spheres, and for this reason studied by separate research groups that are not in communication with each other. In most countries, young people are educated at school and then enter the labour market, with the transition from school to work being merely sequential. A modern vision of relations between education, training and socio-economic development calls for the design and implementation of policies and actions that take account not only of the demand for labour, but also of the quality of the supply. Only a real link between education, training and the world of work, by strengthening placement services and training schemes with an alternation of school and work, will enable us to deal in global and pragmatic terms with youth employment and balanced development of human capital all over the world. Clearly this perspective brings to mind the countries with a dual system (Austria, Denmark, Germany and Switzerland) that have relatively low youth unemployment rates and in which young people make the transition from school to apprenticeships, while they continue to spend one or two days a week in education.

It is well known that in countries such as Austria and Germany apprenticeship systems are built on several mutually dependent features.[51]

---

[49] OECD. 2002. *Employment Outlook 2002. A Better Start for Youth,* Paris: OECD, pp. 31-32.

[50] *Ibid.*

[51] Quintini, G., and S. Martin. 2006. "Starting Well or Losing their Way? The Position of Youth in the Labour Market in OECD Countries", OECD Social, Employment and Migration Working Paper No. 39. OECD, pp. 22-25.

Apprenticeship wages are low (initially about one-third of adult rates, rising to one-half in the final year), which makes apprenticeships attractive to employers. Apprenticeship qualifications have a high value on the labour market, and this makes apprenticeships attractive to young people and their parents. And the institutional basis for these systems is provided by strong and comprehensive industrial employer associations and industrial unions, which define apprenticeship qualifications and seek to maintain their value in the labour market. Hence the strategic role not only and not so much of public bodies, that can provide financial support for these schemes, but above all of the actors involved in the industrial relations system, who have a decisive role to play in relation to these schemes providing for an alternation between work and training.

Drawing on the disappointing results achieved by attempts to support apprenticeship schemes in the countries of Sub-Saharan Africa,[52] a complex problem arises when transposing such schemes from one country to another, that is well known to comparative law scholars, particularly in relation to apprenticeships that derive their strength from particular characteristics that are typical of the national systems in which they operate. It is however the case that only countries that use this tool efficiently have rates of youth unemployment in line with those of the adult population,[53] suggesting a link between apprenticeship schemes and stable employment of good quality.

Recent experience in countries such as Turkey, Malaysia, Tunisia and Egypt[54]—but also Uganda, Zambia and Kenya[55]—shows that, with suitable adaptation, the chances of success are considerable.[56]

---

[52] See Rother, F. 2006. "Intervention to Support Young Workers in Sub-Saharan Africa," Regional Report for the Youth Employment Inventory. Washington: The World Bank, highlighting the fact that apprenticeships are one of the most significant policies in recent years.

[53] Axmann, M. 2004. "Facilitating Labour Market Entry for Youth through Enterprise-Based Schemes in Vocational Education and Training and Skills Development," SEED Working Paper No. 48. Geneva: ILO, 16-40.

[54] Mention should be made in particular of the Mubarak-Kohl initiative in Egypt (a summary is to be found in United Nations. 2005a. *Youth, Education, Skill and Employment.* Addis Ababa: Economic Commission for Africa, p. 25); see also El Zanaty & Associates. 2007. "School to Work Transition: evidence from Egypt", *Employment Policy Paper*, No. 2 Geneva: ILO: according to the study "(...) Egyptian young people face significant challenges in finding decent employment after leaving school. The analysis of the collected data revealed that (in 2007) only 39% of respondents who were economically active (meaning either working or seeking work) or 17% of total respondents had attained employment that they were more or less satisfied with (more information on definitions of transition stages are

At the same time, traditional vocational training schemes, as well as being particularly costly, have not been able to respond to the need for decent work of good quality, nor to the need for developing countries to invest in human capital by providing training for specific occupations.[57] There is a need to devise alternatives to traditional apprenticeship schemes.[58] However, it remains essential, in order to respond to the challenges of globalisation, to rethink traditional systems of education and training, that can no longer be designed and implemented in a self-referential manner, without strong links with the social partners and the labour market. Rather, the combination of practical training with additional theoretical training will increase the qualifications of trainees, and by meeting the needs of enterprises and employers, improve access to decent employment. As underlined by recent studies:[59]

> skills acquired in enterprises are mostly demand-driven as they respond to the needs of the enterprises for qualified workers. Young women and men that have gained working experience during training in enterprises have a good chance to be employed by the company that provided the training or by other companies working in similar branches. They are also much better prepared to start their own business [...]. This approach will also have an impact on the productivity of the enterprise and the quality of the products and services sold. At medium term, the competitiveness of the small enterprise sector will increase and create more and better jobs. It is also expected that improved skills and managerial capacity of the workforce in small enterprises, matched with a better insertion in market niches with

---

provided below). The remaining 61% of economically active youth—more than one-quarter of total respondents (26%)—were still in a period of labour market transition, meaning they had not yet reached their desired goal for decent employment". With reference to Tunisia, see Stampini, M., and A. Verdier-Chouchane. 2011. "Labour Market Dynamics in Tunisia: the Issue of Youth Unemployment," Working Paper Series n.123, African Development Bank, Tunisia.

[55] Grierson, J. 2002. *Enterprise-based Training in Africa: Case Studies from Kenya and Zambia*. Turin: ILO/ITC.

[56] Axmann, M. 2004. "Facilitating Labour Market Entry for Youth through Enterprise-Based Schemes in Vocational Education and Training and Skills Development", SEED Working Paper No.48. Geneva: ILO.

[57] Ibid.

[58] Betcherman, G., M. Godfrey, S. Puerto, F. Rother, and A. Stavreska. 2007. "A Review of Interventions to Support Young Workers: Findings of the Youth Employment Inventory", SP Discussion Paper, No. 715. Washington: The World Bank.

[59] Ibid.

higher value added and demand for labour will, jointly, lead to a sustainable expansion of the small enterprise sector.

Our proposal goes well beyond reforming education and training programmes at national level (though this is clearly an important objective),[60] and calls for the involvement of international organisations and networks of social actors at international and local level in taking a series of initiatives with a global dimension. This includes making provision for the exchange of students, with movement from the developing to the developed countries, in programmes designed at local level together with the institutions and the social partners in the various countries in order to meet training needs.

In the new economy, the main source of the wealth of nations is their endowment with human capital. Indeed, human capital is the key factor for growth and development, and the engine for change. From this point of view, compared to the European countries and the other western nations with a rapid ageing population, the African nations are endowed with enormous wealth. In order to avoid wasting this precious resource, there is a need to manage it not simply by means of legal regulation that may or may not produce results, but above all—in line with developments in many Asian economies in recent years[61]—by means of a reform of the education and training systems on a global scale that should be entrusted to the social partners. The active governance of this system could provide young people in Africa and other developing countries with a realistic alternative to unemployment, work in the hidden economy and migration as undocumented workers. This would require the training provided in the country of origin to meet the needs of the labour market in the most advanced countries, where there is a shortage of skilled workers. Alongside the modernisation of apprenticeship schemes, a decisive role can be played in developing countries by career guidance services that need to be set up inside schools and universities, with the mutual recognition of vocational qualifications.

---

[60] Along this perspective, substantially limited to nationally-based actions and programmes, see the debate developed within the International Labour Organization and summarised in ILO. 2007a. "Informe y conclusiones de la undécesima Reuniòn Régional Africana", Addis Ababa, Ethiopia. April 24-28, 2007, and particularly Annex III and the Conclusions.

[61] See Yusuf, S., and K. Nabeshima, eds. 2007. *How Universities Promote Economic Growth*. Washington: The World Bank. For positive steps in Arabic Countries see http://www.tvet-portal.net/index.php?id=20&L=0.

Bearing in mind that for many of these young people there is no real alternative to migration, as there is a lack of employment in their country of origin,[62] it should be noted that recent international economic studies,[63] have highlighted the fact that the temporary loss of human capital and skilled workers does not necessarily have a negative impact on the country of origin, but can serve as a step towards attracting capital and know-how and for the development of trade between the country of origin and the developed countries.

Today, in an increasingly global labour market, it may be argued that, provided it is properly governed,[64] the outflow of young migrants to the developed world can lead to a number of benefits for both receiving and sending countries.[65] Suffice it to consider the historical experience of many European countries, which after a long period of mass emigration, began to attract migrants from other countries, having benefited from migratory movements in the past.

Clearly, the solution that is proposed is not for the short term, nor is it easy to implement, but requires a considerable effort on the part of education and training, labour market and industrial relations actors, as there appears to be a lack of valid alternatives. There is an awareness among policy-makers "that productive employment for young people cannot be achieved and sustained through isolated and fragmented measures".[66] Rather, it requires long-term, coherent and concerted action

---

[62] International Labour Organization. 2005a. "Youth Employment: From a National Challenge to a Global Development Goal", Background Paper contributed by the ILO to the G8 Labour and Employment Ministers' Conference, London, United Kingdom, 10-11 March 2005, p. 5.

[63] Ratha, D., and X. Zhimei. 2008. *Migration and Remittances Factbook 2008.* Migration and Remittances Team, Development Prospects Group, The World Bank. OECD. 2007. *International Migration Outlook.* Paris: OECD.

[64] Indeed, an ungoverned and not planned migration does not seem suitable for the purpose of providing solutions to this matter, since the lives of those leaving the countries of origin would be made difficult by the lack of integration into the countries of destination (Malmberg-Heimonen, I., and I.Jukunen. 2006. "Out of Unemployment? A Comparative Analysis of the Risk and Opportunities Longer-term Unemployed Immigrant Youth Face when Entering the Labour Market", *Journal of Youth Studies* 9, No.5, pp. 575-592.

[65] International Labour Organization. 2005a. "Youth Employment: From a National Challenge to a Global Development Goal", Background paper contributed by the ILO to the G8 Labour and Employment Ministers' Conference, London, United Kingdom, 10-11 March 2005, p. 8.

[66] Ibid. See also ILO. 2005b. *Resolution on Decent Work for Youth in Africa and the ILO Response, Document GB289/5.* Geneva: ILO.

over a combination of economic and social policies (e.g. modernisation of labour legislation, labour market information, career guidance, education and training for employability in a global workplace).

The school-to-work transition, from this point of view, appears to be the most favourable area in which to work and invest in order to achieve structural results, dealing with the fragile growth of many of the African,[67] while respecting the reciprocal interests of all the regions and economies of the global market.

5. Final Remarks: Theoretical Implications of our Proposal in Terms of Future Developments in the Study of Labour Law and Industrial Relations

Clearly the perspective outlined in the present study requires more in-depth analysis and field work. However, in concluding this preliminary study, it may be said that the school-to-work transition can make a significant contribution to recent strands of research that call for a theoretical reformulation of labour law and industrial relations.

Although the present study is intended to be innovative, and is in need of further development, in theoretical terms it is in line with certain recent proposals by legal scholars aimed at extending and modifying the frame of reference of the study of labour law and industrial relations, in order to ensure that it continues to play a significant role, in spite of international trends that are tending to marginalise these disciplinary fields. Mention should be made of the strand of legal research calling for labour law to be recast as "the law of labour market regulation".[68] highlighting the fact that the dominant paradigm of labour law in the late twentieth century was lacking in "explanatory and normative power" in relation to the changing nature of the labour market (both within the enterprise and on a wider

---

[67] Arbache, J., D. S. Go, and J. Page. 2008. "Is Africa's Economy at a Turning Point?", The World Bank Africa Region, Policy Research Working Paper No. 4519. Angel-Urdinola, D. F., Semlali A., and S. Brodman. 2010. *Non-Public Provision of Active Labor Market Programs in Arab-Mediterranean Countries: An Inventory of Youth Programs*. Washington: The World Bank. ILO. 2007a. "Informe y conclusiones de la undécesima Reuniòn Régional Africana", Addis Ababa, Ethiopia. April 24-28, 2007, 5-10. ILO. 2007b. "The Decent Work Agenda in Africa: 2007–2015", Report of the Director-General to the Eleventh African Regional Meeting, Addis Ababa, Ethiopia, April 2007.

[68] Arup, C., P. Gahan, J. Howe, R. Mitchell, and A. O' Donnell. 2006. *Labour Law and Labour Market Regulations*. Annandale: The Federation Press.

scale), to new economic theories concerning the labour market and its institutions, and to major changes in society arising from the globalisation of the economy and the markets. In this connection, mention should be made of the recent strand of labour law theory which, reflecting on the original paradigm of labour relations, as developed at the beginning of the twentieth century,[69] points to the need to considerable extend its field of observation beyond trade union issues in order to cover all the issues arising from labour relations. This development appears to be essential, if we are to avoid the risk of increasingly marginalising industrial relations in the context of the free market.

An important contribution in this direction could come from the proposal put forward in the present study, to govern the dynamics of supply and demand for labour by strengthening links on a global scale between education and training, and the labour market as a more effective and more realistic solution compared to a regulatory (or deregulatory) perspective, that is becoming weaker and less effective due to the loss of sovereignty on the part of nation states in the governance of the labour market. In this connection, it is not intended to turn away from the traditional protective function of labour law, but simply to highlight the fact that labour law concerns matters of production more than income distribution, in the sense that a lack of growth and development tends to have a negative impact on the potential of the labour market and on workers' protection. This confirms the decisive importance of the method of industrial relations, since no better tool has yet been invented for conciliating the protection of workers with the need for competitiveness on the part of enterprises.

---

[69] Kaufman, B. 2007. "*The Core Principle and Fundamental Theorem of Industrial Relations*", Working Paper 07-01, Department of Economics, W.T. Beebe Institute of Personnel and Employment Relations. Georgia State University. An Italian translation was published in *Diritto delle Relazioni Industriali*, 2006, 4, *Il principio essenziale e il teorema fondamentale delle relazioni industriali.*

References

Online Resources

The following documents are available on the website of ADAPT, School for Advanced Studies in Industrial and Labour Relations (*www.adapt.it*):

A-Z Index, Giovani e Lavoro

Angel-Urdinola, D. F., A. Semlali, and S. Brodman. 2010. "Non-Public Provision of Active Labor Market Programs in Arab-Mediterranean Countries: An Inventory of Youth Programs", Working Paper. Washington: The World Bank.

Annan, K. 2004. "A Global Alliance for Youth Employment: Recommendations to the High-Level Panel on Youth Employment", Report to the Millennium Assembly of the United Nations. United Nations.

Aring, M., and M. Axmann. 2004. "Why Developing Countries Need a School-to-Work System, Now More Than Ever", RTI International. Axmann, M. 2004. "Facilitating Labour Market Entry for Youth through Enterprise-Based Schemes in Vocational Education and Training and Skills Development", SEED Working Paper No. 48. Geneva: ILO.

El Zanaty & Associates. 2007. "School to Work Transition: evidence from Egypt", *Employment Policy Paper*, No. 2 Geneva: ILO.

Conventions and Recommendations Relevant to Work and Young Persons (list of)

Bell, D. N. F., and D. G. Blanchflower. 2010. "Youth Unemployment: Déjà Vu?", IZA Discussion Paper No. 4705. Bonn: IZA.

European Parliament. 2010. "Report on Promoting Youth Access to the Labour Market, Strengthening Trainee, Internship and Apprenticeship Status (2009/2221(INI))", Committee on Employment and Social Affairs.

Garces, E., D. Thomas, and J. Currie. 2000. "Longer-term Effects of Head Start", NBER Working Papers No. 8054. The National Bureau of Economic Research.

Ha, B., C. Mc Inerney, S. Tobin, and R. Torres. 2010. "Youth employment in Crisis", Discussion Paper. Geneva: International Institute for Labour Studies.

International Labour Organization. 2005a. "Youth Employment: From a National Challenge to a Global Development Goal", Background Paper contributed by the ILO to the G8 Labour and Employment

Ministers' Conference, London, United Kingdom, 10-11 March 2005. International Labour Organization. 2006a. *Regional Labour Market Trends for Youth: Africa.* ILO Youth Employment Programme, Geneva: ILO.

—. 2006b. *World Employment Report 2004/2005*. Geneva: ILO.

—. 2008. *It is High Time to Rethink—Youth Employment in 2008.* Addis Ababa: Regional Office for Africa.

Martin, J., and D. Grubb. 2001. "What Works and for Whom: A Review of OECD Countries' Experiences with Active Labour Market Policies", IFAU Working Paper No. 14. Institute for Labour Market Policy Evaluation.

OECD. 2002. *Employment Outlook 2002. A Better Start for Youth,* Paris: OECD.

—. 2010a. *Off to a Good Start? Jobs for Youth*. Paris: OECD Publishing. Quintini, G., and S. Martin. 2006. "Starting Well or Losing their Way? The Position of Youth in the Labour Market in OECD Countries", OECD Social, Employment and Migration Working Paper, No. 39. OECD.

Rother, F. 2006. "Intervention to Support Young Workers in Sub-Saharan Africa", Regional Report for the Youth Employment Inventory. Washington: The World Bank.

United Nations. 2005a. *Youth, Education, Skill and Employment,* Addis Ababa: Economic Commission for Africa.

—. 2005b. *The Economic Report on Africa 2005—Meeting the Challenge of Unemployment and Poverty.* Addis Ababa: Economic Commission for Africa.

A-Z Index, Globalizzazione e lavoro

International Labour Organization. 2010a. *Global Employment Trends January 2010.* Geneva: ILO.

Further References

Arbache, J., D. S. Go, and J. Page. 2008. "Is Africa's Economy at a Turning Point?", The World Bank Africa Region, Policy Research Working Paper n. 4519.

Arup, C., P. Gahan, J. Howe, R. Mitchell, and A. O' Donnell. 2006. *Labour Law and Labour Market Regulations.* Annandale: The Federation Press.

Berg, J., and D. Kucera. 2007. *In Defence of Labour Market Institutions: Cultivating Justice in the Developing World.* Geneva: ILO.

Betcherman, G., M. Godfrey, S. Puerto, F. Rother, and A. Stavreska. 2007. "A Review of Interventions to Support Young Workers: Findings of the Youth Employment Inventory", SP Discussion Paper, No. 715. Washington: The World Bank.

Biagi, M., and M. Tiraboschi. 2000. "The Role of Labour Law in Job Creation Policies: an Italian Perspective", in *Job Creation and Labour Law,* ed. Biagi, M., The Hague: Kluwer Law International, 179-193.

Blanpain, R. 2008. "The End of Labour Law?", in *The Global Labour Market. From Globalization to Flexicurity,* eds. Blanpain, R., and M. Tiraboschi, The Hague: Kluwer Law International.

Booth A. L., M. Francesconi, and J. Frank. 2002. "Temporary Jobs: Stepping Stones or Dead Ends?", *The Economic Journal* 112, No. 480.

Bundesministerium für Wirtschaft und Technologie. 2010. *Nationaler Pakt für Ausbildung und Fachkräftenachwuchs in Deutschland 2010—2014.* Berlin: BMWi.

Diamond, P. A., Massachusetts Institute of Technology, Cambridge, MA, USA, Dale T. Mortensen, Northwestern University, Evanston, IL, USA, Aarhus University, Denmark, and Christopher A. Pissarides, London School of Economics and Political Science, UK. 2011. *The Prize in Economic Sciences 2010 - Press Release. http://nobelprize.org/nobel_prizes/economics/laureates/2010/press.html*

Directorate-General for Employment, Social Affairs and Equal Opportunities, European Commission, The Institute of Population and Labor Economics, and Chinese Academy of Social Sciences. 2010. *New Skills for New Jobs: China and the EU. Shared Labour Market Experiences to Inform the Harmonious and Sustainable Society of the Future*. Brussels: European Commission.

Docquier, F. 2006. "Brain Drain and Inequality Across Nation", in IZA Discussion Paper No. 2440.

European Commission. 2006. *Modernising Labour Law to Meet the Challenges of the 21st Century, COM(2006) 708 final.* Brussels: European Commission.

—. 2007. *Outcome of the Public Consultation on the Commission's Green Paper "Modernising Labour Law to Meet the Challenges of the 21st Century", SEC(2007) 1373.* Brussels: European Commission.

—. 2011. "Tackling Early School Leaving: A Key Contribution to the Europe 2020 Agenda, COM(2011) 18", Communication From The Commission To The European Parliament, The Council, The European Economic And Social Committee And The Committee Of The Regions, Brussels: European Commission.

Grierson, J. 2002. *Enterprise-based Training in Africa: Case Studies from Kenya and Zambia*. Turin: ILO/ITC.

Heckman, J. J., and L. Lochner. 2000. "Rethinking Education and Training Policy: Understanding the Sources of Skill Formation in a Modern Economy", in *Securing the Future: Investing in Children from Birth to Adulthood*, eds. Danziger, S., and J. Waldforgel, New York: Russell Sage Foundation.

Hisashi, T-O., K. Koichiro, I. Koh, H. Park, K. Reiko, S. Tomoki. 2010. "The Labour Issue of Youth: Looking Back over 20 Years", *The Japanese Journal of Labour Studies,* No. 602.

International Labour Organization. 1999. *Convention C182, Concerning the Prohibition and Immediate Action for the Elimination of the Worst Forms of Child Labour.* Geneva: ILO.

—. 2005b. *Resolution on Decent Work for Youth in Africa and the ILO Response, Document GB289/5.* Geneva: ILO.

—. 2005c. *Resolution Concerning Youth Employment.* Geneva: ILO.

—. 2007a. "Informe y conclusiones de la undécesima Reuniòn Régional Africana", Addis Ababa, Ethiopia. April 24-28, 2007.

—. 2007b. "The Decent Work Agenda in Africa: 2007–2015", Report of the Director-General to the Eleventh African Regional Meeting, Addis Ababa, Ethiopia, April 2007.

—. 2010b. *Global Employment Trends for Youth 2010*. Geneva: ILO.

Kalleberg, A. L. 2000. "Non-standard Employment Relations: Part-Time, Temporary and Contract Work", *Annual Review of Sociology* 26.

Kaufman, B. 2007. *The Core Principle and Fundamental Theorem of Industrial Relations*. Working Paper 07-01, Department of Economics, W.T. Beebe Institute of Personnel and Employment Relations. Georgia State University.

Lansky, M. 1997 "Child Labour: How the Challenge is Being met", *International Labour Review* 136 No. 2.

Malmberg-Heimonen, I., and I. Jukunen. 2006. "Out of Unemployment? A Comparative Analysis of the Risk and Opportunities Longer-term Unemployed Immigrant Youth Face when Entering the labour Market", *Journal of Youth Studies* 9, No. 5, pp. 575-592.

Marchand, O. 1999. "Youth Unemployment in OECD Countries: How Can the Disparities Be Explained?", in *OECD Preparing Youth for the 21st Century—The Transition from Education to the Labour Market,* Paris: OECD Publishing.

OECD. 1994. *The OECD Job Study: Evidence and Explanations,* Paris: OECD.

—. 1997. *Implementing the OECD Jobs Strategy: Lessons from Member Countries*. Paris: OECD.
—. 1999a. *Employment Outlook,* Paris: OECD.
—. 1999b. *Implementing the OECD Job Strategy: Assessing Performance and Policy*. Paris: OECD.
—. 2007. *International Migration Outlook*. Paris: OECD.
—. 2010b. *Economic Survey of China: a Labour Market in Transition*. Paris: OECD.
Ratha, D., and X. Zhimei. 2008. *Migration and Remittances Fact book 2008*. Migration and Remittances Team, Development Prospects Group, The World Bank.
Rees, A. 1996. "An Essay on Youth Joblessness", *Journal of Economic Literature* 24, No. 2: 613-28.
Regini, M., and G. Esping-Andersen. "The Effects of Labour Market De-regulation on Unemployment. A Critical Review of the Different Research Approaches and of Empirical Evidence", Paper presented to the European Commission, Brussels, Belgium, 1998.
Ryan, P. 2001. "The School-to-Work Transition: a Cross-national Perspective", *Journal of Economic Literature* 39, No. 1, pp. 34-92. Stampini, M., and A. Verdier-Chouchane. 2011. "Labour Market Dynamics in Tunisia: the Issue of Youth Unemployment", Working Paper Series n. 123, African Development Bank, Tunisia.
United Nations. 2007. *World Youth Report 2007*. New York: Department of Economic and Social Affairs, United Nations
Webb, B., and S. Webb. 1897 and 1926. *Industrial Democracy*. London: Longmans.
Weiss, M. "Realising Decent Work in Africa", Keynote Speech at the Opening Ceremony of the Fifth African Regional Congress of the IIRA in Cape Town, South Africa, 26 March 2008.
Yusuf, S., and K. Nabeshima, eds. 2007. *How Universities Promote Economic Growth*. Washington: The World Bank.

CHAPTER SEVEN

HIGHER-LEVEL APPRENTICESHIP IN ITALY

Introduction

Since the term "higher-level apprenticeship" is the translation into English of an Italian expression describing a new policy and type of contract, first of all a general definition of the concept of apprenticeship seems useful. The Cedefop publication "Terminology of vocational training policy"[1] defines apprenticeships as "systematic, long-term training alternating periods in a school or training centre and at the workplace; the apprentice is contractually linked to the employer and receives remuneration (wage or allowance)".[2] The key feature that distinguishes apprenticeships from other form of alternate training is the fact that the apprentice is an employee, and is paid by the employer.

1. Description of the Main Elements of the Policy

1.1. Background

Apprenticeship contracts and in particular apprenticeship contracts leading to a diploma (high school certificate), university degree or master's degree,[3] known as higher-level apprenticeships, are intended to address the persistent weakness of young people in the Italian labour market.[4]

The unemployment rate for young people (population aged up to 25 years) in 2002, before the introduction of the policy shows that Italy was

---

[1] See Tissot, P. 2004. *Terminology of Vocational Training Policy*, Cedefop.

[2] Ibid., p. 25.

[3] See the annex for the description of the organisation of the education and vocational training system in Italy.

[4] See Tiraboschi, M. 2006. "Young People and Employment in Italy: The (Difficult) Transition from Education and Training to the Labour Market", *International Journal of Comparative Labour Law and Industrial Relations* 22, No. 1.

one of the countries with the worst performance in the European Union, with a rate (23.1 per cent) nearly nine points higher than the average for the EU15 (14.6 per cent). Only Greece and Spain had a weaker performance.

Compared with the total unemployment rate in Italy in 2002 (8.6 per cent, only one percentage point higher than the EU15 rate at 7.6 per cent),[5] the youth unemployment rate was 14.5 points higher. These figures show that the high youth unemployment level was not related to a difficult situation of the labour market and a low labour demand, but to a specific issue of this cohort.

Moreover, young people seem to be more affected by the rigidity of internal labour market as an obstacle to the access to the labour market.[6]

There was an evident need to tackle this problem, that seems to be related to different questions. On the one hand it results from the inefficiency of the education system, reflected in the unusually high average age at graduation, that in 2002 was 28 years,[7] while according to EU regulations concerning state aid and employment incentives, young people are classified as such only up to the age of 25.[8] On the other hand, it is due to the difficult transition from school, vocational training and higher education to work, that to some extent confirms the inefficiency of the Italian education and training system.

---

[5] See Eurostat—Labour Force Survey.

[6] See Freeman, R. B., and D. A. Wise, eds. 1992. *The Youth Labour Market Problem: Its Nature, Causes and Consequences*. Chicago: University of Chicago/NBER, and more recently, van der Velden, R. K. A, and M. H. J. Wolbers. 2003. "The integration of young people into the labour market: the role of training systems and labour market regulation", *Transitions from Education to Work in Europe—The Integration of Youth into EU Labour Markets*, eds. Müller, W. and M. Gangl (Oxford: Oxford University Press).

[7] See Almalaurea, *Condizione Occupazionale dei Laureati—Indagine 2003*. http://www.almalaurea.it/.

[8] This paradox is pointed out by O'Higgins, N. *The Challenges of Youth Unemployment,* cit. § 1.1.1., where he notes that, according to the definition used at a comparative level, the term "young people" is used to refer to those from 15 to 24 years of age, whereas in Italy the concept of "young person" has been extended, also for the purposes of the application of certain legal provisions, to include those up to the age of 32.

Table 2-1. Unemployment Rate of Population up to the Age of 25

Country	2002	2003	2004	2005	2006	2007
EU (27 countries)	17.9	18.0	18.4	18.3	17.1	15.3
EU (25 countries)	17.4	17.8	18.2	18.2	16.9	15.1
EU (15 countries)	**14.6**	**15.3**	**15.9**	**16.3**	**15.7**	**14.7**
Belgium	17.7	21.8	21.2	21.5	20.5	18.8
Bulgaria	37.0	28.2	25.8	22.3	19.5	15.1
Czech Republic	16.9	18.6	21.0	19.2	17.5	10.7
Denmark	7.4	9.2	8.2	8.6	7.7	7.9
Germany	9.1	9.8	11.9	14.2	12.8	11.1
Estonia	17.6	20.6	21.7	15.9	12.0	10.0
Ireland	8.5	9.1	8.9	8.6	8.7	9.1
Greece	26.8	26.8	26.9	26.0	25.2	22.9
Spain	24.2	24.6	23.9	19.7	17.9	18.2
France	19.3	19.1	20.4	21.0	22.1	19.4
Italy	**23.1**	**23.7**	**23.5**	**24.0**	**21.6**	**20.3**
Cyprus	8.1	8.9	10.5	13.0	10.5	10.0
Latvia	22.0	18.0	18.1	13.6	12.2	10.7
Lithuania	22.5	25.1	22.7	15.7	9.8	8.2
Luxembourg	7.0	11.2	16.4	14.3	15.8	15.3
Hungary	12.7	13.4	15.5	19.4	19.1	18.0
Malta	17.1	17.2	16.8	16.2	16.5	13.8
Netherlands	5.0	6.3	8.0	8.2	6.6	5.9
Austria	6.7	8.1	9.4	10.3	9.1	8.7
Poland	42.5	41.9	39.6	36.9	29.8	21.7
Portugal	11.6	14.5	15.3	16.1	16.3	16.6
Romania	23.2	19.6	21.9	20.2	21.4	20.1
Slovenia	16.5	17.3	16.1	15.9	13.9	10.1
Slovakia	37.7	33.4	33.1	30.1	26.6	20.3
Finland	21.0	21.8	20.7	20.1	18.7	16.5
Sweden	11.9	13.4	16.3	21.7	21.5	19.1
United Kingdom	12.0	12.2	12.1	12.8	14.0	14.3
Croatia	35.4	35.8	33.2	32.3	28.9	24.0
Turkey	:	:	:	:	16.0	16.8
Norway	11.1	11.6	11.4	11.6	8.8	7.3
United States	12.0	12.4	11.8	11.3	10.5	10.5
Japan	9.9	10.1	9.5	8.7	8.0	7.7

Source: Eurostat—Labour Force Survey

Another reason for the weakness of young people in the labour market is the mismatch between the skills, competences and knowledge provided by the education system and the vocational requirements of employers, who frequently complain that graduates lack suitable training and skills. Many university degree courses appear to be too general and do not give a specific knowledge providing access to a profession or responding to business needs. The European Council and the Commission[9] underline the fact that in general the Italian higher education system runs programmes that tend not to reflect the needs of enterprises but above all the interests of the faculty members. As a result, many graduates work in a sector or context different from that of their degree, and this highlights the systematic lack of appropriate training and career guidance. There is a lack of employment services supporting young people and graduates seeking access to the labour market. In the debate on youth unemployment and precarious employment, there is clearly a need to consider the question of the school-to-work transition, finding ways to link teaching and training with work.

Furthermore, the level of youth unemployment seems to be affected also by the tendency of enterprises to hire adults rather than young people, since adults are more qualified and experienced, and have a higher level of productivity,[10] while by definition young people need training that means additional costs. This shows the reluctance of companies to invest in vocational training and in human capital.

The difficult school-to-work transition and therefore the high average age at the entry into the labour market also has an impact on the perception of the precarious nature of employment. Whereas young people (up to the age of 25 years) tend not to be acutely aware of a lack of stability in employment, in the same conditions people over the age of 25 are likely to feel more precarious, due the need for greater stability and security relating to their private lives.

1.2. The Goals and Target Groups of the Policy

Higher-level apprenticeships are intended to some extent to address the issues described above, with young people as the target group. However, considering the difficulties for young people in entering the labour market, the policy is applied with reference to young people between the ages of

---

[9] European Commission. 2005. *Joint Employment Report 2004/2005*. COM(2005)13. Brussels: European Commission.

[10] See Caroleo F. E., and F. Pastore. 2006. "La disoccupazione giovanile in Italia", *Scuola, Università, Mercato del lavoro dopo la riforma Biagi*, eds. Gelmini, P., and M. Tiraboschi (Giuffrè, Milano) p. 50.

18 and 29, even though by EU standards those over the age of 25 no longer count as young people.

Designed as a market-oriented training instrument, the main goals of this policy are: earlier access by young people to the labour market, an enhancement of youth employability thanks to the connection between education and employment and, in particular, to the link between educational institutions and enterprises, an improvement of the school-to-work transition and, ultimately, the reduction of youth unemployment and an increase in youth employment.

With regard to the aim of reducing the age of access to the labour market, the reform of the Italian university system is essential.[11] With higher-level apprenticeships, the chance for apprentices to take a diploma, first-level degree or postgraduate degree while working means that they are already employed and active in the labour market.

It is evident that this means of access to the labour market represents a better form of transition from full-time education to employment.

The enhancement of youth employability is linked with the improvement of the skills and knowledge provided by courses. This objective is facilitated by the closer relationship between the educational institution and the working environment, in order for training to achieve the desired aim of providing individuals with the skills required by employers.

In relation to the European Employment Guidelines, it is important to highlight the aim at addressing the priority of improving employability in order to tackle youth unemployment and to prevent long-term unemployment and in particular to "equip young people with the basic skills relevant to the labour market and needed to participate in lifelong learning".[12]

1.3. The Legal and Financial Provisions to Implement the Policy

Under the terms of the apprenticeship contract, the apprentice has the duty to perform his/her work, while the employer is under a dual obligation. On one hand, he/she has to pay the employee (the apprenticeship) and on the other hand to provide training on the basis of

[11] The Italian university system was based on four-year degree programmes. The recent reform introduced a first-level degree courses with a duration of three years and second-level degree courses with a duration of two years. This new system has partly succeeded in reducing the age at graduation.

[12] See *Council Decision of 18 February 2002 on Guidelines for Member States' Employment Policies for the year 2002*, (2002/177/EC), I.

specific training programmes for the purposes of acquiring vocational skills.

With reference to the apprenticeship contract, mention should be made of the fact that the State has exclusive legislative competence in relation to employment contracts, while the Regions have exclusive legislative competence in relation to vocational training.

Higher-level apprenticeships were introduced into the Italian system by Article 50, Legislative Decree No. 276, 23 September 2003. They provide for an apprenticeship contract leading to a diploma, a university or higher education qualification. This means that apprentices obtain the qualification specified in their individual training plan not only by means of off-the-job training (courses and lectures at a school, University or other higher education institution) and individual study, with a periodic appraisal, but also by means of on-the-job training and by the work itself.

It is important to underline the fact that the certificate awarded by the educational institution within an apprenticeship programme has the same form and value as a certificate awarded on completion of a standard school, university or higher education course.

Recently, Article 50, Legislative Decree No. 276, 23 September 2003 was amended by Article 23, paragraph 3, Law No. 133, 6 August 2008, that makes provision for apprenticeship contracts to be utilised also for doctoral research students.

With regard to the field of application of Article 50, this kind of apprenticeship contract can be offered to any young person between the ages of 18 and 29 (and 364 days) in all sectors of production.

Apprenticeships must be based on a written agreement, containing a description of the type of work to be carried out by the apprentice; the individual training plan (*Piano formativo individuale*); and the qualification (diploma, first degree or higher degree qualification) to be awarded at the end of the apprenticeship. Moreover, it is forbidden to pay apprentices piecework and a dismissal before the end of the apprenticeship may be legitimately carried out only when there is a just cause or a just motive of a subjective or objective kind. At the end of the apprenticeship, the contract is turned into an open-ended employment contract except in the case of a dismissal pursuant to Article 2118, Civil Code.

The duration of apprenticeship contracts (related to the duration of education/training programmes) and the regulation of training programmes is delegated to the Regions. These matters are governed by agreements between the Region and trade unions, business organisations, universities and other higher education institutions.

The Region has the power to adopt legal provisions, but an agreement at territorial level is sufficient to regulate higher-level apprenticeships. However, Article 23, paragraph 4, Law No. 133, 6 August 2008, amended Article 50, paragraph 3, Legislative Decree No. 276, 23 September 2003, providing that in the absence of Regional regulation (even an agreement), higher-level apprenticeship programmes may be set up by agreement between employers and universities and other higher education institutions.

Article 53, Legislative Decree No. 276, 23 September 2003 regulates the job classification of apprentices on the basis of the employment grade laid down in the collective agreement. At the time of hiring, the employment grade of the apprentice can be two levels below the employment grade he/she will be assigned to at the end of the apprenticeship.

In cases in which the employer fails to implement the individual training plan, the company has to pay as a sanction the difference between the social security contributions paid and the contributions due corresponding to the remuneration of an employee in the higher employment grade that the apprentice would have been assigned to at the end of the apprenticeship, increased by 100%.

With reference to legal provisions at regional level, the tables below (Table 2-2 and Table 2-3) provide an overview of the state of the regulation and the implementation of higher-level apprenticeships.

Table 2-2. State of the Regulation and the Implementation of the Policy at Regional Level

State of the regulation and the implementation of the policy at regional level	Regions
Higher-level apprenticeships already provided prior to Legislative Decree No. 276, 23 September 2003	Trento, Bolzano (autonomous provinces)
Experimental implementation of higher-level apprenticeships	Lombardy, Piedmont, Veneto, Friuli Venezia Giulia, Liguria, Emilia Romagna, Tuscany, Umbria, Lazio
Legal regulation at regional level, but no experimental programmes	Apulia, Molise, Basilicata, Abruzzo

Lack of legal regulation and lack of experimental programmes	Marche, Calabria, Sicily, Sardinia

Table 2-3 Regional Regulations and Agreements

Regions	Regional regulations
Veneto	Regional Council Resolution No. 262/ 2004: Provisions for the implementation of higher-level apprenticeships also with regional funding Agreement between Region and social parties, 22.11.2004: The duration of the higher-level apprenticeship contract is linked to the duration of the higher-level apprenticeship training programme.
Piedmont	Regional Law No. 2/2007: General provisions for the implementation of higher-level apprenticeships. Regional Council Resolution No. 44-14478/2004: Specific provisions for the implementation of higher-level apprenticeships, with reference to first degree and master's degree courses
Trento (autonomous province)	Regional Law No. 6/2006: Provisions for aspects related to training. Higher-level apprenticeships in operation before Legislative Decree No. 276/2003
Bolzano (autonomous province)	Agreement between Region and social parties, 12.01.2007: Provision for a duration of the apprenticeship contract of three years
Friuli Venezia Giulia	Agreement between Region, Universities and social parties, 05.04.2006: Provisions for: the duration of higher-level apprenticeship training programme, 300/400 hours of off-the-job (school or higher education courses), company tutor training
Lombardy	Agreement between Region and social parties, 20.12.2005: Provision for a duration of higher-level apprenticeship contracts of 30 months

Tuscany	Regional Council Resolution No. 1217/2004: Approval of the agreement on experimental programmes of higher-level apprenticeships Regional Decree 538/2006: Provisions on experimental programmes
Liguria	Regional Council Resolution No. 834/2004: Approval of the agreement between the Region and the social partners on higher-level apprenticeships
Emilia Romagna	Regional Law No. 17/2005: General provisions for the implementation of higher-level apprenticeships Agreement between the Region and the social partners, 11.05.2005: Provision for the higher-level apprenticeship programmes
Marche	*No provisions for higher-level apprenticeships*
Lazio	Regional Law No. 9/2006: Provisions for aspects relating to training
Umbria	Regional Law No. 18/2007: General provisions for the implementation of higher-level apprenticeships
Basilicata	Regional Law No. 28/2006: Provisions for aspects relating to training
Apulia	*No provisions for higher-level apprenticeships*
Abruzzo	*No legal provisions for higher-level apprenticeships*
Molise	Regional Law No. 3/2008: General provisions for higher-level apprenticeships
Campania	*No provisions for higher-level apprenticeships*
Calabria	*No provisions for higher-level apprenticeships*
Sicily	*No provisions for higher-level apprenticeships*
Sardinia	*No provisions for higher-level apprenticeships*

Source: Own Elaboration

Concerning the financial provisions relating to this policy, in general economic incentives for apprenticeship contracts are applied. In particular (pursuant to Law No. 296/2007), the contributions for apprenticeship contracts amount to 10% of gross remuneration (for companies with up to nine apprentices, 8.5% in the first year, 7% in the second year and 10% in further years).

1.4. Institutional Arrangements and Procedures of Implementation

In order to set up higher-level apprenticeship schemes, as noted above, it is sufficient to conclude an agreement at territorial level between the Region, trade unions, business organisations and school, universities or other higher education institutions, establishing the regulation and the duration of the training programmes.

In addition to this territorial agreement, the implementation of higher-level apprenticeship programmes requires an agreement between the school, the university or other higher education institutions and the employer intending to hire the apprentices.

With reference to the professional profile required by the company, the educational institution and the employer jointly define the vocational skills to be acquired by the apprentices at the end of the apprenticeship. Accordingly, the educational institution, with the help of the employer, has the task of designing a training programme responding to the needs of the company. Moreover, it is responsible for off-the-job training, for evaluating and certifying off-the-job (school, university and higher education institutions courses and lectures) and on-the-job training, and monitoring the acquisition of skills.

Concerning the selection of young people to enter the apprenticeship programme, it may be carried out in different ways and depends on the arrangement between the educational institution and the enterprise. The educational institutions can collect CVs and screen the applicants, and then let the enterprise choose the young people to be hired as apprentices. They can decide to carry out the selection and the interviews jointly. In other cases, the enterprise can organise the entire selection. Once the candidates have been selected, they are hired by the enterprise as apprentices.

The educational institution and the employer, and in particular the educational tutor and the company tutor, draft the individual training plan on the basis of a skills audit of the apprentice and the vocational skills required. The tutors are responsible for the achievement of the training objectives.

In general, the regional agreements or regulations specify the minimum duration of the contract and of the training programme in terms of the number of training hours. These include the allocation of time for: courses and lectures provided by the educational institution, formal training provided by the employer (including face-to-face teaching), individual study (including the time required for the drafting of the final research project, if required) and work.

In order to implement the experimental programmes, the Ministry of Labour and the Regions intending to set up higher-level apprenticeship programmes have concluded a number of agreements known as *Protocolli di intesa*. These agreements regulate not only the funding but also the way they are to be run. Provision is made to set up specific courses for each group of apprentices, or to enrol individual apprentices on existing courses.

Specific higher-level apprenticeship courses can be set up with an individual company (with all the apprentices taking part employed by the same company) or with different companies in the same sector for training apprentices who need to acquire the same vocational skills. However, this type of course raises issues relating to the fact that the apprentices attend courses and lectures together, while companies in the same sector are in general competitors and are therefore concerned about the possible exchange of confidential information.

With regard to funding, national funds (based to a significant extent on ESF funds) were allocated by the Ministry to the Regions for the experimental programmes. The Regions issued a tender in order to select the higher-level apprenticeship programmes to be funded. In some cases, the employers co-financed the programmes.

Therefore, the cost of the experimental programmes was covered by State funding and to some extent by employer co-funding. In any case, the employer pays the labour cost (remuneration and other costs) for the apprentices.

2. The Results So Far

2.1. The Quantitative Results of the Policy So Far, in Relation to the Baseline Situation and to the Goals and Targets

According to Ministry of Labour figures, nine Regions (Piemonte, Lombardia, Veneto, Friuli Venezia Giulia, Liguria, Emilia Romagna,

Toscana, Umbria, Lazio) and the autonomous Province of Bolzano have launched experimental programmes[13].

All these higher-level apprenticeships programmes lead to a first degree or postgraduate qualification, and no programmes have been set up leading to a diploma.

The total number of projects activated amounts to 69, involving 1,005 apprentices.

Table 2-4. Overview of the Academic Programmes Relating to the Experimentation on Higher-level Apprenticeships

Region	No. of projects set up	No. of activity	Participants
Piedmont	17	16 Master's degrees 1 Enrolment on a second-level University degree course	211
Lombardy	21	7 Enrolment on IFTS programme in a technical high school 2 Vocational Training Course for high-school graduates 12 Master's degrees	377
Province of Bolzano	3	2 First-level University degree courses (three year degree course)	68
Veneto	1	4 Master's degrees	49
Friuli Venezia Giulia	1	1 Master's degree	14
Liguria	7	6 Master's degrees 1 Enrolment on a IFTS programme	80

[13] The autonomous Province of Trento set up first-level degree programmes before the experimentation introduced by agreement between the Ministry of Labour and Regions. These programmes were funded entirely by the Province.

Emilia Romagna	5	4 Master's degrees Enrolment on another Master's programme	70
Tuscany	3	Enrolment on a Master's degree or a first-level degree course	26
Umbria	1	Enrolment on a Master's degree	5
Lazio	10	6 Master's degrees	105
Total	**69**		**1,005**

Source: Ministry of Labour and the Regions. Data elaborated by Isfol

The experimental programmes consist of 49 Master's degree programmes, seven IFTS[14] programmes, two higher education courses for high-school graduates, two first-level degree courses (three-year degree programme) and the individual enrolment of apprentices on existing first-level degree, second-level degree or, Master's degree courses. With reference to the participants (see Table 2-5), the largest group of apprentices on the experimental programme is to be found in Lombardia, accounting for 37.4 per cent of the total, while the participants in the experimental programmes in Piemonte amount to 21.0 per cent. As a result, more than half the total (58.4 per cent) took part in apprenticeship programmes in these two Regions.

Table 2-5. Number of Participants on Experimental Apprenticeships by Region

Regions	Participants	Percentage
Lombardy	377	37.4
Piedmont	211	21.0

[14] IFTS (*Istruzione e Formazione Tecnica Superiore*) courses are designed for young undergraduates and unemployed adults. The aim is to enable them to acquire vocational skills and abilities thanks to practical work experience programmes. IFTS courses may last from two to four semesters, from a minimum of 1200 hours to a maximum of 2440 hours. They can be adapted to the specific requirements of the apprentice.

Lazio	105	10.4
Liguria	80	8.0
Emilia Romagna	70	7.0
Province of Bolzano	68	6.8
Veneto	49	4.9
Tuscany	26	2.6
Friuli Venezia Giulia	14	1.4
Umbria	5	0.5
Total	**1,005**	**100.0**

Source: The Regions. Data elaborated by Isfol

In comparing these figures with those concerning the residency of the apprentices (see Table 2-6), a certain amount of mobility is to be seen, since all the Italian regions are represented, while only the regions of central and northern Italy have set up apprenticeship programmes. Mobility from the south to the north has long been a trend in Italy both for educational and employment purposes.

Table 2-6. Region of Residency of Apprentices Taking Part in the Experimentation

Residency	No. of Apprentices	Residency	Apprentices
Piedmont	203	Marche	2
Val d'Aosta	1	Lazio	110
Lombardy	261	Abruzzo	3
Province of Bolzano	55	Molise	2
Province of Trento	5	Campania	31
Veneto	66	Apulia	27
Friuli Venezia Giulia	10	Basilicata	6

Liguria	52	Calabria	8
Emilia Romagna	61	Sicily	21
Tuscany	33	Sardinia	8
Umbria	9		

Not specified: 31
Source: The Regions. Data elaborated by Isfol (regions listed in geographical order)

Most of the apprentices (83.6 per cent) took part in first-level Master's (67.4 per cent) or second-level Master's degree programmes (16.2 per cent), while only 9.0 per cent of the apprentices were enrolled on first-level degree programmes, and 7.5 per cent on IFTS work placement schemes.

Table 2-7. Distribution of Apprentices by Type of Programme

Degree	Participants	Percentage
First-level Master's degree	677	67.4
Second-level Master's degree	163	16.2
University Degree	90	9.0
IFTS	75	7.5
Total	**1,005**	**100.0**

Source: The Regions. Data elaborated by Isfol

This distribution of apprentices among the different types of courses shows that most participants in the experimental programmes took Master's courses (49). Universities and employers seem to prefer programmes of this type, since they are shorter than first-degree courses (in general two years instead of three) and they are easier to set up. Another reason for this choice seems to be related to the vocational skills required. Employers prefer courses providing specific vocational knowledge, rather than a basic academic education, and in general Master's degree courses are more suited to achieving this objective.

In relation to the choice of either specific courses for groups of apprentices, or individual enrolment of apprentices on existing academic courses, the experimental programmes under examination consist mainly of courses specifically organised for groups of apprentices. In this way, actually, the educational institution and the employer can decide together when to hold lectures and examinations at the university, in such a way as to respond to the needs of the company.

On the other hand, individual enrolment of the apprentice on existing academic courses appears more appropriate when a specific vocational profile is required by a limited number of companies or just by one company and for this reason it is not possible to set up a specific higher-level apprenticeship programme. Only a small number of apprentices were enrolled on existing academic courses.

As regards the distribution of apprentices by gender, males outnumbered females (see Table 2-8 below).

Table 2-8. Distribution of Apprentices by Gender and Type of Higher Education Programme

Degree	**M**	**F**	**Total**
IFTS	57.3	42.7	100.0
First-level degree	87.8	12.2	100.0
First-level Master's degree	62.9	37.1	100.0
Second-level Master's degree	72.4	27.6	100.0
Total	**66.3**	**33.7**	100.0

Source: The Regions. Data elaborated by Isfol

The preponderance of young men taking part in the experimental programmes can be explained by the distribution of academic subjects among the participants. Table 2-9 shows that the largest group of apprentices consists of engineering graduates and in general these degree courses are attended mainly by young men.[15]

[15] Also some first-level degree courses set up in the engineering subject area: for this reason male participants outnumber females.

Table 2-9. Distribution of the Apprentices Participating in Master's Degree Courses in Terms of their First Degree

Subject	No. Apprentices	Percentage	First-level Master	Second-level Master
Agriculture	4	0.7%	0.7%	0.6%
Architecture	27	4.5%	6.4%	0.6%
Chemistry/ Pharmacy	8	1.3%	1.2%	1.8%
Economics/Statistical Sciences	80	13.5%	13.9%	11.7%
Biology	4	0.7%	0.7%	0.6%
Law	10	1.7%	2.2%	0.6%
Engineering	343	57.7%	52.2%	73.6%
Education Sciences	15	2.5%	3.7%	0.0%
Humanities	21	3.5%	5.0%	0.6%
Modern Languages	7	1.2%	1.5%	0.6%
Political Sciences	41	6.9%	8.2%	3.1%
Psychology	4	0.7%	1.0%	0.0%
Mathematics	30	5.1%	3.2%	6.1%
Total	**594**	**100.0%**	**100.0%**	**100.0%**

Not specified: 31
Source: The Regions. Data elaborated by Isfol

As to the distribution of the apprentices by age at the beginning of the programme, the 26 years age class was predominant (19.9 per cent), followed by the 27 and 28 years age class (respectively 14.4 and 14.1 per cent). This outcome reflects the prevalence of master's degree courses in the experimental higher-level apprenticeships. The younger age classes

(19, 20, 21 years) were more strongly represented on the first-degree courses.

Table 2-10. Distribution of the Participants by Age at the Beginning of the Apprenticeship Programme and Standard Deviation in Relation to the Total Figure of the Participants and the Different Type of Training Programme

Age (years)	Total	IFTS	Degree	First-level Master's	Second-level Master's
19	4.8%	10.7%	33.3%	1.5%	-
20	3.2%	10.7%	18.9%	1.1%	-
21	2.3%	9.3%	14.4%	0.5%	-
22	1.8%	5.3%	11.1%	0.6%	-
23	4.1%	12.0%	6.7%	3.9%	-
24	8.1%	9.3%	5.6%	8.9%	6.1%
25	12.8%	5.3%	4.4%	13.8%	16.6%
26	**19.9%**	14.7%	3.3%	23.1%	18.4%
27	14.4%	5.3%	-	15.5%	22.1%
28	14.1%	6.7%	2.2%	15.9%	16.6%
29	9.9%	6.7%	-	10.7%	13.5%
30	4.5%	4.0%	-	4.7%	6.7%
Total	100.0%	100.0%	100.0%	100.0%	100.0%
Average Age	25.8	23.9	21.1	26.3	26.9
Standard Deviation	2.74	3.31	2.26	2.14	1.66

Not specified: 31
Source: The Regions. Data elaborated by Isfol

These figures reflect the well-known characteristics of the Italian labour market, that is to say the high average age of entry to the regular employment market by young people: the average age of the apprentices taking part in the experimental programmes is 25.6 years old.

Even considering the average age only of the apprentices enrolled on master's courses, the largest age class is 26 years, but in order to enrol on this master's course first-level degree is sufficient, so a 22 year-old could enrol on a master's programme. Clearly, the participants are quite old in relation to the programme, and the first impression is that those who enrol on apprenticeship programmes are graduates who encounter greater difficulty in finding employment. In a small number of cases (about five per cent), the participants graduated four, five or six years before starting their apprenticeships, but for the vast majority of participants this is not the case.

Table 2-11. Years since Graduation (First-level University Degree) at the Beginning of the Experimentation for all the Apprentices and for those Enrolled on Master's Programmes

Years since graduation	**No. Apprentices**	**%**	**First-level Master**	**Second-level Master**
0	167	28.3%	25.5%	35.6%
1	**232**	39.3%	38.6%	41.1%
2	106	17.9%	20.3%	11.7%
3	54	9.1%	10.0%	6.7%
4	22	3.7%	3.3%	4.9%
5	6	1.0%	1.4%	-
6	3	0.5%	0.7%	-
7	1	0.2%	0.2%	-
Total	591	100.0 %	100.0%	100.0%
Average		1.3	1.4	1.0
Standard Deviation		1.20	1.23	1.09

Not specified: 282
Source: The Regions. Data elaborated by Isfol

The majority (67.6 per cent) of the apprentices participating in the experimental programme took their degree one year (39.3 per cent) or less (28.3 per cent) per cent) before starting the programme. It seems that the high average age of the apprentices participating in the experimental programmes does not reflect the quality of the graduates, but rather reflects the high average age at graduation of Italian students in general.

With regard to the final grades of apprentices enrolled on the master's programmes, the average is 101.6/110, suggesting a high level of educational attainment by those taking part in the programme.

Table 2-12. Final Grades of Apprentices Enrolled on Master's Programmes

Disciplines	No. Apprentices	Average final grades
Agriculture	3	103.3
Architecture	27	105.0
Chemistry/Pharmacy	8	106.0
Economics/Statistical Sciences	79	101.9
Biology	4	104.3
Law	10	96.5
Engineering	321	100.5
Education Sciences	15	103.1
Humanities	20	105.5
Modern Languages	7	106.7
Political Sciences	40	103.5
Psychology	4	97.0
Mathematics	30	103.5
Total	568	**101.6**

Not specified: 290
Source: The Regions. Data elaborated by Isfol

As for the companies involved in the experimental programmes, a prevalence of large companies might be expected. However, all company sizes are represented and they are distributed fairly evenly. Only micro companies are under-represented. This is due also to the fact that in Italy small and medium-sized enterprises predominate.

However, as expected, the majority of apprentices were employed by large companies and the number decreases for medium-sized, small and micro companies. The average number of apprentices per company also decreases from large to micro enterprises and table 2-13 shows that the average size is rather small.

These figures show that there are many companies employing just one apprentice, while on the other hand it is known that some higher-level apprenticeship programmes were set up specifically for a single company, employing all those attending the course (first degree or master's degree).

Table 2-13. Distribution of the Companies Involved in the Experimentation by Size and No. of Apprentices Employed by Each Company

Size	Enterprises	Percentage	No. Apprentices	Apprentices per enterprise
Micro	63	17.9%	83	1.3
Small	102	**29.1%**	130	1.3
Medium	88	25.1%	174	2.0
Large	98	27.9%	383	3.9
Total	**351**	**100.0%**	**770**	**2.2**

Not specified: (referring to the employees) 26
Source: The Regions. Data elaborated by Isfol

Moreover, observing the relation between company size and type of higher education programme, it is interesting to note, as expected, that the size of the companies increases as the level of the qualification increases. In other word, large companies participated most of all in second-level master's degree programmes and in first-level master's programmes, rather than in first-level degree programmes, and least of all in IFTS programmes. On the contrary, more than half the micro companies employed apprentices who attended IFTS programmes.

2.2. Other Results and Achievements of the Policy

Taking into consideration the figures for the experimental higher-level apprenticeship programmes, it is difficult to make a final assessment of the achievements of the policy. Evidence of the success of the policy in the integration of young people into the labour market is to be seen in the figures in table 14. The great majority (70.9 per cent) of the participants are still employed in the same enterprise after the conclusion of the apprenticeship; 21.2 per cent are employed in another enterprise and 4.0 per cent are self-employed. Only about 4.0 per cent are unemployed or inactive.

Table 2-14. The Condition in the Labour Market of the Participants after the Conclusion of the Apprenticeship

Condition	**No. Apprentices**	**Percentage**
Employed in the same enterprise	107	70.9%
Employed in another enterprise	32	21.2%
Self-employed	6	4.0%
Unemployed	4	2.6%
Inactive (students, housewives, other)	2	1.35
Total	**151**	**100.0%**

Base: participants after the conclusion of the apprenticeship
Source: Isfol

Although the experimental programmes appear to be successful, it must be underlined that the number of experimental programmes and the apprentices taking part were limited in relation to the overall size of Italian labour market.

However, the advantages for all parties involved in the higher-level apprenticeship programmes are clear. Apprentices have the chance to work and at the same time to continue their education with courses based on specific vocational training, with a view to acquiring particular skills and competences and, in the end, a higher-level education qualification. These higher-level apprenticeship programmes promote earlier access by young people to the labour market, in this way addressing the problem of the high age of entry to the labour market in Italy among graduates.

With these programmes, the employer has the chance to participate, together with the educational institutions, in the design of courses responding to the company's vocational requirements, and to plan training programmes enabling apprentices to acquire key skills and knowledge.

By working together with employers in planning higher-level apprenticeship programmes, school and higher educational institutions can gain a better understanding of the vocational skills, abilities and competences required by the labour market. The information acquired can enable them to update existing courses, in particular at the university level, in order to improve the education and vocational knowledge of graduates and thus facilitate their employability in the school-to-work transition.

As to the results of the policy in relation to the European Employment Guideline objectives, higher-level apprenticeships were introduced in the Italian legal system in 2003 and addressed the priority of the European Employment Guidelines for 2002 (that were in force when it was designed) of improving employability. The aim was to tackle youth unemployment and to prevent long-term unemployment and in particular to "equip young people with the basic skills relevant to the labour market and needed to participate in lifelong learning".[16]

However, higher-level apprenticeships are clearly an appropriate policy instrument to achieve the objectives of the Guidelines for the employment policies adopted in the following years. These apprenticeships are an excellent way "to build employment pathways for young people" as required by the employment guidelines for 2005-2008,[17] confirming the need to reduce youth unemployment. Higher-level apprenticeships also respond to guideline No. 23 *Expand and improve investment in human capital*, calling for "inclusive education and training policies and action to facilitate significantly access to initial vocational, secondary and higher education, including apprenticeships and entrepreneurship training" and the improvement of educational attainment levels and equipping young people with the necessary key competences, in line with the European Youth Pact.[18]

---

[16] See *Council Decision of 18 February 2002 on Guidelines for Member States' Employment Policies for the year 2002*, (2002/177/EC), I.
[17] See *Council Decision of 12 July 2005 on Guidelines for the Employment Policies of the Member States,* (2005/600/EC).
[18] See *European Youth Pact*, in *Annex 1 of Presidency Conclusions of the European Council*, Brussels, 22 and 23 March 2005, (7619/05).

Basically, these objectives are confirmed in the new Integrated Guidelines for Growth and Jobs for 2008-2010,[19] in particular guideline No. 18 *Promote a lifecycle approach to work through,* and guideline No. 23 *Expand and improve investment in human capital*. As a result, higher-level apprenticeships continue to be an effective policy instrument in order to achieve these goals.

2.3. An Assessment of the Obstacles and Constraints Encountered

Mention should be made of the fact that higher-level apprenticeships encountered several obstacles during implementation and experimentation.

First of all it is necessary to underline the lack of "cultural" preparation on the part of all parties (Regions, social partners, higher educational institution) involved, with reference to the design and implementation of the policy and the courses. As already noted, the majority of the experimental programmes were master's degree courses that are considerably easier to organise than degree courses or high school courses.

After the entry into force of Legislative Decree No. 276, 23 September 2003 regulating apprenticeship contracts leading to the award of a diploma, first degree or postgraduate qualification, the Regions had to deal with the regulation of higher-level apprenticeships on the basis of agreement with trade unions, business organisations, universities and other higher educational institutions.

However, the Regions have reacted slowly in terms of the adoption of legal provisions and the conclusion of agreement with the parties involved. This led to a delay in the experimentation of the policy.

At the time of writing, the application of this policy instrument and its regulation are incomplete and uncertain: some Regions have not adopted any provisions, or have not moved beyond the framework regulations. In some cases, the agreements with the parties involved have expired or concern only the experimentation and do not provide a stable organisation of higher-level apprenticeship programmes. This situation gives rise to uncertainty at the level of application, for companies and higher educational institutions that intend to set up new programmes outside and beyond the experimentation, funded by companies themselves.

---

[19] See *Communication from the Commission to the Spring European Council—Integrated Guidelines for Growth and Jobs (2008-2010)*, COM(2007)803, Brussels, 11 December 2007.

Fig. 2-6. Education and Vocational Training in Italy

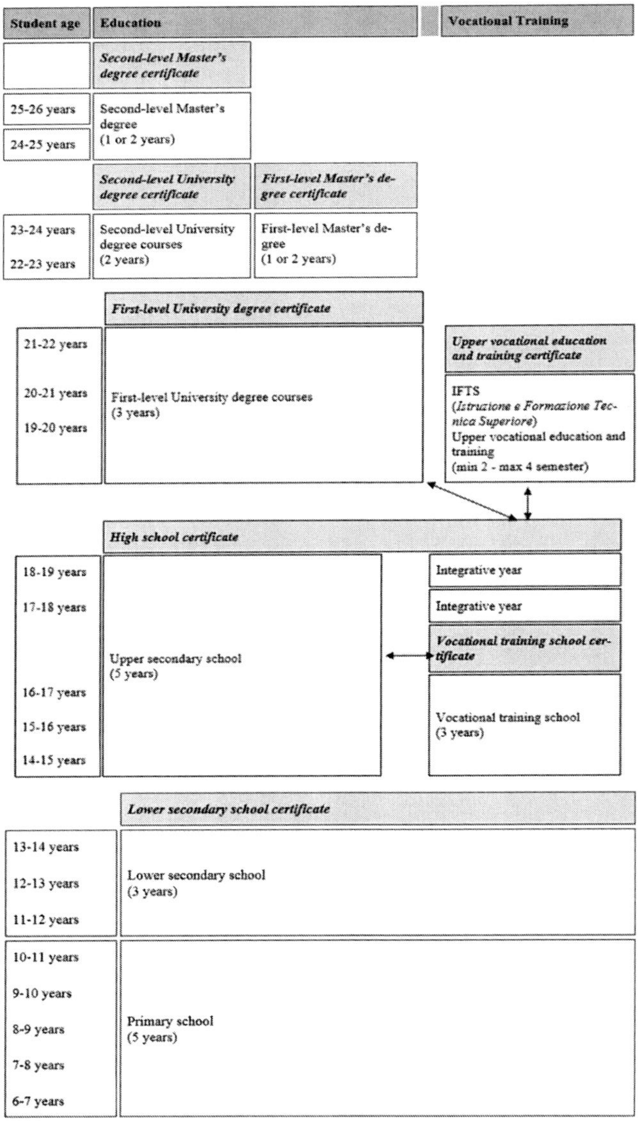

Source: Own Elaboration

The social partners have participated in the agreements at regional level in regulating the policy and the experimentation. In some Regions (Veneto, Emilia Romagna, Lombardia) they have also concluded regional collective agreements on higher-level apprenticeships, regulating for example the duration (in some cases a minimum of 24 months, in other cases a maximum of 30 months).

However, the social partners do not seem to have fully understood the potential of this policy. In some cases, they make no provision for higher-level apprenticeships in the collective agreement, preferring to use the apprenticeships for acquiring specific vocational qualifications (*apprendistato professionalizzante*).

Another constraint that should be mentioned concerns the administrative aspect of the experimental higher-level apprenticeships. It should be underlined that the task of financial monitoring and reporting was onerous in terms of time spent within the overall programme. This monitoring was necessary due to public funding, but it could be organised in a less onerous manner.

In spite of the difficulties mentioned, in some cases higher-level apprenticeships have been adopted as standard practice. In the autonomous Province of Bolzano, the first-level degree course continues beyond the experimentation thanks to an agreement at provincial level and funding by employers and the university, without any public financial support. In Emilia Romagna, a master's degree course has been set up on the basis of an agreement between the employer and the university involved and is completely financed by the company employing the apprentices.

3. The Policy Debate

In Italy there is only a limited debate on higher-level apprenticeships, although such a debate would be useful in order to better understand the functioning of the policy and its potential not only in terms of advantages for young people, but also for enterprises and the economy as a whole (in terms of improved school-to-work transition and lower youth unemployment).

However, the results of experimentation and the obstacles described above have led to an amendment to the law regulating higher-level apprenticeships. In fact, in relation to the difficulties of implementing higher-level apprenticeships due mainly to the absence of regional regulations, Article 50, paragraph 3, Legislative Decree No. 276, 23 September 2003, was recently amended by Article 23, paragraph 4, Law No. 133, 6 August 2008, providing that in the absence of Regional regulation (even a territorial agreement among the parties), higher-level apprenticeship programmes may be set up by agreement between employers and universities and other education institutions.

Thus, higher-level apprenticeships can now be set up all over Italy, either through regional regulations or by means of an agreement between an employer and an educational institution (school, university, higher educational institution), interested in setting up a higher-level apprenticeship programme.

The new regulation should therefore result in a better and more effective implementation of the policy, thanks to the essential provisions for it to operate. Nevertheless, the success of the higher-level apprenticeship in achieving its goal is linked also to the flexibility and adaptability of the regulation. These are key elements for drafting programmes and courses developing the skills and competences required by companies and leading to the award of educational qualifications.

CHAPTER EIGHT

YOUNG PEOPLE AND EMPLOYMENT IN ITALY: THE (DIFFICULT) TRANSITION FROM EDUCATION AND TRAINING TO THE LABOUR MARKET

1. The Employment of Young People in Italy: An Alternative Perspective[1]

One of the central issues that polarises the present debate on the relations between labour law and society is undoubtedly that of young people and the precarious nature of their employment. This issue is not new and is not confined to Italy. All over Europe, and beyond,[2] there is growing concern about the employment prospects (and pension provision)

---

[1] The present contribution was previously published in 2006 in *The International Journal of Comparative Labour Law and Industrial Relations* 22, No. 1, pp. 81-116.

[2] The Japanese debate is particularly interesting, as the public and the Government frame the issue essentially in terms of the "shortcomings" and "faults" of young people. This is the conceptual framework, in particular, of the Government Plan of 2003 to support the spirit of independence and responsibility of young people. See the critique by Inui, A. 2003. "Restructuring Youth: Recent Problems of Japanese Youth and its Contextual Origin", *Journal of Youth Studies,* No. 2:219-233 and the papers of 2005 on "The Transition from School to Working Life Issues", *Japan Labor Review—Special edition,* No. 3, pp. 5-91 and the bibliography therein. For the experience of other countries, see Mortimer, J.T., and R.W. Larson, eds. 2002. *The Changing Adolescent Experience.* Cambridge: Cambridge University Press; and OECD. 1999. *Preparing Youth for the 21st Century—The Transition from Education to the Labour Market.* Paris: OECD, pp. 89-100, available at *www.adapt.it*, index A-Z, under the heading *Università, scuola e mercato del lavoro.*

of the younger generation,[3] also because of the drastic and generalised worsening of the conditions of access to employment of good quality.

Over the past 25 years, taking the most evident and immediate indicators,[4] unemployment levels for young people, including long-term rates, have increased alarmingly in all the industrialised countries, with the main exceptions being the United States, Portugal and the Netherlands, as the only economies to have achieved a slight reduction in youth unemployment.[5]

---

[3] In the French literature, see for example the thought-provoking volume by Bavarez, N., J.-B. de Foucault, A. Minc, and A. Houziaux. 2005. *Le chômage, à qui la faute.* Paris: Les Editions de l'Atelier. With reference to the German and the British cases, O'Higgins, N. 1997. "The Challenges of Youth Unemployment," ILO Employment and Training Papers, No. 7, and in general Furlong, A., and F. Cartmel. 1997. *Young People and Social Change—Individualization and Risk in Late Modernity*, Buckingham: Open University Press; Hammer, T., ed. 2003. *Youth Unemployment and Social Exclusion in Europe.* Bristol: The Policy Press; McNeish, W., and P. Loncle. 2004. "State Policy and Youth Unemployment in the European Union", *Young People and Contradictions of Inclusion,* eds. Blasco, A.L., W. McNeish, and A. Walther, Bristol: Policy Press. In the United Kingdom, two White Papers have been published by the Labour government on skills and employment: see *http://www.dfes.gov.uk/publications/skillsgettingon/* and Tiraboschi, G., Paper *Skill and Education Strategy:* la riforma del sistema educativo e formativo inglese nella prospettiva degli obiettivi di Lisbona,

[4] Though this is probably no longer relevant, as pointed out by Marchand, O. "Youth Unemployment in OECD Countries: How Can the Disparities Be Explained?", *Preparing Youth for the 21st Century etc., cit.*, pp. 329-344 esp. p. 331, who argues that "the unemployment rate becomes less and less appropriate for describing their situation as the length of time they spent in school increases and the average age at which they start working increases". In similar vein see Rees, A. 1996. "An Essay on Youth Joblessness", *Journal of Economic Literature,* pp. 613-628, who suggests using the parameter of joblessness instead of unemployment—undoubtedly more reliable, though not so easy to use in comparative terms—as the main indicator of youth employment problems.

[5] In particular, with regard to the employment of young people in the United States, which cannot be examined solely in terms of the statistical parameter of the unemployment rate, see Lynch, L. M. "The Transition from Initial Education to the Labour Market: Recent Experience in the United States", OECD, *op. cit.*, 289-304 and Klerman, J. A., and L. A. Karoly. 1995. *The Transition to Stable Employment: the Experience of U.S. Youth in Their Early Labour Market Career.* University of California, Berkeley, National Center for Research on Vocational Education.

Table 2-15. Youth Unemployment (Age Range 15- 24 Years) in a Number of OECD Countries

	1977	1987	1997	2003
Australia	12.2	14.6	15.9	12.3
Austria	N.D.	N.D.	6.5	6.3
Belgium	N.D.	21.4	21.3	15.2
Canada	14.3	13.6	16.7	12.6
Denmark	N.D.	8.9	8.1	6.7
Finland	12.3	9.0	23.3	21.6
France	11.2	22.9	28.1	20.7
Germany (a)	5.5	8.5	10	7.7
Greece	N.D.	25.0	31	29.5
Ireland	13.2	24.5	16.1	6.4
Italy (b)	23.9	35.5	33.6	29.7
Japan	3.5	5.2	6.6	9.2
Netherlands	7.3	14.8	9.5	6.6
Portugal	16.3	16.1	16.7	8.6
Spain (c)	11.2	40.2	37.1	25.5
Sweden (c)	4.4	4.6	22.5	11.9
United Kingdom (c)	N.D.	15.8	13.5	11.8
United States (c)	13.6	12.2	11.3	9.3
European Union (25)				18.0

N.D. = no data available
(a) 1977, 1987 data for West Germany; 1997, 2003 data for Germany after unification
(b) age range 14-24 years
(c) age range 16-24 years
Source: Elaboration of OECD Labour Force Statistics (various years)

However, the Italian case presents certain peculiarities, to be examined in the present paper, that are evident even from a superficial comparison of the main employment indicators:[6] in particular, in terms of unemployment among young people, Italy is one of the countries with the worst

[6] For a recent benchmarking study, see European Commission. 2005. COM (2005) 13 final, *Joint Employment Report 2004/2005*. Brussels: European Commission, available at *Boll. ADAPT,* 2005, No. 5.

performances (with a rate 17 per cent higher than the average for the OECD countries), with only Poland and Slovakia reporting slightly higher unemployment rates.[7]

A further peculiarity of the Italian case is that the debate on this issue takes place amid strident or at times apocalyptic tones, as if it were a war of religion. It is significant that some commentators, starting from carefully designed econometric studies that point to the rigidity of internal labour markets as one of the main obstacles to youth employment,[8] speak of a kind of twenty-first century "class struggle" in which the interests and aspirations of young people are opposed to the rights and (at times) the privileges of older ones.[9]

The difficulties encountered by young people in gaining access to employment have recently been highlighted in Italy by the enactment of the complex reform of the labour market generally known by specialists, employment service operators and the general public as the Biagi Law.

---

[7] On the basis of the OECD data for 2003 the international figure for youth unemployment is 12.6 per cent, compared to 29.7 per cent for Italy and 35.2 per cent for Poland and Slovakia. More complete figures are available at www.nationmaster.com, under the heading: Labor—Youth Unemployment. See also Twena, M., and H. A. Aaheim. 2005. *Social Exclusion and Unemployment in the European Union—Current and Future Trends.* Oslo: Center for International Climate and Environmental Research, esp. p. 21, available at *www.adapt.it*, index A-Z, under the heading *Inclusione sociale* and, for Italy, the *Rapporto ISFOL 2004, www.adapt.it*, index A-Z, under the heading *Mercato del Lavoro.*

[8] For the strand of interpretation that sees internal labour market rigidities—and in general the protection of insiders—as one of the main obstacles to access to the labour market by young people, see Freeman, R. B., and D. A. Wise, eds. 1992. *The Youth Labour Market Problem: its Nature, Causes and Consequences.* Chicago: University of Chicago/NBER; see also Garonna, P., and P. Ryan. 1991. "The Regulation and Deregulation of Youth Economic Activity", *The Problem of Youth: the Regulation of Youth Employment and Training in Advanced Economies,* eds. Ryan, P., P. Garonna, and R.C. Edwards eds., (London: Macmillan), pp. 25-81. More recently, Nickell, S. 1997. "Unemployment and Labor Market Rigidities: Europe versus North America", *Journal of Economic Perspectives*, 11, No. 3, pp. 55-74. Van der Velden, R. K., and M. H. J. Wolbers. 2003. "The Integration of Young People into the Labour Market: The Role of Training Systems and Labour Market regulation", *Transitions from Education to Work in Europe - The Integration of Youth into EU Labour Markets,* eds. Müller, W., and M. Gangl, Oxford: Oxford University Press.

[9] See on this point Cazzola, G. 2004. *Lavoro e welfare: giovani* versus *anziani. Conflitto tra generazioni o lotta di classe del XXI secolo?.* Rubettino: Soveria Mannelli.

This reform has given rise to contrasting opinions and considerable opposition, not only at a political and trade-union level, but also in terms of cultural perspectives and values.[10] Some critics have gone so far as to characterise it as a charter for precarious employment and a lack of job security in the labour market.[11]

However, in most cases, and as the present paper will argue, the reform of the labour market has taken the blame for faults that are not of its making. Rather, it would be more accurate to speak of faults for which it could not be responsible, bearing in mind that the debate about unemployment and precarious employment among young people has been going on for over 20 years,[12] and is associated with the difficult transition from labour law for emergencies to labour law for restructuring.[13] In contrast, more than two years after the publication in the *Gazzetta Ufficiale* of Act No. 30/2003 and Legislative Decree No. 276, the implementation of the reform is still incomplete: for the moment, pending the adoption of collective bargaining provisions and regional norms,[14] only

---

[10] An initial assessment of the impact of the reform on the labour market is to be found in my paper ‘The Italian Labour Market after the Biagi Reform’, in *IJCLLIR,* No. 2/2005, where further references are to be found.

[11] See, among others, Romagnoli, U. 2004. “Radiografia di una riforma,” *LD* No. 1:19, and Mariucci, L. 2004. “I molti dubbi sulla c.d. riforma del mercato del lavoro”, *LD*, No. 1:7, in addition to the papers in Ghezzi, G., ed. 2004. *Il lavoro tra progresso e mercificazione—Commento critico al decreto legislativo n. 276/2003.* Rome: Ediesse, and in Perulli, A., ed. *Impiego flessibile e mercato del lavoro.* Turin: Giappichelli.

[12] With regard to the first measures taken to reduce youth unemployment see Garofalo, M. G., and S. Mazzamuto. 1977. “La legge sull’occupazione giovanile”, *RGL* No. 1, 480 ff. See also Olivelli, P. 1981. *Il lavoro dei giovani.* Milano: Giuffrè, and the extensive bibliography therein, and Bruno, S. 1978. *Disoccupazione giovanile e azione pubblica.* Bologna: Il Mulino. In the international literature see the pioneering study by Clark, K.B., and L.H. Summers. 1982. *The Dynamics of Youth Unemployment,* in L.H. Summers, *Understanding Unemployment.* Mit Press, pp. 48-86.

[13] On the transition from labour law for emergencies (De Luca Tamajo, R., and L. Ventura, ed. 1979. *Il diritto del lavoro dell’emergenza.* Napoli: Novene) to labour law for restructuring, see Giugni, G. 1983. “Il diritto del lavoro negli anni ’80”, paper at the AIDLASS Conference on *Prospettive del diritto del lavoro per gli anni ’80,* Bari, 23-25 April 1982. Milano: Giuffrè, 13, esp. pp. 27-30.

[14] For an overview of the many competences and functions assigned by Legislative Decree No. 276/2003 to the Regions and to collective bargaining in the implementation of the reform of the labour market, see the tables published in Tiraboschi, M., ed. 2004. *La riforma Biagi del mercato del lavoro—Il diritto transitorio e i tempi della riforma.* Milano: Giuffrè, pp. 1065-1089.

a limited number of measures laid down by the reform are actually in place.[15] This is especially the case with regard to instruments providing support and incentives for the employment of young people. In this connection, suffice it to mention that, pending the adoption of regional provisions and collective agreements, the new apprenticeship contracts have been introduced in a sporadic manner,[16] with a degree of uncertainty surrounding their application.[17] As a result, with the overall decline in work training contracts,[18] the prevailing norms are those laid down by Act No. 196/1997 and Act No. 25/1955.

Consequently, it cannot have been the recent labour market reform that gave rise to, or even aggravated, the problems of youth unemployment and precarious employment, since these problems date back to several decades, and the reform has been only partially implemented. Similar problems are to be found, to a greater or lesser extent, in all the industrialised countries, and are to be explained not so much in terms of the regulatory framework, but rather in the far-reaching changes taking place in methods of production and work organisation, with the transition from an industrial to a service economy.[19]

In the Italian debate on youth unemployment and precarious employment, little attention has been paid to the difficult transition from school, training and higher education to work.[20]

---

[15] See Ministry of Labour and Social Policy. 2005. *Rapporto di monitoraggio sulle politiche sociali*, available at *Boll. ADAPT*, 2005, No. 32.

[16] In this connection, Treu T., 2005. "L'apprendistato al bivio", *Contratti e Contrattazione Collettiva,* No. 8-9, p. 3.

[17] On the implementation of the three types of apprenticeship for which provision is made in Legislative Decree No. 276/2003, see Tiraboschi, M. 2005. "La messa a regime del nuovo apprendistato tra chiarimenti ministeriali e regolazioni regionali", *DRI,* No. 1:226-231 and for recent amendments and modifications Carollo, L. 2006. "La messa a regime del nuovo apprendistato dopo il "pacchetto competitività'", (legge 14 maggio 2005, n. 80), *DRI* No. 1.

[18] On the predicted demise of work training contracts, see Loy, G. 2005. "I nuovi apprendistati", *Organizzazione del mercato del lavoro e tipologie contrattuali—Commentario ai Decreti Legislativi n. 276/2003 e n. 251/2004,* eds. Magnani, M., and P. Varesi, Torino: Giappichelli, esp. pp. 474-478.

[19] See the recent report on the employment of young people, Honda, Y. 2005. " 'Freeters': Young Atypical Workers in Japan", *Japan Labor Review,* No. 3, esp. pp. 11-12, at http://www.jil.go.jp/english/documents/JLR07_honda.pdf, and Miyamoto, M. 2005. "Prolonged Transitional Period and Policy", *Japan Labor Review—Special edition*, No. 3, esp. pp. 73-75.

[20] Also in the international literature the concept of school-to-work transition is admittedly fairly recent and has not been adequately dealt with by labour law,

Many observers, perhaps oversimplifying, see a contrast between flexibility and precarious employment, or between modernisation and the reduction of labour to a commodity, and tend to overlook or to underestimate the fact that it is the belated entry into the labour market that is the real Italian anomaly in the comparative panorama, though this is essential for an effective analysis of the problem, as shown by the empirical and statistical data.[21]

It therefore comes as no surprise that in Italy there has been little research aimed at moving beyond the sterile debate based on a simple ideological or conceptual opposition between flexibility and precarious employment, with a view to establishing a clear connection between the quality and effectiveness of the education and training system, and the overall efficiency of the labour market.[22]

It is significant, in this connection, that the average age of access to regular employment in Italy is 25 or more. This is the age at which, at least in terms of the EU regulations concerning state aid and employment incentives,[23] young people cease to be classified as such.

---

particularly with regard to legislative measures and institutional structures for promoting youth employment. See Ryan, P. 2001. "The School-to-work Transition: a Cross-national Perspective", *Journal of Economic Literature,* pp. 34-59.

[21] See Istat. 2005. *Rapporto annuale: la situazione nel Paese nel 2004.* Rome, available at *Boll. ADAPT,* No. 20; Istat. 2005. *Università e lavoro—Statistiche per orientarsi 2004/2005.* Rome. in *www.adapt.it,* index A-Z, under *Università, Scuola, Mercato del lavoro;* Istat. 2005. *Inserimento professionale dei laureati.* Rome. in *www.adapt.it,* index A-Z, under *Università, Scuola, Mercato del lavoro;* Almalaurea. 2004. *Condizione occupazionale dei laureati, 7ª Indagine—2004,* in *www.almalaurea.it.* With regard to the work of legal scholars, for an overall assessment, see Cazzola, G. 2005. "Il *placement* dei neo-laureati secondo le più importanti indagini delle forze di lavoro", *Boll. ADAPT,* No. 25, and Accornero, A. 2005. "Valorizzare la qualità del capitale umano per la competitività del Paese", paper at the conference *Le imprese italiane e il mercato del lavoro* organised by the Aspen Institute in Rome on 9 June.

[22] Among the few papers on this issue see Caroleo, F. E., and F. Pastore. 2005. "La disoccupazione giovanile in Italia. La riforma dei sistemi di istruzione e di formazione professionale come alternativa della flessibilità numerica per accrescere l'occupabilità", *Economia e Lavoro,* No. 1, also available at *www.adapt.it,* index A-Z, under *Università, scuola e mercato del lavoro.* By the same authors, in a comparative perspective, see "Youth Participation in the Labour Market in Germany, Spain and Sweden", ed. Hammer, T. *op. cit.,* pp. 115-141.

[23] See for this definition Article 1, Legislative Decree No. 181/2000, as amended by Article 1, Legislative Decree No. 297/2002.

Work experience schemes, temporary employment, and training programmes, all of which are widespread in other countries and acceptable (and also desirable) at a young age, therefore become, or risk becoming, synonymous with precarious employment and social exclusion if they are the only option for those entering the labour market for the first time as adults: that is to say, for individuals who in most cases feel the need for stability and security in material terms as well as in their private lives.

On closer examination, the belated completion of educational and training programmes has a general but rarely examined impact on a vast area of labour law and employment policy concerning young people, and consequently incentives[24] are applied generally with modest results,[25] in a context other than the one for which they were designed.

In Italy an emblematic case is that of work training contracts *(contratti di formazione e lavoro),* the scope of which was initially extended by the national legislator to include "young people" between the ages of 29 and 32.[26] However, this limit has been further extended by regional provisions, for certain categories of workers with particular difficulties in terms of access to the labour market, to the age of 35 in Lazio, 38 in Calabria, 40 in Campania, Abruzzo and Sardinia, right up to the age of 45 in Basilicata, Apulia and Sicily.[27] The obvious result is that this measure no longer

---

[24] For an attempt to systematically reconstruct the incentive measures for youth employment in the light of the limits and conditions laid down by EU competition law, reference may be made to Tiraboschi, M. 2002. *Incentivi alla occupazione, aiuti di Stato, diritto comunitario della concorrenza.* Turin: Giappichelli.

[25] For an assessment of the modest effects of job creation policies for young people, see Ryan, P. *The School-to-Work transition etc.,* cit. esp. § 6, and Grubb, W. N. "Lessons from Education and Training for Youth: Five Precepts", *Preparing Youth for the 21st Century—The Transition from Education to the Labour Market,* cit., pp. 363-383. With regard to the neutralisation of the possible effects of incentive measures due to their proliferation and overlapping, see again my *Incentivi alla occupazione, aiuti di Stato, diritto comunitario della concorrenza,* cit., and the bibliography therein.

[26] With regard to the position prior to the amendments introduced with Legislative Decree No. 276/2003, see Article 16, Act No. 451, 19 July 1994.

[27] This incongruence in relation to the rationale of any youth employment measures is made evident by Advocate General Dámaso Ruiz-Jarabo Colomer, under point 21 of the Conclusions presented on 17 May 2001, in relation to the note on case C-310/99 brought by the Italian Republic against the Commission of the European Communities on the application of competition law to work training contracts. For a reconstruction of this case see Tiraboschi, M. 2002. "Contratti di formazione e lavoro e diritto comunitario della concorrenza", *RIDL,* No. 3. See also Serra, C. "Diritto comunitario della concorrenza e regime italiano di

works as an incentive for the employment of young people with no previous work experience.

The social consequences of the difficult and belated access to the labour market on the part of young people are evident. As confirmed by recent empirical studies,[28] the type of employment contract available, though not appearing to have a significant impact on the decision on when to move away from home, which is taken later in Italy than in other countries, appears to play a major role in establishing stable personal relationships, thanks to an employment status providing the degree of stability normally associated with open-ended employment.

Just as evident are the repercussions on the skills and motivation of young people who risk falling into a vicious circle by extending the transition from full-time education to work over too long a period. The longer the transition, the greater the impact on the chances of entering the labour market with proper training and an adequate level of pay in relation to employment of good quality.[29]

This is also because those with high-school or university qualifications tend to remain unemployed or to enrol for further educational qualifications rather than taking a job that does not match their professional aspirations.[30] At the same time, employers, even when not solely pursuing a policy of reducing labour costs,[31] may find those with

---

incentivazione economica: una lunga querelle tra Governo italiano e Commissione europea", *OGL*, No. 2:23-29.

[28] Salvini, S., and I. Ferro. 2005. "Un difficile equilibrio: i giovani tra flessibilità del mercato del lavoro e scelte familiari", paper presented at the conference on *Famiglie, nascite e politiche sociali*, Rome, Accademia Nazionale dei Lincei, 28-29 April 2005, *www.adapt.it,* index A-Z, under *Università, Scuola, Mercato del lavoro.* For a statistical comparison see Istat. *Rapporto annuale: la situazione nel Paese nel 2004,* cit., esp. pp. 245-248.

[29] Ryan, P. *The School-to-work Transition: A Cross-national Perspective,* cit., § 4.2.

[30] See Checchi, D. 2003. "Scelte di scolarizzazione ed effetti sul mercato del lavoro", Lucifora, C., ed. *Mercato, occupazione e salari: la ricerca sul lavoro in Italia.* Milano: Mondadori, § 1.4, note 33 (*www.adapt.it*, index A-Z, under *Università, Scuola, Mercato del lavoro),* who notes that young people tend to overestimate the earnings premium associated with a degree. See also Blanchflower, D.G. 1999. *What Can Be Done to Reduce the High Levels of Youth Joblessness in the World.* ILO, (*www.adapt.it*, index A-Z, under *Università, scuola, mercato del lavoro)* who rightly notes that "high unemployment encourages young people to stay on longer at school and get more education".

[31] See Bjornskov, C. 2004. "Social Trust and the Growth of Schooling", paper presented at the *First Annual Young Economist Workshop,* Rome, Università "La

advanced educational qualifications to be ill-equipped for the specific needs of the undertaking.

The argument that this belated access to work is one of the chief defects of the Italian labour market is also supported by the fact that Italy has the longest school-to-work transition of the OECD countries: 11 years, against the OECD average of seven.[32]

In Italy students between the ages of 15 and 19 do not normally take up any employment during their studies, unlike many countries, such as the Netherlands, Denmark and Germany, where 30-40 per cent of adolescents in this age range work.[33] The proportion of university students between the ages of 20 and 24 is one of the lowest in the world, less than 10 per cent, whereas in the Netherlands and the United States the corresponding figure is 60 per cent.[34] Just as worrying is the percentage of young people at risk of social exclusion, because they are occupied neither in education and training nor in employment. Almost 35 per cent of adolescents between the ages of 15 and 19 are unemployed but not taking part in any form of training. More than 20 per cent of those aged between 20 and 24 neither work nor study, not counting those who have lost their jobs.[35]

Overall, even without considering factors of geographical variation,[36] it may be said that young Italians have great difficulty in entering the labour market—either due to a lack of education,[37] training, or career guidance,

---

Sapienza", Centro Interuniversitario di Ricerca sullo Stato Sociale, in *www.adapt.it*, index A-Z, under *Capitale sociale.*

[32] See Bottani, N., and A. Tomei. 2004. "Com'è la transizione dalla scuola al lavoro in Italia", paper presented at the international seminar *I percorsi della scuola secondaria: il dilemma dell'istruzione tecnica e professionale,* Bologna 5-6 March (*www.adapt.it*, index A-Z, under *Università, scuola, mercato del lavoro).* See also Bottani, N., and A. Tomei. 2004. "La difficile transizione dalla scuola al lavoro", www.lavoce.info, 9 September.

[33] See Bottani, N., and A. Tomei. "Com'è la transizione dalla scuola al lavoro in Italia", cit., 20.

[34] See Bottani, N., and A. Tomei, *op. cit.,* 20.

[35] On this point, for further discussion, bibliography and statistics, see Sacconi, M., P. Reboani, and M. Tiraboschi. 2004. *La società attiva - Manifesto per le nuove sicurezze.* Venice: Marsilio, esp. 41.

[36] On the relations between youth unemployment and the question of the *Mezzogiorno*, an issue that is beyond the scope of the present study, but which is of particular importance for an effective analysis of the problem, see the insightful paper by Caroleo, F. E., and F. Pastore, *La disoccupazione giovanile in Italia etc., cit.*, esp. § 3.

[37] As highlighted also by PISA, the Programme for International Student Assessment, *www.pisa.oecd.org.*

or because of a clear mismatch between the training provided and the needs of employers[38]—and when they do enter the market, they can no longer be classified as young. Even the age at which they complete their higher education, as shown by the recent surveys carried out by Istat and Almalaurea,[39] is considerably higher than in other European countries: 27-28 years, compared to an average of 22-23.

According to the data provided by the national committee for the assessment of higher education,[40] only 17.5 per cent of degrees are awarded to those aged 24 or less, that is at an age when access to the labour market would be most appropriate. On the other hand, 60.1 per cent of degrees are awarded to those aged between 25 and 29 years, and, remarkably, 22.4 per cent are awarded to students aged 30 or over. Today there has undoubtedly been some improvement on the recent past,[41] but it is still too little compared to the results achieved in other countries. In addition, mention should be made of the variable quality of the teaching programmes, and of the proliferation of degree courses, with first-degree courses totalling 3,817 at the last count, though they are often considered to be inadequate by employers who find themselves hiring "young" people aged 27 or 28 who not only lack work experience, but are considered, rightly or wrongly, to be ill-equipped to make an immediate and effective contribution to production.[42]

It may be seen from a comparison of the examinations in the curriculum (and the related courses) for four-year degree courses that the recent transition to three-year degree programmes has in many cases been carried out by compressing all the contents of the four-year programmes into a three-year time span.[43]

---

[38] On this point, see Accornero, A. "Valorizzare la qualità del capitale umano per la competitività del Paese", *cit.*

[39] *Supra,* note 11.

[40] Available on the website of the national committee for the evaluation of higher education, http://www.cnvsu.it/

[41] See also the figures in the *Sesto rapporto sullo stato del sistema universitario* of the national committee for the evaluation of higher education, Rome, September 2005, in *Boll. ADAPT,* 2005, No. 31 which were not taken into account for the present paper as they were published after the paper was completed.

[42] Confindustria. 2005. *Rapporto Education 2004—Capitale umano, qualità e competitività: quando la formazione anticipa lo sviluppo.* Rome, in *Boll. ADAPT* No. 20.

[43] Conferenza dei Rettori delle Università italiane. 2005. *Rapporto 2005—L'Università vive il Paese. Relazione sullo stato delle Università italiane,* in *Boll. Adapt*, No. 33.

The number of degree programmes still appears to be too high, with too much fragmentation, while in many cases offering little prospect of access to the professions. As a result, in many cases there is a lack of continuity between the degree course taken and subsequent employment.[44] This is not to mention those cases, also statistically significant,[45] in which a degree is not required at all for the type of work undertaken.

Moreover, the figures relating to the methods of access to the labour market are also a matter for concern, providing confirmation of the persistent weakness of public employment services and institutional provision for matching the supply and demand for labour.[46]

In 2003, in an institutional framework that can only be described as antiquated,[47] and that still prohibited universities from engaging in any form of placement,[48] 60 per cent of graduates finding work did so on their own initiative, through vacancy notices in the press or on the Internet, or through family, friends and acquaintances.[49] Only a small percentage made use of public employment services, and, in spite of the concerns of those who believe that precarious employment is caused by the liberalisation of the matching of the supply and demand for labour,[50] even fewer young people entered the labour market through private employment agencies or staff leasing companies.

---

[44] See the figures published by Istat *supra* in note 11.

[45] *Ibidem.* See also Bottani, N., and A. Tomei. 2004. *La difficile transizione dalla scuola al lavoro,* in www.lavoce.info, 9 September.

[46] On these issues see the papers in Olivelli, P., and M. Tiraboschi, ed. 2005. *Il diritto del mercato del lavoro dopo la riforma Biagi.* Milano: Giuffrè and the extensive bibliography therein.

[47] Mention should be made of the case of Japan, where from the early 1980s a mechanism was put in place for the transition from education to the labour market via placement services provided on the initiative of the school. See Kosugi, R. 2005. "The Transition from School to Working Life Issue", *Japan Labor Review,* No. 3, esp 2. See also Ryan, P. "The School-To-Work Transition Twenty Years On: Issues, Evidence and Conundrums", *Preparing Youth for the 21st Century etc.,* pp. 448-449.

[48] See the contributions by Clara Enrico and Paola Olivelli in Gelmini, P, and M. Tiraboschi, eds. 2006. *Scuola, Università e Mercato del lavoro dopo la Riforma Biagi - Le politiche per la transizione dai percorsi educativi e formativi al mercato del lavoro,* Milano: Giuffrè. This issue is dealt with also in Spattini, S., and M. Tiraboschi. "Regimi particolari di autorizzazioni e autorizzazioni regionali", *Il diritto del mercato del lavoro,* cit., esp. pp. 265-271.

[49] See with reference to the Almalaurea figures cited in note 11, the analysis by Cazzola, G. *Il* placement *dei neo-laureati etc., cit.*

[50] See in this connection Angiolini, V., "Le agenzie del lavoro tra pubblico e privato", *Il lavoro tra progresso e mercificazione etc., cit.*, pp. 28-36.

Statistical studies have shown that the impact of private employment agencies continues to be limited in relation to their potential role: private agencies account for just 0.63 per cent of the Italian market, compared to 5 per cent in the UK, 2.6 per cent in the Netherlands and 1 per cent Germany.[51] This is despite the fact that a reliable study recently carried out for the Ministry of Labour and Social Policy[52] reported that "for workers dispatched on temporary assignments the chances of obtaining a permanent occupation within a year and a half are twice those of an individual not taking up an assignment, increasing from 14 to 28 per cent" (our translation).[53] This provides evidence to refute the idea, still widespread in Italy,[54] that temporary agency work and staff leasing result in a lack of stability in employment.

2. The Reform of Labour Market Measures and Policies for Addressing the Chronic Weakness of Young People in the Labour Market: A Critical Overview

Once they have left secondary or higher education, young people in Italy lose contact with formal and institutional employment services, be they public or private. In many cases this has a negative effect not only in terms of the duration and quality of labour market access programmes but also, and this is particular evident in Italy in the comparative context,[55] in terms of the lack of continuity between educational and training and subsequent employment choices. Such choices are made in many cases

---

[51] See International Confederation of Temporary Work Businesses. 2005. *Data elaborated by the International Confederation of Temporary Work Businesses, Boll. ADAPT*, No. 35.

[52] Ichino, A., F. Mealli, and T. Nannicini. 2003. *Il lavoro interinale in Italia—Trappola del precariato o trampolino verso un impiego stabile?* esp. pp. 57-59, *www.adapt.it*, index A-Z, under *Somministrazione di lavoro*.

[53] It is estimated that 51% of temporary workers are told that they may be taken on directly by the user company at the end of their posting. The research by Ichino, A., F. Mealli, and T. Nannicini, *Il lavoro interinale in Italia etc.,* cit., shows that "for 32% of these workers, this prospect becomes a reality. However, even 20% of those who were not told they might be taken on are then hired by the user company". (our translation)

[54] Chieco, P. 2004. "Somministrazione, comando, appalto. Le nuove forme di prestazione di lavoro a favore del terzo", *Lavoro e diritti dopo il decreto legislativo 276/2003,* ed. P. Curzio, Bari: Cacucci, pp. 91-164.

[55] See the Istat and Almalaurea figures cited in note 11.

quite by chance, showing the lack of connection with the normative framework providing career guidance and favouring access to the labour market.

There seems to be widespread agreement among many commentators that reducing the number of young people in a weak position in the labour market depends to a large extent on increasing the percentage of them who complete educational and training programmes at secondary level.[56] However, in Italy not much has been achieved in terms of this objective.

At present it is still too early to say what will be achieved in practical terms by the Moratti Law,[57] though the drop-out rate in secondary education, calculated on the basis of the percentage of 18-24 year-olds who have completed only the first three years of their secondary education without going on to the subsequent stage or into vocational training, reveals the seriousness of the problem,[58] that is particularly significant in comparative terms. In 2003, there was a particularly high drop-out rate in Italy (23 per cent, compared to the European benchmark of 10 per cent by 2010 laid down in the Lisbon Strategy), and the figure was higher still for young men.

A comparison with other European countries shows that Italy is third last (Figure 1), falling below the European average of 18.5 per cent, but also below the new Member States, that, with a drop-out rate of 8.4 per cent, have already reached the benchmark.

A further significant factor is that only 72.9 per cent of young people complete their compulsory secondary education, well below the objective of 85 per cent laid down by the Lisbon Strategy.[59]

Mention should also be made of university drop-out rates, as well as the drop in enrolments between the first degree and postgraduate levels, and the concentration of enrolments in Faculties that do little to facilitate access to the labour market on the part of their students.

---

[56] See Ryan, P. *The School-to-work Transition: a Cross-national Perspective,* cit.; Isfol Report 2005, chapter 4.

[57] Act No. 53, 28 March 2003. See also *L'alternanza scuola lavoro. Ipotesi, modelli, strumenti dopo la riforma Moratti,* CISEM-Franco Angeli, 2003; and in 2004 "Alternanza scuola lavoro le nuove sfide della concorrenza", *Annali dell'Istruzione 2004*. Florence: Le Monnier.

[58] See the figures in Ministero della Istruzione, dell'Università e della Ricerca. 2004. *Indagine campionaria sulla dispersione scolastica nelle scuole statali—Anno scolastico 2003—2004.* Rome, *www.adapt.it*, index A-Z, under *Capitale umano.*

[59] Bulgarelli, A., and M. Tiraboschi. 2004. "Transizione scuola—lavoro: qualcosa è cambiato", www.la voce.info 11.10.

This is indicative of the grave and persistent lack not only of links between educational programmes and work, but also the lack of career guidance during and at the end of secondary education.[60]

Only just over 40 per cent of the adult population aged 25-64 years have a high-school or university qualification. In the age range from 30 to 59 years, 53 per cent of men and 40 per cent of women have only a lower secondary qualification, and one person in 10 has only a primary school certificate.[61]

In a largely unstructured labour market such as Italy these figures are of particular significance also in terms of gender and the extensive category of disadvantaged workers.[62] The labour market participation rate for women, in particular, is closely correlated to qualifications. Only 39 per cent of women without a high-school or university qualification are in paid employment, compared to 61 per cent of those with a high-school diploma and 79 per cent of those with a degree. Low levels of education and training continue to be associated with discrimination against women in the regular and institutional labour market.[63]

---

[60] In addition to the statistical surveys cited above in note 11, See CNEL. 2005. *Educazione e formazione—Osservazioni e proposte.* Rome, 31 March *www.adapt.it*, index A-Z, under *Università, Scuola, Mercato del lavoro.*

[61] For an analysis of these figures see Accornero, A. 2005. *Valorizzare la qualità del capitale umano per la competitività del Paese, op. cit.*, and Bulgarelli, A. 2005. "Verso una strategia di Lifelong Learning: stato dell'arte e evoluzione delle politiche di formazione continua in Italia", *Lo sviluppo del "capitale umano" tra innovazione organizzativa e tecniche di fidelizzazione,* eds. Malandrini, S., and A. Russo, Milano: Giuffrè.

[62] On the basis of the definition in Article 2, letter f) of Community regulation No. 2204, 12 December 2002, now adopted by the Italian legislator in Article 2 (1)(k) of Legislative Decree No. 276, 10 September 2003.

[63] See the figures in the Istat reports cited above in note 11. In the international literature with regard not just to gender but also to other factors such as national or ethnic origin and social background, see Ryan, P. *The School-to-work Transition: a Cross-national Perspective,* cit., § 2.

Figure 2-7. International Comparison of Four Benchmarks for Education and Training

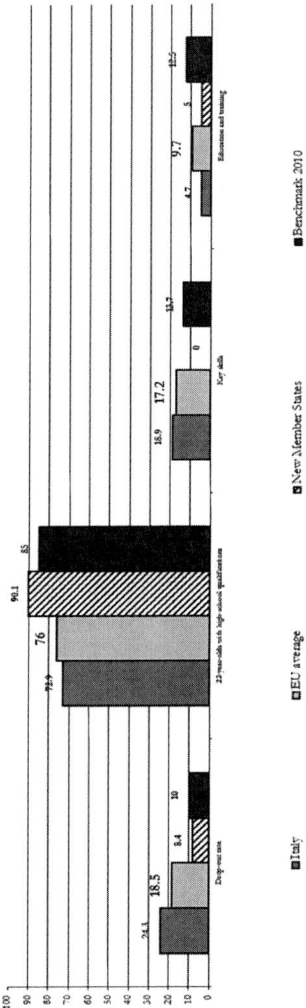

Source: Elaboration of Eurostat, OECD and Istat data

In the light of these considerations, it does not appear that Italy's shortcomings can be resolved simply by means of an increase in funding for training—though a step in this direction was made in Act No.

196/1997[64]—or in financial and other incentives to improve the functioning of the labour market. Rather, it is the structure of training and labour market policies that requires systematic reform and far-reaching innovation to strengthen the position of younger workers and others in a weak position in the labour market.[65]

It is therefore not surprising that Italy is still characterised by low levels of educational achievement among the adult population aged from 25 to 64 years, as shown by the comparison with other countries in Figure 2.[66]

Best practices in the comparative panorama[67] show that the direction to take is not simply a deregulation of the labour market[68] and not even, in contrast with conventional wisdom, the implementation of "job creation" programmes, which practically in all countries[69] but particularly in Italy[70]

---

[64] For a survey of special youth employment measures, especially in the *Mezzogiorno*, see the papers in Biagi, M. ed. 1997. *Mercati e rapporti di lavoro—Commentario alla legge 24 giugno 1997, n. 196.* Milano: Giuffrè esp. 293 ff.

[65] For an in-depth analysis in the light of the EU regulatory framework, see Bulgarelli, A. 2000. *Verso una strategia di lifelong learning: stato dell'arte e evoluzione delle politiche di formazione continua in Italia*, cit. See also Field, J. 2000. *Lifelong Learning and the New Educational Order*. Stoke-on-Trent Trentham Books, 81, and Heidemann, W. 2000. *Lifelong learning and the Employability: is the European Model of Vocational Training in Crisis?* Brussels: European Trade Union Confederation; Jarvis, P. 1999. "Global Trends in Lifelong Learning and the Response of the Universities", *Comparative Education*, 35, pp. 249-257.

[66] Checchi, D. "Scelte di scolarizzazione ed effetti sul mercato del lavoro", Lucifora, C., ed., *op. cit*. The point that the percentage of graduates in relation to the population as a whole is still among the lowest in Europe is also made by Tosi, P. 2005. *Relazione sullo stato delle Università italiane 2005.* Rome, 20 September, in *Boll. ADAPT,* No. 33, esp. 5. See also the Conferenza dei Rettori delle Università italiane. 2005. *Rapporto 2005—L'Università vive il Paese. Relazione sullo stato delle Università italiane 2005.* 20 September, in *Boll. Adapt*, No. 33.

[67] See for an overview and empirical evidence, Ryan, P. *The School-to-work Transition: a Cross-national Perspective,* cit., § 6. Also Gautié, J. "Promoting Employment for Youth: a European Perspective", *Preparing Youth for the 21st Century etc.,* cit., pp. 387-418.

[68] OECD. 1994. *Job Study*, available at *www.adapt.it*, index A-Z, under *Politiche per l'occupazione,* according to which it is the persistent levels of protection and regulation of the labour market that have a negative impact on the level and quality of youth employment.

[69] For an extensive survey of the failure of active policies and subsidies for youth unemployment see Blanchflower, D. G. *What Can Be Done to Reduce the High Levels of Youth Joblessness in the World,* cit., esp. pp. 38-42; Ryan, P. *The School-*

have generally been found to be incapable of providing a structural solution to the problem of youth unemployment.

Fig. 2-8. Percentage of the Population (25-64 years) by Level of Education in a Number of OECD Countries

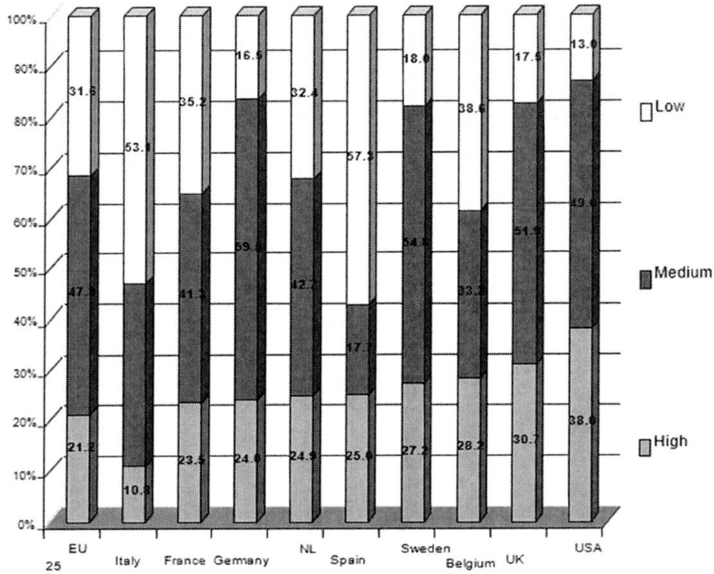

Sources: Eurostat, OECD (USA) 2004

It would seem to be far more important to carry out the reform of education and vocational training,[71] and to improve the functioning of all

---

to-work Transition: a Cross-national Perspective, cit., esp. § 6.2. See also the ILO. 2000. *Employing Youth: Promoting Employment-Intensive Growth,* Geneva: ILO, esp. pp. 47-51, available at *www.adapt.it*, index A-Z, *Università, Scuola, Mercato del lavoro,* and for the labour law aspects, the papers in Biagi, M., ed. 2000. *Job Creation and Labour Law—From Protection towards Pro-action.* The Netherlands: Kluwer Law International.

[70] See Biagi, M., and M. Tiraboschi. "The Role of Labour Law in Job Creation Policies: an Italian Perspective", *Job Creation and Labour Law etc., cit.,* pp. 179-187.

[71] See Caroleo, F. E., and F. Pastore. *La disoccupazione giovanile in Italia. La riforma dei sistemi di istruzione e di formazione professionale come alternativa della flessibilità numerica per accrescere l'occupabilità,* cit.

those bodies intended to promote the employability of young people,[72] also by means of networks, whether formal or informal, between local institutions, educational and training bodies, employers' associations, undertakings or trade unions. In this connection particular attention needs to be paid to the alternation of periods of schooling and work, and especially apprenticeship contracts,[73] as well as institutional mechanisms aimed at promoting the placement of students and in general the transition from education to employment.[74] As recently shown on the basis of the German and Japanese experience, "labor market programs come and go. Institutions develop, adapt and, for the most, endure".[75]

3. Young People and Precarious Employment: The False Problem of Parasubordinate Employment and the Reform of Training Contracts

The most recent empirical findings provide evidence to counter common assumptions about the quality of employment of young people,

---

[72] On this point see Biagi, M. "Università e orientamento al lavoro nel doporiforma: verso la piena occupabilità?", *Marco Biagi—Un giurista progettuale,* eds. Montuschi, L., M. Tiraboschi, and T. Treu, Milano: Giuffrè, pp. 13-31.

[73] Clearly where apprenticeship contracts, and training contracts in general, are not simply considered to be a form of fixed-term contract or entry-level income. From this point of view the German experience is particularly significant: despite recent problems it appears to be the most efficient channel in both qualitative and quantitative terms for the transition from education to employment in a comparative analysis. See Ryan, P. *The School-to-work Transition: a Cross-national Perspective,* cit., § 5 and § 8, and Biagi, M., and M. Tiraboschi. 1999. "La rilevanza della formazione in apprendistato in Europa: problemi e prospettive", *DRI,* esp. pp. 87-89.

[74] For example, the Japanese model of hiring based on selection and placement in schools and universities mentioned below in note 141. See also Ryan, P. *op. cit.,* and the papers in Müller, W., and M. Gangl, eds. 2003. *Transitions from Education to Work in Europe - The Integration of Youth into EU Labour Markets.* Oxford: Oxford University Press.

[75] See once again Ryan, P. *op. cit,* § 8, who, with regard to apprenticeships in Germany and school and university placement services in Japan, rightly notes that "those institutions have allowed Germany and Japan to avoid mass labor market programs and to concentrate instead on institutional development improving general education, vocational preparation and job placement, and making it easier for low achievers to participate. Although Japanese and German transition institutions have come under strain, they have adapted well and they continue—thus far at least—to function largely intact".

according to which young workers are all (or almost all) precariously employed, or engaged in parasubordinate employment as *collaboratori coordinati e continuative.*[76]

According to the INPS report for 2004,[77] the number of young workers in parasubordinate employment is actually much lower than the number of those who enter the labour market as employees in training or with work access contracts that are undoubtedly the best ways to achieve the objective of stable employment in a reasonable period.

At the end of 2004 the number of parasubordinate employees registered with INPS amounted to 3,300,000, with an increase of 493,000 compared to 2003. Of these, the largest group consisted of workers between the ages of 30 and 39, with more than a million workers, over one third of the total. On the other hand, there were relatively few workers up to the age of 25, amounting to 196,000, less than 6 per cent of the total. A considerable number, 853,199, were over the age of 50, accounting for 25 per cent of the total, or four times as many as the number up to the age of 25. In addition, there were almost 370,000 parasubordinate employees over the age of 60, 11 per cent of the total, as shown in Table 2-16.

Table 2-16. Parasubordinate Workers Registered with INPS: Number of Workers Registered by Age Group as at 31.12.2004

Age Range	<20	20-24	25-29	30-39	40-49	50-59	≥ 60	Total
Workers *of which:*	12,509	183,608	477,127	1,092,858	711,018	483,467	369,732	3,339,319
Men	6,198	76,256	196,945	514,921	385,647	306,523	277,633	1,764,123
Women	6,311	107,352	280,182	577,937	325,371	176,944	92,099	1,566,196

Source: Inps Report 2004

[76] For this line of interpretation, which still tends to group together in a simplistic manner those paying INPS contributions under separate management with those in precarious employment, see Rivellini, P., G. A. Micheli, and F. Billari. 2005. "Flessibilità come vincolo e come filosofia: segni di polarizzazione sociale nella formazione delle intenzioni", paper presented at the conference on *Famiglie, nascite e politiche sociali*, Rome, Accademia Nazionale dei Lincei, 28-29 April, *www.adapt.it,* index A-Z, under *Università, Scuola, Mercato del lavoro.* For a reliable study aimed at identifying within the area of parasubordinate employment those who really are in a weaker position, see Accornero, A. 2005. "Nuovi lavori e rappresentanza", *DRI*, 1, 60, and CNEL. 2004. *Rapporto sul Mercato del lavoro 2003,* Rome, in *Boll.* Adapt, No. 43.

[77] *Boll.* Adapt, 2004 No. 20.

It is therefore difficult to imagine, even with the intention of making an ideological interpretation, that parasubordinate employment, reformed by the Biagi Law with the introduction of project work,[78] and in relation to which the debate about precarious employment has now polarised, is a kind of biblical plague, terrible and pitiless, that risks persecuting young Italians for their entire lives, so that even as adults and older persons they will be denied the chance of stable employment.

As shown by the data supplied by INPS (Fig. 2-9), it is clear that the great majority of young people in Italy enter the labour market by means of training contracts of various kinds.

Fig. 2-9. Apprenticeship Contracts, Work Access Contracts, and Work Training Contracts: Monthly Totals

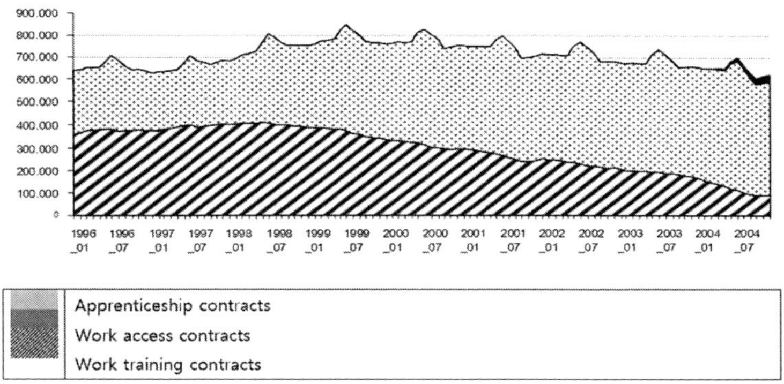

Source: Ministry of Labour calculations based on INPS data

In 2004 there were some 553,000 apprentices working in small businesses or artisan firms, along with some 117,000 employees on work

[78] For an examination of project work that continues to be placed in the area of subordinate employment pursuant to Article 409 (3) of the *Codice di Procedura Civile*, see the circular of the Ministry of Labour and Social Policy 1/2004, in *Boll. ADAPT*, 2004, No. 1. For recent statistical data showing that many of the common assumptions about parasubordinate employment are without foundation, see CNEL. 2004. *Rapporto sul mercato del lavoro 2003,* Rome, 11 November, in *www.adapt.it*, index A-Z, under *Mercato del lavoro;* Istat, "Collaborazioni coordinate e continuative nella rilevazione sulle forze di lavoro", *Boll. ADAPT,* 2005, No. 11. For a summary of the debate among legal scholars see Ichino, P. 2004. "Uno sguardo laico sulla legge Biagi", *RGL*, 655. See also Canavesi, G. 2004. "Il contratto di lavoro a progetto. Profili ricostruttivi e spunti sistematici", *DLM*, 217.

training contracts, and over 30,000 employees hired on the work access contracts *(contratti di inserimento)* introduced by the Biagi Law.

However, it must be pointed out that within a normative and conceptual paradigm reflecting a Ford-Taylorist model of work organisation and production, training contracts providing access to the labour market have long been used as an instrument enabling employers not only to select workers most suited to productive needs in organisational contexts that are largely static and not particularly innovative, but also to benefit from lower labour costs during training, as a result of lower pay scales for trainees, but also due to the generous subsidies made available, often in exchange for minimal or non-existent training programmes, as in the case of many work training contracts *(contratti di formazione e lavoro).*[79]

In many cases, these contracts have consisted almost entirely of work with hardly any training, as defined by legal scholars specialising in the problem,[80] thus highlighting Italy's limited capacity to implement effective training schemes that at a practical level are more than simply a means for making available cut-price labour.[81]

It was the European Union that imposed drastic limits on this irregular form of covert State subsidy ostensibly allocated for training purposes, introducing stricter conditions for the use of public funding and tax and contributions relief for those over the age of 25 (or over the age of 29 in the case of graduates).[82] This matter has been given due consideration by the Italian legislator with the Biagi reform of the labour market, under which work training contracts are replaced by a more flexible access-to-work contract *(contratto di inserimento al lavoro),* not necessarily for the purposes of training, but providing financial incentives in cases in which there is a labour market disadvantage of an objective or subjective nature,

---

[79] On the degeneration and functional overloading of training contracts see Biagi, M., and M. Tiraboschi. 1999. "La rilevanza della formazione in apprendistato in Europa: problemi e prospettive", *DRI,* 85-89. See also Varesi, P.A. 2001. *Contratti di lavoro con finalità formative.* Milano: Franco Angeli.

[80] See Loffredo, A. 2004. "I contratti a finalità formativa: tra un passato incerto ed un futuro difficile", *Mercato del lavoro*, Editoriale Scientifica, eds. De Luca Tamajo, R., M. Rusciano, L. Zoppoli, 489; Tiraboschi, M. 2003. "L'accordo interconfederale di transizione sui contratti di formazione e lavoro", *GL* No. 46:12.

[81] This line of analysis is developed in my paper "La riforma dei contratti a contenuto formativo: il nuovo apprendistato e il contratto di inserimento", *La riforma Biagi del mercato del lavoro etc., cit.,* esp. pp. 191-194.

[82] For a reconstruction of the work training contracts case following the intervention of the European Union, see the authors cited above in note 79.

while making provision for a new kind of apprenticeship contract as the main instrument for alternating training and employment.[83]

The new apprenticeship contract is the first step in a plan which, in keeping with the Lisbon Strategy, initially at a theoretical level but then also by means of assessment of its implementation, is intended to provide strong support for training that continues throughout the working life of the individual, a plan that is intended as a way of bringing together education, training and employment policies,[84] This is clearly on condition that the new apprenticeship contract does not replicate the disappointing experience of the work training contract, characterised not so much by its contribution to training but rather as a channel for tax and contributions relief, and reduced labour costs.[85]

4. The Strategic Role of Higher Education: The Italian Case in the EU and Comparative Context

One of the critical elements of the Italian labour market is the chronic weakness of education and training programmes.[86] The constitutional principle according to which the Republic "takes care of the training and vocational advancement of the workers"[87] has not yet been implemented,

---

[83] For an in-depth analysis, see note 80 *supra*. In the debate among legal scholars, see the paper by Pierantonio Varesi in Gelmini, P., and M. Tiraboschi, eds. *Scuola, Università e Mercato del lavoro etc. op. cit,* and Loy, G. *I nuovi apprendistati,* cit.; D'Onghia, M. 2004. "I contratti a finalità formativa: apprendistato e contratto di inserimento", *Lavoro e diritti dopo il decreto legislativo 276/2003,* ed. Curzio, P., Bari: Cacucci, Bari, p. 271.

[84] For an in-depth analysis see Bulgarelli, A. *Verso una strategia di lifelong learning: stato dell'arte e evoluzione delle politiche di formazione continua in Italia, cit*. On the arduous implementation of the new apprenticeship contracts, see Carollo, L. "La messa a regime del nuovo apprendistato dopo il "pacchetto competitività'", (legge 14 maggio 2005, n. 80), *cit.,* and the bibliography therein.

[85] An *a priori* negative assessment of the new apprenticeship contracts is to be found in Brunello, G., and A. Topo. 2004. "Apprendisti nel tempo", www.lavoce.info, 11 October, according to which "the rules of our country do not provide the parties with sufficient incentives to carry out a training investment of a substantial kind" (our translation).

[86] See Bulgarelli, A., and L. Palomba. 2004. "Istruzione e formazione per promuovere l'occupabilità e la competitività", *Annali dell'Istruzione*, Firenze: Le Monnier.

[87] Article 37 (2) Italian Costitution, discussed in the paper by Mario Rusciano in Gelmini, P., and M. Tiraboschi, eds. *Scuola, Università e Mercato del lavoro etc. op.cit.*

just as references to the EU sources pointing to the need for lifelong learning appear to be largely rhetorical.[88] Moreover, there seems to be a lack of awareness that the economic and social dividend from investment in education and vocational training is particularly significant.[89]

Investing in education and training pays off both for the individual and for society and the economy as a whole, as highlighted by recent estimates released by the EU, which show that raising the level of education by just one year results in five per cent growth in the short term and a further 2.5 per cent in the long term.[90] Moreover, as shown by recent Istat surveys, the unemployment rate and the rates of active participation in the labour market are largely conditioned by the level of educational attainment.[91] Even for the individual worker, the quality and duration of education and training have a decisive impact on earnings.[92]

One particularly critical area in this connection is that of higher education, which also plays a decisive role in the context of the competition, innovation and development policy agreed on by the EU Member States in Lisbon in 2000.[93]

For the European economies that are lacking in dynamism, higher education and investment in human capital are key factors in facing international competition as our main competitors have lower labour costs and more extensive natural resources.

This argument was forcefully underlined by the President of the European Commission, José Manuel Barroso, in a plenary session of the European Parliament in March 2005,[94] during which the mid-term failure

---

[88] See Council of the European Union, Risoluzione sull'apprendimento permanente, 2002/C 163/01, at *www.adapt.it*, Index A-Z, under *Formazione*.

[89] See CNEL. *Educazione e formazione—Osservazioni e proposte,* cit. and OECD. 2005. *Education at a Glance: OECD Indicators*—2005 Edition, Paris: OECD. In the debate among legal scholars see the careful analysis by Checchi, D. "Scelte di scolarizzazione ed effetti sul mercato del lavoro", cit., § 1.3.

[90] CNEL. *Educazione e formazione—Osservazioni e proposte,* cit.

[91] ISTAT. 2005. *Rilevazioni sulla forza lavoro. II trimestre 2005*. Rome: ISTAT in *Boll. ADAPT,* No. 33.

[92] CNEL. *Educazione e formazione—Osservazioni e proposte,* cit. In the debate among legal scholars see Bulgarelli, A. "Verso una strategia di lifelong learning: stato dell'arte ed evoluzione delle politiche di formazione continua in Italia", Olivelli, P., and M. Tiraboschi, eds. 2005. *Il diritto del mercato del lavoro dopo la riforma Biagi*, Milano: Giuffrè, pp. 569-583.

[93] European Commission. 2003. *Il ruolo delle università nell'Europa della conoscenza,* COM(2003) 58 def. Brussels: European Commission, in *www.adapt.it*, index A-Z, under *Università, Scuola, Mercato del lavoro.*

[94] See Barroso, J. M. 2005. "Growth and jobs: a new start for the Lisbon strategy",

to reach the objectives of the Lisbon Strategy was discussed.[95] It was again put forward by the European Commission, in a communication with the emblematic title, *Mobilising European brains*, which pointed out that higher education and research are one of the most critical but neglected areas[96] in a Europe that by 2010 aims to become, as stated in the Lisbon Strategy, the most dynamic and competitive knowledge-based economy.[97]

However, there is still a vast gap between the consensus that there is a need to invest more, and above all in a more effective manner, in human capital and day-to-day reality. This is the case all over Europe, at least for the continental countries. In Europe, just to mention the most evident shortcomings in relation to other economies,[98] the percentage of young people between the ages of 18 and 24 taking part in higher education is less than 25 per cent, compared to 37.7 per cent in the United States. In addition just 21 per cent of the adult population aged between 25 and 64 has a higher education qualification, compared to 43 per cent in Canada, 38 per cent in the United States, 36 per cent in Japan and 26 per cent in South Korea. In Italy, with its high drop-out rates, the levels of participation in training and higher education, public and private investment in training and education, and the levels of lifelong learning are among the lowest in Europe;[99] only Greece and Portugal are at a comparable level.

The fact that the Italian economy continues to have many world-class businesses can partly be explained by the tradition of informal training that

---

Boll. ADAPT, No. 9, 9 March.

[95] See the Conclusions of the Stockholm European Council of 23-24 March 2001, and in particular the *Relazione della Commissione sugli obiettivi concreti futuri dei sistemi di istruzione e di formazione* adopted by the Education Council on 12 February 2001, in Bollettino UE 3-2001.

[96] On the crisis of mass higher education in Europe see the special survey by Adrian Wooldridge in *The Economist,* 8 September 2005, http://www.economist.com/displaystory.cfm?story_id=4339960

[97] For further details see European Commission. 2005. *Mobilising the Brainpower of Europe: Enabling Universities to Make their Full Contribution to the Lisbon Strategy,* COM(2005) 152 final 20 April. Brussels: European Commission, in *www.adapt.it*, index A-Z, under *Università, Scuola, Mercato del lavoro.*

[98] For a detailed analysis see European Commission. 2005. *Annex* to *Mobilising the Brainpower of Europe: Enabling Universities to Make their Full Contribution to the Lisbon Strategy—European Higher Education in a Worldwide Perspective*, COM(2005) 152 final 20 April. Brussels: European Commission, in *www.adapt.it*, index A-Z, under *Università, Scuola, Mercato del lavoro.*

[99] Bottani, N., and A. Tomei. "Com'è la transizione dalla scuola al lavoro in Italia", *cit.*

takes place in companies and at territorial level: this is particularly the case with family-run small and medium-sized enterprises, but in the long run in order to remain competitive it is unlikely to be sufficient.

Investment in higher education in Europe is critical for a variety of factors, including cultural ones. But much depends also on the funding and structure of universities that suffer from a regulatory framework that is highly centralised, and from the idea that education should be run almost exclusively by the public sector, with funding allocated accordingly. According to the European Commission, to match the overall level of spending on higher education in the United States, Europe would need to spend 150 billion euros more every year. The lack of funding and facilities has a strong impact on the level of productivity of the Universities in terms of world-class research, with more modest achievements than the United States in terms of scientific publications, patents and Nobel prizes.

The real problem is that higher education in Europe continues to rely almost entirely on public funding,[100] which is severely limited, whereas in competing countries more vigorous and sustained development is made possible by a wider variety of funding sources, with much more substantial contributions from businesses and private individuals.[101]

This issue has recently been addressed by the European Commission, which laid down three policy objectives for the reform of the universities: i) improving the quality and making them more attractive for young people and for lecturers and researchers from all over the world; ii) improving university governance and administration, also by introducing management practices; iii) increasing and diversifying funding (with or without a substantial contribution from students).[102]

In relation to these objectives, Italy's position is not one of the most favourable. In order to keep pace with Europe, Italian Universities need to speed up the processes aimed at improving the coherence between the educational programmes and the needs of the labour market. This needs to take place in the context of renewed competition between the Universities, based on the capacity to create centres of excellence, by attracting the best students and lecturers—also from abroad, that today is rarely the case—thanks to the quality of the services provided and the prestige that each

---

[100] Psacharopoulos, G. 2004. "Public versus private University systems", *Journal of Institutional Comparison,* No. 4:3-7 and in *www.adapt.it*, index A-Z, under *Università, Scuola, Mercato del lavoro.*

[101] European Commission. *Mobilising the brainpower of Europe etc.,* cit. and Psacharopoulos, G. "Public versus private University systems", cit.

[102] European Commission, *Mobilising the Brainpower of Europe etc.,* cit.

University manages to acquire.[103] One proposal that should be carefully examined in connection with increased competition between Universities, to be discussed in the conclusions of this paper, is that of reconsidering the legal value of university qualifications.

In any case it is clear that an improvement in the research capacity of the Universities needs to be supported by an increase in the opportunities to attract funding (public, but also and above all private) in order to raise the quality of educational programmes and improve the selection of faculty members.

5. The Critical Aspects of the Italian Case and the Reform Proposals in the *White Paper on the Labour Market* of October 2001

Undoubtedly some steps have been taken in this direction. It was 11 years ago, in the Protocol of 23 July 1993,[104] that the Government and the social partners underlined the importance of strengthening University autonomy. This clearly stated objective was to contribute to widening and improving post-diploma and postgraduate programmes, based on the belief that closer collaboration between higher education and the labour market was necessary to facilitate a policy for training and improving human resources in keeping with the needs of productive processes, and the development of small and medium-sized enterprises. However, the idea was not taken any further.[105] It was not until the *Patto di Natale* of 22 December 1998[106] that the current policy for the reform of university education was adopted. For the first time, this agreement, that was intended to pave the way for University autonomy, provided a definition of specific instruments aimed at widening participation in higher education, shortening diploma and degree courses, combating high drop-out rates, and improving links between the Universities and their surrounding territories, resulting in a better match between educational

[103] There is widespread recognition of the well founded nature of the proposals presented by Gagliarducci, S., A. Ichino, G. Peri, and R. Perotti. 2005. "Lo splendido isolamento dell'Università italiana", paper at the conference *Oltre il declino,* Fondazione Rodolfo Debenedetti, Rome, 3 February, in *www.adapt.it*, index A-Z, under *Università, scuola, mercato del lavoro.*

[104] See *www.adapt.it*, index A-Z, under *Concertazione.*

[105] On this point see Biagi, M. *Università e orientamento al lavoro nel doporiforma: verso la piena occupabilità?,cit.*, esp. 19-20.

[106] See *www.adapt.it*, index A-Z, under *Concertazione.*

programmes and emerging vocational needs in the economy and society as a whole.[107]

The reform of degree courses, with the introduction of three-year programmes, has undeniably resulted in a significant increase in enrolments, countering the reluctance on the part of high-school leavers in the late 1990s to enrol at university. But this reform will not produce significant results in terms of the transition from education to work if the trend for students to opt for long rather than short degree programmes is confirmed, thus postponing their entry into the labour market.[108] Indeed, more than 80 per cent of students who complete the three-year degree go on to take a postgraduate degree,[109] thus working against the intention of the reform that was to reduce the time required for the transition from education to work. This is also due to the lack of reform of the professional bodies, which means that in many cases a three-year degree is not sufficient in legal terms.

Mention should also be made of the fact that the recent transformations of the economy mean that employers often prefer high-school leavers to graduates, particularly for companies in the service sector.[110]

The present system does not appear to be capable of responding to a crucial question that is rarely taken into consideration by the competent bodies at national level and in the universities themselves: what realistically is the professional role associated with a three-year degree in, for example, law or engineering?

The autonomy of the Universities—not only in terms of teaching programmes, but also in terms of their legal and financial status—has undoubtedly played a decisive role in the integration of higher education and labour market policies. But it is insufficient if at the same time the conditions are not created for forging closer links between Universities and the enterprises in the surrounding territory.[111]

---

[107] Once again Biagi, M. *Università e orientamento al lavoro nel doporiforma etc., cit.*

[108] For a critical review of the three-year degree programmes, Tosi, P. *Relazione sullo stato delle Università italiane 2005, cit.*, esp. pp. 6-7.

[109] See the figures in Almalaurea. *Condizione occupazionale dei laureati, 7ª Indagine—2004,* cit. In addition the analysis of these figures by Cazzola, G. "Il placement dei neo-laureati secondo le più importanti indagini delle forze di lavoro", *cit.*

[110] For a reliable study of the factors leading to the decline in demand for university graduates, see Hara, H. 2003. "Labor Demand for New High School Graduates in Japan", *Japan Labor Review,* No. 3, pp. 49-72.

[111] Biagi, M. *Università e orientamento al lavoro nel doporiforma ecc.,* cit.

The present system of funding of Italian Universities not only fails to guarantee the provision of educational programmes of high quality, but also, in spite of its pretence at egalitarianism, ends up being iniquitous because it does not effectively promote social mobility.[112]There is a need to reflect carefully on the proposal to liberalise tuition fees, and at the same time to launch large-scale funding programmes, also by means of partnerships with associations representing employers, banks, companies, foundations and other private entities, in order to make available awards, loans and study grants for the most talented students needing financial support.

There is a widespread belief that the Italian higher education system needs more substantial public funding to realise the ambitious objectives for an active society and investment in human capital. But this is not necessarily the case, above all when considering the client-based system often to be seen in the management of public funding allocated to the Universities.[113]

Clearly public funding remains fundamental for free and autonomous research. Nobody imagines that higher education can be transformed into a market just like any other, subject solely to the rules of free competition. It is also the case that the Universities need to fully accept the idea of competition, based mainly on the reputation and quality of their academic staff and research programmes,[114] thus opening up to the market within a clear regulatory framework.

The self-referential nature of the teaching body is undoubtedly a problem in Italian Universities, that is touched on in the Joint Employment Report 2004/2005 by the European Council and Commission:[115] in general the Italian higher education system runs programmes that tend not to reflect the needs of enterprises and the surrounding territory but above all the teaching interests of the various faculty members.

The difference in relation to a system of excellence such as the leading American Universities does not consist mainly in the amount of state funding, but rather in the amount of private funding, and in the capacity of

---

[112] Reference may be made to the statistics published by the national committee for the evaluation of higher education, set up by the Ministry of Education, Higher Education and Research, dell'Istruzione, in the *Sesto rapporto sullo stato del sistema universitario*. Available in *Boll. Adapt*, 2005, No. 31.

[113] See the critical but well founded comments of Lippi, M., and P. Reichlin. 2004. "Critiche fuori bersaglio", www.lavoce.info, 29 January.

[114] Mas-Colell, A. 2004. "La riforma necessaria", www.lavoce.info, 29 January.

[115] European Commission, COM(2005) 13 final, *Joint Employment Report 2004/2005*, in *Boll. ADAPT*, 2005, No. 5.

academic staff and the University administration to attract substantial private resources to allocate to research.

It is for this reason that the *White Paper on the Labour Market* of October 2001[116] called for a programme of local agreements for employability, by means of links between education, training and the labour market, envisaging for the Universities a coordinating and innovating role for the development of the territory.[117] And it is for the same reason that the *White Paper* urged schools and above all Universities to make a special effort to safeguard the employability of all their students, playing an essential role within the overall system in facilitating the transition from education and training to the labour market.[118]

6. The Connections between Secondary/Higher Education and the Labour Market in Act No. 30/2003 and Legislative Decree No. 276/2003

In order to facilitate a new role in career guidance and a closer relationship with enterprises—while avoiding the temptation to make the usual agreements between the social partners characterised by fine promises not supported by practical measures to implement them[119]—the Biagi Law assigns to schools, University foundations, and above all the Universities themselves, three central functions: 1) university-level apprenticeships; 2) placement services to facilitate access to the labour market for students; 3) the certification of employment contracts.[120]

---

[116] See *www.adapt.it*, index A-Z, under *Riforma Biagi.*

[117] In this connection reference should be made to the Modena Pact on Employability of 8 April 2002, available at *www.adapt.it*, under *Mercato del Lavoro*, Index A-Z. See also the paper by Paola Gelmini in Gelmini, P., and M. Tiraboschi, eds. *Scuola, Università e Mercato del lavoro etc., op.cit.*

[118] In this perspective, framing the problem of youth employment in terms of "employability" and not of "the precarious nature of employment" caused by a presumed deregulation of the regulatory framework, see Biagi, M. *Università e orientamento al lavoro nel dopo-riforma etc.,* cit.

[119] In terms of employability and the connections between education and the labour market, there have been many examples of concertation based on agreements that are simply a list of promises and good intentions without any positive impact on the territory concerned. In general, only framework agreements for the design and implementation of work training and career guidance programmes appear to produce any practical results. For a survey of the main agreements see Senatori, I., *Boll. ADAPT,* 2005.

[120] See Zoppoli, L. 2004. "Università e riforma del mercato del lavoro", *DRI,* pp.

With reference to the transition from education and training to the labour market, Legislative Decree No. 276/2003 takes an institutional approach, aimed at consolidating and developing the positive results obtained in terms of access to the labour market with the work experience and career guidance schemes *(tirocini formativi e di orientamento)* introduced by Article 18, Act No. 196/1997.[121] These schemes are intended to promote the employment of young people by actively involving educational and training institutions and, in spite of the criticisms put forward by certain legal scholars,[122] have nothing to do with the deregulation of the labour market. Rather, the reform is intended to reduce the improper use of parasubordinate employment that has so far been one of the main means of access to the labour market for young people. The provisions for project work, as explicitly stated by the legislator,[123] are intended to facilitate the transition, over a period of time,[124] of as many employees as possible from the so-called "grey" or "atypical" area to the various forms of salaried employment, that have now been extended and diversified as part of the overall policy objective of redesigning employment protection by means of regulated flexibility, regulated also by the trade unions, thus promoting employability by enabling workers to adapt to the needs of the enterprise.[125]

This is the perspective within which the far-reaching reform of the system of apprenticeships and training contracts should be seen,[126] with

---

98-112.

[121] See Biagi, M., ed. 2002. "Università e orientamento al lavoro nel dopo-riforma: verso la piena occupabilità?", *DRI,* pp. 343-356, also in *www.adapt.it*, index A-Z, under *Università, scuola, mercato del lavoro.* See also, with reference to pilot schemes, the report on the monitoring of the placement programme at the University of Modena and Reggio Emilia, *www.adapt.it*, index A-Z, under *Università, scuola, mercato del lavoro.*

[122] *Supra,* § 1.

[123] See in this connection Ministerial Circular No. 1, 8 January 2004, *www.adapt.it*, index A-Z, under *Lavoro a progetto.*

[124] See Article 86 (1), regulating the transitory regime. See also the papers in Gelmini, P., and M. Tiraboschi, eds. *Scuola, Università e Mercato del lavoro etc. op.cit.*

[125] For this interpretation of the regulation of project work, reference may be made to my paper of 2004, on "La riforma dei contratti a contenuto formativo: il nuovo apprendistato e il contratto di inserimento", *La riforma Biagi del mercato del lavoro—Prime interpretazioni e proposte del d.lgs. 10 settembre 2003, n. 276*, Milano: Giuffrè, 191 ff., and Tiraboschi, M. 2005. "Il lavoro a progetto", *Studi in onore di Mattia Persiani*. Padova: Cedam.

[126] See the contribution by Pietro Antonio Varesi in Gelmini, P., and M.

the objective of offering: i) adolescents who do not intend to stay at school beyond the minimum school-leaving age the opportunity to take part in vocational programmes, enabling them to get recognised vocational qualifications, and to fulfill the right and obligation to continue their education for at least 12 years, with the option of returning to full-time education; ii) young people who have completed their high-school studies the opportunity to take part in higher-level apprenticeships leading to a diploma or an undergraduate or postgraduate qualification;

In particular, the apprenticeship contract leading to a diploma or associated with higher education,[127] that is currently being implemented by means of experimental programmes run by the Minister of Labour and certain Regions,[128] is characterised by a more innovative approach to training.

Apprentices can obtain the qualification specified in their individual training plan not only by means of off-the-job training, that is essential for any apprentice with an eye to the future, but also by means of training carried out in the workplace. In order to implement this scheme an agreement must be in place between the University and the employer. Moreover, in order for the training provided to be properly assessed, recognised and later certified, there is a need for a third party—in this case, the University or school—to examine the training carried out and the skills acquired by the apprentice.

In a training programme that aims at providing high level qualifications, there appears to be an increasing need for close links with the working environment, in order for the training to achieve the desired aim: the training of individuals who have the skills required by employers.

When the reform becomes fully operational, it will be possible to design programmes in which training includes both structured courses and informal learning. In such schemes the enterprise plans and implements

---

Tiraboschi, eds. *Scuola, Università e Mercato del lavoro etc. op. cit.*

[127] In the debate among legal scholars see Bianchi, F., and M. Trentini. 2004."La riforma del contratto di apprendistato in Italia: alcune valutazioni preliminari", *DRI*, No. 1, 2004; Varesi, P. A. 2004. "Principi, criteri e linee guida per la costruzione del nuovo apprendistato", *Come cambia il mercato del lavoro*, Various Authors, Ipsoa; D'Onghia, M. 2004. "I contratti a finalità formativa: apprendistato e contratto di inserimento", *Lavoro e diritti dopo il decreto legislativo 276/2003,* ed. Curzio, P., Cacucci; Menghini, L. 2004. "Apprendistato", *Contratti di lavoro flessibili e contratti formativi,* eds. Brollo, M., M. G. Mattarolo, and L. Menghini, Ipsoa; Guarriello, F. "Apprendistato", *Il lavoro tra progresso e mercificazione,* ed. Ghezzi, G. Roma: Ediesse.

[128] The experimental scheme is monitored by a ministerial task force set up by Ministerial Decree 12 July 2005.

the training in which the apprentice plays a full role in an awareness of the vocational objectives laid down.

Secondary and university level educational programmes and the transition to employment are therefore supplemented by periods of in-company training with the introduction of innovative learning projects, supported by the experience acquired in recent years of work experience and career guidance programmes.

Monitoring carried out over the past three years shows that companies that provide learning opportunities for students and young trainees improve their growth and development prospects.[129]

Public and private Universities and University foundations set up for the purposes of advanced training and dealing with labour market issues are also authorised *ope legis* to provide placement services *(intermediazione).*[130] For these services, as laid down in the Ministerial Decree of 23 December 2003,[131] they do not need a specific authorisation, but have to comply with the obligation to provide the services on a non-profit basis, to establish a connection with the national employment information system, and to provide the relevant authorities with updated information and figures on the functioning of the labour market.

With regard to the advisability of granting Universities the right to provide placement services, some commentators have criticised the policy of extending the right to provide such services to bodies other than employment agencies. The rationale behind this choice by the legislator is that the increase in the number of bodies engaged in placement and matching the supply and demand for labour can only have a beneficial effect, improving the quality of the matching process, which in certain cases does not appear to be particularly high, also considering the lack of transparency in the labour market as shown by the fact that in many cases in the past the Universities, but also academic staff, played an informal role in matching supply and demand.[132]

It was therefore considered more appropriate to bring these informal processes, that often take place in a manner that is by no means transparent, into a regulated framework linked to the labour market,

---

[129] 11% of undertakings and 53.4% of those with more than 250 employees according to the most recent Excelsior survey for 2003.

[130] See the contributions by Cazzola, G., C. Enrico, P. Olivelli, and G. Pellacani in *Scuola, Università e Mercato del lavoro etc. op.cit.*

[131] Available at *www.adapt.it*, index A-Z, under *Mercato del lavoro.*

[132] On this point reference may be made to Spattini, S., and M. Tiraboschi. "Regimi particolari di autorizzazioni e autorizzazioni regionali", *Il diritto del mercato del lavoro dopo la riforma Biagi*, cit., p. 127.

requiring those involved to connect to the national employment information service, rather than leaving them in the informal sector, providing services that at a formal level were prohibited. This measure has at least two consequences: on the one hand it allows these processes to be regulated; on the other hand, it provides a greater degree of transparency in the labour market through the dissemination of information about vacancies, by means of the obligation on the part of the Universities and University foundations to connect to the national employment information system.

Moreover, it is clear that the granting of authorisation to the Universities *ope legis* is not simply a way to regulate processes that have been going on for some time. The objective is more far-reaching: the intention is to make Universities and University foundations one of the engines for change in the new labour market. In the decree implementing Act No. 30, 14 February 2003, the higher education system, together with the new apprenticeship programmes, serves as the main channel for the development and improvement of human capital,[133] a channel by means of which the performance of the Italian economy can be brought closer to that of the leading European countries, thanks to investment in research and innovation. This choice is clearly dictated by the fact that since Lisbon Europe has made clear its intention to compete as a knowledge-based economy.

Unlike provisions for Universities, in the case of schools the entitlement to provide placement services depends on an authorisation procedure that is to be put in place by the Regional governments,[134] so as to safeguard active labour market policies. The overall aim however is the same, and consists of assigning significant functions to schools in career guidance and external contacts, linked either to higher education programmes or the labour market.

Finally, the Biagi Law allows the bodies set up by public and private Universities and by University foundations to carry out the certification of employment contracts.[135] This function is of particular importance in the

[133] In the debate among legal scholars see Zoppoli, L. 2004. "Università e mercato del lavoro", *DRI,* pp. 98-112; Bulgarelli, A. "Verso una strategia di *lifelong learning:* stato dell'arte ed evoluzione delle politiche di formazione continua in Italia," cit.

[134] See Article 6 of the Regional law of Friuli Venezia Giulia No. 18, 9 August 2005, in *Boll. ADAPT*, 2005, No. 30, and Article 11 of the Regional law of the Marches No. 2, 25 January 2005, *Boll. ADAPT*, 2005, No. 2.

[135] See the papers by Ghera, E., M. Magnani, and S. Magrini in *Scuola, Università e Mercato del lavoro etc. op.cit.* In the debate among legal scholars see Perina, L.

Italian labour market, characterised as it is by the extensive hidden economy or grey labour market.

The entitlement to certify employment contracts is not granted to Universities as such, but to full-time labour law professors who under the terms of agreements with private bodies provide consultancy services and assistance *intra moenia*. It is therefore not an authorisation *tout court*, but for the certification to be legally valid, it has to be carried out in the framework of a specific agreement in favour of third parties. In this sense specific provision is made by Article 76 of Legislative Decree No. 276/2003 that states that University bodies may be authorised "exclusively in connection with relations of collaboration and consultancy carried out by tenured labour law academics pursuant to Article 66, Decree of the President of the Republic No. 382, 11 July 1980".

The University certification centre will therefore operate on the basis of specific collaboration and consultancy agreements for third parties, to be signed by the Rector of the University, the Dean of the Faculty, and the Director of the Department or Institute on the basis of the internal organisation of each University. This means that in setting up a University certification centre, the labour law lecturer needs to procure for the University faculty or department a significant amount of private funding, sufficient to support the work of young scholars, focusing research efforts in sectors that rarely benefit from sufficient funding from the Ministry of Education, Higher Education and Research.[136] Under the terms of the specific agreements, a significant share of the funding is allocated to the faculty or department, to cover general costs and to fund research grants and the cost of administrative staff.

However, there is also another reason why the legislator chose to invest in University certification centres. Whereas the competence of other certification centres (provincial labour offices, provincial bodies, joint bodies) appears to be limited to the application of criteria and indicators provided in the form of codes and forms by the Minister of Labour and Social Policy for the purposes of certifying employment contracts, the contribution of the panels set up by Universities appears to be more

---

2005. "La certificazione nell'impianto della riforma Biagi del mercato del lavoro: finalità, natura ed effetti", *Compendio critico per la certificazione dei contratti di lavoro. I nuovi contratti: lavoro pubblico e lavoro privato,* eds. Enrico, C., and M. Tiraboschi, Milano: Giuffrè.

[136] These considerations appear to outweigh the criticisms put forward by Zoppoli, L. *Università e riforma del mercato del lavoro,* cit., pp. 106-112, that do not appear to take account of the mechanism of agreements with third parties and the consequent funding for university bodies.

specific and systematic, with the result that the opinions they issue, reflecting the specific competence and authoritativeness that the panel members need to bring to their work, will serve as guidelines for the other certification centres, with regard to the proper application of case law decisions, providing an adequate response to the issues raised, thus improving the effectiveness of the certification centres in general.[137] Article 4 of the Ministerial Decree of 14 June 2004 provides that the Ministry of Labour shall hold on file the studies and reports produced by the members of the University certification panels, for the purposes on enrolment on a certification register, allowing access on the part of the general public to the reports, but also and above all contributing to the definition of best practices and indicators relating to employment contracts and tenders.

7. Concluding Remarks

It is by means of these instruments that it appears to be possible to make higher education—as stated in a number of local agreements[138]—the strategic link in a much more complex network of legal and institutional relations which, for the purposes of employability, focuses on the objective of an effective dialogue between education and vocational training, public bodies at a territorial level, and organisations representing the interests of the workers and the local economy.

Without the creation and proper functioning of this indispensable network of formal and informal relations,[139] based on mutual trust and the development of adequate channels of information and communication between the actors present in a particular context, that might be called "social capital"[140] and that promote collective action as part of an overall

---

[137] On this point reference may be made to my paper of 2005. "Le sedi universitarie", *Compendio critico per la certificazione dei contratti di lavoro. I nuovi contratti: lavoro pubblico e lavoro privato,* eds. Enrico, C., and M. Tiraboschi, Milano: Giuffrè. For an opposing view*:* Zoppoli, L. *op. loc. ult. cit.*

[138] See, among others, the Modena Pact for Employability, 8 April 2002, available at *www.adapt.it*, index A-Z, under *Mercato del lavoro.*

[139] On the relevance of the distinction between formal institutions, that are of importance from a legal point of view, and informal institutions, that are of operational significance in a given socio-economic context, see North, D. C. 1994. *Istituzioni, cambiamento istituzionale, evoluzione dell'economia.* Bologna: Il Mulino.

[140] See the classic study by Coleman, J. S. 1988. "Social Capital in the Creation of Human Capital", *American Journal of Sociology,* 94, S95 ff., and more recently,

system, any reference to "human capital" (that is to say the resources relating to the specific vocational skills of those offering their services on the labour market) risks being purely rhetorical in that it would lack the necessary channels for it to play an effective role.[141] This appears to be even more the case—as comparative experience has shown—where suitable institutional channels and schemes for access to the labour market are lacking.

In this connection the Japanese case appears to be emblematic, with its consolidated institutional arrangements and methods for developing social capital and close links with enterprises—such as placement services and liaison offices located in schools and universities—thus, even in the absence of specific regulatory provisions, improving the prospects for labour market access and stable employment, unlike the economies where access to the labour market is managed solely—and inadequately—by networks of friends and acquaintances.[142]

In contemporary economies, that are frenetic and highly unstable, a great deal of social capital is consumed, and often there is a lack of institutions or bodies that take charge of producing or reproducing it, and that are in a position to do so in a context that has a significant international dimension.

Institutions of higher education—and to some extent also schools—can perform this function, enhancing social cohesion in a given territory and creating strong relational and cooperative networks to support social and economic development.

In this connection the position recently adopted by CNEL, the national council for the economy and labour, is significant, pointing out that Italian Universities need to act as catalysts for development at the territorial level,

---

Bagnasco, A., F. Piselli, A. Pizzorno, and C. Trigilia. 2001. *Il capitale sociale. Istruzioni per l'uso.* Bologna: Il Mulino.

141 One of the rare attempts to analyse the relations between social capital and access to the labour market is Seibert, S. E., M. L. Kraimer, and R. C. Liden. 2001. "A Social Capital Theory of Career Success", *Academy of Management Journal.*

142 See Brinton, M. C. 2000. "Social Capital in the Japanese Youth Labor Market: Labor Market Policy, Schools and Norms", *Policy Sciences,* No. 33, pp. 289-306; Mitani, N. "The Japanese Employment System and Youth Labour Market", *Preparing Youth for the 21st Century—The Transition from Education to the Labour Market,* cit., esp. pp. 308-310; Tiraboschi, M. 1993. "Alcune considerazioni attorno al Japanese Employment System", *DRI,* esp. pp. 31-58. With reference to the problem of institutional channels and the lack of access to the labour market by young people classified as NEET (Not in Education, Employment or Training) see Hori, Y. 2005. "Situations of Social Network of Jobless Youth and Assistance Measures", *Japan Labor Review,* No. 3:26.

strengthening strategic alliances with the institutions and the social partners for the purposes of the governance of local systems.[143]

The objective of forming human capital means that secondary schools, the Universities, vocational training bodies and the actors in the labour market need to act in concert as part of an integrated system.

An initial step in this direction could be the strengthening and extension of the experimental programmes that have already been launched,[144] with the setting up of an observatory of the labour market, education and vocational training, with the involvement of all the institutions and the social partners in a given territory. This could be strengthened with reference to the human resources and competition policies adopted in the Lisbon Strategy, making use both of EU indicators relating to the Open Method of Coordination of labour markets,[145] and those recently adopted for the education and employment sector. This appears to be the way forward for the definition of strategic policies for employment, the development of human capital and vocational training.[146]

Careful monitoring of the transition phases from education and training to the labour market is indispensable for the definition of local agreements for employability containing more than just declarations of principle, but leading to practical solutions. The use of EU parameters and indicators, that are authoritative and widely supported, will make it possible to move beyond the close confines of local contexts, which often risk being self-referential rather than promoting an awareness of developments in the international economy. Rather, as often stated, there is a need to think globally but to act locally. The internationalisation of higher education appears to be an essential condition for competing in what is known as the new economy, if we want to avoid this becoming just an empty slogan.

Italy appears not only to be a long way from reaching the objectives of the Lisbon Strategy, that is to say to enable education and training to be of world-class quality by 2010, but also ill-equipped to make its institutions

---

[143] CNEL, *Educazione e formazione—Osservazioni e proposte, cit.*

[144] For the province of Reggio Emilia see the paper by Semeraro F. in *Scuola, Università e Mercato del lavoro etc. op.cit.*

[145] European Commission. 2005. *Indicators for monitoring the Employment Guidelines 2004-2005 compendium.* Brussels: European Union; and the Employment Committee. 2004. *Conclusions of the Employment Committee on the Indicators Group's report indicators to be used in the Joint Employment Report, www.adapt.it*, index A-Z, under *Mercato del lavoro.*

[146] See the Conclusions of the Council of 24 May 2005 on new indicators in the sector of education and training (2005/C 141/04), *www.adapt.it*, index A-Z, under *Università, Scuola, mercato del lavoro.*

of higher education—as stated at Lisbon—the preferred destination for students and researchers from the rest of the world.[147] The complete lack of competition means that Italian Universities are ill-equipped to face the challenges and to take advantage of the enormous potential of internationalisation.

In order to address this strategic issue, it is important not to underestimate the significance of the proposal—mentioned above and now attracting a degree of consensus[148]—to abolish the legal value of university qualifications.[149] This would bring us closer to the model prevailing in the English-speaking countries, with the result that in Italy every University would bear the cost of and take responsibility for the recruitment and selection of its own teaching staff, with a view to eliminating the dubious practices that contaminate the selection process, recently the subject of an open letter by the dean of Italian labour law scholars.[150] It would then be up to the clients making use of educational and research services, that is to say the students, their families and enterprises to take measures in response to abuses of this enormous responsibility, by adopting market mechanisms, voting with their feet for the centres of excellence that reward the best scholars and recognise the talents of our young people.

However, one further point should be made. The central role assigned to Universities in the reform of the labour market seems to be indicative of

---

[147] Particularly emphatic and far removed from reality, from this point of view, the document drafted by CRUI. 2005. "Un anno al servizio del sistema universitario—Le attività della CRUI 2005", Rome 20 September in *Boll. ADAPT,* No. 33, esp. pp. 29-41.

[148] See, in particular, the position taken in the *Manifesto del Gruppo 2003: per una rinascita scientifica in Italia,* in *www.adapt.it*, index A-Z, under *Università, scuola, mercato del lavoro.* See also Maccacaro, T. 2003. "Abolire il valore legale del diploma di laurea", Gruppo 2003, and Gagliarducci, S., A. Ichino, G. Peri, and R. Perotti. "Lo splendido isolamento dell'Università italiana", cit. pp. 26-27. With reference to the Moratti reform proposals, Galli della Loggia, E. 2005. "Trent'anni di rivolte", *Il Riformista,* 29 September. For an opposing view, Accornero, A. "Valorizzare la qualità del capitale umano per la competitività del Paese", *op. cit.,* and the President of CRUI, Tosi, P. *Relazione sullo stato delle Università italiane 2005,* pp. 7-8.

[149] For a balanced analysis of the problem and of possible solutions see Finocchietti, C. "Il valore legale dei titoli di studio", Doc. Cimea 108, March 2002 (*www.adapt.it*, index A-Z, under *Università, Scuola, mercato del lavoro).*

[150] See Giugni, G. "Open letter to labour law scholars on the background to the elections to the selection panels for academic and research posts": English translation available, *Boll. ADAPT*, 2005, No. 23.

an awareness that the success of the reform depends not so much on the specific technical provisions adopted, but rather on an improvement of the quality and the education of the people who, in the coming years, will be called upon to implement the reform measures, as part of a process of governance that is based on a less precarious balance between the various actors than is the case at present. The reforms will be effective only to the extent that those involved are culturally prepared to accompany the processes of change and innovation, and are given the opportunity to perform to the best of their abilities.[151]

---

[151] Biagi, G. "Universitàe orientamento al lavoro nel doporiforma", cit., 16, responding to certain observations by Pera, G. 2001. "Sulla cosiddetta riforma degli studi universitari", *RIDL,* No. 1, pp. 87-93.

CHAPTER NINE

PRODUCTIVE EMPLOYMENT AND THE EVOLUTION OF TRAINING CONTRACTS IN ITALY

1. Overview of the Problem[1]

The new provisions relating to training contracts may be said to be among the most significant features—but probably also the most neglected by legal scholars—of the recent reform of the Italian labour market (the Biagi Reform, Act No. 30, 14 February 2003).[2] The underlying rationale of this reform may be summarised, in this connection, as an attempt to put an end to the ambiguities and grave anomalies in the use and development of "atypical" contracts. There has been an abnormal development, often in the grey area of the law, caused by the refusal to tackle the overall reform of the labour market, and as a result these atypical contracts have become a kind of safety valve for dealing with the persistent rigidities of standard employment contracts. In this perspective, it may be argued that training contracts have become just a form of temporary employment, a kind of fixed-term contract allowing for an exception to traditional labour law standards solely on the basis of age criteria. This form of employment is attractive to employers, not only because it is an additional instrument in relation to the limited range of options made available by the legislator for temporary work, but also because it is accompanied by generous incentives in the form of insurance contributions and tax relief, though it provides no guarantee at all of the effectiveness of training, that in many cases has been inadequate.

---

[1] This contribution was previously published in 2006 in *The International Journal of Comparative Labour Law and Industrial Relations* 22, No. 4, pp. 635-649.

[2] On the reform of the labour market, reference can be made to the documentation and the bibliography on the Marco Biagi Centre for International and Comparative Studies website (*www.adapt.it*), index A-Z, under *Riforma Biagi*.

It may be argued, at least in terms of industrial relations, that it is this improper use of training contracts that has made it possible on a number of occasions to put off the reform of the Italian labour market, thus making younger workers, who tend to be less represented by the trade unions, carry a good deal of the burden of flexibility required by employers. It is therefore not surprising that the problem of youth employment has become a major concern in Italy, due to the high levels of unemployment, without parallel in the rest of Europe, but also as a result of the lack of investment in training that has given rise to widespread precarious employment among young people.[3]

Within a normative and conceptual paradigm reflecting a Ford-Taylorist model of work organisation and production, training contracts providing access to the labour market have long been used as an instrument enabling employers not only to select workers most suited to productive needs in organisational contexts that are largely static and not particularly innovative, but also to benefit from lower labour costs during training, as a result of lower pay scales for trainees, and due to the generous subsidies made available, often in exchange for minimal or non-existent training programmes, as in the case of many work training contracts.

Like other Mediterranean countries, Italy has tended to subordinate training objectives to aims such as cutting labour costs, reducing the rigidity of the labour market in terms of protection for salaried workers, providing income support for young unemployed people and building social consensus. However, this strategy has turned out to be counterproductive, not only because it has failed to reduce the high levels of unemployment and precarious employment among young people. It also appears that the improper use of training contracts has had the effect of diminishing the overall quality of human capital in Italy to the point that there has been a sharp decline in international competitiveness.

It was therefore inevitable that as part of the overall reform of the labour market one of the main objectives was the adoption of a new system of training contracts in order to ensure their proper utilisation.

In this scenario it is possible to see the clear distinction made by the Biagi reform between apprenticeships and access-to-work contracts, that have replaced employment training contracts. Whereas apprenticeship contracts are an effective training instrument for the market, in access-to-work

---

[3] On this aspect, that is beyond the topic of this paper, see Tiraboschi, M. "Young People and Employment in Italy: the (Difficult) Transition from Education and Training to the Labour Market", *The International Journal of Comparative labour Law and Industrial Relations,* No. 1.

contracts training is secondary to the primary goal, which is to promote access to (re)employment for particular categories. This explains why economic incentives are maintained only for apprenticeship contracts and only on condition that the worker is actually given training. For access-to-work contracts, normative provisions are made available for all categories of employees, whereas economic incentives will no longer be granted for those in the 18-29 age group, who are considered to be less disadvantaged.

By means of this reform it will be possible in the coming years to pursue a comprehensive new strategy in the use of training contracts and financial incentives based on a real investment in human capital as a key factor in facing international competition.[4]

2. The Functional Overloading of Training Contracts and their Improper Use

The difficulty of making a rigorous distinction between the training provisions in employment contracts and financial support for employers is not encountered only in the Italian system, though in Italy the improper and instrumental use of training contracts has reached a level of degeneration not found in other systems.[5]

It is evident that apprenticeship contracts and employment training contracts have been improperly used, especially in recent decades, also because of a degree of overlapping in typological and normative terms, which tends to make them even more dysfunctional. The training component has in many cases been neglected due to a kind of functional overload, either for political reasons simply to provide funding for enterprises, thanks to the surreptitious reduction of labour costs made possible by generous grants, which the European Union has started to take action against,[6] or in relation to access to the labour market for unemployed people and income support for the younger members of the labour force.

---

[4] For further details, see Tiraboschi, M. 2005. “The Italian Labour Market after the Biagi Reform”, *The International Journal of Comparative labour Law and Industrial Relations,* No. 2.

[5] For a comparative study see Biagi, M., and M. Tiraboschi. 1999. “La rilevanza della formazione in apprendistato in Europa: problemi e prospettive,” *Diritto delle Relazioni Industriali,* No. 1. p. 87.

[6] For an analysis of the problem, see Tiraboschi, M. 2002. *Incentivi alla occupazione, aiuti di Stato, diritto comunitario della concorrenza.* Torino: Giappichelli, ch. III.

It remains the case that—as in other southern European countries[7]—alongside traditional training objectives, an increasingly important, indeed a predominant, role has been played in recent decades by other functions that are improper, such as cutting labour costs, reducing certain (presumed or real) rigidities in the regulations that protect standard subordinate employment, providing income support for ever larger groups of young workers, attempting to achieve a social consensus, and so on.

All this is by no means surprising but it should be seen in relation to a critical position—which has hardly been applied in practical terms—which for some time now has highlighted the dysfunctional aspects of training policies.[8] These policies, especially in Italy, are often confused with employment policies, and are assigned tasks and objectives that they cannot perform, such as the creation of new employment, the fight against unemployment and social exclusion, and so on. What clearly emerges from this is the ambiguous nature of so-called training contracts which are unable to provide genuine programmes with periods of alternation between work and training but which are actually used as a means to hire workers on lower rates than would otherwise be possible. Once it has been recognised that vocational training is not in itself capable of generating new employment, then it becomes possible to carry out a meaningful analysis of the role to be assigned to apprenticeships and other forms of training contract with an alternation between work and training, without expecting contracts of this kind to become a panacea for the complex problems of the labour market, a fact that was clear in the context of the reform of apprenticeship contracts in the Treu measures in 1997.[9]

In this connection the redesign of training contracts delineated in the Biagi reform must be seen in the light of the complex provisions included in Legislative Decree No. 276/2003, including provisions on adaptability, limiting the improper use of labour flexibility and training policies, and provisions on employability, aimed at strengthening the position of the individual worker in relation to sudden and unexpected changes in the labour market.

---

[7] See again Biagi, M., and M. Tiraboschi, *La rilevanza della formazione in apprendistato in Europa: etc.,* cit.

[8] See also the documentation and bibliography at *www.adapt.it*, index A-Z, under *Formazione.*

[9] See Vittore, A., and F. Landi. 1997. "L'articolo 17 della Legge n. 196/1997: coordinate per la riforma del sistema della formazione professionale", *Mercati e rapporti di lavoro. Commentario alla legge 24 giugno 1997, n. 196,* ed. Biagi, M. Milano: Giuffrè, p. 237.

This is the overall logic that explains the clear functional and normative separation of the two forms of contract. Whereas apprenticeships now become an institutional channel providing young people with access to the labour market, by means of an alternation between employment and training properly speaking, employment training contracts are being phased out (albeit only in the private sector) and in their place the legislator makes provision for a flexible new type of contract, known as the access-to-work contract *(contratto di inserimento al lavoro),* in which the training objective is seen in relation to the primary objective of employment policy, that is the entry or re-entry into the labour market of particular categories of individuals. This is why it is only for apprenticeship contracts that the economic incentives currently made available are maintained. On the other hand, the new access-to-work contracts make use of normative incentives, operating on two distinct levels: the application of normative incentives is provided for all categories of worker, whereas economic incentives will not be granted to the groups of workers considered to be the least disadvantaged, that is to say young people between the ages of 18 and 29.[10]

3. Types of Apprenticeship after the Biagi Reform

Legislative Decree No. 276, 10 September 2003, reaffirms the right and duty to take part in education and training, including the training options providing for the alternation of training and employment adopted in the Moratti reform of the education system, and then identifies three distinct types of apprenticeship contract.[11] In addition to the apprenticeship contract relating to the right and duty to take part in an education and training programme, the reform makes provision also for vocational apprenticeships, for obtaining a qualification by means of on-the-job training and the acquisition of technical and vocational skills, expected to be the type of contract that is most commonly used, and finally an apprenticeship leading to a diploma or specialised training.

The employment provisions for these three types of apprenticeship contract are fundamentally similar, though the training schemes differ considerably for each of them, as a function of the result to be achieved.

---

[10] On this point, also on the difference between economic and normative incentives, see Tiraboschi, *Incentivi alla occupazione, aiuti di Stato, diritto comunitario della concorrenza,* cit.

[11] See the documentation and bibliography at *www.adapt.it*, index A-Z, under *Apprendistato.*

In particular, the employment contract is required to be drawn up in writing and to contain a description of the work to be carried out, the training to be given, and the qualification to be gained at the end of the training period. In addition, it is forbidden to pay the apprentice by piecework, or to terminate the apprenticeship before it has run its full term in the absence of a just cause or justified reason.

The vocational qualifications gained with all the new apprenticeship contracts give rise to an entitlement to credits for further education and vocational training.[12]

In order to harmonise the various qualifications obtained the Ministry of Labour and Social Policy is to set up a register of vocational qualifications. This will be drawn up by a commission set up by the Ministry of Education, Higher Education and Research, the employers' associations and the most representative trade unions at national level, and representatives of the Conference of the State and the Regions.

The national legislator, confirming earlier provisions, has laid down quantitative limits on the use of this type of contract. In particular the percentage of apprentices that may be hired in relation to specialised and qualified staff employed in the firm may not be greater than 100 except in the artisan sector (micro and small enterprises), that are regulated by more favourable provisions as laid down in Article 4, Act No. 443/1985.

Moreover, employers who have no specialised and qualified employees, or fewer than three, are not entitled to hire more than three apprentices. In all cases under the terms of current provisions the employer has the right to terminate the employment relationship upon completion of the apprenticeship, pursuant to Article 2118 of the Civil Code. This latter provision takes on a particular significance in defining apprenticeship contracts. Although opinion is divided among legal scholars, the apprenticeship contract may be said to be a special kind of open-ended employment relationship, which is characterised by the fact that both the employer and the apprentice are entitled to terminate the relationship at the end of the period of training by giving notice to the other party (as laid down by Article 19, Act No. 25, 1955).

Unlike the procedure for fixed-term contracts, which automatically expire at the end of the agreed period, apprenticeship contracts require

---

[12] The procedures for the recognition of training credits are to be established pursuant to Article 51(2), Legislative Decree No. 276/2003, in compliance with the competences of the autonomous provinces and regions and with the provisions of the Unified Conference of State-Regions-Autonomous Local Authorities in the Agreement of 18 February 2000 and the provisions of Legislative Decree No. 174/2001.

notice to be served pursuant to Article 2118 of the Civil Code, a provision expressly entitled "Termination of open-ended contracts". In the event that notice is not served, the employment relationship continues in the same way as a normal open-ended employment contract.

On the basis of these particular provisions for the termination of the apprenticeship contract, it may be considered to be an open-ended contract *(a tempo indeterminato),* as it is not a fixed-term contract in the technical sense, but an employment contract with a maximum duration, linked to particular training objectives: once these objectives have been fulfilled, and in the absence of notice of termination, it is automatically transformed into an open-ended employment relationship.[13]

Especially after the Biagi reform, which aims to strengthen the training component and to provide an institutional channel for access by young people to the labour market, the apprenticeship contract should therefore be considered to be an open-ended employment contract characterised by a deadline by which the parties are free to terminate the contract, coinciding with the completion of the training period.

3.1. The First Level: Apprenticeship Contracts for Exercising the Right and Duty to Take Part in Education and Training

After the age of 15, young people can be hired on apprenticeship contracts for exercising the right and duty to take part in education and training. This contracts lay the foundation for implementing the new right and responsibility to take part in education and training for 12 years, introduced alongside the abolition of obligatory schooling, in compliance with the constitutional principle of labour law, which, pursuant to provisions currently in force on the employment of minors, could not be denied once a young person has reached the age of 15. With the entry into force of the Moratti reform of education, apprenticeship contracts become the only form of employment permitted between the ages of 15 and 18.

This form of apprenticeship, that may be used in any sector of the economy, is intended to lead to a vocational qualification and has a maximum duration of three years. Young people who will be able to take up this form of employment, in principle, are those from 15 to 18 years of age, but not necessarily, because also those over the age of 18 who have not completed a sufficient period of education or training may also be employed on contracts of this type. In addition, the duration of the contract

---

[13] In this connection see Suppiej, G. (heading) *Apprendistato*, in *Enc. Giur*, Giuffrè; Ferraro, *Contratto di apprendistato.*

will be determined on the basis of the vocational qualification to be obtained, the academic qualification, the vocational and training credits awarded, and the skills assessment carried out by the public employment services or accredited private bodies, by means of the recognition of training credits pursuant to Act No. 53, 28 March 2003.

The regulation of the training component of apprenticeship contracts for exercising the right and duty to take part in education and training is the responsibility of the regions and the autonomous provinces of Trento and Bolzano, in agreement with the Ministry of Labour and Social Policy and the Ministry of Education, Higher Education and Research, on condition that they obtain the opinion of the employers' associations and the most representative trade unions at national level.

In order not to interfere with the competences of the regions in training matters, certain fundamental principles are laid down at national level. The definition of vocational qualifications is to be carried out pursuant to Act No. 53, 28 March 2003. Moreover, the total number of hours of training, both on-the-job and off-the-job, considered to be necessary to obtain a vocational qualification, will be established on the basis of minimum vocational standards laid down pursuant to Act No. 53, 28 March 2003.

Once again it is important to note that the decree does not lay down a fixed number of hours, as initially intended in the early drafts of the decree that specified 1200/1800 hours of training.

The extreme flexibility in terms of the number of hours of training, and the means by which training may be carried out, may be explained by the fact that these matters are to be determined by collective labour agreements at national, territorial or company level by employers' associations and the most representative trade unions, with the determination, also by joint bodies (*enti bilaterali*), of the most suitable forms of company training, in compliance with the general standards laid down by the competent regions.

To safeguard the effectiveness of training programmes, a tutor with the necessary training and professional skills is required within the company.

From this overview of the regulation of first-level apprenticeship contracts, it may be seen that there is no risk of the nature of such contracts being radically transformed.

Starting from the principle that the exercise of the right and duty to take part in education and training is a matter of public policy, concerning the training of young people, an alternative system might have been adopted (not proposed by the present author), in which the education system rather than the enterprise would have had to meet the cost of providing training to enable these young people to enter the labour market.

3.2. The Second Level: Vocational Apprenticeships

Young people between the ages of 18 and 29 can be hired in all sectors of the economy on vocational apprenticeship contracts, in order to obtain a qualification by means of on-the-job training and the acquisition of basic, transferable, and technical-vocational skills. Moreover, 17-year-olds can also be hired on such contracts provided they have obtained a vocational qualification pursuant to Act No. 52, 28 March 2003. At least in terms of the definition of those eligible, the historic difference between the artisan sector and other sectors has therefore been eliminated.

The duration of vocational apprenticeships is to be determined by collective agreements concluded between the employers' associations and the most representative trade unions at national or regional level, though in any case the duration must be at least two years and no more than six.

Moreover, it is allowed to add time spent in an apprenticeship for the exercise of the right and duty to take part in education and training, and vocational apprenticeship periods, provided that the total duration is no more than six years.

While safeguarding certain general principles, the regulation of the training component of vocational apprenticeships is the responsibility of the regions, in agreement with the employers' associations and the most representative trade unions at regional level. However, these agreements have been only partially negotiated, and it is for this reason that vocational apprenticeships have been implemented only in a partial and uneven manner, even now, some three years after the entry into force of the Biagi Act.[14]

Unlike the first type of apprenticeship, provision is made for a minimum number of hours, amounting to 120 per annum, for the acquisition of basic and technical-vocational skills. In contrast with previous legislative provisions, such training may be carried out in the company and even in the form of distance learning.

This means the abrogation of the principle introduced by Act No. 196, 24 June 1997, by which the granting of contributions relief to the employer was dependent on the apprentice taking part in training programmes outside the company.

Collective agreements concluded at national, territorial or company level by employers' associations and the most representative trade unions

---

[14] See the documentation and bibliography at *www.adapt.it*, index A-Z, under *Apprendistato*.

are to determine, also through joint bodies,[15] the means by which training will be provided, whether within the company or externally.

Also in this case a company tutor with suitable qualifications and skills is required, and records must be kept of the training provided in the employee's training portfolio *(libretto formativo).*

3.3. The Third Level: Higher Apprenticeships

Young people between the ages of 18 and 29 can be hired in all sectors of the economy on higher-level apprenticeship leading to the award of a high-school diploma, or university and advanced qualifications, as well as advanced technical specialisations pursuant to Article 69, Act No. 144, 17 May 1999.

In this case the regulations laid down in the decree law are minimal, mainly making provision for apprenticeship contracts to be used for advanced vocational training, as in other countries. While no attempt is made to modify programmes that are already operational (the decree law refers to "agreements in force"), the task of regulating and deciding the duration of apprenticeships for the award of a diploma or for advanced training is assigned to the regions, in agreement with the regional employers' associations and trade unions, universities and other training institutions.

4. The Demise of Employment Training Contracts and the Birth of Access-to-work Contracts

On the other hand major changes are planned for employment training contracts, which are to be abolished.[16] The legislator has taken account of the almost total lack of any training component in employment training contracts, and has reconsidered their function with a view to giving priority to access—and above all re-entry to the labour market—on the part of particular groups of workers. As a result, entry-level contracts *(contratti di inserimento)* in the public administration are being phased out.

---

[15] See the documentation and bibliography at *www.adapt.it*, index A-Z, under *Enti bilaterali.*

[16] See the documentation and bibliography at *www.adapt.it*, index A-Z, under *Contratto di formazione e lavoro.*

Under the terms of the new definition,[17] access-to-work contracts are intended to implement an individual plan for the adaptation of the vocational skills of the worker to a specific workplace, in order to facilitate access or re-entry to the labour market on the part of the following categories: a) young people between the ages of 18 and 29; b) those in long-term unemployment between the ages of 29 and 32; c) workers over the age of 50 who are not currently employed; d) workers who intend to start work again after a break of at least two years; e) women of all ages who are resident in geographical areas where the rate of employment for women[18] is at least 20 per cent less than the rate for men, or where the female unemployment rate is at least 10 per cent higher than the rate for men; f) individuals who pursuant to current provisions have a recognised physical disability, learning disability, or psychiatric disorder.

Access-to-work contracts can be issued by: a) public undertakings, enterprises or consortia; b) groups of private enterprises; c) professional, social, cultural or sports associations; d) foundations; e) public or private research bodies; f) sectoral organisations or associations.

Making use of a scheme adopted in the regulations for employment training contracts, it is provided that the use of this type of contract, made more attractive by a mixture of both normative and economic incentives, is conditional on the employer having continued to employ at least 60 per cent of the workers whose access-to-work contracts have run out over the previous 18 months. In calculating this figure, no account is taken of workers who have resigned, those who have been dismissed for good reason, and those who at the end of their access-to-work contracts have rejected an offer to continue in employment on an open-ended contract, those whose contracts were terminated during or at the end of the probation period, and a maximum number of four contracts not converted into fixed-term employment contracts. This provision will take effect as from its entry into force, and therefore will not take into account the conversion of the old employment training contracts expiring during the period of transition to the new regime.

---

[17] See the documentation and bibliography at *www.adapt.it*, index A-Z, under *Contratto di inserimento.*

[18] The employment rate referred to was calculated, pursuant to Article 54(1)(e), with a decree of the Ministry of Labour and Social Policy together with the Ministry of the Economy and Finance (Novembre 2005 at *www.adapt.it*, index A-Z, under *Contratto di inserimento).*

4.1. Vocational Access Plans

An essential component of access-to-work contracts is the vocational access plan. The hiring of workers on access-to-work contracts is conditional on the adoption, by the contracting parties, of an individual training plan aimed at guaranteeing the adaptation of the professional skills of the employee to the workplace.

Collective agreements concluded at national level, or at territorial level by the employers' associations and the comparatively most representative trade unions at national level, and company-level contracts concluded by the company trade union representatives or the unitary trade unions, also through joint bodies, make provision for the regulation of individual access-to-work contracts. They both take into consideration the provision of training, also with the support of multi-sector training funds, for the purposes of improving vocational skills.

4.2. The Regulation of Access-to-work Contracts

Access-to-work contracts are deemed to be equivalent to fixed-term employment contracts, though they are characterised by the presence of an access plan supported by a mixture of economic and normative incentives.

In the absence of different provisions in the collective agreements concluded at national or territorial level by employers' associations and the most representative trade unions at national level, and company-level contracts concluded by company-level or unitary trade union representatives, access-to-work contracts are regulated, wherever compatible, by the provisions of Legislative Decree No. 368, 6 September 2001.[19]

The access-to-work contract is required to be in writing, specifying the individual employment plan. In the absence of a written agreement the contract is null and void, and the worker is deemed to be hired on an open-ended employment contract.

The duration of the contract may be not less than nine not more than 18 months. In the case of individuals with a serious physical disability, learning disability or psychiatric disorder, as defined by legal provisions, the contract may be extended for a maximum of 13 months. Access-to-work contracts may not be renewed between the same parties. Extensions to the contract are allowed up to the maximum duration. In calculating the

---

[19] See the documentation and bibliography at *www.adapt.it*, index A-Z, under *Contratto a termine.*

maximum duration of the contract, no account is taken of periods covered by military or civilian service, or for maternity leave. Percentage limits on the use of this type of contract may be laid down by collective agreements.

5. Economic and Normative Incentives

Both apprenticeship contracts and access-to-work contracts attract a series of economic and normative incentives.

In this connection, in the absence of different provisions laid down by legislation or collective bargaining, no account is taken of workers hired on apprenticeship or access-to-work contracts in the calculation of the limits laid down by law or by collective agreements for the application of specific norms and practices. Moreover, it is permitted to hire a worker in an employment grade two levels below the grade applicable, under the terms of the national collective agreement, to workers carrying out tasks requiring qualifications corresponding to the qualification to be gained at upon completion of the apprenticeship or the access-to-work contract.

However, it is intended to change the economic incentives for these two types of contract. Pending the systematic reform of employment incentives, the economic incentives currently in place are to remain unchanged only for apprenticeship contracts. In the case of access-to-work contracts, on the other hand, the existing economic incentives for employment training contracts will be granted only for workers in the disadvantaged categories.

The Biagi reform extends the range of flexible types of contract, so it was considered to be reasonable to concentrate economic incentives on the one hand on access/return-to-work contracts for disadvantaged workers, and, on the other hand, on apprenticeship contracts, considering that they fully comply with the requirement to provide effective training.

The financial incentives for the old employment training contracts have therefore been concentrated on a more limited range of individuals: formerly these incentives were granted to all those between the ages of 15 and 32, and even to older groups on the basis of regional provisions. The plan to focus financial incentives more sharply is intended to support workers who are far less attractive to employers than those who currently benefit from employment training contracts.

The savings on access-to-work contracts (replacing the old employment training contracts) will be used to compensate the higher costs, when the scheme is fully operational, of the incentives for apprenticeship contracts arising from the increase of the number of possible beneficiaries (by raising the age limit from 24 to 29 years of age).

This increase in costs should be more than offset by the savings achieved, more generally, by the provisions introduced by the decree that are intended to reduce the area of employment in the grey or black market, benefiting not just the workers concerned (in the form of a higher level of protection) but also the public finances (in the form of higher revenues).

In line with the overall aim of redesigning training contracts in order to make the training component effective, the legislator has made provision for sanctions in cases in which the training objectives are not complied with. In particular, in the case of a serious failure to implement the individual access-to-work plan, the employer is obliged to repay the training grant with a 100 per cent surcharge. For apprenticeship contracts, in cases in which no training is provided and the training requirements of the contract are not met, an employer who is solely responsible for non-compliance with the terms laid down in the contract is obliged to repay the training grant with a 100 per cent surcharge.

6. Conclusions: The Impact of the Inadequate Functioning of the Industrial Relations System on the Implementation of Training Contracts

The reform of training contracts was undoubtedly necessary, and there have been repeated calls for such a reform by legal scholars and even by the legislator. Even the Treu reform of 1997[20] contained proposals for a reform of the kind later implemented by the Biagi Act.

However, the reform is making little progress due to the inadequate functioning of the industrial relations system. As a result, the objective that has repeatedly been emphasised of boosting investment in human capital, in support of enterprise and labour productivity, is still far from being reached.

In implementing the Biagi reform, the social partners have simply activated a transition from employment training contracts to access-to-work contracts,[21] without responding to the need to provide norms for apprenticeship contracts. The lack of a collaborative atmosphere between the government and the social partners, both at national and regional level, has led to a paralysis of the reform, resulting once again in an improper

[20] Article 16 (15), Act No. 196, 1997.

[21] Based on two interconfederal agreements, one on employment training contracts in November 2003, and one on work access contracts in February 2004. See also *www.adapt.it*, index A-Z.

use of apprenticeship contracts that increasingly resemble the old employment training contracts rather than the new forms of labour market access with an alternation between education/training and employment.[22]

This is a demonstration of the fact that legislative reforms by themselves cannot achieve a great deal in the absence of an industrial relations system willing to implement them fully and coherently.

---

[22] For updated information on the implementation of the reform of employment contracts, see *www.adapt.it*, index A-Z, under *Apprendistato.*

PART III

NEW JOBS AND ORGANISATIONAL MODELS: THE ROLE OF LABOUR LAW AND INDUSTRIAL RELATIONS

CHAPTER TEN

OUTSOURCING OF LABOUR AND PROMOTION OF HUMAN CAPITAL: TWO IRRECONCILABLE MODELS? REFLECTIONS ON THE ITALIAN CASE

1. Framing the Issue[1]

Starting from the initial reactions to Legislative decree No. 276/2003 (the Biagi law) as supplemented and amended by Legislative decree No. 251/2004[2] it has been rightly pointed out that the regulation of labour intermediation and the outsourcing of labour[3] constitutes one of the most significant innovations of the reform of the labour market.

At times, however, this observation is associated with a highly critical stance towards this particular section of the reform, consisting of Title III and IV of the decree, and of the many innovative measures deriving from it.[4] It has been argued that the new measures dealing with agency work, contracting out, secondment and the transfer of undertakings are aimed solely at increasing the already considerable opportunities for the segmentation of productive processes and for companies to be divided up, "with a view to achieving more advantageous (and legitimate) conditions

---

[1] The present contribution was previously published in Blanpain, R., M. Tiraboschi. 2008. *Global Labor Market: From Globalization to Flexicurity*. The Netherlands: Kluwer Law International BV, pp. 185-208.

[2] See *www.adapt.it*, A-Z index, under the heading *Riforma Biagi*.

[3] The term "outsourcing" is used here in the strict sense, to refer to the practices of subcontracting, contracting out, agency work, and the transfer of undertakings. In this paper it will not be used in the sense of delocalization of offshoring, which is often considered to be a form of outsourcing.

[4] On the new legal framework for agency work, reference may be made to the bibliography and analysis in Tiraboschi, M. "The Italian Labour Market after the Biagi Reform," *The International Journal of Comparative Labour Law and Industrial Relations* 21, No. 2, pp. 149-192.

for the enterprise, in the exchange between labour and economic and normative provisions".[5]

Even legal scholars who are acutely aware of the need for profound change in the regulations governing outsourcing[6] have spoken of a neo-liberal model of organization of the system of production. Such a model is clearly not as strongly connotated as "US neo-liberalism, to some extent taking account of the protection traditionally afforded by Italian labour law" but it still aims at dismantling existing restrictions on the decentralization of production and contracting out, safeguarding the organizational choices and economic interests of business, while restricting the area of illicit activity to "processes based on fraudulent intent and anti-labour practices"[7].

It is hardly surprising that the new legal framework dealing with outsourcing and contracting out has been portrayed as a detonator that in a short period of time could set off a reaction leading to the fragmentation of the organizational structure of companies. The recent legislation would therefore appear to promote management strategies leading to a race to the bottom in terms of wages and legal provisions,[8] rather than the long overdue modernization of productive processes in Italy.[9] The processes of specialization and organizational innovation which, in the intention of the legislator as outlined in the technical report accompanying Legislative

---

[5] In connection with the extensive debate on the new provisions laid down by Legislative Decree No. 276/2003, see Chieco, P. "Somministrazione, comando, appalto. Le nuove forme di prestazione di lavoro a favore del terzo", *Lavoro e diritti dopo il decreto legislativo 276/2003*, ed. Curzio, P., (Bari: Cacucci), esp. p. 92.

[6] See De Luca Tamajo, R. 2004. "Tra le righe del d.lgs. n. 276/2003 (e del decreto correttivo n. 251/2004): tendenze e ideologie," *Rivista italiana di diritto del lavoro (RIDL)*, I, esp. p. 539.

[7] Again De Luca Tamajo, R. *op. ult. cit.*, esp. p. 531.

[8] See Chieco, P. *op. loc. ult. cit.*; see also Romagnoli, U. "Radiografia di una riforma," *Lavoro e diritto (LD)*, 2004, esp. p. 39-38 and Mariucci, L. 2004. "I molti dubbi sulla c.d. riforma del mercato del lavoro," *Lavoro e diritto (LD)*, 11.

[9] Among the legal scholars advocating reform of the legal framework for outsourcing, with a view to providing modern regulations capable of supporting new models of production and labour organisation, see, in particular, Biagi, M. 2003. "Competitività e risorse umane: modernizzare la regolazione dei rapporti di lavoro", *Marco Biagi: un giurista progettuale*, eds. Montuschi, L., M. Tiraboschi, and T. Treu, Milano: Giuffrè, p. 141 ff.; Ichino, P. 2000. "La disciplina della segmentazione del processo produttivo", AIDLASS, *Diritto del lavoro e nuove forme di decentramento produttivo*. Milano: Giuffrè, p. 3 ff. and 361 ff.

decree No. 276/2003[10], should go some way towards combating various forms of speculation on the work of others associated with intermediation in the labour market.

This perspective is not supported by any scientific and objective data and taking this position to the extreme, there have even been critical observations arguing that the new legal framework is not particularly useful for the system of production and for business. It has been claimed, also by those who criticize the Biagi reform due to what they consider to be an excessive degree of flexibility and liberalization of the labour market, that Legislative decree No. 276/2003 not only works to the detriment of labour protection and collective solidarity, but also of the needs for competitiveness of the system and the organizational and managerial efficiency of enterprises.[11]

The overall picture that emerges is decidedly gloomy. In the scenario depicted, not only employees and trade unions, but also employers, human resources managers and company directors are in difficulty due to a pointless reform that is also ill-conceived in technical terms. In support of this argument, reference is made to the exorbitant cost of "what the implementing decree, with a vaguely medical terminology, calls the *somministrazione del lavoro*".[12]

At the same time critics speak of "organizational and managerial chaos" arising from "the co-presence in the same workplace, whether it be a manufacturing facility or an office building, of workers hired on dozens of different contracts" including those classified as "subcontractors, who come into the workplace or office to work alongside employees of the company".[13]

This rhetoric is not only outdated but also in contrast with the findings of historical and legal research,[14] in that it takes the view that modern

---

[10] Available at *www.adapt.it*, A-Z index, under the heading *Riforma Biagi*. The *White Paper on the Labour Market*, October 2001, includes several references to the need for specialisation and innovation in productive processes and work organisation.

[11] See Alleva, P. 2004. "La nuova disciplina degli appalti di lavoro", *Il lavoro tra progresso e mercificazione—Commento critico al decreto legislativo n. 276/2003*, ed. Ghezzi G., Roma: Ediesse, p. 166.

[12] Gallino, L. 2004. "Il lavoro atipico che fa male alle aziende", *La Repubblica*, 5 June.

[13] *Ibid.*

[14] However, this rhetoric is widespread in Italy. Reference may be made of the debate in Parliament on Act No. 30/2003, and Legislative Decree No. 276/2003, in which temporary agency work is still compared in simplistic terms with the exploitation of the work of others, or even with the illegal activity of gangmasters

employment agencies are the *nouveaux marchands d'hommes*—while at the same time, not without a touch of cynicism, reference is made to the commodification of labour in Marxist terms.[15] A further line of criticism, in its most extreme version, seems intent on negating the effects of the reform. However, this is not to be achieved through trade union or industrial action, or by labour policy, but rather on the basis of a simplistic economic rationale casting doubt on the utility for enterprises of the recent labour legislation while at the same time it is said to be excessively neo-liberal—a line of argument that seems to be self-contradictory.

Interacting with hundreds of workers employed by dozens of different enterprises on dozens of different contracts, in the view of those who appear to favour a Fordist model of work organization:[16]

> means having to deal with an infinite variety of interests and approaches, with conflict between interests and groups, and processes associated with a continuous comparison between the terms and conditions of employment of co-workers. In this situation governing company organization and productive processes becomes a task that even Sisyphus would reject.[17]

It becomes difficult, if not impossible, for employers to manage human and material resources in an enterprise undergoing such radical change—as if by magic, it might be said—simply as a result of legislative reform. All this is due to legislation reportedly aiming solely at providing incentives for maximizing the "volatility of those in employment" and not at all due to economic and social processes that have been under way for some time (see below, section 3).

The enterprise therefore loses its innate identity as a "grand construction with sturdy foundations" and turns into a kind of "enormous

---

(*caporalato* in Italian). The Parliamentary debates are available at *www.adapt.it*, A-Z index, under the heading *Riforma Biagi*. Similar remarks were made when Act No. 196/1997 was approved.

15 See Marx, K. 1954. *Il capitale. Critica dell'economia politica*, I. Torino: Einaudi, first ed. 1867, esp. p. 172, with reference to rapacious parasites who position themselves between the real employer and the worker.

16 On the connection between outsourcing and the decline of Fordist factories that carry out 'all the functions required to manufacture their products' see, Supiot, A. 2001. *Beyond Employment: Changes in Work and the Future of Labour Law in Europe—A Report Prepared for the European Commission*. Oxford: Oxford University Press.

17 See Gallino, L. "Il lavoro atipico che fa male alle aziende," cit.

aviary".[18] It also becomes difficult to pursue the objectives of growth, productivity and competitiveness in the Italian economy, although it must be admitted that it is impossible to do without "the specialist contribution of suppliers or subcontractors that are highly qualified, in the productive cycle of the parent company".[19]

In this view the Biagi law embodies labour law and economic policy of limited value since it aims only at the reduction of labour costs. This is to be achieved by means of measures making it possible to "worsen the economic and normative conditions of the workforce, with the material or legal fragmentation of the work-place making it difficult to bring about the aggregation of opposing interests, enabling employers to walk away from their responsibilities towards both individual workers and the trade unions".[20]

Even without taking into account the strong ideological connotation of this position, which loses sight of the innovative potential of the reform, this line of interpretation seems to play a primary role in the study of the legal regulation of the outsourcing of labour. It should however be noted that the official figures,[21] three or more years after the entry into force of Legislative Decree No. 276/2003, reported an increase in stable employment of good quality and a reduction in labour in the hidden economy, thus providing a convincing response to the view that the labour market is undergoing de-structuring, and to the rhetoric of precarious employment,[22]

Rather, it may be argued that the recent labour market reforms, starting from the Treu measures in 1997, have contributed to reining in and governing the insidious forms of flexibility outside the legal framework and devoid of any trade union protection which, in comparative terms,

---

[18] Romagnoli, U. "Radiografia di una riforma," cit., esp. pp. 35 and 37 where he adds that the volatility of the personnel leads, in the case of temporary agency work, to their invisibility, since workers on an assignment are not calculated as part of the workforce of the user undertaking. It must be pointed out, however, that these workers are already calculated as part of the workforce of the employment agency, so it is difficult to see why they should be counted twice. This was the position adopted also in Act No. 196/1997.

[19] Alleva, P. "La nuova disciplina degli appalti di lavoro," cit., p. 166.

[20] Alleva, P. *op. loc. ult. cit.*

[21] See *ISTAT labour force survey*, available at *www.adapt.it*.See also ISFOL, *Rapporto 2006*, CNEL, *Rapporto sul mercato del lavoro 2006*.

[22] On this point see the well documented analysis by Reyneri, E. 2004. *Qualità del lavoro e flessibilità sostenibile, in 1983-2003: la politica locale del lavoro in provincia di Trento compie vent'anni*, suppl. a *OrientaLavoro*, No. 1, pp. 111-118 (available at *www.adapt.it*, A-Z index, under the heading *Mercato del lavoro*).

make Italian labour law one of the most ineffective and deregulated systems in terms of practical application, though on paper Italian legal provisions are among the most rigid. This is the picture that emerges from the shocking estimates of labour in the hidden economy, amounting to some four million undeclared workers, with the result that black market labour is two to three times higher than in other countries.[23]

A more balanced assessment appears to be made by those who, although with some reservations, argue that the Biagi reform of labour protection, at company level, "is left more to the employer than, as was the case in the past, to normative provisions, thus relying more heavily on the employer and at the same time on an increase in the bargaining power of the employees".[24]

In other words it may be said that enterprises now work within a legal framework that is more favourable to organizational innovation and investment in human capital. What may be lacking is a capacity on the part of human resources managers and company directors to implement processes of innovation that appear to be increasingly important to meet the challenges arising from the globalization of markets.

2. The Separation of Labour from the Enterprise: The Sign of a Modern Economy?

In order to carry out a balanced assessment of the new legal framework for outplacement and labour market intermediation there is a need to consider this original and thought-provoking line of reasoning that it is particularly useful in responding to allegations of a de-structuring impact on the Italian labour market of Legislative decree No. 276/2003.[25]

---

[23] See ISTAT. 2004. *La misura dell'occupazione non regolare nelle stime di contabilità nazionale: un'analisi a livello nazionale, regionale e retrospettiva a partire dal 1980*. Rome: ISTAT, in *www.adapt.it*, index A-Z, under the heading *Lavoro irregolare*.

[24] See Rebaudengo, P. A. 2004. "La separazione del lavoro dall'impresa: alcune significative novità," cit., p. 171. In the same perspective see also Russo, A. 2004. *Problemi e prospettive nelle politiche di fidelizzazione del personale—Profili giuridici*. Milano: Giuffrè, esp. Chap. III, sec. II.

[25] The line taken by Perulli, A. 2004. "Introduzione", *Impiego flessibile e mercato del lavoro*, ed. Tiraboschi, M., Torino: Giappichelli, esp. XIII-XIV, who discusses the stated and presumed intentions of the legislator. Considering that this comment appeared a year after the entry into force of the reform, it would have been more useful to examine the early stages of application of the new measures to provide empirical and objective evidence in support of the arguments put forward.

In this analytical perspective the legislator drafting the reform made a more far-reaching attempt than in the past to understand the practical problems of company organization and workforce management.[26] It is significant that the Biagi reform has been favourable reviewed by those who reject the conception of law as a dogmatic and technical body of knowledge as an end in itself:[27] according to this conception, it is the concern of a select group of experts, with scant regard to whether it is effective or enforceable. Today the effectiveness of labour law in Italy is limited in that it fails to meet the needs it is intended to address in terms of the protection of the worker in flesh and blood, though this aim is often stressed by critics of the reform.[28] This lack of effectiveness and enforceability, reflecting the inaccessibility and complexity of legal provisions, works in favour of what Pietro Ichino has quite rightly defined as "the labour law business".[29]

However, turning to the criticism that at first sight is the most penetrating and most effectively presented, it has been suggested that the legislator is at fault for underestimating the consequences of a "rough and ready solution"[30] to the main legal problems concerning work organization. The risk is that Italy will end up with a legal framework that in overall terms is "more oriented towards overcoming critical management issues, hopefully with positive outcomes for enterprises and workers, than towards modernizing labour law with a view to promoting

---

[26] This is hardly surprising, since the reform was subject to intense debate by the social partners and business leaders, in an attempt to identify proposals that were not based simply on legal reasoning, but rather a response to problems at the level of practical application. On this point see D'Oronzo, V. 2004. "La riforma del mercato del lavoro tra concertazione e dialogo sociale", *La riforma Biagi del mercato del lavoro*, ed. Tiraboschi, M., Milano: Giuffrè, pp. 747-771, including the views of the social partners, largely favourable to the reform, in Part II, section C, "La riforma del mercato del lavoro tra concertazione e dialogo sociale: la posizione del governo e il giudizio delle parti sociali".

[27] A different view is taken by Pedrazzoli, M. "La correzione della c.d. riforma Biagi," cit., who defends a static legal system with its own internal logic rather than proposing ways of governing a dynamic situation in continual flux.

[28] On the relations between the Biagi reform and the effectiveness of labour law, see the arguments put forward in Tiraboschi, M. 2004. "Riorganizzazione dei servizi ispettivi e riforma del mercato del lavoro", *La riforma dei servizi ispettivi in materia di lavoro e previdenza sociale*, Monticelli, C. L., and M. Tiraboschi, Milano: Giuffrè, esp. pp. 15-18.

[29] See Ichino, P. *Il lavoro e il mercato—Per un diritto del lavoro maggiorenne*, Mondadori, Milan, 1996, esp. pp. 164-166.

[30] Rebaudengo, P. A. *op. loc. ult. cit.*

human resources; a task that is naturally left entirely to enterprises to perform".[31]

The legal framework for outsourcing should undoubtedly facilitate the transformation of production in the company and also the structural use, within networks of companies increasingly characterized by fragmentation, of employees of other companies, either by means of subcontracting, or by means of staff leasing or the posting of workers. In this way it is possible to deal with the "obsolescence" of the Italian labour law system (in the words of Marco Biagi)[32] which for a long time, due to provisions that were not capable of promoting or even governing outsourcing, resulted in outsourcing being considered not so much an opportunity as "a risk and therefore a constraint".

However, at the same time, the new legal provisions might lead to a worsening of conditions for workers and for their employers. The reason for this, at least in the medium to long-term, is that an employer relying on workers employed by third parties (contractors or staff leasing agencies), instead of the traditional employment contract pursuant to Article 2094 of the Civil Code, has no interest in investing in vocational training, i.e. in identifying suitable training and career plans, taking account of the employees' potential for growth by means of horizontal moves in order to enhance their skills, and providing incentives for them to participate in processes of change and quality schemes in the company. This has a negative impact on management and motivational initiatives that tend to foster a sense of "belonging", "company culture" and "participation".[33]

This line of critical reasoning is directed at the generally recognized principle that has tended to make outsourcing attractive, not only in the eyes of employers: that outsourcing is an essential characteristic of modern economies, favouring organizational and managerial innovation in the employment of labour.[34]

This is the crucial issue for ascertaining the effectiveness or otherwise of the system of outsourcing introduced by the Biagi Law, both in terms of

---

[31] *Ibid.*

[32] Biagi, M. "L'outsourcing: una strategia priva di rischi?", *Marco Biagi: un giurista progettuale*, cit., esp. p. 271. For Biagi, "such are the difficulties, and the numerous risks of a legal kind, that the strategic value of outsourcing may at times be called into question".

[33] See Rebaudengo, P.A. *op. cit;* in the international literature, Autor, D. H. 2003. "Outsourcing at Will: The Contribution of Unjust Dismissal Doctrine to the Growth of Employment Out-sourcing," *Journal of Labor Economics*, esp. p. 9.

[34] On this point see Biagi, M. "L'outsourcing: una strategia priva di rischi?" cit., esp. pp. 284-285.

labour protection measures and in terms of regaining the competitiveness and organizational effectiveness of the Italian economy.

3. Outsourcing of Labour Relations and Organizational Innovation in the New Economy

The issue to be examined is the relation between the competitiveness of the system, labour outsourcing strategies and policies for the promotion of human capital.

In this connection, there is not much to be gained from the rhetoric of the commodification of labour in the examination of outsourcing, staff leasing and employment agency work. This rhetoric, although still firmly rooted in certain academic circles and trade unions, has been defeated by history—as shown not only by the position taken by the International Labour Organization, but also by the developments of the international sources relating to labour issues, and in Italy by Articles 1–11, Act No. 196, 24 June 1997, by which, last of all the European nations, Italy recognized the legitimacy of the use of temporary agency work, on certain conditions and within certain clearly defined limits laid down by law and collective bargaining.

It can also be argued that the early years of implementation of Act No. 196, 24 June 1997 (so called Treu package), showed that the legislator managed to distinguish effectively, in a normative and conceptual framework that was to inform Legislative decree No. 276/2003,[35] between on the one hand fraudulent and parasitic forms of intermediation in labour relations, and on the other hand, highly specialized professional services with a particularly significant role to play in facilitating access to (or a return to) the labour market.[36] In creating additional opportunities for regular and quality employment, these services are useful both for the market and for the workers, who have a better chance of finding stable employment at the end of their assignment.

---

[35] The view taken by Ichino, P. 2004. *Lezioni di diritto del lavoro—Un approccio di labour law and economics*. Milano: Giuffrè, esp. p. 242, note 15.

[36] As indicated in Part III (labour policy) of the Giugni protocol of 1993 on labour costs, thus paving the way for the social legitimization of temporary work agencies in Italy (available at *www.adapt.it*, A-Z index, under the heading *Concertazione*). This aspect is highlighted, among others, by Accornero, A. 2005. "Rappresentanza e nuovi lavori," *Diritto delle relazioni industriali (DRI)*, No. 1 "temporary agency work in Italy is characterised by proper regulation, the certainty of costs, protection of the employee, good quality intermediation, and the chance of a trial period, renewal and hiring for the worker and for the employer."

Mention should also be made of the fact that, according to a survey carried out by the Ministry of Labour and Social Policy,[37] "workers on a temporary work assignment have a reasonable expectation that their chances of gaining permanent employment a year and a half after the assignment will be twice as high, compared to those who have not been placed on an assignment, increasing from 14 per cent to 28 per cent".

Moreover, "some 51 per cent of temporary workers are offered the chance of being hired directly by the user company at the end of their assignment. For 32 per cent of these workers, this becomes a reality. In addition, some 20 per cent of those who are not initially offered the chance of hiring are then hired by the user company".

It is also the case that in many instances, especially in the case of staff leasing on open-ended contracts, the worker may prefer to continue working with the employment agency—that is often a large multinational company—rather than for the user company, due to the terms and conditions of employment and the prospects of continuity of employment and continuing training.[38] This is why the legislator provided incentives, in Article 23(8) and (9) of Legislative decree No. 276/2003, promoting continuity of employment of the worker with the employment agency, permitting the inclusion in the labour supply contract of clauses limiting the hiring of the worker by the user undertaking on completion of the assignment. This is allowed not only in the case of workers hired on open-ended contracts but also, provided the worker receives an adequate salary, in the case of fixed-term contracts.

Empirical research has shown that in any case from the point of view of the undertaking, in labour supply contracts there is a need, over and above the provisions of law, for flexibility of employment and the selection of employees in a perspective of investment in human capital. In addition, the application of the rule of equality of treatment between workers on an assignment and workers hired directly by the user company[39] confirms unequivocally that the net earnings of the employment agency do not represent parasitical income based on the commodification of labour, i.e. simply on the difference between the amount received from the user company for the labour supplied and the amount paid to the worker.

---

[37] Ichino, A., F. Mealli, and T. Nannicini. 2003. *Il lavoro interinale in Italia—Trappola del precariato o trampolino verso un impiego stabile?*, University of Pisa: Edizioni Plus, esp. pp. 57-59, available at *www.adapt.it*, A-Z index, under the heading *Somministrazione di lavoro*.

[38] As pointed out by Ichino, P. *Lezioni di diritto del lavoro*, cit., p. 229.

[39] Art. 23 (1), Legislative Decree No. 276/2003.

Rather, it may be said that the earnings of the employment agency are justified as they are associated with a typical business risk since the employment agency is obliged to supply a service on the market—research, selection, training of the employee and administration of the employment relationship—which, from the point of view of the price of the labour supplied, results in a higher cost than that which the user company would have paid if the workers had been hired directly. This fact undermines the argument of those who see staff leasing and temporary labour supplied by agencies that are expressly authorized by the law, provided they meet certain strict legal and financial criteria, as the embodiment of a policy aimed at the commodification of labour and at promoting precarious employment conditions.

It is, however, the case that the higher cost for the user undertaking making use of temporary employment agencies, together with the fact that not all the normal liabilities of those hiring labour are transferred to the agency, should mean that companies make use of temporary agency work—also in the absence of legal measures and anachronistic constraints, as shown in the case of the United States[40]—only in the presence of objective causes and not simply with a view to reducing labour costs (see below, section 5). In the legal framework put in place by Legislative decree No. 276/2003, thanks to a revised system of sanctions, these technical, organizational and productive reasons, including the substitution of personnel, also in relation to the day-to-day business of the user undertaking, are now intended to govern more effectively the processes of outsourcing and/or insourcing of labour.[41]

As pointed out by the influential *Supiot Report* in 1998 on the transformation of employment and the future of labour law in Europe[42], the tendency to reduce costs and make the employment of the workforce

---

[40] The U.S. case shows that even in the absence of limits laid down by law, as in the Italian system, the recourse to staff leasing and temporary agency work tends to be limited to specialized and niche services, or to labour intensive activities that make it possible to take advantage of economies of scale and external organizational and managerial know-how. In the U.S., it does not involve more than two per cent of the workforce.

[41] For an in-depth treatment see my chapter on Somministrazione di lavoro, appalto di servizi, distacco, in Tiraboschi, M., ed. *La riforma Biagi del mercato del lavoro*, cit., pp. 205-229 and Ichino, P. "Somministrazione di lavoro, appalto di servizi, distacco", *Il nuovo mercato del lavoro—Inserto sulla correzione d.lgs. 6 ottobre 2004, n. 251*, Various Authors, (Bologna: Zanichelli),VII-X.

[42] *Tranformation of Labour and the Future of Labour Law in Europe—Final Report*, 1998, esp. p. 17, available at *www.adapt.it*, A-Z index, under the heading *Statuto dei lavori*. See also Supiot, A. *Beyond Employment etc.*, cit., esp. p. 18.

more flexible has certainly played an important role and can contribute to explaining the outsourcing of functions and tasks that require a low level of skill (cleaning, gardening, deliveries, facility maintenance, catering, transport, etc.). But those who are familiar with recent developments in the system of production and work organization are aware that the outsourcing of functions requiring a high degree of skill is the result of two different factors:

[O]n the one hand technological progress (particularly the role of new information and communications technology), which has increased the level of skills required for certain functions and encouraged the use of outsourcing, while on the other hand there have been significant developments in contracting out techniques, enabling clients to obtain more information about their suppliers, eliminating the risks associated with the outsourcing of crucial phases of the productive cycle (in particular quality standards and ISO 9000 certification).[43]

Moreover, recent empirical studies carried out on behalf of the European Foundation for the Improvement in Living and Working Conditions in Dublin[44] provide evidence that it is misleading to claim, as is often the case in Italy, that the outsourcing of labour is dictated solely by the search for lower labour costs and an attempt to get round labour protection laws.

The reality is decidedly more complex and various factors, not necessarily linked to labour costs and competition between different systems of labour regulation, need to be taken into account in explaining outsourcing, a complex phenomenon that is characteristic of new labour organization processes.[45]

The new economy may be said to be the product of a combination of the increase in technological capital, human capital and organizational capital.[46] Innovation gives rise to the need for investment in technology

---

[43] Supiot, A. *op. loc. ult. cit.* See also Purcell, K., and J. Purcell. 1998. "In-sourcing, out-sourcing e lavoro temporaneo," *DRI,* No. 3, pp. 343-356.

[44] See in particular Huws, U., S. Dahlmann, and J. Flecker. 2004. *Outsourcing of ICT and related services in the EU.* Dublin: European Foundation for the Improvement of Living and Working Conditions, (available at *www.adapt.it*, A-Z index, under the heading *Esternalizzazioni*).

[45] To quote from the Director of the Dublin Foundation, in the preface to the study carried out by Huws, U., S. Dahlmann, and J. Flecker, *Outsourcing of ICT and related services in the EU*, cit.

[46] See the reported presented to the European Commission, edited by Alasoini, T. 2001. *Challenges of Work Organization Development in the Knowledge-Based Economy.* Thematic Paper Presented to DG Employment and Social Affairs by the

providing an adequate return thanks to competent and adaptable human resources and organizational models enabling them to fulfil their potential.[47] In particular, information and communication technologies have resulted in production moving forward from a "vertical" model with an integrated productive cycle in which all the workers carried out rigidly and hierarchically predetermined tasks and were all employed by the same entity, though working in different departments. The digital revolution has made it possible for enterprises to work together as a network—based on a series of contractual relations that are normally stable and standardized[48]—thus favouring the specialization and interdependence of each enterprise.[49]

It thus becomes economically rational for each undertaking to concentrate on its core business and to purchase supplies and services from third parties—often endowed with their own valuable organizational know-how—not only with regard to logistics, facility management, administration, the selection and management of employees, information systems, and the marketing of products, but also, in recent times, with regard to central and highly specialized functions close to the core activities of the company.

This is particularly the case for small and medium-sized enterprises, for which a network approach and the use of organizational and managerial know-how supplied by specialized firms is becoming decisive for survival, in the medium-and long-term, in an economic and social context in continual evolution.[50] This is all the more so in countries like Italy, where it is the particular structure of the productive system—and certainly not the new legal framework introduced by the Biagi law—that makes investment in human resources decidedly problematic, especially in

---

European Work Organization Network, available at *www.adapt.it*, A-Z index, under the heading *Lavoro (organizzazione del)*.

[47] The connection between work organization and the promotion of human capital is clearly shown in the *Green Paper* of the European Commission on *Partnership for a New Organisations of Work*, document drawn up on the basis of COM(97) 128 final, *Bulletin of the European Union*, suppl. 4/97 (available at *www.adapt.it*, A-Z index, under the heading *Lavoro (organizzazione del)*).

[48] See again Supiot, A. *op. cit.*

[49] See Castells, M. 1996. *The Rise of the Network Society*. London: Blackwell, Alasoini, T., ed. *Challenges of Work Organization Development in the Knowledge-Based Economy*, cit.

[50] See the report for the European Commission, Ennals, R. 2002. *The Existing Policy Framework to Promote Modernisation of Work: Its Weaknesses*, October, available at *www.adapt.it*, A-Z index, under the heading *Lavoro (organizzazione del)*.

the field of new technology, with a drift into the hidden economy and informal labour, resulting in what has been termed "the low road to development".[51]

All the changes outlined above have clearly had a strong impact not only on the functioning of national industrial relations systems, but above all on the quality of employment and work organization methods.[52] Labour is characterized not only by greater creativity, initiative taking and specialization—resulting in an increasing demand for services in all sectors but also in a trend towards the distribution of employment across a wider network of companies.

In this perspective, outsourcing becomes the standard approach to the production of goods and services with a view to achieving economies of scale; a relation of reciprocal interest (at a horizontal level) replaces the previous (vertical) hierarchical relations bringing together the various functions. Moving beyond the Fordist model of production enables enterprises to consolidate contractual relations, both with their own employees and with the network of companies operating in the market, which allows them to create added value.[53]

4. More on the Outsourcing of Labour and the Promotion of Human Capital in a Perspective of Competitiveness

The Continental European countries, Italy in particular, present a series of cultural and organizational barriers to the process of change.[54] They are reluctant to face up to uncomfortable facts, also due to the lack of appropriate institutions[55] and in many cases fail to adopt a cooperative

---

[51] See the report of the Work and Technology Consortium on *Work Organisation, Competitiveness, Employment: the European Approach*, CE-V/8-98-001-EN-C, 1998.

[52] See the papers in Blair, M. B., and T. A. Kochan, ed. 2000. *The New Relationship. Human Capital in the American Corporation*, Washington D.C.: Brookings Institution Press.

[53] *Human Resources—Outsourcing in Europe*, ADP Dossier, available at *www.adapt.it*, A-Z index, under the heading *Esternalizzazioni*, esp. p. 9.

[54] See the extensive analysis by the European Commission. 2002. *New Forms of Work Organisation—The Obstacle to Wider Diffusion*, available at *www.adapt.it*, A-Z index, under the heading *Lavoro (organizzazione del)*.

[55] As rightly pointed out by Ennals, R. *The Existing Policy Framework to Promote Modernisation of Work: Its Weaknesses*, cit., esp. pp. 6-7 and also p. 5 where he argues that the European Commission has underestimated the capacity of the social partners to respond to the call (in the *Green Paper on Partnership for a New*

approach to the management of industrial relations.[56] In the presence of an evident expansion in the global economy, their actual rates of growth are below their potential rates. They find themselves under pressure of competition from the Asian economies on the one hand, and the dynamic economies of the English-speaking countries on the other. As a result, the sluggish economies of continental Europe are facing the choice not so much between the high road and the low road to innovation, "but rather between innovation of any kind and no innovation at all".[57]

Supporting those who introduce innovation in the enterprise by making use of the services of human resources professionals that the legislator refers to as "employment agencies",[58] does not mean downgrading the human capital of Italian enterprises and opting for the low road to growth.

Rather, it is a strategy that can make it possible to intervene in a significant manner, at a structural level, to deal with some of the underlying problems of the system of production in Italy "in particular, to provide for continual technological upgrading, to reduce costs by means of increased productivity and more flexible management processes, and to improve the quality of services. In other words, to become more competitive".

This can be the case also when outsourcing takes place by means of the transfer of a part of the undertaking. Not only because, as rightly noted,[59] the transfer of employees to a company providing specialist services can enhance the career prospects of the employees, "offering them opportunities for acquiring new vocational qualifications, thus providing them with a higher degree of job satisfaction than they would have enjoyed in the company of origin". Outsourcing in the form of the transfer of a part of the undertaking can also play an important role in safeguarding employment levels and the quality of employment: "the down-sizing of the workforce in the company can lead to an increase in efficiency and

---

Organization of Work) to take responsibility for the modernization of work organization.

[56] Cfr. The European Work Organisation Network. 2001. *New Forms of Work Organisation—The Benefits and Impact on Performance*, esp. p. 2, available at *www.adapt.it*, A-Z index, under the heading *Lavoro (organizzazione del)*.

[57] Alasoini, T. ed., *Challanges of Work Organization Development in the Knowledge-Based Economy*, cit., esp. p. 8.

[58] On the provisions for temporary work agencies in Legislative Decree No. 276/2003 see Olivelli, P., M. Tiraboschi. 2005. *Il diritto del mercato del lavoro dopo la riforma Biagi.* Milano: Giuffrè, esp. Part I, section B.

[59] Purcell, K., J. Purcell, "In-sourcing, out-sourcing e lavoro temporaneo," *cit.,* p. 351.

competitiveness with the result that the employment of those who continue to work in the company becomes more secure. At the same time, the setting up of a new company, potentially allowing wider margins of flexibility in the management of the personnel (provided it does not take the form of small or extremely small companies) can be a useful measure to save jobs that are at risk".[60] The same may be said of the secondment of workers which, especially within the same group of companies, responds to the needs of the company, contributing to the balanced development of all the companies in the group.

It is also true that the techniques for making use of the labour of others that come under the generic term of "outsourcing of labour", are less and less associated with an irresponsible approach to personnel management.

Temporary agency work gives rise to complex contractual obligations, with an allocation of risks, powers, obligations and responsibilities relating to the employment of salaried employees. This allocation is on the one hand rigorously predetermined by the legislator, with a series of obligations on the part of the enterprise (the obligation to take safety measures, obligations concerning remuneration, social insurance and pensions contributions, the exercise of management and disciplinary rights, civil liability for the actions of the employee, and so on) and which, in the absence of specific legal provisions, are subject to agreement between the parties, in compliance with the principle of equal treatment for temporary workers and permanent employees in the user enterprise[61] and with the general provisions of economic policy.

In relation to traditional salaried employment, in the case of temporary agency work the overall legal position of the worker remains substantially unchanged, both in terms of rights and obligations,[62] and such employees

---

[60] See on this point the authoritative comment of Biagi, M. "L'outsourcing: una strategia priva di rischi?" *cit.,* esp. p. 274. See also Schuler, R. S., S. E. Jackson. 2004. "Human Resource Management in Context", *Comparative Labour Law and Industrial Relations in Industrialized Market Economies*, ed. Blanpain, R., The Hague: Kluwer Law International, esp. pp. 112-116.

[61] In the same way as Act No. 196/1997, Legislative Decree No. 276/2003 makes no provision, for example, in relation to sickness, maternity, postnatal leave, injury, incapacity, unexpected circumstances, or in general the other events that may lead to the interruption of the assignment. In these cases, the allocation of risks and liabilities is left to individual negotiation, or more plausibly, to collective bargaining.

[62] In the sense that the division of risks and liabilities can be taking place only between the temporary work agency and the user undertaking, whereas the transfer of risks and liabilities that are typically the employer's may not be transferred to the temporary agency worker.

carry out "their work in the interest and under the management and control of the user enterprise"[63]. However, the legal position of the employer, although unchanged if considered in its entirety, is divided between two separate entities—the temporary work agency and the user undertaking—giving rise to a duality of employers compared to a traditional employment relationship.

In the perspective of promoting human capital, it should also be noted that employees benefit from a significant allocation of resources in terms of the funding for bilateral bodies provided under Article 12 of Legislative Decree No. 276/2003—aimed at supporting vocational training and retraining initiatives. The objective is to promote continuity of employment and, in the case of employees hired on open-ended contracts, to provide income support in the event of termination. A further aim is to support initiatives aimed at monitoring the use of temporary agency work and its effectiveness also in promoting the emergence of labour in the hidden economy and combating irregular labour contracts.

The employees involved in this kind of insourcing of labour therefore enjoy a higher degree of protection than in the case of the contracting out of services. Only in a very broad and general sense—and in terms that in no way correspond to the majority of atypical employment contracts—can it be argued that temporary agency work makes it possible to transfer a share of the business risk to the employees, in particular "the risk that is intrinsic to every expansion of the workforce carried out with standard open-ended employment contracts".[64]

At least in the framework adopted by the Italian legislator, temporary agency work does not result in the transfer of the risks, obligations and liability associated with salaried employment to entities other than the user enterprise. Rather, it introduces a different arrangement, in keeping with general legal principles, by which the employer can make legitimate use of the goods and services produced by the employee. With temporary agency work, there are two entities benefiting from the labour of the employee, with a type of contract in which two entities share the rights and duties of one contractual party. This type of arrangement may be compared to the practice laid down in US case law,[65] which conceives of the trilateral relation in terms of "co-employment".

---

[63] Article 20 (2), Legislative Decree No. 276/2003.

[64] D'Antona, M. 1990. "Contrattazione collettiva e autonomia individuale nei rapporti di lavoro atipici," *Diritto del lavoro e delle relazioni industriali (DLRI)*, esp. p. 543.

[65] For a definition of co-employment in the United States, see Lenz, E. A. 1994. "Co-Employment—A Review of Customer Liability Issues in the Staffing Services

This accounts for the fact that in the literature there is a conceptual distinction, that more closely reflects the nature of this phenomenon, between outsourcing and insourcing, differentiating between respectively between the use of services supplied on contract or on a subcontract, and the use of agency staff working on the instructions and in the interests of the user undertaking.[66] In practical terms there is an increasing use of forms of co-sourcing, net-sourcing, selective-sourcing, multi-sourcing, back-sourcing, co-specialization and value-added outsourcing[67] providing for an allocation between the parties of risks, obligations and liabilities, in line with general legal principles, as part of a contract of co-employment that is advantageous also to the employee.

As shown by the most highly developed and mature markets[68] there is an evident trend, in outsourcing and insourcing, towards the development of a work-force that is highly qualified and adaptable, which is utilized to cover strategic positions in contractual relations between networks of companies.[69] This confirms the trend, highlighted by the European Commission in the *Green Paper* in 1997, towards a partnership for a new type of work organization,[70] in which the contribution of human capital in the productive process is of key importance, so that the employee becomes the critical factor in creating added value in the network of contractual relations between undertakings.[71]

Industry," *Labor Lawyer*, pp. 195-216. See also Linder, J. 1989. "The Joint Employment Doctrine: Clarifying Legislative—Judicial Confusion," *Hamline Journal of Public Policy*, pp. 321-330; Cooper, S. F. 1995. "The Expanding Use of the Contingent Workforce in the American Economy: New Opportunities and Dangers for Employers," *Employee Relations Law Journal*, p. 525; Siebert, W.V., and N. D. Webber. 1987. "Joint Employer, Single Employer, and Alter Ego," *Labor Lawyer*, pp. 880-883. See also the extensive bibliography in Axelrod J. G. 1987. "Who's the Boss? Employee Leasing and the Joint Employer Relationship," *Labor Lawyer*, pp. 857-871.

[66] Purcell, K. J. Purcell, *op. cit.*, esp., pp. 350 and 351.

[67] Extensive case studies are examined in Millar, J. 2002. *Outsourcing Practices in Europe*, Star Project, No. 27, esp. p. 12 (available at *www.adapt.it*, A-Z index, under the heading *Esternalizzazioni*).

[68] Millar, J. *Outsourcing Practices in Europe*, cit., pp. 28-29, and p. 35.

[69] Huws, U., S. Dahlmann, and J. Flecker. *Outsourcing of ICT and Related Services in the EU*, cit., 3-4, pp.17-18.

[70] European Commission on *Partnership for a New Organisations of Work*, cit.

[71] For an in-depth examination see Golzio, L. 2005. "L'evoluzione dei modelli organizzativi d'impresa", *La riforma del mercato del lavoro: deregolazione o riregolazione?—La 'Legge Biagi' nel confronto comparato*, ed. Serra, C., Milano: Giuffrè.

5. The New Framework for Outsourcing: From the Distinction between Core and Peripheral Employees, to Contractual Integration

The recent changes in the system of production and the organization of labour, with new human resources management strategies, gave rise to the need not only for a radical rethinking at a conceptual level of the model theorized in the literature by Atkinson[72]—with a distinction between core and peripheral employees,[73] but also and above all for the updating of the legal framework. This is particularly the case for a country such as Italy, where outsourcing processes were governed[74] by provisions that were extremely rigid in practical terms but quite ineffective in terms of enforcement. The result was the expansion of unregulated outsourcing,[75] by means of the extensive use of the contracting out of services, but also quasi-salaried or para-subordinate contracts such as *collaborazioni coordinate e continuative* that may be seen as an extreme and individualized form of outsourcing with serious consequences for human capital in the Italian economy.

The core-peripheral employee distinction appears to have been the basis of Act No. 196/1997, serving to overcome the rigid ban on temporary agency work.

Under the terms of Article 1 (1), Act No. 196/1997, agency work was permitted only to satisfy "needs of a temporary nature", and therefore only

---

[72] Atkinson, J. 1984. "Manpower Strategies for Flexible Organisations," *Personnel Management (PM)*, 28-31. See also Atkinson, J. 1985. *Flexibility, Uncertainty and Manpower Management. Institute of Manpower Studies*. Brighton: University of Sussex; and Atkinson, J., and N. Meager. 1986. *New Forms of Work Organisation*, IMS Report 121, IMS.

[73] Purcell, K., and J. Purcell. "In-sourcing, Out-sourcing e Lavoro Temporaneo," *cit.,* 344. On the same point, see also Russo, A. *Problemi e prospettive nelle politiche di fidelizzazione del personale*, *cit.,* esp. pp. 260-264.

[74] See, among others, Ichino, P. "Spazi attuali e prospettive del leasing di manodopera," *Rivista italiana di diritto del lavoro (RIDL)*, 1992, III, p. 119 et seq.; see also Id., *La disciplina della segmentazione del processo produttivo. Introduction and conclusions*. Giornate di studio Aidlass di Trento del 4-5 giugno 1999, available in AA.VV. 1996. *Diritto del lavoro e nuove forme di decentramento produttivo*, Milano: Giuffrè, p. 3 et seq. and p. 361 et seq.

[75] I attempted to argue this point in 1992. "Il lavoro temporaneo in Italia," *Diritto delle Relazioni Industriali (DRI)*, No. 1. On the risks of outsourcing of poor quality, in the absence of an adequate legal framework, see the European Commission. 1993. *White Paper on Growth, Competitiveness and Employment*, esp. Chap. 9.2.

for the exceptional cases laid down by law or by collective bargaining. The consequence of this provision, along with the ban on temporary agency work for low-skilled occupations, was that only a small proportion of the new forms of outsourcing emerged from the hidden economy to become regular employment. Certain legal scholars pointed to the hypocrisy of this Italian form of agency work, describing it as "a new practice totally useless as currently regulated. The harsh truth is that it is simply a duplication of fixed-term contracts, marketed as an important new flexibility measure".[76]

The effect of the measures introduced by Act No. 196/1997 was the reaffirmation of the inderogable abstract norm "coupled with subsequent scrutiny of the courts that has so gravely undermined the certainty of the law and planning by companies in relation to fixed-term contracts".[77]

Moreover, in this perspective temporary agency workers, though covered by far-reaching legislative provisions with the highest degree of rigidity and labour protection in Europe,[78] inevitably ended up in the area of precarious employment.[79] This was the case even when they had been hired on open-ended contracts by a multinational company in the sector, in line with standard employment practice, so that in terms of trade-union representation, they were quite unjustifiably grouped together with para-subordinate workers.[80] This was the case even though Italy, which is characterized by what is usually known as "horizontal" trade unionism, was not characterized by the sharp decline in the Fordist model in the same way as countries in which unionism is mainly or entirely of the "vertical" type.[81]

The framework adopted in Legislative Decree No. 276/2003 moves beyond the core-peripheral worker model in which temporary agency work was seen as a form of precarious and marginal employment, to be permitted only in exceptional cases. Temporary agency work becomes the driving force—in the presence of technical, organizational or productive reasons—for the outsourcing and insourcing of labour in connection with

---

[76] See Vallebona, A. 1997. "L'ipocrisia del lavoro interinale all'italiana," *Argomenti di diritto del lavoro (ADL)*, pp. 135-136.

[77] *Ibid.*, pp. 137-138.

[78] For a comparative overview, see my: 1999. *Lavoro temporaneo e somministrazione di manodopera*. Torino: Giappichelli, Chap. V.

[79] In this perspective, see Vallebona, A. 1996. *La riforma dei lavori*. Padua: Cedam.

[80] The statutes of NIDIL, ALAI. CPO group together parasubordinate workers, temporary agency workers, and those taking part in socially useful work schemes.

[81] On this point, see Supiot, A. *Beyond Employment etc.*, cit., esp. p. 17.

the specialization of production and the organization of work as a network that is the hallmark of the new economy.

In such an economy, Italian companies have more opportunities to legally make use of external labour markets, so that their organizational strategies no longer depend exclusively on the consideration of labour costs, but rather on transaction costs or the cost associated with the various types of labour contracts available.[82]

In the light of the variation in transaction costs in each company and productive sector—i.e. the costs of taking decisions and gaining experience, administrative costs (with regard to the management of contracts and labour relations) the cost of change, and of moving from one contract to another—agency work cannot simply be considered to be equivalent to fixed-term employment. Rather, in the framework of Legislative decree No. 276/2003, it provides a kind of organizational and managerial specialization promoting flexibility in employment but also, and above all, the modernization of the system of production by means of models of contractual integration between enterprises coordinated by qualified employment professional providing a range of services, in employment agencies.

It is in this perspective that it is possible to explain, first of all, the introduction of open-ended agency work (staff leasing). In an attempt to govern and regularize forms of labour which took place in dubious conditions and without any form of protection for the workers, Legislative decree No. 286/2003, laid down a series of reasons relating to technical, productive and organizational matters, which, in competition with the present system of contracting out of services, and quasi subordinate contracts, make it possible *ex lege*, without having to specify particular conditions, to make use of staff leasing. In general it is used for specialized services that can be carried out in a more effective manner, exploiting economies of scale, supplied by those with the technical and vocational requisites laid down by law: cleaning services, storage, facility management; transport services to and from the workplace, and the transport of machinery and goods; the management of libraries, parks, museums, archives, warehouses, as well as general supplies; construction work within the workplace, the installation and dismantling of plant and machinery for particular productive activities, with specific reference to building sites and shipyards, requiring further stages of production; and personnel with different skills from regular employees.

---

[82] Williamson, O. E. 1975. *Markets and Hierarchies: Analysis and Antitrust Implications*. New York: Free Press; see also Golzio, L. "L'evoluzione dei modelli organizzativi d'impresa," cit.

These measures are accompanied by others that are particularly innovative in support of the productive system and organizational innovation of the enterprise, i.e. specialist activities such as management consultancy, certification services, resource planning, organizational development and change, personnel management, selection and recruitment of personnel, information technology consultancy services, including the planning and management of intranet and extranet systems, websites, information systems, the development of software applications, and data entry; marketing, market research, the organization of sales departments, the management of call centres, and all the activities connected with the setting up of new businesses in the Objective 1 areas under EC regulation No. 1260/1999, 19 June 1999, with general provisions on Structural Funds.

These activities can be carried out both by generic temporary work agencies and, with reference to specific activities, by specialized agencies. Compared to contracting out, the undoubtedly higher cost of the services provided by employment agencies (bearing in mind also the four per cent deduction for social insurance purposes and the rule of equal pay and conditions) is in all probability offset by the quality of the services offered, which, in many cases, consist of highly specialized services that can only be carried out by suitably qualified staff with adequate training (also thanks to the training fund under Article 12 of the Decree). Nor should it be forgotten that temporary work agencies are exempt from the procedural requirements for collective dismissals and from the obligation to reserve a fixed number of places for workers with disabilities. Legislative Decree No. 276, 10 September 2003, also makes provision for staff assigned by a temporary work agency to a user undertaking to be excluded from the calculation of the number of staff "for the purposes of legal or collective bargaining obligations".

Also in normative terms, then, temporary agency work is encouraged as an alternative to contracting out. It seems to be paradoxical to consider staff leasing to be "an instrument that combines many of the characteristics of precarious employment"[83] when the employees, in these cases, as well as being able to rely on a dual employer, are often hired on open-ended contracts.

Alongside the different types of employment laid down by law, powers are delegated to collective bargaining, either national or territorial, to identify, also in relation to activities that are by no means marginal to the

---

[83] As argued by Lamberti, M. 2004. "Ragionando di esternalizzazioni: la prestazione di lavoro nei contesti multidatoriali", *Sviluppo e occupazione nel mercato globale*, ed. Ferraro, G., Milano: Giuffrè, p. 408.

productive cycle of the user enterprise, further possible uses of agency work and staff leasing. The task of expanding this type of employment beyond the cases laid down by the legislator is therefore entrusted to the social partners, with a view to reducing the area at present covered by contracting out, that provides much less protection for the employee.

As shown above, except for the establishment of new businesses in Objective 1 areas and the management of regular salaried employment in call centres, it will not be possible, as suggested in some quarters (including those who have spoken of "Chinese boxes") to restructure or empty companies and run them entirely with agency workers. Staff leasing will be allowed only for marginal cases and for jobs that are normally contracted out; in addition to these cases, staff leasing will only be permitted in the cases provided for in collective bargaining (also in this case, as in the decree as a whole, with only the comparatively most representative trade unions able to authorize new types of temporary work).

This situation cannot then be described as an "overblown version of temporary work as provided by the Treu measures".[84] Rather, the new regime—in proposing a unified solution to the problem of labour intermediation[85]—provides not only a significant opportunity for employers, in relation to outsourcing, but also a significant improvement in the protection of employees, particularly those employed by subcontracting firms, or even worse as quasi subordinate contracts, without adequate regulation.

In considering open-ended agency contracts, that normally provide more stable employment and protection for the worker in flesh and blood (and not just on paper), as "a much more dangerous form of employment than temporary agency work",[86] clearly certain legal scholars and part of the trade-union movement have agreed to the legalization of this type of employment contract only insofar as it is classified as precarious and atypical, to be drastically restricted, and allowed only in exceptional cases.

---

[84] Lamberti, M. "Ragionando di esternalizzazioni: la prestazione di lavoro nei contesti multidatoriali," *cit.,* p. 407.

[85] The decision to draft a consolidating act on temporary agency work is supported by Ichino, P. "Somministrazione di lavoro, appalto di servizi, distacco," cit. esp. p. 261, and Bano, F. "La somministrazione di lavoro", *Impiego flessibile e mercato del lavoro*, *cit.,* esp. pp. 13-14.

[86] See, among others, Bonardi, O. 2003. "La nuova disciplina della somministrazione di lavoro", *Il lavoro tra progresso e mercificazione—Commento critico al decreto legislativo n. 276/2003*, ed. Ghezzi, G. *cit.*, esp. p. 124.

However, this highly critical position is indicative of a reluctance to design and implement new organizational and managerial models for increasing the level of protection of workers. Rather, due to ideological reasons and the presumption that the employer and the user should be one and the same entity,[87] there is a tendency to confine workers to contractual arrangements that may well be less gratifying and provide less protection.

In terms of legal provisions, from this point of view there have been significant innovations with regard to temporary agency work, in that it is specified that "temporary agency work is permitted in the presence of technical, organizational or productive factors, or for the substitution of workers, also in connection with the day-to-day business of the organization". This leaves the matter to be dealt with in a flexible manner by employers, within the framework of collective bargaining, enabling them to decide on company organization, based on the needs of the enterprise, the organizational and managerial know-how, the productive sector, and the conditions requiring the enterprise to adapt continually to the market, in line with the life-cycle theory.[88] All of this is based on the belief that in the new economy the legislator cannot decide on the models of work organization, at an abstract level, once and for all, on the basis of meticulous legal classifications.[89]

It is in this perspective that it becomes possible to explain why, subsequently, in the framework of Legislative Decree No. 276/2003 the temporary nature of business requirements[90] ceases to be a key factor, since agency workers may be employed also in relation to "the day-to-day business of the company".[91] In other words, and in line with the provisions for hiring on fixed-term contracts in Article 1 of Legislative decree No. 368/2001,[92] the Italian system once again focuses on combating fraudulent

---

[87] For a critique of the argument that the employer and the user undertaking should be one and the same entity, based on the principle of salaried employment, see Ichino, P. "La disciplina della segmentazione del processo produttivo," cit., p. 24.

[88] Schuler, R. S., and S. E. Jackson. "Human Resource Management in Context," cit., esp. p. 127.

[89] On this point, Ichino, P. *Lezioni di diritto del lavoro*, *cit.*, esp. p. 241, who argues that it is not possible to establish in abstract terms, which model of company management, is preferable: the vertical model or the new network model.

[90] This matter is dealt with in Article 1 (1) of Act No. 196, 24 June 1997. On this point see Biagi M. *Mercati e rapporti di lavoro, Commentario alla legge 24 giugno 1997, n. 196*, cit.

[91] Art. 20 (4), Legislative Decree No. 276/2003.

[92] See Tiraboschi, M. "Apposizione del termine", *Il nuovo lavoro a termine. Commentario al D.Lgs. 6 settembre 2001, n. 368, cit.*

labour practices in the area of temporary work,[93] while moving beyond a rigid approach to the management of the workforce. This is in contrast with certain case law rulings handed down over the years providing an interpretation of Act No. 1369/1960, which tended to place constraints on the flexible management of the workforce.

The delegation of powers in Act No. 30/2003 reflected the anti-fraudulent aim of the new provisions, with a view to prohibiting, or suppressing fraudulent labour practices infringing the rights of workers, by means of the new definition of fraudulent labour intermediation laid down in Article 28 of Legislative decree No. 276/2003. A key objective of the decree, in compliance with the European proposals for regulating agency work, is the repeal of all those provisions aiming to place rigid constraints on the use of agency work, even where they are not required for the purposes of protecting workers' rights. Article 4 of the proposal for a European directive is categorical in stating that restrictions and prohibitions on the supply of labour are permitted only if based on the general interest and, in particular, on the need to protect workers' rights, and that as a result Member States are required to repeal all restrictions and prohibitions that are not justified on these grounds.[94]

This explains why for the purposes of evaluating the reasons laid down in Article 20(3)(4) of Legislative Decree No. 276/2003, that make provision for temporary agency work, judicial control is to be exercised exclusively in compliance with the general principles of the legal system, and limited to ascertaining the existence of the factors that justify the use of this kind of employment contract, and cannot be extended to the examination of the technical, organizational and productive choices of the user undertaking. Just as the legislator cannot establish, in abstract terms, how an enterprise is to be run, nor can the courts intervene in the legitimate choices of management, and they should therefore concentrate on situations in which illegal or fraudulent activity takes place.

In this connection no less importance is given to the provisions on contracting out. Under the terms of Article 29 of Legislative decree No.

---

[93] On the original aim of labour regulations to combat fraud, see Giugni, G. 1978. "Intervento", *Il lavoro a termine, Atti delle giornate di studio di Sorrento AIDLASS,* 14-15 aprile 1978. Milano: Giuffrè, p. 125 and, with specific reference to agency work, Cessari, A. 1961. "In tema di interposizione nelle prestazioni di lavoro," *Il diritto del lavoro(DL)* 1. p.128 et seq.

[94] In general, on the need for EU institutions to provide a favourable environment for businesses, see European Commission. 2005. *Annual Report on Structural Reforms—Increasing Growth and Employment*, Brussels: European Commission, ECFIN/EPC (2004)REP/50550 final.

276/2003, for the purposes of applying the norms relating to temporary agency work, "the contracting out agreement, drawn up and regulated under the terms of Article 1655 of the Civil Code, is to be distinguished from temporary agency work due to the organization of the necessary resources on the part of the contractor, that may also lead, in connection with the needs arising from the work or services to be supplied under the contract, to the exercise of organizational and management powers in relation to the workers employed for the contract, as well as the transfer of the business risk to the contractor". This is in line with the provisions of Article 20(2), which specifies that "for the entire duration of the assignment, the workers perform their tasks under the management and control of the user undertaking".

The framework put in place by Legislative decree No. 276/2003 does not, as some legal scholars have argued, result in radical changes to the regulatory framework. Making use of delegated powers, the legislator simply consolidates and extends certain case law rulings[95] aiming to bring the application of existing legislation into line with changes in the economic and productive system. For some time the Cassazione had recognized as legitimate the contracting out of functions which, though consisting only of labour, were considered to be services carried out under the autonomous management of a contractor.

It must be pointed out that, in the light of the new legal provisions, in order not to engage in illicit intermediation, there is a need to demonstrate the genuine nature of the contract, by means of two key characteristics: the organization of the necessary resources—resources, it is important to note, that may be intangible—and the management of the contract with the contractor taking on the commercial risk.

A particularly important role, with a view to increasing the degree of certainty in outsourcing, can be played by certification bodies. Also because, pursuant to Article 84 of Legislative decree No. 276/2003, employers will soon have the option of adopting codes of good practice and indicators relating to illicit intermediation and genuine contracting out, taking account of the organization of resources and the effective transfer of the business risk from the enterprise to the contractor.

The repeal of Act No. 1369/1960, and the related prohibitions of intermediation in labour relations in Act No. 264/1949, does not in any way result in the abolition of the civil and criminal sanctions laid down in

---

[95] See De Luca Tamajo, R. "Le esternalizzazioni tra cessione di ramo d'azienda e rapporti d fornitura", *I processi di esternalizzazione. Opportunità e vincoli giuridici*, cit., pp. 45-46, including extensive bibliographical and case law references.

cases of violation of the regulations on private intermediation in employment relations. In support of the effectiveness of the new legal framework, specific criminal sanctions are provided in the case of the illegal exercise of private intermediation, with an even stricter set of provisions relating to the exploitation of child labour.

It must be noted that in comparison with the preceding legal framework, the principle of equality of terms and conditions of employment between the employees of the company and those of the contractor in the case of "internal" contracts has been abolished. But as noted, this was a formal provision largely disregarded in day-to-day practice, and was considered to be anachronistic in relation to developments in working methods.[96] What appears to be more effective, and useful for striking a new balance between the demands of the system of production and the need for labour protection, is the principle of joint liability between the principal and the contractor, provided in Act No. 1369/1960, for the remuneration and social insurance contributions due to the employee in all cases of contracting out.[97]

This is a simple rule, but it is of great practical value, and not only with a view to safeguarding a larger number of workers involved in outsourcing. On close inspection, the full implementation of the principle of joint liability, by which also the principal becomes liable for the remuneration and contributions of the employee, means that those who opt for contracting out will tend to look to well-managed, trustworthy and highly qualified companies, and this works to the advantage of the process of specialization of Italian enterprises.

6. Promoting Labour Law in a Human Resources Perspective

The implications of the Biagi reform are undoubtedly far-reaching, especially in terms of human resources management and the proper functioning of the labour market. It has been quite rightly noted in this connection that employers and legal experts are now required to become more aware of the role that they can play: only in this way will it be

[96] De Luca Tamajo, R. "Le esternalizzazioni tra cessione etc.", *cit.*

[97] This principle, initially adopted in Legislative Decree No. 276/2003 only for the contracting out of services, was later extended to all contracting out in Article 6(1) of Legislative Decree No. 251/2004, "with the exception of provisions in national collective agreements concluded between the employers' associations and comparatively most representative trade unions".

possible to "understand the processes set in motion by the new law and to apply the contents in a coherent and balanced way with the intention of improving the functioning of labour markets, both internal and external".[98]

The changes to the framework in place before the reform are undoubtedly numerous, and all of them are far-reaching both at a technical and at a practical and operational level. This is particularly the case with the new system for regulating labour outsourcing. In order to make labour law once again both effective and credible, the legislator chose to provide enterprises with a regulatory framework that is both flexible and enforceable in practical terms, and the implementation of this framework becomes the responsibility of human resources managers, on the basis of technical, organizational and productive factors, in negotiation with the trade unions. This results in an increase in opportunities for enterprises to make legitimate use of the external labour market and as a result to rethink their models of labour organization in the belief—shared by the Community institutions[99]—that only by governing the changes under way will it be possible to maintain and develop the human capital of a given productive system.

From this point of view—as recognized by Tiziano Treu[100]—"the shock resulting from the new provisions may provide a good opportunity to rethink traditional human resources management techniques". What is clear is that a profound change is taking place in thinking about labour law and about the labour protection measures that characterize it.

The Biagi reform provides us with a human resources law that conceives of the employment regulations not simply as an arid set of norms, that are the prerogative of a select group of specialists, but rather as an instrument at the service of employees and enterprises in line with the most recent developments in working and production methods, that place the human factor at the centre of the competitive scenario. In the belief that only by governing real normative processes—and not by means of

---

[98] See Treu, T. "Riforma Biagi e nuove regole del mercato del lavoro", *Sviluppo e occupazione nel mercato globale*, Ferraro, G. *cit.,* 155, esp. p. 169, in which he states that "this objective should be shared by all those concerned, regardless of the reservations and criticisms relating to legislative choices". In a similar vein see my chapter on "Il decreto legislativo 10 settembre 2003, n. 276: alcune premesse e un percorso di lettura", *La riforma Biagi del mercato del lavoro*, ed. Tiraboschi, M., cit., pp. 3-30.

[99] European Commission. 2002. *Anticipating and Managing Change: a Dynamic Approach to the Social Aspects of Corporate Restructuring*, esp. p. 2, available at *www.adapt.it*, A-Z index, under the heading *Lavoro (organizzazione del)*.

[100] Treu, T. "Riforma Biagi e nuove regole del mercato del lavoro," cit., p. 156.

prohibitions and constraints that have become an excessive burden, to the point that they give rise to illegal practices—is it possible to safeguard employment quality and investment in people as the key competitive factor, and therefore as the capital of the enterprise.

CHAPTER ELEVEN

THE CERTIFICATION OF EMPLOYMENT CONTRACTS: A LEGAL INSTRUMENT FOR LABOUR MARKET REGULATION IN ITALY

1. The Legal Context[1]

1.1. Certification of Employment Contracts: The Way it Works

Certification of employment contracts (hereinafter certification) is an Italian legal procedure whose main function is to reduce legal disputes about the classification of employment contracts.[2]

---

[1] This contribution was written in collaboration with Chiara Bizzarro, Flavia Pasquini and Davide Venturi and previously published in 2010 in *The International Journal of Comparative Labour Law and Industrial Relations* 26, No 1, pp. 103-115.

[2] See, for example, Bizzarro, C., A. Corvino, F. Pasquini, and M. Tiraboschi. 2007. "Nuove tecniche di regolazione e certificazione dei modelli organizzativi," *Dossier Adapt*, No. 33; Bubola, G., and F. Pasquini. 2009. "Sanzioni ridotte con la certificazione," *Italia Oggi Sette*, 23 February; Enrico, C, and M. Tiraboschi. 2005. "Certificazione e tipologie di lavoro flessibile nella riforma dei lavori: un primo passo verso lo Statuto dei lavori", *Compendio critico per la certificazione dei contratti di lavoro*, eds. Enrico, C., and M. Tiraboschi, Collana ADAPT—Fondazione "Marco Biagi", No. 7, Milano: Giuffrè; Pasquini, F. 2008. *Autonomia, subordinazione, parasubordinazione: guida pratica alla costruzione di un contratto di lavoro. La certificazione come strumento per la corretta qualificazione del rapporto di lavoro.*Vicenza: IPI Srl; Pasquini, F. 2008 "La Circolare n. 4/2008: una rampa di lancio per la Certificazione?" *Dossier Adapt*, No. 1; Pasquini, F. 2007. "Certificazioni, istanze a quota 1.269," *Il Sole 24 Ore*, 10 October; Pasquini, F. 2007. "Certificazione, primi risultati," *Conquiste del Lavoro*, 28 September; F. Pasquini. 2007. "Lavoro nei call center tra emersione e certificazione," *Bollettino Adapt*, No. 16; Pasquini, F. 2007. "Certificazione per garantire equità," *Il Sole 24 Ore*, 25 aprile; Pasquini, F. 2007. "Due anni di certificazione. Primo bilancio della attività della Commissione di certificazione

In the Italian labour law system, the proper classification of an employment contract is a matter of great importance, as different contracts provide significantly different levels of protection; in other words, the classification has a direct impact on the worker's terms and conditions of employment. This explains why, in the Italian labour law system, the classification of employment contracts gives rise to a considerable amount of litigation.

The classification of contracts is not permitted, by law, to be negotiated by the parties and as a result may not be waived or altered by agreement. This is because classification is mandatory and expressly laid down by law. The matter can be briefly explained by two fundamental judicial rulings. In 1994, the Constitutional Court ruled that: "the

---

istituita presso il Centro Studi Marco Biagi dell'Università degli Studi di Modena e Reggio Emilia," *Dossier Adapt*, No. 29; Pasquini, F. 2007. "La certificazione dei contratti quale strumento deflativo del contenzioso," *Bollettino Adapt*, No. 11; Pasquini, F. 2007. "La certificazione dei contratti di lavoro: l'esperienza dell'Ateneo di Modena e Reggio Emilia," *Bollettino speciale Adapt*, No. 35; Pasquini, F. 2006. "Università e certificazione dei contratti: l'esperienza del Centro Studi internazionali e comparati «Marco Biagi» dell'Università di Modena e Reggio Emilia", *Scuola, Università e mercato del lavoro dopo la riforma Biagi. Le politiche per la transizione dai percorsi educativi e formativi al mercato del lavoro*, eds. Reggiani Gelmini, P., and M. Tiraboschi, Collana Adapt—Fondazione «Marco Biagi» No. 13, Milano: Giuffrè; Pasquini, F., and R. Rakipi. 2006. "I contratti certificati entrano nel bilancio sociale," *Il Sole 24 Ore*, 30 August; Pasquini, F. "Certificazione: stipulata la convenzione Unione Commercio lombarda—Università di Modena, scheda di sintesi della Convenzione tra l'Unione Regionale lombarda del commercio del turismo e dei Servizi e il Centro Studi internazionali e comparati «Marco Biagi»," *Guida al Lavoro*, XII, No. 6 and 7; Pasquini, F. 2006. "Con la certificazione dei contratti di lavoro opportunità e tutele per datori e dipendenti," *Il Sole 24 Ore*, 14 June; Pasquini, F., and R. Rakipi. 2006. "La certificazione dei contratti di lavoro: un nuovo tassello nella responsabilità sociale d'impresa," *Bollettino Adapt*, 30 giugno, No. 38; Pasquini, F. 2006. "Tutele dalla certificazione dei contratti," *Il Sole 24 Ore*, 31 May; Pasquini, F. 2005. "I regolamenti adottati dalle Commissioni di Certificazione costituite presso le DPL," *DRI*, No. 3:842; Tiraboschi, M. 2005. "L'istituto della certificazione tra decretazione ministeriale e circolari interpretative," *DRI*, No. 2,; Tiraboschi, M. 2004. "Nuove tutele sul mercato: le procedure di certificazione", *La riforma Biagi del mercato del lavoro*, ed. Tiraboschi, M. Collana ADAPT—Fondazione "Marco Biagi", No. 2, Milano: Giuffrè; Tiraboschi, M. 2003. "Le procedure di certificazione", *La riforma Biagi. Commento allo schema di decreto attuativo della legge delega sul mercato del lavoro*, ed. Tiraboschi, M., in *Guida al Lavoro*, No. 4; Tiraboschi, M. 2003. "La c.d. certificazione dei lavori «atipici» e la sua tenuta giudiziaria," *Lavoro e Diritto*, No. 1.

principles, the protections and the rights established by the Constitution for the safeguard of employees, are not negotiable between the parties of the contract. Not even ordinary law courts are competent to classify as self-employed contracts those contracts which are objectively ascertained to be employment contracts".[3] The freedom of the parties to classify their contractual relations is thus restricted, as they are required to comply with the models provided by law: employment contracts, quasi-subordinate employment contracts, or self-employment contracts. The proper distinction between employment and self-employed contracts is essential, as the protections provided by the law for employment contracts are a matter of constitutional law.

In 1999 the Italian Supreme Court *(Corte di Cassazione)* stated that "any economically relevant human activity, even the humblest one, can be carried out on the basis of employment contracts or self-employment contracts".[4] Hence, within the limits of classification provided by the law, the parties are free to choose the type of contract underlying the activity performed.

Following on from this, not even certification panels are entitled to endorse derogations from mandatory provisions, by agreement between the parties. Nonetheless, by attesting the lawfulness and the proper classification of the employment contract, certification is the institutional and legal means available to the parties to reduce uncertainty and to ensure compliance with the regulatory framework. In the legal literature, this concept is commonly adopted: certification is regarded exclusively as a form of assisted consensus *ad idem,* and is therefore not viewed in terms of assisted derogation from mandatory rules.

As a result, certification responds to the need for legal certainty expressed by the interested parties who seek to adopt flexible labour relations or to outsource certain stages of production by means of supply chain contracts (using independent contractors).

The bodies that may provide certification services are appointed by law. These certifying bodies are called certification commissions or panels (Article 76, Legislative Decree No. 276/2003). Certification panels may be set up by:

---

[3] Quotation from: Corte Cost., 29 March 1993, No. 121, in *Foro Italiano* 1993, I, p. 2423. The translation is by the authors.

[4] The quotation is taken from: Cass., 28 July 1999, in *Rivista Italiana di Diritto del Lavoro,* 2000, II, p. 280. The translation is by the authors.

- any territorial body of the Ministry of Labour (*Direzione Provinciale del Lavoro* i.e. Provincial Labour Office);[5]
- the Ministry of Labour;
- the Provinces, on the basis of local and territorial autonomy;
- Universities and University Foundations, under the supervision of a professor of labour law;[6]
- bilateral bodies (set up by unions and employers' associations);
- the Professional Association of Labour Advisors.

Each panel has to approve an internal regulation establishing the procedure to be adopted when the parties apply for certification. The internal regulation has to comply with the provisions of law pertaining to certification (Art. 78.2, Legislative Decree No. 276/2003, and Articles 2 and 3, Act No. 241/1990), in accordance with the principles set forth below:

- free determination of the parties: the contract must be submitted voluntarily by the parties to the certification panel;
- duty of disclosure (*dovere di informazione*): as regards the beginning of the procedure, notice has to be given to the Provincial Labour Office, the Social Security Administration and to the tax authorities for all applications for certification;
- duty of motivation. The issuance of certification (or a rejection of the application in case of noncompliance) has to be supported by an adequate and complete motivation, which sets out the grounds of the decision. The motivation has to be consistent with the terms of the contract and with the organizational framework of the employer.[7]
- duty of deliberation: the certification panel is required to take a decision.

---

[5] The Provincial Labour Offices are the territorial bodies of the Ministry of Labour. As a result, they are part of the central Government, and not of the local administration. The province corresponds to a district, and consists of a chief town with the surrounding territory.

[6] See Tiraboschi, M. 2005. "Le sedi universitarie", *Compendio critico per la certificazione dei contratti di lavoro*, eds. Enrico, C., and M. Tiraboschi, Collana ADAPT—Fondazione "Marco Biagi", No. 7, Milano: Giuffrè, p. 107.

[7] As certification is an administrative act, the requirement of motivation is established by the general law for administrative acts Act No. 241/1990, Article 2.

In order to be complete, the certification procedure requires either the issuance of certification or, in case of noncompliance, a duly motivated rejection of the application.

Article 79, Legislative Decree No. 276/2003, establishes that the legal effects of certification, which include the classification of the contract and the regulation between the parties and toward third parties (i.e. Social Security Authorities as regards social security contributions), persist unless a labour court overturns the certification, declaring it void.

Likewise, the actions of the public administration, and in particular of labour inspectors, produce the same legal effects between the parties and before third parties. Generally, if an inspection brings to light a labour law violation, inspectors are entitled to issue administrative orders for the reclassification of employment contracts retroactively to the date of starting work. Certification, however, has a legal effect also in relation to the inspectors, who cannot therefore reclassify a certified contract. Where there is a doubt about the correctness of its classification or of its execution, they can appeal to a labour court for a review of the decision handed down by the panel. In the meanwhile, the certified contract remains in force.

As a result, and considering the careful examination already carried out by the certification panels, the Minister of Labour has issued instructions (General Directive, 18 September 2008) to the labour inspectorate to focus their inspections on non-certified contracts, unless a written claim is filed by workers complaining about a violation of labour protections, or where the improper execution of the contract is immediately ascertained.

Both parties of the contract have the right to bring a civil action against certification, in the case of:

- wrongful classification of the contract (legal error in the certification procedure);
- lack of consent;
- a discrepancy between the content of the contract for which certification was issued and the implementation of the contract.

The first type of annulment requires a judgement on the lawful classification of the contract. It can be claimed by one of the parties, or even by a third party with a legal interest in the contract, in the case of a legal mistake by the parties, for having wrongfully drawn up the contract, and by the Commission, for having incorrectly classified the contract on the basis of a flawed evaluation of the facts. Even though, theoretically, the court has the power to void certification, in practice this is unlikely to happen. Clearly, before deciding the case, the court needs to weigh the evidence and reach conclusions taking into account all the documents acquired and reviewed during the certification procedure and the files in the archives of the certification panel, as certification is the outcome of a prior examination.

The same considerations apply to the second type of annulment, in the case of lack of consent. Even in this case, the labour court must weigh all the evidence acquired during the procedure of certification to ascertain the proper execution of the certification procedure and the validity of the certification issued. Moreover, the consultancy services and the direct assistance given by the panel to the parties (Article 81, Legislative Decree No. 276/2003) in the initial phase in which the terms and conditions are laid down, make it hard to prove in court the lack of consent, or errors of fact or law.

The third type of annulment is much more likely to occur in practice. In fact, it does not concern the certification itself, which is expected to be lawfully executed, but rather refers to the implementation of the contract, and it is envisaged when one or both contracting parties fails to comply with the obligations laid down under the terms of the contract. However, for certified contracts, the parties are not permitted to challenge the certification before the court if they fail to appeal to the certification panel in an attempt at reconciliation. The certification panel is entitled to propose a settlement of the dispute before it is brought to court, but its powers are limited to mediation since, so far, certification panels have not been granted powers of arbitration. If the parties do not reach a settlement, the Commission cannot resolve it by arbitration, and the party filing the complaint has to apply to the labour court.

Finally, the certification procedure is also available for independent contracts (Article 84, Legislative Decree No. 276/2003), that are not labour but business contracts, included in the labour law certification procedure due to the fact that they are ordinary legal instruments by means of which enterprises engage in outsourcing. The way independent contracts are implemented often has a significant impact on working conditions.

1.2. Certification: Micro-level and Macro-level Labour Market Regulation

Certification is a procedure regulating employment contracts. However, it has significant influence also on the labour market. In fact, at a micro-level, certification enables workers to enter the labour market on fair terms and conditions of employment.

The certification of employment contracts presents advantages to both parties. It responds to the needs of the employer by providing a considerable degree of legal certainty as regards the proper classification of the contract, and it does this in advance, before the execution of the contract. At this preliminary stage, the employer can choose any organizational solution for his business, and can opt for outsourcing or flexible labour contracts, with no risk of having to pay damages for abuse of contract. In this regard, certification can be seen as a valuable resource for employers, since in the process of organization or reorganization, it enables them to ascertain the lawfulness of the contracts they intend to issue.

At the same time certification is advantageous also for the workers. In the case of flexible employment contracts, certification grants the worker the best possible protection under the law according to a specific type of contract. This becomes particularly evident in the case of quasi-subordinate (or para-subordinate) employment contracts, often preferred by employers because of their flexibility, but not always implemented in a consistent manner. In the event of a discrepancy between the quasi-subordinate contract and its execution (by way of example: the employer acts as if dealing with a subordinate worker) the contract cannot be certified.

The form, extent and nature of flexible working and the true nature of quasi-subordinate employment contracts require a context of flexible organization. In this respect, certification is a test of contractual lawfulness, intended as substantial (not merely formal) compliance with the law. As a result, certification works as a sort of fairness test[8] concerning the actual execution of the contract. It refers to the effective relation between the organization and the worker, with particular regard to

---

[8] Certification, as a test of substantial lawfulness for the labour contract, may be considered as one of "the modern styles of public regulation", or better of indirect regulation, in the mainstream of the regulatory analysis by Collins, H. 1999. *Regulating Contracts*, Oxford University Press. Specifically about regulation and labour law, see also Collins, H., P. Davies, and R. Rideout. 2000. *Legal Regulation of the Employment Relation.* The Hague: Kluwer Law International; Collins, H. 2001. "Regulating the Employment Relation for Competiveness," *ILJ*, No. 30:17; Arup, C., P. Gahan, J. Howe, R. Johnstone, R. Mitchell, and A. O'Donnell, eds. 2006. *Labour Law and Labour Market Regulation*, Sydney: The Federation Press; Arup, C. 2001. "Labour Law as Regulation: Promises and Pitfalls," *Australian Journal of Labour Law* 14, No. 3; Forsyth, A. 2001. "Re-regulatory Tendencies in Australian and New Zealand Labour Law," *Working Paper,* No. 21, Centre for Employment and Labour Relations Law, in http://celrl.law.unimelb.edu.au/assets/Working%20Papers/celrl-wp21.pdf.

the way a company deals with and complies with the rights and obligations deriving from flexible contracts (flexible organization for flexible employment contracts, traditional vertical organization for traditional employment contracts).

In a comparative analysis, this classification of the employment contract based on substantial characteristics appears to be similar to the procedure formerly adopted in Australia known as the "no disadvantage test".[9] The certification panel carries out consultancy functions and actively assists the parties, helping them to fulfil all the requirements of lawfulness and fairness while reaching their organizational goals. Hence, the contract is evaluated by means of a "no disadvantage" approach: a substantial test of lawfulness and fairness of the terms of the contract, in accordance with the organization of the employer. On account of the peculiar function of enforcement of contractual self-regulation, certification becomes an instrument of regulation of the labour market, both in a micro- and macro-level perspective.

Certification can have a positive impact on the labour market, in quantitative and qualitative terms. It produces a quantitative expansion of the labour market, as it facilitates access to contracts with a legal basis, thus reducing conflict. In addition, it produces qualitative effects on the labour market, as certification results in fair contracts, truly respectful of the workers' rights laid down by each type of contract.

As a legal instrument with a positive impact on the labour market, certification may be viewed as an expression of "legal pluralism": in modern democracies State regulation and self-regulation tend to coexist. Certification, as an expression of enforced self-regulation, is part of a more complex system of labour market regulation that relies partly on private self-regulation, and partly on direct State regulation.

---

[9] In Australia, until 2009, the "no disadvantage test" concerned the substantial correspondence to the legal framework of company collective agreements. It was awarded by the Australian Industrial Relations Commission based on the Workplace Relations Act 1996. For an analysis of the "no disadvantage test" in terms of regulation, see Frazer, A. 2006. "Industrial Tribunals and the Regulation of Bargaining", *Labour Law and Labour Market Regulation*. Sidney: the Federation Press, 223 and 241. The Fair Work Act (2009) is intended to replace the "no disadvantage test" with the "better off overall test", which is awarded by the newly instituted Authority named Fair Work Australia: see Sutherland, C. 2009. "Making the 'BOOT' Fit: Reforms to Agreement-Making from Work Choices to Fair Work", *Fair Work, the New Workplace Laws and the Work Choices Legacy*, eds. Forsyth, A., and A. Stewart, Sydney: The Federation Press, p. 99.

Why is certification a model of enforced self-regulation? Certification is a "self-regulatory" instrument, as it is issued based on the contract the parties intend to draw up. Certification is a voluntary procedure, and the parties of the contract are completely free to apply for certification or not. If they choose not to, the contract still produces its effects under ordinary contract law.

As it is carried out by a third party (the certification panel), as a legal procedure establishing a system of rules for market participants, certification provides "enforcement" for contractual self-regulation.[10] By means of certification, the legal effects of the contract are binding on not only the parties, but also vis-*à*-*vis* third parties. As a result, the Commission acts as a specialized labour market agency. This is why certification can be considered as a form of indirect regulation.

The authority and reliability of the certification panel, along with the expertise of its members and their ability to render a fair and equitable ruling, grant effectiveness to certification[11]. The legal effects of certification are intended to stand between the parties and before third parties and can only be voided by a definitive ruling handed down by a labour court in cases initiated by either of the parties or by a third party. Clearly, the acknowledged effectiveness of the certification procedure is in inverse proportion to the number of annulments received.

In this perspective, the expertise of the Commission is a guarantee of reliability for the parties, but it proves to be also the true benefit of Certification. There are no grounds for jurisdictional annulments if certification is issued in compliance with the principles of fairness, correctness and transparency.

1.3. Certification as an Instrument for Business Organization

As the classification of employment and/or independent contracts is not an abstract test of lawfulness, but a substantial process relating to business organization, certification may be seen as a useful instrument for employers. Employment contracts (or independent contracts) and business

---

[10] It is a sort of soft enforcement, based on advice and moral suasion; see Ayers, I., and J. Braithwaite. 1992. *Responsive Regulation: Transcending the Deregulation Debate*, Oxford University Press. In particular, see the enforcement pyramid, suggesting a range of interventions with increasing intrusiveness, in chapter 2.

[11] On the role of legal advice as an instrument to eliminate economically unacceptable uncertainty in contractual relations, see Suchman, M. C., and M. L. Cahill. 2006. "The hired gun as Facilitator: Lawyers and the suppression of business disputes in Silicon Valley," *Law & Social Inquiry* 21, No.3, p. 679.

organizations are reciprocally linked to another. Thus, traditional vertical business organizations need to substantially redefine their organizational structure if they intend either to outsource production (independent contracts, supply chains) or to employ flexible workers (on quasi-subordinate employment contracts). Flexible labour contracts require flexible business organization. This is why certification turns out to be an instrument of business organization. The certification process is a sort of audit to which enterprises submit their proposals in order to check their consistency in terms of flexibility with the strategies devised by the company management.

The organizational use of certification normally works as follows:

- the company management decides to adopt a flexible strategy;
- the re-organization of the business process is often not quick enough. It follows that the employer decides on flexible contracts without being able to adopt a substantial redefinition of the business organization;
- the company recruits workers willing to work on flexible contracts (or makes arrangements with other companies to carry out stages of the production process) but, as the organization is unprepared to act in a more flexible context, the workers risk losing the protection they would have had under ordinary employment contracts, without gaining benefits in terms of self-organization of their work;
- the parties submit the employment contract for certification;
- where the proper classification of the contract has been ascertained but the organization is deemed inadequate, the certification panel asks the employer to take appropriate measures. Normally this involves exerting a form of pressure towards the enhancement the organization.

At an operational level, all the proposed business organization changes make the organization more flexible and consistent with the business strategies adopted by the management. Gaining flexibility in terms of use of the resources means granting flexibility in terms of organization. As a result, certification can be a useful instrument for Human Resources Management and for business management in general. From a regulatory point of view, companies are free to decide flexible strategies. However, if they do so, their contracts (quasi-subordinate employment or supply chain contracts) need to be implemented in a context of flexible business organization. In this respect, as already underlined, certification is a sort of audit, a test of consistency between strategies and operational organization, between business vision and business practice. Even a rejection of the application for certification is a result of an auditing process, highlighting the inconsistency between flexibility strategies and business organization.

2. The Experience of the Certification Panel at the University of Modena and Reggio Emilia

The following data provide an overview of the cases analyzed by the Certification Panel at the Marco Biagi Centre for International and Comparative Studies at the University of Modena and Reggio Emilia in the first few years of its activity. These statistics are of great interest, revealing how the certification scheme has been applied by experts at the Centre which, since its establishment, has received the highest number of applications in the country. In addition to casting new light on the matter, these data also lay the foundation for the assessment of future developments in this field.

2.1. Number of Applications Received

Table 3-1. Number of Applications Received from July 2005 to April 2009

July 2005—December 2005 (8 months)	33
January 2006—December 2006 (12 months)	448
January 2007—December 2007 (12 months)	1,031
January 2008—December 2008 (12 months)	2,820
January 2009—April 2009 (4 months)	1,104
Total	5,436

Source: Certification Panel at the University of Modena and Reggio Emilia

Particularly noteworthy for this analysis is the number of applications received by the panel, which is equal to 5,436 from July 2005 (when the Commission was set up) to April 2009. As shown in Table 1, during the first year employers were not particularly interested in certification (only 33 applications were received), while after the first year, more consideration was given to the procedure, as confirmed by the number of applications (448, 1,031, and 2,820 applications respectively in the second, third, and fourth years). The total number is likely to increase in the fifth year, as shown by the number of applications received in the first four months of 2009 (1,104). It should also be noted that the certification panel does not operate in August, as the administrative courts are suspended at this time of year.

2.2. Number of Applications Received Divided by Type

Table 3-2. Number and Type of Applications Received from July 2005 to April 2009

Quasi-subordinate employment *(co.co.pro.)**	4,537	83.46%
Apprenticeship *(Apprendistato)*	30	0.55%
Self-employment *(Lavoro autonomo)*	2	0.04%
Joint Venture Partnership *(Associazione in partecipazione)***	10	0.18%
Supply Chain Contract *(Appalto)*	36	0.66%
Internal Cooperative Regulation *(Regolamento di cooperativa)*	1	0.02%
Secondment *(Distacco)*	1	0.02%
Full-time open-ended salaried employment contracts *(Lavoro subordinato a tempo pieno e indeterminato)*	732	13.47%
Quasi-subordinate employment*** *(co.co.co.)*	84	1.55%
On call open-ended labour contract *(Lavoro intermittente a tempo indeterminato)*	3	0.06%
Total	5,436	100%

* work performed personally, on a project basis, with continuity and coordination.
** short-term partnership in which the persons (individuals or businesses) jointly undertake a transaction for mutual profit. Generally each person contributes work or assets and shares risks.
*** work performed personally with continuity and coordination.

Source: Certification panel at the University of Modena and Reggio Emilia

With reference to the type of employment contracts submitted for certification, 4,537 (83.46% of the total) are classified as quasi-subordinate employment contracts (project-based employment), confirming that these agreements are the most likely to raise questions in terms of implementation. The rest of the applications consists of 30 apprenticeship contracts (0.55%), two self-employment contracts (0.04%), 10 joint venture partnerships (0.18%), 36 supply chain contracts (0.66%), one internal cooperative regulation (0.02%), one secondment (0.02%), three on-call permanent labour contracts (0.66%), 84 quasi-subordinate employment contracts (1.55%), and 732 full-time open-ended salaried employment contracts (13.47%). It is also important to consider the differences in the activities of the employers filing applications for quasi-subordinate employment contracts.

Table 3-3. Number and Percentage of Applications Received for Quasi-subordinate Employment (co.co.pro.) by Type of Applicant

Call centres	2,710	59%
Sports betting shops	503	11.1%
Road haulage	1,047	23.1%
Meter reading	115	2.5%
In home care	7	0.2%
Other	155	3.4%
Total	4,537	100%

Source: Certification panel at the University of Modena and Reggio Emilia

2.3. Number of Enterprises Submitting Applications by Region

Table 3-4. Number of Enterprises Submitting Applications by Region from February 2005 to April 2009 Shown in Percentage

Veneto	50	41.32%
Lombardy	19	15.70%
Lazio	14	11.57%
Emilia Romagna	12	9.92%
Sicily	7	5.79%

Piedmont	5	4.13%
Tuscany	4	3.31%
Umbria	3	2.48%
Apulia	2	1.65%
Marche	2	1.65%
Trentino Alto Adige	1	0.83%
Sardinia	1	0.83%
Abruzzo	0	0%
Basilicata	0	0%
Campania	0	0%
Friuli Venezia Giulia	0	0%
Liguria	0	0%
Molise	0	0%
Valley of Aosta	0	0%

Source: Commission for Certification of the University of Modena and Reggio Emilia

The regional figures on applications for certification are also significant. As shown in Table 4, most of the enterprises that filed the application are based in Veneto (50 applications, corresponding to 41.32% of the total), Lombardy (19, 15.7%), Lazio (14, 11.57%), Emilia-Romagna (12, 9.92%), Sicily (7, 5.79%), Piedmont (5, 4.13%), Tuscany (4, 3.31%), Umbria (3,2.48%), Apulia and Marche (two enterprises each, 1.65%), Trentino-Alto Adige, Sardinia, and Calabria (one enterprise each,0.83%).

2.4. Number of Statements of Certification Issued

As for the statements of certification issued, out of a total of 3,710 applications approved, 2,939 were for project-based employment relationships (79.18%), four for apprenticeship contracts (0.11%), two for self-employment contracts (0.05%), six for joint venture partnerships (0.16%), 27 for supply chain contracts (0.73%), 731 for full-time permanent subordinate employment contracts (19.69%), and one for quasi-subordinate employment contracts (0.03%).

Table 3-5. Number of Statements of Certification Issued Divided by Type of Contract and Shown in Percentage

Quasi-subordinate employment *(co.co.pro.)**	2,939	79.18%
Apprenticeship *(Apprendistato)*	4	0.11%
Self-employment *(Lavoro autonomo)*	2	0.05%
Joint Venture Partnership *(Associazione in partecipazione)***	6	0.16%
Supply Chain Contract *(Appalto)*	27	0.73%
Full-time open-ended subordinate employment contract *(Lavoro subordinato a tempo pieno e indeterminato)*	731	19.69%
Quasi-subordinate employment*** (co.co.co.)	1	0.03%
Total	3,710	100%

* work performed personally, on a project basis, with continuity and coordination.
** short term partnership in which the persons (individuals or businesses) jointly undertake a transaction for mutual profit. Generally each person contributes work or assets and shares risks.
*** work performed personally with continuity and coordination.

Source: Commission for Certification of the University of Modena and Reggio Emilia

2.5. Reasons for Non-certification

With reference to the application for certification of an apprenticeship contract, the procedure was suspended, because the employer failed to provide the requested documentation, and it is likely to be approved only for a limited number of cases. Applications for both internal cooperative regulation and secondment were rejected. In the first case, it was due to a lack of competence, while in the second case the applicant did not meet the minimum requirements to apply for certification.

There are additional reasons for non-certification. In 1,332 cases (77.26% of the total), the procedure was suspended by the certification panel pending preliminary evaluation (mostly due to the presence of a number of clauses not complying with the type of contract chosen by the parties). In 321 cases (18.62%) there were other reasons that led to the rejection of the application, such as the inspection process by the Provincial Labour Office, the failure of the parties to attend hearings or to provide the requested information. In 56 cases (3.25%) the procedure was suspended at the specific (joint or unilateral) request of the parties, while in four cases (0.23%) the applications were classified as void. In total, there have only been 11 rejections of applications for certification.

In conclusion, these figures reveal a growing interest in certification, especially once the number of rejected applications is considered, demonstrating that those opting for certification are aware of its high quality and of the value of this regulatory scheme.

Table 3-6. Reasons for Non-Certification

On hold by the certification panel pending preliminary evaluation	1,332	77.26%
Void applications	4	0.23%
Procedures suspended at the specific request of the parties	56	3.25%
Rejection of the application	11	0.64%
Other reasons*	321	18.62%
Total	1,724	100%

* Inspection process by the Provincial Labour Office (DPL), Failure of the parties to attend hearing, Failure to provide requested information, Awaiting replies or additional information.

Source: Certification panel at the University of Modena and Reggio Emilia

CHAPTER TWELVE

WORK ORGANISATION, NEW FORMS OF EMPLOYMENT AND GOOD PRACTICES FOR OCCUPATIONAL HEALTH AND SAFETY: EVIDENCE FROM ITALY WITHIN THE EUROPEAN CONTEXT

1. The Principle of Equal Treatment and the Formal Protection of Non-standard Workers

There is general consensus on the fact that that European legislation has played a crucial role in reforming EU countries regulatory framework for OHS. An example in this connection has been the adoption of a series of provisions (*Individual Directives*) as laid down by the Framework Directive No. 391/1989/EEC, according to which risk assessment has a significant impact on hazard prevention. Subsequently, Directive No. 91/383 was issued, stating that protection should be granted to all categories of workers, with special reference to those regarded as more vulnerable, because of the nature of their employment relationship, viz. precarious and temporary workers.

Regarded as complementary to Directive No. 89/391, Directive No. 91/383 lays down special safeguards for temporary workers aimed to provide them with the same level of protection granted to standard workers. A definition of *temporary agency work* is also provided, that is a tripartite form of employment, with a company (temporary work agency), assigns a worker to a company customer (the user). In this connection, Article 5 of the Directive is significant, as entrusting Member States with the right to resort to temporary agency workers for those activities requiring special medical surveillance, in order to comply with national legislation. Temporary workers should receive *ad hoc* medical surveillance, also to be provided once the employment relationship has terminated. Before starting work, agency workers have also the right to be informed about any risks they might face while carrying out their activities, and, if necessary, to receive adequate training. In this light, an evaluation of their professional qualification is also highly advisable.

Although laying down significant preventive measures, Directive No. 91/383 has been more announced than implemented. It has not produced, according also to statistics for the year 2004 made available by the European Commission, consistent results in practical terms. Nevertheless, there are two main principles laid down by the Directive that are worthy of note, that is the principle of equal treatment between standard and non-standard workers and the risk prevention to be assessed considering workforce diversity resulting from a number of factors (nationality, expertise, psychosocial issues). Equally important is also the implementation of special and supplementary medical surveillance, and information and training based on workers' needs.

Before the passing of Legislative Decree No. 81/2008 and its later amendments,[1] which is the means of transposition of Directive No. 91/383 into Italian legislation, there were a number of difficulties, which had to be faced before implementation could be finalised.

In the context of this chapter, it seems worth pointing out that the definition of "traditional work" in Italian Labour Law encompasses paid employment performed on a full-time and on a permanent basis, which is still the most common form of work in the country.

However, Italy has witnessed major changes within the labour market over the years, especially because of a process of modernisation and flexibilisation resulting from new contractual arrangements. A significant contribution in this connection has been provided by the so-called *Biagi Law* (Law No. 30/2003, and Legislative Decree No. 276/2003), which, in order to fulfil the need for flexibility, redesigned existing employment contracts (part-time work, quasi-subordinate employment) and introduced new forms of employment (staff-leasing, temporary agency work), also

---

[1] To know more about the process of transposition, see Tiraboschi, M. 1996. *Lavoro atipico e ambiente di lavoro: la trasposizione in Italia della direttiva 91/383/CEE*, in *Diritto delle Relazioni Industriali*, 3, 57; Tiraboschi, M. 1997. *La trasposizione della direttiva n. 91/383/CEE nei principali paesi dell'Unione Europea e l'anomalia del caso italiano*, in *DPL*, No. 18, p. 1284 and Tiraboschi, M. 1996. *Lavoro atipico e ambiente di lavoro: la trasposizione in Italia della direttiva 91/383/CEE*, in *Diritto delle Relazioni Industriali* 3, No. 57. A comparative perspective is provided by Javilier, J. C., A. Neal, M. Weiss, J. Saloheimo, U. Runggaldier, and A. Tinhhofer. 1996. *Lavoro atipico/temporaneo e tutela della salute: la trasposizione della Direttiva n. 91/383 in Francia, Regno Unito, Germania, Finlandia e Austria*, in *Diritto delle Relazioni Industriali* 3, pp. 35-50.

giving priority to issues related to OHS as involving a considerable number of employees.[2]

In 1996, the transposition into national law of Directive No. 91/383 was accompanied by strong reservations about its effectiveness, regarded as partial, as putting employees on a fixed-term contract at a disadvantage in terms of health and safety, if compared to those employed on a permanent basis. Since no reference was made to the obligation on the part of the employer to assess the risk considering the workforce diversity, the transposition of the Directive only focused on the need for equal treatment between standard and non-standard workers at a formal level.

In 1997, the Italian Ministry of Labour and Social Policies carried out a survey on the relationship between temporary work, accident prevention and safety measures, pointing out that a number of risks were associated with factors such as isolation, communication and training issues, lack of organization and expertise. The report also argued that questions of this kind called for significant changes in legislation in general terms—therefore not simply reconsidering provisions in health and safety—also in compliance with EU Directives, in particular Directive No. 91/383/EC. A number of proposals have been put forward also at a European level. In France, for instance, it has been demonstrated that temporary workers can be protected by ensuring parity of treatment between this group and those

---

[2] Labour-market reform in Italy has been an incremental process over more than a decade, but the two main provisions have been the Treu and Biagi reforms of 1997 and 2003, respectively. The "Treu package" (September 1996), named after the then Labour and Social Policies Minister Tiziano Treu, aimed to increase employment, particularly among the young, with special measures for the economically depressed south (the *Mezzogiorno*). It eased regulation of new apprenticeships and work-training contracts, and created incentives for on-the-job training, temporary work via private agencies and intra-regional labour mobility. It also legalised worker-dispatching services for the first time and reduced disincentives to the use of fixed-term contracts. Marco Biagi was a labour law professor who drafted the law, one of the most controversial reform of the Italian labour market. Its aim was to increase employment among youth, women, older workers and job-seekers, particularly in the *Mezzogiorno*. The new measures included allowing private employment agencies to compete in the full range of services with public ones; promoting apprenticeships; improving conditions for the use by firms of part-time work; and offering greater opportunities to use other non-standard forms of employment. If previous labour market policies tended to reflect an overriding concern with the protection of employed "insiders", these reforms sought to create greater opportunities for new entrants and other labour-market "outsiders". Both these reforms (as well as a number of other changes to labour legislation adopted in between) were driven by EU-related policy considerations.

employed on a permanent basis. Other proposals—implemented in June 1997[3]—aimed at identifying those occupations requiring special surveillance measures, inclusion of OHS in different levels of education and training and *ad-hoc* initiatives safeguarding workers classified as "unusual". Therefore, at both national and international level, there was a mounting recognition of the OHS problems posed by labour market restructuring and the changes in work organisation, as well as of the need to reconsider regulatory strategies.[4]

Further provisions dealing with OHS for atypical workers are laid down in the Biagi Law, with the latter being of considerable importance in the modernisation of the labour market as representing a legislative intervention aimed at liberalising the emerging forms of atypical contracts, as well as facilitating the national implementation of Directive No. 91/383. Before the entry into force of this provision, health and safety at the workplace mainly dealt with traditional employment relationships. Today, also by promoting cooperation between health and safety authorities and labour market actors, the aim is for the Biagi Law to combat joblessness, and to promote access to regular and quality employment, in accordance with the Community goals laid down in the Lisbon Strategy.

Although no specific reference has been made to OHS, the Decree has provided a definition of *worker*[5] according to which protection granted to traditional workers has been extended also to those who already exit labour market, or to those employed under new forms of contract (agency work, intermittent work, job-sharing, out-sourcing, quasi-subordinate employment etc.). As for quasi-subordinate employment, the law provides that workers operating within the employer's premises be entitled to full protection, therefore in line with case law decisions, whereas a more detailed definition for OHS is provided for agency workers, especially referring to obligations on the part of the user enterprise. In terms of health and safety, the awareness of special needs for some categories of workers, as well as the adoption of new criteria in the definition of the employment status represent the first significant attempt to provide effective safeguards to atypical workers.

---

[3] Law No. 196 of 24 June 1997, called "Treu package".

[4] Quinlan, M., C. Mayhew. 1998. *The Implications of Changing Labour Market Structures for Occupational Health and Safety*, paper presented to Policies for Occupational Health and Safety management Systems and Workplace Change Conference, Amsterdam 21-24 September.

[5] Article 2 par. 1 sub. J.

1.1. Tackling Personal Factors of Vulnerability

There are usually four personal factors to consider while analysing workers' vulnerability in Italy: age, sex, nationality, and physical condition, with the regulatory approach mainly oriented towards policies aimed at controlling, preventing and prohibiting discriminatory practices at a systematic level. Such policies usually deal with working time patterns, skills development and maintenance, access-to-work programmes and hazardous tasks, with workers who need to be also instructed and further trained about their equipment, machinery and personal safety, especially regarding the exposure limits to dangerous substances (in accordance with Directive No. 92/85/EC and Directive No. 94/33/EC). It should be pointed out, however, that risk assessment processes identify hazards resulted from personal factors *de facto*, classified them as "particular risks", for which further measures have been adopted in relation to organizational issues, equipment, emergency situations and so on.

Significantly, no special provision applies to workers with disabilities, even though the employer is under the obligation to ensure their health and safety and work accessibility (through staircases, showers, etc.). In this respect, although introducing a number of innovative measures, domestic safety legislation has been regarded as affected by major shortcomings in the implementation of provisions at a practical level.

It should be worthy pointing out also that psychosocial factors, such as mobbing and burnout have been largely neglected by safety legislation, with relevant case law showing that such phenomena have been dealt with by resorting to general provisions included in the Civil Law Code (Article 2087). Instead, special attention has been given to work-related stress, for which *ad hoc* guidelines have been adopted by the Ministry of Labour and Social Policies, as a result of the transposition of the European Framework Agreement into national law.[6]

[6] See Italian Ministry of Labour and Welfare. 2010. *Indicazioni della Commissione consultiva per la valutazione dello stress lavoro-correlato*, published on 18 November: *http://www.lavoro.gov.it/Lavoro/Notizie/20101118_stresslavorocorrelato.htm.*

2. A New Approach to Health and Safety Culture

2.1. The Consolidated Act

In compliance with Community Directives, the passing of the Consolidated Act on occupational health and safety has resulted in a major overhaul of relevant legislation, with its implementation being rather difficult due to the fact that preventive measures needed to be adopted called for a review of labour organization models *in toto*, also because of a rise in non-standard employment relationships. In this connection, the enactment of Legislative Decree No. 81/2008 raised awareness of the issue, as an instrument to identify atypical workers' needs regardless of contractual arrangements, and to modernize labour market in organisational terms. As a matter of fact, while applying to such categories of workers, as being characterized by high rates of occupational injuries, the Decree makes provision also to individuals engaged in apprenticeship and voluntary work, as well as to those performing under more flexible forms of work (ex. quasi-subordinate employment), provided that they operate at the employers' premises.

2.2. Risk Assessment

In the context of the new law, the risk assessment process is of fundamental importance to identify the areas of vulnerability[7] and their related occupational hazards at the workplace and adopt preventive measures to safeguard workers' health and safety.[8] The new structure of risk assessment is based on a workforce diversity management approach.[9] In particular, according to Article 2, par. 1, sub. Q of Legislative Decree No. 81/2008 such processes aimed at "providing an overall and certified evaluation of work-related risks within the establishment they operate, in order to put in place appropriate preventive measures and draw up

---

[7] For further information on the new approach to risk assessment in Italy, see Ferrua, S., M. Giovannone, M. Tiraboschi. 2009. *Gruppi di lavoratori esposti a rischi particolari e tipologie di lavoro flessibile: la valutazione del rischio*, in *Il Testo Unico della salute e sicurezza sul lavoro dopo il correttivo (d.lgs. n. 106/2009)*, eds. Tiraboschi, M., L. Fantini, Milano: Giuffrè, pp. 569-584.

[8] See Court of Justice of the European Communities, C-49/00, 15 November 2001 dealing with the employer obligation to assess particular risks within the Italian framework.

[9] European Agency for Safety and Health at Work. 2009. *Workforce Diversity and Risk Assessment: Ensuring Everyone is Covered.*

guidelines with the view to improving health and safety in the workplace". This definition consists of three phases: assessing the risks, identifying effective safety policies, and improving worker's protection through legislation. Accordingly, companies need to face the new issue of vulnerability by implementing new policies in terms of work organization and the environment, also increasing public awareness of the issue, moving beyond stereotypical views and promote safety training in any stage of life.

It is also advisable to improve job satisfaction by means of specific training and retraining initiatives designed also to consider differences among workers—also making use of personalized programs and small study groups—which will result in higher levels of productivity, innovation, occupational development and mobility between companies. In light of the above, there is a need for innovation in cultural terms to be carried out by all actors involved in the labour market, and to reconsider links between environment, health and age in the workplace over the entire working life. In this light, apart from the draft of the ordinary risk assessment report it was also established that in cases of contracting, subcontracting, supply and installation of materials and provision contracts, the principal employer promotes cooperation and coordination with the contractor and drafts a Unified Interference Risk Assessment Document (DUVRI) which must be dated and must contain the following compulsory elements:

- a report on the assessment of all health and safety risks, which specifies the criteria adopted for the assessment;
- indication of the prevention and protection measures implemented and the persona protective equipment adopted;
- the program of measures necessary to improve safety levels over the time;
- identification of the procedures to implement the measures to be taken and the roles of the company organization that must apply these procedures;
- the name of the prevention and protection service manager, the workers' safety representative;

- the identification of the tasks that expose workers to specific risks, which require recognized professional know how, specific experience, adequate training and preparation.[10]

3. Vulnerable Workers[11]

The new risk assessment process is the key for the definition of vulnerability, both at personal and contractual level. The definition adopted for vulnerable workers in the context of Occupational Safety and Health (OHS) refers to those workers who are more likely to suffer from industrial injuries as a result of environmental, physiological, and personal factors (e.g. young people, people over 50, women, and migrant workers), though this does not necessarily depend on the type of employment contract. It seems to be useful to provide an overview of relevant legislation in order to frame the issue. Pursuant to Legislative Decree No. 81/2008 (Article 28, par.1, as amended by Legislative Decree No. 106/2009), it falls to the employer to assess the employees' level of protection, especially for those who are more vulnerable, viz.:

- workers suffering from work-related stress;
- pregnant women;
- workers who are discriminated against because of their age, gender, nationality, and employment status.

3.1. Workers Exposed to Risks Arising from Gender Inequalities and Pregnant Workers

As mentioned earlier, Legislative Decree No. 81/2008 (Article 28, par.1, as amended by Legislative Decree No. 106/2009), sets forth that the process of risk assessment should *inter alia* consider gender inequalities and hazards that are specific to some categories—e.g. pregnant women—as laid down also by Legislative Decree No. 151 of 26 March 200. The aim is to provide women with employment protection considering also their commitment to family and children, taking into account differences with male workers. In this sense, it is worth pointing out that, for instance,

---

[10] Castriotta, M., F. Grosso, and A. Papale, *The European Campaign on Risk Assessment: A New Concept for a Successful Model, in Prevention Today* 5, No. 1/2, ISPESL, January-June 2009.

[11] For further information on the different degrees of vulnerability, see Sargeant, M. 2009. *Health and Safety of Vulnerable Workers in a Changing World of Work,* Working Paper ADAPT, 101, 2009.

exposure to chemicals, vibrations, and radiations has a different impact on women and men's health.[12] Therefore, while identifying preventive measures and good practices to be adopted to safeguard working women, the employer should take such "diversity" into account.

Among the aspects to consider for a *women-friendly* approach in terms of health and safety, mention should be made of the following:

- certain hazards are specific to certain occupations;
- women and men are clearly different, especially in terms of reproduction;
- they take responsibility for different household chores, with women regarding them as an extra working activity.

Women should be granted safeguards in terms of work-life balance, and protected as *human beings* in all different stages of life (pregnancy, maternity and so on).[13] In this connection, a number of actions should also be taken especially concerning work organization, in order to provide women with flexible working time and better career prospects. In addition, equal opportunities should be granted to women in terms of adequate training, career advancement, fair remuneration, also preventing them from direct and indirect discrimination. Special attention should also be paid to measures adopted to tackle discrimination on the grounds of sex, together with offensive and persistent behaviour leading to sexual harassment. With reference to pregnant workers and their legal protection, Article 11 of Legislative Decree No.151/2001 sets forth that it is up to the employer to assess risks for women employees during pregnancy, considering their exposure to chemicals and biological agents, and other factors with the results of such evaluation to be communicated to workers and their representatives.

Measures of this kind might include the assignment of the worker to another task, if necessary at a lower level in terms of the employment grade, especially if an adjustment to working hours is not possible, with the employer being under the obligation to provide notice of the new assignment to the inspectorate of the Ministry of Labour in writing. Otherwise, the Provincial Labour Office (*Direzione Provinciale del*

[12] European Agency for safety and Health at work, *Mainstreaming gender into occupational safety and health*, 2005.

[13] For further details on risks arising from gender inequalities, see Legislative Decree No. 198 of 11 April 2006, which regulates the Code of Equal Opportunities between men and women.

Lavoro) might provide for parental leave lasting three months prior to and seven months following the expected date of childbirth.

Furthermore, working women, both during pregnancy and up to seven months following childbirth, cannot be employed in hazardous tasks that are physically demanding and that require the lifting of heavy loads, pursuant to Article 7 of Legislative Decree n. 151/2001.

Otherwise, they must be immediately re-assigned to a new task, regardless of the risk assessment. Jobs defined as dirty, demanding, and dangerous are listed in Article 5 of Presidential Decree No. 1026 of 25 November 1976, also appearing in Annex A of Legislative Decree 151/2001, while Annex B of the Decree provides a list of those tasks deemed to be hazardous due to their exposure to chemicals and unsafe working conditions.

Measures of this kind should be adopted also in the event that an inspection carried out by the Ministry of Labour—on its own initiative or upon the party's request—certifies that working and environmental conditions pose serious health risks to working women. In addition, they should not be employed in the event of poor state of health or complications in pregnancy, and when a new assignment is not available. Hence, they are required to communicate their medical condition to the employer by providing a medical certificate. If the employee does not present the medical certificate within the required period, the implementation of the measures mentioned above can be delayed until such certification is provided.

Article 8 of Legislative Decree n. 151/2001 deals with exposure to ionizing radiations, setting forth that "pregnant workers cannot be engaged in activities involving a significant risk for the child to be born, with the provision also applying to breastfeeding mothers. In this case, women are under the obligation to submit a declaration of pregnancy to the employer, who has to promptly assign them a new task, more compatible with their health status. If this is not possible, the worker is prohibited from performing the current working activity.

Further measures have been introduced also to protect the health and safety of pregnant workers, dealing with night work that is from midnight to 6 am. In this connection, they cannot be assigned to night shifts during pregnancy, or for 12 months following childbirth.

In addition, the following categories are exempt from performing night work:

- female and male workers with care-giving responsibilities with children younger than three years old;
- primary carers with children younger than 12 years old.

The provisions mentioned above dealing with night work are included in Article 11 of Legislative Decree No. 66/2003, also specifying that failure to comply with such measures may result in two- to four-year prison sentence and a fine between 516 and 2,582 euro.

3.2. Risks Associated with Migrant Workers

People working overseas face major challenges, particularly related to language barriers and a reduced perception of occupational risks. They are also more likely to take up hazardous and unskilled jobs, characterized by unfavourable working conditions, excessive working hours and unsocial shifts resulting in mental and physical fatigue that undermines alertness levels. It is also relevant that rotating shift workers, as well as night workers, tend to underperform their dayshift counterparts because of an attenuated brain response, with lack of sleep resulting in a general fatigue and tiredness often leading to occupational injuries. Poor language skills are another major issue, representing an obstacle to adequate training opportunities in OHS.

Migrant workers often come from countries with low levels of awareness of risks in the workplace, developing a different approach to occupational hazards. Therefore, the focus should be on information and training as a way to improve migrants' capacity to assess risk. As mentioned earlier, Legislative Decree No. 81/2008 (Article 28, par.1) specifies that immigrant workers are classified as being more vulnerable: employers should take responsibility for their health and safety and adopt specific measures to safeguard them. Article 36., par. 4 of the decree also makes provision for the workers' right to be informed properly about health and safety risks at work, setting forth that content must be easily accessible to workers—especially migrants—enabling them to gain necessary knowledge. Article 37 also lays down that the onus is on the employer to provide occupational and language training, with par. 13 reasserting that the content should be understandable by all workers.

In addition to assessing language skills, measures should be adopted to increase awareness of workers' rights and duties in terms of OHS, also by way of the implementation of good practices.

Finally, there is a need to take into great consideration occupational risks involving the followers of Islam, especially during *Ramadan*, the Islamic month of fasting according to which participants refrain from eating and drinking from 5 am to 5 pm. In this light, the employer should provide more flexible time arrangements in order to safeguard their health and safety, as well as their freedom of religion.

3.3. Age-related Risks

Pursuant to Article 28, par. 1, of Legislative Decree No. 81/2008, the burden is on the employer to assess and adopt measures to prevent risks associated with age for both young and older workers.

In this connection, Law No. 977/1967—as amended by Legislative Decree No. 345/1999, which was itself supplemented by Legislative Decree No. 262/2000—lays down special provisions for minors. In particular, Article 7 sets forth a number of factors to be considered while assigning them a new assignment, such as their physical development, lack of expertise, low risk perception, and the need for health and safety training and information. Young workers face additional challenges, as, unlike older workers, they are unfamiliar with the working environment, and unaware of risks and their rights and duties. Not to mention the working conditions and the employment status they operate in. This is often on a temporary basis with inadequate safety training (a case in point is young people working in call centres). In addition to being precarious, young workers—especially those aged 15 to 24 years—are more likely to undertake physically demanding jobs and to work to tight deadlines and at very high speed and this may result in musculoskeletal disorders. In addition, young workers are also more likely to take on jobs characterized by repetitive motion, rapid movement, vibration, the handling of toxic chemicals, exposure to high temperature, and, as newly hired, to harassment and bullying. In order to cope with those questions, the employer needs to adopt a set of measures in terms of health and safety, training, information, also appointing mentors within the company to help newly hired workers in their routine activities.

In order to safeguard young people the company must disseminate relevant information on potential risks and preventive measures before they start to work, as statistics show that in the first month of work they are five times more likely to suffer from occupational injuries than their older counterparts do.

Furthermore, supervisors should oversee their work to evaluate the effectiveness of training programmes and to make sure they carry out their tasks properly. Supervisors should also be provided with adequate training themselves, and be instructed on what actions need to be taken in the event of injuries suffered by young workers. More specifically, their task consists of:

- ensuring the implementation of good practices in terms of health and safety;

- making sure that safety measures have been designed also in practical terms;
- promoting a strong "culture of health and safety";
- reporting any changes and problems;
- providing advice for younger workers.

In the same way, young workers must report to their supervisor any perceived risks, comply with OHS rules and regulations, be instructed and trained properly about their equipment, machinery, and personal safety devices.

A case can be made for the inclusion of risk education as part of educational programmes. In this respect, schools and colleges need to play a major role in increasing the awareness of hazards among young people, and in the planning of specific measures to be adopted in the years to come. Specific risk assessment should involve also older workers, due to their vulnerability arising from lower levels of adaptability and reduced physical strength.

3.4. Workers Experiencing Stress at Work

Legislative Decree No. 81/2008 (Article 28, par.1) sets forth that work-related stress is a factor to be considered in the evaluation of occupational risks. In doing so, reference is made to the Autonomous Framework Agreement of 8 October 2004, which was transposed on 9 June 2008 by way of an inter-business collective agreement between employers' associations and trade unions. The main goal of the Agreement is to provide employers and workers with an instrument to identify, prevent and manage issues associated with work-related stress, therefore contributing to the improvement of employees' efficiency and working conditions, with a considerable impact also in economic and social terms. However, the Agreement does not envisage any measure to deal with workplace bullying, harassment, and post-traumatic stress disorder, therefore disregarding phenomenon such as *mobbing* and *straining*. As a result, the focus is on work-related stress, that is defined as a medical condition—accompanied by physical, psychological or social complaints or dysfunctions—resulting from individuals feeling unable to keep up with the requirements expected of them. Individuals may be well adapted to cope with short-term exposure to pressure, which can be considered as positive, but have greater difficulty in coping with prolonged exposure to intense pressure. Moreover, different individuals can react differently to similar situations and the same individual can react differently to similar situations at different times of his/her life. It should be pointed out, however, that work-related stress does not include all manifestations of stress at work, although stress originating outside the working environment can lead to changes in behaviour and reduced effectiveness at work. In this connection, the employer is under the obligation to provide protective measures only with regard to work organization, working conditions and environment. This entails the identification of those factors that are stress inducing and actions to be taken to reduce them, with the duty to report and evaluate the results on a regular basis.

In addition to the risks mentioned above, reference should be made also to those associated with precarious employment, as workers engaged in precarious jobs—characterized by low income, inadequate opportunities in terms of training and career advancement—usually operate in more dangerous working conditions, without necessarily receiving training in occupational safety and health, and with higher levels of stress due to uncertainty over the continuity of employment.

In this connection, it is up to the employers to prevent, reduce or eliminate issues arising from work-related stress. They should work to determine appropriate measures to be implemented together with workers and their representatives. Such measures might also include an overall process of risk assessment, or *ad-hoc* initiatives aimed at identifying stress factors. Furthermore, measures in terms of management and communication such as those clarifying the company's objectives and the role of workers should be adopted, ensuring suitable management support for individuals and team, matching responsibility and control over work, and improving work organisation and processes, working conditions and environment.

This should also be followed by adequate training for both managers and workers, awareness-raising campaigns aimed at increasing understanding of the issue and how to deal with it, and the adoption of an "award system" for those complying with health and safety regulations. In addition, a number of actions should be taken to address questions dealing with:

- working hours;
- participation and management;
- workload;
- work content;
- role within the organization;
- working environment;
- career prospects.

Once implemented, anti-stress measures should be reviewed on a regular basis to assess their effectiveness, in order to verify their appropriateness.

With reference to the employer's obligation to evaluate risks associated with work-related stress, Legislative Decree No. 207/2008, converted into Law No. 14/2009, deferred the date of the enforcement of this obligation to 16 May 2009.

Subsequently, Legislative Decree No. 81/2008 (in particular Article 28, par.1) was amended by Legislative Decree No. 106/2009, which specifies in this regard that, from 1 August 2010, the assessment of the risks linked to work-related stress should be carried out in compliance with the conditions laid down by the Advisory Panel on Health and Safety at Work. This obligation, applying to both the public and the private sector, was further deferred to 31 December 2010.

The guidelines on risk assessment, which are normative in character, were issued by the Advisory Panel on Health and Safety at Work set up by the Italian Ministry of Labour and Social Affairs on 18th November 2010. In order to comply with European legislation, and to deal with questions arising from its interpretation, Article 28, par. 8 of Legislative Decree No. 81/2008 specifies that the assessment of risk must be carried out also considering work-related stress. With the issuing of par. 1-*bis*, the Panel was also entrusted with the task of performing an advisory function, helping employers, advisers and supervisors to fulfil the necessary requirements not later than 31 December 2010, also backed by a tripartite committee. Far from being taken for granted, the issuing of the guidelines on 2 November 2010, was a subject of a heated debate between the government, the social partners, experts in the field and inspection bodies at a local level. In this connection, strong reservations were expressed about the transposition into national law of the Framework Agreement via the inter-business Agreement of 9 November 2008, to which Legislative Decree. 81/2008 referred, as methodology to assess the risk is subject to a variety of interpretations. Furthermore, considerable doubts were raised about the adoption of mandatory minimum standards to be reliable, fair in evaluating the individual's state of health and cost-effective for the companies, since they pay for the medical surveillance.

The long-awaited much-discussed provision was the result of months of talks among the actors involved, and it aims at meeting everyone's interest and providing employers with minimum requirements to be improved on a voluntary basis.

3.5. Occupational Risks Associated with Contractual Arrangements

Legislative Decree No. 106/2009, which amended Legislative Decree No. 81/2008, makes provision for the risks associated with the nature of the employment relation, focusing particularly on atypical workers and temporary workers, who are more exposed than other groups to hazards. This is due to a number of factors: the short duration of the assignment, job insecurity, inadequate training, the nature of the tasks to be carried out, low bargaining power, and low levels of union and legal protection.[14] The new provision is in this regard an attempt to safeguard those workers who are more vulnerable in contractual and individual terms. The categories of workers who are more likely to suffer from occupational risks (e.g. young people, women, and migrant workers) are often employed under these forms of contracts, although the individual risk is not necessarily associated with the type of employment contract.

4. The Role of Information and Training

Decree No. 81/2008 codified the notions of training and information by fully embracing the current case law and doctrinal standpoint; it also introduced the fundamental principle that every subject playing a role related to safety and security in a company needs a training path, tailored to his/her responsibilities and tasks within that specific organization.[15] The latter statement clearly extends the duty of training and information on safety and security to managers and other roles in the company (not only for employees). As for training, it has been defined as the educational process through which employees (and other subjects of the safety and security system) acquire knowledge and procedures useful to perform their duties in security and to identify, reduce and manage risks.

---

[14] Messineo, A., A. Bruschi, G. Di Martino, A. Imperatore, O. Rossi, and N. Serretti. 2006. "I lavori atipici: rilievi di attualità, sorveglianza sanitaria, vigilanza", *GIMLE* 28, No. 3, 307, see also Kompier, M., Fekke Ybema, J., J. Janssen, and T. Taris. 2009. "Employment Contracts: Cross-sectional and Longitudinal Relations with Quality of Working Life, Health and Well-being", *Journal of Occupational Health*, 51, pp. 193-203.

[15] See OECD. 2007. *Activity on Recognition of Non-Formal and Informal Learning Italy Country Background Report*, and Ecotec *European Inventory of Informal and Non-formal Learning,* which investigates the evolution of a new approach to training policies.

The initial aspect to stress is that of the educational process, as it is not of a generic kind (i.e. general skills concerning safety and security), but rather, it is specific in the sense that it comprises of the risks, procedures, and actions relative to the office carried out by the employee in his company. This point relates to a fundamental condition to evaluate the adequacy of the training process.

Other rules tend to further reinforce the concept of specific training as a mandatory requisite to tackle factors of vulnerability by a specific approach. The result is that, for instance, the mere participation of employees and other roles to basic and generic courses on safety and security, without any reference to the real situation of the company and the specific tasks carried out, makes the training process extremely inadequate, because it does not provide the necessary skills to prevent accidents and professional illness.

Descending from this principle, the employer not complying with this duty, as defined by the law, is liable both from the penal standpoint (for inadequate training) and from the contractual standpoint. An employee, not adequately trained (e.g. one who only attended a course of a few hours and only about general topics), can refuse to carry out his office (Articles 15, 18 and 44), in compliance with the principle of self-protection, and he keeps the right to remuneration and to preserve his position of employment. He can also resign "for good reasons", according to Article 2119 of the Civil Code. Among the inadequacy parameters of the training process, we can certainly include "undifferentiated training", i.e. the fact that heterogeneous groups of workers, of different office, sex and age, can attend the same lesson. Another inadequacy parameter is the planning of the training process that does not take into account the behavioural aspects and the specific needs of the trainee. An inadequate training process is moreover one that lacks proper interaction and collaboration with the local "Organismo Paritetico" (joint bodies), and training courses to migrant workers, performed without an evaluation of their level of understanding of the language.

Another relevant point is the teacher's qualification: Article 106 of Decree 2009 has assigned to the so called Advisory Panel on Health and Safety at Work set up by the Italian Ministry of Labour and Social Affairs the task of identifying a list of criteria to assess teacher's qualification. Recently, it was discovered that teachers were too young and/or lacked any experience on the specific topic themselves. The result was that those lessons were carried out as a formality, rather than being of any substance. It is surely relevant to our study that risks evaluation should comprise all risks for employees. On the other hand, it should be noted that the

Ministry of Labour is working on the redesign of training subjects and tools in order to include new risks and organisational models.

5. The Participatory Model

One of the leading principles in the new regulatory context is the strengthening of the role of the workers' representatives and the revisiting in the role of third joint bodies, as a means to give stronger voice to vulnerable workers.

This has been an important precondition for the generalisation of the participatory model of worker representation, deepening the roots of the principle of tripartism, stated by the International Labour Organisation, which implies an involvement of representative organizations (not only employers but also employees)

Legislative Decree No. 81/2008 is distinguished by particular cultural openness to the participatory model, knowing that participation, even more than consultation, is a relationship model, a style of confrontation and constant relation.

Recently there have been a number of signs of openness towards greater attention to collective protection, in particular through the consolidation of the thought that recognizes the legitimacy of unions as the civil party in trials related to violations of accident prevention regulations, the liability for workplace accidents and occupational diseases, the liability for sexual offences made in the workplace.

In the same connection, there is the innovative provision, which recognizes that trade unions hold the power to exercise rights on behalf of the person offended by the crime of manslaughter or offences.

The desirability of a trade union's involvement in a criminal trial is meaningful as long as they are able to contribute to what is being informed to the court. As it has been recognized, the new role of the union should move organizations toward less conflictual behaviour and onto a greater focus on a new style of industrial relations, to affirm the viability of an increase of safeguards, including the increase of protection levels.

The participation of workers and their representatives is invoked in many regulations concerning the management of safety and security prevention; starting from: the general measures of protection; the obligations of the employer and the manager, with particular attention to the risk assessment and its implementation modes; the obligations of the competent physician, related to the innovative works contracts, up to the organization of prevention services, regular meetings, training of workers, of their representatives, and of the ones responsible for checking the implementation of effective models of organization and management of safety and security.

Participation takes the form of information, consultation, and right of access and concerns mainly the representatives of workers' safety, the joint bodies and in some cases bilateral bodies and trade unions, in most cases, trade unions. As for the workers' representatives the new law, enhances the role of workers and their representatives.

The criteria followed was the revision of requirements, safeguards, the functions of subjects in the company prevention system, with particular reference to the strengthening of the role of representative of workers for territorial security and the introduction of the concept of safety representative of the production site. This concept was developed in two directions: on the one hand, guaranteeing a certain figure of reference for employees for each working reality (company representative /area/ production site), on the other hand strengthening the powers of the workers' representative for safety and security. It thus appears that the figure of a specialized representation, an exponent of collective security as a common interest of several people operating in the same working environment, with a specificity which distinguishes it from other figures of the prevention system in the company (the incompatibility with the manager or employee appointed to the prevention and protection system is now explicit) and from those trade unions which also can be part of the process.

These measures meant the renewed emphasis of the participatory philosophy, which is stipulated in European law. This particular Italian law is an implementation of the European law, which deems essential that workers and their representatives are able to contribute with a balanced participation in the adoption of the necessary preventive measures.

6. Best Practices and Future Evolution: Certification of Labour Contracts and Qualification of Enterprises

With the prospect of a dynamic evolution of the regulatory framework, the Consolidate Act introduced the principle of consolidation of best practices development and dissemination, as a soft law mechanism to improve health and safety standards. Indeed the definition of good practice varies between Member States due to different OHS systems and legislation, culture, language and experiences. In addition, different groups with different interests and levels of knowledge have different points of view on good practice in the workplace.

In the past, the EU-OHSA highlighted the difficulty in finding an exact definition of good practice and gave the following definition: Good practice information should provide persons with OHS duties the information to allow them to reduce the health and safety risks to workers at enterprise level in the EU.[16] This information should be of sufficient quality and quantity to produce, following an appropriate assessment of the hazards and risks present, a permanent and verifiable reduction in the whole potential to cause harm to all person affected by the enterprise and ensure that relevant occupational health and safety legislation is met. The information should be relevant, ethical and effective, focusing where possible on preventing exposure to hazards at source. It is implemented most effectively with the strong involvement of all relevant parties and in particular those workers and their representatives who will be directly affected by the action taken.

In Italy the concept of good practice was established for the first time by the Consolidated Act (Article 2) as:

> organisational or procedural solutions, which are compliant with current legislation and employ good technique; are adopted voluntarily and are aimed at promoting occupational health and safety by reducing risks and improving working conditions; are developed and collected by the regions, the National Institute for Occupational Safety and Prevention (ISPESL), the National Institute for Insurance against Occupational Accidents and the joint bodies; they are approved by the Permanent Consultative Committee as per Article 6, subject to a technical review by ISPESL, which ensures its broadest possible dissemination

In this light, the Advisory Panel on Health and Safety at Work set up by the Italian Ministry of Labour and Social Affairs is working on behalf of the law (Article 27) on the definition of a system of qualifications of enterprises as a means of selection of virtuous employers within the market. Obviously, OHS standards are at the top of the selection criteria. This system is based on the identification of economic sectors and the set organizational criteria which should be based not only on formal compliances and certifications, but on the constant application and monitoring of requisites of professional capacity in terms of: training activities, effective respect of sectoral collective agreements, use of genuine individual labour contracts and tenders, accompanied by the certification set in the Biagi Law.

---

[16] European Agency for Safety and Health at Work. 2000. *Guidelines on the Collection, Evaluation and Dissemination of Good Practices Information on the Internet,* Bilbao.

The system has immediately focussed on vulnerable sectors, which included construction, temporary agency work, and work in call centres. In the field of construction, this instrument has been defined as a sort of licence, which assigns the employer and the enterprises a score based on the application of the previous standards. This score is subject to deduction in cases of OHS violations and related crimes, up to final elimination from the market. Furthermore, in contracting and subcontracting all the stakeholders in value chains associated with these requisites will receive preferential treatment concerning access to public tenders and to the public funding.

On the other hand, in cases of private contracting and subcontracting purchasers, apart from the traditional documental requisites, they are obliged to check the tenure of these requisites for the selection of contractors, subcontractors and self-employed workers engaged for their activities.

The Biagi Law certification is going to be the cornerstone and the most innovative element of the system. It is a voluntary administrative process played by the Commissions of Certification (neutral public bodies established within public universities, the local labour inspectorates and bilateral bodies) whose task, as is clear from the wording regulatory, consists of a reduction of the use of litigation in labour law matters. On the base of a preliminary investigation of the formal content of the contract and an eventual investigation on its development in practice, a judgment is issued by the same Commissions of Certification. This judgment, which can be positive or negative, aims to check and test the genuineness of the contracts.

It has a legal effect in case of litigations on labour matters even if not binding. At a certain stage, it can also stop and postpone the inspections in the workplace. Certification of labour contracts is an Italian legal procedure whose main function is to reduce legal disputes concerning the qualification of labour contracts.

With reference to the Italian labour law system, the correct qualification of a labour contract is a process of great importance, as different contracts provide considerably different levels of protection to the worker; in other words, the qualification has direct impact on the worker's salary. This explains why, within the Italian labour law system, contractual qualification continually gives rise to a considerable amount of litigation.

In fact, qualification is excluded, by law, from the contractual terms under the power of variation of the parties and, therefore, may not be waived or altered by agreement. This is because qualification is mandatory and expressly established by law.

Following from this, not even Certification is entitled to endorse variations of mandatory provisions, pursued or introduced by the agreement of the parties. Nonetheless, Certification, by attesting the lawfulness and the correct qualification of the labour contract, is the institutional and legal means available to the parties to reduce uncertainty and ensure compliance with the regulatory framework. In legal literature, this concept is widely expressed: Certification, in fact, is exclusively regarded as a form of "assisted consensus ad idem", and is therefore not viewed in terms of "assisted variation" to mandatory rules.

Thus, Certification meets the need for certainty felt and expressed by interested parties who seek to perform flexible labour relations or to externalize stages of the production process by means of supply chain contracts (independent contractors). The subjects in charge of Certification are appointed by law. These certifying bodies are called "Commissions/Boards for Certification" (Article 76, Legislative Decree No. 276/2003).

Commissions for Certification (from now on: "Commissions") shall be set up:

- by each territorial body of Ministry of Labour (Direzione Provinciale del Lavoro, Provincial Labour Direction (4));
- by the Ministry of Labour;
- by Provinces, as expression of the local and territorial autonomies;
- by Universities and University Foundations, under the supervision of a professor of Labour Law;
- by Bilateral Bodies (Unions and Employers Associations);
- by the Professional Association of the Labour Advisors.

The law (Article 79, Legislative Decree No. 276/2003) establishes that the legal effects of Certification, which enforce the qualification and the regulation between the parties and toward third parties (i.e. Social Security Authorities as regards social security contributions), persist unless the judge of labour overturns Certification declaring it void.

Likewise, the actions of the public administrations, and in particular of the inspectors of labour (as a general rule, if an inspection confirms a labour law violation, inspectors are (4) The Provincial Labour Direction is the territorial organ of the Ministry of Labour. Therefore, they are part of the Government, and not organs of the local administration. The province, which is the territorial partition where they have competence in, corresponds to a district, and consists of a chief town with its territory around. (5) Being Certification an administrative act, the requirement of motivation is established by the general law for administrative acts Law 241/1990, Article 2.4 entitled to issue administrative orders for the re-qualification of labour contracts retrospectively to the starting date of work), produce the same legal effects between the parties and before third parties. Certification, though, produces its legal effects also before inspectors, who cannot therefore re-qualify a certified contract. Where there is a doubt about the correctness of its qualification or of its execution, they can appeal to a judge of labour for a review of the decision handed down by the Commission. In the meanwhile, the certified contract still produces its legal effects.

Because of this, and due to the close examination already carried out by the Commissions, with the General Directive of the Sept.18 2008, the Minister of Labour has requested the inspectors of labour to focus their inspections on non-certified contracts, unless a written claim is filed by workers complaining about a violation of rightful labour protections, or where the incorrect actual execution of the contract is immediately ascertained.[17]

Certification seeks to enforce labour standards through a proper use of contractual models, as to manifest the true intention of the parties and fully suit their interests. Certification is addressed from a regulatory perspective. Firstly, all labour and supply chain contracts are eligible for certification. Although apparently different, these contracts share a common origin: the global process of "vertical disintegration" of the firm. Secondly, certification is a form of labour market regulation, which does not fall among compulsory provisions nor is the expression of pure self-regulation. It rather represents an enforced self-regulation, or better a "co-regulation" willingly undertaken by the parties, availing of and relying on the competence and expertise of the members of the board of certification, who act impartially. Employers are not compelled by law to defer their contracts to the board of certification, but if they do so and receive positive feedback, "certification" gives the contract a legal presumption of fairness, certifying its conformity to the principles of law as to prevent future disputes. The theoretical framework of the paper views certification as a tool to promote regulatory compliance and responsibility, along with a more conscious use of contractual models.

---

[17] A deeper analysis on certification is provided in Bizzarro, C., F. Pasquini, M. Tiraboschi, and D. Venturi. 2009. *Certification of Labour contracts: A Legal Instrument for Labour Market Regulation in Italy*, paper presented at the International Society for Labour and Social Security Law, XIX World Congress of, 1st—4th September, Sydney, Australia.

As for OHS this new system, which has to be developed and implemented by the help Permanent Consultative Committee (a Ministerial body), could bring to the extension of the voluntary certification systems of labour contracts and tenders, introduced by the Biagi Law (Legislative Decree No. 276/2003) in the field of OHS organisation standards. In the field of OHS this could lead to the implementation of quality in OHS management standards, where it remains that in this matter a preponderant role should be assigned to risk assessment, specific training and of collective and individual protection for use by workers.[18]

In a broad sense, it can be also be interpreted as a modern and soft law mechanism to validate from the outside the quality of policies and product of a company in terms of: customer orientation and satisfaction, professional reliability, economic stability leadership, staff policies, corporate reputation and better management. This evolutionary perspective of the managerial model of labour relations applies a management process that has the characteristics of transparency and of the absence of negative externalities for the worker. Therefore it could be hypothesized—to use an image dear to those who, like Marco Biagi, envisaged the establishment of a "Worker's Statute"—a certification of concentric circles, which, starting from the analysis of compliance with the rules of law and the collective agreement applications (minimum standard of legal and formal coherence), extending to measures, for successive circles and therefore beyond mere legal requirements, the compliance with certain standards of quality and optimal management of staff along the lines of certification of excellence and good practice, evidently still to be defined. Alternatively, on the contrary, one could imagine the reverse path, enabling the achievement of excellence only to companies that perhaps matches the certification of a limited number of reports that have embarked on a path of change.

Finally, concerning the criminal persecution prospect, the new law has revised the pattern of offences and penalties, on the other hand it introduced, for the first time in our system, the principle of corporate social responsibility and the voluntary adoption of compliance programs in the field of occupational health and safety.

---

[18] On the evolution of certification in OHS field Barboni, A., C. Bizzarro, M. Giovannone, F. Pasquini, and M. Tiraboschi. 2009. "Mutamento dei modelli di organizzazione del lavoro, gestione della sicurezza, certificazione", *Il testo Unico della salute e sicurezza sul lavoro dopo il correttivo* (d.lgs. n. 106/2009), eds. Tiraboschi, M., L. Fantini, Milano: Giuffrè, pp. 67-94.

The implementation of this regulatory pattern is supposed to be strengthened within the context of the system of qualification of enterprises.

7. Conclusions

From the analysis of above mentioned indicators (risk assessment, participatory models, information and training and consolidation of best practices), it is evident that risks related to precariousness and vulnerability must be faced not only through the recognition of equal treatment between vulnerable and non-vulnerable workers and traditional compensation/social security systems. Equal treatment must be balanced by including age, sex, nationality, psychosocial conditions and contractual position in a special mandatory process of risk assessment and by the use of special training programmes.

At the same time, all these organizational instruments must be accompanied by legal instruments of quality, certification of labour contracts and models of organization of work, and the enforcement of compliance systems.

References

Barboni, A., C. Bizzarro, M. Giovannone, F. Pasquini, and M. Tiraboschi, "Mutamento dei modelli di organizzazione del lavoro, gestione della sicurezza, certificazione," in *Il Testo Unico della salute e sicurezza sul lavoro dopo il correttivo (d.lgs. n. 106/2009)*, eds. Tiraboschi, M., L. Fantini, Milano: Giuffrè, pp. 67-94.

Bizzarro, C., F. Pasquini, M. Tiraboschi, and D. Venturi. 2009. *Certification of Labour Contracts: A Legal Instruments for Labour Market Regulation in Italy, Paper Presented at the International Society for Labour and Social Security Law*, XIX World Congress of, 1st-4th September, Sydney, Australia.

Castriotta, M., F. Grosso, and A. Papale, *The European Campaign on risk assessment: a new concept for a successful model*, in *Prevention Today*, Volume 5, No. 1/2, ISPESL, January-June 2009.

Court of Justice of the European Communities, C-49/00, 15 November 2001 dealing with the employer obligation to assess particular risks within the Italian framework.

Ecotec. 2007. *European Inventory of Informal and Non-formal Learning.*

European Agency for Safety and Health at Work. 2009. *Workforce Diversity and Risk Assessment: Ensuring Everyone is Covered*, Bilbao, October.

—. 2005. *Mainstreaming Gender into Occupational Safety and Health.*

—. 2000. *Guidelines on the Collection, Evaluation and Dissemination of Good Practices Information on the Internet*. Bilbao.

Ferrua, S., M. Giovannone, and M. Tiraboschi. 2009. *Gruppi di lavoratori esposti a rischi particolari e tipologie di lavoro flessibile: la valutazione del rischio*, in *Il Testo Unico della salute e sicurezza sul lavoro dopo il correttivo (d.lgs. n. 106/2009)*, eds. Tiraboschi, M., and L. Fantini Milano: Giuffrè, pp. 569-584.

Italian Ministry of Labour and Welfare, *Indicazioni della Commissione consultiva per la valutazione dello stress lavoro-correlato*, http://www.lavoro.gov.it/Lavoro/Notizie/20101118_stresslavorocorrelato.htm, 18 November 2010

Javilier, J. C., A. Neal, M. Weiss, J. Saloheimo, U. Runggaldier, and A. Tinhhofer. 1996. "Lavoro atipico/temporaneo e tutela della salute: la trasposizione della Direttiva n. 91/383 in Francia, Regno Unito, Germania, Finlandia e Austria," in *Diritto delle Relazioni Industriali*, No. 3, pp. 35-50.

Kompier, M., J. Fekke Ybema, J. Janssen, and T. Taris. 2009. "Employment Contracts: Cross-sectional and Longitudinal Relations with Quality of Working Life, Health and Well-being," in *Journal of Occupational Health*, No. 51, pp. 193-203.

Messineo, A., A. Bruschi, G. Di Martino, A. Imperatore, O. Rossi, and N. Serretti. 2006. "I lavori atipici: rilievi di attualità, sorveglianza sanitaria, vigilanza," in *GIMLE* 28, No. 3, p. 307.

OECD. 2007. *Activity on Recognition of Non-Formal and Informal Learning Italy Country Background Report*. Paris: OECD.

Quinlan, M., and C. Mayhew. 1998. "*The Implications of Changing Labour Market Structures for Occupational Health and Safety,*" paper presented to Policies for Occupational Health and Safety management Systems and Workplace Change Conference, Amsterdam 21-24 September.

Sargeant, M. 2009. "Health and Safety of Vulnerable Workers in a Changing World of Work," Working Paper ADAPT, No. 101, 27 November.

Tiraboschi, M. 1996. "Lavoro atipico e ambiente di lavoro: la trasposizione in Italia della direttiva 91/383/CEE," in *Diritto delle Relazioni Industriali*, No. 3. p. 57.

—. 1997. "La trasposizione della direttiva n. 91/383/CEE nei principali paesi dell'Unione Europea e l'anomalia del caso italiano," in *Diritto e Pratica del Lavoro*, No. 18. p. 1284.

CHAPTER THIRTEEN

EMPLOYMENT PROSPECTS IN THE GREEN ECONOMY: MYTH AND REALITY

1. Framing the Issue[1]

The issue of the employment opportunities provided by the "green economy" has been much debated among the experts in the field in recent years.[2] In this connection, the 1997 White Paper on renewables issued by the European Commission marked a turning point at European level.[3] In planning a set of measures aimed at promoting renewable energy,

---

[1] The present contribution was written in collaboration with Lisa Rustico and previously published in 2010. *The International Journal of Comparative Labour Law and Industrial Relations* 26, No. 4, pp. 369-387.
This study was based on the international research project Women in Renewable Energy Sector (WiRES) led by ADAPT—the Association for International and Comparative Studies in Labour Law and Industrial Relations, in collaboration with the Faculty of Law of the University of Szeged Hungary and the Union for Private Economic Enterprise (UPEE) Bulgaria and co-funded by the European Commission, DG Employment, Social Affairs and Equal Opportunities, Budget heading 04.03.03.01, Industrial Relations and Social Dialogue. Sections 3 and 4 were written by Lisa Rustico, while 1, 2, and 5 were written by Michele Tiraboschi.

[2] For literature review about green jobs, see ADAPT, *Employment Perspectives of the Green Economy and the Impact on the Labour Market—Literature Review Updated in 2010*, at *www.adapt.it*, *Green Jobs*.

[3] European Commission. 1997. *Communication from the Commission, Energy for the Future: Renewable Sources of Energy. White Paper for a Community Strategy and Action Plan*, at *www.adapt.it*, *Green Jobs*. The European Commission argues that 'the development of renewable energy sources can actively contribute to job creation, mainly among small and medium enterprises', p. 4, and that 'a proactive move towards such energy sources will lead to significant new employment opportunities', p. 13.

policymakers were aware of its potential in terms of employment, although the concept of the green economy was not yet widely established.

Whereas, in the past, green jobs were not widely promoted, except in Spain[4] and Germany,[5] they have now become a key objective, and public awareness has been raised. The US administration[6] publicly acknowledged the importance of the green economy as an instrument to tackle the financial crisis starting in 2008, and since, then more and more consideration has been given to the sector, viewed also as a means to promote employment.

In addition to its potential in terms of employment, the green economy responds to other major concerns to be faced by policymakers in the coming years, such as the need for renewable energy sources and the control of pollution, reflecting their commitment to combat climate change.

Accordingly, the measures in the Kyoto Protocol, as well as those laid down in the 2000 Millennium Development Goals of the United Nations, focus on the environment at a global level. In Europe, the "20–20–20" provision contained in the Climate and Energy Package[7] lays down mandatory norms aimed at reducing greenhouse gas emissions and

---

[4] With reference to Spain, see Fundación Biodiversidad, Observatorio de la Sostenibilidad en España. 2010. *Empleo Verde en una Economía Sostenible*, at *www.adapt.it*, *Green Jobs*. The Spanish government started to address the issue of the employment impact of sustainable development policies about ten years ago. See the study commissioned by the Spanish Ministry of Environment in 1998 when Spain had more than 219,382 employees in 'green' activities, 1.55% of the Spanish working population at that time: Ministerio de Medio Ambiente y Medio Rural y Marino. 2000. *Estimación del Empleo Ambiental en España*.

[5] DB Climate Change Advisors. 2010. *Creating Jobs and Growth—The German Green Experience*, at *www.sustainableprosperity.ca/files/German%20Green%20 Experience%20Jobs%20and%20Growth.pdf*, last accessed on 30 Sep. 2010.

[6] See the American Recovery and Reinvestment Act 2009. See also Barboni, A., M. Zagordo, eds. *Gli effetti della crisi economica sul mercato del lavoro statunitense. Proposte e soluzioni per il rilancio dell'occupazione*, *Special Adapt Bulletin*, 5 February 2009, No. 3. For an assessment of the effects of the Clean Energy Jobs and American Power Act on the labour market, see Congressional Budget Office, S. 1733, Clean Energy Jobs and American Power Act, *www. adapt.it*, *Green Jobs*, 16 December 2009.

[7] The Energy and Climate Package, adopted by the European Parliament on 17 December 2008, responds to the commitment undertaken by the European Council to tackle climate change and promote renewable energies. The Package, based on an EU system of exchange emissions quotas, sets binding targets in terms of CO_2 emissions reduction in the sectors not included in the European emissions quota exchange system and utilization of the renewable energy sources.

encouraging a more efficient use of energy, as specified also by the Directive on energy from renewable sources in 2009.[8] In addition, with the European institutions[9] renewing their commitment in this respect, national governments have made an effort to harmonize environmental policies and employment programmes,[10] also with regard to taxation.[11]

---

[8] Directive 2009/28/EC of the European Parliament and the Council of 23 April 2009 on the promotion of the use of energy from renewable sources and amending and subsequently repealing Directives 2001/77/EC and 2003/30/EC, in GUUE, 5 June 2009, L 140/16, at *www.adapt.it*, *Green Jobs*. The Directive sets a common framework for the promotion of renewable energy sources and establishes binding national targets for the share of energy from renewables in relation to gross energy consumption and for the share of energy from renewables in transport.

[9] The Commission started promoting climate actions and strategies some twenty years ago, and the first Community strategy to limit CO_2 emissions and improve energy efficiency dates back to 1991. However, Member States and the European Union are called to significant efforts to comply with the Kyoto Protocol's requirements and those set out by the Commission in 2000 and 2005, through the *Climate Change European program*, *http://ec.europa.eu/environment/climat/eccp.htm*. See also Green Paper from the Commission to the Council, the European Parliament, the European Economic and Social Committee, and the Committee of the Regions. 2007. *Adapting to Climate Change in Europe—Options for EU Action*, COM (2007) 354, 29 June 2007; European Commission, White Paper. 2009. *Adapting to Climate Change: Towards a European Framework for Action*, COM (2009) 147, 1 April 2009.

[10] European Commission. 2005. *Commission Staff Working Document on the Links between Employment Policies and Environment Policies*, SEC 2005, 1530, at *www.adapt.it*, *Green Jobs*, 17 November. See also European Commission. 1997. *Environment and Employment: Building Sustainable Europe*, COM 97 592 final. The key points of this communication were later transposed into the Employment Guidelines of 1998. European Council, *Employment Guidelines*, Resolution of 15 December 1997.

[11] On this point, the Commission, by regarding the environmental tax reform as a possible driver for the creation of new jobs, used the expression 'double dividend' to highlight the trade-off between employment and environmental targets; in European Commission, Commission Staff Working Document on the links, etc., *supra*. On the relation between environmental/energy taxation and job creation, see Heady, C. J. et al. 2000. *Study on the Relationship between Environmental/Energy Taxation and Employment Creation*, study prepared for the European Commission, Directorate General XI, at *www.adapt.it*, *Green Jobs*. The Environmental Programme of the United Nations defines "double dividend" as the positive result of reaching environmental targets and creating employment. See United Nations Environment Program (UNEP), International Labour Organization (ILO), *supra*, 10. The International Labour Organization adopted the same expression with reference to environment and employment. Cf. ILO. 2009. "Green Policies and

In the coming years, environmental policies are expected to promote the creation of high-quality jobs and the setting up of green companies using either traditional or innovative technology.[12]

However, differences in the implementation of standards can cause cost differentials to widen in the European countries. In this connection, the European[13] Trade Union Confederation (ETUC) estimates that a considerable number of businesses that are more exposed to international competition will resort to outsourcing, with negative effects on employment and the quality of the work.

However, a number of studies undermine this argument. Spain, for instance, is regarded as a reference point in the quest for renewable energies, despite some critical research findings. According to a survey carried out by the Rey Juan Carlos University in Madrid on the effects that alternative sources of energy have on employment, every "green job" created in Spain resulted in the elimination of 2.2 other jobs.[14] The research also showed that in 2000, the Spanish government allocated EUR 0.5 million to fund the creation of each job in the green economy and EUR 1 million for each new job in the wind energy sector.

The promotion of "green" job opportunities has been widely supported by public funding and by a number of measures aimed at tackling the

Jobs: A Double Dividend?", *World of Work Report 2009, The Global Jobs Crisis and Beyond*, ILO, Ch. IV, 97 et seq., at *www.adapt.it*, *Green Jobs*.

[12] See, among many, Stern, N. 2007. *The Economics of Climate Change: The Stern Review*. Cambridge: Cambridge University Press, esp. summary of conclusions xvii, on based on "action on climate change will also create significant business opportunities, as new markets are created in low-carbon energy technologies and other low-carbon goods and services. These markets could grow to be worth hundreds of billions of dollars each year, and employment in these sectors will expand accordingly".

[13] European Trade Union Confederation (ETUC), ISTAS, SDA, Syndex, Wuppertal Institute. 2007. *Climate Change and Employment 2007. Impact on Employment in the European Union-25 of Climate Change and CO_2 Emission Reduction Measures by 2030* (hereinafter 'ETUC, *Climate Change and Employment*'), *www.adapt.it*, *Green Jobs*. See also ITUC. 2009. *Trade Unions and Climate Change. Equity, Justice & Solidarity in the Fight Against Climate Change*; *Les syndicats et le changement climatique*, *www.adapt.it*, *Green Jobs*, November.

[14] Calzada, G. A., R. M. Jara, and J. R. Rallo Julián. 2009. *Study of the Effects on Employment of Public Aid to Renewable Energy Sources*. Madrid: Universidad Rey Juan Carlos, *www.adapt.it*, *Green Jobs*.

international financial crisis,[15] which will soon entail growing competition, affecting not only levels of employment but also pay scales and legislation regulating work. As pointed out by the International Labour Organization (ILO),[16] major concerns about green jobs refer to developing countries and the ongoing phenomenon of dumping, which might lead to an increase of existing social inequalities with industrialized countries. As a result, future research[17] should focus on the real employment impact of the green economy.

In order to lay the foundations for further investigation, the aim of this paper was to provide an overview of the debate-taking place at an international level on the relationship between the green economy and the labour market, also considering industrial relations perspectives.

2. The Problem of the Definition of Green Jobs and their Impact on the Labour Market

The expression "green jobs" is used to refer to occupations that promote the protection of the environment. This also means considering the effects on the labour market of company restructuring as the result of investment in the green economy and the subsequent process of adaptation.[18]

---

[15] In relation to measures in response to the economic crisis, see UNEP. 2009. *Global Trends in Sustainable Energy Investment*; HSBC. 2009. *A Climate for Recovery*; Deutsche Bank. 2008. *Investing in Climate Change 2009. Necessity and Opportunity in Turbulent Times*; Edenhofer O., and N. Stern. 2009. *Towards a Global Green Recovery Recommendations for Immediate G20 Action.* Foreign Office of the German Government; UNEP. 2009. *Global Green New Deal*. See also Organization for Economic Co-operation and Development (OECD). 2009. *Green Growth: Overcoming the Crisis and Beyond.* Paris: OECD, *www.adapt.it*, *Green Jobs*.

[16] See, among the others, the United Nations Environment Program report, UNEP, ILO report. 2008. *Green Jobs: Towards Decent Work in a Sustainable, Low-Carbon World*, *www.adapt.it*, *Green Jobs*.

[17] See Rossi, G. *Premesse economiche: perché investire nei settori eco-sostenibili? Presentazione delle ragioni economiche che promuovono l'occupazione nei settori verdi*, *www.adapt.it*, *Green Jobs*.

[18] It is important to note the difference between, on the one hand, 'mitigation' strategies, which include all measures addressed to the mitigation of the negative impact that human activities have on the environment, by reducing the intensity of the coal energy use, for instance, establishing industrial standards to increase energy efficiency in production processes—definition was taken from OECD. 2008. *Climate Change Mitigation.* Paris: OECD, 11—and on the other hand,

The ILO and the United Nations Environment Programme (UNEP) adopt the following definition of green jobs:

> positions in agriculture, manufacturing, construction, installation, and maintenance, as well as scientific and technical, administrative, and service-related activities, that contribute substantially to preserving or restoring environmental quality. Specifically, but not exclusively, this includes jobs that help to protect and restore ecosystems and biodiversity; reduce energy, materials, and water consumption through high-efficiency and avoidance strategies; de-carbonize the economy; and minimize or altogether avoid generation of all forms of waste and pollution. But green jobs... also need to be good jobs that meet long standing demands and goals of the labour movement, i.e., adequate wages, safe working conditions, and worker rights, including the right to organize labour unions.[19]

The international literature[20] shows that green jobs can be classified on the basis of the area and the sector, with a focus on building, transport, and manufacturing,[21] as well as food, agriculture, and forestry. However, the literature does not provide a universally recognized definition of the term, covering all production sectors and employment grades and a wide range of skills relating to environmental protection,[22] also due to a blurring of boundaries[23] between some occupations.

'adaptation' strategies, including actions undertaken to reduce the inevitable negative consequences of climate change and to exploit positive opportunities, e.g., the use of scarce water resources—definition was taken from OECD, *Economic Aspects of Adaptation to Climate Change: Costs, Benefits and Policy Instruments,* Paris: OECD, 2008, p. 1.

[19] UNEP, ILO. *Green Jobs: Towards Decent Work, op. cit.*

[20] See literature review in No. 1.

[21] For an in-depth examination of the eco-industry, see European Commission, DG Environment. 2006. *Eco-industry, Its Size, Employment, Perspectives and Barriers to Growth in an Enlarged EU*, Ernst and Young.

[22] The US Bureau of Labor Statistics has recently undertaken a series of interviews with researchers and experts, aimed at defining green jobs based on the firm's economic activity, evaluating whether and how the economic outcome of work can be aimed at the protection or restoration of the environmental balance.

[23] Some authors talk of an "irradiation" effect for which "green" economic activities have the potential of greening other economic sectors. In other words, "the creation of green employment in key parts of the economy has the potential to 'radiate' across large swaths of the economy, thus greening commensurately large sections of the total workforce", UNEP, ILO, 2008, *op. cit.* p. 38.

The lack of a shared definition, together with different approaches to the data,[24] highlights the difficulty of making a quantitative or qualitative assessment of the effects of the green economy on employment. Most of the studies make a positive assessment,[25] alternatively opting for a neutral position,[26] suggesting that negative effects are less likely.

The Organization for Economic Co-operation and Development (OECD) has conducted a series of studies[27] that are worthy of note, focusing on the outcomes of a more recent investigation dealing with the employment impact of the green economy, according to which the effects of the environmental policies were slightly significant.[28] A 2004 survey[29] highlighted the fact that, although they have a considerable impact in the

---

[24] For a comprehensive analysis of the environmental impact assessment measures, see Rossi, G. "Job Creation and Job Losses Related to Green Investments: An Overview of the Current Debate", Stagnaro C., ed. 2009. *The Impact of Green Investments on Labour Market*, Dossier ADAPT, No. 9, *www.adapt.it*, *Green Jobs*.

[25] In this perspective, see WWF. 2009. *Low Carbon Jobs for Europe. Current Opportunities and Future Prospects*. See also among many, Fankhauser, S., F. Seheiler, and N. Stern. 2008. *Climate Change, Innovation and Jobs*, *Climate Policy* 8, pp. 421-429.

[26] See, for a different view, among many, Morgestern, R. D., W. A. Pizer, and J. S. Shih. 2002. "Jobs Versus the Environment: An Industry-Level perspective," *Journal of Environmental Economics and Management* 43, pp. 412-436; see also the OECD. 1997. *Environmental Policies and Employment* Paris: OECD) confirmed in OECD. 2004. *Environment and Employment: An Assessment*, Working Party on National Environmental Policy, ENV/EPOC/WPNEP200311/ FINAL, *www.adapt.it*, *Green Jobs*.

[27] Since the 1970s, the OECD has carried out a number of studies on the employment impact of environmental policies: the first literature studies date back to 1978: OECD. 1978. *Employment and Environment*. In the 1990s, Member States encouraged a new study, due to the high employments rates *www.oecd.org/document/55/0,3343,en_2649_34405_35142967_1_1_1_1,00.html*.

[28] OECD. 1997. *Environmental Policies and Employment*. Paris: OECD. The outcomes of which are confirmed in OECD, *Environment and Employment etc.*, *supra*, where the lack of macroeconomic studies that consider employment as an important indicator for the evaluation of environmental policies is also highlighted.

[29] This research considers the results of a 1997 study, which investigated the effects of the environment on employment. It distinguished between positive and negative effects, direct and indirect effects, short- or long-term effects, temporary and sustainable effects, effects leading to part-time or full-time jobs, effects that create new jobs while maintaining the old ones, OECD, *Environment and Employment etc.*, *supra*, 9.

short-run at sectoral level, the results of CO_2 reduction policies are uncertain.[30]

According to ILO, estimates[31] in 2005 restructuring associated with mitigation policies involved 38% of workers in high-energy intensity sectors,[32] for a total of 600,000 workers worldwide. In confirming the existing data, the study found that green policies could increase employment rates by 0.5 to 1.1 percentage points over a period of five years,[33] thus having only a marginal impact.

However, the combination of environmental policies and measures supporting innovation in technology could provide higher levels of employment: 2.6 million new jobs in the most industrialized countries, 14.3 million worldwide.[34]

The adoption of legislative provisions,[35] as well as the allocation of public funds, should drive innovation further. It could also contribute to raising aggregate demand for goods and services and to a positive effect on employment.[36] In this connection, the energy sector seems to offer the brightest prospects in terms of job opportunities.[37]

---

[30] OECD. *Environment and Employment, op. cit.*, p. 73.

[31] ILO, Institute of Labour Statistics. 2009. *World of Work Report 2009. The Global Jobs Crisis and Beyond*, Geneva: ILO, IILS, 100.

[32] For a classification of the high carbon intensity sectors, see ILO, IILS. 2009. "Annex A. Estimating the Size of the High Carbon Intensive Sectors", *World of Work Report 2009, op. cit.,* ILO, Institute of Labour Statistics.

[33] *Ibid.*, p. 102.

[34] For a classification of the high carbon intensity sectors, see ILO, IILS, Annex A. *Estimating the Size of the High Carbon Intensive Sectors*, *op. cit.*, p. 104.

[35] On the risks arising from the interaction of different instruments in environmental policy packages, see OECD. 2009. *Green Growth: Overcoming the Crisis and Beyond*. Paris: OECD, 11, *www.adapt.it*, *Green Jobs*.

[36] See Torres, R. 2008. "The Social Impact of Policies to Address Climate Change: A Review of the Issue," *International Labour Review* 147, No. 2-3.

[37] Among the studies on the energy sector, see Kammen, D., K. Kapadia, and M. Fripp. 2004. *Putting Renewables to Work: How Many Jobs Can the Clean Energy Industry Generate?* Energy Resources Group, Goldman School of Public Policy, University of California, Berkeley. For the wind energy sector, see Blanco M.I., and G. Rodrigues. 2009. "Direct Employment in the Wind Energy Sector: An EU Study," *Energy Policy* 37:2847-2857. However, econometric analysis underlines the moderate impact of renewable energy sector policies on economic growth in Europe, attributing positive employment effects to the increase of energy costs caused by a greater technology use to produce energy from renewable sources. See Fraunhofer ISI Germany, Ecofys the Netherlands, Energy Economics Group EEG Austria, Rütter + Partner Socioeconomic, Européenne d'Économie SEURECO France. 2009. *EmployRES. The Impact of Renewable Energy Policy on Economic*

UNEP[38] provided different figures, suggesting that in 2030, there will be 20 million workers employed in the energy sector worldwide, compared to 2.3 million in the sector in 2006, of which 300,000 were in wind energy; 170,000 were in photovoltaic energy; 600,000 were in solar thermal energy; and 1.2 million were in the biomass sector.

According to the European Commission,[39] the number of employees in the renewable energy sector was 1.4 million, with 640,000 in the biomass sector; 180,000 in wind energy; and 55,000 in photovoltaic energy, amounting to 0.64% of the total workforce. In Europe, a million new jobs are expected to be created in renewable energy by the end of 2010.[40]

Other studies by European institutions have predicted that 240,000 additional jobs will be created by 2020, taking into account a number of factors including higher levels of unemployment in the traditional energy sectors, together with 0.24% growth in GDP.[41]

However, research by Greenpeace and the European Renewable Energy Council suggests that technological innovation in renewable energy production will contribute to the creation of 2.7 million new jobs in the sector over the next twenty years.[42]

Despite these optimistic forecasts, there is still a good deal of scepticism about the impact of the green economy on employment.

A research group set up at the Rey Juan Carlos University in Madrid and supported by the Bruno Leoni Institute[43] recently published some statistics questioning the overall impact of the green economy on employment growth.[44] The study found that certain "green" programmes

---

Growth and Employment in the European Union, Karlsruhe, *www.adapt.it*, *Green Jobs*.

[38] UNEP, ILO. 2008, *op. cit.*, p. 127.

[39] European Commission. *Meeting the Targets & Putting Renewables to Work*. Overview Report, Monitoring & Modelling Initiative on the Targets for Renewable Energy (MITRE), at *www.ewea.org/fileadmin/ewea_documents/documents/policy/external_documents/040330_MITRE_overview_-_Meeting_the_targets_and_putting_renewables_to_work.pdf; MITRE, http://mitre.energyprojects.net*.

[40] European Commission, EU Citizens' summary.

[41] Fraunhofer ISI, Ecofys, EEG, Rütter + partner, LEI, SEURECO, EmployRES, *op. cit*.

[42] Rutovitz, J., and A. Atherton. 2009. *Energy Sector Jobs to 2030: A Global Analysis, prepared for Greenpeace International by the Institute of Sustainable Future*. Sidney: University of Technology.

[43] See Lavecchia L., and C. Stagnaro. 2010. *Are Green Jobs Real Jobs?* Milan: Istituto Bruno Leoni, p. 8.

[44] See Calzada, G. A., R.M. Jara, and J.R. Rallo Julián. *Study of the Effects on Employment*, *op. cit*. For a comprehensive explanation of the Spanish debate

actually destroy more jobs than they create. In Spain, renewable energy resulted in the loss of 2.2 jobs for every green job created in the traditional sectors, without taking into account the jobs that might have been created by private investment.[45] In France, the employment forecasts by the government, according to which 600,000 jobs would be created by fifteen environmental protection programmes under the Grenelle de l'Environnement, have attracted considerable criticism,[46] mainly because of shortcomings in data collection methodology. In Italy, the Bruno Leoni Institute has cast doubt on the potential of the green economy to make a significant contribution to employment growth.[47]

The Institute takes issue with the optimistic view that the green economy will increase employment rates in Italy, maintaining that investments of this kind are not part of an effective policy for the creation of jobs.

In the same vein, a number of studies conducted in the United States have focused on the risks of overestimating the employment predictions,[48] pointing out the doubts among scholars.[49] Although public support for the green economy is strong, the jobs that are created in this sector are not necessarily of good quality.[50] There has even been talk of a "green

---

started after the publication of this study, see Rossi, G. "Job Creation and Job Losses Related to Green Investments: An Overview of the Current Debate," *op. cit.*

[45] See Calzada, G.A., R.M. Jara, and J.R. Rallo Julián. *Study of the Effects on Employment*, *op cit.*, p. 29.

[46] The study commissioned by the Minister of the Environment Jean-Louis Borloo and carried out by the Boston Consulting Group BCG has been criticized by Beaudet, M.B. 2009. "Doutes sur la création des 600 000 emplois verts, » *Le Monde*, 30 July. However, the focus on the employment impact of environmental policies is not present in the most recent French government strategy for sustainable growth; see Premier Ministre. 2009. "Stratégie nationale de développement durable 2010-2013. Vers une économie verte et équitable, 2009," *ADAPT Bulletin*, September 2010.

[47] Lavecchia L., and C. Stagnaro. *Are Green Jobs Real Jobs?*, *op cit.*. 40.

[48] See Bezdek, R. H. 2009. *American Solar Energy Society, Estimating the Jobs Impacts of Tackling Climate Change*, *www.adapt.it*, *Green Jobs*, 21 October.

[49] Michaels, R., and R. Murphy. 2009. *Green Jobs Fact or Fiction? An Assessment of the Literature, Institute for Energy Research*, *www.adapt.it*, *Green Jobs*.

[50] Morriss, A., et al. 2009. "Green Jobs Myths," Law and Economics Research Paper No. LE09-001. University of Illinois; and Research Paper Series No. 09-15. Case Western Reserve University, *www.instituteforenergyresearch.org/issues/green-jobs-resources/*.

bubble",[51] and some researchers have argued that environmental protection measures may result in a loss of jobs.[52] Even shifting from a quantitative to qualitative approach, the doubts remain. The influential study by ILO and the UNEP[53] looked at four possible outcomes. In some cases, new jobs will be created, in occupations dealing with technological instruments related to pollution control or updating existing tools and machinery.

In other cases, the workforce will be replaced, as a result of the shift from fossil fuels to renewable power or in order to comply with waste management guidelines. In certain other cases, some jobs will no longer be regarded as necessary. This is particularly true for those occupations relating to materials and procedures that are no longer allowed under the most recent regulations. Finally, the provision of further training for existing occupations also needs to be considered, as well as the emergence of new occupations to meet the market demand and to comply with new environmental protection rules.

As for the classification of workers, in the United States, green jobs may be seen in terms of "green collar jobs", which are reasonably well-qualified occupations providing opportunities in terms of career advancement and wages.[54] However, trends in the European labour market over the last decade suggest that the green sector includes both low-paid unskilled jobs and highly skilled occupations.[55]

At a European level, policies could be adopted to create new forms of green employment, to cope with the increasing polarization of the labour market, and to mitigate the impact of such measures on women in the workforce. According to the literature,[56] green jobs are increasing in male-dominated industries and occupations.

Another aspect to consider is the skills mismatch, that is, the lack of qualifications that means that workers are unable to keep up with changes

---

[51] Bell, R. 2009. *Speech at the Brooklyn College*. New York: City University of New York, *http://robertibell.com/thegreenbubble.html*.

[52] See Babiker, M., and R. S. Eckaus. 2006. "Unemployment Effects of Climate Policy," MIT Joint Program on the Sciences and Policy of Global Change, Report No. 137. Cambridge: MIT. The authors argue that emission restrictions would have a negative effect on employment and on growth rates in the United States.

[53] See UNEP, ILO. 2008, *op. cit*, pp. 43-44.

[54] *Ibid.*, 288. See literature review in No. 1.

[55] OECD. 2008. *Environment and Employment*, *op. cit.*, pp. 20-21; see also the European Commission in ECORYS. 2008. *Environment and Labour Force Skills. Overview of the Links between the Skills Profile of the Labour Force and Environmental Factors*, p. 27.

[56] See literature review in No. 1.

and innovation in the economy. Several studies highlight a lack of "green" competencies, see section 4 below.[57] In the green economy, there is a need for new vocational skills and occupations.[58]

With many European countries adopting measures to tackle climate change, unskilled and unqualified workers may not see any benefit in terms of employment.

3. Implications for Women Workers

While the impact of green jobs on employment is uncertain, the need to evaluate the risks and the difficulties for women in gaining access to the green economy is widely acknowledged. This is because most green sectors, such as renewables, transport, building, and agriculture, are traditionally male-dominated.[59] The different needs of male and female workers in the green economy have been given scant consideration.[60] At an international level, there is a lack of reliable data about the gender

---

[57] See ECORYS. *Environment and Labour Force Skills. Overview of the Links between the Skills Profile of the Labour Force and Environmental Factors*; for an overview of the relation between skills, productivity, employment growth, and development, ILO, *Report v. Skills for Improved Productivity, Employment Growth and Development*, International Labour Conference, 97th Session, 2008.

[58] See Rustico, L. *Le competenze: focus sui fabbisogni formativi dei lavoratori impiegati nei settori eco-sostenibili. Presentazione delle strategie per l'analisi delle competenze nei settori verdi*, *www.adapt.it*, *Green Jobs*.

[59] See the WiRES project, *Women in Renewable Energy Sector*, co-financed by the European Commission, DG Employment, Social Affairs and Equal Opportunities budget heading 04.03.03.01, Industrial Relations and Social Dialogue, promoted by ADAPT together with UPEE, Union for Private Economic Enterprise Bulgaria and the Faculty of Law of the University of Szeged Hungary. The project analyses and promotes social dialogue to raise the employment rates of women employed in renewable energy in Europe and to improve the working conditions in a perspective of gender mainstreaming. See Rab, A., L. Rustico, and S. Terzimehic, eds. 2010. *Women in the Green Economy. A Human Capital Perspective*, ADAPT Dossier No. 12, Rossi G., and S. Terzimehic, eds. 2010. *Social Dialogue, Renewable Energy, Female Employment*, ADAPT Dossier, No. 4; Gospodinova, R., J. Hajdú, and L. Rustico, eds. 2010. *Green Jobs: nuove opportunità o nuovi rischi?*, ADAPT Dossier No. 4; Rossi, G., ed. 2010. *The Economic and Occupational Impact of Green Economy*, ADAPT Dossier No. 2; Mattioli, F., ed. 2010. *Green Economy and Female Employment: More and Better Jobs?*, Special Adapt Bulletin, No. 3.

[60] In the EU-27 from 2000 to 2008, the female employment rate increased by 5.2%, reaching 59.1% in 2008.

impact of the green economy,[61] except for a survey in Spain[62] that pointed out the risks of the exclusion of women in the transition to the green economy, in spite of what appears to be a greater awareness of green issues[63] compared to men. Most new green jobs will be created in the industrial sector,[64] where women are underrepresented. In the energy industry, for which encouraging employment statistics were recorded in 2007, 20% of the workforce were women: 6% of them were employed in technical occupations; 4%, in decision-making positions; and less than 1%, in management.[65] More generally, recent statistics show that women still tend to be employed in (or relegated to) clerical work.[66]

---

[61] In the United States, good practices have been developed for the promotion of the female employment in green jobs; see Wider Opportunities for Women (WOW). 2009. *Women and the Green Economy. An Opportunity for Economic Security*, Washington: WOW. In Europe, some research has dealt with the relation between women and environmental issues, mainly referring to access to resources by women; with reference to energy resources, see Clancy, J., S. Oparaocha, and U. Roehr. 2004. *Gender Equity and Renewable Energies*, paper discussed during the International Conference for Renewable Energies. Other studies have proposed a gender analysis of the mitigation and adaptation policies to climate change. See Terry, G. 2009. *No Climate Justice without Gender Justice: An Overview of the Issues*. Gender and Development 17, No. 1, pp. 5-18.

[62] International Labour Foundation for Sustainable Development (Sustainlabour). 2009. *Green Jobs and Women Workers. Employment, Equity, Equality*. Sustainlabour.

[63] OECD. 2008. *Gender and Sustainable Development: Maximising the Economic, Social, Environmental Role of Women*. Paris: OECD.

[64] Sustainlabour, *Green Jobs and Women Workers*, *supra*, 8. In particular, one-third of the total employment created in the building trade sector through reconstruction and building activities in accordance with environmental standards will contribute to the fulfilment of the energy efficiency targets. In the same way, transport system will contribute to green employment growth, in particular through the planning and the production of low-emission vehicles, infrastructure, and public transport. Finally, new occupations will be created in the manufacturing sector in relation to low environmental impact technologies, materials, instrumentation, and techniques. These sectors employed less than 25% women workers in 2009, with peaks of 38% in agriculture and 30% in manufacturing, based on EUROSTAT data. For an overview of the European labour market, see Rossi, G. "The State of the Art in the European Labour Markets", *Social Dialogue, Renewable Energy, Female Employment*, *op. cit.*

[65] Sustainlabour, *Green Jobs and Women Workers*, *op cit.*, p. 9.

[66] For a recent classification and analysis of the women's segregation in the labour market, useful to understand the trends also in green jobs, see European Commission Expert Group on Gender and Employment EGGE. 2009. *Gender*

Women risk finding themselves without the necessary qualifications to take advantage of opportunities in the green economy due to a lack of skills and expertise. A recent empirical study[67] suggests that the requirements for occupations in renewable energy tend to exclude women. A survey of the gender of graduates in different subjects[68] found that women were underrepresented in science, technology, engineering, and mathematics.[69] Vocational training programmes are seen as increasingly male-oriented. At the same time, the renewable energy sector requires workers with a certain level of expertise in the electric/energy sector and who are willing to travel, both factors that tend to discourage working women.

The needs of women workers[70] are not limited to access to the labour market but also concern other factors, such as working conditions, career paths, wage differentials, access to training contracts, and health and well-being at workplace that may be a male-dominated environment.

All the factors mentioned above may increase the level of female employment in the green economy, as long as effective support is provided. The need to adopt measures aimed at promoting equality between men and women in the labour market is widely acknowledged. This is particularly true in the emerging sectors of the economy, where there is an attempt to move beyond gender equality in theoretical terms.

In Italy, an initiative launched by the Minister for Equal Opportunities together with the Minister of Labour, Health and Social Policy[71] aims to

---

Segregation in the Labour Market: Root Causes, Implications and Policy Responses in the EU.

[67] Rustico, L., and S. Terzimehic. "Women in the Green Economy: A Snapshot", *Women in the Green Economy. A Human Capital Perspective*, *op. cit.*, pp. 2-9.

[68] This refers to data from the OECD database in Rustico, L., and S. Terzimehic. "Women in the Green Economy: A Snapshot," *op. cit.*, pp. 4-5.

[69] This trend excludes the more highly qualified female workforce; UNESCO, Institute for Statistics. 2009. *Global Education Digest: Comparing Education Statistics across the World.* The green jobs challenge might result in the promotion of equal opportunities in high-profile positions.

[70] Recent European studies continue to highlight the challenges and the problems connected to the quality of the women's work. See European Commission. 2010. *Report on Equality between Women and Men*; Eurofound. 2009. *Patterns of Recent Employment Growth in the EU: Implications for Gender Equality.*

[71] Ministry of Labour, Health and Social Policy, Ministry for Equal Opportunities. 2009. *Italia 2020: Programma di azioni per l'inclusione delle donne nel mercato del lavoro*, *www.lavoro.gov.it*, in *ADAPT Bulletin* No. 37. See also Bettoni, M., and C. Bizzarro, eds. 2010. *Parità di genere: i progressi e le sfide*, Special Adapt Bulletin No. 8.

promote the social inclusion of women and facilitate their access to the labour market by means of green employment. The programme focuses on two main objectives. First, it aims to encourage greater participation by women in non-traditional employment, for example, the energy sector, promoting working conditions allowing for work-life balance, supporting programmes to ensure equal opportunities in terms of vocational training and retraining in line with the needs of the labour market, and providing information about job opportunities in these fields.

Second, it aims to strengthen female employment in the sectors traditionally employing a high percentage of women, such as education, health, and social services, by creating high-profile positions to promote energy saving and environmental protection.

In order to cope with the challenges posed by the labour market, gender issues should be dealt with by means of gender mainstreaming, which appears to be the only approach reflecting the complexity of the problems associated with gender equality.

4. Skills for the Green Economy: Towards a New Concept of Education and Training

One of the major challenges in the green economy is to provide a practical evaluation of quantitative and qualitative factors associated with green jobs, particularly the skills needed in the labour market to achieve a better match between supply and demand. The need to develop skills for employment in the green economy is widely acknowledged at an international level, as shown by the reports issued by the European Commission,[72] the UNEP,[73] and OECD.[74] The literature on the issue is extensive.[75] The demand for specific green skills has also been analysed in

---

[72] European Commission. 2008. *New Skills for New Jobs—Anticipating and Matching Labour Market and Skills Needs*, COM (2008) 868, *www.adapt.it*, *Green Jobs*, 16 December. Also EMCO Working Group. 2010. "The Employment Dimension of Tackling Climate Change," Progress Report, Draft, 24 June.

[73] UNEP, ILO. *Green Jobs: Towards Decent Work in a Sustainable, Low-Carbon World*, *op. cit.*

[74] OECD. *Environment and Employment*, *op. cit.*; OECD. 1999. *Seminar Social and Environment Interface Proceedings*, Paris: OECD, *www.adapt.it*, *Green Jobs*.

[75] TNO Netherlands Organization for Applied Scientific Research, SEOR Erasmus University Rotterdam, ZSI Centre for Social Innovation. 2009. *Investing in the Future of Jobs and Skills Scenarios, Implications and Options in Anticipation of Future Skills and Knowledge Needs. Sector Report: Electricity, Gas, Water and Waste*, *www.adapt.it*, *Green Jobs*.

a more general view, in terms of the ability to deal with restructuring and ongoing changes.[76]

An aspect that is not given much consideration in Europe is the harmonization between the education and training system and the green labour market, although an increasing number of authors are focusing on the strategic role of social dialogue and industrial relations in providing innovative placement services.[77]

Climate change is expected to have two main consequences in terms of skills development. Policymakers will come under pressure to develop new policies and to assess the skills needs of the labour market, as well as the effects of environmental policies on employment.[78] The definition of green skills has been the subject of heated debate at an international level, with scholars holding divergent positions, giving rise to considerable uncertainty.

If the focus is on the content of the work performed, a widely used definition is the one adopted by the OECD, according to which skills and qualifications for green jobs are similar to those required in more traditional occupations.[79] This view is confirmed if we consider the US labour market, taken as a reference model in this connection. In this case, occupational requirements comprise basic skills that do not differ from traditional ones, in terms of education and working experience.[80] In the

---

[76] Turok, I, and P. Taylor. 2006. "A Skills Framework for Regeneration and Planning," *Planning Practice and Research* 21, No. 4, pp. 497-509.

[77] Szovics, P., M. Tessaring, and A. Zukersteinova—Cedefop. "Skills for Green Jobs: The Pathway is Green", *Green Jobs: nuove opportunità o nuovi rischi?*, *op. cit.* American experiences in the construction of network and shared paths for the workers' green jobs training in the green economy. See White, S., and J. Walsh. 2008. *Greener Pathways. Jobs and Workforce Development in the Clean Energy Economy*. Madison: Center on Wisconsin Strategy, University of Wisconsin, *www.adapt.it*, *Green Jobs*.

[78] Scott, J. 2008. *Future Skills Needs for the Green Economy: Some Starting Points*, Third Generation Environmentalism, 3G, London, *www.adapt.it*, *Green Jobs*, 5 October. For a bibliography review on the impact of climate change on skills policies, GHK. 2009. *The Impacts of Climate Change on European Employment and Skills in the Short to Medium-Term: A Review of the Literature*, Final Report—Volume 2, *www.adapt.it*, *Green Jobs*.

[79] OECD. 2000. "Seminar Social and Environment Interface Proceedings," *op. cit.* See also Institut fur Wirtschaft und Umwelt, and A. K. Wien. 2000. *Environment and Employment: Sustainability Strategies and Their Impact on Employment*, *www.adapt.it*, *Green Jobs*.

[80] Clearly, J., and A. Kopicki. 2009. *Preparing the Workforce for a 'Green Jobs' Economy*. New Jersey: John J. Eldrich Center for Workforce Development,

same vein, studies in Australia suggest that green skills should be acquired at the same time as or soon after the main skills needed for a given occupation.[81]

Green skills may be regarded as generic, as argued by the OECD, since they are difficult to define and acquire, but at the same time, they are essential,[82] considering in particular the concept of sustainability, its implementation in management and production, an awareness of innovative technology and standards and green manufacturing processes, as well as sustainable procurement, which has been promoted by the European Commission by means of a specific programme.[83]

Soft skills refer to a range of skills, such as the ability to ensure compliance with safety standards during production; a willingness to change jobs; teamworking skills; the ability to strengthen motivation in the workplace, to raise awareness of environmental issues, to carry out a product life-cycle analysis, and to adopt environmentally friendly technology; as well as the ability to communicate and to sell goods and services within the eco-business. More generally, those taking up new occupations in green employment require various kinds of knowledge, which should include an awareness of the legal provisions and instruments dealing with environmental issues, and the ability to determine resource availability on the basis of the sector and the geographic area. Furthermore, depending on the economic background, further skills should be gained aimed at ensuring and managing sustainable development and becoming aware of the processes associated with sustainability, in economic, environmental, political terms.[84]

In recent publications, however, the OECD seems to move away from its initial position, maintaining that the green economy calls for traditional

---

Rutgers, 2, *www.adapt.it*, *Green Jobs*. For case studies, see Environmental Defense Fund, Ella Baker Center for Human Rights, Apollo Alliance, Oakland Partnership. 2009. *Green Jobs Guidebook. Employment Opportunities in the New Clean Economy.*

[81] This approach, by significantly reducing the costs in terms of economic and time resources for green skills training, could also make the business world, for which environmental protection is mainly a cost, aware of the need to upgrade the skills of the workforce in view of environmental challenges. Goldney, D. et al. 2007. *Finding the Common Ground: Is There a Place for Sustainability Education in VET?*, p. 2.

[82] Down, C. 2004. *Employability Skills: Revisiting the Key Competencies or a New Way Forward?* Brisbane: Australian Academic Press, 2004.

[83] European Commission at *http://ec.europa.eu/environment/gpp/index_en.htm*.

[84] Rigg, M. 2008. *Skills for Sustainable Development: Necessary but Not Sufficient?*, Policy Study Institute, p. 12.

and new skills,[85] including an understanding of sustainable materials, an ability to carry out environmental impact assessments, and an understanding of carbon footprinting, as stated by the European Commission.

According to a survey carried out by Cedefop,[86] skills in the green economy will be characterized by their interdisciplinary nature, moving beyond a particular position or sector. Communication and problem solving in relation to environmental issues, as well as the use of appropriate technology, are key instruments for employees in the green economy.[87]

Communication skills play a significant role in the green economy, as there will be a growing need for professionals who are able to explain to managers, enterprises, and consumers how to implement and benefit from new technologies, on the basis of a process known as cascade communication. Researchers from Cedefop and ILO[88] argue that green skills have given rise to a new concept that moves beyond the traditional distinction between "basic" and "transversal" competences. The new approach highlights the need for a wealth of knowledge that combines traditional and new skills, consisting of "shades of green".[89] While some experts point out the innovative nature of green skills, such as the assessment of environmental impact and knowledge of environmental

---

[85] Martinez Fernandez, C., C. Hinojosa, and G. Miranda. 2010. *Greening Jobs and Skills, The Local Labour Market Implications of Addressing Climate Change*. Paris: OECD.

[86] Cedefop. 2010. *Skills for Green Jobs. European Synthesis Report* (Luxembourg: Publications Office of the European Union, *www.ilo.org/wcmsp5/groups/public/—ed_emp/—ifp_skills/documents/publication/wcms_143855.pdf.*

[87] Szovics, P., et al. 2009. *Identification of Future Skill Needs for the Green Economy*. Cedefop.

[88] Cedefop. *Skills for Green Jobs*, *op. cit.*. The International Labour Organization, together with Cedefop, is carrying out research on skills needs in the green economy. The research, published in 2010, is based on fifteen countries, outlines good practices, and highlights the fact that national policies for green energy are inevitably integrated with the identification of vocational needs and effective responses to these requirements.

[89] The expression is mainly used with reference to the different extent to which product sectors, in different regions, are affected by the economic and political change arising from the green economy; this term was adopted in UNEP, ILO.2008, *op. cit*, 40. Further considerations about the political implications of stimulus packages can be found in Nikolova, M. 2009. *Light Shades of Green. Climate-Friendly Policies in Times of Crisis*. ETUI.

protection laws,[90] the majority maintains that these are existing skills that have been adapted to sustainability and new trends in the labour market, to construct a new society based on information and knowledge. In this connection, a UNEP report[91] states that a wider range of skills will be required in the green economy, with an educational background and training also in green-related activities, not only in eco-industries, strictly speaking.

The level of employment is another matter to consider in defining green skills, with the OECD[92] and the European Commission[93] arguing that employment is becoming more and more polarized. The ILO, in its research on decent work, points out that the risks arising from low-qualified occupations in the green economy are closely related to inadequate education and training.[94]

The US case shows that workers in the green economy may be classified as having low to mid-range qualifications,[95] generally provided by community colleges, offering higher vocational education, usually over a period of two years.

A United Nations survey suggests that all occupations may be regarded as green and that skills associated with such positions will affect unskilled workers, professionals, business people, engineers, craftsmen, managerial staff, and so on.[96] There may also be a positive impact on female employment, considering that skills development and adaptation will be required in all economic sectors.

Research carried out by Cedefop[97] points out that all working activities should somehow be characterized by a "green factor", with a need for training programmes and courses for those who are willing to acquire new

---

[90] Cedefop. 2008. *Future Skill Needs for the Green Economy*, Seminar 6-7 October. Papers available at *www.cedefop.europa.eu/etv/news/default.asp?idnews ¼3800*.

[91] UNEP, ILO. 2008, *op. cit.*, p. 4.

[92] OECD. *Environment and Employment*, *op. cit*.

[93] European Commission. 2005. *Commission Staff Working Document on the Links between Employment Policies and Environment Policies*.

[94] Evans-Klock, C., and P. Poschen. 2011. *ILO Green Jobs Initiative and Implications for Skills Development. On Decent Work and Climate Change*, cf., International Labour Office. 2009. *The Social and Decent Work Dimensions of a New Agreement on Climate Change.* Geneva: ILO.

[95] Workforce Alliance. 2009. *Oregon's Forgotten Middle-Skill Jobs, Meeting the Demands of a 21st Century Economy*.

[96] Degryse, C., and P. Pochet. 2009. *Paradigm Shift: Social Justice as a Prerequisite for Sustainable Development*. ETUI.

[97] Cedefop. 2010. *Skills for Green Jobs-European Synthesis Report*.

skills. In this connection, there is a need to distinguish between human resource management taking into account sustainable development[98] and the need to (re)train adult workers on the basis of labour market needs.

Training needs have been investigated in a number of studies, including those on Education for Sustainable Development and the 1987 Bruntland Report, which examined evidence from national cases in Europe.[99] A new field of research, the greening economy, is now developing, focusing on academic programmes, teaching methods, and bio-construction, on the assumption that environmentally related education and training programmes might result in a new learning approach leading to a more sustainable society, supporting the individual in the transition from school to university and in lifelong learning.

Moreover, several international forums[100] and some studies in Australia[101] have predicted that, especially in the short run, vocational training in the green economy will have a decisive impact on educational policies.[102] This will concern not only entry-level workers but also experienced workers in need of retraining due to company restructuring, and therefore, at risk of being forced out of the labour market. In Europe, training and retraining programmes may also be a means to increase the levels of flexibility, save jobs, and tackle gender inequalities, as in the case of the electrical power industry.[103]

With regard to sustainable development, further research may be carried out on the impact of occupational skills on productivity,

---

[98] Renwick, D., et al. 2008. *Green HRM: A Review, Process Model, and Research Agenda*, University of Sheffield Management School, Discussion Paper No. 2008; Haddock, J., et al. 2009. *Green HRD: The Potential Contribution of HRD Concepts and Theories to Environmental Management*. London: Education against Climate Change Programme, Middlesex University.

[99] Danish Ministry of Education, Department of Higher Education and International Cooperation. 2009. *Education for Sustainable Development. A Strategy for the United Nations Decade 2005-2014*.

[100] See *World Summit on Sustainable Development*, 2002.

[101] Goldney, D., et al., *Finding the Common Ground etc.*, *op. cit.*

[102] The potential widening of the focus of vocational training deserves further consideration. See Goldney et al., *op cit.*, p. 19 et seq.

[103] Tarren, D., H. Potter, and S. Moore. 2009. *Restructuring in the Electricity Industry: A Toolkit for Socially Responsible Restructuring with a Best Practice Guide*. A Report for EURELECTRIC, EPSU, and EMCEF, Working Lives Research Institute.

competitiveness, organizational models, and health and safety in the workplace.[104]

It has been suggested[105] that this impact is dependent on the way skills are developed, on the effectiveness of education and vocational training programmes, and on the provision of alternative solutions in terms of skills development, by including networks and partnerships. This approach appears to be useful in promoting social dialogue and innovation in industrial relations, providing a contribution to the setting up of research centres in the field of greening education and training in the workplace[106] based on the principle of subsidiarity.

On the basis of these considerations, the question arises as to whether the traditional education and training system will prove effective in responding to the challenges posed by the changing labour market in the green economy. An increasing awareness of the inadequacy of formal learning for occupations regarded as "green" points to the need for innovation in learning strategies, focusing on the acquisition of soft skills, which include more general knowledge, which is decisive in green employment. The acquisition of these skills should take place in the workplace, regarded as the most suitable environment for the acquisition of further abilities,[107] allowing for economically sustainable on-the-job experience.

The implementation of alternative education strategies should be associated with a different perception of learning methods, in order to respond to market demand while promoting a sound pedagogical approach to environmental issues.[108]

---

[104] A possible skills classification for green jobs, with reference to their potential for reducing carbon emissions, distinguishes between leadership, innovation, process, and technical application skills.

[105] New South Wales Department of Education and Training. 2007. *Skills for Sustainability*.

[106] See Lloyd, C., and J. Payne. 2002. "Developing a Political Economy of Skill," *Journal of Education and Work* 15, No. 4:365-90. See also Stern, N. 2007. *The Economics of Climate Change: The Stern Review*. Cambridge: Cambridge University Press.

[107] Virgona, C., and P. Waterhouse. 2004. *Two Dimensional Work: Workplace Literacy in the Aged Care & Call Centre Industries*. In Italy, in the White Paper of 2009, at *www.adapt.it*, *Welfare*, the Ministry of Labour considered the enterprise as the most appropriate place for learning and skills development.

[108] In the Italian case, the traditional approach to vocational training, connected with state-sector education, should be replaced by the modern concept of learning based on skills and learning outcomes, closer to production processes and to technological innovation.

Following the example of United States and Australia, a solution might be found in the setting up of networks and partnerships among educational bodies, training providers, universities, enterprises, and the actors involved in social dialogue and industrial relations, to develop sector-specific skills and to share new ideas on training programmes responding to market needs.[109] Green employment can make a major contribution in terms of environmental protection, as in every occupation there is a "green factor". In addition, awareness of green issues begins in primary school, as shown by the research focusing on greening education, and continues throughout life. Green skills are the result of a lifelong learning process, with the concept of workplace learning or work-based learning becoming increasingly relevant. In addition, work-based learning serves as a response to changes in the green sector in terms of job opportunities, the development of which are difficult to forecast,[110] especially in a financial downturn, when it becomes harder to plan production in the medium and long term.

5. The Role of Industrial Relations and Social Dialogue

In the coming years, the demand for vocational training and retraining in the green economy will increase significantly, together with the need to provide effective guidance on the skills needed in the labour market.[111] It will be necessary to increase and adapt the workforce, providing workers with higher levels of qualifications, also in an attempt to reduce gender inequalities. To be effective, this strategy should not involve state intervention, often ambitious and unrealistic, aimed at overseeing and managing the reorganization and restructuring process.

---

[109] Newman, P., et al. 2004. *Training for Sustainability: The Vocational Education and Training Sector*. Perth: Green Skills Inc., Centre for Learning, Change and Development and Institute for Sustainability and Technology Policy, Murdoch University.

[110] Degryse, C. 2009. *What's in the Sustainable Development Strategy for Workers?*. ETUI Benchmarking Working Europe 2009. Brussels: ETUI.

[111] See Cedefop. 2009. *European Guidelines for Validating Non-formal and Informal Learning*; Campbell, M. et al., for the European Commission. 2010. *New Skills for New Jobs*. See the Italian agreement on the *Linee guida per la formazione nel 2010* signed by the Government and Region representatives and social partners on 17 February 2010 in Bellezza, E., and L. Rustico, eds. 2010. *2010: l'anno della formazione*, ADAPT Bulletin No. 6, 18 February. See also Bellezza, E., and L. Rustico, eds. 2010. "Formazione e dialogo sociale: l'intesa Governo, Regioni e parti sociali del 17 febbraio 2010," *Diritto delle Relazioni Industriali*, No. 2.

Rather, based on the principle of subsidiarity, it should entail the participation of all those actors, including the social partners, who can help to address the mismatch between supply and demand in the green economy.[112] The industrial relations system can play a leading role in an economy with a lower environmental impact, supporting the reorganization and the restructuring of production. Particular attention should be paid to the most vulnerable workers, who are more exposed in the event of restructuring and the transition to a more sustainable economy.

Collective bargaining could develop further techniques providing incentives to support the transition towards the green economy, vocational training and retraining (also for women workers), and inclusion in the green sector.[113] Although regarded as a priority in the green agenda of many countries,[114] measures encouraging good practices are still rare (see Table 1), especially with regard to the employment and gender impact of environmental policies.[115]

Although it is clearly difficult to identify a common instrument to manage the economic crisis, the social partners have agreed on some priorities, even in times of recession.[116] Apart from the recognition of workers' rights to information, consultation, and participation in the green economy and at company level, there is also a need to provide employees with adequate training to face employment transition and changes in the labour market. Effective skills retraining should help respond to economic fluctuations during recession.[117]

---

[112] See ETUC. *Climate Change and Employment*, *op. cit.*

[113] Scott, J. *Future Skills Needs for the Green Economy etc.*, *op. cit.*

[114] Eurofound, Greening the European Economy: Responses and Initiatives by Member States and Social Partners. 2009. *www.adapt.it*, *Green Jobs*. See ETUC. 2006. *Climate Change and Employment*; ETUC, *Mid-term Review of the 6th Community Environment Act Programme*, Position of the European Trade Union Confederation ETUC, *www.etuc.org/IMG/pdf/6th_EAP_mid-term_Review11.pdf*, 2006.

[115] A review of *http://ec.europa.eu/social/main.jsp?catId¼521&langId¼en* shows the lack of joint texts, documents, and agreements on the topic.

[116] Hurley, J. et al. 2009. "Restructuring in Recession, European Restructuring Monitor (ERM), 2009", *Elder Employees during Restructuring: Stress and Well-Being*, eds. de Vita, P., and M. Giovannone, 2010. Special ADAPT Bulletin No. 7.

[117] On the importance of investing in education and training in times of crisis, see Cedefop. 2009. *Learning in Crisis Times*, *www.adapt.it*, *Green Jobs*, See also Council Decision on *Guidelines for the Employment Policies of the Member States*, 7 July 2008 10614/2/08 REV 2.

Social dialogue in Europe can provide a major contribution to the implementation of the green agenda, also in terms of training and retraining programmes,[118] as shown by the initiatives of employers' associations and trade unions in Table 3-7.

More generally, social dialogue and industrial relations have to focus on rethinking education and training in the light of future occupational requirements. Educational institutions, with the social partners, should promote a multidisciplinary learning environment within the company, including internships to help young people gain access to the labour market. Trade unions and employers' associations could provide written certification of the skills acquired in non-formal and informal contexts, with the support of educational experts. Training should be provided also for teachers, with a special focus on the specific needs of women teachers.

The European Commission and Cedefop have highlighted the need to establish a stronger link between the needs of the enterprise and the education and training system, in order to raise awareness of environmental issues, which is essential for sustainability in the green economy. Accordingly, the industrial relations actors should develop the potential of the green economy in full, transforming risks into opportunities for all those involved.

Table 3-7. Initiatives by the Social Partners at European Level in the Field of Vocational Training and Retraining in the Green Economy

Country	Practices
Ireland	The employers' confederation IBEC provides environmental training for members; this includes a Foundation Course in Environmental Management for managers wishing to get up to speed on current environmental performance trends, standards legislation, and solutions.
Norway	The Norwegian Association of Local and Regional Authorities along with the Confederation of Unions for Professionals and the Norwegian Union of Municipal and General Employees have organized a conference for safety representatives and trade union representatives, in order to develop their knowledge and expertise in relation to green issues. The trade union confederation LO and its member unions have set up courses on climate change for shop stewards.

[118] Eurofound, *Greening the European Economy*, *op. cit.*

Belgium	Regional plans: research and training in green technologies. National social dialogue structures—namely, the National Labour Council and the Central Economic Council—are currently active in relation to environmental issues and are preparing a joint statement on green jobs. An innovative scheme exists in Belgium, whereby long-term jobseekers are trained to carry out energy assessments and help advice on energy-saving measures. These people are called "energy trimmers" and help to implement energy-saving measures in buildings through "energy trimming companies", which are not-for-profit organizations. The schemes exist in all regions of the country.
Spain	Social dialogue on green issues is carried out within the framework of the country's standard tripartite social dialogue structures and is linked to the debate on the modernization of the economy.
Italy	The government has set up a fund to finance research projects on energy efficiency and the use of renewable energy sources in urban areas. The trade fair SolarExpo and the employment agency Adecco have developed training and retraining courses for technicians in the solar panel and wind farm industry. Under this scheme, skills that are particularly relevant to these industries are taught. The Association of Energy Producers from Renewable Sources organizes company training and information courses on European and national regulations in the energy and environment sector.
Finland	The National Commission on Sustainable Development acts as an important tripartite forum where different stakeholders can present their ideas, goals, and programmes, as well as engage in a broad debate about ecological sustainability. The employer organization EK has published a guide on corporate responsibility, which contains tools for self-evaluation and development for companies. The construction industry branch and the biotechnology industry association Finnish Bio industries have also published their own principles on corporate social responsibility, business ethics, and sustainable development.
Hungary	Regional operational programmes, provisions for the setting up of regional crisis management funds to help in cases of company restructuring and to support vulnerable enterprises by providing exemptions from payroll taxes to enable companies to maintain their workforce.

Denmark	Environmental Economic Council—economic advisory body, established by law in 2007. Twenty-four members representing trade unions, employers, non-governmental organizations (NGOs), independent experts, and the Danish government.
Slovenia	Seminars have been held for business representatives to help them prepare for legislative changes related to the green economy.
Austria	National and local governments have launched a joint initiative, known as Masterplan Environmental Technology, aiming to set up a joint strategy for policymakers, business, and relevant research institutions to improve the competitiveness of the Austrian environmental technology industry. The government is looking at reforming the country's vocational training scheme in order to meet increasing business demand for skilled workers in the environmental technology sector. On the employer side, courses are run by the Austrian Federal Economic Chamber to help members reduce energy consumption.
Luxembourg	A conference to debate climate protection and economic and employment prospects was organized by government ministries and the Chamber of Employees in February 2009.
Estonia	Much effort has been invested in raising public and consumer awareness of green issues through a variety of means—including the development of a network of local environmental education centres, the provision of training days and seminars, and the holding of national and international conferences.
Poland	The celebration of Earth Day 22 April 2009 included information campaigns, educational initiatives, and workshops. Government training courses are offered in order to train technicians in environmental management, as well as in health, safety, and environment at the workplace.
Portugal	The General Workers' Union is preparing to introduce environmental issues into its training activities for collective agreement negotiators.

The UK	The employer organization, the Confederation of British Industry (CBI), highlights that skills are needed in areas such as science, technology, engineering and maths, technical competencies, and a range of new business skills. The CBI makes a range of recommendations on how to increase the number of workers with these skills: these include encouraging a greater focus on such skills in schools and proposing ways to encourage education providers to work with business to meet the demand for these types of skills. The CBI has been running regular events on issues related to climate change for its members. For example, in 2009, it is running a series of three breakfast seminars on the subject of environmental legislation for people involved in property management and leasing. The TUC operates a range of courses for trade union representatives, helping them to address the following issues: identify environmental changes that affect the workplace; research and identify appropriate environmental legislation, policies, and information; and identify environmental problems and opportunities for trade union action.
Germany	The Confederation of German Trade Unions and affiliates participate in two working groups—one on energy and the other on the environment—within the country's tripartite "Alliance for jobs, training and competitiveness" initiative. A joint body has been established to provide information and training to work councils on environmental protection issues. The trade union confederation DGB, in cooperation with the educational institution DGB Bildungswerk and the German Ministry for the Environment, Nature Conservation, and Nuclear Safety, runs a project in German entitled "Resource Efficiency in Firms". The project trains work council members and employees in detecting and implementing ways to improve energy efficiency. The training is part of a programme that leads to a certified degree as an "efficiency expert". The metalworking trade union IG Metall cooperates with the employer association of the aluminium industry in implementing this project at workplace level.

Source: Eurofound, Greening the European Economy: Responses and Initiatives by Member States and Social Partners, 2009.

PART IV

BILATERALISM AND EMPLOYEE PARTICIPATION

CHAPTER FOURTEEN

BILATERALISM AND BILATERAL BODIES: THE NEW FRONTIER OF INDUSTRIAL RELATIONS IN ITALY

1. Bilateralism as a Way to Enhance Workers' Participation in Italy[1]

Bilateralism has been increasingly regarded as the new frontier for the rebirth—or at least the profound renewal—of industrial relations in Italy. Originally established only in the building sector, bilateral bodies were considered as instruments for the joint administration of financial resources collected by employers' associations and trade unions for the allocation of benefits in some critical circumstances (illness, occupational injuries, mutual assistance in the event of stoppage or reduction of working hours, and so on). In addition to the building sector, a system of bilateral bodies was set up starting from the early 1980s in other sectors as well where industrial relations were weak, and where there was a prevalence of micro enterprises, unstable employment, high turnover of employees, a widespread use of atypical and undeclared work, and limited trade union presence. This is the case of the artisan sector, commerce and tourism and—more recently—liberal professions.

Accordingly, bilateralism has developed in these sectors as a cooperative method of stabilizing both products and markets and as a form of protection of workers by means of the joint administration and governance of the entire labour market, becoming the paradigm of a new system of cooperative and collaborative industrial relations. This should come as no surprise. Indeed, these committees are well-established bodies in the industrial relations arena, characterized by a "dynamic" nature, yet are far less regulated—particularly in the Anglo-Saxon countries. In addition to collective bargaining, bilateral bodies are usually administered

[1] This contribution is published in 2013 in the *E-Journal of International and Comparative Labour Studies* 2, No. 1.

by committees consisting of representatives of both employers and trade unions. As joint bodies, they perform their duties on a cooperative and participative basis, for they *per definitionem* constitute the manifestation of the contractual intent of the parties setting up the bilateral bodies, as laid down in collective agreements. They can be seen as a traditional cooperative device within the Italian industrial relations system, particularly if considered in terms of regulations set forth in collective agreements.

Yet, their innovation lies in the bilateral and participatory approach, which makes a clean break with the past. In this connection, the Italian case is noteworthy. Unlike the other countries in continental Europe, the dialogue among social partners is less institutionalized—also because of a lack of trade union legislation—and this aspect is traditionally associated with high levels of industrial conflict at both individual and collective levels.

Accordingly, bilateralism is seen as an instrument to create more participatory labour—management relations in Italy, also taking into account recent developments concerning legislative issues and contractual arrangements. Nevertheless, bilateralism presents some distinguishing features that seem to be specific of the Italian legal and trade union systems—which, for instance, differ considerably from German co-management, particularly with regard to the employees' involvement in management decision-making. Although sharing similar views on decision-making, the distinctive trait of the Italian case lies in that joint bodies comply with regulations laid down in collective agreements, making provision for both the internal and external labour market to supplement statutory rules and protect and resolve all workers' claims.

For this reason, bilateralism can be viewed as a form of employees' participation to economic and social processes which goes beyond the management of decision-making and the effective oversight of the company, as it helps to devise a shared strategy to stabilise the labour market and provide protection to workers by means of the joint administration of the entire labour market. In this sense, bilateralism has been reported to be increasing in Italy—also thanks to the devising of ad-hoc legislation—as it has been considered the most influential and reliable device to bring about a change of the antagonistic attitude within the production processes. Through a renewed sense of trust and cooperation, it would also be possible to further enhance the fruitful relationship between capital and labour with regard to economic growth, productivity and social justice.

From 2003 onwards, that is after the enforcement of the Biagi Law, the Italian legislator entrusted the bilateral bodies with more powers—following on from some successful outcomes in terms of governance and regulation—as contributing to the creation of a system of industrial relations which is more appropriate in keeping up with economic and societal changes. Due to major developments in the market economy (the growth of the service economy, globalization, and delocalisation), profound economic changes in demography and their impact on welfare states in terms of sustainability, it has been necessary to resort to alternative measures of social protection. Significantly, the central government has downplayed its role as an administrator of financial resources—providing its contribution only in an indirect way—by setting forth a set of framework provisions serving as reference legislation for those operating in the private sector. In this sense, the role of bilateral bodies is relevant, all the more so following the resounding impact of the crisis on the world economies, which called for private investments to sustain a welfare state that proved to be inadequate.

2. Bilateral Bodies: Juridical Nature and Functioning

In the context of the Italian system of industrial relations, the expressions "bilateral bodies" or "joint bodies" are used to refer to entities that are set up and regulated by means of collective bargaining and that have three main features:

1) they consist of representatives from social partners who conclude collective agreements through which such bodies are governed;
2) they provide (employment) services and protection to both workers and employers, in accordance to what is laid down by collective agreements and by statutory laws. Funds to such activities are collected by means of contributions paid by employers and—to a minor extent—by workers;
3) upon the free choice of the parties that comprise them, bilateral bodies are autonomous legal entities.

From a legal and technical viewpoint, bilateral bodies are therefore entities consisting of the signatories to a collective agreement that take the form of unincorporated/voluntary associations or associations with legal personality. By signing the accord, its associates, that is employers' associations and trade unions, express their willingness to constitute the joint body. In technical terms, it is the collective agreement that lays down the obligation to establish the joint body. It follows that all bilateral bodies are committees having a contractual nature—upon approval of its article of association—need to comply with a contractual obligation, the expression of private collective autonomy. The juridical nature of these entities becomes apparent if one considers that they are entrusted with special functions by law. In this case, the willingness to constitute the body is still regarded as resulting from private autonomy which is manifested through the collective agreement. The law only allows for some tasks and functions to be fulfilled by bilateral bodies, with the establishment of the body itself that is left to private and collective autonomy.

Unlike other voluntary associations, the main characteristic of bilateral bodies is their joint nature (*pariteticità* in Italian) at managerial level, a typical feature of collective bargaining, from which they originate. Besides appointing a president serving as a legal representative, these committees set up bodies consisting of both representatives from employers' associations and trade unions with decision-making, executive and executive powers, who remain in office for three years and can be re-elected. Decisions are made on a unanimous basis so as to avoid cleavage among union's representatives or issues arising from employers becoming the minority. Bilateral bodies are also independent in financial terms, for they can rely on their own resources collected through membership fees which are paid on a regular basis. They are also entitled to tax incentives and contribution relief. The services provided by these entities to workers (e.g. supplementary health services, supplementary retirement schemes, income supports, and the co-funding of public income support, pursuant to Art. 19 of Legislative Decree No. 185/2008 as subsequently converted into Law No. 2/2009) are forms of protection that in some cases are deemed to be contractual rights, provided that some conditions are met.

2.1. Funding Bilateral Bodies

The question as to whether one should be under the obligation to join bilateral bodies needs to be investigated considering the negative freedom of association. In this sense, Art. 39 of Italian Constitution provides that individuals—be it employers or workers—have the right to refuse to associate with others in collective organizations, as in the case of bilateral bodies. It is important to point out that one of the main problems to deal with in this connection, is the difficulty arising from including clauses for the setting up of the committees among the binding clauses of the collective agreements (known as economic and regulatory clauses).

Further, Italian legislation does not provide for the *erga omnes* effect of collective agreements, that are treated as private agreements—pursuant to the section of the Civil Code that deals with contracts and obligations—and therefore cannot apply to a third party (non- signatory trade unions and companies). Thus, since the provisions laying down the establishment of this committee are included among the obligations set in the collective agreement, there is no requirement on the part of employers in terms of funding and membership. Such an obligation would induce them into joining the union—yet in an indirect manner—therefore violating the foregoing principle of negative freedom of association, according to which no obligation to join the bilateral body can be imposed on employers who are not enrolled in unions that have set them up. The same holds true for associates, as only signatories need to comply with provisions for the setting up of the bilateral bodies, as included in obligations set in the collective agreements.

However, what has recently emerged from the debate among legal scholars is that such an interpretation of relevant legislation is somehow objectionable, as the section containing obligations in collective agreements only refers to the set of provisions regulating the relationship between unions that are signatories to the accord, without any consequences for the workers. Arguing for the obligatory nature of the provisions concerning the bilateral bodies is like stating—so to say—that they fall outside the legal sphere of the workers. Reality is usually different, at least in cases whereas signatories to collective agreements that set up the bilateral body provide otherwise.

In cases where contributions are not paid by the employers to the bilateral body, workers will not be entitled to benefits as specified in the contract. In this sense, the failure to become an associate—particularly the failure to comply with the payment of contributions to the body—will translate into fewer benefits and lower levels of protection for the workers, placing them at an economic disadvantage. It is therefore apparent that workers are affected—yet in an indirect manner—from such non-payment. On the basis of these considerations, it might be argued that the provision of services offered by bilateral bodies, both at national and local level, should be regarded as contractual rights whereas expressly laid down by the collective agreement, a type of "deferred earnings" that workers should also be granted if operating under employers who have not joined the body.

The issuing of Circular No. 43/2010 by the Italian Ministry of Labour makes provision for the obligation in terms of membership and contributions to join the bilateral bodies. The document specifies that membership is not mandatory. However, workers working for employers who did not sign the collective agreement setting up the body, should be entitled to the same rights of those working for the signatories. In the former case, employers should fulfil their obligation by adhering to these committees, or by paying an amount of money in accordance to what is laid down in the collective agreement or providing them with equivalent benefits. This only happens if the applicable collective agreement states that a certain benefit provided by the bilateral body represents contractual rights, on the assumption that such benefit is regarded as a "fringe benefit" or "additional remuneration". As a result, Circular No. 43/2010 points out that workers performing for employers who did not join the body are entitled to contractual rights that take the form of additional remuneration.

Therefore—and in accordance to what is set by collective bargaining—these rights can be fulfilled by paying a sum of money or granting a service that amounts to that provided by the bilateral bodies. In complying with the rights that are guaranteed by the Italian Constitution, this mechanism provides an alternative system of funding as contributions are paid directly to the bilateral bodies, preventing cases of a "race to the bottom" that might reduce the levels of protection granted to workers. There is no doubt about the constitutional legitimacy of this financing system, as it is up to the employers to choose whether to join the bilateral body or not, by paying the amount due. However, even though they may opt out of the committee, they are still under the obligation to pay the corresponding sum to workers, because of the *erga omnes* effect of collective agreements, in the sense that they extend to all employers in the industries covered. Arguably, the freedom of choice on the part of employers should be distinguished from their free will, particularly when this undermines or clashes with the rights of workers to receive services provided by bilateral bodies or equivalent benefits. This is the case insofar as such benefits are considered as a form of remuneration entitled to workers—either directly or indirectly—in proportion to the quantity and quality of their work and in all cases sufficient to ensure them and their families a free existence as laid down by Art. 36 of the Italian Constitution. It is worth pointing out that Art. 36 also allowed the Italian judiciary to determine the remuneration criteria for non-unionized workers or those operating for employers who were not a member of the bodies that signed the collective agreement.

Accordingly, such a mechanism seems to reconcile opposite interests. On the one hand, employers would have the right to refuse to join the body. On the other hand, employees would be granted an extra sum of money, the amount of which corresponds to contributions not paid to the body. This functioning seems consistent with collective bargaining practices in this sector, that are intended to promote new arrangements to enhance the productive system and safeguard workers' rights.

3. Bilateral Bodies and Their Main Functions

Bilateral bodies played an active role in renewing the labour market. In this sense, the Biagi law purposely included them among the sources of labour law, classified as a "privileged channel" for the regulation of the labour market (Art. 2, par. 1, sec. H of Legislative Decree No. 276/2003). Bilateral bodies have been set up in different industries not just as a mere service provider, but rather as a means for assisting labour market stability and protecting workers by way of the joint administration and governance of the entire labour market.

Accordingly, bilateralism is regarded as an established instrument to enhance cooperative dialogue among social partners and the full implementation of mechanisms of protection for workers, such as the provision of benefits as laid down in the collective agreement. On the basis of such a successful experience in terms of governance and joint administration, the legislator entrusted bilateral bodies with a new and wider set of powers. The special—yet not exhaustive—nature of the functions these committees are empowered to perform pursuant to Art. 2, sec. h of Legislative Decree No. 276/2003, allows for the experience of bilateralism to handle issues other than those universally regarded as relevant and long- lasting. Indeed, bilateral bodies carry out a number of important functions. In general, they are set up to

- promote more stable and quality jobs;
- provide placement services;
- devise programmes for training, particularly by means of on-the-job learning;
- disseminate good practices against various discriminatory practices, favouring the integration of disadvantaged groups into the labour market;
- set up and administer mutual assistance funds for income support;
- certificate employment contracts and their compliance with norms and contributions schemes;
- develop actions and initiatives relating to occupational health and safety;
- undertake other activities assigned to them by collective agreements.

With regard to the last point, the attempt has been to free and provide bilateral bodies with more leeway to maneuver with regard to the joint regulation of the labour market.

In Italy, it is collective bargaining that makes provision for the setting up of joint bodies, although in some cases this is done by making reference to a special legislative framework. The reason for this distinction lies in the difference between the services provided by these bodies and the functions they carry out. Some of them are established via collective bargaining on an exclusive basis, while others are recognised by law, although being the result of private bargaining autonomy. If bilateral bodies were not expressly assigned, the foregoing functions by relevant authorities, services that are "authorised" and "recognised" by law could not be provided in any case—or they would not produce specific effects within the Italian legal system. Conversely, the services specified in the collective agreements originate directly and autonomously from collective bargaining and, as such, are of a different type and are provided in a number of ways, depending on the functioning of the bilateral bodies and some contractual arrangements.

3.1. Occupational Health and Safety

The role played by bilateral bodies in terms of occupational health and safety is relevant, as they are legally assigned special functions and need provide some special services.

Legislative Decree No. 276/2003 and, more recently, the consolidating legislation on health and safety at work (Implementing Decree No. 81 of 9 April 2008, subsequently amended by Legislative Decree No. 106 of 3 August 2009), view the joint bodies as a channel to promote, steer, and support both employers and employees which should lean on a participatory model to develop strategies concerning health and safety.

In practical terms, such legislative support is evident if one considers two funding schemes. Art. 52, sec. C provides for a special fund set up by the National Institution for Insurance against Accidents at Work (INAIL) that supports activities carried out by joint bodies. Further, Art. 51, par. 3-bis allows for the usage of ad-hoc funds (*fondi interprofessionali*), or funds for temporary agency workers in order to finance health and safety training programmes.

Of relevance is also the fact that—pursuant to Legislative Decree No. 106/2009—employers can be awarded with a certificate showing that effective OHS management practices and organizational models have been adopted. The fulfilment of these tasks on the part of bilateral bodies also ensures their involvement in terms of health and safety governance, on the assumption that such a participatory model contributes to building a safety culture in the company, increasing the minimum levels of protection in the working environment.

3.2. Training

On the subject of training, the Italian legislator has provided a significant number of provisions to allow bilateral bodies to carry out activities with regard to vocational training. Art 118 of Law 388/2000 sets forth the establishment of some special funds for life-long learning (called interprofessional joint funds for life-long training—*fondi paritetici interprofessionali per la formazione continua*), that are to be laid down in interconfederal agreements among the largest employers' associations and trade unions at a national level. The money allocated amounts to 30% of contributions paid by each worker to employers who join the fund—and corresponds to the mandatory insurance against unemployment. In cases when the employers join the fund on a voluntary basis, it is the National Institution for Insurance against Accidents at Work that is under the obligation to pay such amounts of money. The strengthening of the role of the bilateral bodies as training provider also within the company results from the view shared by the parties that training is a common good and can help to promote employability and competitiveness.

3.3. Matching Supply and Demand in the Labour Market

The provision of placement services is among the most relevant functions assigned to bilateral bodies by law. Such an activity can be carried out upon authorization released by the Ministry of Labour pursuant to Art. 6, par. 3 of Legislative Decree No. 66/2003.

The idea to authorize trade unions to serve as placement providers—also indirectly via bilateral bodies—arises from the assumption that they can protect workers not only by negotiating the best working conditions, but also by administering some services that help the unemployed and first-time job-seekers to access or re-enter the labour market.

3.4. The Certification of Labour Contracts

Undoubtedly, one of the major developments that has recently taken place in labour legislation—particularly with regard to the employment relationship—is the appointment of bilateral bodies as a subject for certification of a labour contract. Not only can bilateral bodies certify contractual schemes regarded as atypical and flexible, but also all the other contractual arrangements, in order to determine the rights and obligations deriving from them, as well as the ensuing forms of protection. This aspect will also help to clarify issues in terms of transactions as laid down by Art. 2113 of the Civil Code, and promote soundness with regard to contributions as a means for transparency in the labour market and employment services.

In legal terms, the involvement of bilateral bodies in the certification of labour contracts is relevant in promoting bilateralism as an instrument to ensure that employers fulfill some duties (e.g. payment of social security contributions, the identification of the employment relationship—whether autonomous work or salaried employment—particularly for tax, social security, and even administrative purposes). The peculiarity of this function lies in that certification also involves an inspection and validation process of employers that join the bilateral bodies that adds to that carried out by public institutions—e.g. the National Social Welfare Institution (INPS) and the National Institution for Insurance against Accidents at Work.

3.5. Income Support

Bilateral bodies also provide a decisive contribution in terms of income support measures, by administering the mutual assistance of funds that support workers operating in those industries that do not envisage wage guarantee funds. With a view to safeguard workers' rights, the function of bilateralism in this area is twofold: experimenting with practices of co-management, yet still referring to forms of welfare (public aid) provided by the government. It is therefore pivotal to devise some innovative welfare schemes that match public measures and non-state sources. To this end, social safety net measures could be supplemented with well-established funds run by bilateral bodies.

In an awareness of this state of affairs, the legislator has laid down a number of provisions—Art. 2 of Legislative Decree No. 276/2003, subsequently amended and repealed by Art. 5 of Law No. 196 of 24 June 1997 and more recently, which, in turn, has been amended by the set of provisions labeled as *Collegato Lavoro*—in order to govern and regulate the setting up of funds for income support and the provision of training on the part of relevant authorities. The enactment of the *Collegato Lavoro*, has attributed a decisive role to the bilateral bodies—particularly by envisaging unemployment allowances to maintain continuity of income in cases of prolonged unemployment. In this sense Art. 19 of Law Decree No. 185 of 29 November 2008—which was subsequently converted into Law No. 2 of 28 January 2009 and which refers to a scheme laid down by Art. 13, par. 8 of Law Decree No. 35 of 14 March 2005, subsequently converted into Law No. 80 of 14 May 2005—makes provision for income supports to be paid by bilateral bodies in the event of stoppage in those sectors that are not covered by wage guarantee funds, *de facto* increasing the levels of protection. In a similar vein, the direct involvement of bilateral and joint bodies in the provision of lifelong learning constitutes an attempt to experiment with and further develop supplementary welfare schemes, the result of the relationship between active and passive labour market policies, in order to guarantee that workers are offered adequate protection.

In the context of this paper, it seems worth pointing out that the increasing attention given to income support measures on the part of actors involved in collective bargaining led to the establishment of bilateral bodies operating at a national level on matters concerning the healthcare system and the system of supplementary pension. The latter is of relevance, as regulated by some special provisions (Legislative Decree No. 124 of 21 April 1993; Legislative Decree No. 243 of 23 August 2004; Implementing Decree No. 252 of 5 December 2005).

4. Concluding Remarks

The fact that in the future bilateral bodies might perform all activities and functions assigned to them statutorily or by applicable collective agreements upholds the intention of the legislator to rely on joint bodies and bilateralism to modernize trade unions—who are more and more involved in practices at company and local level—and to the establishment of a new and alternative social model.

In this perspective, there are reasons to question the view that regards the set of provisions promoting bilateralism as a "Trojan horse" to be used only to transform the role of trade unions, without considering the function of bilateral bodies as a tool to reflect the interests of those concerned, seeing them simply as service providers. For this viewpoint, one of the major concerns is that bilateralism might take the place of trade unions in dealing with some issues, especially by giving priority to dialogue over the traditional conflictual methods and downplaying the role of collective bargaining. As a result, trade unions would no longer be the interpreters of social conflict and the representatives of common interests, but they would just provide employment services and deprived of their autonomy.

In reality, bilateralism should be considered as another activity carried out in the context of unions, as it functions on the basis of what is laid down by the rules of the collective agreements, as referred to by the legislator. Clearly, there are different functions. In some cases, they administer mutual assistance funds, dealing with resources financed by social partners on an exclusive basis. In other cases, they carried out general functions assigned by law, without managing financial resources. In some other cases bilateral bodies are legally responsible for the management of public resources. In the case of the latter, it is reasonable on the part of the government to carry out a monitoring function on the basis of agreed upon criteria.

In Italy, the involvement of trade unions in financial and management issues—both in a direct and indirect manner—is established (the authorized centres of fiscal assistance—CaF—and organizations affiliated with leading trade unions that offer a wide range of services dealing with special issues—*patronati*—are some suitable examples in this connection).

The development of bilateralism—which should take place gradually but steadily—also through a range of provisions that promotes the setting up of bilateral bodies, is consistent with a new and practical system of industrial relations based on cooperation, and with ongoing societal and economic changes which result in the need to set new priorities in terms of labour market policies. The decline of the manufacturing sector that favoured the growth of the service sector and small enterprises, the dissemination of productive processes at a local level, ongoing changes in technology, the widespread use of atypical work and, more recently, the *debacle* of the economic system highlighted the weaknesses of the domestic production system, which might lead to a global crisis and increase unemployment levels. For this reason, there is a need to devise a new welfare system that takes account of the shortcomings of financial resources available and promotes the participation of individuals and groups concerned (the notion of horizontal subsidiarity).

The aim of bilateralism is to put forward a range of solutions and measures that provides protection in terms of remuneration and social security, the costs of which could not be borne by a system characterized by shortcomings and wastes.

Evidently, the fact that bilateral bodies reduce the level of conflict and enhance social cohesion represents a surplus value.

Indeed, these committees are bodies operating in the context of industrial relations on a participatory and cooperative basis.

Although performing their duties autonomously, they comply with rules and procedures laid down by the founding parties in the collective agreement. For this reason, Ten years ago the accompanying report of the Biagi Law referred to bilateral bodies as privileged channels for enhancing social justice and competitiveness that might contribute to providing a more cooperative approach to industrial relations, thus promoting more stable and quality jobs.

5. Essential Literature Review

As a typical and, to some extent, unique institution of the Italian industrial relations system, bilateral bodies have been mainly the subject of investigation carried out by Italian scholars. English-language literature on bilateralism is therefore limited to few contributions written by Italian academics, including an introduction to bilateral bodies in the artisan sector by S. Ciuffini, G. De Lucia, "The System of Bilateral Bodies in the Artisan Sector: The Italian Experience in the Context of European Social Dialogue", *The International Journal of Comparative Labour Law and Industrial Relations*, 2004 and a focus on bilateralism as a form of employee involvement in Italy by M. Tiraboschi, F. Pasquini, W. Bromwich, 'Employee Involvement in Italy', in M. Weiss, M. Sewerynski (eds.), *Handbook on Employee Involvement in Europe*, Kluwer Law International, 2004 and M. Tiraboschi, 'Employee involvement in Italy', in Various Authors, *Employee Involvement in a Globalising World. Liber Amicorum Manfred Weiss*, Berliner Wissenschafts-Verlag, 2005.

Regarded as the new frontier for the rebirth (or at least the profound renewal) of labour relations in Italy, bilateral bodies are organisations set up jointly by employers' associations and trade unions on the basis of a collective agreement. In order to distinguish them from other forms of joint institutions, L. Bellardi, "Le istituzioni bilaterali tra legge e contrattazione collettiva: note di sintesi e prospettive", L. Bellardi, G. De Santis (eds.), *La bilateralità tra tradizione e rinnovamento*, Franco Angeli, 2011, recently proposed a more detailed definition according to which the expression "bilateral or joint bodies" is used to refer to entities that are set up and regulated by means of collective bargaining and that have three main features: 1) they consist of representatives from social partners concluding collective agreements through which such bodies are governed; 2) they provide (employment) services and protection to both workers and employers, in accordance to what is laid down by collective agreements and by statutory law. Funds to such activities are collected by means of contributions paid by employers and—to a minor extent—by workers 3) upon the free choice of the parties that comprise them, bilateral bodies are autonomous legal entities. Bilateral bodies were originally widespread only in the building sector as a strategy for the joint administration of financial resources collected by employers' associations and trade unions for the allocation of benefits to employees in certain critical circumstances (illness, accidents at work, mutual assistance in case of stoppage or reduction in working hours, etc.). Starting from the earlier contribution, a first historical analysis of the origins of bilateralism in the Italian building sector is carried out by L. Bellardi, *Istituzioni bilaterali e contrattazione collettiva: il settore edile (1945/1988)*, 1990.

From the early 1980s, in addition to the building sector, a system of bilateral bodies was set up also in other industries characterised by weak industrial relations and a limited presence of trade unions such as the craft sector, commerce and tourism, not only for the joint administration of financial resources but also as a new paradigm of a cooperative system of industrial relations. A cross-sectoral description of bilateralism in Italy is provided by M. Cimaglia, A. Aurilio, "I sistemi bilaterali di settore", L. Bellardi, G. De Santis (eds.), *La bilateralità tra tradizione e rinnovamento*, Franco Angeli, 2011.

Taking into account the classical demarcation between static and dynamic collective bargaining systems proposed by O. Kahn-Freund, "Intergroup Conflicts and their Settlement", *The British journal of sociology*, 1954, there is large consensus among academics to frame bilateral bodies under the dynamic model. Bilateralism therefore represents a refusal of the traditional conflictual method of labour dispute resolution based on static collective bargaining, which is not well suited to the peculiarities and characteristics of certain sectors (prevalence of small and micro enterprises, fragmentation of the workforce, high turnover of employees, rapid and continuous changes in the labour market, etc.). In other words, according to M. Tiraboschi, "The reform of the Italian labor market over the past ten years: a process of liberalization?", *Comparative Labor Law & Policy Journal*, 2008 bilateralism does not eliminate conflict, nor does it alter the function of the trade union with a shift toward a liberal approach to labour market regulation, but may be useful for implementing the terms and conditions negotiated during collective bargaining. In this connection, M. Biagi, "Cultura e istituti partecipativi delle relazioni industriali in Europa", L. Montuschi, M. Tiraboschi, T. Treu (eds.), *Marco Biagi un giurista progettuale*, Giuffrè, 2003 regarded bilateralism in Italy and Europe as a cooperative and participative model of industrial relations aimed at protecting workers in small and micro enterprises through the joint administration and governance of the entire labour market. The bilateral approach is therefore associated with an industrial relations model of a collaborative and cooperative type, promoting territorial development and regular employment of good quality.

As far as the legal nature of bilateral bodies is concerned, a comprehensive analysis is provided by L. Bellardi, "Contrattazione collettiva ed enti bilaterali: alcune osservazioni",*Lavoro informazione*, n. 1/1997, G. D'Aloia, "Sindacato e enti bilaterali. Spunti da una ricerca", *Quaderni di Rassegna sindacale*, n. 4/2005, D. Garofalo, 'Il bilateralismo tra autonomia individuale e collettiva', in Aa.Vv., *Autonomia individuale e autonomia collettiva alla luce delle più recenti riforme*, Giuffrè, 2005 and M. Napoli, "Diritto del lavoro e riformismo sociale", *Lavoro e diritto*, 2008. Unanimously academics recognize that bilateral bodies have a contractual origin, even in cases where their establishment is foreseen by the law.

Linked to their legal nature, the funding system of bilateral bodies has been widely debated among scholars during the last decade in relation to the nature of collective agreements in Italy, which are not provided with *erga omnes* power. The thesis under which the financial contribution to bilateral bodies is not compulsory for those companies unaffiliated to the employer's association that signed the collective agreement was mainly supported by F. Stolfa, "Enti bilaterali artigiani e benefici contributive", *Diritto e pratica del lavoro*, 1997. On the other hand, P. Ichino, "Estensione dell'obbligo di adesione ai fondi di sostegno al reddito", *Diritto e pratica del lavoro*, 1994, p. 3424; A. Bellavista, "Benefici contributivi ed enti bilaterali artigiani", *Rivista italiana di diritto del lavoro*, 1998, p. 476; M. Miscione, "Le prestazioni degli enti bilaterali quale onere per sgravi e fiscalizzazioni", *Diritto e pratica del lavoro*, 1997, p. 3347, M. Lai, "Appunti sulla bilateralità", *Diritto delle Relazioni Industriali*, 2006 and more recently M. Tiraboschi, "La contribuzione alla bilateralità: il modello del settore artigiano", *Guida al lavoro*, n. 37/2010 defended the opposite thesis, which is now reinforced by the administrative act No. 43/2010 issued by the Italian Ministry of labour according to which the contribution to bilateral bodies is binding for all the companies irrespective of their affiliation to the signatory employers' associations. This interpretation is basically grounded in the fact that if the companies could opt-out to pay contribution to its relevant sectoral bilateral body, their employees would therefore be discriminated against those workers that benefit of the services provided by it.

The reform of the labour market regulation enacted in 2003 (known as the Biagi reform) strengthened the role played so far by the bilateral bodies, assigning them new and extended functions. In this perspective bilateralism is proposed by the legislator as a privileged channel for the regulation of the labour market not only in the building, craft, commerce and tourism sectors, but also as the paradigm of a new system of labour and employment relations in order to create more participatory relations in all sectors. In positive terms, extensive analysis on the effects of the Biagi reform on bilateralism is provided by a number of Authors in M. Tiraboschi (eds.), *La riforma Biagi del mercato del lavoro, Prime interpretazioni e proposte di lettura del d.lgs. 10 settembre 2003, n. 276. Il diritto transitorio e i tempi della riforma*, Giuffrè, 2004. On the other hand, criticism on the strengthening of bilateral bodies was expressed by G. Martinengo, "Enti bilaterali: appunti per una discussione", *Lavoro e diritto*, 2003, L. Mariucci, "Interrogativi sugli Enti Bilaterali", *Lavoro e diritto,* 2003; Id., "Commento sub art. 2 lett. h)", E. Gragnoli, A. Perulli (eds.), *La riforma del mercato del lavoro e i nuovi modelli contrattuali*, Cedam, 2004, S. Leonardi, *Bilateralità e servizi: quale ruolo per il sindacato?*, Ediesse, 2005, which rejected the emphasis of the reform on bilateralism as a sort of Trojan horse that risks destroying the role of trade unions by transforming them into a para-public institution. Against this idea, a large part of academics, including F. Carinci, "Il *casus belli* degli enti bilaterali", *Lavoro e diritto*, 2003; R. Del Punta, "Gli enti bilaterali e modelli di regolazione sindacale", *Lavoro e diritto*, 2003; P.A. Varesi, "Azione sindacale e tutela del mercato del lavoro: il bilateralismo alla prova", *Diritto delle Relazioni Industriali*, 2004; G. Proia, "Enti bilaterali e riforma del mercato del lavoro", *Argomenti di diritto del lavoro*, 2004; A. Vallebona, "Gli Enti bilaterali: un seme di speranza da salvaguardare", *Diritto delle Relazioni Industriali*, 2006; M. Lai, "Appunti sulla bilateralità", *Diritto delle Relazioni Industriali*, 2006; M. Napoli, "Riflessioni sul ruolo degli enti bilaterali nel decreto legislativo 10 settembre 2003, n. 276", *Jus*, 2005; A. Reginelli, "Gli enti bilaterali nella riforma del mercato del lavoro: un primo bilancio", *DRI*, 2006 and E. Ghera, "La certificazione dei contratti di lavoro", Id., *Il nuovo diritto del lavoro*, Giappichelli, 2006, argue that the new functions recognized to bilateralism do not affect the role and the identity of the trade unions insofar as bilateral bodies continue to be the expression of the collective autonomy of the workers' organizations.

CHAPTER FIFTEEN

EMPLOYEE INVOLVEMENT IN ITALY

1. Introduction[1]

1.1. Definition

The term "employee involvement" has appeared only recently in the Italian debate since the promotion of the involvement of employees in company decision-making has become an essential part of the Community's mainstreaming strategy in its social policy agenda. This term is used as the equivalent of "workers' participation" and "employee participation", and both are used to refer to all forms of employee involvement in the management of an enterprise, as well as "employee involvement" in the capital of the enterprise and in profit sharing.

To speak of participation or of the influence of employees on management decision-making in the private sector in Italy takes on a different meaning according to which of the two concepts is being emphasised. If viewed in a participatory perspective in the sense commonly accepted at a comparative level (i.e. the cooperative involvement of workers in the running of a company), the Italian system presents a rather limited range of experience. If, on the other hand, the focus is on the level of influence that can be brought to bear on the exercise of what have traditionally been managerial powers, the range of cases becomes far more interesting.

1.2. Purpose

The purpose of this paper is to provide a national survey of the channels (i.e. instruments) and functions (and therefore of the activity carried out with these instruments) through which workers influence management other than in a perspective of conflict. It would be too simple

---

[1] This contribution was written in collaboration with Flavia Pasquini and was previously published in Weiss, M., and M. Sewerynsky eds. 2004. *Handbook on Employee Involvement in Europe*. Kluwer Law International.

to argue that industrial conflict is the means by which workers in many countries (Italy included) are able to limit management prerogatives. This report will focus on the ways in which influence is exerted in a participatory perspective, i.e. on the assumption that there is employee involvement in the decision-making process (even if, in fact, such involvement may be weak, sometimes so weak as to be appear to be entirely absent).

1.3. Historical Overview

1.3.1. The Structural Perspective

When speaking of forms of employee representation in private-sector undertakings in Italy, it is necessary to make a clear distinction, between not only a structural and a functional perspective, but in structural terms, between the period before and after the end of the 1960s. Until then, the system of representation could be defined as dual: on the one hand, *sezioni sindacali aziendali* (associative bodies, an integral part of the trade-union structure taking part in bargaining activity and conflict), and on the other hand, *commissioni interne* (elected bodies, representing all the employees, even if they were not union members, dealing with the employer on collaborative and participatory terms).

However, the *autunno caldo* or hot autumn (the profound upheaval of Italian trade unions and society coinciding with the 1968-69 bargaining round, involving university students as well as factory workers) had the effect of replacing this system that was becoming less and less effective and rooted among the workers, with a completely new one. It was based above all on representatives known as *delegati*, elected by groups of workers with common occupational interests or at least employed in the same productive unit in a company.

From the beginning of the 1970s, the *delegati* began to form a new system of representation within bodies known as *Consigli di fabbrica* or *Consigli di delegati.* Basically, this is a single-channel system that is still in operation today.

The originality of this system is undoubtedly based on its uncertain nature. From a technical point of view the *Consigli* are the same body as the *rappresentanze sindacali aziendali* (known as RSA, to be dealt with below), regulated by the *Statuto dei diritti dei lavoratori* (Act. No. 300/1970), in the sense that in most cases the trade unions affiliated to the most representative confederations (CGIL, with a mainly Communist/post-Communist membership, CISL, with an originally

Catholic background, and UIL, with a mainly Socialist membership) waived their right to form representative bodies (RSA) separately, while conferring on the *Consigli* the powers granted by Act No. 300/ 1970.

The RSA are plant-level representative bodies that may be set up in productive units of industrial and commercial enterprises (head offices, establishments, branches, offices and independent workshops) employing over 15 workers. The same provisions apply to agricultural concerns employing over five workers and to industrial and commercial enterprises employing over 15 workers within the same municipality, and to agricultural concerns that employ more than five workers within the same geographical jurisdiction, even if the productive units do not reach this figure when considered individually.

Until 1995 Article 19 of the *Statuto dei lavoratori* regulated the establishment of trade union representation (that could be set up exclusively by the most representative trade unions), but the referendum of 11 June of that year repealed letter a) and part of letter b). As a result, this Article no longer lays down the concept of the most representative union at national level, and the right to set up representative bodies is granted to workers in the framework of the organisations signing the collective labour agreements applying in the productive units.

Since then Italian legislation has upheld the principle of comparative representativeness, with reference to the concept for example in the provisions governing part-time working (Legislative Decree No. 61/2000) and temporary work (Act No. 196/1997).

The *Consigli di fabbrica* to all intents and purposes left the associative phase behind them in the sense that they also started to represent employees who were not union members, yet considered the representative bodies (RSA) to be their agents in the workplace. In fact, these bodies were elected based on procedures that were sometimes laid down by the statutes of the *Consigli* themselves and in other cases were simply based on practice.

In the 1980s the unitary relationship between the three trade-union confederations, CGIL, CISL, and UIL, was considerably weakened. One of the consequences was the break-up of some *Consigli di fabbrica* when a trade union decided to set up a separate and autonomous representative body (RSA). This situation gave rise to intense debate about the urgent need to introduce clearer and more definite rules on employee representation in the workplace. However, this debate did not call into question either the unitary nature of the system of representation or its general function, i.e. the fact that it was expected to give voice to the employees' expectations in the undertaking on all matters, both in a collaborative and in a conflictive perspective, according to the circumstances.

1.3.2. The Functional Perspective

Concerning the functional perspective, to be dealt with below, there is no doubt that, concerning collective bargaining, in the Italian case participation is more highly developed at macro than at micro level, and in this connection mention should be made of the attempts at "social concertation" (tripartite negotiation) at the end of the 1970s and the beginning of the 1980s. In particular, the 1983 agreement on labour costs was explicitly tripartite, in the sense that it was made with the active participation of the Government not only as a political mediator but also as a signatory to the agreement, based on a three-way exchange between the Government, the employers' associations and the trade unions.

The 1983 agreement was followed by others, each of them with their own particular characteristics. The first of these was in February 1984, the St Valentine's Agreement, that CGIL, the most important trade-union federation in terms of membership, refused to sign, unlike CISL, UIL and a series of smaller associations. Due to this refusal, the Government decided to turn an essential part of the agreement into a decree law.

The interconfederal agreement of 8 May 1986 on labour costs and industrial relations adopted a different approach in that the social partners gave *ex post facto* approval to a system that had previously been governed by legislative provisions.

The subsequent phase of industrial relations in Italy was characterised by a moderate degree of conflict, but also by a serious economic recession, that resulted in a return to a tripartite bargaining model aimed above all at financial restructuring.

In the wake of the tripartite agreements of 6 July 1990 and 10 December 1991, the Protocol of 31 July 1992 was signed by 26 representatives of the social partners, laying down certain obligations and a series of policy statements by the Government, mainly concerning the adoption of measures aimed at combating inflation, improving competitiveness on the international markets and reducing the public deficit. The dual nature of this agreement gave rise to problems of interpretation, since it was by no means easy to distinguish the policy statements from the commitments negotiated, and therefore to establish to what extent the obligations were binding on the social partners.

Faced with the public finance crisis and the risk that European Economic and Monetary Union might leave Italy behind, the unions, employers and the government negotiated a major tripartite agreement on 23 July 1993 known as the Social Pact.

This agreement introduced tripartite bargaining in order to achieve wage restraint as a final, formal step in the process by which industrial relations in Italy could be brought into line with the new European climate of economic and social convergence. The incomes policy agreement was based on the same guiding principles that characterised the gradual approach to European integration: inflation in line with the average in the soundest Community economies, and a reduction in the public debt and deficit. Therefore, it may be said that the 1993 agreement laid down a new constitution for Italian industrial relations.

The main objective of the 1993 agreement was to contain inflation and labour costs. Furthermore, it contained a series of institutional innovations affecting company-level interest representation structures on the one hand and the system of collective bargaining on the other.

The cross-sectoral protocol of July 1993 gave enterprise bargaining a complementary role to industry-wide bargaining, and set out the information needed for such bargaining as well as information, consultation and supervisory procedures.

At the end of the first four-year cycle of collective bargaining, an assessment of the 1993 agreement was carried out by the parties involved, i.e. the trade unions, employers' associations and Government. This process was concluded at the end of 1998. In the view of the trade-union confederations, CGIL, CISL and UIL, the tripartite agreement was fairly effective, as it contributed to the containment both of the inflation rate and the public deficit, making it possible to meet the convergence criteria of Maastricht, while the purchasing power of wages was defended. Furthermore, the 1993 agreement permitted a substantial renewal of the structures of interest representation at company level (RSU). A negative outcome, however, was the relatively low level of decentralised bargaining.

Nevertheless, the trade unions' policy on the matter of bargaining levels was to extend and consolidate the model laid down by the agreement of 1993, extending the use of second-level bargaining (company and territorial).

The trade unions were interested in using the assessment and updating the central tripartite agreement of July 1993 to press ahead with an enforcement of participation rights.

The tripartite agreement of July 1993 has so far been the most advanced case of institutionalisation of industrial relations, especially with regard to the system of trade-union representation and collective bargaining that provides the structural basis of participation in Italian industrial relations. By defining bargaining levels and their function, the 1993 agreement succeeded in providing the industrial relations system with a degree of stability.

Even if participation was not explicitly regulated, the 1993 agreement offered a new starting point for participatory experience at the company level in the form of "performance-related pay increases negotiated at company level, to be linked to the results of development programmes agreed between the parties. These programmes were aimed at improving productivity, quality and other aspects affecting the competitive position of the company. In general, trade unions preferred to link this performance-related pay increase to quality and productivity parameters but not to profits, as it was more difficult to control and influence them.

In 1994, with the advent of a centre-right Government, tripartite bargaining slowed down considerably. In particular, the breakdown of negotiations between the social partners in relation to financial policy choices, together with a possible reform of the pension system, forced the Government to eliminate from the annual budget legislation the proposed measures relating to social insurance, and to deal with these matters as part of a general reform of the pension system.

Considering that Italy's economic situation had deteriorated, an agreement was concluded on 12 April 1995, albeit only between the Government and the unions. The employers' association, Confindustria, refused to take part in this agreement, the main purpose of which was to make provision for supplementary pensions, that were intended to make up for the reduction in state pensions.

The agreement of 24 September 1996, on the other hand, mainly focused on the need to combat unemployment by means of a preliminary reform of the labour market. This represents an example, as has rightly been noted, of the preliminary negotiation of provisions that were to become almost entirely legislative (partly transformed into Act No. 196/1997, containing measures for the promotion of employment, and Legislative Decree No. 469/1997, that devolved powers relating to the labour market to the regional and local authorities, based on a model in keeping with information and consultation procedures). The aim of the agreement was above all to reduce passive support measures for employment (tax incentives, early retirement, generalised state funding of enterprises), in order to adopt more active policy measures, including a range of provisions mainly aimed at promoting access to the labour market by means of the introduction of flexibility measures. This was also the purpose of the decision to bring to an end the public monopoly on placement, and the reform of public employment services.

The social pact of December 1998 was concluded by the Italian government and 32 organisations representing the social partners. The primary aim of the agreement was to create employment by reducing labour costs and taxes on the one hand and reforming the system of vocational training on the other. Moreover, the trade unions managed to defend the two-level collective bargaining system. However, participation issues were not discussed at all.

It is important to underline that with this agreement the regional and local institutions started to play a role in tripartite bargaining, that was therefore strengthened.

In October 2001, the Government presented a White Paper, drafted by a group of experts, outlining its reform policies for the labour market and industrial relations. After talks with the social partners on the contents of the White Paper, in November and December 2001 the government issued proposals for the reform of the labour market, the tax system and pension provisions. These reforms were to be introduced by means of "delegated legislation", by which Parliament delegates to the Government the power to legislate on a particular issue.

The three main trade-union confederations reacted in different ways to these proposals: CGIL was highly critical and expressed its total opposition to the reforms, whereas CISL and UIL also criticised the Government positions, but expressed their willingness to continue negotiations.

Negotiations with the social partners over the Government's proposals continued, but were broken off many times. On 5 July 2002, the Italian Government and the main employers' organisations and trade-union confederations, with the exception of CGIL, signed a Pact for Italy (*Patto per l'Italia*), dealing with the labour market, the tax system, the South of Italy (*Mezzogiorno*) and irregular work.

The lack of unity among the union confederations reflected their contrasting views on the Government's proposals. Meanwhile, at its annual assembly in May 2002 the employers' confederation, Confindustria, reiterated its position, stressing the importance of reform of the labour market and the tax system in order to increase competitiveness.

The Pact for Italy recognised that the tripartite national agreement of 1992 and that of 23 July 1993 on incomes policy and bargaining had played a key role in Italy's ability to take part in EU Economic and Monetary Union (EMU). The social dialogue practices and the incomes policy resulting from these agreements made possible the recovery of

Italy's public finances and the control of inflation. In the Pact the Government also explicitly recognised the importance of concertation among the social partners, something that it had previously questioned, and stated that it considered this method fundamental to achieving the employment and modernisation objectives agreed at the Lisbon EU summit.

2. The Structural Perspective

2.1. Sources

The Italian legislative framework for workers' participation is not highly developed. However, the Constitution lays down in Article 46 that: "For the purpose of raising the economic and social level of labour, and subject to the requirements of production, the Republic recognises the right of the workers to participate, in ways and within limits established by law, in the management of undertakings".

Not only has this constitutional provision never been brought into force from a technical point of view, in the sense that Parliament has not enacted legislation referring explicitly to Article 46, but the Italian system of industrial relations as a whole has not developed historically along the lines foreseen at the time of the Constitution. In fact, the role exercised by Italian trade unions in the workplace has, been for a long time mainly interpreted in an adversarial perspective, and until recently, in an ideological sense of conflict between different social classes that were irremediably antagonistic towards each other.

The law has naturally intervened also in Italy to regulate collective labour relations, though to quite a limited extent. Arguably, the most important intervention to date is the *Statuto dei diritti dei lavoratori* (Act No. 300/1970). This legislation gave great importance to supporting and strengthening the so-called "most representative" trade unions, i.e. those affiliated to the three major confederations, CGIL, CISL and UIL.

Thanks also to this legislation, trade unions in the workplace enjoy a good deal of protection and, because of this, a kind of "participation through conflict" is given considerable support. The *Statuto* not only prohibits any form of discrimination on trade union grounds (or for any other reason) but also gives express protection to the rights of the *rappresentanze sindacali aziendali* (RSA). This is the case for the right to call meetings of employees (whether union members or not), to hold ballots, to make use of notice boards for displaying trade union material, to take paid or unpaid leave for carrying out trade union duties outside the workplace, and to be protected against transfers from one unit to another without the approval of the trade union to which the official belongs. This is not to mention the special protection that union activists enjoy in cases of unlawful dismissal.

Although at micro level it is possible to identify this type of legislation that indirectly concerns the capacity of workers' representatives in a company to influence management decision-making, it may be said that at macro level a legislative framework favouring employee participation is almost entirely lacking.

Overall, it may therefore be argued that, from the point of view of the sources, by far the most important role is carried out by collective bargaining. In other words, the conditioning of management initiative takes place by means of bargaining, typically carried out by the trade unions.

In this connection, it must be borne in mind that the Italian Constitution (Article 39) provides for collective agreements applying to all those belonging to the economic sector in question, but so far this provision has not been implemented by Parliament. However, the universal effect of collective agreements, making them binding even for employers and workers who are not affiliated to the bargaining agents, has partly been enforced by case law.

On the basis of Article 36 of the Constitution (the principle of fair remuneration), the courts have declared null and void those clauses in individual contracts of employment that set lower levels of pay than those laid down by the applicable collective agreement. More recently, legislation has laid down an obligation on the part of undertakings in receipt of state grants or awarded public works contracts to ensure that conditions applied or made to apply for workers must not be worse than those set by collective agreements for the relevant category and area (Article 36, Act No. 300/1970).

On other occasions, as a prerequisite for employers applying for relief on social security contributions, legislation has laid down that the remuneration paid to the workers must not be lower than the minimum set by the collective agreement in force.

Apart from these technical points, important as they may be, with regard to the application of collective agreements it must be underlined that in Italy the system of collective bargaining is highly developed. Originally, it consisted of several levels (national agreements for each category, company agreements, as well as intermediate levels such as regional agreements) and applied to all workers. It was quite varied also because of the considerable diversity on the employers' side.

There are in fact several employers' associations, characterised both on the basis of the type of company in the association (small or large, private or state owned, cooperative, artisan, local authority-owned, etc.) and of the political and ideological orientation (e.g. for artisan or co-operative firms). The fact that there are a number of associations is explained by the traditional political allegiances that are to be found in the trade union movements, Socialist, Communist and Catholic. This is why at times there are several national industrial agreements for workers employed in the same sector but in companies of different kinds.

As mentioned above, the Italian system of collective bargaining was redesigned by the agreement of 23 July 1993 between the trade union confederations, the employers' associations and the Government. The system is now based on two levels of bargaining: industry-wide bargaining at national level and a second level that can be either company or territorial (region, district) level. Pursuant to the 1993 reforms, industry-wide agreements are negotiated for four-year periods with regard to normative matters and for two-year periods with regard to pay.

Although collective bargaining is by far the most important source for the regulation of participatory forms, it is by no means the only one. There is a tendency towards the expansion of participatory forms that have not been formally defined in agreements but that are being experimented with at the initiative of management.

The management of human resources by means other than trade union negotiations is no longer anomalous or infrequent, especially in medium to large undertakings. Quality circles and similar strategies for favouring employee participation for the purposes of achieving greater productivity at work no longer meet with a hostile response from the trade unions, that was often the case until not so long ago.

2.2. Channels and Institutions of Representation

2.2.1. Autonomous Representative Bodies and Unified Representative Bodies

At present, in Italy representation chiefly takes place through a single channel, the methods of which were clarified and standardised following the cross-sectoral agreements of 1991 and 1993.

In 1991, under pressure from Parliament, the trade-union confederations drew up joint plans for representatives to be elected by all workers every three years from trade union lists. The protocol of 1 March 1991 changed the name of this form of representation, and it became the *Rappresentanze Sindacali Unitarie* (RSU), i.e. unitary trade-union representative bodies. The dual nature of representation was retained: the RSU were considered to be trade-union institutions, while elections were open to all workers (albeit from trade union or independent lists).

The draft protocol of 1991 was fleshed out by the cross-sectoral protocols and agreements of 23 July 1993 and 20 December 1993.

The agreement of July 1993 redesigned trade-union representative bodies at company level, the so-called RSU. They are unitary structures of plant representation, elected for a three-year term of office by employees and, for the first time, recognised by employers.

It is important to note that there is an explicit mention of the requirement for contact between the trade-union organisations that negotiate the national agreements and the unitary trade-union representatives (RSU) set up under those agreements, reflected in the composition of the RSU: two-thirds elected by the entire workforce, and one-third appointed or elected by the unions that are party to the national agreements. This clause was strongly favoured by the employers, who wanted an assurance that these bodies would be dominated by the same unions as those signing the sectoral agreement. The "one-third rule" also acts as a safeguard for the smallest of the confederations, or for the one least favoured by the electorate.

A typical problem of Italian industrial relations, based on the single-channel model, regards the overlapping in a single representative body of both bargaining prerogatives and participatory activities. The RSUs are the only workers' representative bodies legitimised at company level. Although they have in certain cases the possibility to delegate their rights to other participatory bodies (e.g. joint committees) set up by agreement, this does not overcome the basic contradiction that RSUs continue to hold a power of veto over the activity and decisions of such participatory bodies.

With regard to the public sector, Decree Laws No. 421/1992 and No. 29/1993 brought the system of collective bargaining more or less into line with the methods used in the private sector. Legal provisions drawn up in Legislative Decree No. 396/1997 laid down the reference framework for the introduction of RSUs. Two framework agreements on RSUs, electoral rules and guidelines for the use of trade-union time, signed on 7 August 1998 by ARAN (the Italian advisory, conciliation and arbitration service) and the three confederations CGIL, CISL and UIL, followed on from these provisions.

Still with reference to the public sector, pursuant to Article 43, Legislative Decree No. 165/2001, sectoral collective agreements may be concluded only by trade unions that are considered to be "representative", that is to say those that in a given sector represent at least 5% of the workers, considering for this purpose the average of the membership and the election results. Membership is calculated as the percentage of authorisations for the deduction of trade-union dues in relation to the total number of such authorisations in the workplace or establishment concerned. The election results are considered as the percentage of votes obtained in the elections for the RSU, in relation to the total number of votes cast in the workplace or establishment concerned.

Efforts are made to ensure that the various categories of workers are fairly represented through the composition of the lists or the establishment of separate electoral colleges. Some collective agreements (such as for the chemical sector) make provision for separate representation for managerial staff. Moreover, electoral methods, a source of disagreement in the past, have been more clearly defined in the agreements concluded since 1993.

After the elections, a list of representatives has to be forwarded to the employer, so that those elected can benefit from statutory provisions (i.e. the right to time-off).

2.2.2. Joint Committees

The Italian system also includes several examples of joint committees, normally consisting of equal numbers of representatives of each side. Once again, it is collective bargaining that increasingly defines arrangements at company level, often providing for contractual matters (e.g. information rights, to be dealt with below) to be dealt with by joint committees.

Especially in state-owned industry (IRI, ENI groups, etc.) there have been "bilateral committees" since the mid-1980s. These are bodies on which representatives of the two sides of industry sit, and that may be defined as specialised, distinct, but not separate, from (and therefore not in opposition to) general representative bodies. In this connection, it is significant that at company level the appointment of members is the prerogative of the *Consiglio di fabbrica* or, as the case may be, of the RSA. They are specialised in terms of the matters dealt with and not in terms of their composition. They are in fact standing committees for information and consultation, with a duty to evaluate proposals and to issue an opinion that is obligatory, but not binding on the employer.

2.2.3. Bilateral Bodies

This type of concerted action in industrial relations is to be found not only at company level. Some interconfederal agreements and national industry-wide collective agreements for certain sectors have introduced bodies for the joint management on a territorial basis of vocational training, a subject about which there is a considerable and interesting convergence of views between the two sides of industry.

These joint bodies, known in the Italian system as *enti bilaterali* or bilateral bodies, were first set up, in an embryonic form, in the 1950s, as *casse edili*, mutual funds for the building industry.

However, it was only in the 1970s that collective bargaining introduced joint bodies that were similar to those that are now widespread, aimed at dealing with certain matters, such as the examination and resolution of labour disputes, and the interpretation and classification of labour agreements. The real turning point for bilateral bodies came in the mid-1990s, when the social partners strengthened them, redefining their functions and area of operations.

This period saw the conclusion of a number of cross-sectoral agreements between workers and employers, laying down the competences of these bodies, not just in the coordination of services and vocational training systems (introducing a certification process for the quality of the services provided), but also as a means of providing support for workers involved in restructuring processes leading to the termination or suspension of the employment relationship, and providing services favouring technological and organisational innovation in the enterprise.

The most significant agreements are those with the employers' association Confindustria, the one in the artisan sector, the one concluded by Confapi in 1993, and finally the interconfederal agreement of 23 July 1994 for the cooperative sector. From an analysis of these agreements and their implementation, it can be seen that the first services to be developed were those providing mutual support, as opposed to those providing vocational training. Measures were taken in support of employment, in an attempt to make up for the inadequacy of social security "shock absorbers" or safety-net measures that have never been extended to cover small enterprises.

These measures consist mainly of funds supported by the enterprises, and in certain cases also by the employees, by means of small contributions, and subsequently the payment of subsidies to firms at critical moments.

The legislator has also underlined the importance of bilateral bodies, in particular by means of Article 9, Act No. 236/1993, that provided for the setting up of these bodies in implementation of agreements between the most representative trade unions and employers' associations at national level, making provision for them to sign agreements with autonomous regions and provinces for the analysis and in-depth study of local employment markets and surveys of vocational training needs.

The tripartite agreement of 23 July 1993 that opened up a new phase in industrial relations in Italy makes various references to bilateral bodies, especially with regard to training. In particular, in the sections devoted to youth employment and training, the parties to the agreement recognise the fundamental powers of the bilateral bodies in the design, implementation and certification of employment contracts with a training element. These bodies are given powers relating to course planning, the organisation of training plans, surveys at local level of the supply and demand for training services, the implementation of measures facilitating access to the labour market on the part of certain categories of workers and for promoting the employment of those at risk of exclusion from the labour market. Finally, the Pact for Labour of September 1996 recognises the role of bilateral bodies, once again with particular reference to vocational training policies.

With regard to the form that these bodies generally take on, in most cases, they are set up as non-recognised associations pursuant to Articles 36 et seq. of the Civil Code, on the basis of an agreement between the trade unions and the employers' associations. However, they may also be set up as limited liability companies, as consortia pursuant to Article 2615 of the Civil Code or as non-profit organisations pursuant to Section III, Title II, Book I of the Civil Code and generally without the distribution of earnings. Bilateral bodies may in general be defined as "associations of associations" in which the parties are, for the trade unions, the confederal associations—CGIL, CISL, UIL—each with its own autonomy and separate identity, while for the employers the signatories may be individual associations (for example, Confindustria) or pluralist associations (Confartigianato, Can, Casa, Claai).

Bilateral bodies may have an internal structure consisting of an ordinary and extraordinary general meeting of the members, a board of directors or management, and an audit committee. All the management and administrative bodies are appointed on the basis of the principle of joint representation of the employers and the trade unions, generally for a renewable three-year term of office. The chair of the bilateral body, in particular, as the legal representative, is normally appointed by the employers' association, whereas his or her deputy is normally appointed by the trade unions. With regard to internal management procedures, the unanimity rule is prevalent, and is applied for all major decisions, to underline the consensual approach that these bodies are intended to take.

The system of bilateral bodies is strongly decentralised to regional and, in certain cases, provincial level. The four national bodies (Bilateral body for the artisan trades, for Confindustria, Confapi and Cooperation) are cross-sectoral and confederal. In addition there are bilateral bodies for tourism and commerce that in spite of the particular characteristics of this sector, are defined in the same way.

From an analysis of certain legislative provisions recently enacted (Act No. 30/2003 and Legislative Decree No. 276/2003, implementing this Act), there emerges an intention on the part of the Italian legislator to provide incentives, by means of a range of measures, for bilateral bodies and methods. In these legislative provisions, the role played in the past by these bodies is considerably strengthened, on the one hand promoting the tasks that they have traditionally performed, and on the other hand assigning new competences and functions. This strengthening concerns three areas of bilateral action, in particular the regulation of the labour market (with future prospects for the management of supplementary measures or measures replacing the general obligatory system of income support), the matter of the reorganisation of training contracts, and finally, the certification of employment contracts, transactions and contracting out, conferring on the bilateral bodies an important role, in order to avoid the use of fictitious job descriptions, that in many cases are intended to circumvent employment protection measures.

In particular, Article 2 (1) (h) of Legislative Decree No. 276/2003 lays down a definition of bilateral bodies, that on the whole confirms that they may be set up in various ways, and lists in a non-exclusive manner the functions they may perform. The long-standing practice in Italian industrial relations is therefore confirmed, by which bilateral bodies are "set up at the initiative of one or more employers' associations and the most representative trade unions", that are destined, from this legislative provision onwards, to become the preferred forum for the regulation of the labour market "by means of the promotion of regular employment of good quality; the matching of the supply and demand for labour; the promotion of training initiatives and the identification of ways of providing in-company training; the promotion of best practices against discrimination and for the inclusion of the most disadvantaged groups; the joint management of funds for training and income support; the certification of employment contracts and of regular and proportionate remuneration; the development of actions relating to health and safety at work" and, perhaps even more important, "any other activity or function assigned to them".

It should be noted that this measure provides for bilateral bodies to be set up only by the most representative trade unions, and is therefore not of general application, but only for those bodies that intend to perform the functions laid down.

In this report it is not possible to provide an exhaustive account of the functions laid down for bilateral bodies by the legislator. However, it is clear that they will be able to play a fundamental role with regard to the participation of workers in management decision-making in small enterprises.

In this connection there is a fundamental aspect to take into consideration: the instruments that the Italian system has provided in the past, in an uncoordinated manner, to promote employee participation in the broad sense depend on the enterprise reaching certain employment thresholds, with only a few marginal exceptions.

One of the exceptions that should be mentioned is the provision in Article 43 of the *Legge Finanziaria* for 2004, applicable to all companies regardless of the number of employees, and legislative proposal C. 2778, to be discussed below, expressly designed for small companies, that is limited to profit-sharing.

Consequently, it has generally been impossible for employees in small and medium-sized enterprises to take advantage of participation schemes, in spite of the benefits that these schemes clearly could provide, in an area in which there would not be any reason for conflict with representative bodies in the company.

It is at this point that the "bilateral" system of joint bodies can play an important role. In fact, in the productive sectors in which the social partners have set up bilateral bodies, with an equal number of representatives of each side, the employees of very small companies have seen the emergence of participatory mechanisms in the broad sense. However, these mechanisms can clearly not be considered in formal terms to be procedures of information and consultation or employee participation in company decision-making strictly speaking.

One example in this connection is to be found in the tourist sector where, following the issue of Legislative Decree No. 626/1994 on health and safety at work (to be dealt with below), the interconfederal agreement of 18 November 1996 gave rise to the setting up of a special section of the national bilateral body, to take over the functions of the joint national body for health and safety at work, and provided that the functions of the provincial joint body for health and safety at work are to be carried out by territorial bilateral bodies. The numerous activities carried out by these territorial structures as joint bodies dealing with health and safety at work have produced positive results, providing support for the argument that Legislative Decree No. 276/2003, entrusting the bilateral bodies with the development of actions relating to health and safety at work, takes full advantage of the strategy adopted in the tourist sector.

In fact, the artisan sector has also moved in the same direction, setting up a fund for territorial health and safety representatives under the auspices of the bilateral body.

Another example goes farther back in time, and for this reason is even more innovative. A scheme was developed in the 1980s in the artisan sector, where, for companies with up to 15 employees, permanent forums were set up to enable the employers' representatives and the "territorial" trade-union representatives to meet, in order to deal with individual grievances and collective disputes not resolved at company level. In this way, as noted in, "conflict" was moved outside the company and trade-union representation was able to play a full role, exercising the workers' rights in the bilateral or joint bodies set up for this purpose.

In this connection, mention should be made of the provision included in the national agreement for the tertiary sector, the retail trade and services (concluded on 20 September 1999 by Confcommercio and the sectoral organisations, Filcams-Cgil, Fisascat-Cisl e Uiltucs-Uil), by which, in cases in which flexible working hours are introduced, the territorial bilateral body must always be notified, in the absence of company-level collective bargaining (in other cases, however, notice must be given to the RSU).

There is therefore a widespread belief that, albeit with an operational form that is manifested "outside" the company, bilateralism is the form that participatory schemes take on in territorial contexts with small and medium-sized enterprises since it provides a channel for the permanent development of convergent strategic interests. Moreover, bilateralism is also one of the most appropriate means for small enterprises to make up for their asymmetrical position compared to large companies, probably mainly due to their ability, by means of interaction and continuous exchanges between the social partners, to promote reciprocal trust.

It is for this reason that the promotion of the system of bilateral bodies, first introduced in Act No. 30/2003, and more recently implemented with Decree No. 276/2003, must be seen also as a contribution to and an incentive for worker participation in the broad sense.

2.3. "Specialised" Participation (via Collective Forms): Health and Safety

Collective bargaining has in many cases set up joint bodies at company level for the protection of the health and safety of workers, a tendency partly in contradiction with legislative provision on the subject, that was originally to be found only in Article 9 of the *Statuto dei diritti dei lavoratori*. This norm lays down that the initiative in monitoring these matters as well as in proposing new measures for the prevention of accidents is to be taken by the employees through their "representative bodies". Whereas at first legal opinion considered such representative bodies to be distinct and separate from the RSA (and moreover not bound to the most representative trade unions), case law (supported by subsequent legislative modification) has since held that the two forms of representation are one and the same thing. Therefore, the law has in the final analysis been corrected by case law, leaving no room for specialised bodies in this area.

However, this contrast has not been too evident. As mentioned above, collective bargaining has reconsidered the matter, often setting up joint bodies with a view to achieving close collaboration between the parties.

At present, the transposition of Directive 89/391/EC by means of Legislative Decree No. 626/1994 makes provision for the appointment of specific representatives as regards health and safety, with rights of information, consultation, supervision and proposal.

In particular, hazard prevention and protection services have been set up, consisting of the human resources, technical systems and internal and external resources of the company (from Article 2 of Legislative Decree No. 626/94) aimed at providing prevention and protection from occupational hazards in the company or the productive unit. This is an operational instrument that the employer can make use of to comply with the obligations laid down by law.

With regard to the organisation of these services, there are three possible approaches. They may be organised within the company or productive unit by the employer, who is required to appoint a health and safety officer in charge of prevention and protection from among those with the aptitude and skills, as well as safety stewards who are also required to have the appropriate skills and to be allocated the resources and the time necessary to carry out the tasks assigned to them. It is also possible for such services to be outsourced. In addition, in this case, however, those outside the company appointed by the employer to provide the services are required to be in possession of the necessary skills. Finally, the employer may opt to perform these tasks directly (pursuant to Article 10 of the Legislative Decree under consideration, this is possible only in certain cases and prior notice to the workers' health and safety representative is required: these cases are generally correlated to the size of the company or the type of activity carried out).

The health and safety officer must be appointed (pursuant to Article 8(2) of the Legislative Decree under consideration) from among the employees involved in health and safety services, and is distinct from the health and safety "delegate" (or health and safety representative) who is required to monitor compliance with safety regulations; he or she does not have the power to adopt safety measures in practical terms and does not have power to allocate resources, but carries out a largely consultative but obligatory role. Consequently, the law does not lay down specific sanctions for the health and safety representative, nor for the safety stewards, for failure to comply with safety measures, since they do not have power to take practical measures and are therefore not liable to prosecution if these measures are not implemented.

One of the tasks of the health and safety service (Article 9, Legislative Decree No. 626/94) is to draw up proposals for a plan of information and training for the employees, as well as to take part in consultations on health and safety issues (periodic meetings for hazard prevention and protection) and to provide employees with the necessary information for the protection of their health and safety.

The former is in fact one of the most significant and innovative aspects of Legislative Decree No. 626/94, in that it represents the main forum for participation in health and safety matters on the part of all the individuals concerned by the legislative provisions, as well as the channel for the information, training, consultation and participation of the workers, through their representatives. There is an obligation to hold such a meeting periodically, at least once a year, only in companies with at least 15 employees. In companies or productive units below this threshold, such a meeting is held only at the request of the health and safety representative, and only if circumstances arise that justify calling such a meeting. The employer is in general responsible for convening a meeting of this kind, where necessary through the health and safety representative.

The employer, on the other hand, is required to provide the health and safety service with information relating to the nature of hazards and work organisation, and the design and implementation of preventive and protective measures; a description of the productive installations and processes; information from the register of accidents and occupational diseases, and finally the measures taken by the monitoring bodies.

A fundamental role is played by the workers' health and safety representative, who is defined (Article 2(1)(f) of Legislative Decree No. 626/94) as the person, or persons, elected or appointed to represent the workers in relation to aspects of health and safety at work.

This representative is not expected simply to put forward trade union demands. He/she is a worker who is able to interact with the employer in a competent and well informed manner, thanks to the fact that the health and safety provisions guarantee on the one hand the right to information and consultation on matters relating to the protection of health and safety at work, and access to the relevant company documents, and on the other hand the right to receive (at the expense of the employer) the necessary training to carry out the tasks for which he/she was appointed, in relation to health and safety legislation and the specific hazards in the workplace represented (pursuant to Article 22(4) of Legislative Decree No. 626/94).

For the first time in the workplace, a specific and institutionalised form of worker representation on health and safety has been set up, to which specific prerogatives and participatory rights are granted in connection with significant decision-making processes.

The general principle (laid down by Article 18 of Legislative Decree No. 626/94) is that in all companies or establishments there is a requirement to elect or appoint a health and safety representative. With regard to the appointment or election of the representative, as well as the means for the exercise of his/her specific functions, the law refers the matter explicitly to collective bargaining.

Among the main functions assigned to the health and safety representative, mention must be made of the right of access to places where work is carried out; the right to be consulted in advance and in a timely manner about risk assessment; the identification, planning, implementation and monitoring of prevention in the company or the productive unit; to be consulted about the appointment of health and safety stewards, measures for fire prevention and first aid services and the evacuation of workers; to be consulted about the organisation of training for the workers appointed to take charge in an emergency; to receive company information and documentation relating to the assessment of risks and the related preventive measures, as well as information about hazardous substances, processes, machines and equipment, the organisation of the working environment, occupational injuries and diseases; to receive information from the health and safety monitoring service; to promote the drafting, design and implementation of preventive measures for protecting the health and physical integrity of the workers; to report any relevant facts during visits and inspections carried out by the competent authorities; to take part in regular meetings to discuss health and safety matters; to make proposals relating to preventive measures; to notify the company health and safety officer of hazards identified at work; and to refer matters to the competent authorities when it appears that the measures of prevention and protection adopted by the employer and the resources allocated to implement them are not sufficient to safeguard health and safety at work.

Finally, Legislative Decree No. 626/1994 lays down that among the trade unions joint bodies may be set up (pursuant to Article 20, Legislative Decree No. 626/94) involving the employers and the workers, with a view to providing guidance and promoting vocational training for the workers. These bodies are also the first port of call for resolving disputes arising from the application of rights of representation, information and training laid down by the health and safety legislation.

2.4. Quality Circles and Direct Communication Techniques

The discussion so far should not overshadow the growing importance of communication strategies aimed directly at employees in order to give them an incentive to participate and therefore to cooperate. Normally these are experiments in forms of active and explicit involvement of the employees with regard to certain aspects of production. In this regard, it is worth mentioning not only quality circles but also more generally the use of direct communication techniques (by means of various forms of information and/or meetings) between management and employees in order to increase their awareness of company aims and perspectives.

It may be stated in this respect that these are not always alternatives to traditional forms of worker representation (trade union or otherwise). In fact, from this point of view, the tendency of companies to cooperate with the unions appears to be more marked where the unionisation rate is higher and, more generally, where there is greater willingness on the part of management to take into serious consideration the views put forward by the formal representatives of employees in day-to-day management.

3. The Functional Perspective

3.1. Collective Bargaining

Also in a functional perspective, as well as in terms of sources, collective bargaining must be considered the means which, more than any other, makes employee participation possible, at the same time exerting a strong influence over decision-making in private-sector companies. This is even more the case when considering the fact that bargaining does not always lead to collective agreements in the strict sense. On the contrary, it quite often leads to informal accords, i.e. to arrangements that are made without signing an official agreement, but that are no less important in practical terms as instruments for the regulation of labour relations.

The intensity of bargaining in Italy can clearly not be explained by a general obligation to negotiate that is not laid down by legislation at least in the terms provided in the United States or France, though management may only exercise certain powers after having initiated a negotiating process with the RSA at company level. The reference here is to Articles 4 and 6 of the *Statuto dei lavoratori,* that lay down two instances of what might be called a "duty" to negotiate. These statutory provisions state that the use of television and other equipment for the remote monitoring of workers' activity as well as personal searches of the worker (considered indispensable for safeguarding the property of the undertaking) may only take place after negotiations have been attempted between the RSA and the employer. Only if these negotiations fail ("in the absence of an agreement" the Act says) may the employer ask the Labour Inspectorate to issue the necessary authorisation.

However, statutory legislation plays a role in the wide variety of negotiating that takes place in Italy also at micro level. A considerable part of the *Statuto dei lavoratori* (Title III), that confers powers on the RSA, undoubtedly has the effect of promoting bargaining activity, though it does not deal with other questions such as the identification of bargaining agents. While only a few years ago the powers of the *Consigli di fabbrica* could not be seriously brought into question, more recently Italy too has begun to suffer from the problems typical of rival unionism.

In the private sector this is due to the break-up (albeit not complete and not everywhere) of the unitary relationship between CGIL, CISL and UIL but another important factor is the ambition of middle-managerial employees to have their own representative bodies and therefore their own agreements. There is also a risk that the fragmentation of the trade-union front, with the proliferation of unions in the public sector spreading to the private sector.

Significantly, private-sector employers have proposed statutory intervention to clarify which bodies have the right to bargain collectively.

However, the key element of the Italian bargaining system is to be found at macro level in relation to national negotiations for each category. This level has traditionally tended to unify working conditions in each sector and guaranteed certain minimum terms relating to fundamental issues such as job classification, work organisation, wages, working hours, trade union rights and, of great importance in the perspective analysed here, information and consultation rights. With regard to the relations between collective agreements at various levels, as seen above they have been characterised by alternating phases of centralisation and decentralisation.

3.2. Information and Consultation Rights

3.2.1. Consultation Rights in the Broad Sense

In Italy it is necessary to distinguish between information and consultation rights in the broad sense and in the strict sense. Traditionally, in the broad sense these rights depend above all on the size of the company (whether public or private), whereas, in the strict sense, it is possible to refer to these rights only in state-owned industry (the IRI, ENI, EFIM groups, etc.).

Collective bargaining has played a significant role in the implementation of information and consultation rights. For example, the collective agreement for private-sector metalworkers of 18 January 1987 laid down that information in an undertaking must be supplied by the management of establishments with more than 200 employees to the RSA (therefore to the *Consigli di fabbrica*) "with regard to substantial modifications in the productive system affecting in a decisive manner the technology adopted so far or the overall organisation of work or the type of production carried out and overall levels of employment".

Different provisions are made by the same collective agreement with regard to "information about the options and forecasts for productive activity as well as about plans involving new industrial establishments or significant extensions of existing ones", as well as the "foreseeable implications of the above-mentioned investments on employment, environmental and ecological conditions, and the criteria for the selection of sites". In this case companies with more than 350 employees are required to inform the trade unions on an annual basis, at a meeting to be held at the headquarters of the employers' association in question (the Federmeccanica, affiliated to the Confindustria, in the case of the collective agreement taken as an example) in the area where the head office of the undertaking is located.

In some cases, the unions have tried to introduce performance-related pay schemes based on the improvement of quality and productivity by developing autonomous proposals with regard to new forms of work organisation. In theory, the trade unions have the chance to play a part in changes in work organisation and the definition of quality programmes aimed at strengthening the company's competitive position. This means that these agreements, like those in restructuring processes, also serve to define participatory models, based in general on the setting up of joint technical committees, to monitor the most significant aspects, such as economic and employment strategies and company prospects, work organisation, product quality, vocational training, and health and safety. In general, these joint committees have a technical advisory role rather than a direct negotiating function. As noted above, there are also cases in which joint committees include outside experts.

The introduction of company-level participation is mainly to be found in the agreements of large groups (e.g. Zanussi, Galbani-Danone, Nestlé, Ferrero and Fiat).

Zanussi has implemented one of the most highly developed participation systems, characterised by joint technical committees. Additionally, in this case participation focuses on influencing central enterprise decision-making. In a 1997 agreement, Zanussi introduced a supervisory board consisting of six trade-union representatives that meets three times a year with the management and whose role is to consider the group's results and to examine in advance any industrial and organisational decisions under consideration.

Moreover, since the 1996 agreement at Alitalia that was intended to promote cooperation and to restructure the company, three of the 17 members of the Alitalia Board of Directors have been employee representatives. Two of these seats are allocated to representatives of the CGIL and the CISL, while the third seat is reserved for a representative of pilots who have one-third of the 20% of shares allocated to company employees. In March 2002, an agreement was reached by management and trade unions on the restructuring of Alitalia, supporting the company's business plan for 2002-2003 and providing for a joint procedure for monitoring the implementation of the plan. To this end, the agreement made provision for monitoring by the monitoring committee, the technical secretariat and the adviser.

The monitoring committee is set up on a joint basis, including one representative for each union signing the agreement. The work of the committee is supported by an advisor and the technical secretariat, to provide information and opinions on market developments, and on trends in air traffic and demand in relation to the business plan forecasts. The monitoring committee is convened every month, and holds periodic meetings with the technical secretariat every two months and the advisor every three months. The committee may submit written proposals and requests to the company relating to measures intended to consolidate and develop the company in relation to the business plan for 2004-2006.

The technical secretariat consists of two independent experts, one appointed by the company and one by the unions, and coordinated by a member of the senior management (the senior vice-president for finance and control). It has the task of monitoring trends in markets, air traffic and demand, and of drawing up reports and technical papers for each session of the committee and providing the information required to accompany the requests put forward by the monitoring committee.

The *super partes* advisor is appointed jointly by the company and unions. Should they not agree, the advisor is nominated by the Minister of the Economy and Finance. The advisor expresses opinions on trends in markets, air traffic and demand, and on the proposals made by the monitoring committee. The parties take the advisor's assessments and opinions as the final stage of the monitoring procedure, and they are then submitted to the company board. Alitalia makes available the facilities and resources required by the monitoring bodies.

In other cases, for example Italtel, a system of participation has been introduced in order to deal with processes of reorganisation and in particular aspects such as the allocation of production, working hours, and workloads.

With regard to participation in small and medium-sized enterprises, we find the most advanced participatory experiences in the Emilia-Romagna region. In the mid-1980s, the metalworkers' unions started to negotiate the introduction of new forms of work organisation and define new models of employee participation. In these cases, there was a clear separation of functions: while the trade union bodies negotiated the introduction of joint technical committees, the members of the committees were workers chosen according to their particular skills. This principle has not always been adopted in other sectors and regions. In many cases, appointments to joint technical committees have been decided by the trade unions at company level based on political criteria.

Since industrial relations in Italy are characterised by the single-channel system, the involvement of the RSU implies a strong position also for external trade unions.

Among the experiments carried out in Italy in recent years, mention should be made of the national collective agreement for railway workers, concluded on 23 November 1999. Part 5 of this agreement, dealing with industrial relations and participation, viewed the participatory approach as not just a useful but as a necessary instrument for improving relations between the two sides and promoting the involvement of workers in the process of company transformation. For this reason, the agreement specified that the system of participation in the company covered three areas: the right to information, consultation mechanisms and the setting up of joint bodies.

With regard to the first matter, it was laid down in particular that matters relating to information rights should be dealt with by making a distinction between rights relating to bargaining and those relating to consultation, and these rights are assigned to two separate bodies, with the participation of representatives of the employer and those of the trade unions signing the agreement.

The first of these bodies is the standing bilateral committee, set up for consultation purposes, that is called upon to give a prior opinion, obligatory but non-binding, on matters of strategic importance for the company, without encroaching on the powers of the company decision-making bodies, and fully respecting the autonomy of the participatory organisations. This committee took over the powers of the Participation Committee set up under Article 5 of the previous collective agreement of the same company signed on 6 February 1998.

Secondly, a series of joint bodies were set up with a consultative and monitoring function in matters relating to the working environment, health and safety (taking over the functions of other joint bodies previously dealing with these matters), job mobility, quality and training, with the task of monitoring training initiatives linked to restructuring processes and with the aim of improving training quality, as well as examining training programmes for newly recruited staff, on the basis of agreements regulating access to employment and training for various employment grades. In addition these bodies can deal with any other activities considered useful for enhancing participation.

Provisions of this kind are also to be found in Article 12 of the national collective agreement for textile workers of 19 May 2000, that lays down a series of procedures for information, consultation and monitoring, for the purposes of sharing information between the social partners and defining the aims of collective bargaining, with a view to improving the competitive position of the enterprise, as well as the development of the industrial relations system. To this end, provision is made for the workers' and the employer's representatives to hold meetings at company level to evaluate the future development and productive needs of the company, in relation to the need for profitability and efficiency, together with working conditions and employment prospects.

While the company-level agreement remains in force, the implementation of the programme must be monitored on the basis of performance indicators, in discussions that may take place also in the form of information meetings pursuant to Article 22 of the agreement, to be discussed below. At company level, methods may be determined for improving the exchange of information and the monitoring activities.

Article 22 makes provision for an information system organised at various levels. In particular, at provincial level the employers' associations are required, at the request of the trade unions in a given territory, to provide annual aggregate figures for the entire sector and where appropriate for individual units, with information about any problems arising and measures proposed to deal with them.

Moreover, they are expected to provide information about economic and employment trends, investment and diversification plans, new industrial establishments and their location; initiatives aimed at energy saving and ecological conditions relating to industrial processes; the application of equal opportunities legislation and positive action programmes, the laws relating to the employment of young people and interconfederal agreements on employment training contracts. Further matters to be dealt with include the most significant trends in the local labour market and their relation to future training needs. A joint examination is also carried out of the likely implications for employment levels and job mobility, the working environment and ecological matters, and vocational training issues, for the purposes of providing workers with adequate knowledge and skills in connection with technological and organisational change and of enabling companies to make optimal use of their human resources in relation to emerging needs and to deal with issues relating to the employment of women.

Any practical proposals relating to these matters dealt with by mutual information and consultation are submitted to the competent public authorities and the joint industry-wide bodies, so that the planning and implementation of initiatives can take account of the expected requirements of the clothing and textile sector.

In addition to the provisions for information systems at local level, the various territorial organisations are authorised to jointly determine the timescale, methods and techniques for gathering information (for example, by setting up Observatories) and the means for carrying out the information process.

These examples are perhaps sufficient to give at least an idea of the complex provision for this matter in collective agreements.

Below the employment levels indicated by way of example above, sometimes information need not be given, while in other cases a system of information is provided at territorial level. This consists of meetings between the employers' associations and the trade unions at local level where matters such as new technologies and the overall trends in employment levels in the area are discussed. An information system also exists at central level, where, for example, the national industry-wide agreement provides for the setting up of a "database of new technologies".

3.2.1.1. The Ordinary and Special Wage Guarantee Funds

Measures relating to workers' information and consultation rights are also to be found, first of all, in the legal provisions regulating one of the most important social "shock absorbers" in the Italian system, the *cassa integrazione guadagni* or wage guarantee fund, that provides direct support in the form of 80% of overall earnings for workers who have been laid off or made redundant due to the closing down or scaling back of production in the enterprises where they work.

The *cassa integrazione guadagni ordinaria*, or ordinary wage guarantee fund, intervenes in the event of partial suspension of production of a temporary or transitory nature in manufacturing (except for the artisan sector and regardless of the number of employees), in the construction industry and in agriculture (in the event of adverse climate conditions).

The *cassa integrazione guadagni straordinaria,* or special wage guarantee fund, provides support in the case of total or partial suspension of production resulting from processes of restructuring, reorganisation or transformation of a company, as well as in the event of company crisis, insolvency or bankruptcy. This fund may be used to support industrial companies with more than 15 employees and commercial undertakings with more than 50 employees, as well as publishing companies.

In connection with the procedure to be implemented by undertakings applying for support from the wage guarantee fund, Act No. 164/1975 and No. 427/1975 lay down an obligation to carry out prior consultation and negotiation with the unions. Trade union information and consultation are therefore seen as necessary conditions to be met prior to an application for support from the wage guarantee fund, as the employer is obliged to specify that these requirements have been fulfilled when submitting the wage guarantee fund application. The same procedural requirements are laid down for the ordinary wage guarantee fund.

In cases in which for objective reasons production has to be stopped as a matter of urgency and negotiations cannot take place prior to the stoppage, provision is made for notification to be made at a later date to the representative bodies, the RSA or the RSU, or alternatively to the most representative trade unions for the sector at provincial level. In addition, the trade unions have the right to request joint negotiations (to be held within five days of the request being made) regarding any suspension or reduction in working hours of more than 16 hours per week.

In other (non-urgent) cases of a reduction of working hours or total stoppage, the employer is required to give prior notice to the representative bodies, the RSA or the RSU, and to the most representative trade unions for the sector at provincial level. In addition, the trade unions have the right to request joint negotiations (to be held within 25 or 10 days of the request being made, depending on whether the number of employees is greater or less than 50).

With regard to the special wage, guarantee fund, in all cases prior notification is required, which the employer is obliged to give in a timely manner to the RSU, or in the absence of such a representative body, to the trade unions that in comparative terms are most representative at provincial level. Moreover, at the request of the employer or the above-mentioned representative bodies, within three days of the notification a joint examination must be carried out of the situation of the company in the presence of the competent regional authorities or the Ministry of Labour (in cases of productive units located in a several different regions), once again to be held within 25 or 10 days of the request being made, depending on whether the number of employees is greater or less than 50).

After completing the trade-union consultation process, in the case of the ordinary wage guarantee fund the application for redundancy measures and any further renewals must be submitted to INPS, the social insurance board. However, in the case of the special wage guarantee fund, the application, including the plan that the undertaking intends to implement, must be submitted to the Ministry of Labour (Directorate General for social insurance and social assistance) accompanied by supporting documentation provided by the Regional authorities.

The notification and the joint negotiations with the unions are required to deal with the selection criteria for the workers to be laid off and a system of rotation. Where the employer claims that there are objective reasons for not adopting a system of rotation, these reasons must be notified to the trade unions and specified in the wage guarantee application. If considered justified, the Ministry of Labour will seek an agreement between the social partners, or in the absence of such an agreement will issue a decree laying down a system of rotation on the basis of the proposals of the social partners.

3.2.1.2. Collective Redundancies and Mobility Schemes

Another instance of information and consultation procedures is to be found in Act No. 223/1991, as amended by Legislative Decree No. 151/1997 that lays down two kinds of collective redundancy: one consisting of a reduction in staffing levels, and the other of mobility schemes.

These provisions uphold the power of the employer to reduce staffing levels in the enterprise, but require the employer to adopt a procedure, known as a mobility scheme, intended primarily to enable the trade unions to ascertain the validity of the reasons given for the reduction in staffing levels, and secondly to promote the conclusion of trade-union agreements preventing redundancies, or at least reducing the number of workers to be made redundant, also by the adoption of alternative measures.

In order to dismiss employees as part of a redundancy package, it is necessary for the employer to have at least 15 employees, and to intend to dismiss at least five of them in the same province within a 120-day period. The cause of redundancy is required to be the same in all cases, and associated with a reduction or transformation of production in the undertaking. This definition is taken to include those cases in which the reduction in the number of workers depends on the introduction of new technology without reducing the level of production or activity (known as technological redundancy).

An undertaking with more than 15 employees may implement a mobility scheme when, during or at the end of a period of support from the special wage guarantee fund, the employer is not in a position to rehire all the suspended workers or to take alternative measures. For this type of redundancy, there are no quantitative or time limits.

A mobility scheme takes effect by means of the written notification that the undertaking is required to submit to the representative trade-union bodies in the company and the sectoral associations affiliated to the most representative confederations stating the technical and organisational reasons giving rise to the need to dismiss the redundant workers. This notification must be detailed and complete, and in any case provide the basis for negotiations with the trade unions. It is required to specify the number, company position and job classification of the employees to be made redundant, as well as of the workers usually employed, the time scale for the implementation of redundancies and any measures designed to deal with the social consequences of the plan.

The procedure that begins with the written notification may be implemented in two stages. The first phase, known as the trade-union phase, is preliminary, and gives the trade unions the right to request within seven days of receiving notification a joint examination of the factors leading to the excessive staffing levels and of possible alternatives for the workers at risk of redundancy. In this way, there can be an open discussion between the trade union and the employer, in which the employer is free not to take on board the trade union proposals, in cases in which they are not considered acceptable. If no agreement is reached during these discussions, the administrative phase begins, and the examination of the situation continues in the presence of the provincial labour directorate in order to reach a negotiated settlement.

Once the entire procedure has been completed without having reached an agreement, over a period that may not be more than 75 days, the employer has the right to dismiss the redundant employees.

The selection of the employees for redundancy must be carried out on the basis of the criteria laid down in the collective agreement, in the absence of which the legal criteria must be applied, based on technical, productive and organisational requirements, number of dependants and seniority.

In case of a failure to comply with the selection criteria, the redundancies can be declared null and void. However, in this case, the employer is allowed to dismiss a number of employees equivalent to the number reinstated, without having to implement a new procedure, but in compliance with the trade union or legal criteria of selection, giving prior notification to the trade-union representative body in the company.

3.2.1.3. Transfer of Undertakings

Finally, a particular procedure for trade-union information and consultation was introduced by Article 2112 of the Civil Code, as amended by Article 47 of Act No. 428/1990 (implementing Directive No. 77/187/EC) in the event of the transfer of an undertaking. These provisions were further amended and supplemented by Legislative Decree No. 18/2001, implementing Directive No. 98/50/EC) and by Legislative Decree No. 276/2003 (implementing Act No. 30/2003), amending the provisions relating to the transfer of part of an enterprise with Article 32. This reform needs to be considered in the light of the explicit reference in the above-mentioned delegated legislation to the recent Directive No. 2001/23/EC, concerning the approximation of the legislation of the Member States in relation to the safeguarding of workers' rights in the case of the transfer of an undertaking. However, it had no effect on the information and consultation procedures to be discussed below.

On the basis of the above-mentioned provisions, when it is intended to transfer an undertaking employing more than 15 workers overall (though the same provisions apply also in the case of the transfer of a branch of an undertaking), the transferor and the transferee must give written notification at least 25 days prior to the execution of the transfer or prior to a binding agreement between the parties, if such an agreement is made prior to the transfer.

The bodies entitled to exercise such information rights are the unitary trade union representative bodies (RSU) or the plant-level trade union representative bodies (RSA) set up in the establishments concerned (of both the transferor and the transferee), as well as the employers' associations and trade unions signing the collective agreement applied in the undertakings involved in the transfer. In the absence of representative bodies in the undertaking, notification must be given to the employers' associations and most representative trade unions in comparative terms at national level.

In essence, the implementation of the trade-union procedure during negotiations is required in order to allow the unions to intervene in what is seen as a crucial phase, in which the future of the workers employed is still uncertain, and to verify the ability (both technical and financial) of the new owner of the undertaking to manage and/or restructure the company, with regard to investment plans, production goals and above all guarantees concerning employment levels and working conditions.

The notification must include such information as the date of the transfer, the reasons for the planned transfer, the legal, economic and social consequences for the workers and any measures planned in relation to the workers. However, the notification does not need to include economic and financial information that is of a confidential nature for reasons of competition between enterprises.

At the written request of the plant-level representative bodies or the sectoral trade unions, submitted within seven days of receiving the notification, the transferor and the transferee are under an obligation to carry out, within seven days of receiving the request, a joint examination with the trade unions submitting the request. This consultation is considered complete when a 10-day period of negotiation has gone by and no agreement is reached.

The obligation to provide information and to carry out a joint examination must be fulfilled also in cases in which the decision over the transfer has been taken by a parent company. The failure on the part of a parent company to supply the necessary information cannot be used to justify non-compliance with these obligations.

The failure on the part of the transferor or the transferee to comply with the obligation to supply information, as well as the obligation to carry out a joint examination, is deemed to be anti-trade union behaviour pursuant to Article 28 of the *Statuto dei lavoratori*. Moreover, it should be noted that it does not invalidate the transfer negotiations, since compliance with the above-mentioned trade-union procedures cannot be considered to be a necessary precondition for the validity of the transfer.

Finally, it must be underlined that the information and consultation procedures pursuant to Article 47 of Act No. 428/1990 are applicable, in the absence of special provisions, also in relation to public employees in the case of the transfer of a public-sector business to other entities, whether private companies or public bodies (pursuant to Article 31,

Legislative Decree No. 165/2001). This provision was introduced due to the serious repercussions on the employment relationship that such a transfer may have.

3.2.2. Consultation Rights in the Strict Sense

As regards consultation rights in the strict sense, once again it was collective bargaining (starting in the IRI group in 1984) that set up a system based on joint consultative committees at various levels (group, sector territorial, company, etc.). The general duties of such committees (with equal numbers of representatives of the IRI group and of CGIL, CISL, UIL) are as follows:

- to examine and carry out a preliminary investigation, at the planning stage, of economic and industrial policy options, major operational plans for restructuring and development and the most significant matters concerning labour policy and industrial relations;
- to issue a formal opinion, obligatory but not binding, on these questions, as well as indications for any alternative options and plans;
- to inspect and monitor the operational stages of the overall policy plans examined;
- to draft proposals for strategies for work organisation, industrial relations and the labour market.

The collective agreements specify more exactly and in greater detail the matters that the various joint committees may deal with at the different levels. Meetings are normally held every four months but further meetings may be held at the request of one of the parties.
In order to be able to form the opinions they are required to express, the committees must be given information by management on the following subjects (by way of example):

- production goals classified by sector, geographic area and undertaking;
- global investment and disinvestment goals and plans;
- plans for technological innovation and of a technical and organisational character;
- investment and financial goals and staff numbers in the field of research;
- plans relating to environmental and ecological conditions and employee health protection;
- employment structure classified by sector, geographic area and undertaking specifying sex, age group and job classification.

It is clear from this brief outline that this is really a separate and distinct model of industrial relations, quite different from the model in use in the private sector. Moreover, state-owned industry in Italy has always had a pioneering role in the search for collaborative solutions in labour matters. The results of the first years of application may, on the whole, be said to be of some interest, even though there has obviously been (and this applies also to information rights) no lack of disputes that are at times resolved by the courts on the basis of complaints filed under Article 28 of the *Statuto dei lavoratori* (anti-trade union behaviour on the part of the employer).

It is worth specifying that this system of consultation is different from that existing in other countries, for example Germany: in Italy, these committees do not have the right to take binding decisions.

However, a unitary statement by both parties expressed as a "formal opinion" might take on a certain importance at a practical level even though it is not legally binding. In other words, it becomes difficult for management and the trade unions to adopt strategies different from those supported by their representatives on the joint consultative committee.

4. Employee involvement In Transnational Corporations

4.1. European Works Councils

Finally, it is necessary to underline the importance in Italy of the recent Legislative Decree No. 74, 2 April 2002, that implemented the Directive of the Council of 22 September 1994, 94/45/EC relating to the setting up of a European Work Council or, alternatively, a procedure for the information and consultation of workers in enterprises or groups of enterprises with a European dimension (provisions on this matter were made in the interconfederal agreement of 6 November 1996, that resulted in the partial transposition of the Directive as a result of negotiations, but that was considered to be insufficient for the purposes of full transposition.

This represented a step towards the implementation of a series of Directives of the European Council, that are linked by the intention of laying the foundations for a more extensive and effective involvement of workers in company decision-making. This was the case of Directive 2001/86/EC, that supplemented the European Company Statute with regard to employee involvement, Directive 2002/14/EC, that laid down the general framework for employees' information and consultation rights, and most recently Directive 2003/72/EC, that supplemented the European Cooperative Company Statute, once again with regard to employee participation. As regards the EU Directive on national information and consultation rights, EU Member States have until 23 March 2005 to comply with its requirements. Under the Directive, all undertakings with at least 50 employees (or establishments with at least 20 employees) must inform and consult employee representatives about business developments, employment trends and changes in work organisation. However, in Italy the only measure taken so far has been Act No. 14/2003 (Community Act for 2002), which delegated legislative powers to the Government to issue a legislative decree implementing the Directive within one year of the entry into force of the Act, a time limit that is about to run out.

The field of application of the above-mentioned decree continues to be rather limited, since it applies only to enterprises employing at least 1000 employees in the European Union, or at least 150 workers per Member State in at least two EU countries, as well as to groups of enterprises employing 1000 workers in the Member States, with two enterprises in the group located in two different Member States and with at least two companies in the group employing not less than 150 workers in two Member States. The companies and groups of companies covered by this definition are not required to apply Legislative Decree No. 74/2002 in cases in which they had concluded agreements before 22 September 1996 setting up transnational information and consultation rights with the trade unions signing the national collective agreement applying in the company or group of companies.

Directive 94/45/EC did not assign negotiating powers to the European Works Councils (EWCs), but at the same time it did not specify that they cannot have such powers. They can therefore operate as co-ordination centres for trade-union activities in the various countries in which companies covered by these norms operate, especially in cases in which some of their members are appointed by the trade unions (as laid down by the Italian transposition norm, in keeping with the national model of single-channel representation). The Directive left it to the individual states to determine the methods for appointing the members of the EWCs, but also of the Special Negotiating Delegation that has the task of setting up the EWC.

It is possible to identify certain divergences between the EWC Directive and the Italian transposition norms, though in this report it will be possible to examine only the most salient ones. First of all, whereas Directive 94/45/EC consists of three sections, Legislative Decree No. 74/2002 consists of just two parts, reflecting the interconfederal agreement of 1996. Like this agreement, the transposition norm differs from the

Directive in the order given to the three criteria of presumption for the purposes of identifying the parent company. In particular, priority is given to the power to appoint more than half the members of the Board of Directors. Moreover, unlike the Directive, the Decree defines not only the concept of consultation (the exchange of opinions and the setting up of a dialogue between the parties) but also information (that is to say, the provision of data, figures and news). Although the Community source made provision in setting up the Special Negotiating Delegation for the coordinated and negotiated involvement of workers employed by the company or the group with a European dimension in at least two states, the Italian decree gave powers of initiative also to the trade-union organisations signing the applicable national collective labour agreement.

For the purposes of defining the scope, composition, powers and term of office of the EWC, the Directive lays down an obligation on the part of the central management of the company to deal with the Special Negotiating Delegations which, on the basis of the transposition provisions of the Italian legislator, can also avail itself of the services of experts. Legislative Decree No. 74/2002 introduced a series of additional measures to be adopted in the absence of an agreement between the parties, laying down a series of indications providing the minimum provisions that may be agreed upon during negotiations, since it is unlikely that the Special Negotiating Delegation would agree to less favourable provisions than those that would automatically apply without an agreement. Some of these measures contain interesting additions in relation to the corresponding Annex to the Directive, for the purposes of improving the functioning and effectiveness of the EWC.

Finally, certain matters must also be mentioned, that Legislative Decree No. 74/2002 failed to address. In particular, it is not clear what is supposed to happen to the Special Negotiating Delegation once the EWC has been set up, given that its function has thereby been fulfilled. Considering that it is laid down that when their term of office runs out, the EWCs themselves are to renegotiate the agreements setting them up, presumably the Special Negotiating Delegation ceases to exist when the EWC has come into existence. Nor is it specified whether the Special Negotiating Delegation has the right to gather prior to the meeting with the management of the multinational company, but this may be taken to be implicit, to enable the members of this body coming from different countries to get to know each other and to draw up a joint negotiating strategy in advance of the negotiations.

4.2. European Company

Together with the Regulation of the European Council No. 2157/2001, on 8 October 2001 the European Council finally approved a Directive (2001/86/EC) integrating the regulation setting up the European Company (hereinafter simply referred to as EC), from the point of view of the involvement of employees and of their representatives. It is therefore necessary for Member States to take action for the transposition of the Directive into their legal systems. They have been granted a three-year period in which to do so. Until the Directive has been transposed into the Member States' national legislations, it will not be possible to envisage a European Company Statute.

The regulation clearly states that the fundamental prerequisite for the setting up of an EC is the solution of question of employee involvement.

A distinction must be made, however, between involvement and participation, as the Directive uses "participation" as a synonym for the presence of employees and their representatives in management bodies of the EC, while in Italy "participation" corresponds more closely to the concept of co-management.

In Italy Article 1(1) of the Community Act for 2001 (Act No. 39, 1 March 2002) delegated powers to the Government to issue, within one year of its entry into force on 10 April 2002, a legislative decree implementing Directive 2001/86/EC. However, the time limit for this authorisation ran out on 10 April 2003, without the implementation taking place. Considering that the final deadline for implementation is laid down by the Directive as 8 December 2004, it is expected that the Government will take the necessary steps in the coming months to implement this Directive. To this end, reference will be made to the guidelines drawn up by the group of experts appointed by the European Commission (that met in Brussels on 27 June 2003), with a view to avoiding contrasts between the different national systems in the transposition process.

5. Self-Employment and Workers' Participation

5.1. The Case of Workers' Co-operatives

This paper on the Italian system would not be sufficiently wide-ranging without at least a mention of a type of self-management that has been in use for over a century, i.e. workers' co-operatives. Indeed, it may be argued that in this model employee involvement and influence over management is to be found in its most advanced form.

It is possible in this context to speak of a self-management model. The majority of workers employed in these co-operatives are also shareholding members. They invest not only their physical energy but also part of the capital. They therefore have the right to elect the board of directors and to approve the financial statement at the annual general meeting. The originality of this model consists of the fact that they do not lose their prerogatives as employees: they join trade unions and their working conditions are laid down by national collective agreements for each sector negotiated by associations representing the co-operative companies and the trade unions. Moreover, there is a considerable amount of plant-level collective bargaining.

This may therefore be seen as a separate system of industrial relations properly speaking (i.e. a system in which trade unions and collective bargaining are to be found) in self-managed companies. What at first sight seems to be a contradiction is actually proof that an advanced model of participation is not incompatible with the role and activity of trade unions. Moreover, this trade union presence guarantees that the self-management model does not degenerate into bureaucratic or authoritarian forms. This is an important force also from an economic point of view: suffice it to mention that some of the most important Italian construction companies, operating both in Italy and abroad, are workers' co-operatives.

The law on this matter was amended by Act No. 142, 3 April 2001, introducing a "Reform of the legislation relating to the cooperative sector, with particular reference to the position of the worker member".

This law is highly significant, in that it introduced clear and consolidated regulations on a matter on which current legal opinion and case law had produced conflicting views and rulings, both with regard to the definition of the nature of the relationship between the worker member and the cooperative, and concerning the provisions to be applied to such workers.

The matter may be summarised as follows. The new law made clear that the provisions are applicable not only to production and labour cooperatives, but to all cooperatives in which mutual support takes the form of employment.

With regard to worker members of cooperatives, the law clearly laid down that they take part in two different and distinct legal relationships: not only as members of an association, but also as workers (with the member becoming an employee either at the time of joining the association or at a later date).

The question of membership is dealt with in Article 1(2): "The worker members of a cooperative: a) participate in the management of the undertaking by participating in the governing bodies and in the definition of the management or administrative structure of the company; b) take part in the drafting of development programmes and decisions concerning strategic choices, as well as in the implementation of productive processes in the undertaking; c) contribute to the formation of the capital stock, and share the commercial risk of the undertaking and company earnings, and take part in decisions about the distribution of such earnings; d) make available their vocational skills also in relation to the type of business carried on, as well as the quantity of labour dedicated to the cooperative".

With regard to the employment relation, this is governed by the provisions of Article 1(3), based on which work may be carried out "in the form of salaried employment or self-employment or in any other form, including quasi-salaried employment not of an occasional nature, in order to contribute to the achievement of the aims of the undertaking".

The new law makes detailed provisions for the various types of labour relationship of the cooperative member in relation to individual and collective rights (Article 2), remuneration (Article 3), social insurance matters (Article 4), the assignment of a general charge on the assets of the cooperative and of rights relating to legal procedures (Article 5), and matters relating to the internal regulation of the cooperative (Article 6).

With reference, in particular, to the exercise of trade-union rights, the new law lays down that "In relation to the special nature of the cooperative system, specific forms for the exercise of trade-union rights may be negotiated under collective agreements". However, the agreements that can regulate these rights in the cooperative sector were only those at national level, concluded by the comparatively most representative associations.

Article 9(1)(b) of Act No. 30/2003 laid down that the rights under Title III of Act No. 300/1970 are to be exercised in a manner compatible with the status of the worker member, as laid down in the collective agreements negotiated by the national associations of the cooperative movement and the most representative trade unions in comparative terms.

5.2. Past and Future Developments

Overall, it may be said that the Italian industrial relations system is characterised by more extensive participation than in the past, for example in the 1970s. From this point of view, in the 1980s some progress was undoubtedly made, above all in the area of information and consultation by means of what is known as the IRI model, that was briefly referred to above as a model that seems likely to be consolidated in public-sector companies.

It seems much less likely that such a model will be "exported" from this area and taken up in collective agreements in the private sector, regardless of the employers' association taking part in negotiations. Indeed many years after they were first introduced, trade union information rights have yet to be shown to be successful. On the contrary, some observers have concluded that they are a complete failure.

Several reasons may be given for this. Unlike management in public-sector industry, private-sector management in Italy is still reluctant to accept the logic of fair collaboration with trade unions.

Moreover, the unions continue to give much more importance to the bargaining process as the instrument for exerting real influence over the decision-making powers of management. It is therefore unlikely that the IRI model will spread beyond public-sector companies.

Meanwhile, it is necessary to take account of an element that only a few years ago could not have been foreseen, namely the marked decline in the representativeness of the CGIL, CISL and UIL trade union confederations. The question therefore arises as to what is the most useful channel for favouring employee participation.

In any case, the decline of trade union power, at both micro and macro level again raises the question of employee participation on a new basis in which the scope for management initiative is considerable. It is therefore foreseeable that, at least in the short term, it will be the companies themselves that take the initiative to achieve a style of human resources management capable of involving employees to the greatest possible extent in order to increase productivity and company profitability.

Moreover, some tentative steps in this direction may be seen in the case of certain initiatives relating to worker participation in company management. First, mention should be made of legislative proposal No. 2023, presented on 23 November 2001, containing "A delegation of powers to the Government for the adoption of a 'participatory statute' for companies aimed at worker participation in company management and profits".

This proposal was intended to implement Article 46 of the Constitution, Articles 21 and 22 of the European Social Charter, which lay down the right of workers to information, consultation and participation, and Recommendation 92/443/EEC of the Council, concerning the promotion of participation by salaried workers in company profits.

This is intended to be achieved by a mechanism that requires above all the determination of minimum conditions for enterprises intending to adopt a "participatory statute", so that they can implement such a statute by means of an agreement concluded with the representative bodies of the unions signing the collective labour agreements applying in the companies or with the respective coordinating bodies, or by means of a company proposal, subject to the approval by secret ballot of a majority of the salaried employees on open-ended contracts. Moreover, it is laid down that the benefits deriving from the adoption of the "participatory statute" are to be specified.

With regard to the minimum requirements, they should include the option of setting up joint bodies consisting of representatives of the enterprise and workers' representatives elected or appointed for this purpose by the representative trade union bodies, endowed with adequate powers of planning, control, decision-making and management of matters relating to the organisation of work, equal opportunities, vocational training, job security, health and safety in the workplace, performance-related pay and the regulation and resolution of collective disputes, or the adoption of formal binding and guaranteed procedures to provide information and consultation in advance as well as control by the workers' representatives over the most significant company decisions, also by setting up trade-union bodies to which these rights may be conferred.

Moreover, the proposed legislation provides for three methods of participation in company profits by employees. One method is the distribution to the employees of a share of profits above a certain threshold, another is the allocation of shares in the company, and a third method is "collective access by salaried workers to the capital stock of the company, by setting up workers' associations with the aim of using the shares in a non-speculative manner and by collective representation at company level".

Finally, it is proposed to set up at the Ministry of Labour and Social Policy (also known as the Ministry of Welfare) a Central Participation Committee, for certifying the requisites specified above, consisting of at least one representative of the same Ministry, of the Ministry of Economic Activity, the Ministry of Economics and Finance, and the national committee for equality and equal opportunities between men and women, and representatives of the employers' associations and the trade unions.

The legislative proposal outlined here is not the only one put forward in this connection. Parliament still has to examine Legislative Proposal No. 3926 (presented on 22 April 2003) containing "Provisions for promoting employee participation in the management of companies implementing Article 46 of the Constitution", and Legislative Proposal

No. 4039 (presented on 4 June 2003), also containing provisions relating to workers' information and consultation rights.

The tendency that can undoubtedly be observed in Italy to dedicate particular attention to participation issues is also shown by Article 43 of the annual budget legislation or *Legge Finanziaria* for 2004, that provides for the setting up under the Ministry of Labour and Social Policy of a special fund providing incentives for the participation of workers in their companies, intended to act "in support of programmes drawn up for the implementation of trade-union agreements or company statutes aimed at promoting the participation of employees in the profits or management choices of companies".

The Fund has an initial allocation of 30 million euros, and is to be managed by a joint committee set up by ministerial decree consisting of 10 experts, including two representing the Ministry of Labour and Social Policy, and eight representing the employers' associations and the most representative trade unions at national level. The Committee will elect a Chair from among its members, and will draw up its own operational rules autonomously. The decree will lay down the fundamental management criteria of the Fund. On the basis of the adoption of interconfederal agreements or joint notices between the social parties, and in compliance with the policy objectives of the European Union, the Minister of Labour and Social Policy may make further provisions for the management of the Fund by means of decrees issued at a later date. Finally, the joint committee will draw up an annual report containing details of the monitoring of allocations by the Fund, to be presented by the Minister of Labour and Social Policy to the competent parliamentary committee and the National Council for the Economy and Labour (CNEL).

6. Employee Financial Participation

6.1. The Legal Framework

In Italy, the financial participation of employees in the enterprise is deeply rooted, though it continues to be a controversial matter. The issue of "economic democracy" was the object of a lively economic and juridical debate even at the beginning of the 1900s, before the emergence of the solidarity and non-conflictive approach to labour relations that was typical of corporatist ideology and the social doctrine of the Catholic Church. It emerged in the Italian political debate for the first time in the late 1920s, when certain legislative proposals were put forward concerning employee share ownership and profit sharing, though these proposals were never enacted.

The matter was again considered, though not too enthusiastically, by the Civil Code, and later by the Constitution. This issue has therefore been through different phases, periodically surfacing in academic, trade union and political debate, yet without giving rise to legislative provisions suited to its increasing importance.

Council Recommendation No. 92/443/EEC, of 27 July 1992, concerning the financial participation of employees in enterprise results and profits (including share ownership), required Member States to adapt their national frameworks to the promotion of employee financial participation, also by means of financial or tax relief. However, these recommendations have not been followed up by any action, except for Legislative Decree No. 314/1997, which was not sufficient on its own to support or develop this concept.

Furthermore, the spread of employee financial participation has not been facilitated by the industrial relations climate, characterised by strong opposition on the part of employers (Confindustria) and by a significant part of the trade union movement and, in particular, by CGIL, despite strong support by CISL. The main fear, expressed by many parties, was that it would undermine the pluralistic and conflictive rationale of the traditional industrial relations model, which has been in place in Italy throughout the post-war period.

As already mentioned, the main regulatory tenets relating to employee financial participation are to be found in the Constitution of 1948 (Articles 46 and 47) and in the Civil Code of 1942. Although these two articles are generally cited in relation to employee financial participation in enterprise capital, no specific indication is found in the rules and regulations that have been issued.

Moreover, no significant measures have been taken to implement Article 46, where only the issue of employee cooperation in management has been highlighted; or Article 47, paragraph 2, where the references to favouring direct or indirect investment in the country's main industries are generally taken as references to savings in general, without any specific restriction to employees' savings or to investment in the capital stock of a company by individual employees.

Therefore, the most important elements of the regulatory framework are to be found in the Civil Code, that governs the different forms of profit sharing and employee share ownership.

In particular, it is Article 2099(3) of the Civil Code that makes provision for employees to be remunerated in whole or in part by means of profit-sharing, though Article 2102 of the Civil Code lays down that the share of profits is to be determined, in the absence of an agreement to the contrary, on the basis of the net results reported in the annual financial statement. As a result this provision is only applicable in cases in which workers are employed in joint-stock companies.

With regard to the shareholding schemes laid down in Italian company law, provision is made in Article 2349 of the Civil Code (as recently amended by Legislative Decree No. 6/2003). On the basis of this provision, the general shareholders' meeting may, as an exceptional measure, allocate a share of the profits to the employees of the company (or of subsidiary companies) by means of the issue, for an amount equivalent to the profits to be distributed, of special categories of shares to be allocated to company employees on an individual and free basis (in other words by means of a free or nominal increase in capital). In contrast with this far-sighted provision the legislator now appears to intend to limit the issue of shares to employees to those cases in which there is an explicit provision for such profit-sharing in the company statute. The Civil Code also specifies that by means of this procedure special categories of shares may be allocated "with particular norms concerning the form, the method of transfer and the rights of shareholders". The shareholders' general meeting therefore has not only the task of determining the number of shares to be given to the employees but also of regulating the allocation of shares and the related rights. It should be noted that Article 2349 of the Civil Code grants the shareholders' meeting the right to allocate to employees of the company or of subsidiary companies financial instruments other than shares, with rights that do not include the right to vote at the shareholders' meeting (instruments of this kind are provided on a general basis by the new clause 6 of Article 2364 of the Civil Code).

In this case particular norms may be laid down regarding the conditions for the exercise of the rights assigned, the conditions for the transfer and any reasons for the expiry of shareholding rights or of redemption. It must be underlined that the employees are in any case free to accept or reject the offer of free shares.

As well as a free allocation of shares, the Italian Civil Code makes provision for employees to purchase shares on favourable terms. This arrangement is more widely used by enterprises, and is regulated by Article 2441(8) of the Civil Code (as amended by Legislative Decree No. 6/2003), on the basis of which the company may pass a resolution for an increase in share capital with a corresponding increase in the number of shares issued at a given price to employees of the company or of the parent company or subsidiary companies. The same clause allows for the suspension of the stock option rights of existing shareholders, for up to one quarter of the new shares issued, by means of the approval of the majority required for extraordinary general meetings. For the suspension of stock option rights above this level, an absolute majority is required.

The particularly favourable conditions consist in the derogation from the general principle laid down in Article 2441(1) of the Civil Code, on the basis of which, in the case of an increase in social capital, any new shares issued must be offered as an option to the shareholders in proportion to the number of shares held. Moreover, in this case the price of the new shares issued does not have to be calculated by taking account of the net worth of the company, but may be based on the nominal value, that in general is much lower.

A further arrangement by which workers are given preferential treatment for the purchase of shares in the company consists of the sale of company shares as laid down in Article 2357 et seq. of the Civil Code. In this case, the allocation of shares does not take place by means of an increase in capital stock, but by the redistribution of existing shares. Unlike the two schemes described above, this is not a particular form of employee shareholding, since in principle the employees are in the same position as investors in general. The particular nature of this arrangement depends on the special terms of purchase, comparable to the sale of shares to the public but with the employees having an option on the shares.

All the schemes so far outlined result in the individual allocation of shares to the employees. However, there are no legal provisions for the allocation of shares on a collective basis, so schemes of this kind may be considered to be an atypical form of share ownership.

The most widespread and representative form of collective investment is the unit trust fund. By means of this instrument the company does not allocate shares to individual employees, but places them in a professionally managed unit trust fund, and the employees have a share in the fund based on the number of units allocated. It is important here to distinguish between trust funds of a collective nature, including unit trust and pension funds, and employee shareholding schemes set up for the workers in a company. Whereas the unit trust is based on the collective management of shareholdings, the employee shareholding scheme is a collective arrangement for those participating in the shareholding plan. This structural difference is reflected also in the difference in the aims of these funds. First of all, unit trust or collective funds tend to interact closely with company management, exerting pressure for efficient and sustainable governance, and secondly, they operate as independent investors, diversifying their financial portfolios in order to minimise the risks arising from a crystallization of their shareholdings. On the other hand, employee shareholding schemes operate with a view to promoting the identification of the employees with management objectives, acting as collective incentive schemes in order to promote efficient practices within the company in both productive and organisational terms.

It must be noted that at times such schemes give rise to forms of control over management, albeit in embryonic form. In this connection mention should be made of the agreement of 22 July 1998 for promoting employee shareholding in Dalmine S.p.A., that made express provision for the presence of an employee representative on the Board of Directors in the event that the shares held by the employees amounted to 10 per cent of the capital stock.

Although Italy is still far from achieving the level of employee shareholding envisaged when provisions were first made (as mentioned above), it must be noted that the pension fund law is a highly significant development along the way towards greater "economic democracy". Although enacted with some delay in relation to developments in the main industrialised countries, the legislation on complementary social security (Legislative Decree No. 124/1993 and, especially, the changes introduced by Act No. 335/1995) made possible interesting developments, allowing employees to try out new institutional forms of "collective" investment, with an impact on the financial market, and significant repercussions on the Italian industrial relations system.

Among the most widespread forms of shareholding participation, mention should be made of stock option schemes. In this case the company gives the employee the right to purchase shares at a later date at a price determined when the stock option is made available. This is therefore an atypical form of share ownership, in which the transfer of shares to the employee does not take place when the scheme is launched, but after a set period when the employee can opt to purchase the shares. Such schemes are clearly not aimed at raising capital from the employees, but rather at increasing loyalty to the firm and productivity on the part of certain employees (nearly always senior management). For those benefiting from the stock option scheme, the correlation between their earnings and the value of the company shares at set intervals, known as vesting, provides a strong incentive for the employee to promote the interests of the company, intended to result in greater loyalty and higher productivity.

However, since these schemes do not have a collective dimension, it is doubtful whether they can be included among participation schemes in the strict sense (unlike employee shareholding schemes for which all the company employees are eligible).

Finally, mention should be made of a legislative provision, relating only to tax and contributions, that is particularly advantageous for the companies that make use of it, introduced by Legislative Decree No. 505, 23 December 1999. This decree, amended and supplemented by Article 48, Decree of the President of the Republic No. 917/1986, relating to the transfer of shares to employees, provided tax exemptions for stock options for individual or certain categories of employees.

Other incentives are provided for employee shareholders by Legislative Decree No. 58/1998, for companies listed on the Stock Exchange, and in order to facilitate the sale and repurchase of shares in employee shareholding schemes in which the ownership of shares is planned for a period of time that is sufficient to maximise earnings and capital gains (Article 132).

In conclusion, it may be argued that recent legislative measures have tended to confirm the individual character of employee shareholding in Italy. Employee shareholders are not considered as an organised group, and do not have organisational autonomy, nor a functional position within the company, enabling them to exert pressure on management. However, it must be said that Legislative Decree No. 6/2003 lays down certain regulations with regard to supplementary agreements between the two sides of industry, laying the foundations for forms and procedures for organising the votes of small shareholders (and therefore also of employee shareholders).

It is evident that a number of schemes of considerable interest, at least from the industrial relations point of view, have been implemented in Italy, especially since the privatisation of public bodies and the transformation of State-owned companies into joint stock companies. However, it should be underlined that the level of employee shareholding is insignificant, even in those cases where this form of financial participation has been introduced. The only significant exceptions that might be mentioned in this scenario are the cases of Telecom and Alitalia. Since the privatisation of the company, Telecom employees have purchased shares amounting to more than 3 per cent of the entire share capital, becoming the major private shareholders, whereas in the case of Alitalia, employee shareholding amounts to more than 20% of the share capital.

Concerning Alitalia, the 2002 agreement underlines the value of employee shareholding and the company's commitment to enhancing employee involvement, with a view to moving towards profitability. It also highlights the need to find ways to recognise the contribution made by employees to the company's recovery. To this end, Alitalia undertook to give free warrants (or options) to employees. These warrants were intended to enable workers to purchase shares issued by means of an *ad hoc* capital increase. The warrants are to be taken up three years after their issue (a condition introduced in order to benefit from tax incentives).

The beneficiaries are to be flight crew, cabin crew and ground staff. Each category is to receive a share of warrants proportionate to their contribution to the labour cost reduction for the period 2002-3. Pilots will thus receive 32.19% of the warrants, flight technicians 3.1%, cabin crew 25.85%, and ground staff 38.86%. Moreover, in view of the importance of employee shareholding for the company, Alitalia undertook to find statutory means to promote workforce representation on its governing bodies. However, it must be noted that the implementation of these plans depends on negotiations that are still in progress.

6.2. Future Developments

The social partners have taken up different positions in relation to the financial participation of employees. As mentioned above, with the exception of CISL, the trade unions have expressed their lack of interest, if not their hostility to this issue.

A tentative move towards systematic regulation was nevertheless made on 23 December 1998, with the signing of the "Agreement on concertation policies and on new industrial relations policies for the European integration and transformation of the transport system" by the Government and the social partners.

The signatories to the agreement stated their intention to "enable the industrial relations system to evolve towards new participation models in the ways envisaged by collective bargaining, aimed at involving all the workers' representatives in strategic decisions in the enterprise" (clause 4.6). To support this plan, "the Ministry of Transport was to submit a specific bill to the National Transport and Logistics Council to support and foster employee shareholding in transport companies".

What appeared to be just a sectoral initiative, planned for the critical and restless transport industry, was actually an attempt to re-launch employee shareholding in general. By concluding this agreement, the social partners showed for the first time that they were willing to overcome their traditional lack of interest if not hostility towards this issue. However, with the change in the legislature, this draft reform was not followed up by any concrete action.

The idea of employee shareholding was re-launched in the Government White Paper on the Italian labour market in October 2001. In particular, the White Paper highlighted the need to "verify financial participation formulas aimed at enhancing key workers' loyalty within small and very small-sized enterprises, including tourist businesses and craft firms. From this point of view, it is necessary to re-establish a participation agreement, i.e. to resort to other forms of profit-sharing, supporting these instruments also through adequate economic and tax incentives" (section III.3).

There appears to be a need above all for a legislative intervention regulating not only individual shareholding, but also collective shareholding schemes, since it may be argued that it is primarily through such collective schemes that it is possible to implement effective forms of economic democracy.

With regard to legislative proposals under examination by Parliament, as mentioned above, on 21 May 2002 a legislative proposal was presented, No. 2778, regarding profit-sharing among salaried employees in artisan firms and agricultural enterprises with up to 10 employees, hired on open-ended contracts and with at least six years of continuous employment with the same employer.

Based on this proposal, the extent, forms and means of profit-sharing are to be determined by agreement between the parties, in compliance with the provisions of Article 2102 of the Civil Code and without prejudice to the economic and legal rights accrued by the worker. In sharing out profits, the employer is required to take account of the different levels of seniority of the employees, and unless the parties agree otherwise, to pay out a share of the profits on an annual basis, as severance pay to be paid in advance, to be made by the company to the employee, on the basis of an overall sum determined by prior agreement between the parties.

Employers deciding to pay out or set aside sums of money in favour of employees as part of a profit-sharing scheme would be entitled to relief on social insurance contributions proportionate to the amount of profit paid out or set aside.

Finally, the draft legislation provides for the drawing up of guidelines for the proper use of profit-sharing agreements, and compliance with these guidelines would be a decisive factor in the case of a dispute between the parties.

As further confirmation of the renewed attention of the Italian legislator for employee participation (including financial participation), it must be underlined that the proposal outlined above is just one of several currently before Parliament. Mention should also be made of Legislative

Proposal No. 1003 (presented on 21 June 2001), containing "Measures for the participation of employee shareholders in the governing bodies of joint-stock companies"; Proposal No. 1943 (presented on 13 November 2001), containing "Measures for promoting widespread shareholding on the part of salaried workers" Proposal No. 3642 (presented on 5 February 2003), "Measures promoting the participation of employees in the capital stock of enterprises", and finally Legislative Proposal No. 4039, mentioned above, containing measures relating to share ownership by salaried workers.

In effect it appears that in the absence of an agreement between the social parties to set up a system of financial participation based on trade-union practice the legislator has suddenly recognised the urgent need to regulate this matter "from the top down" as it were. However, with the failure to take significant steps in this direction in Legislative Decree No. 6/2003 (the reform of Italian company law), it may be argued that the most appropriate opportunity for systematic reform of this matter has been missed.

References

Alaimo A. 1998. *La partecipazione azionaria dei lavoratori*. Milano: Giuffrè.

Ales E. 2000. "Dal conflitto alla partecipazione: le nuove relazioni sindacali nei trasporti," *Riv. giur. lav.* 1, p. 81.

Arrigo G. 2000. "La partecipazione dei lavoratori nel diritto comunitario tra armonizzazione normativa e competizione di modelli," *Dir. lav.* 1, p. 381.

Baglioni G. 1997. *La partecipazione dei lavoratori alle decisioni dell'impresa*, in *Giornale dir. lav. e relaz. ind.*, No. 1, p. 223.

Bellardi L. 1989. *Istituzioni bilaterali e contrattazione collettiva: il settore edile (1945-1988)*. Milano: Franco Angeli.

Biagi M. 1983. "Workers' Cooperatives and Labor Relations: An Example of Industrial Democracy in Italy," Occasional Paper No. 42. Bologna Center: The Johns Hopkins University. Reprinted in: Tiraboschi M., ed. 2003. *Marco Biagi: Selected Writings*. The Hague: Kluwer.

—. 1990. "Forms of Employee Representation at the Workplace," in *Comparative Labour Law and Industrial Relations in Industrialised Market Economics*, ed. Blanpain, R., (Deventer), p. 202.

—. 1990. *Rappresentanza e democrazia in azienda. Profili di diritto sindacale comparato*, Rimini.

Carabelli U. 1996. "Le r.s.a. dopo il referendum, tra vincoli comunitari e prospettive di partecipazione," *Dir. relaz. ind.*, p. 21.

Cella G. P., Treu T. 1989. "La contrattazione collettiva," *Relazioni industriali. Manuale per l'analisi dell'esperienza italiana*. Bologna: Il Mulino.

Cesos. 2000. *Le relazioni sindacali in Italia, Rapporto 1997-1998*. Rome: Cnel.

D'Antona M. 1992. "Partecipazione, codeterminazione, contrattazione," *Riv. giur. lav.*, p. 137.

De Lucia G., and S. Ciuffini. 2004. *Il sistema degli enti bilaterali nell'artigianato: una esperienza italiana al servizio del dialogo sociale europeo*, in M. Tiraboschi (ed.), *La riforma Biagi del mercato del lavoro*, Giuffrè, Milan, 2004, p. 679.

Dondi G. 2003. "Comitati aziendali europei: il d. lgs. n. 74 del 2002 per l'attuazione della direttiva n. 94/45/CE," *Arg. Dir. Lav.*, No. 1, p. 103.

Earle, J. 1986. *The Italian Cooperative Movement*. London.

Fiorillo, L. 1998. *Le relazioni sindacali nel lavoro pubblico (informazione, consultazione, partecipazione): esame della attuale normativa e ipotesi di rivisitazione*, in *Foro it.*, *Rep.* Section: *Impiegato dello Stato e pubblico*, No. 151.

Ghera, E. 2003. "Azionariato dei lavoratori e democrazia economica," *Riv. It. Dir. Lav.*, No. 4, p. 413

Giugni, G., and F. Mancini. 1974. *Worker Participation in the Management of the Enterprise. Italian National Report to the IX Congress of Comparative Law*. Teheran.

—. 1984. "Recent Trends in Collective Bargaining in Italy," *International Labour Review* 123, No. 5. p. 599.

—. 1987. "Social Concertation and Political System in Italy," *Labour 1987* 1, No. 1, p. 3.

—. 2003. *La lunga marcia della concertazione*. Bologna: Il Mulino.

Giugni, G. *et al.* 2003. "*Relazione finale della Commissione per la verifica del Protocollo del 23 luglio 1993*," in *La lunga marcia della concertazione*, ed. Giugni, G., Bologna: Il Mulino.

Guaglianone, L. 2003. *Individuale e collettivo nell'azionariato dei dipendenti*. Torino: Giappichelli.

Klug, G., and W. Daubler. 1987. "Protocollo IRI: in Germania dicono che...," *Lavoro e Diritto* 1, No. 4, p. 701.

Manghi, B. 1999. "Sindacato e partecipazione tra cautela e pigrizia," *Lavoro e diritto* 1, p. 7.

Merli, G. 1985. *I circoli della qualità: filosofia, organizzazione, gestione*. Rome.

Montalenti, P. 1994. "Partecipazione dei lavoratori alla gestione dell'impresa," *Digesto comm*. Torino: Utet 10, p. 472.

Montuschi, L. 1986. *Diritto alla salute e organizzazione del lavoro*. Milano: Franco Angeli.

Paparella, D. 2002. "La bilateralità nel sistema di relazioni industriali italiane," Working Paper Cesos, available at *http://www.cesos.org/doc/bilatera.doc.*

Paparella, D., and V. Rinolfi. 2002. *Firmato il Patto per l'Italia*, available at http://www.eiro.eurofound.ie/2002/07/feature/IT0207104F.html

Parrotto, R. 1996. "Competitività d'impresa e governo delle dinamiche sociali: la partecipazione negoziata in Telecom Italia," *Dir. relaz. ind*., p. 119.

Pasquini, F. 2004. "Il ruolo degli organismi bilaterali nel decreto attuativo della legge 14 febbraio 2003, n. 30: problemi e prospettive," in *La riforma Biagi del mercato del lavoro*, ed. Tiraboschi, M., Milano: Giuffrè, p. 650.

Pedrazzoli, M. 1991. "*A*lternative italiane sulla partecipazione nel quadro europeo: la cogestione," *Giornale dir.lav. e relazioni ind*., 1.

Pichot, E. 2001. "Employee Representatives in Europe and their Economic Prerogatives," Report conducted for the European Commission, p. 122.

Regalia, I. 1989. "Le relazioni industriali in azienda: l'esperienza lombarda," *Lavoro e Diritto* 3, No. 3.

Ricci, M., and B. Veneziani, eds. 1988. *Tra conflitto e partecipazione. Un'indagine empirica sul protocollo IRI e sui diritti di informazione*. Bari.

Ricciardi, M. 1999. "Il protocollo di partecipazione in Telecom Italia Mobile," *Lavoro e diritto* 1, p. 17.

Russo, A. 2004. *Problemi e prospettive nelle politiche di fidelizzazione del personale*. Milano: Giuffrè.

Schlesinger, P. 2001. "Un fenomeno con un significativo rilancio, ma senza rilevanti sviluppi, in L'impresa al Plurale," *Quaderni della partecipazione*, No. 7/8, pp. 380-381.

Sciarra, S. 1987. "Plant Bargaining: The Impact of Juridification on Current Deregulative Trends in Italy," *Comparative Labor Law Journal* 8, No. 2, p. 126.

Telljohann, V. 2000. *The Italian Industrial Relations System and New Forms of Participation*, in *Fourth International Progressive Policy Conference - Track B: Globalisation, Industrial Relations and the Future of Trade Unions - Session 8: Impact of Globalisation on Labour Participation in the Workplace I*, available at *http://www.ipielle.emr.it/ita/index.html*

Tiraboschi, M. 2004. "Il sostegno alla contrattazione collettiva e alla bilateralità nella riforma Biagi: alcune osservazioni critiche sull'art. 10 della legge 14 febbraio 2003, n. 30," in *La riforma Biagi del mercato del lavoro*, ed. Tiraboschi, M. Milano: Giuffrè, p. 717.

—. 2003. *Le prestazioni di disoccupazione in Europa. Spunti di riflessione per il caso italiano.* Study carried out for CNEL.

—. 2004. "Il sistema degli ammortizzatori sociali: spunti progettuali per un progetto di riforma," *La riforma Biagi del mercato del lavoro*, ed. Tiraboschi, M., Milano: Giuffrè, p. 1105.

Treu, T., and S. Negrelli. 1985. *I diritti di informazione nell'impresa.* Bologna: Il Mulino.

—. 1987. "Workers' Participation and Personnel Management Policies in Italy," *International Labour Review* 126, No. 1, p. 81.

Treu, T. 1987. *Centralization and Decentralization in Collective Bargaining*, in *Labour 1987*, No. 1, p. 147.

—. 1987. "Ten Years of Social Concertation in Italy," *Labour and Society* 12, No. 3, p. 355.

—. 1992. "Informazione, consultazione, partecipazione—Prospettive comunitarie e realtà italiana," *Foro it.*, *Rep.* Section: *Comunità europee e Consiglio d'Europa*, No. 229.

Zoli, C. 1989. *L'obbligo a trattare nel sistema di relazioni industriali.* Bologna.

Documentation in Italian available at *www.adapt.it*
(Click on Indice A-Z, then *Partecipazione*)

Raccomandazione n. 92/443/CEE del 27 luglio 1992.

Accordo interconfederale del 6 novembre 1996.

Libro Verde della Commissione Europea del 1997 (Partenariato per una nuova organizzazione del lavoro).

Risoluzione del Parlamento Europeo del 15 gennaio 1998.

Relazione della Commissione Europea riguardante la promozione della partecipazione dei lavoratori subordinati ai profitti e ai risultati dell'impresa.

Direttiva 94/45/CE del Consiglio, del 22 settembre 1994, riguardante l'istituzione di un comitato aziendale europeo o di una procedura per l'informazione e la consultazione dei lavoratori nelle imprese e nei gruppi di imprese di dimensioni comunitarie.

Direttiva 2001/86/CE del Consiglio, dell'8 ottobre 2001, che completa lo statuto della società europea per quanto riguarda il coinvolgimento dei lavoratori.

Direttiva 2002/14/CE del Parlamento Europeo e del Consiglio, dell'11 marzo 2002, che istituisce un quadro generale relativo all'informazione e alla consultazione dei lavoratori.

Direttiva 2003/72/CE del Consiglio, del 22 luglio 2003, che completa lo statuto della società cooperativa europea per quanto riguarda il coinvolgimento dei lavoratori.

Proposta di Legge n. 1003, presentata il 21 giugno 2001: Disposizioni per la partecipazione dei dipendenti azionisti agli organi delle società per azioni.

Proposta di Legge n. 1943, presentata il 13 novembre 2001: Disposizioni per favorire l'azionariato diffuso dei lavoratori dipendenti.

Proposta di Legge n. 2023, presentata il 23 novembre 2001: Delega al Governo per l'adozione di uno "statuto partecipativo" delle imprese finalizzato alla partecipazione dei lavoratori alla gestione e ai risultati di impresa.

Proposta di Legge n. 2778, presentata il 21 maggio 2002: Norme in materia di partecipazione agli utili da parte dei lavoratori dipendenti delle piccole imprese.

Proposta di Legge n. 3642, presentata il 5 febbraio 2003: Norme per favorire la partecipazione dei dipendenti al capitale d'impresa.

Proposta di Legge n. 3926, presentata il 22 aprile 2003: Disposizioni per favorire la partecipazione dei lavoratori alla gestione delle imprese in attuazione dell'articolo 46 della Costituzione.

Proposta di Legge n. 4039, presentata il 4 giugno 2003: Disposizioni in materia di informazione e consultazione dei lavoratori, nonché di partecipazione azionaria dei dipendenti.

Documentation in English available at *www.adapt.it*
(Click on Indice A-Z, then *Participation*)

European Council. 1992. *Council Recommendation of 27 July 1992 Concerning the Promotion of Participation by Employed Persons in Profits and Enterprise Results (Including Equity Participation) 92/443/EEC*. Available at: http://europa.eu.int/infonet/library/f/92443 ce/en.htm.

European Commission. 1997. *Green Paper—Partnership for a new Organisation of Work. COM(97) 128*. Available at: http://europa.eu.int/comm/employment_social/soc-dial/social/green_en .htm.

European Parliament. 2002. *European Parliament Resolution on the Commission Green Paper on Promoting a European Framework for Corporate Social Responsibility (COM 2001 366—C5-0161/2002—*

2002/2069 (COS)). Available at: http://www.cleanclothes.org/ftp/eu_res.pdf.

Van Den Bulcke. 1999. *A Company Perspective on Financial Participation in the European Union. Objectives and Obstacles.* Brussels: Research Centre for Financial Participation, Catholic University Brussels. Available at: http://europa.eu.int/comm/employment_social/labour_law/docs/finpartobjobs_en.pdf.

Poutsma, E. *Recent Trends in Employee Financial Participation in the European Union.* The Netherlands: Nijmegen Business School, University of Nijmegen; for the European Foundation for the Improvement of Living and Working Conditions and the European Commission, Directorate-General for Employment and Social Affairs, 2001. Available at: http://europa.eu.int/comm/employment_social/labour_law/docs/financialpartdublinreport_en.pdf.

European Council. 1994. *Council Directive 94/45/EC of 22 September 1994 on the Establishment of a European Works Council or a Procedure in Community-scale Undertakings and Community-scale Groups of Undertakings for the Purposes of Informing and Consulting Employees.* Available at: http://europa.eu.int/comm/employment_social /labour_law/directive9445/9445euen.htm.

European Council. 2001. *Council Directive 2001/86/EC of 8 October 2001 Supplementing the Statute for a European Company with Regard to the Involvement of Employees.* Available at: http://europa.eu.int/eur-lex/pri/en/oj/dat/2001/l_294/l_29420011110en00220032.pdf.

European Parliament. 2002. *Directive 2002/14/EC of the European Parliament and of the Council of 11 March 2002 Establishing a General Framework for Informing and Consulting Employees in the European Community—Joint Declaration of the European Parliament, the Council and the Commission on Employee Representation.* Available at: http://europa.eu.int/eur-lex/en/lif/reg/en_register_05202030.html.

European Council. 2003. *Council Directive 2003/72/EC of 22 July 2003 Supplementing the Statute for a European Cooperative Society with Regard to the Involvement of Employees.* Available at: http://europa.eu.int/comm/employment_social/labour_law/docs/directive2003_72_en.pdf.

European Industrial Relations Observatory. 2001. *Government presents White Paper on Labour Market.* Available at: http://www.eiro.eurofound.eu.int/print/2001/10/feature/it0110104f.html.

ILO. 2002. *Report on the Pact for Italy, Infocus Programme on Social Dialogue, Labour Law and Labour Administration* Available at:

http://www.ilo.org/public/english/dialogue/ifpdial/sd/social_pacts/it_pact_5.htm.

CHAPTER SIXTEEN

FINANCIAL PARTICIPATION OF EMPLOYEES: THE ITALIAN CASE

1. Deep Roots[1]

Employee financial participation has rightly been compared to "a seemingly underground stream of the Italian industrial culture".[2] Yet it reveals deep—although controversial—roots in the history and experience of Italian industrial relations.[3]

The notion of "economic democracy" became the subject of a lively economic and legal debate at the turn of the last century, even before the emerging of the harmonious and non-conflictual perspective underpinning capital and labour relations, which was typical of corporatism and Catholic social teaching. This aspect clearly emerged for the first time in the Italian political arena in the late 1920s, when a number of bills—which were never converted into laws—were put forward concerning employee share ownership and profit sharing.

This aspect was again considered—although not too enthusiastically—by the Civil Code, first, and by the Constitutional Charter, afterwards (cf. next §). Therefore, this issue has undergone different phases, periodically surfacing in the academic, union and political debate, yet without so far becoming a well-established law discipline.

---

[1] The present contribution was produced in 2002 in collaboration with Marco Biagi and was previously published in *Quality of Work and Employee Involvement in Europe*. The Hague: Kluwer Law International.

[2] On this subject, see cf. Pessi, R. 1996. "L'azionariato dei dipendenti ed il sistema italiano delle relazioni industriali", *Le azioni del futuro. Privatizzazione partecipazione responsabilità*, Various Authors, (Rome: Ufficio Studi delle Relazioni Industriali e Amministrazione, Telecom Italia), p. 237.

[3] A similar consideration holds true also at a European scale. In Germany and the United Kingdom, in particular, the first bills date from the mid-19th century. Cf., Gabaglio, E. 2001. *Foreword. Lavoratori e capitale d'impresa in Europa.* Roma: Edizioni Lavoro, p. 11.

In spite of a significant number of tests and experiences—which undoubtedly point to a revived interest towards the issue—practice shows that no progress has been made,[4] at least in comparison with other national legal systems.[5] It lacks a modern statutory framework, which would be necessary to support its effective dissemination and establishment in our country, as also urged at a community level.

Council Recommendation No. 92/443/CEE of July 27th 1992, concerning the financial participation of employees in enterprise results and profits (including employee share ownership),[6] required Member States to amend their national legal frameworks in order to promote employee financial participation, also through any form of financial or tax allowances. Yet this recommendation has not been followed up by any action, save for a 1997 provision, which was not sufficient to support or to further develop the concept.[7]

Furthermore, if one considers the industrial relations actors, the recourse to employee financial participation was met with strong opposition by employers (Confindustria) and most of the trade union movements, chiefly Cgil, in spite of being backed by Cisl. The fear was that of questioning the pluralistic and conflictual rationale featuring the traditional industrial relations model, which was in place in Italy since the post-war period. This is useful to understand the ambiguous attitude on the part of trade unions towards employee financial participation, in Italy as elsewhere.[8]

---

[4] As recently and authoritatively stated by Schlesinger, P. 2001. "Un fenomeno con un significativo rilancio, ma senza rilevanti sviluppi,"*L'impresa al Plurale, Quaderni della partecipazione,* No. 7/8, p. 379 ff.

[5] Cf. Poutsma, E. 2001. *Recent Trends in Employee Financial Participation in the EU.* The European Foundation for the Improvement of Living and Working Conditions—European Commission. Cf. also for a brief overview, the European Foundation for the Improvement of Living and Working Conditions. 2001. *Recent Trends in Employee Financial Participation in the EU.* Dublin: Eurofound.

[6] In *GUCE* n. L 245 dated August 26 1992, pp. 53-55. Cf. also, at a Community level, the *European Parliament Resolution dated January 15 1998 on the Commission Report on PEPPER II—The Promotion of Employee Participation in Enterprise Results and Profits (including Employee Share Ownership) in the Member States* (COM(96)0687—C4-0019/97).

[7] See Legislative Decree No. 314/1997 and successive *infra §*.

[8] See Gabaglio, E. *Foreword*, p. 11.

2. The Legal Framework and its Limits

The main regulatory principles concerning employee financial participation are laid down in the 1948 Constitution and in the 1942 Civil Code. Article 46 of the Constitution sets forth that:

> The Republic recognises the rights of workers to collaborate in the management of enterprises, in the ways and within the limits established by law.

Article 47 continues:

> The Republic encourages and safeguards savings in all forms. It regulates, coordinates and oversees the operation of credit. The Republic promotes the access through citizens' mutual savings to the ownership of housing and of directly cultivated land, as well as to direct and indirect investment in the equity of the large production complexes of the country.

Although these two articles are generally referred to when it comes to employee financial participation in the enterprise profits, no specific indication is found in the rules and regulations that have been enforced.

No follow-up can be tracked on Art. 46, where only the employees' support to the running of the enterprise is dealt with. Similarly, Art. 47, paragraph 2, refers to *favouring direct or indirect share investments in the country main sectors* concerning *people's savings as a whole,* therefore without specifying if we are dealing with employees' savings only, or with an investment in the company's capital made by employees individually".[9]

It is also true that the Constitutional bills are too vague and do not contribute to solve the practical and theoretical moot points regarding employee shareholding. They mirror a deeply rooted disagreement among the main schools of thought over the way in which employee participation in the enterprise results works, as well as how the notion of "capital" should be conceived. This controversy has not been settled so far, and even though it was never turned into open opposition, it characterised the perspective of the major political parties and trade unions. As a result, the issue of economic democracy is now one of the most controversial and ambiguous subjects among the Italian industrial relations actors.

Hence, the backbone of the regulatory framework lies in the Civil Code. Pursuant to Article 2349, "In the event of an employee who

---

[9] Schlesinger, P. 2001. *Un fenomeno con un significativo rilancio, ma senza rilevanti sviluppi,* in *L'impresa al Plurale, Quaderni della partecipazione,* No. 7/8, pp. 380-381.

participates in profit-sharing on an off-and-on basis, special forms of share schemes can be issued, the value of which corresponds to the profits themselves, to be distributed directly among the workers, according to special rules regulating their rights and the way shares are transferred".

Par. 8 of Article 2441 provides that: "employees' right to share options is not to be applied when concerning a quarter of the newly- issued shares, if they are made available to employees by way of subscription, upon the decision made by the majority of shareholders, as required for extraordinary meetings. If the exclusion from share option schemes concerns more than a quarter of the newly issued shares, it must be approved by a majority vote as set out in the fifth paragraph".

Yet these provisions may not provide for the development of employee financial participation. The insufficient ground provided by Article 2349 and par. 8 of Articles 2441 of the Civil Code has often been pointed out by legal opinion—either by chartered accountants and labour law experts. It is commonly held that, although allowed by the regulatory provisions, any employee participation in a company share scheme requires both incentives (tax and credit allowances) and sound and transparent legal rules, in order to help it become more and more established, socially relevant and "significant for the improvement of the participatory dimension of industrial relations".[10]

It is also true that complex draft reforms concerning the legal framework have been put forward recently, an aspect that fuels the doctrinal debate and points to the diverse but renewed interest in the issue of financial involvement of employees and shareholding.

Lawmakers have also tried to re-launch the idea of large-scale employee share ownership plans. The new wording of par. 2 of Article 48, of the Consolidated Act on income tax, as amended by par. 1, article 3 of Legislative Decree No. 314/1997, introduced a provision which in fiscal terms is particularly favourable to those companies issuing new shares for their own employees.[11] This addition was confirmed with the enforcement

[10] See, Treu, T. 1993. "L'accordo del 23 luglio 1993: assetto contrattuale e struttura della retribuzione," *RGL,* p. 232.

[11] This article provides that, in the event of a subscription for new shares pursuant to the last paragraph of articles 2349 and 2441 of the Civil Code, even if issued by controlled and controlling companies, the value of the foregoing shares does not contribute to make up the holder's income. Furthermore, article 6 of Legislative Decree No. 314/1997 provides that the amount paid for the shares should be deducted from the social contributions. On this subject, see cf. Artina, V. 1999. "*L'emissione di stock options,*" *Amministrazione & Finanza,* No. 3, spec. 5-9.

of a rule supporting listed enterprises, in order to promote the recourse to stock option plans, i.e. employees' rights to buy new shares.

Legislation on pension schemes is likewise important in order to promote the notion of "economic democracy". Long overdue, recent legislation on complementary social security[12] now provides new perspectives, allowing employees to opt for new institutional forms of "collective" investment, which might have an impact on the financial market and their savings, with important repercussions also on the Italian industrial relations system.

However, no structured rules and regulations have been put in place so far, as recommended by the European Union, to support and untangle this knot.

It is not therefore surprising that employee shareholding in Italy has not fully developed to date, as lacking modern regulatory basis providing the kind of support already supplied in many other countries.[13]

This is one of the reasons why, along with the traditional distrust expressed by trade unions and employers, and save for a few exceptions, the recourse to employee shareholding has to be considered limited.

3. The Modest Italian Experience

The importance and, in some cases, the uniqueness of the Italian experience—especially after the recent privatisation process of a number of public bodies shifting from State-owned companies to joint stock companies[14]—cannot be overlooked, at least from an industrial relations perspective. It should be highlighted how employee shareholding does not deserve the name actually, even in those cases where this financial

[12] See Legislative Decree No. 124/1993 and, especially, the changes introduced by Law No. 335/1995. In this regard, it should be recalled that par. 15, article 2 of this provision excluded from taxable remuneration for contribution purposes «the difference between the market price and the privileged price granted to employees for the allotment of shares of their enterprise, the controlling or controlled enterprises, according to the law in force».

[13] A comparative review has been provided by the authors of this paper, in the framework of a research project funded by the European Commission during the first semester of 2001, aimed at the creation of a *forum* on the financial participation of employees. See the website: http://www.financialparticipation.org.

[14] Cf. Pedersini, R. 2001. "L'azionariato dei dipendenti nelle privatizzazioni italiane", *L'impresa al Plurale, Quaderni della partecipazione,* No. 7/8, p. 257 ff.

participation formula has been put in place.[15] The only significant exceptions that might be mentioned in such a complex and heterogeneous framework are the recent cases of Telecom and Alitalia.

After being privatised, employees at Telecom purchased shares amounting to more than 3 per cent of the company's share capital, thus becoming the majority shareholder. In the case of Alitalia, instead, employee shareholding was not less than 20% of share capital.

4. The Little Impetus of Trade Unions and the Clear Indications of the *White Paper*

As already mentioned, social partners took up different stances with reference to the issue of the financial participation of employees. Apart from Cisl, all the other trade unions expressed a lack of interest, if not their hostility, towards this issue.

A feeble attempt towards the systematic regulation was nevertheless made in 1998, with the conclusion between the Government and the social partners of the "Agreement on Concertation and New Trade Relations Policies for the European Integration and Transformation of the Transport System", on 23 December 1998.

As laid down by clause 4.6, the signatories agreed to "allow trade relations to evolve towards new participatory models in the ways envisaged by collective bargaining, aimed at involving all the workers' representatives in business decision-making". To support this initiative, "the Ministry of Transport *was supposed to submit* a specific bill to the National Transport and Logistics Council to promote and foster employee shareholding in transport firms".

What apparently seemed just a timely initiative at a sectoral level in order to help a critical and yet very active sector, was instead a major effort to re-launch the whole employee shareholding project.

By undertaking this commitment, social partners proved for the first time to be willing to overcome their traditional disregard towards this issue, if the following conditions were met:

- the development of a reference legal framework;
- employee involvement in the setting down of the objectives and the management of the economic strategies.

---

[15] Cfr. the cases presented in the review under note 12 are also available at: http://www.financialparticipation.org.

As far as industrial relations is concerned, two closely interrelated issues have to be taken into account: the amendment of the legal framework concerning the involvement of employees in business shareholding is not an end to itself, but in the views of the social partners and the Government, it was the juridical and institutional precondition for increasing the involvement of trade unions at the time of devising guidelines for the enterprises, while redistributing and widening the scope of share ownership.

From a methodological point of view, the perspectives referred to by the foregoing agreement implicitly contained some major indications that were already included in Council Recommendation No. 92/443/Cee of 27 July 1992, which admittedly urged Member States to "acknowledge the potential advantages deriving from a greater individual and collective use of a wide variety of employee participation in enterprise results and profits, such as profit sharing, share ownership, or a combination of different formulas".

It is true that the instrument adopted by the Council soon proved to be ineffective, if one considers the legally binding character of the provisions in different Member States.

Nevertheless, this does not mean that the foregoing recommendation was not right in highlighting two essential prerequisites for the effective implementation of employee shareholding in Europe.

In this connection, it is essential to review the existing regulations and ensure the involvement of social partners. These prerequisites had been made clear in the 1988 Agreement on the transport system. At a further stage of the project carried out at an experimental level, they could be extended to all the other sectors.

The amendments in legislation were not followed by any practical action. What remains is a draft project set up by the authors of this paper on behalf of the pro-tempore Minister of Labour Tiziano Treu.[16] It might now provide the basis for further discussion concerning any initiative carried out by lawmakers in the field.

Employee participation was given fresh momentum in the Government White Paper on the Italian labour market in October 2001. The European Commission itself has recently launched a new initiative, by submitting a working paper to the Member States, with the Italian Government that has also been urged to express its opinion on it.[17]

---

[16] See *Diritto delle Relazioni Industriali,* 2000, No. 1.

[17] European Commission. 2001. *Financial Participation of Employees in the European Union,* SEC(2001) 1308. Brussels: European Commission.

The issue should be taken into due account. From this point of view, an awareness-raising campaign is necessary to tackle what the Community paper defines a "cultural issue" and a "cultural deficit", in the sense that employees and their representatives feel excluded from financially participate in the company they operate.

In particular, in the White Paper, the Government has highlighted the importance to

> verify financial participation formulas aimed at enhancing key workers' loyalty within small and small-sized enterprises, including tourism businesses and the artisan sector. From this point of view, it is necessary to re-establish joint venture partnerships, namely to resort to other forms of profit sharing, supporting these schemes also through adequate economic and fiscal incentives (item III.3).

5. Key Theoretical and Legal Issues

The issues associated with employee participation illustrated in the previous paragraphs, confirm once again the difficulties related to this question from the industrial relations point of view, rather than from the legal and the institutional one.

There are several and different objectives concerning employee shareholding. Arguably, profit sharing may be seen: as a tool to collect risk capital, as a privileged channel during privatisation and/or restructuring to foster the renewal of the company (also from a cultural point of view), as an alternative to collective dismissals, as a flexible wage system, as a way to reduce the risks associated with employees exiting the business, and as a means to strengthen workers' involvement in decision-making. Similarly, there may be several and different ways to resort to employee shareholding. The ambivalent nature of this instrument, as well as the variety of strategies that can be put in place both by the enterprise and trade unions, cannot but increase the feeling of distrust on the part of social partners, which run the risk of being circumvented by financial participation schemes, which are unilaterally defined by the enterprise and developed on an individual basis.

6. A Possible Hypothesis

It is precisely this aspect that confirms the need for a regulatory intervention to support employee shareholding. It is not to be intended as a means to stiffen employee participation in profit sharing, nor to predict the choice of both stakeholders and social partners. Here, a set of rules would be desirable only if aimed at stimulating the dialogue among social partners within the industrial relations arena, which would also encourage the setting up of experimental schemes.

Undoubtedly, legislative action, now and in the years ahead, shall concern the traditional tools intended to promote employee shareholding – such as tax allowances – as well as the adoption of innovative and farsighted policies, like those that have recently been enforced by the French and British governments.

From this point of view, the scope for tax-deductible expenses might be taken into account within the framework of the financial participation plan at the time of purchasing convertible bonds and shares according to set annual thresholds, as already experienced in some major foreign companies.[18] Like the allocation of bonus issues, public offerings or sale of shares in view of the implementation of a financial participation scheme, the employer overseeing this plan should be allowed to deduct the following items from taxable income:

- the interests, as well as the capital shares, accrued on loans granted to employees to buy or subscribe for shares;
- the difference between the share value, calculated on the basis of the enterprise net worth resulting from the last balance sheet duly approved, and the price at which shares have been offered to the employees for sale or for subscription;
- in the case of an offer of free additional shares (bonus issue), the whole share value shall be reckoned on the basis of the enterprise net worth resulting from the last balance sheet duly approved;
- the amount paid to financial institutions, credit institutions or pension funds to reimburse employee's expenses concerning the purchase or the subscription for shares;

Following the international experience, the entitlement to tax allowances might be dependent upon the inalienability of those shares sold within a financial participation scheme for a certain number of years starting from the actual transfer, as decided by the ordinary assembly meetings. Prior to the agreement with the employees' representatives, the

---

[18] In some European countries, such as Denmark, France, and the UK, there are limits set for the amount of the annual allocation of bonus shares and the total amount of shares that can be bought by the employees. On the provisions regulating this issue, see cf. the EU Commission Report on Pepper II, *La promozione della partecipazione op. cit.* and also Poutsma, E. *Recent Trends in Employee Financial Participation in the EU, op. cit.*

financial participation schemes might provide for longer periods for the inalienability of shares to take place.

Furthermore, by means of an *ad hoc* rule, the legislator, in agreement with the stakeholders involved in collective bargaining, might have also laid down the conditions to purchase or subscribe for shares within the framework of a financial participation scheme, also envisaging an advance on severance pay, the use of wage quotas or portions, the use of credit mechanisms and pension funds, derogating from the provisions set forth in article 6, paragraph 5, letters a) and b) of Legislative Decree No. 124/1993.

Taking into account the major changes occurred in the organisation of work, the involvement of all employees in financial participation schemes, including those working in controlling, controlled or associated enterprises, should not be underestimated. The same might be said also of the former employees who still have shares in the company as well as of those employed in quasi-subordinate employment.

From this point of view, and as implied by the statutory general principles, a specific provision might be useful to explicitly rule out any form of discrimination when taking part in forms of participation, in compliance with the principle of equal opportunities, based on the employees' status, assignment or length of service.

7. A Matter of Choice

It is clear that given a *de iure condendo* perspective, the actual question to be tackled is that of an alternative between individual and collective shareholding, as it is often pointed out by legal opinion. This alternative is a "political moot point for the future development of the financial participation of employees in profit sharing".[19]

If this objective was pursued by the employer on a merely individual basis, the financial participation schemes would not only have little to do with the issue of economic democracy, but indeed the role of trade unions, as well as their ability to represent, would be called into question.

Yet this question should necessarily be tackled by lawmakers rather than by social partners from an industrial relations perspective.

In defining its scope of action, any future legislative intervention should indeed restrict itself to recognise the legitimacy of a wide range of financial participation schemes, either unilaterally defined by the enterprise or agreed upon with trade unions. Once this broad definition of

---

[19] Ghera, E. 1997. "L'azionariato dei lavoratori dipendenti,"*ADL,* 20.

"financial participation schemes" has been approved, lawmakers should regulate the forms of representation of the employee shareholders, as well as the rights to information and control.

If this perspective is taken, the features of the associations consisting of both employees and shareholders should be redefined, in order to:

- pursue the exclusive goal of representing their members, by promoting information concerning the enterprise, the shareholders, the rights deriving from financial participation schemes and any other relevant information;
- explicitly set out in the memorandum of association and in the articles of association that the right to vote and those related to participate in the association of each member should be based on the *per capita* principle rather than on the capital shares within the association;
- include the employee shareholders of the enterprise, either in employment or retired, as well as former employees still possessing company shares;
- establish a minimum number of employee shareholders, each of whom owning a certain number of shares up to a maximum percentage of the share capital, including shares granting them the right to vote and represent themselves in the assembly meetings.

In compliance with the provisions set forth by article 141 of Legislative Decree No. 58/1998, these associations of employee shareholders would be entitled to enjoy the rights enshrined in articles 20-27 of the Workers' Statute, once the necessary adjustments have been made. The ways in which these rights should be enforced might be laid down trough collective bargaining.

However, the real knot to unravel is that concerning forms of representation in decision-making and/or regulatory bodies. From this point of view, we fully agree with the assumption that "such a legal change—far from having disruptive effects on the company governance—would be consistent with the transformation process of the large joint stock companies started up by Legislative Decree No. 58/1998, which is aimed at empowering shareholders *without control* so that they have their *voice* heard within the enterprise".[20]

From a *de iure condendo* perspective, the point would rather be that of deciding whether to support a form of representation within the board of

[20] Alaimo, A. 1998. *La partecipazione azionaria dei lavoratori. Retribuzione, rischio e controllo*. Milano: Giuffrè, pp. 210-211.

directors or the board of auditors, through a specific piece of legislation, that might have either a promotional if not a legally binding effect.

PART V

THE COURAGE TO REFORM

CHAPTER SEVENTEEN

MARCO BIAGI: THE MAN AND THE MASTER[1]

On the days immediately following the tragedy which took place on the evening of 19 March 2002, I repeatedly resisted the idea of writing a tribute to Marco, fearful that I could not pay due respect to my mentor. Yet it was not merely rejecting the idea of writing a commemorative piece in his memory. Perhaps Marco, just like his own Master,[2] would not have appreciated it. It was not even the vain attempt to stem the flood of intense and painful emotions and grief by someone who, like me, would have liked to wake up from a terrible nightmare. Someone who still today, whenever the phone rings, thinks it might be him, someone who thinks of him. I believe it was rather a sense of reticence towards my private and intimate suffering that needed to remain as such. It was as though talking about Marco would mean more than just severing the bond that closely tied us for more than a decade and that allowed us to rejoice in each other's achievements. In fact, it would also mean washing away part of our deepest feelings, memories and sacrifices that, day after day, gave rise first to a unique and unequalled friendship, and then to a professional relationship which would otherwise be lost forever. Marco Biagi had a profound impact on my life, and I believe I somehow too had an impact on his. My inspiration to write did not arise out of normal circumstances, but I felt compelled to do so following numerous requests. Political manipulations, rhetorical memorials, reams of fine words did not impress

---

[1] The present contribution was published in *The International Journal of Comparative Labour Law and Industrial Relations* 18, No. 3:231-249.

[2] In this regard, Marco and I exchanged a few comments that seemed to me at the time to be light-hearted, when he was writing his tribute to Federico Mancini to be presented at the John Hopkins University in March 2001, cf. Biagi, M. 2008. *Federico Mancini: un giurista "progettuale"*, The Johns Hopkins University Bologna Centre, No. 8:3. As he then told me, I would have been precluded from writing any kind of tribute given the age limitations and his intention—as he often repeated—to remain in charge of our Centre for International Studies in Modena for the next twenty years or so and, possibly, even more.

me at all. Early feelings of anger soon turned into pain and then into sadness and loneliness. Only through commitment to slowly and silently putting back in motion the Centre for International Studies at the University of Modena—founded by Marco in 1991—could Marco's "children" (Riccardo Salomone, Alberto Russo, Olga Rymkevitch, Carlotta Serra and I) respond to so much injustice and manipulation. This would have been the only way Marco would have chosen to keep on living and to let others talk about his work as well as this little miracle, which took place over the past few years—referred to by Roger Blanpain[3] as the "Mecca of Comparative Studies". As a young boy having already mourned the loss of a loved one, I thought I had already paid a high price. Unfortunately I was wrong. Today, as a mature man, I am not only left with a sense of emptiness concerning a past event, but also with the regret of arising from a new experience; the regret of having been interrupted in the middle of a conversation; the regret of a hurried goodbye at the railway station; the regret of a broken dream and so many projects swept away all of a sudden and with no reason; the regret of realizing what happened, which I did not experience when I was young. Now what? I am left with a new life, with a little girl who is about to born; a daughter teaching me that I have to look ahead one more time, who gives a new sense to my life to fill the void that I had as an adolescent, which Marco helped me to overcome and that now inexorably tends to re-emerge. I hope—indeed I am sure—that along with feelings of anger, sadness and loneliness, Marina, Francesco and Lorenzo will very soon learn to feel and nurture a kind of love which is extraordinary: the love that is fed and nurtured in memory of Marco and all those little day-by-day events that apparently seem so trivial and taken for granted, but that actually make up our lives.

No, I do not want to yield to the temptation of thinking that everything is now meaningless—and I am saying this not only to myself but also to Lorenzo. If we had never existed it would have been worse, because we would not have had the good fortune to meet and know Marco; we would have never had the privilege of laughing, playing, rejoicing and also arguing with him. And this—I am sure—is something that we will all understand with the passing of time.

In spite of our marked differences in temperament and personality, I shared with Marco a deep and instinctive faith in God. The explanation of what happened remains a mystery—and the same is true of our lives, of the great and small things of our daily routine, the precariousness of our

---

[3] See Blanpain, R. 2002. "From the President of the International Society for Labour Law and Social Security," *The International Journal of Comparative Labour Law and Industrial Relations*, 18, No. 2.

existence, all the sacrifices made that now seem useless and meaningless. Yet I am certain that one day we will meet again! In the meantime, although from far away, I am sure, Marco, that you will follow us while riding who knows what sort of bike (because no doubt you must by now have already found a new bike!),[4] and from there you will accompany all of us: your family, your students from the Modena Centre for International Studies and all those who have truly loved you!

There have been at least two articles that moved me and prompted me to write a tribute to Marco as a Man and as a Master.

The first one is a powerful editorial by Gianpaolo Pansa in *L'Espresso*. I immediately felt a pang of nervousness in my stomach, as soon as I started reading its title: "Biagi, who was he?"[5] Pansa reveals a bitter truth when he states: "Taliercio, Rossa, Casalegno, Tobagi: all names and stories that no longer have any resonance today. It will soon happen also to Prof. Marco Biagi and, thus, people will ask "Biagi, who was he?". Massimo D'Antona's murder is clear evidence of that;[6] he left his family, his most intimate friends and his most extraordinary students with an everlasting memory, yet a sense of general indifference towards him can be felt among the public opinion at large, perhaps among many labour law experts too, not necessarily the youngest ones.

Even more significant to me was reading various drafts, submitted to my attention, of the magnificent article written by Marcello Pedrazzoli as a tribute to Prof. Biagi for the *Rivista Italiana di Diritto del Lavoro.*[7] It was not merely because Pedrazzoli—beyond any academic reason—showed kindness and a paternalistic attitude when he invited me to face my responsibilities as one of Marco's disciples and friends. It was first and

---

[4] The bike: another regret. It was a common passion, although we never had the pleasure of cycling together.

[5] Published in *L'Espresso*, No. 14, 2002.

[6] One of my most beautiful memories of Marco is linked to Massimo D'Antona. I still remember the simplicity and discretion with which Marco reacted—during one of the sessions at the 6th European Congress of the Labour Law and Social Security International Association (Warsaw, 13-17 September 1999), outside any official protocol or tribute (which had not been envisaged in that venue). While sitting at the centre of the panel, between Paul Davies, on his left, and Alain Supiot, on his right, he suddenly asked the audience to stand up and be silent for one minute to pay tribute to Massimo D'Antona. It was a spontaneous and sincere gesture in front of a totally foreign audience (apart from Matteo Dell'Olio and one of his young collaborators), for whom the memory of the name and history of D'Antona had already faded away.

[7] Pedrazzoli, M. 2002. "Marco Biagi e le riforme possibili: l'ostinazione del progetto"*RIDL [Rivista italiana di diritto del lavoro]*, No. 2.

foremost because the task to write a tribute in memory of Prof. Marco Biagi was undertaken by someone who was undoubtedly close to him, although being an "outsider".

At this stage, I feel not only able but obliged to put in writing the memory of Marco Biagi as a Man and as a Master from the point of view of an "insider", thus completing what Marcello Pedrazzoli wrote so effectively and what others will likewise write. No doubt this will contribute to provide a different perspective from which Marco's personality and academic contribution can be viewed and appreciated. I was persuaded that this might be a further way of recalling a name and a story, which goes far beyond listing his series of astounding academic and professional achievements. And this might be especially effective if recounted from the point of view of someone—like me—who worked side by side with him (as Gigi Montuschi pointed out to me, by arousing and freeing my emotions, thus healing a wound as though by the touch of a magic wand). This might be an unavoidable starting point to give a new sense to Marco's life and also to the lives of the people who as 'insiders' have lived and worked with Marco on a daily basis, by sharing with him joys and sacrifices that have laid the foundations for his extraordinary working method, in other words[8], his forward thinking.

1. Marco Biagi and Federico Mancini: Forward-thinking Labour Lawyers

> "2-4-86
> To Marco, the student who has walked in my footsteps at a close distance, a book in which the liberal minded can find the explanation of his liberalism: namely in his respect for the societies that simply aims at decency. The Founder of the Labour Law School of Bologna".

In this dedication by Federico Mancini—the Founder of the Labour Law School of Bologna—which appears in the first page of *A Theory of Justice* by John Rawls,[9] much can be found about Marco. Above all, his relationship with his Master. But also a pragmatist approach to reforming, longed for someone who, only with tenacity, obstinacy and a great deal of patience, aims at impacting the institutions and mechanisms governing a complex democratic and pluralistic society. Marco, just like Federico Mancini, was a forward-thinking labour lawyer and this "professional"

---

[8] As Marcello Pedrazzoli foretold perfectly, *op. cit.*

[9] Rawls, J. 1984. *Una teoria della giustizia*, Feltrinelli.

side can be considered as the completion of the work initiated by the Founder of the Labour Law School of Bologna.

In consideration of the various methodologies and inclinations, every member of the Labour Law School of Bologna is the follower of the work commenced by Federico Mancini. Unlike other students, Marco followed his footsteps not only in terms of methodology—that of comparative legal studies—but mainly as a political passion (as intense as their well-known liking to the Bologna football team) and more recently through his involvement in new projects, also thanks to the fundamental contribution by Tiziano Treu. Marco, too, was a jurist "with a project in mind" as he used to define himself.

Marcello Pedrazzoli has already written a brilliant article about Marco Biagi and some possible future reforms. In this regard I will add a few more things later on. Now I would rather draw a parallel between Federico Mancini and Marco Biagi. Not only because Marco always told me about his Master and what he would have done under similar circumstances. In this connection, one might find it useful to read the article titled *Federico Mancini: un giurista "progettuale"*[10] to understand how Marco felt being Federico Mancini's living follower—in spite of a clear and unequivocally different personality and of what he defined the "uniqueness" of his Master.

By recalling Prof. Mancini, Marco saw—as a natural consequence—a reflection of himself and of his human and academic development: first of all, the comparative scholar, but also the Master of the school of Modena and then, the innovator, the modernist, the protagonist.[11] Just like Federico Mancini, Marco Biagi was also a combination of all these aspects which turn a jurist into a forward-thinking jurist. And this is how I like remembering him.

2. Marco Biagi: The Comparative Lawyer

It is not for me to say whether or not Marco was a great labour law and industrial relations comparative scholar. My view would not only be predictable, but also biased. Furthermore, the recent and increasingly less veiled controversy about the way Marco resorted to comparative analysis still echoes in my mind. Marco did not only know Otto Kahn-Freund's classics on the use and abuse of comparative law, but he also humbly

---

[10] Biagi, M. *Federico Mancini: un giurista "progettuale"*, cit.

[11] These are the paragraphs around which the tribute to Mancini had been written. Cf. Biagi, M. *Federico Mancini: un giurista "progettuale"*, cit.

borrowed that methodological approach: i.e. making a national system simply one of the various systems under comparison, in order to be analyzed solely on the basis of its intrinsic characteristics[12]—and that was unequalled experience in the Italian labour law arena.

It became natural to Marco to shift away from the centrality of the national legal system, not because of intellectual arrogance but due to his inborn farsightedness—that was also acknowledged by Federico Mancini—to look ahead and to foresee in advance future scenarios and events. Under certain circumstances, this attitude might have probably contributed to fuelling divergent views among those who, more or less consciously, were reluctant to walk away from the narrow focus provided by the national labour law perspective. Yet this is undoubtedly the precious legacy left by Marco Biagi as a comparative lawyer.

The increasingly pervasive European and community labour law dimension, the internationalisation of markets and the complex processes that have recently led to the substantial loss of national sovereignty over the rules regulating the production and distribution of wealth did not worry those like Marco, who had long left the narrow perspective of national labour law. Indeed, it was thanks to his moving away from the different national systems that it was particularly easy for him to engage in benchmarking activities, which became a fixture of Marco's thinking and planning and ability.

Marco was not simply interested in transplanting overseas models. At least over the past decade, he believed that comparative analysis was the only possible way to foresee the implementation outcomes of regulatory mechanisms that are still at the preliminary stage.[13] Moreover, he contributed to dispel some misconceptions and ideological resistance towards the modernization of the employment relationship. The last joint work that we were involved in concerned new fixed-term work regulations.[14] It is a clear example of how the comparative approach should lead to the analysis and to the pragmatic solution of labour market problems.

As Rodolfo Sacco wrote in one of his books—which is particularly dear to us—"Comparison is history: it is this history that sweeps false concepts away and thus leads to knowledge".[15]

---

[12] Cf. in particular, Biagi, M. 1990. *Rappresentanza e democrazia in azienda. Profili di diritto sindacale comparato*, Maggioli, 3.

[13] Biagi, M. *Federico Mancini: un giurista "progettuale"*, 5.

[14] Biagi, M. 2002. *Il nuovo lavoro a termine. Commentario al D.Lgs. 6 settembre 2001, 368*. Milan: Giuffrè.

[15] Sacco, R. 1990. *Introduzione al metodo comparato*. Giappichelli, 18.

From this point of view, Tiziano Treu's contribution has also been fundamental. If Gigi Montuschi—Marco's other Master—strongly supported and encouraged him in adopting the comparative method, starting from the memorable 1983 Kyoto conference, Tiziano Treu represented an ideal guide for the practical application of the method itself[16]. Marco often told me about his willingness to help Tiziano Treu prepare his contribution for that congress: a feeling that was no less strong than the one accompanying him fifteen years later when he organized, once again in collaboration with Tiziano Treu, the 11th World Congress of the International Industrial Relations Association (IIRA)[17] in his capacity as President.

At the Kyoto conference, he also met Roger Blanpain for the first time: a jurist and a man who was in many respects very different from Marco, but who has been for many years the repository of a highly sophisticated organizational method that has substantially influenced our working method at the Modena Centre. From this point of view, Marco considered himself also to be one of Roger Blanpain's "disciples" and over the coming years he would have written something comparable to the monumental *International Encyclopedia for Labour Law and Industrial Relations* edited by Blanpain for Kluwer.

The overall picture that I have just outlined might probably appear less emblematic and significant than the legendary sea journey made by Federico Mancini and Gino Giugni to the United States to study the American model, which would deeply affect the development of our national labour law over the next few years. Yet, on close inspection, Marco's cultural itinerary was likewise fascinating and outstanding, as one would expect from a talented comparative scholar as he was, most notably from someone who did not restrict himself to study other systems and experiences simply at a theoretical level, but who realized that a true comparative study can never be an activity to be carried out in isolation.

As Marco wrote, comparative research requires that "most of the work (collecting bibliographical information and, above all, understanding how

---

[16] Cf. Treu, T. 1994. "L'internazionalizzazione dei mercati: problemi di diritto del lavoro e metodo comparato", *Studies in Honour of R. Sacco*, (Milan: Giuffrè), 1:1117, which represented a sort of cultural manifesto for all those who were committed in the activities of the Modena Centre of International Studies set up by Marco.

[17] *Sviluppare la competitività e la giustizia sociale: le relazioni fra istituzioni e parti sociali*, Proceedings of the 11th World Congress of the International Industrial Relations Association, Bologna 22-26 September 1998, Sinnea, Bologna, 1998.

a system actually works) must be conducted in collaboration with other colleagues".[18]

A cursory look at the programme of one of his traditional meetings in Modena, or at one of numerous introductory comparative contributions[19] are enough to appreciate Marco's extraordinary ability, resulting from his well-known reliability and seriousness, to bring together a varied group of authoritative labour law experts, among whom his 'brother' Yasuo Suwa, Lammy Betten and Alan Neal, to whom he succeeded in the management of the *International Journal of Labour Law and Industrial Relations*.

Finally, another important figure has been that of Manfred Weiss, another great Master, akin to Marco in his rigorousness and reliability, and with whom Marco had launched one of his several international projects. Under Manfred Weiss's Presidency at the International Industrial Relations Association, Marco enjoyed the fleeting pleasure of being appointed as one of the five speakers at the international IIRA congress that was held in Berlin in September 2003. The congress would also have been different from the previous ones because, for the first time, not just Marina—who is usually reluctant to fly—but also the whole Modena team would have taken part in it.

Yet it would not be fair towards Marco if I did not mention another talent of his, typical of a true comparative scholar. A comparative scholar is never afraid of differences between models and systems, no matter how significant they are.[20] In the same vein, Marco never posed barriers in terms of academic status, geographic origins, and cultural background. His Summer Schools, his lectures at the students of the John Hopkins and Dickinson University, the many international meetings, initially organized at Sinnea International and then, starting from 1994, at the new venue of the Centre for International Studies at the University of Modena, were above all a thriving think tank. It is there that graduates and students could meet prestigious international scholars, government ministers, EU commissioners, etc., in an extraordinarily informal atmosphere that cannot usually be found in any other Italian academic circle. This allowed students and scholars to make a "live comparative analysis" as Marco had defined it.[21]

I still remember one warm summer evening in July 1996, when during the ceremony for awarding attendance certificates at the Summer School

---

[18] Cf. Foreword to Biagi, M. *Rappresentanza e democrazia in azienda etc.*, cit.

[19] A list can be found at the website of the Modena Study Centre: *www.economia.unimo.it/Centro_Studi_Intern/home.htm* [n.d.r.].

[20] As rightly pointed out by Sacco, R. *Introduzione al metodo comparato*, cit., 23.

[21] Biagi, M. *Federico Mancini: un giurista "progettuale"*, cit., 4.

in Labour Law and Industrial Relations, along with the all-present Tiziano Treu, Mr. Romano Prodi—the then Italian Prime Minister—suddenly arrived and did not hesitate to go and shake hands first with the younger foreign guests and students even before welcoming the authorities. One of Marco's pictures, showing him surrounded by Tiziano Treu, Romano Prodi, a young Japanese researcher, our first Modena student, Giulia Moretti, and a Canadian colleague, Véronique Marleau, still hangs at the entrance of his office in via Valdonica, close to the bed which had for a long time provided accommodation to his "brother" Yasuo Suwa, and later on to myself for almost one year and a half while I was still trying to find my own place in Bologna. Enrico Traversa's guitar and songs, which turned that event into a magical evening, still echo in my mind, overcoming the melancholy of these past few years with sounds and feelings.

3. Marco Biagi, the Master

Whereas extreme informality marked both Marco Biagi and Federico Mancini's relationships, the same cannot be said of his role as "Master". Marco Biagi never had his own School and perhaps only now conditions in Modena have been adequate to make it possible for the creation of an extremely ambitious and important project to be completed in a few years. It was not until 2000 and 2001 that a group of young scholars began to emerge, among others Riccardo Salomone, Alberto Russo, Olga Rymkevitch and Carlotta Serra.

Until then, Marco's dimension has always been like that of the "craftsman's workshop". He liked this expression and frequently repeated it, proud of the fact that, although assisted by an inexperienced apprentice from Bergamo, he was nevertheless able to carry out an incredible number of studies, both at a national and international level, thus giving the impression that he could indeed avail himself of a long-established Modena School. But this was far from the case. We were supported only by some students in political economics and business economics who were in their final year and were attracted by Marco's fascinating human qualities.

Our office soon became well-known within the whole faculty. Different factors proved to be successful, such as the informal nature of the relationships, the professor's renowned availability, the careful supervision of dissertations, the opportunity to use a few computers thanks to the support of a talented computer engineer, Vincenzo Salerno, always ready to give a hand, Marco's ability to make conections with employers, thus testing pioneering attempts of the company-based apprenticeship system, which would help so many young graduates to gain access to the labour market. All these factors allowed us to set up an extraordinary group of people, willing to help and devote their precious time and energy to support our project on a voluntary basis. These included Serena Vaccari, Giulia Moretti, Emanuela Salsi and Ylenia Franciosi, as well as Giorgia Verri, Silvia Spattini, Elisa Pau, Barbara Maiani, Gianluca Nieddu, Anna Simonini, Francesca Crotali, Paolo Fontana, Federica Rossi, Federica Gambini, Alessandra Lopez, Federico Bacchiega, Cinzia De Luca, Lucia Mangiarelli, Luana Ferraro, Sabrina Guerzoni, Giuseppe Bertoni and Massimo Morselli.

At the end of their academic career, these students have continued to attend our offices and to collaborate with us for months, a year, or even more. Yet, the relationships that have been established have often gone far beyond the informal collaboration and some of them still continue in the more genuine form of friendship. From this point of view, Marco was a true Master: not just the 'founder of the school' strictly speaking, but a guide who has always tried to be surrounded by a group of young people who shared mutual esteem and the involvement in the project. Furthermore, one of Marco's greatest qualities was his ability to rejoice with sincerity at these youngsters' early achievements, either as a group or individually.

I would not do justice to Marco and to the people who have worked with us if I overlooked the fact that this form of group work could sometimes degenerate, causing disillusion and tension, and sometimes giving rise to a number of misunderstandings. At times, the obstinacy put in our work led to certain insensitiveness towards the undeniable merits of some of our younger collaborators. In this case I take full responsibility for it, because I always yielded to the temptation of believing that every collaborator might be turned into a budding scholar, thus unconsciously fuelling academic expectations that could not be met, probably either because of Marco's particular position within the Bologna School, or because of the fragile legal background of our students at the Faculty of Economics. It is from this awareness that early and more stable collaborations came about, beginning with Nicola Benedetto and Giuseppe Martinucci and then with some of my latest students in Milan, and in particular with Giuseppe Mautone and Marina Mobilia. It is from there that the idea of setting up a group originated, as soon as Riccardo Salomone was appointed researcher and Alberto Russo received a research grant. Olga Rymkevitch joined us later from St. Petersburg, full of hopes and enthusiasm, followed by Carlotta Serra, who soon became the

Master's favourite, thanks to her strong personality, and then a little later by Flavia Pasquini. It was therefore easily foreseeable that it would not have taken much longer for a true Modena School to be set up. It was just a matter of time.

Marco has certainly been a Master in the true sense of the word, at least for me. I owe him a lot, and not just in the academic field. It was he who believed in me and in 1992, on Stefano Liebman's advice, brought me to Modena from Milan, after a year-long stay at the Labour Law Institute of the Catholic University of Leuven under the supervision of Roger Blanpain. It was he who taught me the job in his 'craftsman's workshop' and encouraged me day after day, by entrusting me with increasingly demanding and stimulating tasks. Our collaboration then turned into a strong friendship, into a kind of symbiotic relationship that did not allow for any rest or indecision. I believe that we complemented each other perfectly, or this is at least what I thought. We were friends. But I knew well that this bond of friendship, like all the relationships that matter in one's life, could not simply be defined in these terms.

As a Master he astonished me not only because of his scrupulous reading of my papers, but especially because of his extreme clear-sightedness in assigning me a task, foreseeing well in advance the issues that a few years later would have become topical. For instance, temporary agency work was already pivotal in 1991, when this form of employment was not only prohibited by law in our country but totally unknown, except for a few experts in the field. Or in 1998, well ahead of completing my first monograph, when he asked me to start working on such issue as employment incentives and the European law on competition. After a thorough revision and reading by Tiziano Treu and Mario Rusciano, I sent it to press on Monday 18 March. On the previous day, Sunday afternoon—alongside the scheduling of the following week's agenda, which I was usually sent after the football match—Marco delivered an attachment containing his introduction to my book.

He used to send me detailed memos to supplement the weekly schedule of the Sunday. This was one of the things which characterized our working method. I received his last memo by fax on 19 March at 10.50 a.m., a few hours before leaving home to join us in Modena. He replied to my message concerning me sending the book to press simply with: "Excellent!" This is the last memory I keep of Marco as a Master. Yet I have also been left with a legacy. As usual, he had already long entrusted me with a third monograph on the "Workers' Statute", on which

I had started working with him in 1997, as part of our collaboration with Tiziano Treu.[22]

4. Marco Biagi, the Innovator

If Federico Mancini was one of the first examples of modern labour law experts, Marco Biagi can certainly be regarded as his ideal follower, although in a completely different social, economic and institutional context. He too was firmly determined in changing the direction taken in this area, particularly by providing a fundamental contribution to the Europeanization process of Labour Law.

The challenge posed by the recent reform of Title 5 of the Constitution would have undoubtedly been a further and decisive turning point in his work of re-examining and modernizing labour law, as shown by an unpublished—and not yet complete—work that appeared in one of the next issues of the journal *Diritto delle Relazioni Industriali.*[23] This paper should not be mentioned simply because of his attempt to refine some sections of the October 2001 White Paper on the labour market, drafted and supported principally by Marco, but rather because of some deep-rooted convictions of European and federal origins. Marco, just like Mancini, was also convinced that a more just—or at least more "decent"—society could be created only in a broader context, such as the European and federal legal institutional framework. As usual, time will prove him right on this issue as well.

In this sense, especially over the past few years, Marco's commitment was to prove that, unlike what commonly held, it is not a lack of ideas and projects that prevents the launch of a complex labour law reform. "What still needs to happen"—he recently wrote[24]—"is to overcome ideological prejudice and blinker that slow down for no good purpose the evolutionary process that is taking place as well as necessary reforms, in order to prevent de-structuring and deregulating mechanisms from spreading throughout the labour market: these phenomena are, in turn, the cause and

---

[22] Cf. Biagi, M. 2001. "Progettare per modernizzare", *Politiche del lavoro. Insegnamenti di un decennio*, ed. Treu, T. (Bologna: il Mulino), 269-280 and also Biagi, M., and M. Tiraboschi. 1999. "Le proposte legislative in materia di lavoro parasubordinato: tipizzazione di un *tertium genus*o codificazione di uno Statuto dei lavoratori?" *LD [Lavoro e diritto]*, 4.

[23] Biagi, M. 2002. "Federalismo e lavoro. Il lavoro nella riforma costituzionale," *DRI [Diritto delle Relazioni Industriali]*, No. 2:157-164.

[24] Cf. for a synthesis, Biagi, M. "Progettare per modernizzare", *op. cit.,* 270.

the result of an emerging hidden economy in our country, which is two or three times bigger than in other countries".

Marco was motivated by his desire to prove that simple and effective ideas are indeed in place to promote the necessary reforms in Labour Law; it was with this spirit that, though fully involved in his activity as legal advisor for the centre-right Government, he once again agreed to collaborate with Tiziano Treu. Along this collaboration, he gathered and classified the main labour market modernization projects that had characterized the last seven years of a hectic activity of project developments. With different roles and attitudes, they have both played a pivotal role in shaping the national labour policies.

"It was a really fascinating and unique experience"—Marco wrote[25]—"marked by important successes (such as the case of Act n. 196, dated 24 June 1997, on employment incentives)",[26] "but also by inevitable compromises (e.g. the case of work regulations for members of co-operatives) and sometimes even by certain disillusionment (e.g. in the case of a reform bill for the 35-hour week that prematurely put an end to the government coalition led by Romano Prodi)".

Much has been said and written about Marco, the innovator and the reformist, though not always correctly. However, his several articles are there to speak for him, and any further word would be superfluous. Once the rhetoric and sensationalism of the first few months after his passing died away, I was convinced that his thinking and planning activity would be fully acknowledged. No resistance to change and modernization—just like the false problem of the reform of Article 18 of the Workers' Statute—can prevent Marco's enlightened and effective proposals from emerging.

From the vantage point of an "insider", let me highlight one innovative side of Marco's character: his exquisite aptitude for dialogue enabled him to communicate easily with many different people, from the most authoritative officer to the youngest student here in Modena. Marco was an innovator also in terms of style: elegant and simple at the same time,

---

[25] *Ibidem*, 271.

[26] Strong evidence of this success can be found in the note to Act No. 196/1997 entitled *Markets and Labour Relations*, edited by M. Biagi for Giuffrè in 1997. This again is a true methodological innovation in the academic domain in Italy and beyond, for the fact that—as can be read in the introduction by Marco Biagi—"for the first time, a provision is assessed and discussed by authors within relevant authorities who are also in charge of its preparatory work. In addition, these authors work at the Ministry for Employment and Social Security engaged in the implementation and enforcement of the law itself".

direct, without any cultural or mental prejudice or barrier. I still remember how during the breaks at the courses held at the various Summer Schools organized by Sinnea International, he would sit on a low wall or on a desk eating a sandwich while chatting with his students.

In my view this was a true innovation—the ideal way to establish first of all a human and then a professional relationship, as a precondition leading to the establishment of a community, beyond any academic or educational logic.

Over time I also learnt to appreciate his simplicity of language as well as his natural ability to be brief– two basic qualities that should govern the innovation processes underlying the 21st century labour market regulatory mechanisms which, at the beginning of my career, I had substantially underestimated. I was then firmly convinced—as can be seen all too frequently in my work—that jurists needed by necessity to use a complex and long-winded style, along with a large number of references. This shows the readership the wide range of interpretations and exhaustive thinking behind each individual sentence or idea. But I was wrong. Marco's essential and clear style was the expression of the enlightened ideas of an intellectual, put at the service of society. Marco was a true innovator because he went straight to the heart of the problems, in search of their solution. The legal and conceptual system was not seen as an obstacle to dialogue, but only a necessary starting point in his work as a forward-thinking jurist.

As an innovator, Marco was first and foremost a great communicator, more than a forward-thinking reformer. His great skills in establishing a dialogue with political leaders and industrial relations practitioners stemmed from his immediate and simple language, as well as from the modesty with which he addressed his readership and audience—despite his long-standing experience as a jurist and an advisor—whether through an Editorial or an academic paper. Complex reform projects and articulated reform bills were made incredibly easy to understand also to non-specialists. That is why Marco soon became one of the columnists for the newspaper *Il Sole 24 Ore*. In addition to his well-known ability to foresee, with certain reliability, forthcoming events that would become central in the political and trade union debate, Marco also distinguished himself for his plain and direct writing style that helped people understand problems and fuel debate. He was not the kind of person who loved abstruse conceptual arguments or complex analytical historical and legal reconstruction. He was instead a simple and pragmatic person.

That is why in 1999 Marco was invited to go to Milan to participate in a daring and ambitious reform project, which eventually led to the well-known "Milan Employment Pact". He was involved in this project because he made his point clearly and never stepped back, while always ready to experiment and innovate. This is also why Marco has been one of the few Italian labour law jurists who were able to communicate easily not only with overseas colleagues but also with the most prestigious European and international institutions, be they the International Labour Organisation, the European Commission, the Dublin European Foundation or the Aspen Institute.

He was also an innovator in the way he ran his Journals (*Diritto delle Relazioni Industriali* and, more recently *The International Journal of Comparative Labour Law and Industrial Relations*), and its Associations (since 1994 the *Associazione Italiana di Studio delle Relazioni Industriali* (AISRI) and, since 2000, also ADAPT, an association started from scratch, which soon pooled together a large number of enterprises and all the main employers and employees' associations, except for CGIL). But his true innovative nature emerged in his management approach: he had an extraordinary ability to assign precise tasks to everyone and to make anyone feel important, but also a master of maieutics, being able to draw the best out of each one of us.

Despite the idea one might have from the outside[27]—which can nevertheless be partly justified—Marco was not in favour of the revision of Italian labour law to be carried out 'within the closed circles of the Ministry, rather than by opening a debate that might involve all the experts in the field'. Working with him side by side I realized how indefatigable he was. He was animated by inexhaustible energy, the fruit of a true passion or vocation, which led him to move relentlessly back and forth Rome, Milan, and Brussels, patiently engaged in weaving a network of consensus around the goal to modernise labour law, yet without never neglecting any of his academic commitments. Not only did he join the activities of our Faculty, but he was also one of those jurists who attended several meetings, without missing important national or international events.

Hence, his reform project stemmed, indeed, from serious—although not always fruitful—talks with the various experts in the field. The AISRI and ADAPT membership is clear evidence of that.

In opposition of many people claimed or thought, there was no tacit agreement between the "prince's counsellor" and the "prince" himself. This was often said to raise the tone around the reforms or simply out of

[27] Cf. i.e. Carinci, F. 2002. "Dal Libro Bianco alla Legge delega," *Dir. Prat. Lav. [Diritto e pratica del lavoro]*, No. 11:732.

provocation, in order to question Marco's power and the undeniable heightening of reputation. This is because Marco while writing about Federico Mancini was thinking to himself, and was not the "prince's lawyer", but indeed—as he himself put it—a "lawyer with a project in mind".[28] It is enough to go through the White Paper, with his grand project carried out in collaboration with the Prodi Government[29] to realize Marco's absolute consistency. Just like Federico Mancini, Marco Biagi, too, gave his sword to the service of the projects he believed in, be they right or wrong, but never to the service of any individual, political party, or Government.

Marco has always worked with an approach based on forward thinking—helped in this task by the patent fragility of political and institutional bodies that in turn addressed themselves to him—without ever yielding to the temptation of pleasing those in charge. We have never been influenced or pressured while carrying out our projects. And if one of our assumptions did not work we were always ready to start anew, motivated by our usual patience, passion and enjoyment, qualities which are few and far between in any other working environment.

5. Marco Biagi, the Modern Man

Marco's objective was to devise new projects with a view to modernize.[30] Although he never relinquished his academic rigour, Marco was never obsessed with the perfect presentation. Instead he was obsessed with promptness, care for detail and the quality of the overall project. His modernity mainly lies in his pragmatic approach. Marco was not keen on complicated and abstruse projects that were an end in themselves, nor did he ever like to indulge in self-celebration for whatever had been accomplished so far, no matter how significant the results were. He never allowed himself rest, or time to celebrate, as he indeed deserved. His continuing dissatisfaction sometimes really exasperated us. But that was his way of being modern: he had fully accepted the challenge launched on a daily basis by our hectic and irrational modern times.

Marco did not fully master technology and the Internet, but he immediately understood its huge potential. It was he who advised us on how to use it effectively and who set the pace for our work. His close relationship with young people, his daily exchange with the American

---

[28] Biagi, M. *Federico Mancini: un giurista "progettuale", op. cit.* 9.
[29] Cf. Treu, T. *Politiche del lavoro. Insegnamenti di un decennio*, *op. cit.* 269-395.
[30] Biagi, M. "Progettare per modernizzare", *op. cit.*

students from the Dickinson Institute and his love for his two sons made him a man who was particularly attentive to social changes and a talented interpreter of the legal developments underlying the social and economic processes currently underway. His fondness of soft-laws and his enthusiasm for Europe and federalism are a clear indication of a renewed concept of law as a technique for regulating society and managing conflict in complex post-modern societies.

Marco was a precursor in the present labour law trends. He humbly tried to put his visions of the future at the service of a project. Of course, Marco, just like any other man, had a combination of passions and instincts and perhaps was also ambitious. Yet one thing is certain: he applied the method that he had developed and passed it on to all of us. The meticulous way in which he always gathered the documentation and the accuracy through which he worked on even the less important projects were typical of a young scholar who is fully aware of his limits when faced with demanding academic tasks and tries to overcome them. I do not know whether he truly believed it or not, but he often told me about his wish to withdraw to Pianoro to become a full-time scholar, just like the old days.

Once again it is his modernity that explains the difficulty to interact with other experts in the field and, in particular, with CGIL. Marco would complain about the real matter, rather than the tones—often inexcusably violent—of the controversy. An example is the decision on the part of CGIL not to take part in any of his conferences and meetings, and even before that the sudden withdrawal of CGIL from the academic arena, chiefly from *the Associazione Italiana di Studio delle Relazioni Industriali*. It is not up to me to say whether Marco or his opponents were right or wrong and I am also aware many of the historical reasons and political argument that may lead CGIL to resist change. Yet, I know that rejecting dialogue, the lack of respect for one's opponent are the opposite of modernity, but also of those traditional values that are at the basis of a democratic and pluralistic society, which help us make cohabitation among human beings slightly more 'decent'.

To him, the present frontiers of modernity consist in the issues of the federal reform of the State, techniques for building a relationship of trust with employees and the 'Workers' Statute'.

6. Marco Biagi, the Protagonist

Marco has therefore been a major figure in our times and certainly not a mere spectator. Over a relatively short period he completed works of great value and significance, as will become evident over the next few years, when the importance of his work has been properly assessed. Many people, some with an abrupt turn of opinion, have already emphasized Marco Biagi's powerful and fruitful dialogue with political authorities and institutions, at a community, national and local level.

What I would like to point out is that Marco Biagi has been a protagonist in our lives. Our encounter has profoundly changed us and left a seed that will soon bear fruit. Continuing our work as 'protagonists', each one of us following our own inclinations and commitment, is the response we must give to his death, and even more so, given the brutality and absurdity with which a still young life has been torn away from the love of his beloved ones and students. As he himself wrote in his tribute to Federico Mancini[31], 'this is what our Master would have expected from all of us'.

Not only that. I think that Marco Biagi also helps us understand much more than that, going beyond the issue of labour law and its modernization. I really wish that his sacrifice will not be useless for us, as people, as human beings, all too often affected by petty and selfish feelings, which do not let us fully appreciate the beauty of life and the people who surround and love us. I really wish that the look of sadness on all our faces might be turned into practical and humble commitment to continue making our own lives and the lives of those who accompany us along this mysterious and often too cruel pathway slightly more decent.

[31] Biagi, M. *Federico Mancini: un giurista "progettuale", op.cit.*, 11.

INDEX